JAMES G. BLAINE

A POLITICAL IDOL OF OTHER DAYS

James G. Blaine

JAMES G. BLAINE

A Political Idol of Other Days

By
DAVID SAVILLE MUZZEY

KENNIKAT PRESS, INC./PORT WASHINGTON, N. Y.

PREFACE

IF HISTORY is the "distillation of innumerable biographies," it is equally true that every biography worthy of record is a composite of innumerable factors of history. A paradox of the genealogical table furnishes the biographer with an interesting analogy. For just as an individual name there stands both at the apex of a pyramid whose base broadens downward through descendants and at the apex of an inverted pyramid whose base broadens upward through ancestors, so every significant career stands at the waist of the hour-glass of history. It is focal. It gathers the experience of the past, passes that experience through the lens of a distinctive intellectual, emotional and moral endowment, and sends forth widening rays of influence for good or evil, to grow steadier and more penetrating or to fade into feebleness, according to the inexorable judgments of time.

The task of a biographer is to appraise as accurately as he can the conditioning endowment of his subject and to calculate the resultant of the forces furnished by that character and the problems of the times in which he lived. Conscious both of the difficulty of sounding the depths of another's personality and of the limitations which fragmentary knowledge, scanty or conflicting sources, and the inevitable margin of error in the historian's judgment place upon even the most conscientious efforts to understand a past age, I have tried in the following pages to present a faithful delineation of one of the most conspicuous figures in American political life in the last half of the nineteenth century. I have approached the man *sine ira ac studio*, seeking neither to establish nor to demolish any preconceived thesis of his merit or demerit, and equally removed from the solicitation to hagiography or denunciation. By most of his biographers James G. Blaine has been portrayed either as a corrupt politician whose public rascality was partially redeemed by amiable traits of geniality, generosity and domestic fidelity, or as a paragon of virtue pursued by the lying slanders of jealous detractors. Both of these interpretations reveal the bias of their authors. And both are false.

With the passing of the issues which were fought over with such heat in the decades following the Civil War, it is possible to get a much bet-

PREFACE

ter perspective on the life of Blaine. While far less important men have been the subject of careful research and elaborate portrayal by scholars in recent years, only one biography of Blaine has appeared in more than a quarter of a century—and that one (Charles Edward Russell's *Blaine of Maine,* 1925) less a careful, dispassionate estimate of the man in his times than a journalistic portrayal. It is surely time that the statesman who was the idol of millions of the American people, the acknowledged head of his party for a quarter of a century and in five successive national Republican conventions a contestant for the nomination to the presidency of the United States should be recalled to the memory of a generation which preserves only an astonishingly meager knowledge of his life and work.

It would be impossible for me to acknowledge in detail the help and counsel which I have received from colleagues, friends and strangers in the preparation of this biography. Some instances of my indebtedness appear in the footnotes. While asking many who have answered my queries or have volunteered valuable information to accept this "blanket" acknowledgment of their kindness, I must record my special gratitude to a few upon whom I have called for special favors: first of all to Blaine's daughters, Mrs. Walter Damrosch and Mrs. Harriet Blaine Beale, who put at my disposal hundreds of letters and other valuable manuscript material without which my book could hardly have been written. Further, I owe thanks to Blaine's two secretaries, Thomas H. Sherman of Gorham, Maine (now past his 90th milestone) and Louis A. Dent of Washington; William Allen White of the Emporia (Kansas) *Gazette;* William Gorham Rice of Albany; Rowland B. Mahany of Washington; P. Tecumseh Sherman of New York; Mrs. Benjamin Harrison of New York; Professor George F. Howe of the University of Cincinnati; Professor A. T. Volwiler of Wittenberg College, Ohio; Professor Allan Nevins of Columbia University, New York; Professor J. Franklin Jameson of the Manuscripts Division of the Library of Congress and his assistants; and the ever obliging staffs of the Archives of the State Department at Washington, the American Chancellery at London, the Maine Historical Society and the Libraries of Columbia and Harvard Universities.

DAVID SAVILLE MUZZEY

Columbia University, July, 1934

TABLE OF CONTENTS

TABLE OF CONTENTS

TABLE OF CONTENTS

ILLUSTRATIONS

JAMES G. BLAINE
A POLITICAL IDOL OF OTHER DAYS

THE ADMONITION of the genial Autocrat of the Breakfast Table that a man should exercise care in the selection of his ancestors was evidently heeded by James G. Blaine; for he came of five generations of emigrants to the New World of that happy mixture of Scotch and Irish stock in which the Caledonian's inexorable granite of conviction was tempered with the entreatable amiability of the Celt—the stock which has contributed to our richly composite American society many a leader of distinction, including Jackson, Calhoun, Grant, and McKinley.

The first of the Blaines, James by name, came over from Londonderry, Ireland, in 1745, and settled at Donegal, Westmoreland County, Pennsylvania, removing later to Toboyne, Cumberland, on the banks of the Juniata. His great-great-grandson, the subject of this biography, seems not to have had an absorbing interest in his more remote ancestors. However, toward the end of his life, when he was Secretary of State in Harrison's Cabinet, he happened to mention to a Scotchman who had called on him for an introduction to Secretary Noble of the Interior, "in connection with a matter then pending before the Land Office in Washington," that he believed that his forebears had come from Ayrshire. On his return to the old country, this visitor, "thinking that it might possibly interest Mr. Blaine to know something about" these putative Scotch ancestors, had the records of the various parishes in Ayrshire searched, but "found no record of any entry of the name of Blaine under any spelling," though the name of MacBlaine was "somewhat frequent in the district of Galloway." He enclosed in his letter to Blaine from Edinburgh, Sept. 11, 1890, a note furnished by the antiquarian who had made the search, to the effect that the muniments of the Burgh of Irvine contained a charter dated August 18, 1477, in which John Blaine was mentioned as the owner of a tenement; that a Mr. Blaine appeared as the proprietor of lands in the shire of Wigmore in a valuation of 1667; and that Patrick Blaine was listed in McKerlie's *Galloway Families* as the recipient, in the sixteenth century, of a grant by the Countess of Moray of "the half of the ten merk

1

lands of Meikle Wig," whatever that may mean. But that the busy Secretary of State could have been much interested in these sporadic references to his supposititious forebears is difficult to believe.

The first James Blaine brought with him from Londonderry in 1745 a four year old son Ephraim, who was destined to play an important rôle not only in the Province of Pennsylvania but also in the history of the American colonies as a whole. As a stripling he bore arms in the French and Indian War, and when the redoubtable Ottawa chieftain Pontiac in the summer of 1763 hurled his painted warriors against the frontier posts from Detroit to Erie, in a last desperate effort to preserve the barbarism of the forest against the encroaching tide of civilization, Ephraim Blaine was busy from the Susquehanna to the Monongahela stiffening the courage of the Pennsylvania settlements. The danger past, he settled in Carlisle, married Rebecca Galbraith of the same sturdy stock as his own, and, taking advantage of Governor Penn's proclamation reopening the Indian trade, speedily amassed a considerable fortune by sending his pack-trains over the rude trails of western Pennsylvania with which he had become so familiar during the distressful years of the Indian raids. When the quarrel with the mother country came to its crisis, he was already one of the most influential citizens of Pennsylvania. He embraced the American cause with ardor, playing a conspicuous part in the meeting of the patriots of Cumberland County, on July 12, 1774, to register an indignant protest against the closing of the port of Boston, and serving on the Committee of Correspondence there organized "to coöperate in every measure conducing to the welfare of British America." He was ready to serve on the battlefield too, as colonel of a battalion of Cumberland militia; but his complete knowledge of the routes and resources of the Province marked him for the no less important service of supplying the troops with food and drink. The Continental Congress appointed him Commissary of Provisions in the spring of 1776, promoted him four months later to the post of Deputy Commissary of Purchases, and, as a reward for his indefatigable exertions to keep the wolf of starvation from the doors of the huts of Valley Forge, made him, at the request of Washington himself, Commissioner General of Purchases for the Northern Department. To the duties of this exacting office Colonel Blaine devoted not only his executive talents and his unrivaled knowledge of the country's sources of supply, but also his private credit, again and again advancing from his own full purse the sums necessary to secure the delivery of the flour, beef, pork, and spirits which his insistent importunity had obtained from the reluctant farmers. His travels carried him from New England to North Carolina, and his forthright correspondence is punctuated with sentiments of dutiful independence toward his superiors and scathing denunciations of the least sign of incompetence or malfeasance in his deputies and agents. He was rewarded with the gratitude which is proverbial in republics. As late as the Administration of President Monroe, his sons James and Robert were still pressing their ineffectual claims upon Congress for the large sums of money which he had advanced from the family fortune.

After the war Colonel Blaine returned to his home in Carlisle and resumed his extensive business in land speculation, brokerage, and trade, eschewing the political career which might have taken him to Philadelphia as a member of the Congress or of the State legislature.[1] He grew gracefully and affluently into a middle-aged patriarch, delighting in gathering his relatives about him and providing his sons and daughters-in-law with lands and houses. When President Washington rode with Hamilton at the head of the militia levies to put down the Whisky Rebellion in 1794, it was at Colonel Blaine's home in Carlisle that he was sumptuously entertained—and decided that it was unnecessary for him to proceed farther with the troops. The strong friendship formed between Blaine and Washington during the dark winter of Valley Forge remained unbroken until Washington's death in 1799. Colonel Blaine lived five years longer.

No other ancestor of James G. Blaine attained such emience or deserved so well of his country as this great-grandfather. A stout file of cards in the catalogue of the Division of Manuscripts of the Library of Congress, under the rubric Ephraim Blaine, testifies to the importance of his public papers. His oldest son James, after a sojourn in France, returned to America at the age of seventeen, with the reputation, according to the Chief Justice of the Province, of being "among the most accomplished and finest looking gentlemen of Pennsylvania." Neither the attractions of the boulevards of Bordeaux, however, nor the more somber rectangular gayety of Franklin's Philadelphia could wean him from the love of the sparkling rivers and the broad farms, meadows and

[1] The capital of Pennsylvania was not moved to Harrisburg until 1812.

woodlands of the western country. He settled at Carlisle and enlarged the family fortune by steady acquisitions of land and wider ambits of trade. In 1793 he came back from a business trip to New Orleans to experience the swift vicissitudes of sorrow and joy. His charming young bride, Jane Hoge, had died during his absence, and in his anguish over her grave he moaned that life for him too was over. But the resiliency of twenty-seven years is proof against the most cruel blows of fate. The disconsolate widower recovered his interest in life with unexpected and perhaps a bit humiliating promptness. He entered with zest into the festivities attendant upon his father's entertainment of President Washington in 1794, and next year married the presiding hostess of these festivities, his accomplished cousin Margaret Lyon, thereby introducing a third strain of Scotch-Irish blood into the inheritance of the family. For Margaret was the granddaughter of Samuel Lyon, who, like James Blaine and James Galbraith, had come from the Scotch colony of Ulster to the Pennsylvania wilderness. Young James Blaine also continued another tradition of the family by moving westward, settling successively at Brownsville on the Monongahela, at Sewickly a few miles south of Pittsburgh, and at Washington, the first town in America named for George Washington.

Ephraim Lyon Blaine, the son of James, had the advantage of an education at Washington College, the first of the many educational institutions named after the great President, and the most appropriately named, since a part of the land on which it was situated was donated by Washington himself. After enjoying a European trip, like his father, and studying law in the office of a Mr. Watts, Ephraim was admitted to the bar soon after the family moved from Carlisle. The attraction of business, however, proved stronger than the lure of the law or of politics, to which the law was then as now the most frequent way of entrance. He settled at Sewickly to contribute the talents of a fourth generation to the conservation and enlargement of the family patrimony.

While the Blaines were thus consolidating their interests and extending their influence over Pennsylvania from the Susquehanna to the western border, still another family from Ulster was establishing itself in the far corner of the State. Neal Gillespie, a rare combination of shrewd judgment and adventurous enterprise, brought his bride from old Donegal to this land of promise soon after the Revolutionary War, and, journeying across the State of Pennsylvania, fixed his desire upon

an ample farm known as Indian Hill, on the western bank of the Monongahela, where Michael Cresap's ferry crossed the river from Redstone
Old Fort on Braddock's Road. The deed conveying the land from the
heirs of "Indian Peter" to Neal Gillespie was signed in January, 1787,
four months before the Convention met at Philadelphia to frame the
Constitution of the United States. Redstone Old Fort, renamed Brownsville, had already become a thriving center of trade. Here the long
overland route from Baltimore via Fort Cumberland reached the "western waters," and the far longer journey down the Monongahela, the
Ohio and the Mississippi, by the cumbrous flatboat or ark, began. The
younger Neal Gillespie, inheriting his father's winning personality as
well as his business ability, built up a prosperous trade with New Orleans, married a Virginia belle, and brought up a talented family at
Indian Hill. The oldest son John, a distinguished scholar, died in his
early thirties, leaving a daughter who became a mother superior (Mother
Angela) of the Sisters of the Holy Cross and the author of a series of
Catholic textbooks. Another son was educated for the priesthood, but
took his vows at the altar of matrimony instead, leaving it to his son to
enter holy orders and become a professor at the Catholic University of
Notre Dame. In Neal Gillespie's daughter Maria were united the ex-
quisite beauty of face and sweetness of character of her Virginia mother
and the good judgment and genial practicality of her paternal ancestors.

In the summer of 1820 Ephraim Lyon Blaine drove the fifty miles of
forest-lined road from Sewickly to West Brownsville to wed Maria
Gillespie at the "palace" which her grandfather had built on Indian
Hill. The Rev. Father Maguire came down from Pittsburgh to perform
the ceremony. For while the Blaines had clung (with diminishing devotion, it must be confessed) to the stern Presbyterian creed of the great
majority of the Scotch-Irish immigrants, the Gillespies were Roman
Catholics. This divergence of religious belief, however, was never allowed to disturb the harmonious relations between husband and wife.
Neither had the slightest trace of intolerance or bigotry, and the children who came in rapid succession grew up in the happy unconscious-
ness of confessional strife. By an accommodation quite commonly
practiced at the time, the boys followed the father's religion and the
girls the mother's. Years later, when one boy had attained great eminence in public life, his political enemies of both creeds attempted to
discredit him by accusations of religious treachery. Bigoted Protestants,

led by Bishop Haven of the Methodist Church, charged him with being a "crypto-Catholic," and bigoted Catholics branded him as an "apostate." The Baltimore *Catholic Mirror*, for example, in an editorial of January 29, 1876, when Blaine was the most prominent candidate for the approaching presidential nomination, declared that "Squire (Ephraim Lyon) Blaine became a convert to the religious faith of his wife and lived and died a firm believer in it"; that "all the children were raised as Catholics"; that James G. Blaine "emigrated from his family home shortly after his majority" to attend Washington College, "where his religion was not popular and he changed it . . . for the sake of politic preferment and an evanescent popularity." Every phrase of this statement is false, except the bare fact that Blaine went to Washington College. The editorial closes with the pious hope that "Mr. Blaine may not, like Mr. Lincoln, meet with a sudden death, but that God, in His infinite mercy, may give him the grace to repent of his apostacy before his demise."

Shortly before the tenth anniversary of their marriage, Ephraim Lyon and Maria Gillespie Blaine left Sewickly with their four children to return to the wife's home at Indian Hill, West Brownsville. And here, on the last day of January, 1830, James Gillespie Blaine was born.

One need not be a disciple of the extreme school of eugenists to recognize the immense influence which the cumulative force of tastes, habits, occupations and traditions, followed for a number of generations, must exercise upon the character of any man, especially when the family has been molded by the relatively homogeneous culture of the frontier, rather than exposed to the distracting solicitations of our rootless urban life. Although the subject of this biography, like Abraham Lincoln—or, for that matter, like any leader in history—developed talents which could be neither predicted nor explained on the ground of heredity, he nevertheless showed many a trait of his Pennsylvania ancestors. A readiness to shift his residence to incur new hazards of fortune was one such trait. From the first James down, there was not a Blaine who continued to live in the place of his birth and early childhood. The family migrated in successive stages across the Colony and State of Pennsylvania, founding homes in Donegal, Conestoga, Carlisle, Sewickly, Brownsville and Washington. Lancaster, Westmoreland, Alleghany and Washington counties felt the imprint of their personalities. Moreover, in this progressive invasion of the Pennsylvania frontier, they had a keen eye for the location and development of choice tracts of land as well as a flair for the strategic points for their real estate transactions and trading ventures. A goodly share of the spirit and methods of the "promoter" entered into the inheritance of James G. Blaine. Neither the exacting demands of political leadership nor the burdens of high office, nor even the menace of exposure to the obloquy which attaches to the statesman who is suspected of using his public influence to advance his private interests, could wean him from the lure of business schemes and speculations. He acquired large interests in iron and coal mines in Pennsylvania and West Virginia; he entered enthusiastically, and persuaded his friends to enter, into roseate but somewhat risky enterprises for the financing of Western railroad construction; he cultivated the friendship of the great bankers and promoters, like the Cookes, from whom he sought and to whom he gave advice which derived an enhanced value from the political influence which he wielded at Washington. What bitter discomfiture was caused him by this inheritance of the lure of the market place, later pages will show. It was a veritable shirt of Nessus for him, consuming some of his fondest hopes in its tormenting, indivestible grasp.

A happier legacy bequeathed to Blaine by his Pennsylvania ancestors was a genial and comprehensive hospitality. He would have been in his element entertaining President Washington at Carlisle or doing the convivial honors at Neal Gillespie's "palace" on Indian Hill. He was a born host. Among his papers are carefully checked lists of frequent dinner parties, with diagrams of the seating arrangements. Mrs. Blaine's delightful letters, published by her daughter Mrs. Harriet Blaine Beale, tell how she had to be ready always to put on extra plates for the guests her husband might bring home for luncheon or dinner, and reveal the tireless enthusiasm with which he followed every detail of the construction of his Washington mansion at Dupont Circle and his villa at Bar Harbor, designed not only to provide room for his growing family, but also to furnish ample entertainment for his guests. "You may have the land," wrote his friend W. W. Phelps, from whom he obtained the Washington site, "provided you build an ample dining room." To partake of good cheer was the least of the joys of sitting at his table. Interesting anecdotes, apposite historical information, illuminating political comment, brilliant repartee flowed from his inexhaustible store of wit and memory; and the humdrum trivialities of conversation were silenced in willing deference to the unobtrusive dominance of the master host.

But had Blaine been nothing more than an epitome of his ancestors, he would never have emerged from the comparative obscurity of their provincial careers. He was the first of his family to realize fully the value of a higher education. To be sure, his father had graduated from Washington College and served his apprenticeship in a law office. But he was not a scholar in the true sense of the word. The library was less attractive to him than the Squire's office. He did not feel

> The thirst to know and understand,
> The large and liberal discontent

which impelled his son to explore varied fields of learning with unquenchable curiosity. Few of our public men have equaled James G. Blaine in the amplitude and accuracy of their knowledge of European and American history, or in the skill to use that knowledge effectively in political debate and formal treatise. Nor is it easy to find in the literary remains of our statesmen passages to compare in depth of sentiment, beauty of imagery, and purity of diction with the closing paragraph of Blaine's eulogy of President Garfield. The two volumes of his *Twenty Years of Congress*, composed in the intervals between absorbing executive duties, bear witness to the high place he might have occupied in American historiography had he devoted himself wholly to that profession.

Not even the delightful labors of scholarship, however, could tempt Blaine to forsake the one great and dominant pursuit of his life—a political career. In this ambition, too, as in his love of learning, he shows a decided departure from the traditions of his ancestors. We have seen how persistently they shunned any reward of political office for their service in war or in the development of the Pennsylvania frontier. Blaine's father did occupy for a few years the modest position of prothonotary (a pretentious Byzantine word meaning "chief clerk") of Washington County, but that trifling deviation into office was the exception to the rule of family abstention from politics.

Politics, however, was the very breath of life for James G. Blaine. He entered with equal zeal into a contest for a seat in the Maine legislature or in the White House. He canvassed votes as a miser counts his gold pieces. Year after year his predictions of the outcome of the elections in Maine were confirmed with uncanny accuracy. A remarkable memory for facts, faces, names and figures was an invaluable asset in his political popularity. Many a story is told of his instant greeting by name of an acquaintance whom he had not met for years. When reference was once made in a dinner conversation to the make-up of Congress at the beginning of President Taylor's Administration, it is said that he recited the entire roll of the Senate without a slip. Though he gave and took hard knocks in the arena of debate, he neither inspired nor cherished resentments. With the exception of the imperious Roscoe Conkling, it is doubtful whether any of his colleagues in Congress allowed a passage at arms on the floor to harden into a personal enmity. Moreover, few of our public men have risen to political leadership with so little adventitious aid. Representing a comparatively insignificant State, he had no extensive patronage at his disposal, nor could he exploit, like a Conkling or a Platt in New York or a Cameron or a Quay in Pennsylvania, the power of a great political machine. Of the five Republican Presidents who occupied the White House between the inauguration of Grant in 1869 and his own death in 1893, he enjoyed the full confidence and friendship of only one—and that one, Garfield, was laid low by an assassin's bullet four months after his inauguration. In a word, Blaine owed his commanding position in the Republican Party not to the support of the political organization, but to the intellectual talents and ingratiating amiability with which he appealed to the imagination and affection of the masses of the people.

Though he left his Pennsylvania home before his eighteenth birthday, to return only for an occasional visit to look after business affairs or to appear as an honored guest at the graduating exercises of his *alma mater*, Blaine always kept an affection for his native State. Nor did Pennsylvania ever quite wholly relinquish him to his adopted State of Maine. The Republican State Convention at Harrisburg, in August, 1891, recorded its pride in "the brilliant administration of the State Department by one of Pennsylvania's native sons, whose superb diplomacy has electrified the hearts of all Americans"; and, while deeming it too early to "express the hope that the Republican National Convention of 1892 may place him in unanimous nomination for the Presidency," took occasion "to reaffirm the loyalty and devotion of the Republicans of Pennsylvania to her most distinguished son, James G. Blaine." [1]

[1] New York *World*, Aug. 20, 1891.

10   JAMES G. BLAINE

The attachment on Blaine's part, however, was rather retrospective. "You and I," he wrote to a compatriot in later life, "are the descendants of five generations of Scotch-Irish ancestry." But of his contemporary relatives we hear little. The large family was scattered, and Blaine seems not to have followed the fortunes of his brothers and sisters with much interest. In 1859 he wrote to a sister: "You and Ma could not do me a greater favor than to send me all your family letters from Lancaster, Washington and wherever else you may think worth while. I am so far out of the circle of my own kith and kin that I hear no more of them directly than though I was in Siberia." [1] Occasionally a letter turns up from a relative like his "old schoolmate and cousin," John Gillespie, who writes from Texas in 1870 to ask aid in the removal of his political disabilities; [2] or from Mrs. Minor of Louisiana, "a grand-daughter of Sarah Blaine," who pleads for a loan from Congress in 1873, for the rehabilitation of the cotton industry; [3] or a quaintly pious and mis-spelled letter from his "dear friend and kinsman," President John H. Ewing of Washington and Jefferson College, thanking him for a dona-tion of a thousand dollars (1874), and reiterating the hope that his many warm friends in the little college town might soon have the pleas-ure of welcoming him and his "lady," who, the gallant old gentleman thinks, "would do the honors of the White House with much credit." [4] Blaine's mother lived to see him rise to the high position of Speaker of the House of Representatives. Her death in 1871 severed the last tie that bound him to the homeland of the Galbraiths, Blaines, Lyons and Gillespies, and thenceforth there remained only the impressions of the early years in his retentive memory and the impress of the family heri-tage upon his receptive character.

[1] Quoted in Gail Hamilton's *Biography of James G. Blaine*, p. 133.
[2] John Gillespie to Blaine, Dec. 27, 1870.
[3] Mrs. R. A. Minor to Blaine, Dec. 10, 1873.
[4] John H. Ewing to Blaine, May 4, 1875.

Genealogical Table

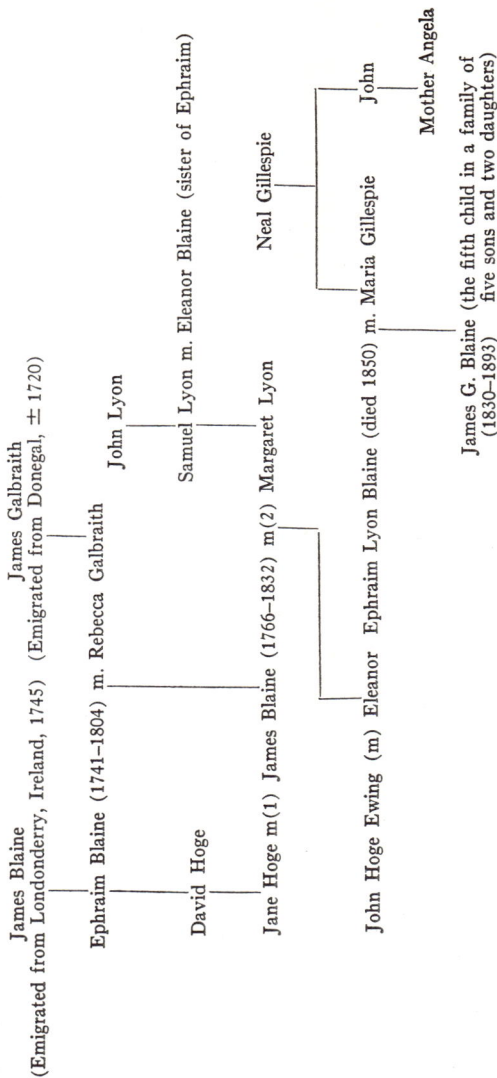

James Blaine
(Emigrated from Londonderry, Ireland, 1745)

James Galbraith
(Emigrated from Donegal, ± 1720)

Ephraim Blaine (1741–1804) m. Rebecca Galbraith

John Lyon

Samuel Lyon m. Eleanor Blaine (sister of Ephraim)

David Hoge

Jane Hoge m(1) James Blaine (1766–1832) m(2) Margaret Lyon

Neal Gillespie

John Hoge Ewing (m) Eleanor Ephraim Lyon Blaine (died 1850) m. Maria Gillespie

James G. Blaine (the fifth child in a family of
(1830–1893) five sons and two daughters)

John

Mother Angela

Chapter II   The Formative Years (1830–1854)

IT WAS a carefree, sun-filled childhood that the boy "Jim" Blaine lived with his brothers and sisters and cousins on the old Gillespie farm on the banks of the Monongahela. The family was harmonious and its fortunes equally removed from the affluence which tempts to idle self-indulgence and the poverty which casts a shadow of premature responsibility over the spirit of youth. There was nothing precocious about the lad, as an early omen of genius. He was seven years old when he learned to read, and it was not hard then to lure him from his books for a game or a swim or a berrying party. Both the time and the place of his birth had a marked influence on his early years. The first decade of his life coincided almost exactly with the "reign" of Andrew Jackson. It was the period of the exciting controversy over nullification in South Carolina, the slaughter of "Nick Biddle's monster" the National Bank, the Specie Circular and the collapse of the pet banks, the devastating panic which put an end to the fictitious prosperity based on speculative paper values. It was the period when Clay and Webster rallied the various forces of opposition to the "tyranny" of "King Andrew the First," and organized them into the new party which adopted the old remonstrant name of Whig. The Whigs stood for the "rescue" of the Constitution of the fathers by the subordination of the executive power to the will of the representatives of the people and the States in House and Senate. They advocated a national bank to stabilize the currency and guarantee commercial honor by sound methods of finance. They favored a high tariff for the protection of American industry and the upbuilding of an extensive consumers' market through the purchasing power of generous wages. They approved the expenditure of national funds for the development of roads, rivers and canals to facilitate the settlement of the West and the transportation of its produce to the Eastern markets and seaports. This "American System," declared Clay, would bind the sections of the country together by ties of mutual benefit, and increase the devotion of each to the common welfare of all.

The Blaines and the Gillespies, as befitted the descendants of Pennsylvania pioneers, were ardent followers of Henry Clay. Young James must

12

have heard his father and his Uncle William engage in many an argument with the Locofocos in defense of the American System, or have listened attentively when they read with triumphant comment the report of the senatorial onslaught of their hero upon the "military chieftain in the White House." At ten the boy was a dyed-in-the-wool Whig, and incidentally began his long career as a political campaigner. It was the year of the boisterous Whig campaign to seat William Henry Harrison in the White House in the place of Van Buren. James had spent the winter and spring in Lancaster, Ohio, visiting Hugh and Tom Ewing, whose mother was his own mother's cousin, and whose father, Thomas Ewing, had been United States Senator from Ohio (1831–1836) and was to be a member of the Cabinets of the two Whig Presidents, Harrison and Taylor.[1] The three boys were driving from Lancaster to Columbus when they passed a flagpole from which the banner of Van Buren was fluttering. James immediately jumped up in his seat and saluted the obnoxious emblem with his thumb to his nose. Repeating the unseemly gesture on the way back, against the warning of Hugh, he was promptly ejected from the buggy and forced to trudge several miles across the fields to the home of the nearest relative. But he never revised his opinion of the Democrats.

Though West Brownsville was as insignificant a town as Bethlehem Ephrata of the Scriptures, its situation brought it into touch with one of the liveliest currents of American life. For it lay on the route of the great National Road, which had been built over the grass-grown traces of the "narrow swath of a road cut through the darkling Alleghanies" by Braddock's axmen half a century before; which, in turn, followed the old Indian trail of Necomalin that Washington had used when he carried Governor Dinwiddie's warning to the French forts on the Alleghany River in 1753. As Braddock's Road was the first thrust of the British attack to pierce the French encirclement which would have confined the English colonies to the narrow strip between the Alleghenies and the Atlantic, so the National Road was the first of the great high-

[1] It is impossible to resist recording the striking parallel between Ewing's relations to these two Whig Presidents and Blaine's relations to two Republican Presidents exactly forty years later. In 1841 Ewing was appointed Secretary of the Treasury by Harrison; in 1881 Blaine was appointed Secretary of State by Garfield. Harrison died and Garfield was assassinated soon after their respective Administrations were installed, and in the reorganizations of the Cabinets both Ewing and Blaine were retired to private life. Ewing was made Secretary of the Interior by Taylor in 1849; Blaine was again made Secretary of State by the second Harrison in 1889. Ewing left his second Cabinet office after two years of service, and Blaine his after three.

ways by which the new West was opened up to the stream of American migration. Altogether, the hundred mile stretch between Will's Creek (Fort Cumberland) and the Monongahela, connecting the Potomac with the "western waters," was the most important road in American history. Over it went an endless succession of wagons and coaches, carrying goods and passengers out to furnish the new States of the Ohio Valley. It was not uncommon to see a score or more of the great blue-bodied, red-wheeled Conestoga wagons standing in the courtyard of one of the numerous inns that lined the road.

The year of Blaine's birth his father became one of the incorporators of a company to build a bridge over the Monongahela to take the place of Neal Gillespie's ferry between the Brownsvilles. Naturally, the boy James shared the village excitement when the "June Bug" or the "Pioneer" or the "Monkey Box" came dashing down the Brownsville hill to the bridge, proud of making its schedule to the minute. And what distinguished Senator or Cabinet officer or even President himself might not be aboard, on his way to a new session of Congress at Washington! Clay, Jackson, Polk, Harrison, Corwin, Ewing, Crittenden, Bell and a host of other notables from the trans-Allegheny country were frequent travelers over the National Road; and it is certain that Blaine's boyish interest in politics was stimulated by the noted men who came and went before his wide-open eyes.

In 1842 Ephraim Lyon Blaine took his family westward on the same road to the town of Washington, there to assume his office of prothonotary of Washington County. And in 1843 James, at the age of thirteen, entered Washington and Jefferson College, from which he graduated four years later as the youngest member of what the authorities were pleased to call "a large and respectable class of thirty-three." The advantages offered to the student at Washington and Jefferson were not exceptional. The small faculty was undistinguished and the curriculum was heavily weighted, as in small denominational colleges generally, on the side of rhetoric, the ancient languages and moral philosophy. Of history and political science there was hardly more than a smattering. Psychology was a minor branch of metaphysics, and the social studies which bulk so largely in a modern curriculum figured not at all. As for the laboratory sciences, biological or physical, poverty of equipment in both material facilities and professorial training made impossible any respectable results. Mathematics remained a purely formal drill.

In spite of his youth Blaine found no difficulty in meeting the modest requirements for the bachelor's degree and in sharing the highest honors with two of his classmates. On his graduation the president and several members of the faculty signed a rather fulsome testimonial to his general proficiency, to serve as a recommendation for a teaching position. But if any of his teachers won his lasting gratitude, by virtue of sympathetic personal inspiration or stimulating professional guidance, the records fail to show it. In his correspondence after leaving college there is no mention of professors or courses. It was the association with his fellow students that had interested him. His letters to "Countee" Clark or "Tom" Searight recall the pranks, the parties and the heated political discussions of their college days. His attitude was like that of the average "old grad"—an ardent but somewhat unfocused attachment to the "dear old college" where he had spent "four glorious years" the like of which he "would never see again."

There is evidence, too, that Blaine in his college days was already developing the deep but unobtrusive interest in theology which he kept all his life; though there is no sign of the adolescent religious crisis so frequent in more introspective youth. Dr. James King, who had been on the faculty of Washington and Jefferson College thirty years before, wrote in the Pittsburgh *Gazette* of January 19, 1876, that Blaine from his entrance to his graduation "was a constant attendant upon the services of the Presbyterian Church, which had and still has the exclusive control of the college." But regularity in attendance, compulsory as it was, was no guarantee of regularity in doctrine. The inquisitive, disputatious young student was already speculating on the fundamental tenets of the orthodox faith. "What are your views now on the Trinity?" his uncle William Gillespie, himself a gloved iconoclast, wrote to Blaine at the close of his junior year; "are they as wild and infidel like they were when we conversed upon the subject?" And a few years later his devoted mother, in a Christmas letter, ventured an apologetic hope to see him "a practical Christian." "You haven't told me how you spend your Sunday. Not, I fear, as I wish, attending church. But this, Jim, is an unpleasant subject and one you think I have no right to speak of." [1] Whether he conquered his religious doubts or suppressed them, Blaine did become a "practical Christian" ten years after leaving college, when

[1] Gail Hamilton, *Biography of James G. Blaine,* p. 96.

he joined the Congregational Church at Augusta, Maine, and even taught a Bible class for a season. He was never a conspicuous pillar of the church, however, nor was there a trace of proselytizing zeal in his nature. Religion he regarded as a personal affair between man and his Maker. He was always averse to any display of religion, and especially to the least exploitation of religious sectarianism in politics.[1]

While in college Blaine decided on a legal career and planned to spend two postgraduate years at the Yale Law School, but he had to forego his hopes for a season. The family finances were not in the best of conditions when he finished his college course. Ephraim Lyon Blaine had inherited his forebears' hospitable and open-handed generosity to a greater degree than their business acumen. Not only did he "make the money fly," as his neighbors said, but he yielded to the besetting temptation of kind-hearted men of means to become surety for the financial obligations of importunate friends. Though somewhat reduced in fortune, he was able and willing to send James to Yale, but the young man decided that he would be asking more than his fair share of the family income by prolonging the expense of his education another two years. So, instead of traveling eastward to study law under the quiet elms of New Haven, he turned his steps westward in the autumn of 1847, to find such employment as fortune had in store for him.

Along the National Road and down the Ohio he went, visiting Cincinnati, Maysville, Louisville and Lexington, Kentucky. At the latter place, on a rainy November day, he sat entranced, "pencil and note-book in hand," at the feet of his hero Henry Clay, listening to the great Whig statesman's denunciation of the Mexican War in particular, and of the fortune-favored policy of his successful rival for the presidency, James K. Polk, in general. At Lexington also Blaine read in a newspaper of a vacancy on the faculty of the Western Military Institute at Georgetown, about a dozen miles to the south. He immediately hired a horse and buggy, drove down to Georgetown to make personal application, and was immediately accepted.

[1] When the religious issue was raised in connection with his candidacy for the presidential nomination in 1876, Blaine wrote to a friend: "My ancestors on my father's side were, as you know always identified with the Presbyterian Church. . . . But I will never consent to make any public declaration on the subject, and for two reasons: First, because I abhor the introduction of anything that looks like a religious test or qualification for office in a republic where perfect freedom of conscience is the birthright of every citizen; and, second, because my mother was a devoted Catholic. I would not for a thousand presidencies speak a disrespectful word of my mother's religion." Chas. W. Balestier, *James G. Blaine*, p. 6.

In January, 1848, a few weeks before his eighteenth birthday, "Professor" Blaine entered upon his duties as a teacher of mathematics and the ancient languages. The Institute was patterned on the military college at Lexington, Va., and had several graduates of the older institution on its faculty. Blaine's academic work was not burdensome, for the classes in Vergil, Cicero and algebra were on the level of the upper forms of a preparatory school of today. From the meager records of his three and a half years at Georgetown that have come down to us, we can gather that he was a successful teacher and a popular personality with the students, faculty, and citizens of the town. Though many cadets were old enough to be sitting beside him as classmates rather than under him as students, their respect for his dignity and ability needed no reinforcement from the military discipline of the institution; while the same qualities commanded the cordial recognition of equality by the older members of the faculty. For example, he had been in the Institute only six months when he was delegated by his colleagues to convey the following invitation to the Rev. Robert J. Breckenridge of Lexington, whom he had once heard preach:

Saturday, July 1st, (1848)

Dr. R. J. Breckenridge,
Dear Sir:

A month or two since, the Literary Society of our Military School resolved to have an address delivered to them at the close of the present session. As we had not yet aspired to any great standing, we thought it more becoming to invite a townsman, and accordingly the Reverend Mr Baird was selected. He has been compelled (on account of indisposition) to decline; and we are consequently without anyone to address us. At this late hour it occurred to us that you would probably consent to deliver us a lecture upon the subject of the Common Schools, as you are the General Superintendent. The Georgetown people have been long expecting an address from you upon this subject, and I think there could be no time more favorable than the present. I am instructed to tender you the invitation in behalf of the Faculty and the Literary Society of the Military Academy, and the citizens of the town.

We would offer you an apology for so late a notice, but I am well aware that you require no time to prepare for such an occasion. Would you be kind enough to reply to this this evening, and I will instruct the omnibus driver to call for your note tomorrow morning. You can designate the hour that would best suit you, forenoon, afternoon, or evening. We can accommodate our other exercises to your convenience. We will have a conveyance ready for you at whatever time you wish to start.

In the hope, sir, that you will consent to favor us this time, I remain most respectfully,

Your obedient servant,
J. G. Blaine.[1]

That this mature-minded "professor" of eighteen was able at the same time to sympathize fully with the spirit of youth, we learn from a letter written in the midst of the presidential campaign of 1884 by Wm. M. Johnson, city engineer of Dallas, Texas, and a graduate of the class of 1847 of the Western Military Institute. Mr. Johnson asks Blaine if he remembers being roused by sounds of revelry one night and coming to the door of a student's room to find who was breaking the rules of the Institute. He discovered two gentlemen beyond his jurisdiction seated at a table evidently spread for four. At their invitation he partook of the excellent food and wine, and bade them a courteous good-night without taking the slightest notice of the protruding boots of the two students who had sought a hasty refuge under the bed.

Blaine's genial adaptation to the social customs of the communities with whom his lot was cast is noticeable even in these early years at Georgetown. He always thought that he was attached to places with an undying devotion, but it was people that really captured his sympathies. He was at home wherever he lived because he quickly appraised the minds of his fellow citizens, for hearty coöperation in case of agreement and honorable battle in case of opposition. His disposition was incurably social. So, in spite of his protestations to one of his college mates soon after leaving Washington and Jefferson, "I never can nor shall I ever be anything else in feeling than a Pennsylvanian," we find him at the same time writing another college chum enthusiastic descriptions of the country and people (including the belles) of "old Kentucke," which would be "hard to beat." He was proud to be living in a place which could count within the radius of a few miles the homes of Clay, Crittenden, Bell, Breckenridge and R. M. Johnson. He eagerly anticipated attending the Constitutional Convention to be held at Frankfort in 1849, and speculated on the political opinions of the delegates, especially on the great issue of slavery. He thought that three fourths of the delegates at least would be opposed to emancipation, and wrote as though he rather agreed with them in combating the "mischief" which the agitation of

---

[1] This letter was kindly furnished to the author by Dr. J. Franklin Jameson, of the Library of Congress.

the Garrisonians was causing: "So the Abolitionists of the North may console themselves with the reflection that their ultra course has created this reaction (from Clay's policy) in the public pulse of Kentucky." [1] Indeed, his sympathy with the beat of the public pulse of Kentucky in 1849 caused him some embarrassment in later years, when he had made his home among the Abolitionists of the North and was himself a champion of their cause. Professor Parish of the University of California at Los Angeles tells the following amusing incident in his biography of Senator G. W. Jones of Iowa. The old ex-Senator visited Washington early in 1875, when Blaine was Speaker of the House, to secure the passage of a land bill in the interests of his State. He was instantly recognized by Blaine and introduced to a number of Congressmen standing near the Speaker's desk. "Do you not recall my having been introduced to you in 1850 by Mr. Clay at Blue Lick Springs, Kentucky?" asked the Speaker. "I educated your sons Charles and William at the Western Military Institute." "Well," replied the blunt old ex-Senator, "you played the Devil educating them, for you made two of them secessionists." Whereupon Speaker Blaine denied any such intention and promptly changed the subject. [2]

Satisfactorily as he performed his academic duties at Georgetown, it was not education but politics that absorbed Blaine's attention. His letters to college mates are filled with amazingly shrewd comments on the political situation in Pennsylvania, Kentucky and the nation at large. He correctly and regretfully assessed the decline of Clay's influence in Kentucky after his defeat by Polk in 1844, and analyzed the factors in the campaign of 1848 which convinced him of the certain election of General Taylor. He read the presidential messages and the reports of the heads of departments at Washington with all the eagerness that a modern youth in his late teens would devote to a magazine story or the sporting pages of the newspaper. He felt himself almost a participator in the stirring debates in Congress over the organization of the new territories taken from Mexico, the admission of California, and the parlous state of the Union revealed by the powerful speeches of Calhoun, Webster, Seward and Chase in the Senate. And once more he was permitted to thrill with admiration for his hero Henry Clay, when that aged statesman, his form racked with the ravages of consumption, re-

[1] Blaine to T. B. Searight, Apr. 8, 1849.
[2] John C. Parish, *George Wall Jones*. Iowa Biography Series, 1912, pp. 286–7.

turned to the Senate to urge mutual concession and reconciliation upon the rapidly diverging sections of the country by his great compromise program of 1850. He even thought for a moment, after the inauguration of Taylor in the spring of 1849, of applying for a clerkship in one of the departments at Washington, in order "to be at the center and see how the machinery of government worked." But the wise advice of his mother's cousin, Thomas Ewing, who had returned to the capital to enter Taylor's Cabinet, dissuaded him from this premature venture into practical politics. He was still like a ship carrying an immense spread of political sail, but lacking the necessary ballast of education and experience. Nevertheless, he had the voyage and the port already in mind. When he read that Robert C. Winthrop was elected to the Speakership of the House in December, 1849, he immediately announced himself as an eventual candidate for the position: a prophecy which was fulfilled just 22 years later, as he humorously wrote to a friend, "as a remarkable instance of faith, patience and despatch harmoniously combined."

At Millersburg, twenty miles from Georgetown, there was a "Female Seminary," as girls' schools were called in those days, presided over by Mrs. Johnson, the wife of the head of the Western Military Institute. Naturally, the relations between the two institutions were intimate, and the members of the faculties were well acquainted with one another. Two sisters, Caroline and Harriet Stanwood, were teachers at the Millersburg Seminary. The younger, Harriet, was older by two years than "Professor" Blaine, but not in looks or dignity of manner. Their friendship rapidly ripened into love, and on the last day of June, 1850, they were united in a marriage which was blessed by a perfect mutual devotion and understanding during the more than forty years of their life together. Mrs. Blaine's keen and educated mind enabled her not only to share her husband's problems but also to offer helpful criticism at times, while her gracious amiability and domestic efficiency made her a hostess equal to every social demand of his high public positions. Gamaliel Bradford in his volume entitled *Wives* has shown what an invaluable asset Mrs. Blaine was to her husband, although he is led by his obvious bias against the latter (see his sketch of Blaine in *Damaged Souls*) to set the wife's virtues in bright relief against the dark foil of the husband's faults.

The Stanwoods were of simon-pure New England stock. A Philip Stainwood is listed in the town records of Gloucester, Massachusetts, in 1654, as owning "four acres in Anasquam between Lobster and Goose Coves." His descendants, all marrying descendants of the mid-seventeenth century English immigrants, continued to live in Essex County until well into the nineteenth century. Jacob Stanwood, of the fifth generation from Philip, moved from Ipswich, Massachusetts, to Augusta in the new State of Maine, in 1822, and there Harriet, the fifth of his six daughters, was born. Jacob's sister Hannah was the mother of Mary Abigail Dodge. This cousin of Mrs. Blaine's made her winter home with the family in Washington, and from her intimate association of many years gathered the valuable material for her rather ponderous biography of Blaine, published under the pseudonym of "Gail Hamilton," two years after the statesman's death (1895). Daniel Stanwood, a nephew of Jacob's, followed his uncle from Ipswich to Augusta in 1825, and became the father of Edward Stanwood (1841–1922), the well-known author of *The History of the Presidency* and *The Tariff Controversies of the Nineteenth Century,* as well as of the shorter biography of Blaine in the American Statesmen Series. As a schoolboy in his early teens Edward remembered the visits of his second cousin Harriet's brilliant young husband to Augusta, and later told how the Philadelphia schoolmaster would make him stand between his knees while he quizzed him on his Latin lessons.[1]

Blaine had not abandoned but only postponed his purpose to study law when he renounced the idea of going to Yale in the autumn of 1847. We find him writing to Tom Searight in April, 1849: "I intend to commence the study of law regularly this summer. My preceptor will be Judge Robertson, one of the first lawyers of the State." [2] But evidently such time as the demands of the classroom left free he preferred to use driving the twenty miles to Millersburg to practice the *ars amatoria* rather than the dozen miles to Lexington to study the *ars aequi ac boni.* And we hear no more of Judge Robertson. Blaine's marriage in June, 1850, and his father's death the same month increased his sense of the need to be at the business of preparing for his chosen profession. The teaching position had been only a stop-gap. He could not go on indefinitely teaching quadratic equations and the orations of Cicero. Besides, complications arose in the management of the Institute which resulted in the resignation of Colonel Johnson and convinced the young pro-

[1] C. K. Bolton, "Memoire of Edward Stanwood," in the *Proceedings of the Massachusetts Historical Society,* December, 1923, p. 5.
[2] Quoted in Gail Hamilton, *Biography of James G. Blaine,* p. 96.

fessor that he had nothing more to give to the institution, even as it had nothing further to give him. He resigned at the close of the school year 1851.

His father's death had broken up the old Pennsylvania home, but the doors of the Stanwood house in Augusta were always open to the young couple. Thither they went on leaving Kentucky, and there their oldest child, Stanwood, was born. He should have been named Ephraim, to continue the family custom of a century of naming the eldest son after his grandfather; but the Hebrew names of the Old Testament worthies were beginning to sound queer by the middle of the nineteenth century, and no more Ephraims appeared in the Blaine family.

To support his wife and infant son, without at the same time sacrificing his hope of preparing for a legal career, Blaine now found what seemed to him an ideal opening. The Pennsylvania Institute for the Education of the Blind, at Philadelphia, wanted an instructor in English and literature. Blaine applied in person for the position, as he had done at Georgetown, and was selected out of a large number of competitors. The salary was considerably larger and the teaching hours fewer than at the Western Military Institute, and the city of Philadelphia offered adequate facilities in its law libraries. Mrs. Blaine accompanied her husband to the Quaker City and entered into his work with enthusiasm, often reading the English classics to groups of students in her home in evening meetings.

But again fortune barred Blaine's path to his chosen profession. The weekly Kennebec *Journal* had been established in Augusta in 1825 by Luther Severance and so effectively edited by him and his associates Eaton and Dorr for a quarter of a century that it had become the leading Whig newspaper in Maine. When Severance retired in 1850 the proprietors of the *Journal* were on the lookout for a suitable successor to assume the chief burden of editorship. Blaine was returning from his vacation in Augusta, late in August of 1853, to resume his classroom work and his legal reading in Philadelphia, when he was joined on the train by John Dorr, and, to his surprise, was invited to move to Augusta and assume editorial charge of the Kennebec *Journal*. The proposal, sudden as it was to him, had been carefully considered by Mr. Dorr and his associates. They had come to know Blaine during his frequent visits to Augusta and to appreciate his brilliant qualities. He lacked journalistic experience, to be sure, but he was genial in character, persuasive in argument, versed in politics and ardent in his devotion to the Whig Party and principles. There seems to have been no hesitancy in Blaine's acceptance of the offer. As soon as arrangements were made for filling his place at the Pennsylvania Institute and the necessary capital for the enterprise was advanced by his brothers-in-law, Eben and Jacob Stanwood, he started on his new career. The issue of the Kennebec *Journal* of November 16, 1854, carried a notice that the paper had been sold to Joseph Baker and J. G. Blaine, who thenceforth would conduct its editorial and business affairs.

With the exception of his persistent refusal to take the Republican nomination for the Presidency in 1888, Blaine's acceptance of Dorr's offer was probably the most important decision of his life in its effect on his public career. In the first place, it meant that at the age of twenty-four he was established as a prominent resident of New England. With characteristic promptness he became acclimated to his new environment and more or less consciously absorbed the influences of its long historical tradition. Henceforth he was "Blaine of Maine." The tentative *Wanderjahre* were over. From his New England station he looked now upon "old Kentucke" not as a land of brilliant statesmen and charming women "hard to beat," but as a State afflicted with the social and economic curse of slavery. There were no more complaints from him of the "ultra course" of the Abolitionists of the North; there was no more danger that he would educate any young men to be "secessionists." Had he remained a Kentucky schoolmaster or even a Philadelphia lawyer, what a vast difference would it not have made in his whole attitude toward the great questions of the moral justification of slavery and the legal rights of the Southern States which were then rapidly moving toward their crisis!

Furthermore, his ready identification with the economic interests of his adopted State molded or confirmed his opinions on a number of important political questions, like taxation, the tariff, the currency, the fisheries, maritime policy and foreign relations. The largest and most sparsely populated of the New England States, with an extensive agricultural and forest hinterland, Maine was still largely a frontier community. The greenback heresy flourished here more vigorously than in any other Eastern State. In the absence of industrial centers, the tariff was less a subsidy to the manufacturer than a protection to the farmer and lumberman against Canadian competition. The perennial contro-

versy over the rights of the New England fishermen, under the treaties
and conventions which marked practically every decade from 1783
down, made it almost impossible for a Maine leader to view the British
Foreign Office in any other light than as the abettor of Canadian aggres-
sions upon the privileges of the American cod and haddock takers under
international law and treaty guarantees. The preponderance of the
extractive products of the sea, the soil and the forests demanded markets which were to be found through the encouragement of a strong
merchant marine and reciprocal trade with our South American neighbors. How such conditions of his Maine environment affected Blaine's
economic theories and public policies we shall see illustrated in many a
chapter of his political career—in his fight for hard money, his arguments for the benefits of a protective tariff, his advocacy of reciprocity,
his Pan-American program, his concern for the interests of "those who
go down to the sea in ships," his jealousy of admitting Canada to un-
requited privileges in the American market and his rather intransigeant
attitude toward European chancelleries in general and the British Foreign Office in particular.

Of equal importance with the change of residence involved in the
acceptance of Mr. Dorr's offer was the change in vocation. Blaine's
ambition for a legal career, cherished with intermittent devotion for
seven years after his graduation from college, was now definitely abandoned. He was destined to enter public life through the horn gate of
journalism, not the ivory gate of the law. For a man endowed with
qualities of confidence and conviction, with a mind extraordinarily alert
in the acquisition of knowledge, clear in exposition, persuasive in argument, and merciless in irony, journalism, in the days when the newspaper was a sounding board for the editor's opinions, offered a wonderful
opportunity for political influence. At the same time, it offered to that
type of man certain temptations.

From the comparative immunity of the editorial sanctum he could
speak in a language of assertiveness and iteration. His arguments were
prepared not for submission to an attentive jury, but for immediate
influence upon a public generally more impressed by pontifical pronouncements than by close arguments. This does not mean that Blaine
was in any degree a patron of "yellow journalism." He was sincere in
his political convictions and honest in his exposition of them. Nevertheless, a tendency to speak in a tone of finality grew out of his editorial

writing. In later years, when he had become head of the State Department, his opponents accused him of addressing foreign cabinets in language more fitting for a political campaign than for decorous diplomatic intercourse. Whatever truth there was in this charge of "jingoism" was probably due to the habit of confident statement and controversial vigor developed by his journalistic experience.

Finally, Blaine's removal to Augusta coincided with stirring events in our history which immediately enlisted his zeal and gave ample scope for his aggressive talents. The Whig Party was breaking up. Its two great leaders Clay and Webster had died in 1852, and the same year it made its last bid for the Presidency with its third military hero, General Winfield Scott, who miserably failed to repeat the triumphs of Harrison and Taylor. Scott carried only four States against the Democratic candidate Franklin Pierce, and the Whig vote was cut from 138,369 to 81,775 in the seven cotton States of the lower South. The questions of internal improvements, the bank, the tariff, the public lands, and resistance to executive "tyranny," on which the Whigs had fought their former battles, had all lost their timeliness. The issue of slavery had not yet become acute enough to split either of the major parties. The Abolitionists, the Free-Soilers, and the Native Americans (a new party founded on hostility to the Irish immigrants and the Catholic Church) were bidding for the votes of the dissatisfied "regulars" of both parties. Political opinion was in solution. Only a shock was needed to crystallize it into new and sharply defined forms. That shock was given in the spring of 1854 by the passage of Douglas's Kansas-Nebraska bill, which repealed the Compromise of 1820 and opened the whole Louisiana Purchase to the slaveholder—a bill which James Ford Rhodes characterized as the most momentous measure that passed Congress from the day that the Senators and the Representatives first met until the outbreak of the Civil War.[1]

Note the effects of the Kansas-Nebraska bill that followed in rapid succession in the very months that Blaine was completing his arrangements to take charge of the Kennebec *Journal*. On May 30, 1854, President Pierce signed the bill. On July 6 a group of protestors, meeting at Jackson, Michigan, launched the new Republican Party, agreeing to sink their political differences and to "coöperate in the fight against the

---

[1] J. F. Rhodes, *The History of the United States from the Compromise of 1850*, Vol. I, p. 490.

extension of slavery until the contest be terminated." The same month a score of Abolitionists started from Massachusetts for the plains of Kansas, the vanguard of the throng of emigrants who were determined to make the new territory free soil. "Pierce and Douglas," said Horace Greeley in the New York *Tribune,* "have made more Abolitionists in three months than Garrison and Phillips could have made in half a century." The congressional elections of November (held less than a fortnight before Blaine assumed the editorship of the *Journal*) sent 117 anti-Nebraska men to the House and reduced the Administration Democrats from 159 to 79. Only seven of the 42 Northern Democrats who had voted for the Kansas-Nebraska bill were reëlected. In Maine the September election had resulted in the choice of Anson P. Morrill, the fusion candidate of the anti-Nebraska Democrats and Whigs, aided by the temperance and the Native American vote. The Kennebec *Journal* had forthwith hailed the election as a Republican victory. "We did not know the exact political stripe of many of them" (the Morrill supporters), it said, "but the term Republican has come to have a well defined meaning and informs everyone that the person thus designated sympathizes with and belongs to the new fusion movement or People's party that is springing up throughout the free States to resist the encroachments of slavery and maintain the rights of the North."

Such was the crisis in our national politics when Blaine took up his residence in Augusta, and such were the sentiments of the newspaper to which he came, in full sympathy with its crusading purpose. He had left Clay and Webster and Scott behind him now, as he had left Kentucky and Pennsylvania. The Whig past was dead and buried. Blaine of Maine was henceforth a perdurable Republican.

Chapter III   Journalism and Politics in Maine (1854–1863)

THE PARTNERSHIP of Messrs. Joseph Baker and J. G. Blaine in the ownership of the Kennebec *Journal* lasted only a few weeks. Mr. Baker's increasing practice as a prominent lawyer of Augusta left him little time to devote to the paper, and early in 1855 he sold his interest to the Rev. John L. Stevens—the same Stevens who was to step for a moment into the limelight of national prominence thirty-eight years later, when, as minister to Hawaii, he had marines landed from the warship *Boston* to support the revolution which put Queen Liliuokalani off her throne and established the provisional Hawaiian Republic under American auspices. At the time Stevens joined Blaine in the ownership of the paper he was in the middle thirties, with sufficient local reputation as a politician to be chosen chairman of the State Republican Committee. His widening activities in this post again, as in the partnership with Baker, threw upon Blaine's shoulders most of the burden of editorship. It was Blaine's articles that gave the tone to the paper and that were frequently quoted or copied by other news sheets in New England.

The Kennebec *Journal* under Blaine and Stevens was first of all an organ for disseminating the principles of the new national party, which it confidently declared to have been established in Maine by the election of the previous September, with "elements of permanence such as no party has had since the birth of our State." If it seems strange that so ardent a partisan as Blaine had been should, in this early manifesto, have spoken of Republicanism as "the exaltation of principle above party," it must be remembered that it was precisely through men's forsaking of their allegiance to the Whig and Democratic Parties, for the sake of a compelling moral principle, that the Republican Party was formed. And so long as that principle remained dominant, the partisan note in Republicanism was subdued. Even the name Republican was suspended in 1864 in favor of the appellation "Union Party."

Blaine's versatile energy as an editor was by no means confined to political propaganda. Education, literature, temperance, and various measures of social reform claimed his attention. He supplemented each of the weekly lectures given at the Augusta Lyceum during the winter

months with discriminating articles of appraisal and criticism in the
Journal. He wrote a fourteen column memorial of Luther Severance,
the founder of the paper. He filled the position of reporter of the
debates of the Maine Senate with signal success, his remarkable powers
of concentration and memory enabling him to reproduce the substance
of a speech or to repeat a roll call without taking a note. The Democratic rival of the district, the *Age,* was conducted by Messrs. Fuller and
Fuller, uncle and nephew. The latter, Melville W. Fuller, reported the
debates of the Senate for it, as Blaine did for the *Journal*. And the two
young men who were thus associated in the capitol at Augusta came
together again thirty-five years later at Washington, one as Secretary of
State and the other as Chief Justice of the Supreme Court.

Between the Democratic *Age* and Republican *Journal* there was a
running fight, sometimes conducted with good-natured raillery, but
more often with vituperative vigor. The *Age* had enjoyed the privilege
of printing all the laws, resolves, orders and public notices of the State
for thirteen years, before the victory of the Morrill coalition in the
autumn of 1854 ousted the Democrats from the control of the legislature, which promptly awarded the State printing to the *Journal*. This
good fortune, added to the profits which Blaine's skillful editorship was
earning, made the *Journal* a highly remunerative enterprise. Looking
back to those halcyon days, Blaine wrote to a friend in 1868: "Was I
not then State printer, making $4000 a year and spending $600, a ratio
which I have never since been able to establish and maintain. Bless me,
how rich I should grow if I should now come into the annual receipt
of seven times my outlay." He invested his surplus in coal lands in
Pennsylvania and later in West Virginia, which rapidly appreciated in
value and brought him a good income. As early as 1863 we find him
signing a contract calling for a royalty of sixty cents a hundred bushels
on coal taken from his mines in western Pennsylvania, with a clause
providing for a minimum delivery of three hundred thousand bushels a
year. In later days Blaine was accused of having amassed a large fortune, even "millions," by prostituting his political influence as Speaker
of the House in certain questionable railroad deals. Without anticipating here the discussion of these charges, it is fair to state that Blaine
never amassed a fortune remotely approaching a million dollars, and
that, in spite of his income from investments, he was frequently in
rather serious financial straits.

On June 17, 1856, the first national nominating convention of the Republican Party met at Philadelphia. Though Blaine had been a resident of Maine for only twenty months, he was chosen one of the three delegates to represent his district and was made one of the secretaries of the convention. He had already predicted that neither Seward nor Chase could obtain the nomination, the former because of his radical utterances on Abolition and his intense Whig partisanship, the latter on account of his Democratic antecedents. The situation called for a compromise candidate, a man without too prominent political affiliations, yet sound on the main doctrine of the platform: namely, the right and duty of Congress to abolish slavery in the Territories. The American or Know-Nothing Party was still strong. Representative Israel Washburn of Maine had stated the case in a letter to Blaine from Washington as early as February, 1856: "The quest for as small a modicum of Republicanism as will answer and as large an infusion of Know-Nothingism as will be safe has put all the first-class men out of the ring and left the nomination possible only to second or third raters. Frémont may be the best man that we can take. I do not feel sure that he is not, but I must feel sure that we can tie to him on the slavery question." [1] Blaine did feel sure that the romantic "pathfinder" and "conqueror of California" was not the best choice. He was for Justice John McLean of Ohio, a member of the Supreme Court for twenty-six years, whose name had been suggested for the nomination in every one of the Whig conventions since the formation of the party. Among the reasons given by Blaine for his preference was one that seems strange from the pen of the aggressive young editor, namely, "a kinship of feeling" with Judge McLean's "conservatism." The movement for Frémont, however, was irresistible. He was nominated on the first ballot, with 520 votes to 37 for Justice McLean and one for Seward. Blaine supported the ticket with whole-hearted zeal both in the *Journal* and on the stump, contributing more than any other man to the splendid majority of 25,000 which the State gave Frémont in the November election.

The next autumn Blaine received the flattering offer to become editor-in-chief of the Portland *Advertiser,* the most influential Republican daily in Maine, at a salary of $2000. By the terms of the contract, no editorial article was to appear "without the inspection and assent of said Blaine," except by order of the owner of the *Advertiser,* Con-

[1] Israel Washburn to Blaine, Feb. 14, 1856.

gressman J. M. Wood; and even then, "said Blaine" had the right to express his dissent in the columns of the paper. During his connection with the *Advertiser* Blaine was pledged to spend five days of each week in Portland, except when he was reporting the sessions of the legislature at Augusta. He "thought a good deal about moving to Portland," as he wrote his mother in the spring of 1858. "The city is a very beautiful one, of 30,000 inhabitants, situated directly on the ocean, and possesses many attractive points as places of residence. I think, however, that upon the whole I prefer the quiet and retirement of Augusta." [1] Here was the grave of his firstborn son, Stanwood, who had died in infancy; here his two boys, Walker and Williams Emmons, had been born in 1855 and 1857; and here were the Stanwood relations and a large circle of devoted friends. So the "quiet" little capital on the Kennebec remained the home of the Blaines until the mother's death early in the twentieth century.

Although work was more exacting on the daily Portland *Advertiser* than on the weekly Kennebec *Journal,* Blaine still found time for active political life. His talents were too valuable to the party to allow him to be tied to the editorial desk. In the autumn of 1858 Governor Morrill appointed him special commissioner to investigate the Maine prisons, which were costing the State far too much money. After an extended examination of the prisons in Maine and other States, he presented a report which revealed gross mismanagement, waste of material, and "doctored" accounts, and led to a thorough reform of the system. He visited Illinois in the course of his investigations and attended two of the famous debates between Lincoln and Douglas on the slavery issue. In that experience he found a hero to replace Henry Clay.

Politics now proceeded rapidly to eclipse journalism in Blaine's career. He was elected to the lower branch of the Maine legislature in September, 1858, and in the three following annual campaigns was nominated by acclamation and elected by large majorities. At the close of two years in the legislature, he was unanimously chosen Speaker, and presided over the sessions of 1861 and 1862 with an expertness in parliamentary usage and an impartiality which foreshadowed his brilliant conduct of the national House of Representatives a few years later. For a while he tried to combine his new political responsibilities

[1] Gail Hamilton, *Biography of James G. Blaine,* p. 124.

with his editorship. His contract with the *Advertiser* was so modified in February, 1860, as to require only three leaders and one letter each week during the legislative session, for which he was to receive the munificent sum of twelve dollars. But this arrangement did not satisfy the owners of the paper, and in August they made a final effort to secure Blaine's full services. His friend Senator William Pitt Fessenden tried again to wean him from Augusta. "Now can you and will you become identified with Portland?" he wrote; "I have heretofore given you my views as to the proper place for *you*. My opinion remains unchanged. This is the point of strength for you in every aspect, political and pecuniary. Let me know what you think about it soon, as our action will be influenced by your decision." [1] But Blaine's decision between the careers of journalism and politics had already been made. He had committed himself still further to the latter by accepting the chairmanship of the Republican State Committee, which Mr. Stevens had resigned in 1859. This position he held for twenty-two years, until he entered Garfield's Cabinet as Secretary of State. So his connection with the *Advertiser* came to an end, and, except for a momentary resumption of the editorship of the Kennebec *Journal* in the autumn of 1860, his journalistic career was closed. When he entered Congress, however, three years later, his occupation was listed as "editor."

His four years in the legislature at Augusta coincided with the outbreak of the "irrepressible conflict" which Seward had predicted in his Rochester speech the month after Blaine's election as chairman of the State Committee. At the moment when he was taking over that office, John Brown's raid at Harper's Ferry occurred. While he was attempting to adjust his legislative duties to the editorial demands of the *Advertiser,* the Republican nominating convention of 1860 met at Chicago and filled the "wigwam" with wild cheers for "honest Abe" Lincoln. Blaine was not a delegate, but he went to the convention, pleading all the way out to Chicago with his companion, Governor Lot M. Morrill, to support Lincoln's candidacy. He also tried his best to persuade his former partner on the *Journal* to vote for Lincoln, but Stevens remained an ardent Seward delegate to the end. It was probably due to Blaine's persistent canvassing, however, that a half dozen of the unpledged Maine delegates reputed to favor Seward swung over to Lincoln. Enthusiastic over the nomination, Blaine accompanied the

[1] Fessenden to Blaine, Aug. 15, 1860.

committee of notification to Springfield and heard Lincoln's brief and modest speech of acceptance. He did not in the least share that mingled feeling of mistrust and contempt for Abraham Lincoln which was so widespread among the politicians and publicists of the East. "I think the nomination the very best that could have been made in every way, and I have no more doubt of the election of the ticket than I have that Maine will be carried by the Republicans," he wrote home from Springfield. He thought Mrs. Lincoln "a very ladylike and good-looking person," and, while he admitted that Lincoln was "an awkward looking man," he added that one realized at once that it was "the awkwardness of genius." [1] When Blaine returned to Augusta he threw himself heart and soul into the campaign, the first of a half dozen presidential contests in which, as chairman of the State Committee, he marshaled the Republicans to victory. Stevens, sorely disappointed at Seward's failure to win the nomination, sulked in his tent. He would not even go to the office of the *Journal*. "Here, you have got your man," he said to Blaine; "now take your damned old paper and run it." And Blaine did run it for three months as the most powerful Lincoln organ in the State.

From the first the new member from Augusta took an active part in the legislature. He had familiarized himself thoroughly with the history and economic resources of the State. He had become acquainted with many of its important political figures through his reportorial duties in the Senate. He had competently discussed its current problems—temperance, railways, shipping, fisheries, forests, schools and prisons—in the columns of the *Journal* and the *Advertiser*. He was prepared to move easily from the editorial chair to a seat in the House, to advocate by speech and support by vote the policies which he had commended in the press. There is a touch of irony in the fact that the first important duties of the man who was himself destined to be a defendant in bitterly prosecuted investigations by committees of Congress were the investigations of two cases of mismanagement and fraud —that of a State Treasurer who attempted to hide his defalcations by false entries in the books, and a clergyman who disgraced his cloth by embezzling public funds to repair his losses in land and lumber speculations.

Blaine's devotion to the welfare of his adopted State was not con-

[1] Blaine to his family, May 20, 1860. Gail Hamilton, *Biography of James G. Blaine*, p. 129.

fined to the four years in which he served in the legislature at Augusta. During his entire career in the Federal House and Senate he was quick to defend the interests of Maine whenever they seemed to be involved in any proposed legislation. Still his eye was on the broader field of national politics from his youth up. He was nationally, not parochially, minded. It was once said of him that he was "born under the rotunda of the Capitol at Washington." It took the crucial questions of America's policy and destiny to kindle his imagination and arouse his utmost energies.

Such a question came to its crisis in the outbreak of the Civil War, when he was Speaker of the Maine legislature. From the moment the shot was fired on Fort Sumter he gave unfaltering support and aid to the Union cause, in the appropriation of funds, the recruitment of regiments, the selection of officers and the procurement of military supplies. He visited Washington to learn the most pressing needs of the government, and was the trusted adviser of Governor Israel Washburn in devising the methods by which Maine could best supply its share of those needs. Late in October, 1861, he received a long letter from the Governor at Augusta, filled with the details of military requisitions, and concluding with the request that he should "visit all our Maine camps and report condition, etc." [1] That Blaine did not at the age of thirty-one volunteer to carry a musket in the war, and that he provided a substitute when drafted were facts cited by his opponents in the presidential campaign of 1884 to prove his lack of patriotism—though his rival, Mr. Cleveland, several years younger, had taken exactly the same course. But the reproach cast upon both these unmilitary gentlemen was pure political propaganda. The commutation of military service was a perfectly honorable practice, and highly profitable to the government. Besides, nobody, from the Governor down, doubted that Blaine was infinitely more useful to the cause in the position which he filled than he could have been in the ranks.

In addition to the military disaster at Bull Run, the Lincoln government had many trials in the early weeks of the war. The extraordinary powers assumed by the Executive provoked widespread protest in the name of the preservation of the liberties and immunities guaranted by the Constitution. There was a sharp difference of opinion between the civil authorities and some of the commanders in the field on the ques-

[1] Israel Washburn to Blaine, Oct. 30, 1861.

tions of the emancipation of the slaves and the confiscation of the property of persons in rebellion against the government. There was resentment against Great Britain on account of the Queen's hasty recognition of the belligerency of the Confederate States, and for a moment it looked as if the Trent affair of November 8, 1861, might lead to war with England. President Lincoln was denounced by some as a tyrant overriding the law and the Constitution, and by others as a cowardly weakling letting the Union go to ruin. On Februay 7, 1862, before the heartening tidings from Fort Donelson had come to offset the inaction of McClellan's army, the Senate of Maine, by a vote of 24 to 4, passed the following resolutions relating to national affairs:

RESOLVED: That we cordially endorse the Administration of Abraham Lincoln in the conduct of the war against the wicked and unnatural enemies of the Republic, and that in all its measures calculated to crush this rebellion speedily and finally the Administration is entitled to and will receive the unwavering support of the loyal people of Maine.

RESOLVED: That it is the duty of Congress, by such means as will not jeopard the rights and safety of the loyal people of the South, to provide for the confiscation of estates real and personal of rebels, and for the forfeiture and liberation of every slave claimed by any person who shall continue in arms against the authority of the United States, or who shall in any manner aid and abet the present wicked and unjustifiable rebellion.

RESOLVED: That in this perilous crisis of the country it is the duty of Congress, in the exercise of its constitutional power to "raise and support armies," to provide by law for accepting the services of all able-bodied men of whatever status, and to employ these men in such manner as military necessity and the safety of the Republic may demand.

RESOLVED: That a copy of these resolutions be sent to the Senators and Representatives in Congress from this State, and that they be respectfully requested to use all honorable means to secure the passage of acts embodying their spirit and substance.

When these resolutions reached the House for concurrence, they were combated in a two-day speech by Mr. Gould of Thomaston, an able lawyer and for many years a Democratic member of the legislature. Whereupon Speaker Blaine called Wm. P. Frye of Lewiston to the chair and took the floor in reply to Gould (March 7). The main points of Gould's argument had been: (1) that Congress had no constitutional power to conduct the war, that power residing in the President alone as Commander in Chief of the army and navy; (2) that the Southern

States, being still in the Union (as Lincoln contended), were under the protection of the Constitution, and that hence their citizens could neither be punished for "treason" beyond the penalties prescribed in Article III, section 3, nor be deprived of their property without "due process of law." Blaine made short work of the first argument by citations from the Constitution itself, buttressed by appropriate passages from Alexander Hamilton's pen in the 23rd number of the *Federalist,* and by references to Lincoln's own acknowledgment of the subordination of his military powers to the will of Congress. In answering the second point as to the constitutional privileges and immunities of citizens of States in revolt against the national government, Blaine buried his opponent beneath a mass of historic precedents, unanswerable logic and merciless sarcasm.

Mr. Gould had denied that the war was a "rebellion" or even a civil war, because Jefferson Davis was not trying to oust Lincoln from the Presidency, but only to establish his own presidential power over eleven States detached from the rest. But, argued Blaine, since Lincoln was constitutionally elected President of the *United* States, defiance of his authority in Georgia or Louisiana was as truly rebellion as defiance in Pennsylvania or Maine. The government at Washington had perforce treated those in revolt in arms against its authority as belligerents, because they were too numerous and powerful to be dealt with by the ordinary judicial procedure. The only *posse comitatus* that could deal with them was a national army. But as belligerents in arms they could not claim the protection of a Constitution which they were leagued together to destroy. As belligerents in arms, whatever property of military value they had was subject, by the rules of war, to confiscation by the enemy. "Due process of law" was for the protection of the property and lives of citizens acknowledging obedience to the law, and was applicable where the courts of justice were regularly functioning. The secessionists could not have both the protection of the Constitution as law-abiding citizens, and the status of belligerents fighting against the authority established by the Constitution. "The argument of the gentleman," said Blaine, "gives every advantage to the rebels and imposes every disability on the Federal Government. And by assuming this ground I charge the gentleman with having advocated the cause of Jefferson Davis just as effectually as if he had appeared here as his avowed champion with a retainer in his pocket from that Prince of

Rebels."

Irony was mingled with invective in the speech. Gould, on being asked what kind of war was going on if not a civil war, had defined it as a "domestic war." To this the Speaker replied, amid laughter: "I have heard of domestic woolens, domestic sheetings and domestic felicity, but a domestic war is something new under the sun. . . . Vattel will, I suppose, have a new edition with annotations by Gould, in which 'domestic war' will be defined and illustrated as a contest not quite foreign, not quite civil, but one in which the rebellious party have at one and the same time all the rights of peaceful citizens and all the immunities of alien enemies." "I have only to say," he continued, "that the argument which maintains that the States would have to be out of the Union before a contest with their rebellious citizens could be conducted as a civil war is nothing short of an Irish bull of the most grotesque description. . . . The very essence of a civil war consists in its being a strife between members properly subject to the same sovereign authority."

But Blaine did not stop with the vindication of the legality and expediency of the confiscation policy advocated by the Maine Senate. He made the issue the opportunity for a hearty endorsement of the sorely beset President. "I am for the Administration through and through," he asserted, "being an early and unflinching believer in the ability, the honesty, and the patriotism of Abraham Lincoln." He declared his confidence that the struggle would end with victory for the Union. He confessed "boldly" that if the life of the nation seemed to demand the violation of the Constitution, he would violate it, agreeing with the sentiment of Lincoln's message that "it were better to violate one provision than that all should perish," and with Thomas Jefferson's declaration that to "lose our country by a scrupulous adherence to written law would be to lose the law itself, together with life, liberty and property, thus absurdly sacrificing the end to the means."

We have dwelt with what may seem disproportionate emphasis on this speech, not only because it was Blaine's first official discussion of national affairs, but also because, in form, content and purpose, it was the model of his subsequent speeches. All the characteristics of his mature mind appear here—intense patriotism, a thorough knowledge of American history, acquaintance with authorities in international law, a flair for the weak points in an opponent's logic, a gift, sometimes to

prove embarrassing, for withering sarcasm, and an unshakable conviction of the sacredness of the Union. The Mr. Frye of Lewiston, who
listened from the chair, and who, fifteen years later, was to be his colleague in the United States Senate, thought that Blaine never in his
long congressional career spoke with greater power or persuasion.

It was inevitable that a man of Blaine's ability should find a wider
field of influence than the legislature of Maine, and that his services to
the Republican Party in the State should be rewarded with the opportunity to serve it in its national responsibilities. This opportunity was
offered early. In the summer of 1860 there was a movement on foot to
send him to Congress. On the twenty-third of June, hardly a month
after Lincoln's nomination at Chicago, he received a letter from a
prominent Republican of Maine asking whether he was going to allow
his name to be presented at the convention of the district, and pledging
"hearty support" and the vote of "every Republican of this town" in
the event of his nomination. Knowing that ex-Governor Anson P. Morrill wanted the nomination, Blaine immediately declined the proffered
support. "You can readily see," he wrote, "how unbecoming it would
be in a man of my years to contest the nomination with him, even if I
desired to do so. Its effect would only be to divide the hitherto harmonious ranks of the Republicans of Kennebec. I shall therefore most cheerfully support Governor Morrill for the nomination, and shall urge all
my friends to do the same." Two years later, however, the path was
clear, and, incidentally, Blaine's prestige was greatly enhanced by his
reply to Gould on the seventh of March, 1862. In the district convention
at Waterville the following July, he received the first of seven consecutive unanimous nominations to represent the third Maine district in the
national House. His platform as announced in his speech of acceptance
was terse and single-minded: "If I am called to a seat in Congress, I
shall go there with a determination to stand heartily and unreservedly
by the Administration of Abraham Lincoln. In the success of this Administration, under the good providence of God, rests, I solemnly believe, the fate of the American Union. . . . The case is one, in the
present exigency, where men loyal to the Union cannot divide. The
President is Commander in Chief of our land and naval forces, and,
while he may be counseled, he must not be opposed."

The President, however, was bitterly opposed in the elections of
1862. The military situation was distressing for the North. Grant's suc-

cesses at Forts Henry and Donelson had been followed by the terrible slaughter and doubtful victory at Shiloh. Despite Farragut's capture of New Orleans, the Confederates still held control of the Mississippi from Port Hudson up to Vicksburg. The summer had brought a series of disasters to the Union armies in Virginia: McClellan, with superior forces, baffled in his half-hearted attempts to take Richmond; the boastful Pope soundly beaten at Manassas and his supply train burned in a bonfire whose ominous glow in the skies could be seen from the windows of the White House; Shields, Banks, and Frémont outwitted and defeated in the Shenandoah Valley by the wizardry of Stonewall Jackson; Lee and Jackson, united at Richmond, planning the great offensive to detach Maryland from the Union, strike panic into the bankers of Philadelphia and New York and send the Lincoln Administration down in defeat. True, Lee's invasion was checked in mid-September by McClellan at Antietam, but the dearly bought victory was spoiled when the Union general, with characteristic dilatoriness, allowed Lee to get his entire army, with the exception of ten thousand who fell in the battle, across the Potomac to Virginia and safety. The Emancipation Proclamation, which followed the victory at Antietam, seemed likely to prove a boomerang to the Administration. Thousands of hitherto loyal supporters of the President in the North regarded it as at best a blunder and at worst a debasement of American citizenship. In the South it was universally interpreted and abhorred as an incitement to servile insurrection. The middle and upper classes in England, already resentful over the Trent affair and Minister Adams' protest against the building of commerce destroyers in British shipyards, condemned it as an illegal and inflammatory manifesto. "The American law-giver," said the London *Saturday Review,* "not only confiscates his neighbors' slaves, but orders them to cut their masters' throats!"

The mounting cost of the war and the ill fortune of the Union arms were nourishing a widespread spirit of defeatism. Men were beginning to assert openly that the conquest of the South was an impossibility. Constitutional purists were criticizing Congress for its "illegal" acts and the President for his "despotic" edicts. Councils were divided. The political animosities which had been sunk in a common devotion to the preservation of the Union and the defense of the flag at the beginning of the war, were revived. The influential editor of the New York *Trib-*

une was scolding Lincoln for not immediately freeing the slaves, and Postmaster General Blair was declaring in Cabinet meeting that the Emancipation Proclamation would wreck the Administration. Thousands of Northern Democrats who had rallied, with their great leader Stephen A. Douglas, to Lincoln's support in 1861, turned against him now. Other thousands, Republicans as well as Democrats, grew coldly critical of the Administration, which they believed had not only failed to win the war but also to preserve the "liberties" of American citizens. The States of New York, Pennsylvania, Ohio, Illinois, Indiana, and Wisconsin, all of which had voted for Lincoln in 1860, went Democratic in the elections of 1862. The Democrats gained 32 seats in Congress, reducing the Administration majority to a bare 20. Indeed, had it not been for a solid Republican delegation returned from the border States of Maryland, Kentucky and Missouri, where the voting was conducted under the supervision of Federal troops, President Lincoln would have been confronted with a hostile majority in the Thirty-eighth Congress.

As chairman of the Republican Committee of Maine, it was Blaine's first duty to assure the national Administration of the support of the State. His own candidacy was a minor incident of the campaign. On his shoulders rested the responsibility of supervising the personnel of the State ticket, arranging the dates and places of the political rallies, providing speakers, and procuring funds. The fight was a hard one. In the September elections, which came at the moment when Lee was launching his invasion of Maryland, the State ticket, with Abner Coburn at its head, won by only 4000 majority instead of the 15,000 or 20,000 usually given to the Republican candidates. One Democratic Congressman was elected, but the Kennebec district gave Blaine an ample majority. Before he took his seat in Congress in December of the following year, he had another opportunity to prove the sincerity of his pledge to "stand heartily and unreservedly by the Administration of President Lincoln."

The disaffection of the autumn of 1862 deepened into a discouragement akin to despair in the following spring. It was the darkest moment of the war for the Union cause. Volunteering had almost ceased. Desertions were rife. Carloads of civilian clothing were being sent through the lines of the Army of the Potomac to furnish the renegades a change for their uniforms. Early in March Congress passed a Conscription Act and authorized the President to suspend the writ of habeas corpus at his discretion. But the first measure was evaded and resisted, even to violence, and the second was opposed as a further evidence of Lincoln's "tyranny." Richard H. Dana wrote to Charles Francis Adams, Jr., a cavalry commander in the Army of the Potomac, on March 9: "As to the politics of Washington, the most striking thing here is the absence of personal loyalty to the President. . . . He has no admirers, no enthusiastic supporters, none to bet on his head. If a Republican canvass were to be held tomorrow, he would not get the vote of a State. He does not act or talk or feel like the ruler of a great empire in a crisis. . . . He is an unutterable calamity to us where he is. Only the army can save us." Clement L. Vallandigham, the famous "copperhead" from Ohio, was scolding the government, on the floor of the House, for prolonging the war: "You have not conquered the South; you never will. . . . Money you have expended without limit, and blood poured out like water. . . . Defeat, debt, taxation and sepulchers—these are your only trophies." The expenses of the war had mounted to $2,500,000 a day, or five times the revenue raised by duties, excises and taxes. Only $25,000,000 of the $500,000,000 five-twenty bonds authorized had been sold by the first of November, 1863, when a new issue of ten-forties was voted.

"By a common instinct," wrote Joseph Medill of the Chicago *Tribune*, "everybody feels that the war is drawing to a disastrous and disgraceful termination. Money cannot be supplied much longer to a beaten, demoralized, and homesick army." There were even threats of secession in the Northern States, as in New England in the War of 1812. Indiana and Illinois, so Governor Morton telegraphed from Indianapolis to the Secretary of War, Stanton, were considering a joint resolution of their legislatures, "acknowledging the Southern Confederacy and urging the States of the Northwest to dissolve all constitutional relations with the New England States."

In order that his own State might give the harried Administration the first endorsement of the autumn of 1863, Blaine organized a strenuous campaign for the September elections. Anticipating the course of the national managers in the presidential campaign of 1864, he substituted the name Union for Republican; while he selected a loyal Democrat, Samuel Cony, to replace the rather inefficient Coburn as Governor. He conducted the canvass with untiring energy, raising an exceptionally large fund, enlisting the most effective speakers, and distributing vast amounts of campaign literature. The results fully justified his optimistic labors. The Union ticket was successful all along the line and Governor Cony was elected with the normal Republican majority.

Already Blaine had become so conspicuous in his services to the party that demands were being made for his presence and voice at political rallies in various parts of the country—demands which were to come with increasing persistence for the rest of his life. A month after the victory in Maine he received a pressing invitation from the Union State Committee of New York, signed by Governor Edwin D. Morgan, Thurlow Weed, Preston King, and Ira Harris, to come over and help the Empire State in its election. "Our defeat here," they said, "would be more disastrous to the country than the loss of a battle. . . . Give us all the time you can possibly spare." But even if Blaine had had the time for campaigning in New York, it is little probable that it would have hindered the reëlection of the Democratic candidate, Horatio Seymour, which he foresaw and predicted, and which, if not as serious as "the loss of a battle," was at least as annoying as the interruption of a march.

So, at the age of thirty-three, a tall and robust figure, with a commanding poise and presence and penetrating brown eyes which bespoke at once intellectual alertness, amiable dignity and kindly humor, Blaine went to Washington to play his part on the national stage.

WHEN BLAINE took his seat in the House of 183 members who represented the twenty-four loyal States, the crisis of the Civil War was passed. Gettysburg and Vicksburg had assured the eventual triumph of the Union arms. The "Father of Waters" flowed again "unvexed" to the Gulf of Mexico. The resistance to the Conscription Act had been overcome, and the draft of a million men in 1864 was filled with ease. Secretary Chase's new system of national banks had provided a market for the government's bonds; and, as the President gratefully acknowledged in his message of December, 1863, the huge expenses of the war were being "cheerfully borne" by the people of the North. The slight danger of foreign intervention in behalf of the Confederacy was over, and the British government had made a tardy disavowal of its negligence in allowing ships to be built in its yards to prey on the commerce of a friendly nation. Not that there were not plenty of serious problems left to confront the Administration, military, political and financial; and still more serious problems to meet when the assassin's bullet removed the "kindly-earnest, brave, foreseeing" Lincoln from the control of Reconstruction.

In the discussion of all these problems Blaine came to take a part commensurate with his wide knowledge, cogent logic, and exceptional clarity of presentation. At first, as befitted a new member, he listened much and spoke little. The *Congressional Globe* for the first few weeks of the Thirty-eighth Congress contained only occasional references to his name, a sentence or two, here and there, interpolated to clear up a misunderstanding or correct a misstatement; a few brief resolutions. His committee assignments were insignificant, except for a place on the Committee on Military Affairs. His name was next to last on that committee, but his advocacy of the assumption by the national government of all the debts of the States "incurred in their efforts to aid in suppressing the rebellion" led to his appointment as chairman of a select committee to deal with this matter.

A bill had been introduced into the House by Thaddeus Stevens for the reimbursement of Pennsylvania in the amount of $700,000 spent in calling out the militia, on June 26, 1863, to resist Lee's invasion. In a brief speech of January 12, 1864, Blaine, while not questioning Pennsylvania's claim, cited a prior unsettled claim of Maine for money spent to protect the United States navy yard at Kittery. He hoped that, instead of "piecemeal legislation" on the subject of reimbursement, "some general and equitable system for all the States" would be adopted. On April 21 he proposed a substitute for the Stevens bill, providing for a commission of three, to be appointed by the President, to ascertain the total indebtedness of the loyal States incurred in the prosecution of the war, and to report to Congress on or before the first Monday of December, 1865, when the Thirty-ninth Congress would meet. He followed the motion with his first set speech in the House. He cited as precedents the assumption of the State debts incurred in the Revolutionary War, the War of 1812 and the Mexican War, and dwelt especially on the ability of the national government to discharge its obligations without impairment of its credit. He showed how trifling a matter the assumption of, say, $150,000,000 in State debts would be for a nation whose wealth was approaching $20,000,000,000, as compared with the assumption of $21,500,000 in Hamilton's day, when our national wealth was not more than $600,000,000. Estimating that if the war lasted until the midsummer of 1865 our debt would reach approximately $2,500,000,000, or one eighth of our national wealth, he demonstrated that with the maintenance of our normal rate of increase in population and prosperity, this apparently staggering sum would amount to less than three per cent of our national wealth at the close of the century. Great Britain's debt of $4,300,000,000 at the close of the Napoleonic wars totaled nearly half her wealth, and she had to sell her bonds at less than fifty cents on a dollar to raise money to fight the decisive campaign of Waterloo. Yet in less than fifty years since Waterloo her wealth had tripled and her per capita taxes had been nearly halved. What, then, of our own country, with its "varied, magnificent and immeasurable" resources in agriculture, commerce, manufacture and mining? By the close of the nineteenth century our population would reach 100,000,000 and our wealth $85,000,000,000. Forty new States would be carved out of the vast western wilderness. The grandest future reserved for any people awaited us. "With such amplitude and affluence of resources, and with such a vast stake at issue, we should be unworthy of our lineage and our inheritance if we for one moment distrusted our ability to maintain ourselves a united people with one Country, one Constitution, one Destiny." [1]

It was for the last sentence that the speech was written. Its ostensible object was the assumption of a six per cent increase in the national debt; its real object was the demonstration of the infrangible strength of the United States. It was the redemption of Blaine's preëlection pledge to "stand heartily and unreservedly by the Administration of Abraham Lincoln." And it was timely. For the promise of the autumn of 1863 seemed to be fading. The President's ten per cent plan for the reconstruction of the seceded States, announced in December, was meeting determined opposition in Congress, which culminated in the pocket veto of the Wade-Davis bill on July 4, 1864, and the fierce Manifesto of the authors in the New York *Tribune* accusing the President of a "studied outrage on the legislative authority of the people." Political antagonism to the influence of the Blairs in the Administration increased until Lincoln was forced in September to ask for the resignation of the Postmaster General, Montgomery Blair, from the Cabinet.

Twelve days after Blaine's speech General Grant crossed the Rapidan to hammer Lee's army into submission and capture Richmond, intending to "fight it out on this line if it takes all summer." But his terrible losses in the battle of the Wilderness, at the "bloody angle" of Spottsylvania and at Cold Harbor compelled him to abandon the frontal attack in midsummer and resort to the slow operation of the siege of the important railroad junction of Petersburg, just at the moment when Jubal Early's cavalry crossed the Potomac and threatened the defenses of Washington. July and August were months of profound discouragement at the North. Defeatism again raised its head. The Democratic National Convention at Chicago, on August 29, nominated General McClellan for President on a platform containing Vallandigham's plank declaring that "after four years of failure to restore the Union by the experiment of war . . . justice, humanity, liberty and the public welfare demand that immediate efforts be made for the cessation of hostilities." Lincoln himself thought it "extremely probable" that he would be defeated in the November election. The victories of Farragut at Mobile Bay, of Sherman at Atlanta and of Sheridan in the Shenandoah Valley saved the Administration. But Blaine's April

[1] *Cong. Globe,* 38th Cong., 1st sess., pp. 1796–7.

speech was a heartening influence during the troubled summer.

By a strange whim of fortune the amiable new member from Maine, in his middle thirties, was destined again and again to pit his opinions against the grim and cynical old dictator of the House, Thaddeus Stevens. And in spite of the almost uniform prevalence of Blaine's contentions, the mutual friendship and esteem of the ill-mated colleagues continued unimpaired till Stevens' death in 1868. The disagreement began, as we have seen, in Blaine's successful opposition to the "piecemeal legislation" proposed in Stevens' bill for the reimbursement of Pennsylvania for expenses incurred in helping to check Lee's invasion. On May 30, 1864, he clashed again with the redoubtable member from Pennsylvania. In order to keep the new national banks entirely free from State control, Stevens sponsored a measure prescribing a uniform rate of seven per cent interest charges for loans and accommodations by said banks. Blaine, deeming it unfair that the credit of the national banks should not be available on as favorable terms as that of the State banks, proposed an amendment allowing the national banks to charge interest "at the rate established by law in the State where the association (the national bank) is situated." The Blaine amendment prevailed.[1]

The most spectacular contest between the two men, however, came early in the second session of the Congress, when Stevens introduced a bill (Dec. 5, 1864) permitting contracts made payable in gold to be discharged in paper and "preventing any note or bill issued by the United States, and being made lawful money and legal tender, from being received for a smaller sum than is therein specified." The bill calls for a word of explanation. In the emergency of war the government had been driven reluctantly and as an avowedly temporary expedient, to resort to a paper currency not based on actual deposits of gold or silver in the treasury. Beginning with an issue of $150,000,000 in February, 1862, Congress had caused to be printed and put into circulation by the autumn of 1864 United States notes (later nicknamed "greenbacks") to the amount of $449,338,902. As lawful money these greenbacks were valid for all business transactions (unless payment in gold was specified in the contract), and were receivable by the government for all dues and taxes except customs duties. The latter had to be paid in gold in order to meet the interest on the government bonds,

[1] *Cong. Globe*, 38th Cong., 1st sess., p. 1353.

which was payable in "coin." It was inevitable, as our bitter experience with the continental currency at the time of the American Revolution showed, that the universal law of the depreciation of unsupported ("fiat") paper money should affect the value of the greenbacks. Gold became an object of speculative bidding, reaching a premium of 285 in July, 1864. How costly this was for the government may be seen by a simple calculation in arithmetic. A premium of 285 on gold meant that a paper dollar was worth but 35 cents in coin. Therefore, on the sale of each $1000 bond for lawful money (greenbacks) the treasury would receive the equivalent of only $350 in gold, while it was obliged to pay $60 a year in interest in gold on the same $1000 bond. In other words, the government was paying interest at the actual rate of 17.1 per cent in the summer of 1864.

It was with the laudable desire to put an end to this speculation in gold that Stevens introduced his bill punishing with fine and imprisonment anyone who exchanged greenbacks for gold at less than their face value. He was ever an advocate of coercion. Accustomed to bearing down opposition by a cynical and dictatorial display of force, he flouted the power of social opinion and economic law. Blaine rose on December 4, 1864, to combat the Stevens bill. Even in the brief twenty-four hours that it had been "allowed to float before the public mind as a measure seriously entertained by this House," he said, it had been "productive of great mischief," as witnessed by the sharp rise in the premium on gold in Wall Street. Were it not for his respect for the distinguished gentleman who introduced the bill, he would say that its provisions were "absurd and monstrous." If passed it would render liable to fine and imprisonment all the people of the Pacific coast, where the paper currency was held in scorn. "You cannot make a gold dollar worth less than it is nor a paper dollar worth more than it is by congressional legislation." In spite of his sarcastic jibe at his "friend from Maine," who had "an intuitive way of getting at a great national question . . . which has exercised the thoughts of statesmen of several countries for many years," Stevens failed, by a vote of 51 to 68, to get his bill reported to the Committee on Ways and Means; although such important members of the House as Robert Schenck, Henry Winter Davis, Justin S. Morrill, R. P. Spalding, Samuel Hooper and James A. Garfield voted with him against Blaine. After the Christmas recess, Stevens returned to the charge with new shafts of irony in his quiver:

"My excellent friend from Maine," he said, "in an alarmed and excited manner informed the House that the bill was fraught with innumerable mischiefs. He modestly stated that it was an absurdity. The House, partaking of the magnetic manner of my friend from Maine, and wishing to escape the evils of this gunpowder plot, immediately laid the bill on the table." [1] Stevens was not able to resuscitate the bill; but incidentally he furnished in the phrase "magnetic manner" the adjective which has ever since been applied to the Maine statesman.

Besides these tilts with Stevens, there were several other instances of Blaine's activity in his first congressional term. He defended the commutation clause of the Conscription Act against James F. Wilson of Iowa, who advocated the absolute enforcement of the draft.[2] He suggested an amendment to the Constitution which would permit Congress to levy a tax on exports, reviewing the debates in the Constitutional Convention on the subject, and pointing out that moderate taxes on tobacco, naval stores and cotton would bring $100,000,000 into the Treasury, without injury to our foreign markets for those commodities.[3] He opposed the imposition of an excise tax on sailing vessels, on the ground that the materials used in the construction of the ships were already heavily taxed, and that vessels could be built in New Brunswick thirty per cent cheaper than they could in the shipyards of Maine.[4] He caused to be laid on the table, by a vote of 69 to 63, a resolution of the Chairman of the Committee on Foreign Affairs, Henry Winter Davis, declaring that it was "the constitutional right of Congress to define our foreign policy and the constitutional duty of the President to respect that policy." And in defense of the Lincoln Administration, he adduced many instances, from Washington's day down, to confirm the concurrent power of the President in the conduct of foreign affairs.[5] On the expiration of the Thirty-eighth Congress, in March, 1865, he returned to his family in Augusta, and to his management of the State campaign, already recognized by the country at large as an influential leader of the Republican Party.

During that spring and summer of 1865 came events of momentous import. The Southern armies laid down their arms, and the tattered

[1] *Cong. Globe,* 38th Cong., 2d sess., p. 117.
[2] *Ibid.,* 1st sess., p. 434.
[3] *Cong. Globe,* 38th Cong., 1st sess., p. 1261.
[4] *Ibid.,* p. 1907.
[5] *Ibid.,* 2d sess., p. 49.

flag which Major Anderson had lowered in April, 1861, was again raised above the ramparts of Fort Sumter. Lincoln was murdered, and Andrew Johnson entered the White House, breathing vengeance upon the "rebels and traitors" of the South. State after State was ratifying the Thirteenth Amendment, which had been passed by Congress in January, declaring slavery forever banished from the United States and all places subject to their jurisdiction. Under the moderating influence of Secretaries McCulloch, Welles, and especially Seward, whom he had retained along with the other members of Lincoln's Cabinet, President Johnson soon executed a complete *volte face* in his policy toward the South. He dropped the language of punitive reprisals and spoke in Lincoln's tones of reconciliation and healing. He issued a proclamation on May 29, granting amnesty to all who had been in rebellion against the authority of the United States, except the military and political leaders and certain citizens of influence in the communities; and even they might recover their full rights of citizenship by applying to the Executive for the pardon which would be "liberally extended." He recognized the Lincoln governments established in Louisiana, Arkansas, Tennessee and Virginia, and appointed provisional Governors in the other seven States of the secession, to summon constitutional conventions and provide for general and local elections under the same, the only conditions imposed being the repudiation of the secession ordinances and the acceptance of the emancipation measures.

When the Thirty-ninth Congress assembled in December, 1865, these "Johnson Governments" were fully organized in all the States of the late Confederacy except Texas, and the full quota of Representatives and Senators from the ten States had come up to Washington to take their seats in the national legislature.

It was a critical moment, not only for the fortunes of the South, but also for the fate of our balanced constitutional government, when Thaddeus Stevens rose at the opening of the session to move that the names of the Representatives-elect from the Southern States be omitted from the roll call of the House, and that a joint congressional committee of fifteen be appointed to determine the conditions on which the States lately in rebellion should be readmitted to the Union. It meant the repudiation of President Johnson's summer work, the commencement of reconstruction *de novo*, and the initiation of a dozen years of rule by a congressional oligarchy. Many reasons lay behind this drastic reversal of the presidential policy of both Lincoln and Johnson—the claim of Congress, already put forth in the Wade-Davis bill, to prescribe the terms of reconstruction; resentment against the "accidental" President Johnson for having proceeded with his program during the recess of Congress, when its leaders were fuming in impotence at home; indignation with the South for having sent up to Congress many of the conspicuous leaders of the "rebellion," including the Vice President of the Confederacy, Alexander H. Stephens; condemnation of the Johnson legislatures, in which many a Confederate officer sat in his gray uniform, because they had passed stringent laws (the so-called "black codes") regulating the social and economic status of the newly enfranchised Negroes; and, finally, anxiety lest the Democratic members from the South, combined with their fellow partisans from the North, should wrest the control of Congress from the Republicans.

Before the seceded States could be readmitted, the question of their equitable representation in Congress must be settled. Since the beginning of the government under the Constitution three fifths of their slaves had been counted in the population upon which representation in the House was based. By virtue of this provision, they had in 1860 twenty-one more members than they would have had if the slaves (who, of course could not vote) were not counted at all. And now, if the freed Negroes (whom, of course, they would not allow to vote) were all counted in the population, the South would have an excess of 35 representatives in the House and 35 presidential electors.

The remedy proposed for this inequality by the joint committee early in 1866 was a constitutional amendment basing representation in the House on the number of voters instead of the number of persons in the several States. Blaine was not a member of the committee. He took the lead in opposing their proposition. He pointed out the injustice that would result for certain States of the Union from basing representation upon the voting population. California and Vermont, for example, with total populations of 358,000 and 314,000 respectively, each had three members in the House. But the voters in the "man's country" of California numbered nearly two thirds of the population (207,000), while in Vermont they were hardly more than one fourth of the population (87,000). California, then, according to the committee's plan would have eight Representatives in Congress to Vermont's three. By the same token Indiana would have a fifty per cent larger representation than Massachusetts, instead of the actual ten per cent excess.

Moreover, Blaine thought that the committee's plan would tempt the States to "cheapen suffrage requisites" in order to increase their delegations to Congress. He favored retaining the total population as the basis for representation, but excepting from the count all persons "to whom civil or political rights or privileges are denied or abridged by the constitution or laws of any State on account of race or color." And he ventured to predict that the Southern States, faced with the penalty of a sharp reduction in the number of their Congressmen, would grant the right of suffrage to the Negroes "in a very few years." [1] Apparently Blaine had no objection to seeing the States of the South "cheapen suffrage requisites" for securing a larger representation in Congress! His proposition was embodied in substance in the second section of the Fourteenth Amendment, which, with other sections conferring inviolable citizenship on "all persons born or naturalized in the United States and subject to the jurisdiction thereof," depriving all persons who had engaged in rebellion after having taken the oath to support the Constitution of holding national or State office until their disabilities should be removed by a two-thirds vote of Congress, and providing for the validity of the United States debt and the repudiation of the Confederate debt, was submitted to Congress on April 30, 1866, passed by the required two-thirds vote, and on June 13 sent to the several States for ratification.

Blaine believed that it was "as clear as day" that the amendment need be submitted only to the loyal States actually represented in Congress, which would have secured its speedy ratification. But the majority of Congress were not ready at this time to force the amendment on the South. They thought that its terms were generous and hoped that the late seceded States would accept them (as Tennessee promptly did) as a fair basis for their restoration to the Union. It was a fond delusion. Outraged especially by the disqualifying clause, State after State in the South, with the encouragement of President Johnson, who was now engaged in a bitter personal and political struggle with the Republican leaders in Congress, rejected the amendment. Not a vote was cast for it in the legislatures of Mississippi, Louisiana and Florida,

[1] *Cong. Globe,* 39th Cong., 1st sess., pp. 141–2.

only one in South Carolina and Virginia, and two in Arkansas and Georgia. Texas gave five votes in its favor, Alabama ten, and North Carolina eleven. Had Blaine and those of like mind foreseen the indignation with which the South was to spurn the amendment, or the utter futility of his prophecy that they would voluntarily extend suffrage to the freedmen in order to increase their representation in Congress, he probably would never have opposed the committee's original plan of basing representation on the voting population. His illustrations of the injustice such a system would cause in the representation of the Northern States were after all rather exceptional cases, and, as for "cheapening the suffrage," it is hard to see what specific measures could have been adopted to increase the number of voters in States where virtually unrestricted manhood suffrage already prevailed. But it is certainly not true that Blaine's proposition was indirectly responsible for the "scandal of the carpetbag State governments" and the "horrors of the Ku Klux Klan" in the South, as Edward Stanwood implies in his biography (p. 79).

The Southern States would have rejected the Fourteenth Amendment just as decisively had it provided for representation on the basis of the voting population alone. Its main offense in their eyes was not the suffrage clause, but the section which excluded from office all their former political and military leaders, until they should petition a Republican Congress for what they regarded as a supererogatory pardon. They preferred remaining out of the Union to coming back on terms which seemed to them harsh and humiliating.

When, to use the language of Representative James A. Garfield, "the last of the sinful ten" had "with contempt and scorn flung back into our teeth the magnanimous offer of a generous nation," Congress substituted coercion for invitation. President Johnson, by his exhibition of egotism and pugnacity, had lost whatever chance he had of winning sufficient conservative support to put through his essentially sound Lincolnian policy of reconstruction on a conciliatory and constitutional basis. The "radicals" were in the saddle. They carried the congressional elections of 1866 by a more than three to one majority; and, under the lead of the grim, implacable Stevens, they devised a punitive program for the South, culminating in the Reconstruction Acts of March and July, 1867, described by John W. Burgess as "the most brutal proposition ever introduced into the Congress of the United States by a responsible committee."

The Johnson governments were swept aside and the "sinful ten" States were put under the rule of five major generals supported by 20,000 soldiers of the regular army, under whose supervision they were to frame new constitutions. Negroes were enrolled, 703,000 of them to 627,000 whites, to participate with full political rights in every step of the process of reconstruction. When the new constitutions should have incorporated the unrepealable grant of Negro suffrage and otherwise secured the endorsement of Congress, and when the legislatures elected under them should have ratified the Fourteenth Amendment, then the States, with the permission of Congress, might reënter the Union. Thus began the orgy of Reconstruction under carpetbagger, scalawag and Negro domination, which lasted from two to eight years, and which it is needless to describe again in its sickening details.

Blaine took only a minor part in the debates on the reconstruction measures, though he approved of them in general and voted for the March bill—being absent on his first European trip, with Justin S. Morrill of Vermont, when the July bill was passed.[1] He was veering toward the radicals. In March, 1866, he had spoken strongly against an amendment to an army bill closing the doors of West Point to any cadet from the seceded States. He was willing to trust the President to appoint the sons of Southern loyalists. The proscription proposed was "illiberal and narrow-minded": "its logic can only be justified on the ground taken by my distinguished friend from Pennsylvania [Stevens], who holds that the entire population of the Southern States are alien enemies." [2] Which drew a sarcastic snarl from his "distinguished friend." But the events of the succeeding twelve months had changed Blaine's attitude. He shared the general indignation of the North at the rejection of the Fourteenth Amendment. He lost his last shred of confidence in Andrew Johnson after the latter's disgusting exhibition of demagogy on his "swing around the circle." He believed the exaggerated reports of "Negro massacres" in the South. He interpreted the sweeping radical victory in the November elections of 1866 as the mandate of the people for the enfranchisement of the

[1] Evidently Blaine had some thought of going to South America at this time, for we find among his letters one from J. K. Agassiz, written on April 29, 1867, in reply to a query as to the climate in Brazil: "You could not select a better season for a visit to Rio than the month of June or July, and at no time is the climate more healthy or agreeable."

[2] *Cong. Globe*, 39th Cong., 1st sess., p. 1206.

Negro. "You must protect the loyal man at the South," he declared, "by the gift of free suffrage—the most far-sighted provision against social disorder, the surest guarantee for peace, prosperity and public justice." [1]

Nevertheless, while yielding his assent to compulsory Negro suffrage, he still feebly opposed the Reconstruction Act in its original form, which would have given the Southern States no promise of eventual delivery from military rule. He said that he would vote for the bill anyway, but he begged his "venerable friend" from Pennsylvania to allow an amendment assuring the States of restoration when they should have complied with its terms. John Sherman, who had charge of the bill in the Senate, agreed with him; and the compromise bill which was hurried through Congress in time to prevent a pocket veto, contained, as we have seen, elaborate conditions on which the States might come back into the Union.

In other words, outrageous as the conditions were, Blaine still preferred to keep the States out until they voluntarily accepted them, while Stevens was ready to force the States to accept them at the point of the bayonet. But Blaine receded from this quasi-liberal position also, and approved the radical coercive measures of the Grant Administration, such as the Force bills and the Ku Klux Act. His course was dictated neither by vindictiveness (of which he had not a trace in his nature) nor by partisanship (of which he had more than a trace), but by his inability to regard the leading men of the South as anything else than unrepentant "rebels."

Contrasting sharply with his opportunistic attitude on the reconstruction measures was Blaine's firm stand on the other main question that occupied the attention of Congress in the years immediately following the Civil War—namely, the preservation of the public credit. The war meant much more than the military triumph of Grant over Lee or the constitutional triumph of Webster over Calhoun; it marked also the definitive economic victory of Hamilton over Jefferson. The government's unprecedented demands for food, clothing, munitions, horses, blankets, rifles, cannon and the hundred other requisites of the commissary and quartermaster departments had enormously stimulated the production of the farms, factories, mills and mines. The high tariffs, necessitated by the heavy internal revenue taxes, ensured

[1] *Cong. Globe,* 39th Cong., 2d sess., p. 53.

golden profits to the manufacturer. The issue of hundreds of millions of new currency in the form of greenbacks and national bank notes provided a volume of fluid capital sufficient to finance the industries of extraction, conversion and transportation, which now began for the first time to exploit seriously the illimitable natural resources of the country.

During the decade of the sixties 13,000 miles of railroad were added to the 31,000 operated at the beginning of the war. The value of manufactured products rose from $1,800,000,000 to $4,500,000,000; and the bank deposits from $200,000,000 to over $600,000,000. Business had adjusted itself to the "currency" (paper money) basis, and the question at issue was whether the government should disturb that adjustment by restoring the specie basis, either suddenly or gradually. A group of inflationists, headed by George H. Pendleton of Ohio and Benjamin F. Butler of Massachusetts, advocated a continued issue of paper by the government and even the payment of the principal of the five-twenty bonds in greenbacks. "The return to specie payment," said Butler, "would be equivalent to confiscation by legal action of one-third the value of all the property in the country, excepting only that held by the creditor class. . . . We want a money based not only upon the gold in the country, but upon every other source and element of the national prosperity, emancipated from the control of all other nations." Bryan was to make the same plea for free silver a quarter of a century later.

Blaine was the first man in Congress to attack the repudiation theory of Butler and Pendleton as both morally dishonorable and financially disastrous. On November 26, 1867, he made a masterly speech (followed by others of like tenor in March and June, 1868) to prove that the nation's faith was pledged to the redemption of the five-twenty bonds in coin, even though it was not stipulated on the face of the bonds themselves. Gold had been the recognized currency of the country for years before the bonds were issued. The authorization of $150,-000,000 of greenbacks contemporaneously with the bond issue was purely an emergency measure to save the Treasury from bankruptcy. It was expected that the greenbacks would all have been retired long before the bonds became due, and they were made convertible into bonds to hasten their absorption. At the time of the twin authorization of the bonds and the greenbacks, not a person in Congress, not even

Pendleton himself, had expressed a doubt that the former were payable in gold; and the provision in the law of issue that custom duties
must be paid in coin, in order to provide a sinking fund for the ultimate redemption of the bonds as well as for the payment of the interest on them, showed that it was the intention of the government to
pay the principal in coin also. If an express provision to that effect had
been put into the law authorizing the issue of the ten-forties, it was
only because in the interval "covert insinuations" had been made that
the principal of the five-twenties might be paid in paper. Even Thaddeus Stevens, who in 1862 had spoken of "redemption in gold in
twenty years as one of the special inducements to capitalists to take
the bonds," had now turned to the support of the Butler-Pendleton
heresy. Moreover, when the ten-forties were issued in March of 1863,
only $25,000,000 of the $500,000,000 five-twenties had been sold. It
was only after the victories of Gettysburg and Vicksburg that Jay
Cooke and Company were able to dispose of the rest.

Would any sensible man, argued Blaine, have bought a dollar's
worth of these five-twenties if he had remotely suspected that they
might be redeemed in paper currency, while the ten-forties, specifically
redeemable in coin, were on the market on equally advantageous terms?
He not only showed the illogicality of the Butler-Pendleton theory and
condemned its supporters out of their own mouths, but he cited the
explicit statements of two Secretaries of the Treasury to fortify his position. On April 18, 1864, Secretary Chase had written to Representative Harper of Massachusetts: "The five-twenty sixes are considered
as belonging to the funded or permanent debt. . . . These bonds therefore, according to the usage of the government, are payable in coin."
And Secretary McCulloch had written even more definitely to the New
York banker, Levi P. Morton, on November 15, 1866: "I regard, as
did also my predecessor, all bonds of the United States as payable in
gold. . . . The bonds which have matured since the suspension of
specie payment (a twenty year loan of $3,000,000 in 1842) have been so
paid. . . . The five-twenty bonds of 1862 will either be called in five
years from their date and paid in coin or permitted to run until the
government is prepared to pay them in coin."

So much for the obligation of the government as understood by both
buyer and seller. As to the expediency of paying the principal of the
bonds in paper, that would require the emission of hundreds of mil-

lions more of greenbacks, which would constantly depreciate in value. The government, to be sure, would have no difficulty then in paying its debt so long as "rags and lampblack held out," but in the process it would lose its credits in the markets of the world. The burden imposed by the war could not be discharged by any facile resort to nostrums or by the easy sophistry of Representative S. F. Cary of Ohio, to the effect that "the value of money has no relation to or dependence upon the material of which it is made: if it has the properties of representing measuring or exchange value it is money, and these properties are conferred upon any chosen material by the sovereign power." So the United States might "confer" the properties of money upon linoleum or lozenges, and go its way defiant of the rest of the world.

The true and sensible way to restore our finances, argued Blaine, was to "direct our efforts toward the resumption of specie payment," reducing our military and naval expenditures, reorganizing our revenue system, and stopping the "innumerable leaks and gaps" in our national economy. Above all, no repudiation of our obligations, "in any form, either open or covert, avowed or indirect." "It will doubtless cost us a vast sum to pay that indebtedness," he concluded, "but it would cost us incalculably more not to pay it." [1]

The numerous set speeches in both Houses of Congress on the currency added little in information and nothing in force to Blaine's masterly analysis of the situation in November, 1867. Though "Gentleman George" Pendleton, the champion of the "Ohio idea" of rag money, failed to get the Democratic nomination for President the next year, the party platform contained the declarations that "where the obligations of the government do not expressly state on their face, or the law under which they were issued does not provide, that they shall be paid in coin, they ought in right and justice to be paid in the lawful money of the United States" (i.e. greenbacks); that the government bonds should be taxed; and that there should be "one currency for the producer and the bond holder."

The greenback heresy died hard. Its advocates, often joining with discontented labor groups to form independent parties, were able to get a bill through Congress in 1874 for the inflation of the currency by raising the issue of greenbacks to $400,000,000. President Grant vetoed the bill, and the following year the act was passed providing for re-

[1] *Cong. Globe,* 40th Cong., 1st sess., pp. 799–802.

sumption of specie payment (or the redemption of the greenbacks in gold) on January 1, 1879. Still the soft money men fought for the repeal of the Resumption Act, polling over a million votes in the elections of 1878. The distress of the panic years 1873 to 1878 furnished recruits for their ranks. But with the brightening of the economic skies and the complete success of the resumption policy, the Greenback Party suffered a rapid decline. It polled only a little over 300,000 votes for General James B. Weaver in the campaign of 1880, and four years later it could muster but a meager 175,000 in support of its last presidential candidate, Benjamin F. Butler, a political weathercock who might have aroused the envy of Talleyrand by his rapid changes of party livery.

One act of his congressional career Blaine never ceased to regret. That was his vote cast on February 24, 1868, for the impeachment of Andrew Johnson. For more than a year he had opposed the attempts of Ashley, Boutwell, Stevens, Butler and other extreme radicals to bring the President before the bar of the Senate, challenging Butler to name twenty-five of the two thousand Republican newspapers of the country that advocated "the impeachment movement as one seriously to be undertaken by Congress at this time." He knew that the President's use of his constitutional prerogative of the veto, however exasperating it might be to the congressional "oligarchy," and that his attacks on radical Senators and Congressmen, however unbecoming they were in the chief magistrate of the Republic, did not render him subject to the charge of "treason, bribery or other high crimes and misdemeanors," specified in the Constitution as the grounds for impeachment. He knew that even in the dismissal of Secretary Stanton, in the face of the Tenure of Office Act, the President was not only exercising the privilege of controling his own Cabinet, always accorded to the Executive, but also, in the opinion of the best constitutional lawyers, not even violating the letter of the act itself.

All this Blaine freely confessed in his *Twenty Years of Congress,* published nearly twenty years after the event. Ashley's charges against the President, he says, "were gross exaggerations and distortions of fact" which "could not be sustained by legal evidence or indeed by reputable testimony of any kind." Three times he declares that "the Senate was in the wrong" in its attempt to force upon the President a Cabinet officer who was "personally distrusted and disliked by him."

He commends the seven Senators "of spotless character" who voted for Johnson's acquittal, and declares that "a similar course (to that of Johnson) by Lincoln, Grant or any other President in harmony with his party in Congress would not have been followed by impeachment or censure or even dissent." [1] It is true that every Republican vote cast in the House on February 24, 1868, was in favor of impeachment, and that, aside from casting his vote, Blaine did nothing to help the bad cause. He neither participated in the vituperative tirades against the President which fill 200 columns of the *Congressional Globe* for that day, nor did he serve on the committee to draw up the articles of impeachment and present the accused at the bar of the Senate. Nevertheless, he knew as well in 1868 as he did in 1885 that the charges against Andrew Johnson "could not be sustained by legal evidence or indeed by reputable testimony of any kind"; and that the impeachment proceedings were, as the grim old Thaddeus Stevens boastfully confessed, a purely partisan manoeuvre to get rid of an embarrassing President.

Partisan zeal would have led Blaine in any case to support the Republican nominee in the presidential campaign which opened a few days after the acquittal of President Johnson. But his praise of General Grant as a man than whom "none more highly gifted with executive talent could be found within the limits of the United States," and with whom there would come "a higher standard of American citizenship, with more dignity and character to the name abroad and more assured liberty and security attaching to it at home," [2] would certainly have been modified had he foreseen the depths of degradation and the "nadir of national disgrace" to which American public life was to sink during the Presidency of the victor of Appomattox. Nor would he perhaps have pitched his premature eulogy of Grant so high if the Democratic challenge to policies which he believed vital to the country's welfare had been less defiant. For not only did the platform on which Governor Seymour and General Blair were nominated contain the offensive soft money plank which we have noted, but it also repudiated "the Reconstruction Acts, so-called, of Congress . . . as usurpations, and unconstitutional, revolutionary and void."

Furthermore, just before the convention met, General Blair had written a letter to one of the delegates declaring that "the real and only

[1] *Twenty Years of Congress*, Vol. II, pp. 342, 354, 379.
[2] From a speech at a Republican meeting at Augusta, July 11, 1868. See Blaine's *Political Discussions, Legislative, Diplomatic and Popular*, p. 95.

question," compared with which bonds, greenbacks and the public credit were all "idle talk," was the liberation of the South from congressional coercion. He would have the President "declare the Reconstruction Acts null and void, compel the army to undo its usurpations at the South, dispossess the carpetbag State governments, and allow the white people to organize their own governments and elect Senators and Representatives. To Blaine such a course would be tantamount to abandoning the freedmen to enslavement by their former masters and fomenting a new "rebellion." He never believed, or at least never acknowledged in his public utterances, that the Southerners had ceased to be "traitors" and "rebels."

Still, he could be fair and even generous to the South in matters which did not threaten the reconstruction settlement and Republican domination below Mason and Dixon's line—which he rationalized as the "protection" of the freedmen. We have already noted his objection to visiting the sins of the fathers on the children by the exclusion of Southern lads from the academy at West Point. He was also interested in the economic rehabilitation of the South. In 1866 three fourths of the nearly $20,000,000 of internal revenue collected from the States of the late Confederacy was derived from a tax on cotton. Blaine made a strong plea on February 22, 1867, for the repeal of this tax. Not only were the prosperity of the South and the fate of the Negroes bound up with cotton, he said, but the return to a specie basis depended upon our "exporting something else than gold eagles and five-twenty bonds to pay our balances in Europe." "Put the cotton region in a position to produce 5,000,000 bales," he continued, "and I warrant you we shall be on a specie basis at once. . . . The idea which some gentlemen advance that we are punishing the South by this tax is utterly delusive, if it were not indeed unworthy. . . . Resentment is always an unsafe basis for legislation, and especially unsafe when applied to business and financial questions." [1]

Again, when Ignatius Donnelly and others were urging that the pre-war land grants to the Southern States for railroad construction be confiscated and divided into 40-acre homesteads for destitute loyalists in the South, instead of being left in the hands of "rich rebel stockholders," Blaine vigorously objected in a speech of January 28, 1868. He asked that no action be taken on the subject until the Southern

[1] *Cong. Globe,* 39th Cong., 2d sess., p. 1479.

States were represented in Congress, as they would be "in a few weeks." He pointed out that there were 46,000,000 acres of public land, exclusive of the railroad grants, available for homesteads in the South. He "put the rebels out of the account." His concern was for the economic prosperity of a great section of our country. "I say there is no hope for the growth of cotton and grain down South on the part of the loyal men there, unless we furnish them with the magnificent facilities for transportation to market afforded by those very lines of railroad. . . . The interest of the country demands their speedy completion." [1] This speech was made long before Blaine had any personal financial interest in the building of any of these railroads.

When Blaine was serving his second term in Congress, an incident occurred, so trivial in its political significance as to be soon forgotten, but destined to be of sinister importance for his future career. On April 24, 1866, Roscoe Conkling of New York, a towering colossus of conceit, with a handsome haughty mien crowned with "Hyperion's curls," and an imperious manner that bore down opposition as a personal insult, rose to attack a section of an army bill providing for a permanent Provost Marshal's Bureau, and at the same time to cast aspersions on the prospective head of the bureau, General James B. Fry. The bill, he said, "creates an unnecessary office for an undeserving public servant." Blaine, who was a member of the Committee on Military Affairs. immediately came to the aid of the bill and the General. The passage at arms developed into a bitter quarrel, in which Blaine accused Conkling of misrepresenting General Grant's views on the subject, of seeking personal revenge against General Fry for having "come out second best" in several altercations with that officer, of having violated his oath by accepting a fee of $3000 as judge advocate while serving as a member of Congress, and of having altered his truculent language on the floor of the House for publication in the *Congressional Globe*. Instead of confining himself to the difficult task of refuting these charges, Conkling resorted to his characteristic device of crushing his opponent under an avalanche of vituperative scorn. "If General Fry is reduced to depending for vindication upon the gentleman from Maine, he is to be commiserated indeed. If I have fallen to the necessity of taking lessons from that gentleman in the rules of propriety or of right or wrong, God help me! . . . If the member from Maine had the least idea how profoundly

---

[1] *Cong. Globe,* 40th Cong., 2d sess., pp. 810–811.

indifferent I am to his opinion on the subject which he has been discussing, or upon any other subject personal to me, I think he would hardly have troubled to rise here and express his opinion."

This was a little too much for Blaine's equanimity. Turning to Conkling, who was busily writing at his desk in order to show his "profound indifference," he flung at him an impromptu retort which has become a classic in the annals of Congress: "As to the gentleman's cruel sarcasm, I hope he will not be too severe. The contempt of that large-minded gentleman is so wilting, his haughty disdain, his grandiloquent swell, his majestic, supereminent, turkey-gobbler strut has been so crushing to myself and all the members of the House, that I know it was an act of the greatest temerity for me to venture upon a controversy with him. But, sir, I know who is responsible for all this. . . . That gifted and satirical writer, Theodore Tilton of the New York *Independent*, published in that paper a little jocose satire, a part of which was the statement that the mantle of the late Winter Davis had fallen upon the member from New York. The gentleman took it seriously and it has given his strut additional pomposity. The resemblance is great. It is striking. Hyperion to a satyr, Thersites to Hercules, mud to marble, dunghill to diamond, a singed cat to a Bengal tiger, a whining puppy to a roaring lion. Shades of the mighty Davis, forgive the almost profanation of that jocose satire!" [1] Blaine's ill feeling was wholly blown off in this unpremeditated outburst of sarcasm. He was ready to consider the incident closed and resume amicable relations with his colleague.[2] But Conkling, whose remarks had been fully as insulting if not so picturesque as Blaine's, would neither forgive nor forget. He repelled every overture from Blaine's and his own friends for reconciliation, and to the end of his life used his tremendous power as boss of the Republican machine in New York State to thwart the political ambitions of the Maine statesman. "No, thank you," he replied when asked to take the stump for Blaine in the campaign of 1884, "I don't engage in criminal prac-

---

[1] *Cong. Globe,* 39th Cong., 1st sess., pp. 2151–2299.

[2] The two men, however, were so antagonistic in temperament that they never could have become close friends. They had already had several tiffs in Congress and out, in which Conkling's bad disposition was shown. The trouble began, it is said, at a dinner party, over the authorship of a couplet which had greatly taken Conkling's fancy, because he represented the Utica district in New York:

"No pent up Utica contracts our powers,
But the whole boundless continent is ours."

Conkling insisted that the lines were in Addison's *Cato,* and Blaine bet him a basket of champagne that they were not. Conkling lost the bet and sent the champagne, but he refused to attend the dinner which Blaine gave to open it.

tice." His home county of Oneida, which had given Garfield a plurality of 1946 in 1880, went for Cleveland in 1884. This defection alone cost Blaine nearly double the votes he needed in the final count to carry New York and the election.

The election of Schuyler Colfax of Indiana as Vice President on the ticket with Grant in 1868 created a vacancy in the Speakership of the House. Blaine was an aspirant for the position. Immediately after the election he wrote from Augusta to his friend Garfield, who was being mentioned for the place, calling his attention to the fact that, since both the presidential and vice presidential candidates were from the West, and the Speakership had been held for the past six years by a Western member, it was only fair that the East should have the honor. "I infer from this series of facts," he continued, "that you will probably not allow your name to be used. If not, I desire your most active sympathy and support for myself." He based his request upon "sympathy of views, identity of age, contemporaneous service in the House and an unshaken and cordial friendship for the past six years." [1] Henry L. Dawes of Massachusetts was also a candidate for the office, but when the Forty-first Congress met in March, 1869, Dawes withdrew and himself nominated Blaine, who was elected by the unanimous vote of the Republican members. He was reëlected with the same unanimity in the two succeeding Congresses, and retired from the Speakership in 1875 to become the minority leader on the floor, when the Democrats came into control of the House for the first time since the outbreak of the Civil War.

By common consent of Republicans and Democrats, friends and foes, Blaine ranks with the very greatest Speakers of the House. He was eminently fitted for the position. The vigor of the early forties animated his tall, commanding figure and radiated from eye, voice and gesture. His courtesy was unfailing, his temper unruffled, and his command of parliamentary law and procedure unimpeachable. His committee appointments, over which he labored for weeks during the recesses of Congress, were wisely and fairly made.[2] His rulings, even in the heat of bitter partisan strife, were invariably sustained by the House. His con-

---

[1] Blaine to Garfield, Nov. 10, 1868; *Garfield Papers* in the Library of Congress, Vol. 20, item 99.

[2] For example, recognizing the sentiment for tariff reform in the elections of 1870, and ignoring the protests of the high protectionists, he appointed two revisionists out of the six Republican members of the Ways and Means Committee, who, with the three Democratic members, gave the tariff reformers a majority of five to four on the committee.

ception of the Speakership differed from that of Henry Clay, with whom he has been most frequently compared. For, while Clay often left the chair to debate issues and join controversy on the floor of the House, Blaine seldom did.[1] Since he thus sank his political privileges as a member in his parliamentary duties as presiding officer of the House, the six years of his Speakership, in contrast to his previous six years in Congress, furnished little material for the columns of the *Congressional Globe* or the *Congressional Record*.[2]

Probably the years of the Speakership were the happiest period of Blaine's life. Not only did he find the duties and responsibilities of the position congenial, but the hundreds of letters of commendation that poured in upon him must have been extremely gratifying to his receptive nature. Carl Schurz, who later was to be a thorn in his flesh, wrote to him from St. Louis in January, 1869: "I hope soon to have the occasion to congratulate you on the promotion you desire and deserve." The Democratic Congressman S. S. ("Sunset") Cox, with whom he had had many a set-to on the floor, wrote from New York in November 1873: "To miss your face in the House and at its Head would be to miss the House itself." And a year later Michael C. Kerr, who was to be his Democratic successor, wrote from New Albany, Indiana, to thank him for his letter of congratulation, and added: "If it (my election) should happen, no reflection would give me more disquiet than that which makes me realize the essential difficulty there would be in an untried hand attempting to preside over such a body, *after* one who has per- formed that duty with such signal ability and success as you have done."

Blaine's delightful family life, which was founded on a mutual devotion of parents and children which far transcended all the vicissitudes of political fortune, was also enhanced in these years by the gratification of certain social ambitions. Early investments in coal and iron lands had brought him a moderate fortune. In 1862, finding the old Stanwood homestead in Augusta inadequate for his growing family, he had pur-

---

[1] On one occasion, in March, 1871, when he descended from the chair to administer a stinging rebuke to the redoubtable Benjamin F. Butler, Blaine explained his conception of the Speakership in these words: "Mr. Speaker, in old times it was the habit of the Speaker of the House of Representatives to take part in debate. The custom has fallen into disuse. For one, I am very glad that it has. . . . The Speaker should, with consistent fidelity to his own party, be the impartial administrator of the rules of the House; and a constant participation in the discussions of the members would take from him that appearance of impartiality which it is so important to maintain in the rulings of the chair." *Cong. Globe,* 42d Cong., 1st sess., p. 125.

[2] It was during Blaine's Speakership, in December, 1873, that the name of the journal of Congress was changed from *Globe* to *Record*.

chased from the heirs of Greenwood Child the spacious mansion and grounds at the corner of State and Capitol Streets, just across the way from Charles Bulfinch's capitol building.[1] When he became Speaker he bought a comfortable house on Fifteenth Street, between H and I, in Washington, with the aid of a $30,000 mortgage loan by Jay Cooke & Co. He was able now to have his whole family with him at Washington during the sessions of Congress, and to utilize to the full his wife's brilliant social talents. Senator Buckingham of Connecticut and Representative Swann of Maryland were his next-door neighbors. Fernando Wood of New York lived two doors away, and across the street Secretary of State Hamilton Fish. Near by, on I Street, was the home of his cousin Ellen Ewing Sherman, wife of the General and sister of his boyhood chums at Lancaster, Pennsylvania, Tom and Hugh Ewing. He gathered about his hospitable table distinguished guests who often forgot to finish their courses as they became absorbed in the feast of reason which he set before them from his wonderful store of historical and political knowledge. Other men gave more elaborate dinners, but no other could furnish a more delightful and profitable evening. He was the most popular man in Washington and was rapidly becoming the recognized leader of the Republican Party in the nation.

Though the years of the Speakership witnessed the revelations of the scandals which disgraced the Grant Administration, it was not until after he had left the Speaker's chair that Blaine himself was charged with any impropriety in the conduct of his office. When the Crédit Mobilier compelled the attention of the Congress which met in December, 1872, Blaine called S. S. Cox to the chair and himself moved the appointment of a committee of investigation, which, under the efficient chairmanship of Luke P. Poland, conducted the examination without fear or favor. When the "Salary Grab" act was passed in March, 1873, Blaine refused to be a beneficiary of the "back pay steal," and read

---

[1] The Blaine mansion, enlarged and refitted for the purposes of state, is now the residence of the Governor of Maine. It was bought from the Blaine heirs by Truxton Beale and given to his son Walker Blaine Beale on his twenty-first birthday, March 22, 1917. Early in the next year Walker Beale offered the house to the State of Maine for use during the war. Lieutenant Walker Blaine Beale fell on the battlefield of St. Mihiel, and Mrs. Beale deeded the mansion to the State in memory of her son. The memorial tablet, with its courageous motto, *Laetus sorte mea,* stands on the wall of the entrance hall, between the portraits of Lieutenant Beale and his grandfather. The most interesting room in the house is Blaine's little study, with the old furniture (the gas chandelier, square clock, leather covered sofa, and high bookcases filled with the historical and political classics of the last century) left as it was in the days when he retired from the friendly confusion of the household to devote himself to his arduous tasks.

into the bill a phrase exempting the Speaker from the retroactive provision which gave Senators and Representatives a bonus of $5000 for their service in the Congress which was just coming to an end. "Mr. Blaine," said the Baltimore *American* of March 2, 1875, "has never been smirched with the corruption prevalent around Washington. The man possesses an integrity above such temptation, and with this character, united to his intellect and independence, he is marked for further prominence in American politics."

Indeed, the flavor of clover was so stong that the presidential bee began to buzz about Blaine's bonnet, if not in it. He was too good an Administration man to dream of contesting the renomination of Grant in 1872, whatever misgivings he might have had about the superlative blessings which he had declared four years earlier were certain to result from the election of the "highly gifted" victor of Appomattox.[1] Of course, also, he was too good a party man to have anything but scorn for the bolting "Liberal Republicans" who assembled in mass meeting at Cincinnati on May 1, 1872, under the leadership of Carl Schurz, to make an end of "Grantism" and all its evil works—the perpetuation of bayonet rule in the South, corruption in the civil service, venality, graft and plunder in high office. The Liberal Republicans, with a platform commendable in many respects, nominated an impossible candidate in the person of Horace Greeley of the New York *Tribune,* who was a high protectionist, an ardent advocate of the spoils system, and the most vituperative persecutor of the Democrats in the whole country. In fact, his only qualification to run on the Cincinnati platform was his policy of amnesty to the South, his adjuration of his fellow countrymen to "clasp hands across the bloody chasm" of the Civil War.

The Republicans renominated General Grant on the first ballot, at

---

[1] Mrs. Blaine, whose lively letters to her absent children (published by Mrs. Harriet Blaine Beale in 1908) reflect the opinion of the household, has little good to say of Grant. On October 19, 1871, she wrote to her son Walker in Paris: "Father is in Bangor, accompanied by the President. . . . There was a great crowd and Grant was as miserable as is his wont on such occasions. . . . Joe (Manley) says there were many comparisons drawn between the bearing of the President and the Speaker. Probably the latter never stood so high in the affection of his fellow citizens as he does at this moment." (Vol. I, p. 48–49). In her letter of February 18, 1872, she says: "Friday we had our Presidential dinner. O, how glad I am to have it over! The President is so heavy in everything but feeding—there he is very light. He talked incessantly about himself. I have a certain sympathy with him, for I think him an honest man, and indeed he feels dreadfully assailed." (*Ibid.*, p. 90.) And again, on May 15, she writes: "Just now people are constantly coming to (your father) to talk on the presidential question. What can be done with the situation occupies all heads, and some few good people put their hearts over the bars. But no politics in home letters." (*Ibid.*, p. 126.)

Philadelphia, June 5. The Democrats, a few weeks later at Baltimore, in their desperate desire to "beat Grant," stultified themselves by accepting the Cincinnati platform, and, with a very wry face, ate the dish of "boiled crow" set before them in the nomination of Horace Greeley. Ninety-five per cent of the delegates at Baltimore endorsed the candidacy of the man who had never picked up his powerful pen to write of the Democrats without dipping its point in gall.

Blaine had harbored no ambition to secure the nomination either at Cincinnati or at Philadelphia. Still the presidential bee continued to buzz about his head. Richard Smith of the Cincinnati *Gazette* wrote to him on May 4, 1872: "Certain it is, if Grant should get out of the way and you should be nominated, the Republican Party would sweep the country. The breach in the West would be promptly and effectively healed. Our liberal Republicans and our liberal press, German and English, would wheel into line. These are disgusted with the result of the Cincinnati convention, and would gladly avail themselves of the opportunity to get back, but there is so much feeling against Grant that I do not see how it is to be overcome. . . . The whole German press of the West repudiates Greeley. I feel satisfied Schurz is perfectly disgusted and that he would support you."

Blaine worked zealously during the summer to "kindle enthusiasm on the Grant side" by a decisive Republican victory at the September elections in Maine. "As Maine goes, so goes the election," had long been a political proverb. So important were the returns from this lead-off State that Greeley in person invaded Blaine's stronghold on a stumping tour, and the Greeley press made Blaine an even more conspicuous target for their abuse than Grant himself. On September 4, just on the eve of the Maine election, Charles A. Dana filled more than half the columns of the New York *Sun* with a tale of "colossal bribery" perpetrated by the Crédit Mobilier corporation, formed for the construction of the Union Pacific Railroad, and composed of an inner ring of the stockholders of the road who awarded themselves lucrative fraudulent contracts at the expense of the government and the taxpayers of the country. A disgruntled member of the ring, one Henry S. McComb, who thought he had not got the share of the loot due him, furnished Mr. Dana with a list of public men who had been bribed by the gift of Crédit Mobilier stock, together with a letter from Congressman Oakes Ames of Massachusetts, the directing spirit of the shady enterprise, to the effect that he had placed the shares of stock "where they would do the most good."

At the head of the list stood the name of James G. Blaine, followed by a dozen others, including Vice President Colfax, Secretary of the Treasury Boutwell, two United States Senators, and eight members of Congress. Blaine contented himself for the moment with a denial of the accusation. But after he had brought the Republican State ticket in Maine through with a majority of 15,000, the opposition press redoubled its efforts to fasten the charges of corruption upon him. The New York *Tribune,* on September 28, published another story under the caption "Proof of Blaine's Frauds," to the effect that he had accepted as a gratuity, in order to influence his votes in Congress, stock to the value of nearly $2,000,000 in the Leavenworth, Pawnee and Western Railroad, which had been merged into the Eastern Division of the Union Pacific. Declining the advice of his friends to sue the *Tribune* for libel, Blaine took occasion in a campaign speech delivered at Cleveland, Ohio, the next month, to demolish the story completely. "In 1862, when the act (incorporating the Union Pacific) was passed," he said, "I had not taken my seat in Congress, I had not been elected to Congress, I had not even been nominated for Congress. When the act to which the *Tribune* refers became a law, I was a member of the Maine legislature and Speaker of the lower House. I had no more to do with congressional legislation than the fish-wardens and tide-waiters on the Kennebec River." [1] The ridiculous mouse that came out of the labor of this mountain of accusation was the discovery that Blaine's brother, John E. Blaine, one of the early settlers of Kansas, had owned $10,000 of stock in the L. P. and W. Railroad before its merger into the Union Pacific. The *Tribune,* with its tongue in its cheek, then "took pleasure in withdrawing in the promptest and fullest manner the imputations upon Mr. Blaine."

So much for the canard of the two millions. But there remained McComb's list of the prominent recipients of the incriminating Crédit Mobilier stock. As Blaine's name was the first on the list, he was the first to appear before the Poland investigating committee, which, as we have seen, was appointed on his own motion (p. 64). After his categorical denial that he had ever accepted a single share of the stock, he turned to Oakes Ames with the question: "Is it not so, Mr. Ames?"

[1] Gail Hamilton, *Biography of James G. Blaine,* p. 277.

and Ames replied, "It is so, Mr. Blaine." [1] Others came out of the investigation less fortunately. Vice President Colfax, after involving himself in a mass of contradictions and tergiversations, descended from the witness stand thoroughly discredited, and soon after retired into deserved obscurity. James A. Garfield, confronted with Ames' inexorable memorandum book showing a cash payment to him of $329 which represented the excess of dividends over the purchase price of the stock, tried to pass the sum off as a "loan" from Ames which he was not asked to repay! This lame explanation, however, did not prevent Garfield's return to the House or his election later to the Presidency. [2]

Other defendants brazened it out, declaring that there was nothing wrong in accepting the highly profitable stock and that they would have taken more if they had had the chance. [3] Senator James W. Patterson of New Hampshire was the only man on the McComb list to be publicly reprimanded for participation in the scandal. A committee of his colleagues, reviewing his perjured testimony, recommended his expulsion from the Senate. But, as his term was about to expire, the Senate did not act on the case. Two scapegoats were provided, however, to appease the popular indignation. The Poland Committee recommended the expulsion of Oakes Ames and James Brooks (a Democrat from New York) from the House. Brooks' guilt was clear. As a government director of the Union Pacific, he had broken the law by the surreptitious acquisition of 240 shares of the railroad's stock, and he had been hand in glove with the men who were seeking to debauch his fellow congressmen. [4] As to Ames, the judgment was, and still is, divided. His testimony certainly sounds more honest than that of some of the men who emerged from the ordeal without rebuke. Again and again he avowed that he had not had the remotest idea of "bribing" his friends in Congress by offering them a good bargain in Crédit Mobilier stock. Why should he bribe them? Bribes were for enemies, and all these men were friends

---

[1] The Poland Committee, *Testimony,* p. 17.

[2] In its report of Feb. 18, 1873, the Poland Committee, without censuring Garfield, adopted Ames' version of the transaction. "He (Garfield) agreed with Mr. Ames," it read, "to take ten shares of Crédit Mobilier stock, but did not pay for the same. Mr. Ames received dividends . . . which together paid the price of the shares and interest and left a balance of $329. This sum was paid over to Mr. Garfield." Poland *Report,* p. vii.

[3] In the 32 months from April, 1867, to December, 1869, the Crédit Mobilier declared dividends of 615% in Union Pacific stock, 280% in U. P. first mortgage bonds, and 60% in cash. Reckoning the stock and bonds at the conservative market value of 19 and 80 respectively, the yield to the holder of $1000 of Crédit Mobilier stock would amount to $4008.50.

[4] Poland Committee, *Testimony,* pp. 164, 176, 242, 426.

of the Union Pacific. To which the obvious reply is: If they were friends, why the need to distribute the stock among them "where it would do the most good"?

For one who was so eager on the witness stand to deny the acceptance of any of the Crédit Mobilier stock, Blaine's treatment of the men who proffered it was, to say the least, indulgent. He must have known that Ames was not making gifts of stock which paid fabulous dividends to members of Congress, without expecting any favors in return. Yet he went out of his way to give his private sympathy and public approval to his fellow congressmen under suspicion, and even to Ames himself. Gail Hamilton paints a pathetic picture of "Oakes Ames—a man of honored ancestry and stainless name, the modest hero of the great Pacific Railroad, the man whose energy had wrenched it from failure when to a less patriotic insight the nation itself seemed a failure (!), and had made its final link a guaranty of national peace and union— sitting silent, stunned into immobility before Mr. Blaine's library fire with his head bowed on his breast, while the younger man (Blaine), alert and intent, applied himself indefatigably in and out of the House, arranging for his defense as for that of the other men who were im- plicated with him, and who were equally guiltless of bribery." [1] When an amendment before the House to substitute a vote of censure for the expulsion of Ames and Brooks was on the point of being defeated, Blaine held up the vote until enough of Ames' friends could be summoned to the floor to ensure the passage of the amendment. But a vote of censure could hardly be interpreted as an exculpation! And the fact that the vote of censure was passed on February 27, 1873, by 182 to 36, showed that the great majority of the House were convinced of Ames' guilt.

Five days after this closing incident in the Crédit Mobilier investiga- tion, General Grant entered upon his second term, with the following highly inappropriate expression of personal feeling in his inaugural ad- dress: "I have been the subject of abuse and slander scarcely ever equaled in political history, which today I feel that I can afford to dis- regard in view of your verdict, which I gratefully accept as my vin- dication." Had he known what trials and humiliations the next four years were to bring, his "gratitude" would have been left unspoken. For the Crédit Mobilier was only the first of a series of sordid revela-

[1] Gail Hamilton, *Biography of James G. Blaine*, p. 286.

tions of greed, graft and corruption in high places which led Henry Adams to remark that "Grant's Administration outraged every rule of ordinary decency: the moral law had expired—like the Constitution." [1] The "salary grab," the festering sore of racial strife in Louisiana and South Carolina, the whisky frauds, the abandonment of the civil service to the basest use of the Butlers, the Mortons, the Chandlers and the Conklings, the complicity of Secretary of War Belknap and his dashing wife in the sale of Western post traderships, the náusea that the names of Simmons, Shepherd and Sanborn brought to the stomachs of honest men—all put an increasing load of obloquy on the Administration.

Neither the successful outcome of the arbitration of the Alabama Claims at Geneva, nor the President's courageous veto of the inflation bill could save the Republicans from a crushing defeat in the mid-term elections of 1874. Massachusetts, Pennsylvania, Ohio and Indiana elected Democratic Governors, and for the first time since the Southern Congressmen had left their seats at Washington to join the Confederacy, in the closing days of Buchanan's Administration, the Democrats secured control of the House of Representatives, replacing a Republican majority of over a hundred by a Democratic majority two thirds as large. Economic distress reinforced political upheaval. The severe panic which broke out in September, 1873, with the failure of that reputed Gibraltar of American finance, Jay Cooke, continued unrelieved through Grant's second Administration. The country had fallen on evil days, indeed.

In the centennial year of 1876, Senator George F. Hoar of Massachusetts summed up the scathing indictment in his speech before the Senators sitting as judges in the impeachment trial of Secretary Belknap: "My own public life has been a very brief and insignificant one, extending little beyond the duration of a single term of senatorial office. But in that brief period I have seen five judges of a high court of the United States driven from office by threats of impeachment for corruption or maladministration. . . . I have seen in the State in the Union foremost in power and wealth four judges of her courts impeached for corruption, and the political administration of her chief city become a disgrace and a by-word throughout the world. I have seen the chairman of the Committee on Military Affairs in the House

[1] *The Education of Henry Adams,* p. 280.

rise in his place and demand the expulsion of four of his associates for making sale of their official privilege of selecting the youths to be educated at our great military school. When the greatest railroad of the world, binding together the continent and uniting the two seas which wash our shores, was finished, I have seen our national triumph and exaltation turned to bitterness and shame by the unanimous report of three committees of Congress . . . that every step of that mighty enterprise had been taken in fraud. I have heard in the highest places the shameless doctrine avowed by men grown old in public service that the true way by which power could be gained in a republic is to bribe the people with the offices created for their service, and that the true end for which it should be used when gained is the promotion of selfish ambition and the gratification of personal revenge. I have heard that suspicion haunts the footsteps of the trusted companions of the President." [1]

Still, Blaine's withers were unwrung. The scandals of the Administration passed him by. His stock never stood higher than in the closing days of his Speakership. Recruits to what Charles Edward Russell calls "the Blaine legion" were coming from all parts of the country. Congratulatory letters were pouring in upon him: from George W. McCreary in Iowa, "The West will be for your nomination in 1876"; from Governor Garland of Arkansas, "May you live long to serve and to honor our common country"; from the Harpers in New York (to Gail Hamilton), "We like Blaine. He is as independent as any man we ever knew. . . . As your western friends say, we can safely 'go blind on him.' *O, si sic omnes!*" A group of liberal Republicans called on him at his house in Washington in the winter of 1875 to try to get him to head a movement for a new reform party.[2] The press reflected the growing sentiment of congratulation and approval. The powerful New York *Tribune* passed after Greeley's death in 1872 into the control of Whitelaw Reid, one of the staunchest of the Blaine supporters. Even Dana in the *Sun* gave grudging approval to some of "Brother Blaine's" rulings, while the caustic *Nation* said (March 11, 1875), "Mr. Blaine's rise to a position of prominence among the leading men of his party is a gratifying sign, for he has obtained his powers not by unscrupulous partisanship, but by hard work in a difficult office, and has increased

1 George F. Hoar, *Autobiography of Seventy Years*, Vol. I, p. 307.
2 Gail Hamilton, *Biography of James G. Blaine*, p. 319.

his popularity not by buncombe speeches or the low arts of the demagogue, but by the exhibition of those qualities of firmness, good sense and respect for the rights of others which ought to make a man popular. He has his faults, no doubt, but, compared with Morton, Logan and the present leaders of the Republicans, he seems like an ancient Roman for virtue."

The closing scene of the Forty-third Congress marked the apogee of Blaine's popularity. He was later to receive louder partisan acclaim, but never again to enjoy so great a measure of esteem in the eyes of his countrymen, regardless of section, party or creed, as when he arose on the fourth of March, 1875, to deliver his brief valedictory address as Speaker of the House. He spoke with modest dignity of the honor and responsibility of the position which he had held for a period surpassed in length by only two of his predecessors, and made gracious acknowledgment of the "generous courtesy" with which the Democratic minority of the House had always treated him. When he brought down the gavel to mark the adjournment of the House *sine die,* the floor and crowded galleries broke into prolonged applause. "No such ovation," says an eyewitness, "was ever before given to a retiring Speaker. No other since Henry Clay has been so popular as he, in his six years of service. Tears came into the good man's eyes as he stood silently contemplating this tribute to his justice and equity, his unflinching rectitude and admirable tact. The Democratic side cheered as lustily as the Republican. The exuberant Cox looked as if nothing short of a somersault would adequately express his feelings. Then came the prolonged handshaking, till I wondered how the firm right hand could stand the strain." [1] The Maine delegation brought forward a present of several articles of solid silver, which he received quietly and sent directly home by a page. "Mr. Blaine," said the Boston *Advertiser,* the day after the adjournment, "has proven himself equal to all the requirements of his high office, and, in laying down the gavel at the close of his six years service, he does so with the universal respect of the whole country and with the admiration and respect of all who have served in Congress under his Speakership."

It was the cloudless, sun-drenched hour before the storm.

[1] Emma James in the Cleveland *Daily Herald,* March 11, 1875.

"Mr. Blaine," continued the editorial quoted at the close of the preceding chapter, "is a member-elect of the next Congress, so that the country will not lose the benefit of his ability and long experience. He will, of course, take high position as leader of the Republican minority in the next House." This prophecy, amply fulfilled, came perilously near to nonfulfilment. In the late evening of June 12, 1875, the train on which he was riding from Boston left the tracks about ten miles from the New York terminal, and his car was overturned. "There we were," he wrote to his anxious family from the Fifth Avenue Hotel the next day, "an indistinguishable mass of men, women, chairs, sofas, carpetbags, umbrellas and so forth. . . . On attempting to rise I found my right side so lame and so painful that I certainly thought some ribs were broken. I am very stiff today and full of aches and pains; but I have great cause for thankfulness that I got off without any real injury. . . . The train was running 35 miles an hour in the dark and rain, so that no element was lacking to make the accident fearful. . . . Had the car taken fire, I don't see how any one of us could ever have got out, but fortunately there was no kerosene, the Boston line using large candles." [1] By the end of the month Blaine was well enough to attend the commencement exercises at his *alma mater* at Washington, Pennsylvania, and there to be hailed as the next Republican nominee for the Presidency. During the summer letters came to him from all parts of the country, assuring him of enthusiastic support for the honor.

But the Republican Party did not share the popularity of its brilliant son. It was not enough that one scandal followed on another's heels, like the procession of specters which passed before Macbeth's fear-haunted eyes. Bullying and blundering had to be added to the score. President Grant had entered his second term with the declaration that "the States lately at war with the general Government are now happily rehabilitated." Yet the history of South Carolina, Mississippi, Arkansas, and Louisiana in the two years that followed pre-

---

[1] Gail Hamilton, *Biography of James G. Blaine*, p. 372.

sents a sickening record of race wars, massacres, assassinations, election riots, rival governments, mounting taxes, vanishing property values, official rascality and rapacity exploiting ignorance and prejudice. To meet these anarchic conditions in the South, the Administration resorted to the grim enforcement of the very policy that had produced them. President Grant was doubtless sincere when he wrote to the Attorney General, Edwards Pierrepont, on September 14, 1875, in reply to the request of the carpetbag Governor Ames of Mississippi for Federal troops: "The whole public are tired out with these annual autumnal outbreaks in the South, and the great majority are ready now to condemn any interference on the part of the Government." [1]

But it was a late repentance—on the eve of a presidential year. Before that he had been deaf to the voices of conciliation. The noble eulogy of Charles Sumner, delivered by L. Q. C. Lamar of Mississippi in the Senate chamber on April 27, 1874, with its closing appeal, "My countrymen, know one another and you will love one another," had left him cold. The apostles of vengeance, force and narrow partisan advantage had his ear, and they egged him on to measures of repression, such as the proclamation of martial law, the dispatch of Federal troops to the South and the support of every carpetbag and scalawag official whose ascendency gave promise of more Republican votes. The "bloody shirt" was frantically waved in the attempt to flag Democratic success in the elections of 1874. The Republican State Committee of Indiana, under the orders of Morton, sent a circular to the Republican editors of the State to give chief prominence, until after the election, to "the horrible scenes of violence and bloodshed transpiring through the South." [2] Benjamin Butler's Force Bill, giving the President the right to suspend the writ of habeas corpus for two years in the States of Alabama, Louisiana, Mississippi and Arkansas, thus converting Grant into "a sort of tawdry Caesar," [3] was passed by the House in February, 1875, though Congress expired before it came to a vote in the Senate. Three days before the close of the session, however, the President signed a Civil Rights Bill (passed in deference to the memory of Charles Sumner [4]), forbidding the exclusion of Negroes from jury

---

[1] *Appleton's American Cyclopaedia*, 1875, p. 516.
[2] W. D. Foulke, *The Life of Oliver Morton*, Vol. II, p. 350.
[3] The phrase is used by the New York *Nation*, Feb. 18, 1875.
[4] J. F. Rhodes, *History of the United States from the Compromise of 1850*, Vol. VII, p. 90.

service and giving them equal rights with whites in hotels and inns, public conveyances, theaters, concerts and other amusement places.[1]

The object of all this solicitude of the radicals that the reconstruction laws "be faithfully executed" was, of course, the salvaging of the diminishing Republican majorities. The *National Republican* of Washington, the Administration organ, made no concealment of the fact. Commenting on the Force bill of 1875, it said (February 27), "The passage of this bill is required to preserve to the Republican Party the electoral vote of the Southern States. Remember that if the Democrats carry all the South, it will require only fifty electoral votes from the Northern States to elect a Democratic President."

Not only was it necessary to elect a Republican President in 1876, but that President, according to the plans of the radical junto, must be General Grant. The movement for a third term for the "strong silent man" in the White House was assuming threatening proportions. It was stated that 80,000 Federal officeholders, including the whole force in the South, were working for it. Grant himself met the suggestion in a letter of May 29, 1875, with the equivocal statement: "I do not want a third term any more than I wanted a first. . . . I would not accept a nomination unless it should come under such circumstances as to make it an imperative duty." [2] The circumstances of the whisky frauds and the Belknap graft were little likely, however, to persuade the American people to depart from the precedent set by Washington and Jefferson. And the "third term bogy" was laid to rest soon after the assembling of the new Congress by the overwhelming adoption (233 to 18) by the House of a resolution declaring that a third term would be "unwise, unpatriotic and fraught with peril to our free institutions." That ended the incipient boom for Grant. His name was not presented at the nominating convention of 1876.

It was significant that Blaine did not vote on the anti-third-term resolution. It would have looked too much like Prince Hal trying on his father's crown.[3] He had returned to Congress after his seventh easy victory in the Kennebec district, to devote his talents to the leadership of the Republican minority in the House, and as the leader of the op-

[1] This legislation was declared unconstitutional by the Supreme Court in 1883. 109 U. S. 3.

[2] *Appleton's American Cyclopaedia*, 1875, p. 743.

[3] The report was telegraphed to the West that when Grant was informed of Blaine's failure to vote, he blurted out, "He is not in anybody's way, so he needn't be so damned careful." W. E. Niblack of Indiana to Blaine, Dec. 19, 1875.

position to prove himself as formidable as ever a Fox or a Peel or a Gladstone had been in the British Parliament. He was forty-five years old, at the height of his mental and physical vigor, at once winsome and aggressive, reasonable and resolute, with a complete mastery of parliamentary finesse. The session had no sooner opened than he proceeded to stand the Democratic majority on its head.

The anarchic condition of Louisiana had resulted in the election of rival governments in 1874, and a piebald delegation had come up to Congress from the State. Most of the members-elect had certificates signed by the heads of both factions, but one had a certificate signed only by the radical claimant to the Governorship, Kellogg, while one had a certificate signed by the conservative McEnery alone. The latter seat was contested, and Fernando Wood, Democrat, of New York, moved that the contest be referred to the Committee on Elections, which was, of course, predominantly Democratic. By the so-called "Wheeler Compromise" of 1874, it had been agreed that the conservatives should be restored to their seats (and therewith a majority) in the Louisiana legislature, on condition that they would not eject the radical Kellogg from the Governorship. Blaine now attacked Wood's motion, declaring that it involved a recognition of the claim of McEnery, who was "no more Governor of Louisiana than Fernando Wood was Governor of New York." S. S. Cox of New York and Lamar of Mississippi tried to answer him; but he soon had the whole Democratic side of the House floundering in such a maze of bewilderment that Speaker Kerr sent down word from the desk asking Wood to withdraw his motion.[1]

Throwing the Democrats of the House into confusion, however, much as it might delight his colleagues, was not Blaine's chief task. The Democratic tide in the nation must be stemmed before it should carry a "rebel" sympathizer into the White House. Blaine's opportunity came when, on December 15, the same day that the anti-third-term resolution was passed, Samuel J. Randall of Pennsylvania introduced a bill to restore to their full political rights all the Southerners who were still suffering under the disabilities imposed by the third section of the Fourteenth Amendment. It was not a new proposition. An identical bill had received the unanimous approval of the Committee on Rules, of which Speaker Blaine was chairman, in December, 1873, and had passed the House by a vote of 141 to 29, without the formality of

---

[1] *Cong. Record,* 44th Cong., 1st sess., pp. 168–173.

a roll call.[1] But that was in the days when the Republicans had a two-thirds majority in Congress, before the "tidal wave" of 1874 had brought up sixty brigadier generals from the South to sit with their Democratic colleagues. It was one thing for Republicans to extend amnesty to the South by an act of grace; [2] it was a quite different thing for Democrats to remove disabilities as a simple matter of justice.

On January 6, 1876, Blaine gave notice that he intended to propose an amendment to Randall's bill to the effect that "all persons now under disabilities imposed by the Fourteenth Amendment to the Constitution of the United States, with the exception of Jefferson Davis, late President of the so-called Confederate States," should be relieved of those disabilities upon taking an oath of allegiance to the Constitution before a judge of a United States court.[3] Whether or not we credit the sincerity of Blaine's protestations in favor of amnesty, it is certain that he did not want to have the Democrats credited with the passage of the measure. And his amendment put them in an extremely embarrassing position. For, while the Northern Democrats would vote readily enough for an amnesty bill which included Jefferson Davis without specific mention, many of them would hesitate to go on record as opposing an amendment which specifically excluded him. Blaine had skillfully shifted the question from the relief of 750 Southerners to the full political rehabilitation of Jefferson Davis. Randall tried in vain to shut off debate on his motion and the amendment to it. He was outgeneraled by Blaine on the parliamentary points involved, and when his motion came to a vote on January 10 it failed of the two-thirds majority necessary to remove disabilities. Blaine voted for the motion in order that he might move reconsideration, and thus superseded Randall as the member in charge of the measure. His speech reopening the debate was perhaps the most effective appeal to partisan solidarity in the name of righteous indignation that has ever

---

[1] *Cong. Record,* 43d Cong., 1st sess., p. 91.

[2] As they had done for example by the law of March 22, 1872, which relieved of disabilities all participant in the "rebellion," except those who had been members of the Thirty-sixth and Thirty-seventh Congresses, or had served as judicial, military or naval officers of the United States, or had occupied positions as cabinet officers or foreign ministers of the United States. Of perhaps 20,000 Southerners originally disqualified by the Fourteenth Amendment, this bill left only about 750 still under disabilities; and only in a single instance had Congress refused an application for pardon. Added to the fact that none of the Southern leaders had been condemned for treason, as they would have been in the European countries, this record was, in the eyes of the Northerners, a remarkably generous one.

[3] *Cong. Record,* 44th Cong., 1st sess., p. 303.

been made in Congress.

After reciting the "large-minded magnanimity and mercy of Republican Congresses, far beyond any that has ever been shown before in the world's history by conqueror to conquered," he continued: "In my amendment I have excepted Jefferson Davis from amnesty. I do not place his exclusion on the ground that Mr. Davis was . . . the head and front of the Rebellion, because on that ground I do not think the exception would be tenable. Mr. Davis was in that respect as guilty— no more so, no less so—as thousands of others who have already received the grace of amnesty. Probably he was far less efficient as an enemy of the United States, probably he was far more useful as a disturber of the councils of the Confederacy, than many who have already received amnesty. It is not because of any particular and special damage that he above others did to the Union, or because he was personally or especially of consequence, that I except him. But I except him on this ground, that he was the author, knowingly, deliberately, guiltily and wilfully, of the gigantic murders and crimes at Andersonville."

Those crimes against thirty-five thousand Northern prisoners of war in Southern prisons Blaine described as more hideous than the deeds of the Duke of Alva in the Low Countries, the massacres of Saint Bartholomew or the tortures of the Spanish Inquisition. He cited the report of a congressional committee in 1867, concurred in by the Democratic members, describing such conditions of filth, disease and starvation within the stockade at Andersonville as made "the bravest and the best of the grand armies that ever carried the flag of their country to final victory" realize "in the studied torments of their prison house the ideal of Dante's Inferno and Milton's Hell." He cited the testimony of a Catholic priest of Georgia who had appealed in vain to General Howell Cobb for the parole of these "living skeletons," and quoted the order of the commander of the district, General Winder, in July 1864, when General Sherman's army was invading Georgia, that if the Northern troops should approach to within seven miles of Andersonville, the Florida artillery should "open fire upon the stockade with grapeshot." He was not calling for vengeance or punishment, he said. Jefferson Davis was a free man—free to come and go as he pleased, to buy and sell, to cast his vote, and even to occupy a large number of minor offices. But it was asking too much to open the door of the White House itself to the man who "by the wink of his eye, by the wave of his hand, by the nod of his head could have stopped the atrocities at Andersonville." "Some of us had kinsmen there, most of us had friends there, all of us had countrymen there, and in the name of these kinsmen, friends and countrymen I here protest, and shall with my vote protest, against calling back and crowning with the honors of full American citizenship the man who organized that murder." [1]

Blaine always maintained that his arraignment of Jefferson Davis was prompted solely by the righteous indignation which appears in his speech; that it had nothing to do with the immanence of a presidential election or the presence of the Southern brigadier generals in the Democratic Congress. But this interpretation was shared neither by his supporters nor by his opponents. The former hailed the speech as a successful, the latter as a desperate bid for the presidency; the former were jubilant, the latter incensed, because he had revived the flagging spirit of sectional strife. Cox of New York immediately took the floor to rebuke him for "raking up again the embers of dead hate," at the beginning of the centennial year. Whether he was "led like Macbeth by the dangerous vision of the crown," or hoped to revive the life and vigor of his party "by diverting public scrutiny from the maladministration of the government," it was "a bad, malicious purpose, which will never elect him to the presidency if he lives a thousand years." [2] On the following day General Benjamin H. Hill of Georgia replied to Blaine's charges in a speech in which truth and falsehood, wisdom and folly, protestations of loyalty to the union and praise for the noble aims of the Confederacy were strangely blended. He absolved President Davis from any responsibility for the sufferings at Andersonville, declared that most of the soldiers who perished there had died of homesickness, and threw upon the North the reproach of inhumanity in shutting off supplies of medicine by the blockade of the Southern ports and refusing to exchange prisoners of war. Then, warming to his subject, he made the outrageous charge that the Southern prisoners at Elmira, New York, and other Northern prison camps were treated worse than the Federal prisoners at Libby and Andersonville.

James A. Garfield replied to Hill the next day in a speech of better temper and less dramatic quality than Blaine's, furnishing incontrovertible proof of the falsity of the charges of General Hill. He produced

[1] *Cong. Record*, 44th Cong., 1st sess., pp. 323–326.
[2] *Ibid.*, pp. 326, 329.

the official documents of the Confederate government showing that two assistant adjutant and inspector generals of the Southern army, Colonels Chandler and Chilton, had reported to President Davis the horrible conditions at Andersonville and had recommended the removal of General Winder; and that, instead of dismissing this brutal officer, Davis had promoted him to the post of Commissioner General of all the Confederate prisons. Garfield yielded the floor for a moment to Thomas C. Platt, who read a dispatch from General B. F. Tracy of Brooklyn, who had been in command of the prison at Elmira during the war, stating that the Southern prisoners had been well cared for in every respect. Another dispatch came from General J. J. Elwell of Cleveland, attesting that he had furnished the fifteen thousand prisoners at Elmira with the same quality of provisions that he supplied to the Northern soldiers, that they had had the same clothing and medical care and that their dead had been decently buried in a special cemetery with white wooden crosses over their graves. Representative Walker of New York declared that he had frequently visited the prison camp at Elmira during the war, and could corroborate the testimony of Generals Tracy and Elwell. Hill rose to disclaim any intention of accusing the Union authorities of inhumanity, but Garfield confronted him with his own words of the day before: "The atrocities at Andersonville did not begin to compare with those of Elmira." [1]

On January 13 Proctor Knott of Kentucky again reported the Amnesty Bill, containing the provision for the oath of allegiance, but not excluding Jefferson Davis. It narrowly failed of the necessary two-thirds majority, by a vote of 182 to 97. Blaine then asked unanimous consent to bring his amendment to vote, only to be met with cries of "I object!" from the Democratic side of the House. He thereupon withdrew his motion to reconsider Knott's bill, and the debate in Congress on the amnesty issue came to an end. It was not until the United States were engaged in another war, in which the men from the North and the men from Dixie fought side by side in the jungles of Cuba, long after Jefferson Davis had gone to his grave as a "man without a country," that a Republican Congress passed the act of June 6, 1898, restoring to full citizenship the few survivors of the Confederacy who were still unpardoned.

[1] For Hill's speech see *Cong. Record*, 44th Cong., 1st sess., pp. 345–351; for Garfield's reply, *Ibid.*, pp. 382–389.

If Blaine intended, as his opponents insisted, to stir into flame the dying embers of sectional hate, to provoke the Southern brigadiers into defiant justification of the "rebellion," to rally the sons of the North to their old war enthusiasm, and to "wring another Republican President from the bloody flag," he certainly accomplished his purpose. He was swamped with messages of congratulation for having, as Colonel Ingersoll was to express it a few months later, "snatched the mask of Democracy from the hideous face of the Rebellion." Newspapers in the Northern States printed scores of letters from soldiers who had survived the horrors of Andersonville, Libby and Belle Isle, execrating the name of Jefferson Davis and excoriating Hill for his defense of "the arch-rebel." One correspondent, signing himself "a surviving Andersonville skeleton," found prose inadequate to express his emotion and sent the following lyric to the Cincinnati convention:

> Thanks for heart and voice and vote,
>   Blaine of Maine!
> Thanks for Freedom's flag afloat,
>   Once again!
> Thanks for treason quick to threaten,
> Boldly met, and balked and beaten;
> Thanks for heart and voice and brain,
>   Blaine of Maine!

And so on for five more stanzas of impassioned doggerel.

Jefferson Davis himself added fuel to the flames by writing an acrimonious letter to Judge Lyon (Jan. 27), in which he denounced the story of cruelty at Andersonville as a malicious fiction and reiterated General Hill's charges of the inhumanities of the Northern "horde of invaders." He wanted no "spurious amnesty." He scorned the idea of "pardon." It was for the South to forgive, and not the North. The imposition of disabilities by the Fourteenth Amendment was a violation of law and justice; their removal by Congress "an empty gesture of usurpation." "Under the mellowing influence of time," concluded the ex-President of the Confederacy, "and occasional demonstrations at the North of a desire for the restoration of peace and good will, the Southern people have forgotten much, have forgiven much of the wounds they bore. If it has been less so among their invaders, it is but another example of the rule that the wrongdoer is less able to forgive than the man who has suffered causeless wrong." The letter was published and drew sarcastic comments from the North. What the South had "forgotten" was the generosity of a government which they had sought to destroy and which had nevertheless restored to them the rights which they had forfeited; what the South had "forgiven" was the folly and wickedness of their own leaders in carrying them into secession and rebellion. "The perverse ingenuity of the ex-President of the Southern Confederacy," said the New York *Tribune*, "was never more characteristically exercised than in his angry letter. When Mr. Blaine proposed to distinguish Jefferson Davis by refusing to include him in a general amnesty, a majority of the Republicans of the North believed he had made a great mistake. *More than half of Davis' letter, however, is taken up in showing that Mr. Blaine was right.* Whatever may be the feeling of the rest of the South, it is plain that Davis at heart is unchanged . . . and the comment at the North will be: *Well, Blaine knew Davis best after all.* . . . He will be marching through the country in a little while as the champion of the disabled Union prisoners, just as he did a month ago in the character of champion of the public schools." [1]

The amnesty debate was of great importance not only in furnishing the country with a popular issue for the campaign of 1876, but also in its effects on the political fortunes of James G. Blaine. Hitherto he had had friends, supporters, admirers; now he had devotees. The masses, who had little understanding of his speeches on the tariff or the currency, hailed his denunciation of the "rebel chieftain" and his defense of the "boys in blue" with shouts of enthusiasm. State after State in the North, beginning with his own State of Maine (Jan. 20, 1876), declared him their choice for the coming nomination for the Presidency. It was freely predicted that he would win on the first ballot. Some said that he would be nominated by acclamation. The "Blaine legion" increased to millions. Their hero was already taking on the legendary proportions of an American idol. He was becoming the Republican Party

---

[1] The reference is to controversy over the danger of the permeation of the public schools by religious and sectarian influences—one of those periodical waves of suspicion of Roman Catholic propaganda which appeared in the Know-Nothing movement, the American Protective Association of the 1880's, and the savage opposition to Governor Alfred E. Smith in the presidential campaign of 1928. The question was prominent in the Hayes-Allen campaign for the governorship of Ohio in 1875, and Blaine wrote a letter on October 3 to the chairman of the Ohio Republican Committee, in which he said: "The issue forced upon you in regard to the public schools may have far reaching consequences. In a government where every citizen is entrusted with political power, the importance of free education cannot be exaggerated. The schools must be kept free, free in every sense, and especially free from sectarian influence or domination. The bitterest of all strifes is the strife between religious sects; and if that strife be permitted to cross the threshold of our public schools, free education in this country is at an end."

incarnate. Moreover, the very hostility which he had provoked by his amnesty speech contributed to his emergent eminence. Heretofore he had had critics, opponents, adversaries in debate, but (always excepting the implacable Conkling) no real enemies.

Now, however, he was overtopping the surrounding summits to such a degree that he brought the lightning down on his own head. The Democratic opposition was becoming centered on him. To defeat the Republicans meant to defeat Blaine. His political adversaries could no longer afford to treat him with the courteous consideration of other days. The same "Sunset" Cox who had written him in 1873 that to miss his face in the House would be to miss the House itself, in January, 1876, called him "the honorable hyena from Maine" (words expunged from the *Congressional Record*), and ironically bade the House "bow down before his Majesty from Maine." Hitherto, moreover, Blaine had had warm friends in the South, on account of his conciliatory position on such questions as the limitation of the penalties of the Reconstruction Acts, the reception of Southern cadets at West Point, the renewal of land grants to the Southern railroads, and the defeat of Butler's Force Bill in the closing days of the Forty-third Congress. Blaine's secretary, Thomas H. Sherman, tells how he met two Southern Congressmen on the steps of the Capitol as they were going home after the heated debate of January 10, 1876, and overheard one of them say to the other: "Now there's Blaine, damn him! but I do love him." [1] They could not love him much after he had, in the words of James Ford Rhodes, "stolen the thunder of Morton and Conkling, who were the residuary legatees of Grant, and who favored a harsh policy toward the South." [2]

Along with the letters of congratulation which poured in upon Blaine after the amnesty debate,[3] there was one letter of sinister import. On February 28, 1876, a friend wrote him that Mr. J. S. C. Harrison of Indiana, a government director of the Union Pacific Railroad Company was responsible for the statement that there were seventy-five practically worthless bonds of the Little Rock and Fort Smith Railroad in the treasury of the Union Pacific, and that these bonds had been received from James G. Blaine as collateral for a loan of $64,000 which he had never been asked to repay. In other words, the Union Pacific had taken

[1] Thomas H. Sherman, *Twenty Years with James G. Blaine*, p. 39.
[2] J. F. Rhodes, *History of the United States from the Compromise of 1850*, Vol. VII, p. 181.
[3] Samples are given in Gail Hamilton's *Biography of James G. Blaine*, pp. 378–384.

the bonds off Blaine's hands at a price many times in excess of their value. Harrison cited E. H. Rollins, an officer of the Union Pacific as authority for the statement that the money had been paid to Blaine on the order of Thomas A. Scott, the president of the railroad, through the banking house of Morton, Bliss and Company of New York. Blaine immediately replied to the letter, denying any connection with the transaction. But the rumor would not down. An Indianapolis editor got the story and published it on April 11, with the prefatorial comment: "A prominent banker of the city is in possession of a secret the exposure of which will forever blast the prospects of a certain candidate for the Presidency." With the accusation thus become public, and with the threatening hints from various quarters that Harrison was about to ask the Judiciary Committee of the House for an "immediate investigation," Blaine could no longer remain silent. He might himself have demanded the investigation, as he did in the Crédit Mobilier case, but he chose another course, dictated both by his own nature and by the political situation. He was a man of Dantonesque "audacity." Conscious of his power in debate, he preferred to move to the attack to confound his enemies rather than wait their attack behind the walls of defense. Furthermore, the Republican nominating convention was but two months away, and he was certain that an investigating committee appointed by a Democratic Speaker would, whatever evidence of his guilt or innocence might be produced, refuse to lift the cloud of suspicion from his name in time to allow it to go before that convention. Blaine therefore decided to take the bull by the horns.

On the twenty-fourth of April he rose to a question of personal privilege and read a carefully prepared statement to a House which, in spite of the storm of wind and rain outside, was filled to capacity. He produced a letter from E. H. Rollins, written at his request, and dated March 31, 1876, in which Rollins said: "I have been treasurer of the Union Pacific Railroad since April 8, 1871, and have necessarily known of all disbursements made since that date. During that entire period, up to the present time, I am sure that no money has been paid in any way or by any person by the company in which you were interested in any manner whatever. I make this statement in justice to the company, to you and to myself." Blaine also read two letters from Morton, Bliss and Company, dated April 6 and 13, testifying that no draft, note, check or any other evidence of value had passed through their books, nor had anything been paid by them "in any form or at any time to any person or any corporation in which you were known, believed or supposed to have any interest whatever." Furthermore, to corroborate his assertions that he had "never had any transaction of any kind with Thomas A. Scott concerning bonds of the Little Rock and Fort Smith Railroad or the bonds of any other railroad . . . directly or indirectly, immediately or remotely," and that he never had any business transactions with the Union Pacific Railroad, and "never in any manner received from that company, a single dollar in money or stocks or bonds or any other form of value," Blaine put in evidence letters from Scott and his successor, Sidney Dillon. One of these letters from Dillon to Scott, dated April 21, 1876, contained the passage: "In these days of public scandal, from which few men in public life seem to be exempt, I feel it my duty to state: that the Little Rock and Fort Smith bonds purchased by the Union Pacific Railroad in 1871 were not purchased or received from Mr. Blaine directly or indirectly, and that of the money paid by the Union Pacific Railroad Company, or of the avails of the said bonds, not one dollar went to Mr. Blaine or to any person for him or for his benefit in any form." "This closes the testimony I have wished to offer," said Blaine after reading the Dillon letter just quoted.[1]

If Blaine had been content to rest his case on these explicit letters of exoneration from the witness quoted against him in the accusation, it would have been well. But, in his zeal to clear himself of any shadow of suspicion, he continued with a lengthy exposition of his relations with the Little Rock and Fort Smith Railroad, in which he made statements in regard to the road which were open to historical objection, and gave an explanation of his own financial transactions with the road that did not contain the whole truth. As to the first point, he maintained that since the road had received its charter and its grants of public land from the legislature of Arkansas, its policies or privileges were matters of State and not congressional control. This was technically true, but actually misleading. For Congress had granted and regranted to the State of Arkansas the land which the State in turn granted to the railroad. And Blaine himself, while Speaker of the House, on April 10, 1869, had secured the renewal of the land grant to Arkansas and thereby

[1] *Cong. Record*, 44th Cong., 1st sess., pp. 2724–2725.

saved the railroad (though at that time he had no pecuniary interest in it). Six months later, when he had received and accepted from Warren Fisher, Jr., of Boston "a most liberal proposition" to share in the resuscitation of the railroad, Blaine wrote Fisher asking him to inform Josiah Caldwell, another of the promoters of the railroad, that he (Blaine) had "unwittingly" done Caldwell "a great favor" by his ruling of the previous April. This hardly squares with the doctrine insisted upon by Blaine that "the Little Rock derived all it had from the State of Arkansas and not from Congress."

Furthermore, Blaine's statements of his own financial relations with the Little Rock and Fort Smith road are open to still more serious criticism. At the close of his speech he summarized his defense in three categorical denials; first, he had never received $64,000 or any other sum of money from the Union Pacific; second, no Little Rock bond of his had ever been sold to the Atlantic and Pacific or the Missouri, Kansas and Texas railroads; third, to quote his exact words, "instead of receiving bonds of the Little Rock and Fort Smith Railroad as a gratuity, I never had one except at the market price, and instead of making a large fortune out of that company, I have incurred a severe pecuniary loss from my investment in its securities, which I still retain." In a word, there is no hint in Blaine's carefully prepared apologia that he had had any other business with the Little Rock and Fort Smith than that of an ordinary investor, "in common with hundreds of other people in New England and other parts of the country," as he said, who had bought a not very large number of the bonds of the road, "paying for them at precisely the same rate that others paid." "My whole connection with the road has been open as the day," he asserted. "If there had been anything to conceal about it I should never have touched it. Whenever concealment is desirable avoidance is advisable, and I do not know any better test to apply to the honor and fairness of a business transaction." [1]

Those persons who believed that the story of the worthless Little Rock bonds in the treasury of the Union Pacific would "forever blast the prospects of a certain candidate for the presidency" seem to have missed their guess completely. Blaine's statement was generally hailed as a conclusive answer to his political persecutors. More letters of congratulation came; more State conventions declared him their choice

[1] *Cong. Record,* 44th Cong., 1st sess., p. 2725.

for the coming nomination.[1] "I have just read your vindication of yesterday," wrote Judge Noah Davis of New York, on April 25; "it is clear, explicit and complete. I never had a doubt of the utter falsity of the charges against you, and hereafter no honorable man can have one." His old Democratic opponent Gould of Thomaston, Maine, wrote the same day: "Allow me to congratulate you on your complete vindication of yourself in the House yesterday. . . . The charge was an improbable one; but in these days of general corruption almost any charge against a public man is credited by many. I trust that the attempt to defeat your nomination by such foul means will advance your prospects, as it ought. I am of that number of Democrats who would prefer your success to that of any other person yet named as the probable nominee of the Republican Party." John Hay congratulated him on his "immense success before the people"; J. G. Whittier was gratified by his "complete vindication." Even the *Nation*, voicing the critical views of the political "Independents," conceded that, "as far as allegation can go, Mr. Blaine has vindicated himself. The only thing further he could do would be to submit his proof to an investigating committee; but this does not seem necessary, as there is nothing cloudy in the statement." [2]

However, the House was not satisfied to drop the investigation of the Union Pacific Railroad, nor were Blaine's political adversaries ready to acquiesce in the opinion of his exoneration. On January 31, 1876, Representative John K. Luttrell of California had submitted a long resolution asking that the Judiciary Committee be instructed to inquire and report to the House whether the several Pacific railroad companies had complied with the laws of Congress giving them franchises and powers, or whether there had been fraudulent negotiations in their construction and financing, which might establish claims of the government upon them. Now, on May 2, Representative Tarbox of Massachusetts made the inquiry more pointed and specific in the following resolution:

"Whereas, it is publicly alleged and is not denied by the officials of the Union Pacific Railroad Company that the corporation did, in the year 1871 or 1872, become the owner of certain bonds of the Little Rock and Fort

[1] When a telegram came to the Blaine home announcing that Washington territory had elected Blaine delegates, he jocosely remarked, "Well, Maine is for me and Washington is for me; now all that is necessary is for my friends to fill up the little space between." Gail Hamilton, *Biography of James G. Blaine*, p. 384.
[2] The New York *Nation*, April 27, 1876.

Smith Railroad Company, for which bonds the said U. P. R. R. Co. paid a consideration largely in excess of their actual or market value, and that the board of directors of said U. P. R. R. Co., though urged, have neglected to investigate such transaction: therefore, Be it resolved that the Committee on the Judiciary be instructed to inquire if any such transaction took place, and if so what were the circumstances and inducements thereto, from what person or persons said bonds were obtained and upon what consideration, and whether the transaction was from corrupt design or in furtherance of any corrupt object; and that the committee have power to send for persons and papers." [1]

Mr. Tarbox's resolution was adopted, and the subcommittee appointed by Chairman Knott of Kentucky consisted of two Democratic members, Hunton of Virginia and Ashe of North Carolina, and one Republican, Lawrence of Ohio.

Up to the end of May the pertinent points in the large mass of testimony taken by the committee were as follows: (1). On May 15 J. S. C. Harrison stated under oath that he had moved at the September (1872) meeting of the board of directors of the Union Pacific the appointment of a committee to find out and report how the road had come into possession of the Little Rock and Fort Smith bonds. "Thereupon," he continued, "E. H. Rollins the Secretary took me to one side and told me that I must withdraw the motion . . . as it would involve James G. Blaine. He said the fall elections were at hand, and Blaine was a candidate for reëlection to Congress in Maine. An exposure of the transaction just at that time would be sure to defeat him.[2] With that I withdrew the motion." [3] (2). On May 16 Rollins testified: "As near as I can recollect, prior to this meeting of the board, I had heard a report— I cannot now recollect the source from which I heard it—that these bonds in question were the bonds of Mr. Blaine." [4] And a few moments later, in reply to the question whether he was still of the opinion that an investigation might involve Blaine, he replied: "I think the most thorough investigation of the matter would show that the bonds were not Mr. Blaine's." [5] (3). On May 15 Thomas A. Scott testified that he had purchased the seventy-five Little Rock bonds under question from

---

[1] The resolution and hearings may be found in *House Miscellaneous Documents,* 44th Cong., No. 176, Serial 1706.
[2] Blaine had actually been reëlected to Congress by a very large majority on September 9, 1872, two days before this meeting of the board of directors of the Union Pacific.
[3] *House Misc. Doc.,* No. 176, p. 18.
[4] *Ibid.,* p. 26.
[5] *Ibid.,* p. 31.

Josiah Caldwell, one of the reorganizers of the road, at eighty cents on the dollar, and that the Union Pacific Railroad had purchased them from him for $64,000, in consideration of a "very considerable service I had rendered them." [1] "Mr. Blaine never had anything to do in any way, directly or indirectly, with the matter—never was interested in it or connected with it in any manner whatever." [2] (4). On May 31 Warren Fisher, Jr., of Boston, who had taken a contract for building the Little Rock and Fort Smith Railroad, testified, in reply to the question; "Did you ever let Mr. Blaine have $130,000 of the bonds of the Little Rock and Fort Smith Railroad without any consideration?" "No, sir."

Q. Or any other amount?
A. I let Mr. Blaine have some bonds in his hands, but they were for other parties.
Q. Without consideration?
A. No; I got my pay for them.
Q. From Mr. Blaine or from the parties for whom he bought them?
A. From the parties for whom he bought them. [3]

(5). On May 31 Elisha Atkins, a director and member of the executive committee of the Union Pacific, answered the question, "Have you any knowledge as to the person to whom the Little Rock and Fort Smith Railroad Company sold those bonds which were afterwards held by the Union Pacific?" "No sir, I have not." "Did you ever hear that an investigation of the ownership of those seventy-five bonds would involve Mr. Blaine?" "No, sir." [4]

It is evident that the testimony quoted above gave no support to the charge that the Union Pacific had taken the worthless Little Rock bonds off Blaine's hands in return for actual or anticipated favors from the Speaker of the House. Blaine himself had followed the testimony with eager attention, sometimes interrupting to question a witness who, he surmised, might have a prejudice against him, and once or twice reasserting his complete innocence of the $64,000 transaction. Then, on May 31, a bomb was thrown into the committee room. A new witness, James Mulligan of Boston, was sworn and examined. Mulligan had formerly been a clerk in the employ of Jacob Stanwood, Blaine's brother-

[1] *House Misc. Doc.*, No. 176, p. 48.
[2] *Ibid.*, p. 57.
[3] *Ibid.*, pp. 89–90.
[4] *Ibid.*, p. 93.

in-law. He and Stanwood had had a disagreement when their association was severed, and Blaine, called in as arbiter, had decided the dispute in favor of Stanwood. Blaine was convinced that Mulligan cherished a grudge against him for this, and that Mulligan was coming to Washington "loaded" with ammunition to disgrace him and defeat him for the presidential nomination. As soon as Mulligan and Fisher reached the capital, on May 30, Blaine asked them to come to his house for a conference. Mulligan declined the invitation, but Fisher went and told Blaine that Mulligan had a number of letters in his possession which Blaine had written to Fisher over a number of years—letters which Blaine believed had been destroyed when he and Fisher had settled their accounts in 1872. The next morning, before the hearing opened, Blaine went to the Riggs House, where he found Mulligan in the barber shop, and, after shaking hands with him said: "James, they report that you are here as an enemy of mine." But apparently, nothing was said of the letters then.

When Mulligan took the witness stand a little later he testified that he, as Fisher's bookkeeper, had kept the accounts of the Little Rock and Fort Smith transactions; that through Blaine as agent Fisher had sold $130,000 worth of the Little Rock bonds "to parties in the State of Maine," and that Blaine had received for his commission $130,000 land-grant bonds and $32,500 first-mortgage bonds of the road. Mulligan furthermore directly controverted the testimony of Atkins (above, paragraph 5) in respect to the seventy-five bonds held by the Union Pacific: "Mr. Atkins told me that Mr. Blaine gave the bonds to Tom Scott and that Tom Scott made the Union Pacific take them" at the price of $64,000.[1] According to Hunton, the chairman of the subcommittee, Mulligan was testifying "very quietly" when he "happened to mention that he had in his possession certain letters written by Mr. Blaine to a Warren Fisher, Jr. The mention of these letters seemed to have a remarkable effect on Mr. Blaine, for in a moment or two afterward he whispered to Mr. Lawrence, the Republican member of the committee, 'Move an adjournment.' It so happened that I heard the suggestion. Mr. Lawrence got up with great solemnity on his countenance and said, 'Mr. Chairman, I am very sick and I hope the committee will adjourn' (Laughter). It was half past twelve o'clock, a half an hour later than the usual time for the adjournment of the committee in

[1] *House Misc. Doc.*, No. 176, pp. 94, 95, 105.

order to allow the members to attend the regular session of the House." [1]

The same afternoon Blaine went to the Riggs House, where Mulligan, Fisher and Atkins were staying, in order to get the letters. He asked Mulligan to deliver them either to him or to Fisher, claiming that they were private letters having no relation to the subject of the committee's inquiry, and that they were the rightful possession of only the author or the receiver of them. Fisher declined to demand them of Mulligan, and Mulligan refused to give them to Blaine. He must keep them, he said, to protect himself; but he promised that he would not make them public unless his testimony before the committee was impugned or his character attacked. Blaine then asked to be allowed to examine the letters, and Mulligan handed them to him after exacting a pledge that they would be returned. Blaine looked them through and gave them back, remarking that there was but one letter that bore upon the Union Pacific investigation. Then Mulligan went upstairs with the letters to Fisher's room, and Blaine followed him, leaving Fisher and Atkins in the parlor below.

As to what went on between Mulligan and Blaine alone in the upper room we have utterly different accounts given by the two men in their testimony before the committee the following morning. According to Mulligan, Blaine abjectly begged for the letters, declaring that if they were published or came into the hands of the committee it would "ruin him for life." "He prayed, almost went on his knees . . . and implored me to think of his six children and his wife . . . He contemplated suicide." Then, the appeal to sympathy failing, Blaine had turned to the bait of political office and "asked me if I would not like a consulship." But bribery proved no more effective than supplication. Blaine then asked to be allowed to see the letters again, although he had looked them through carefully a few minutes before in Atkins' parlor; and Mulligan again handed him the package on condition that it should be returned. This time, however, Blaine refused to give the letters back, and left the room with them in his pocket.[2]

Blaine's statement under oath of what went on in Fisher's room contradicted Mulligan's in every respect: "I talked with Mr. Mulligan I think the better part of an hour, but the form he gives the interview, about my offering him a consulship and about my being ruined

[1] *Cong. Record,* 44th Cong., 1st sess., p. 3611.
[2] *House Misc. Doc.,* No. 176, pp. 98, 102.

and all that sort of thing, is mere fancy. . . . I talked as calmly as I am talking at this moment." It was Mulligan, according to Blaine, who was excited and afraid, and who "repeated with a good deal of emphasis and a good many *By God!'s*," that he was going to hold the letters for his vindication, in case anyone "impugned" his motives. Blaine had made no promise to return the letters the second time, and he retained them because they were "strictly private letters" which Mulligan had no right to have, and because (with the exception of the one which he would allow Mulligan to retain) they had "no more connection or relationship with the examination now going on before the Judiciary Committee than the man in the moon." [1] Blaine fortified his position by showing the letters to two eminent lawyers, J. S. Black a Democrat and Matthew Carpenter a Republican, who gave him a signed opinion (June 2) that "the letters and papers aforesaid have no relevancy whatever to the matter under inquiry," and that "it would be most unjust and tyrannical, as well as illegal" for the committee to demand their production. "We advise Mr. Blaine," the lawyers concluded, "to assert his rights as an American citizen and resist any such demand to the last extremity." [2]

The subcommittee was in a quandary. The full Judiciary Committee had no advice to give as to the way out. A proposition that the matter be referred to the whole House was rejected. The subcommittee, after discharging Atkins, Fisher and Mulligan as witnesses on June 3, adjourned over the week-end, actually to meet again on Wednesday, June 7. However, Blaine's position was far from enviable. His friends might congratulate him that he had "made a most gallant and satisfactory fight and triumphed in every encounter with the unprincipled dogs" who were striving to cry him down.[3] Nevertheless, certain ugly facts remained. Blaine had seized the letters (whether in violation of his pledged word or not, it made little difference) from a witness subpoenaed to appear before a committee of the House of Representatives. It was for the committee, and not for Blaine or his private lawyers, to decide whether the papers which the witness brought were relevant to the case or not. He had refused to deliver the letters to the committee, even with their guarantee that they would not be made public. If there was "nothing in those letters" that he would have "occasion to blush

[1] *House Misc. Doc.*, No. 176, p. 106.
[2] *Ibid.*, p. 110.
[3] General James Kilpatrick to Blaine, June 5, 1876.

over," [1] why, it was asked, should he be so determined to recover and retain them; why did he not emulate Senator Allison, who had declared at the time of the Crédit Mobilier investigation, "I have no interest in any matter covertly that I am not willing the public at any time should know all about"? [2] Moreover, there were rumors spread abroad that Blaine had "bulldozed" the committee,[3] and that the Democrats intended to move his expulsion from the House for tampering with witnesses and sequestering their papers. Clearly, with the Republican nominating convention less than a fortnight away, the most prominent aspirant for the Presidency could not afford to let these clouds of suspicion rest upon him. He decided again, as on the twenty-fourth of April, to take the matter out of the hands of committee or subcommittee, and to vindicate his innocence on the floor of the House.

The news spread rapidly that Blaine would take advantage of the Monday (June 5) hour for questions of privilege to reply to his accusers. That morning the galleries of the House were packed to suffocation and scores of unauthorized persons defied the doorkeepers and crowded upon the floor of the House. They were tense with expectant emotion when Blaine rose to deliver the most important and sensational speech of his life. At the outset he secured the sympathy of a large part of his audience by insisting that he had been made a victim of persecution. The Tarbox resolution of May 2, he said, in spite of the disclaimer of its author, had been aimed solely and only at him; it was evident from the moment that the subcommittee was designated that it was not the Union Pacific Railroad Company that was to be investigated, but James G. Blaine. Chairman Knott, in selecting the two majority members of the subcommittee, had passed over the seven Northern Democratic members of the Judiciary Committee and named the two "who were from the South and had been in the rebel army." [4] Without making the direct charge, Blaine indicated clearly that the appointment of Hunton and Ashe as his inquisitors was an act of revenge for his speech of the preceding January on the exclusion of Jefferson Davis from the benefits of the Amnesty Bill. Moreover, the witness Mulligan had been summoned with a hostile purpose; he had come "loaded" and "primed"

---

[1] *House Misc. Doc.*, No. 176, p. 107.
[2] Poland Committee, *Report*, p. 308.
[3] See the attack on Blaine for "terrorizing" the committee in the New York *Sun* of June 8, 1876.
[4] Mr. Ashe declared in a meeting of the subcommittee two days later that he had never been in the Confederate army.

with material which he had no right to have in his possession and which had no more to do with the investigation than "with the North pole." Would any gentleman allow his private correspondence for the last eight or ten years to be scanned over and made public? Did it imply guilt or wrongdoing for a man to insist upon the inviolability of his intimate personal business correspondence? Surely not. And he was "ready for any extremity of contest or conflict in behalf of so sacred a right."

Then followed a startling dramatic scene. Drawing himself up to his full height and sweeping the hall with his flashing eye, Blaine thrust his hand into the breast pocket of his coat, drew out a package, held it up for a second at arm's length, and then brought it down upon his desk with a bang, shouting: "I am not afraid to show the letters. Thank God Almighty! I am not afraid to show them. There they are. There is the very original package. And with some sense of humiliation, with a mortification which I do not pretend to conceal, with a sense of outrage which I trust any man in my position would feel, I invite the confidence of 44,000,000 of my fellow countrymen while I read those letters from this desk." With his audience still under the spell of this dramatic appeal, and with no sign of "humiliation" or "mortification" in his mien or voice, Blaine proceeded to read the letters, making brief comments on them as he went along. He did not read them in chronological order, as they were listed in Mulligan's memorandum, but began with letters dated in the summer of 1872 dealing with his difficulty in coming to a settlement with Fisher, then inserted a letter of 1864, then read two dated 1869. Sometimes he prefaced the reading with the simple remark, "Here is one dated May 2, 1864" or "the next letter to which I refer is dated Washington, April 28, 1872," or, "I read these letters now somewhat in their order." One listening to them as read would have difficulty in getting any clear idea of the inception and development of the transactions with Fisher, especially as there were no letters written from Fisher to Blaine. It was like listening to one end of a conversation over the telephone.

But Blaine did not intend that the hazy impression left by the reading of the letters should remain uppermost in the minds of either the members of the House or the 44,000,000 of his fellow countrymen. He had another *coup de théâtre* ready for the final scene. We quote the words of the *Congressional Record*, which can convey no idea of the tense and breathless excitement of the throng on the floor and in the galleries of the House when Blaine advanced to hurl a challenge at Proctor Knott, the chairman of the Judiciary Committee:

BLAINE: There is one piece of testimony wanting. There is but one thing to close the complete circle of the evidence. There is but one witness whom I could not have, to whom the Judiciary Committee, taking into account the great and intimate connection he had with the transaction, was asked to send a cable dispatch—and I ask the gentleman from Kentucky (Knott) whether that dispatch was sent to him.
FRYE (who was acting for Blaine as prompter): Who?
BLAINE: To Josiah Caldwell.
KNOTT: I will reply to the gentleman that Judge Hunton and myself have both endeavored to get Mr. Caldwell's address, and have not yet got it.
B: Has the gentleman from Kentucky received a dispatch from Mr. Caldwell?
K: I will explain that directly.
B: I want a categorical answer.
K: I have received a dispatch purporting to be from Mr. Caldwell.
B: You did?
K: How did you know I got it?
B: When did you get it? I want the gentleman from Kentucky to answer when he got it.
K: Answer my question first.
B: I never heard of it till yesterday.
K: How did you hear it?
B: I heard you got a dispatch last Thursday morning at eight o'clock from Josiah Caldwell, completely and absolutely exonerating me from this charge, and you have suppressed it.[1]

The tumult of applause from the floor and galleries drowned the Speaker's voice and gavel as he vainly called for order. Business was suspended amid the wild jubilation. When he could be heard the Speaker ordered the floor to be cleared of intruders and threatened to clear the galleries if the demonstrations were repeated. But the doorkeepers reported to the Chair that it was impossible to clear the hall and the throngs remained in the galleries to cheer again. Blaine, now master of the situation, pressed his victory home by a resolution that the Judiciary Committee be directed to report forthwith to the House whether "it has sent any telegram to Josiah Caldwell in Europe and received a reply thereto. And if so to report said telegram and reply,

[1] *Cong. Record,* 44th Cong., 1st sess., p. 3608. For Blaine's whole speech, *ibid.,* pp. 3602–3617.

with the date when said reply was received, and the reasons why the same has been suppressed."

It was in vain that Judge Hunton rose to rebuke Blaine for his "un-exampled conduct" of appealing to the House and the public by "under-taking to anticipate" what the action of the subcommittee should be while it was still in the midst of its investigation; and to plead that the committee had been fair to Blaine, not "prolonging" its hearings with a view to keeping him under suspicion until after the nominating con-vention should have met, but even "postponing" them at Blaine's own request, in order to allow him to attend the celebration of Centennial Week at Philadelphia or to recover from illness. It was in vain also that Chairman Knott followed with a legal argument that Blaine had no right to the possession of the Mulligan letters, and to explain that he had not "suppressed" the Caldwell telegram, but was holding it secret only because he suspected that it was "a fixed up job." These apologies fell upon the excited audience as dead as the radio announcer's review of the plays of a football game after the whistle has blown for the end of the last quarter and the sons of victory have swarmed out on the field to tear up the enemy's goal posts.

The Blaine resolution was referred to the Judiciary Committee and the House adjourned, while scores of excited members rushed up to shake Blaine's hand. Like a stag at bay, he had fought off what General Kilpatrick called "the unprincipled dogs" who were striving to bring him down; but not without moral lacerations which were to cause him suffering in the days to come. He still refused to give the Mulligan let-ters to the committee and they were published only in the form in which he had read them in the *Congressional Record*. This alone was enough to start rumors that he had transposed, garbled and even sup-pressed parts of them in the reading. But even as they stood in the official record, they contained embarrassing passages for the man who six weeks earlier had told the House that his transactions with the Little Rock Railroad had been "open as the day," and that he was only an ordinary investor who had purchased some bonds of the road "on precisely the same terms" as any other man might buy them in the market. If so, asked his critics, why such sentences in his correspond-ence with Fisher as: "You urge me to make as much as I can out of the arrangements into which we have entered. It is natural that I should do my utmost to this end" (Oct. 4, 1869); or, "I do not feel that I shall prove a dead-head in the enterprise if I once embark on it. I see various channels in which I can be useful" (June 29, 1869); or, "I can not make a settlement until I receive bonds due on your articles of agreement with me" (Aug. 9, 1872).

Blaine had acted as agent in selling the Little Rock bonds to several of his friends in Maine and had received a commission in bonds and cash therefor. He had honorably incurred heavy losses by paying their subscriptions back to these parties when the investment turned out to be worthless. There is no evidence that he ever used his official position as Speaker of the House to favor the road when he himself was interested in its success, for the "various channels" in which he could be "useful" may be fairly interpreted as his agency in selling the bonds to his Maine friends. The thing that undermined confidence in Blaine's integrity in the minds of many who had been his admirers was that he had denied any privileged connection with the Little Rock and Fort Smith Railroad in his declaration before the House on April 24, 1876, and a few weeks later had sequestered as purely private correspondence letters which made that privileged (but unprofitable) connection perfectly clear.

The Caldwell telegram, too, which Blaine used with such dramatic effect as the climax of his defense, falls far short of a "complete and absolute exoneration." The Judiciary Committee had *sent* no telegram to Josiah Caldwell, for the reason that they did not know his address in Europe. But Chairman Knott had received a telegram from Caldwell, unsolicited, and dated "London," without street or house address. Under these circumstances, Knott said that he suspected that the telegram was a "fixed up job." A former secretary of Caldwell's, J. C. Reed, who knew his address in London, had cabled him, at the request of Blaine's friends, asking him to send Chairman Knott a dispatch worded as follows: "Have just read in New York papers Scott's evidence about our land transactions and can fully corroborate it. I never gave Blaine any Fort Smith railroad bonds directly or otherwise. I have three foreign railway contracts on my hands which makes it impossible for me to leave without great pecuniary loss, or I would gladly voluntarily come home and testify. I can make an affidavit to this and mail it if desired." The dispatch therefore, much as it surprised Knott, was no surprise to Blaine's friends, who had dictated it.[1] Moreover, the contents of the dispatch contained nothing new or valuable for the inquiry. They simply confirmed Scott's testimony (see page 88 above) that he had purchased the seventy-five Little Rock bonds from Caldwell, who had sold them to the Union Pacific for $64,000, and that Blaine had had nothing to do with that transaction; [2] and added the statement that Caldwell had never given Blaine any Fort Smith bonds. The dispatch did not absolve Blaine from having received bonds from Fisher as a commission, nor cast any light on the disposition which Blaine had made of such bonds. Finally, the dispatch was inadmissible as testimony, since it was neither sworn to nor witnessed.[3]

But revelations which were to appear months and even years later could not stem the tide of rejoicing that followed Blaine's triumph of June 5. He had risen and scattered his enemies before him like chaff in the wind. The Republican press waxed lyric in praise of his power and reiteration of his innocence.[4] Benjamin H. Bristow wrote him from Philadelphia, June 6: "This minute I have laid by your speech of yesterday. You have macerated these scamps. With head erect and defiant tone you have scattered the wretched crew of calumniators and spies on private life and private intercourse." John Greenleaf Whittier, the Quaker poet, was exultant: "How splendidly Mr. Blaine held himself in his fight with the ex-Confederates of the Committee! I hope thee saw it. . . . He has cleared himself of all the charges against him." [5] Blaine's nomination by the convention which was to meet at Cincinnati the next week now seemed assured. "Mr. Blaine," says his ecstatic biographer Gail Hamilton, "had made his own report to the great tribunal, to the highest Court of Appeal on earth, the people; and received from them forever not only the reward of innocence, but the plaudits of righteousness. Thenceforth he became, and as long as he

---

[1] William P. Frye of Maine sat near Blaine during his challenge to Knott, with a copy of the Caldwell telegram in his pocket.

[2] A letter of January 26, 1871, from Blaine to Fisher (not published till 1884) suggests a meeting between Blaine, Fisher and Caldwell in Washington, at which, says Blaine, he is "very sanguine" that Caldwell could "do something" with Scott. This seems to disprove Scott's testimony that Blaine "had nothing to do in any way, directly or indirectly, in the matter" of the disposal of the bonds.

[3] For the justification of Knott, see debate on the report of the Judiciary Committee on the Blaine resolution on August 3 nearly a month after Blaine had left the House for the Senate.

[4] See, for example, the New York *Tribune* for June 6, under the caption, "Mr. Blaine's Enemies Disarmed."

[5] Gail Hamilton, *Biography of James G. Blaine,* pp. 388–393.

lived remained, the one prominent Republican candidate for the Presidency, more eagerly desired by a larger number than any President has ever been, and followed and loved as a leader with an ardor that had relation to no place except that which he had made in the hearts of the people." [1]

The subcommittee reconvened on June 7, but all interest in its proceedings had been killed by Blaine's "anticipation" of its report. It wrangled with Blaine and his friends Frye and Hale over the Caldwell dispatch, and examined some witnesses in regard to complicated charges of Blaine's dealings with the Kansas and Pacific Railroad. Then it adjourned, at Blaine's request, on the morning of Saturday, June 10, to meet the following Monday—after a final attempt of Judge Hunton to get Blaine to surrender the Mulligan letters and memorandum.[2] Before Monday came, however, a tragic event occurred which suspended the work of the committee and postponed its report to the Greek kalends.

Blaine had been under a tremendous strain. Gail Hamilton pictures him "endlessly pacing back and forth through the long suite of rooms" in the Fifteenth Street house, and once, when lying on the sofa ill with malaria, "raising his clenched hand high and exclaiming in a voice thick with emotion: 'When I think, when I think, that there lives in this broad land one single human being who doubts my integrity, I would rather have stayed' . . . leaving the sentence unfinished." [3] Mrs. Blaine wrote to Emmons at Harvard, June 4, anxious to hear that he is "enduring like a good son the fiery ordeal through which your father is passing. . . . I have been afraid you might go to Boston and do something to Mulligan; but you have sense enough to know that nothing could be worse for your father than notoriety of that kind." [4] And to the old family friend Joseph H. Manley of Maine she wrote the same day: "You must not think, dear Joe, from the tone in which I write that we are cast down. . . . We are full of courage, though perfectly aware that now is the crisis. . . . I have never been enthusiastic for the nomination. . . . But now I want Mr. Blaine to have it and to go to it, as it were on men's shoulders." [5]

[1] Gail Hamilton, *Biography of James G. Blaine*, p. 394.
[2] *House Misc. Doc.*, 44th Cong., 1st sess., No. 176, pp. 135–174.
[3] Gail Hamilton, *Biography of James G. Blaine*, p. 395.
[4] *Letters of Mrs. James G. Blaine,* edited by Harriet Blaine Beale, Vol. I, p. 135.
[5] *Ibid.,* pp. 136–137.

Sunday, June 11, was a hot sultry day. Blaine came to the breakfast table in good spirits, carrying a child perched on each shoulder. When it was suggested that the carriage should be called to take the family to the Congregational Church about a mile away, he said that he preferred to walk. He was mounting the broad stone steps to the church when suddenly he raised his hand, crying "My head, my head!" and sank unconscious into his wife's arms. A passing omnibus was hailed and he was taken to his home, where he was laid on the floor in the open hall to catch such little air as was stirring. The report of the tragedy spread quickly. Friends flocked to the house. General Sherman bent over the prostrate form crying, "Blaine, Blaine, don't you know me?" For two whole days he lay unconscious, now and then mumbling a word; but on Tuesday his mind cleared, and that afternoon he telegraphed to Hale and Frye at Cincinnati, waiting for the convention to open on the morrow: "I am entirely convalescent, suffering only from physical weakness. Impress upon my friends the great gratitude I feel for the unparalleled steadfastness with which they have adhered to me in my hour of trial."

Report had gone out that Blaine was dying; that he was dead. But, recalled from "that bourne from which no traveler returns," he was able to write with his own hand an assuring message to his supporters at Cincinnati. Their relief and joy were great. But his enemies saw in the tragic incident only another piece of play-acting to win the sympathy of the gullible masses. The Washington correspondent of the New York *Sun* sent his story to his sardonic chief, Charles A. Dana, under the heading: "Blaine Feigns a Faint."

IN THE second week of June, 1876, Cincinnati, the "Queen City of the Ohio," was seething with excitement and intrigue. A motley host of politicians, high and low, officeholders and office seekers, hard-boiled bosses and ardent reformers, together with the crowds of the curious who hang upon the edges of great enterprises, purveyors of vice, and all those who make and love a noise were flocking to the sixth quadrennial nominating convention of the Republican Party. The streets of the city were filled with shouting paraders marching behind brass bands, flaunting banners and transparencies, carrying dripping kerosene torches which feebly reinforced the flickering gas lights at the street corners. Ramshackle hotels and moribund boarding houses were filled to and beyond their capacity. Whisky and oratory flowed in an unquenchable stream. And meanwhile, in corners of hotel lobbies or in smoke-filled headquarters rooms above, the powerful ones were canvassing prospects and discussing deals to further the fortunes of their respective candidates.

The convention was called to order at high noon of Wednesday, June 14, by the Chairman of the National Republican Committee, ex-Governor Edwin D. Morgan of New York, who had performed the same service at Philadelphia at the first national Republican convention twenty years before, and again at the conventions at Chicago and Baltimore which had nominated and renominated Abraham Lincoln. Exposition Hall, which housed the 756 delegates, the alternates and the thousands of eager spectators, was a huge wooden structure with twin towers, facing on Washington Park, and resembling in its architecture "an ambitious and disappointed railroad depot." It had been built in 1869 for the national *Saengerfest,* and had been used in 1872 for that heterogeneous mass meeting of political reformers known as the Liberal Republicans. That something of the spirit of '72 still hovered among the bare beams and rafters above the heads of the delegates might be inferred from the tributes paid to honest government in the speeches and resolutions of the convention. More potent, however, was the "Spirit of '76." For it was the centennial year of the birth of the American nation. The great exposition at Philadelphia was attracting its tens of thousands of visitors daily, to view with pride the triumphs of American inventive genius, its progress in manufacture, mining, transportation and agriculture during the century. In the midst of our magnificent material achievements we should not fail to take stock of our political and moral ideals. How was it with the health of the Republic? Surely, this was the moment for rededication to the vision of the founding fathers, for rebaptism by the cleansing power of American democracy—a Pentecostal season.

There were plenty of signs in this centennial year of the working of the spirit of reform. A tongue of flame descended even upon the rather frigid head of Henry Adams. In the early months of 1876 he left his customary seat on the sidelines of politics, from which he watched the sordid struggle in a mood of boredom and cynicism, to enter the arena itself. He wrote a long letter to Carl Schurz on February 14, urging the support of a candidate who would "purify party machinery by depriving it of the means of corruption," and enclosed a draft of a circular letter to be sent to "about 200 of the most weighty and reliable of our friends," inviting them to attend "a conference of gentlemen independent of party ties," to meet about a week after the convention to "decide whether they could support the nominee," and if not, "to place before the people candidates of our own selection." [1] Letters of similar tone were sent to Henry Cabot Lodge.[2] But the reformers did not wait until the Republicans had made their nomination. A month before the convention the 200 "weighty and reliable" men met in a conference at the Fifth Avenue Hotel in New York to take measures to "prevent the national election of the centennial year from becoming a choice of evils." The group, under the leadership of Carl Schurz, contained such prominent figures as William Cullen Bryant, Thomas W. Higginson, Charles Francis Adams, Theodore Roosevelt, Sr., Mark Hopkins, Julius H. Seelye, Horace White and James Freeman Clark. Theodore Woolsey, the president of Yale, was the chairman, and Henry Cabot Lodge secretary. They were not agreed upon a candidate, some favoring Grant's Secretary of the Treasury, Benjamin H. Bristow, who had courageously prosecuted the "whisky ring" at St. Louis; others, including Schurz, preferring Charles Francis Adams, whose very name would be a guarantee of rededication to the ideals of 1776. But all agreed to

[1] *The Letters of Henry Adams,* ed. Worthington C. Ford, p. 273.
[2] *Ibid.,* pp. 278–283.

the pledge voiced in Schurz's stirring address of May 16 to support no candidate, "however conspicuous his position or brilliant his ability, in whom the impulses of the party manager have shown themselves predominant over those of the reformer." [1] The administration papers abused these reformers as "soreheads," "Pharisees" and "traitors" to the Republican Party; but Reid, in his New York *Tribune,* which had not yet become an out and out partisan of Blaine and the regular Republican organization, called them "the saving element in American politics." [2] It was with fair warning, then, to set their house in order that the Republicans met in mid-June at Cincinnati.

In his opening address Governor Morgan reminded the delegates that for the first time in sixteen years the convention would be faced with the responsibility of actually choosing a standard bearer, and not merely ratifying a choice already designated by public opinion, as in the case of the renomination of Lincoln at Baltimore in 1864 and the unanimous nominations of Grant in 1868 and 1872. "Such a state of things no longer exists," continued the speaker. "There appears to be at the present time no one to whom the unerring finger points as the only candidate. There seems to be no one man rising so far above all others as to cause exultant voices to exclaim, 'Thou art the man!' Therefore . . . greater responsibilities rest upon this Cincinnati convention than upon any or all that have preceded it." [3]

After the "keynote" speech by the temporary chairman, T. M. Pomeroy of New York, lauding the accomplishments of the party in spite of some "want of harmony," and declaring that no platform was "buoyant enough to float an unworthy candidate," the convention proceeded to the composition of the committees on credentials, permanent organization, rules and order of business and resolutions (the platform). At two o'clock it reconvened to listen to a strong appeal from the National Republican Reform Club of New York, read by George W. Curtis, assail-

[1] Claude M. Fuess, *Carl Schurz, Reformer,* p. 222.
[2] The New York *Tribune,* May 17, 1876. Reid had written to Blaine on January 23, after the latter's speech on the exclusion of Jefferson Davis from amnesty: "I cannot help thinking that the debate which your Andersonville charge provoked has damaged you with the class of men whose support you most wanted in New England." Royal Cortissoz, *Life of Whitelaw Reid,* Vol. I, p. 334. Again, on Nov. 14, 1876, Reid wrote to Hay, at the time of the indignation caused by the Belknap scandal: "Why doesn't Blaine protest against the evils of the party? . . . If he had only done one or two plucky things instead of being forever a partisan." *Ibid.,* p. 337.
[3] *Proceedings of the National Republican Convention . . .* 1876. Officially reported by M. A. Clancy and William Nelson. Republican Press Association, Concord, New Hampshire, 1876, pp. 6–7.

ing the New York Republican machine under the domination of Senator Roscoe Conkling as "an odious and intolerable oligarchy which menaces the very system of our government," scoring "the flagrant decay of official faith and integrity which has occurred during the present Federal Administration," and beseeching the convention to "put no man in nomination who is responsible in any degree for the repudiation or evasion of the unfulfilled promises" of reform.[1] The motion to adopt the address as the sense of the convention was lost, and it was simply referred to the Committee on Resolutions. General John A. Logan of Illinois followed with an ardent defense of the party against the Democrats and the unreconstructed Southerners, who were ready to "plunge the dagger of detraction . . . into the very vitals of the men who stand firm against the storms that have been rolling against liberty and freedom in this country"—a wave of the bloody shirt to shoo the spirit of '72 back to the beams and rafters.[2] Several others responded to calls to take the platform; ex-Governor Hawley of Connecticut, ex-Governor Noyes of Ohio, William A. Howard of Michigan, and Frederick Douglass, the noted leader of the colored race. Except for a brief paragraph in Governor Hawley's speech, however, the note of reform sounded by Mr. Curtis was not stressed. The pervading *motif* was the duty of maintaining the ascendancy of the Republican Party.[3] At the end of the afternoon, the organization having been completed, the permanent chairman, Edward McPherson of Pennsylvania, took the chair with a brief speech of defiance against the "enemy" (the Democracy) which was "striped all over with treason and malignity and hate of everything that is national," and declared the convention ready for business.

The next morning, after the presentation of a petition for woman suffrage and the reports of various committees, the platform was read by Governor Hawley, chairman of the Committee on Resolutions. Its seventeen sections contained the usual encomiums of the Administration and the usual pledges of unique devotion to the ideals of the Republic. It made no mention of corruption or dissension in the party, but "rejoiced in the quickened conscience of the people concerning political affairs." "The invariable rule for appointments," said the section

[1] *Proceedings of the National Republican Convention* . . . 1876, pp. 16–18.
[2] *Ibid.*, pp. 18–21.
[3] *Proceedings*, pp. 21–27.

(5) on the civil service, "should have reference to the honesty, fidelity and capacity of appointees, giving to the party in power those places where harmony and vigor of administration require its policies to be represented, but permitting all others to be filled by persons selected with sole reference to the efficiency of the public service (!) . . . We will hold all public officers to a rigid responsibility, and engage that the prosecution and punishment of all who betray official trusts shall be speedy, thorough and unsparing." [1] Well for them could they have put the last sentence in the past and not the future tense! Still, political platforms, in the large and highly organized parties, are not taken with embarrassing seriousness, being made, as a cynical witticism puts it, "not to stand on but to run on." The real and absorbing business is the nomination of the candidates for President and Vice President of the United States. It was toward three o'clock of the afternoon of June 15 that the secretary began to call the roll of the States alphabetically for the presentation of candidates for the nomination. Connecticut, Indiana, Kentucky, Maine, New York, Ohio and Pennsylvania responded as the call progressed, and sixteen speakers advanced to the platform during the next two hours to make or second the nomination of candidates from these seven states.

Two of the candidates put forward, Postmaster General Marshall Jewell of Connecticut and Governor John F. Hartranft of Pennsylvania, were merely "favorite sons," with no support outside their own States. There was not the slightest chance that either of them would be nominated, but their votes, especially the fifty-eight of the Pennsylvania delegation, would be worth bargaining for when the choice should be narrowed down to the final contenders. Two others, Senator Roscoe Conkling of New York and Governor Rutherford B. Hayes of Ohio, had claims to somewhat wider support. Conkling was supposed to be the favorite of the Administration: "the residuary legatee of Grantism," the commander of the "bread and butter brigade," and "Grant's lackey" were phrases applied to him by the opposition press. His overbearing manner and contemptuous conceit had made him so many enemies that the Union League Club of New York asked him to withdraw his candidacy in March and its resolution was endorsed by the New York *Times.* Yet his control of the State machine was so complete that the Republican convention which met at Syracuse on March 22 chose a

[1] *Proceedings,* pp. 56–57.

virtually solid Conkling delegation for Cincinnati. George W. Curtis was the only recalcitrant among the seventy delegates, and he thereafter was treated with the utmost scorn by Conkling. Although President Grant's first choice for the nomination was his Secretary of State, Hamilton Fish,[1] he preferred Conkling to any other of the actual contestants. But the paucity of support for Conkling outside of New York suggests that the approval of the Administration was rather a millstone about his neck than a medal of mascotship.

Hayes, while regarded at the outset as merely Ohio's favorite son, nevertheless had advantages which won him increasing support in the convention. He was acceptable to the reformers, without having offended the conservatives by any breach of party regularity. He had successively defeated three of the strongest Democratic candidates for the Governorship of Ohio—George W. Pendleton, Allen G. Thurman and William Allen. He had defended the cause of "sound money" and the resumption of specie payment. He had a group of remarkably able men, including ex-Governor Noyes, Senator Sherman, James A. Garfield, Charles Foster and Stanley Matthews, working for his nomination. And the fact that the convention was held in the leading city of his own State, where the press was friendly and his friends numerous, was a powerful, and in the opinion of some the determining, element in his eventual success.

The three other names presented to the convention commanded a more widely distributed support. Senator Oliver Morton of Indiana, the famous war Governor of the State, was a stalwart Administration man, who would have had equal claim with Conkling to the favor of the President if his views on the currency had been equally sound. He had the misfortune to be nominated by R. W. Thompson in the feeblest and most trivial speech of the afternoon, and to be seconded by a disreputable politician from Louisiana named Pinchback, who declared that Morton's elevation to the Presidency would "strike terror to the hearts of those monsters in the South who are driving away capital from that section . . . and persecuting and murdering black and white Republicans." [2] Pinchback's bravado was the true index of Morton's strength, for the Indiana Senator had been diligently gathering the Republican delegates from the South to his banner. Outside the thirty

---

[1] John Russell Young, *Around the World with General Grant,* Vol. II, p. 275.
[2] *Proceedings,* p. 68.

votes of the Indiana delegation, he did not have support from a single one of the States north of Mason and Dixon's line which must be counted on to furnish the electoral votes in the Republican column; and, though he stood next to the top on the first ballot, his vote steadily declined until his name was withdrawn.

The candidate upon whom the hopes of the reformers were pinned, the "residuary legatee" of the Liberal Republican movement of 1872, was Benjamin F. Bristow of Kentucky. Bristow had an unimpeachable record as soldier and administrator. He had fought as lieutenant colonel of infantry under Grant at Fort Donelson and Shiloh, had served as Solicitor General of the United States when the new Department of Justice was formed in 1870, and in June, 1874, had been appointed Secretary of the Treasury by President Grant. It was his zeal in following the President's famous instructions to "let no guilty man escape" in the prosecution of the whisky frauds (until the trial led too close to Grant's own intimates) that recommended him to the reform elements of the party. Following John M. Harlan's enthusiastic presentation of Bristow's name, ex-Congressman Luke P. Poland of Vermont, George W. Curtis of New York, and Richard H. Dana of Massachusetts seconded the nomination in speeches emphasizing the critical condition of the party and the confidence of the country in the integrity and courage of the Secretary of the Treasury. "Let us understand," said Curtis, "that this government must be purified if the party is to be saved, and that Benjamin F. Bristow is the one man who stands before the country as the embodiment of governmental purification." But, in spite of these glowing credentials, and of the activities of Adams, Schurz, Lodge and other "weighty and reliable" friends of reform, it was impossible to galvanize Bristow into a winning candidate. His support was widely distributed, but thin. His rather heavy, prosaic nature lacked appeal to the emotions which sway conventions and carry candidates to victory on a wave of contagious tumult. Besides, he came from the wrong side of the Ohio River for a Republican nomination. Kentucky went Democratic in the ensuing election by 62,000, a majority which Bristow might have reduced somewhat, but which he certainly could not have wiped out.

"The only other candidate who had an active support was Mr. Blaine of Maine," writes the said candidate in one of the very few passages in which he mentions himself in his history of *Twenty Years of*

Congress.[1] As a matter of fact, Blaine was by far the most popular candidate, commanding support and rousing enthusiasm in every part of the country. His delegates had been chosen before that dramatic day in the House when he had appealed to the confidence of his 44,000,000 fellow citizens as he read the Mulligan letters from his desk. But it is certain that neither their number nor their ardor would have been diminished if they had been chosen on that issue. Murat Halstead, then bitterly hostile to Blaine, reprinted the letters in his Cincinnati *Commercial* on the eve of the convention—with the sole result of strengthening the sympathy for the popular idol who had been "malignantly assailed by a Democratic Congress." Blaine has been generally portrayed as a man consumed with ambition for the Presidency during the last twenty years of his life. He did figure prominently in four successive Republican conventions, and less prominently in a fifth; but the testimony of his family and friends corroborates that of his own letters and public utterances that it was only in 1876 that he really desired the nomination. He stood for it in 1880 chiefly to block the movement to make Grant President for a third term, and was gratified by the choice of Garfield. The nomination came to him in 1884 (after he had privately urged General Sherman to run) with less effort on his own part than most defeated candidates have put forth. He declined the nomination in 1888, when it was his not for the asking but for the accepting. And if he really wanted it in 1892, all one can say is that he acted in a way which a man of a tithe of his political acumen must have known would ensure his defeat.

There is no doubt, however, of Blaine's desire for the nomination at Cincinnati.[2] It was in the logic of his career. It would mean the recognition of his eminence as a great national leader, the reward of his brilliant championship of the Republican Party and principles, the capstone of his vindication from the slanders of his political enemies. In spite of his collapse on the church steps, he was at the height of his physical and mental powers. He was in fighting trim, and was receiving hundreds of letters from all parts of the country hailing him as the people's choice and pledging him enthusiastic support. And he made

[1] James G. Blaine, *Twenty Years of Congress*, Vol. II, p. 569.
[2] He even tried to win the support of that chronic bolter and inexorable critic of the regular Republican organization, Carl Schurz, who in happier days had sent him such hearty wishes for higher political honors "richly deserved" (p. 63). Meeting Schurz on the street one day in the spring of 1876, Blaine put an arm about his shoulder and said, "Carl, you won't *oppose* me, will you?" Claude M. Fuess, *Carl Schurz, Reformer*, p. 220.

no secret of his ambition. "He is not a coy candidate," wrote J. W. Forney in an article comparing him with Henry Clay. "It is an honest aspiration, and he indulges it like a man. If he gets the nomination, he will arouse young America from Canada to California, and put rapture in the strife that will once more make the public heart throb with joy under a great intelligent leadership." He welcomed the news of each accession to the ranks of the "Blaine legion," and calculated, without apprehension, the chances of his chief rivals. In a conversation with Jeremiah D. Black shortly before the convention met, he said that he had no fear of Morton, who did not "represent a single sure electoral vote"; nor of Bristow, whose support was not organized; nor of Conkling, whose candidacy was "an absurdity," since he could not even carry his own State of New York. "Is there anybody you are afraid of?" asked Black. "Yes," replied Blaine, "there is the Great Unknown." [1] Did the capitalized abstraction refer to some possible "dark horse" or to the inscrutable ways of Providence?

When the State of Maine was reached in the roll call, Colonel Robert G. Ingersoll of Illinois rose to present Blaine's name. Ingersoll was a majestic figure. Authority emanated almost visibly from his Jovian brow. It was said that he had only to stand in his splendid silence before the most turbulent audience to command and captivate it. But when he spoke he carried his hearers to the heights of delirious assent. His magnificent voice played on the whole range of human emotions as the harpist's fingers sweep the strings. Ingersoll's opening sentences were a clever piece of strategy. The ears of the delegates were still ringing with the praises of Bristow's unblemished honor and unquestioned integrity. Though Blaine had not been mentioned by name, it was obvious enough that his suspected reputation was the foil against which the virtues of Bristow were set. "I tell you, gentlemen of the convention," Dana had cried, "I know no other name which is sure to carry the old commonwealth of Massachusetts next November. . . . Massachusetts is satisfied with the loyalty of Benjamin H. Bristow."

"Massachusetts may be satisfied with the loyalty of Benjamin H. Bristow," began Colonel Ingersoll, in measured tones which reached to the farthest corners of the hall. "So am I. But if any man nominated by this convention cannot carry the State of Massachusetts, I am not satisfied with the loyalty of Massachusetts. If the nominee of this con-

[1] Royal Cortissoz, *The Life of Whitelaw Reid,* Vol. I, pp. 329–331.

vention cannot carry the grand old commonwealth by 75,000 majority,
I would advise them to sell out Faneuil Hall as Democratic headquarters." Having thus skillfully shifted the emphasis from the virtues of
Bristow to the merits of the Republican Party, Ingersoll went on to
describe the kind of leader that the party demanded, in terms which
pointed unmistakably to the experienced statesman from Maine.

The candidate must have a "political reputation spotless as a star,"
but he need not have a "certificate of moral character signed by a Confederate Congress." "This is a grand year," said the orator as he warmed
to his subject, "a year in which the sons of freedom will drink from the
fountain of enthusiasm; a year in which the people call for the man who
has preserved in Congress what their soldiers won upon the field; a year
in which they call for the man who has torn from the throat of treason the
tongue of slander, the man who has snatched the mask of Democracy
from the hideous face of the rebellion. . . . Like an armed warrior,
like a plumed knight, James G. Blaine marched down the halls of the
American Congress and threw his shining lance full and fair against
the brazen forehead of every traitor to his country and every maligner
of his fair reputation. For the Republican Party to desert that gallant
man now is as though an army should desert their general upon the
field of battle. . . . Gentlemen of the convention: In the name of the
great republic, the only republic that ever existed on the face of the
earth; in the name of all her defenders and supporters; in the name
of all her soldiers living; in the name of all her soldiers that died upon
the field of battle; and in the name of those that perished in the skeleton clutch of famine at Andersonville and Libby, whose sufferings he so
vividly remembers—Illinois, Illinois nominates for the next President
of this country that prince of parliamentarians, that leader of leaders,
James G. Blaine." [1]

It was magnificent, but it was not—exactly true. Transported by the
Colonel's eloquence, the delegates and audience failed to detect the
flaws in his argument. He had out-Danaed Dana and out-Curtised Curtis in praise of the one candidate indispensable to the success of the
Republican Party. The railroad investigations in which Blaine was
implicated were not instigated by Southerners, but Ingersoll represented his hero as battling against the slanders of "treason" and "rebellion," masquerading as Democracy. Moreover, Blaine himself was

[1] *Proceedings*, pp. 73–75.

not pleased with the simile of the plumed knight. He thought that the plume might suggest the white feather as well as the helmet of Navarre.[1]

Had the balloting begun while the convention was still under the spell of Ingersoll's eloquence, Blaine might have been nominated, if not on the first ballot, at least after several scores of delegates had fulfilled their duty by casting a complimentary vote for the favorite sons of their States. But New York, Ohio and Pennsylvania followed Maine on the roll call, and by the time the sponsors of Conkling, Hayes and Hartranft had finished their speeches it was after five o'clock. There were still more than two hours before sunset in Cincinnati on that day in mid-June, but according to Blaine, "The hastening shades of evening compelled an adjournment to the next morning." [2] William P. Frye, eager to capitalize the enthusiasm which Ingersoll had aroused, asked if the hall could not be lighted. But the chairman was informed that the gas lights could not safely be kindled, and the balloting went over until half past ten the next day.

On the first ballot Blaine received 285 votes from thirty-five States and Territories, and was within less than 100 votes of the necessary majority of 378. He was far ahead of his nearest rivals, Morton and Bristow, who had 124 and 113 votes respectively. Furthermore, two thirds of Blaine's votes came from the States of the North and West, which might be counted upon to swell the Republican electoral column, while three fourths of Morton's were from the South, which was certain to go Democratic so far as it had recovered home rule. Bristow also proved as weak as Blaine predicted he would. He received only forty-nine votes from States north of Mason and Dixon's line, seventeen of them from Massachusetts. From the three largest delegations in the convention (New York, Pennsylvania, and Ohio) Blaine did not receive a single vote on the first ballot, nor was he able through the five succeeding ballots to detach a single delegate from Conkling or Hayes, though he got a few Pennsylvania votes from the second ballot on.[3] The support of any two of these three great States at any time during the convention would

---

[1] *Letters of Mrs. James G. Blaine,* Vol. I, p. 129, note.
[2] James G. Blaine, *Twenty Years of Congress,* Vol. II, p. 571.
[3] There was a lively debate after the second ballot, when the chairman of the Pennsylvania delegation tried in vain to get the presiding officer of the convention to uphold the "unit rule," which requires that the solid vote of the delegation be cast for the candidate approved by the majority of the delegation. The unit rule has never been applied in Republican conventions.

have given Blaine the nomination. It was clearly a case of Blaine against the field from the beginning, and it was also clear that, in spite of his huge lead, Blaine could not win so long as the field held firmly against him. His managers offered both Bristow and Hayes the second place on the ticket, only to have their advances spurned. They knew that there was no use approaching the implacable Conkling. It was only a question of whether and when the anti-Blaine forces could unite on an acceptable compromise candidate. That moment came on the sixth ballot, on which Blaine jumped from 286 to 308 votes, while his nearest competitor had but 113. But it was significant that that competitor, Governor Hayes, had gained on every ballot while all the others (except Blaine himself) had declined. Obviously Hayes was the man of destiny. The seventh and final roll call had proceeded as far as Illinois, showing 105 votes for Blaine to 19 for Hayes, when the fireworks began. Indiana withdrew the name of Morton and gave 25 of her 30 votes to Hayes. Then Kentucky withdrew Bristow and cast her solid vote of 24 for Hayes. Massachusetts transferred 14 Bristow votes to Hayes. New York, "in the interests of amity and victory," dropped Conkling and gave 61 of her 70 votes to Hayes. Pennsylvania withdrew Hartranft and divided her vote almost equally between Blaine and Hayes (30 to 28). When the total was cast up, the Blaine vote had risen to 351, but Hayes had gone up from 113 to 384 and won the nomination by a margin of six votes.[1] His skillful managers, the most skillful at the convention, had exactly carried out the succinct program of James A. Garfield: "We should give you the solid vote of the Ohio delegation, and await the break-up which must come when the weaker candidates drop out."[2] They knew how to win the support of the Bristow reform element (chiefly through promises made to them by Stanley Matthews) without alienating such staunch Administration men as Conkling and Morton. They had exploited their colorless candidate as a guarantee of "all things to all men," and persuaded a convention "two thirds of whose members knew nothing of Hayes, to ac-

[1] The following condensed table shows the result of the balloting for the most serious contenders;

	range of votes on first six ballots	vote on seventh
Hayes:	61–113	384
Blaine:	285–308	351
Bristow:	126–111	21
Morton:	124–85	0

[2] Garfield to Hayes, March 2, 1876. H. J. Eckenrode, *Rutherford B. Hayes, Statesman of Reunion*, p. 122.

cept him instead of the man of their desire." [1]

Blaine, sitting in his library at Washington, listened to the results of the balloting, which came to him over a private wire from his managers, Hale and Frye, at Cincinnati. He noted the steady gain of Hayes on each ballot, and, on the fifth, he predicted that the Governor of Ohio would be nominated. His telegram of congratulation to Hayes was most cordial. He offered him whole-hearted support during the campaign and hoped to continue that support when Hayes entered the White House.[2]

It is perhaps idle to speculate on whether Blaine could have been elected if nominated in 1876. The charge of having used the influence of his official position for his private enrichment would undoubtedly have been a handicap; but the dramatic and apparently successful refutation of that charge might have been a still greater asset. Only the test of the polls could have told what proportion of the rank and file of the Republican voters believed with Carl Schurz that Blaine was both guilty and vulnerable,[3] or with John Hay that he was both innocent and invulnerable,[4] or with George F. Hoar that he was innocent but vulnerable.[5] But, even granted that the first opinion was widespread, it must be remembered that Blaine was an aggressive defendant, resourceful, brilliant and wary, persuasive in eloquence and "magnetic" in personal appeal. Would he not have captured the electorate as he

---

[1] H. J. Eckenrode, *Rutherford B. Hayes, Statesman of Reunion,* p. 135.

[2] The relations between Blaine and Hayes were most cordial up to the time of the latter's accession to the Presidency.

[3] Some years later Schurz wrote to Hayes: "I oppose Blaine because I believe that the election to the presidency of the United States of a man who wrote the Mulligan letters, and who stands before the country as the representative of the practices they disclose, would be a precedent fraught with incalculable evil, a fatal blow at the moral foundations of our republican government. It would be a terrible thing to teach our young people that such a record does not disqualify a man for the highest honors and trusts of the Republic." Quoted from the Hayes papers by Eckenrode, *Rutherford B. Hayes, Statesman of Reunion,* pp. 120–121.

[4] "The (Mulligan) letters show absolutely no wrong, but some imprudence." Hay to Reid. Cortissoz, *Life of Whitelaw Reid,* Vol. I, p. 341. "Twenty men are ready to work for Blaine to one for Bristow. Blaine has shown positive capacity for government, Bristow has not." *Ibid.,* p. 336.

[5] "I was satisfied then (1876) and I am satisfied now," wrote Hoar in 1903, "that the charges against Mr. Blaine of any corruption or wrong doing were totally unsustained. . . . Yet he erred when he thought it proper to embark in such a speculative investment (as Little Rock bonds) . . . I did not think it wise, under the circumstances, to nominate Mr. Blaine either in 1876 or later. I believed then, and now believe that he would have been an admirable President of the United States. But I did not think it wise to put at the head of a movement for reform . . . a man whose supporters must defend him against such charges, and who must admit that he had most unwisely and of his own accord put himself in a position where such charges were not only possible but plausible." G. F. Hoar, *Autobiography of Seventy Years,* Vol. I, pp. 280–281, 379–380.

had captured the House? Besides, the issue which he would have championed with consummate skill—namely, the maintenance of the Republican measures of reconstruction against the danger from a Democracy still tainted with "rebellious" sentiments—was far more vital in 1876 than it was eight years later. The Republican Party still depended largely upon the "soldier vote." As Eckenrode says, "The election of 1876 was the last scene in the drama of the Civil War." [1]

At any rate, Blaine's failure to win the coveted nomination in 1876 was as significant an incident in his career as his failure to win the hotly contested election in 1884. And the reasons given for the former failure are as numerous and various as those alleged for the second. Rhodes says that Blaine "would unquestionably have been the nominee had not the charge of personal corruption been fastened upon him." [2] T. C. Crawford, who reported the convention for the Blaine press, says that he would have won on the sixth ballot had not Eugene Hale rejected Don Cameron's offer to throw the Pennsylvania delegation to Blaine in return for the promise of a place for a Pennsylvania man (presumably himself) in the Cabinet.[3] George F. Hoar thought that Blaine could have had enough votes from the Bristow delegation to put him over when the break came, if he had not snubbed the Secretary of the Treasury.[4] John Hay wrote to Blaine the day after the balloting: "It is a bitter disappointment to us all. . . . You not only had your 351 votes, but also the cowardly good-will of the Ohio and Pennsylvania delegations, who would have voted for you if they had dared to defy the machine lash." [5] John Sherman declared that, it was Conkling's bitter antagonism which held the New York delegation

---

[1] H. J. Eckenrode, *Rutherford B. Hayes*, p. 146.

[2] J. F. Rhodes, *History of the United States from the Compromise of 1850*, Vol. VII, p. 207.

[3] T. C. Crawford, *Life of James G. Blaine*, p. 392.

[4] The story is that Blaine accused Bristow of instigating attacks upon him in the Kentucky papers, and that when the Secretary called at the Blaine house to present his message of sympathy after the tragic incident of Sunday, June 11, the door was closed in his face. The news was sent to Bristow's manager at Cincinnati, John M. Harlan, who swung the Kentucky delegation solidly to Hayes. G. F. Hoar, *Autobiography of Seventy Years*, pp. 381–382.

[5] Quoted in Rhodes, *loc. cit.*, Vol. VII, p. 211. Edwin Cowles of the Cleveland *Leader*, one of the few Blaine delegates from Ohio, wrote to Hayes on June 27: "To be candid, I feel almost conscience-smitten at my having apparently (!) gone back on Blaine after having announced to him three years ago in his library that I was going to trot him out for the presidency and fight for him to the bitter end. . . . He is a noble fellow and the best abused man in America. . . . My heart was for him, but my head was for you." C. R. Williams, *Life of Rutherford B. Hayes*, Vol. I, p. 453, note.

solid against Blaine to the end, and "probably defeated him." [1] Eckenrode believes that the followers of Bristow and Morton were responsible for Blaine's defeat. Bristow was for Hayes because the latter was
a "quasi-reformer," and Morton wanted to keep the Presidency in
the Middle West. "Men stood together in the Corn Belt." [2] Others attributed Blaine's discomfiture to the astuteness of the Ohio managers,
to the ineptitude of the permanent chairman, McPherson, and even to
the deficient lighting system of the convention hall, which prevented
the balloting on Thursday evening, after Colonel Ingersoll's rousing
speech for the "Plumed Knight."

Whatever its cause or combination of causes, however, the elimination of Blaine from the contest of 1876 accomplished the purpose of
his inquisitors. "Mr. Knott and his allies," said the Philadelphia *North
American,* "succeeded in keeping Mr. Blaine from the Presidency, but
Knott at least has covered himself with ineffaceable dishonor." [3] Once the
decision was made at Cincinnati, the subcommittee of the Judiciary had
no further reason to continue the investigation of the charges against
Blaine. But even had they wished to do so, they would have soon
found him removed from the sphere of their jurisdiction. Three days
after the convention closed, Bristow resigned the Treasury portfolio,
and President Grant chose Senator Lot M. Morrill of Maine to succeed him. On July 10 Governor Selden Connor appointed Blaine to
the vacant seat in the Senate, and when the Maine legislature met in
the autumn, it not only ratified the appointment without a dissenting
voice, but also unanimously elected Blaine for the six-year term beginning March 4, 1877. So the Maine statesman went to join his old
enemy Conkling in the Senate of the United States, but the two men
never gave a sign of recognition of each other in that august chamber.

The Democrats, meeting at St. Louis, June 28, nominated Governor
Samuel J. Tilden of New York and Thomas A. Hendricks of Indiana.
Tilden had amassed a fortune as a corporation lawyer. It was said that
in the years of business depression just preceding the Civil War, the
affairs of half the railroads between the Hudson river and the Mississippi were in his hands. During the war he had been a staunch Union-

---

[1] John Sherman, *Recollections,* Vol. I, p. 550.
[2] H. J. Eckenrode, *loc. cit.,* p. 134.
[3] *Cong. Record,* 44th Cong., 1st sess., p. 5126.

ist, albeit, like Governor Seymour, bitterly opposed to many of President Lincoln's policies. He combined public spirit with private business enterprise, serving in the New York Assembly at the age of thirty-two (1846), assuming the chairmanship of the Democratic State Committee in 1866, and reëntering the legislature in 1872, chiefly for the purpose of aiding in the prosecution of the corrupt judges Barnard and Cardozo of the "Tweed Ring." For this service he was rewarded in 1874 by the election to the Governorship, where he continued his reforming activities by the prosecution of the Erie Canal ring. Though his Republican opponents averred that his zeal for the purification of politics was both belated and insincere,[1] his reputation as "the great reformer" was solidly established in the Democratic Party; and his hold upon the organization was remarkable, considering his lack of the traditional qualities of political leadership—geniality, bold initiative and the joy of battle.

The Democratic platform, composed by Manton Marble of the New York *World,* in coöperation with Tilden, and characterized by George W. Curtis as "a vast wash of words," stressed reform in the currency, the tariff, public expenditures, the "carpetbag tyrannies" of the South, the civil service, and "even more" the purification of the higher branches of the public service. It denounced the "abuses, wrongs and crimes" of the Republican Party in general, and attacked a number of Republican officials in person, including "a late Speaker of the House of Representatives marketing his rulings as presiding officer." Thomas Ewing, a kinsman of the "late Speaker," vainly attempted to get this "shameful attack on Mr. Blaine" stricken out of the platform.[2]

About a week after the convention Blaine was able to leave Washington with his family for a period of rest and recuperation at his home in Augusta, before devoting himself to the campaign. In spite of his efforts, however, he was not able to redeem his promise to Hayes in his telegram of congratulation, that Maine would give the national ticket

[1] "During all Tweed's ascendency and control of the Democratic Party in the State of New York," said *Harper's Weekly* of August 15, 1876, "Mr. Tilden as chairman gave the weight of his name and official action to Tweed's nominations." Blaine, in his *Twenty Years of Congress* (Vol. II, p. 575) says of Tilden: "He understood better than any other man the art of appropriating to himsef the credit for events which would have come to pass without his agency, and for reforms already planned by his political opponents."
[2] Ewing wrote to Miss Dodge (or Mrs. Blaine) from St. Louis, June 30, 1876: "I was a member of the Committee on Resolutions, and moved to strike out that clause of the platform, which had been brought out from New York by the Tildenites. . . . My motion led to an angry debate . . . and was lost at last by a vote of 18 to 20."

as hearty support as if he himself were the candidate. The September elections showed the usual Republican majorities for the State ticket; and Hayes wrote Blaine on the fourteenth: "How gloriously you have done! I congratulate you and thank you. This will give heart and life to our friends everywhere." But in the presidential election Maine gave the Hayes and Wheeler ticket a majority of only 17,500, as against 28,000 and 32,000 for Grant in 1868 and 1872. The defection was attributed largely to the inroads of the "greenback heresy," which became threatening in several of the Eastern States during the depression of the middle seventies.

The Maine State canvass over, and, his "amazing vitality" fully restored, Blaine joined the large and able group of orators, including Schurz, Ingersoll, Evarts, Logan, Garfield, Harrison, Curtis, Sherman and Depew, who were enlisted to avert the "calamity" of a Democratic victory. He spoke to great audiences in New York City and Newark, New Jersey, toured New York State according to an itinerary prepared by A. B. Cornell, and roused the enthusiasm of packed houses in a dozen cities of Ohio and Indiana. He did not need the hint of Hayes: "Our strong ground is the dread of a solid South, rebel rule, etc., etc. I hope you will make these topics prominent in your speeches. It leads the people away from 'hard times' which is our deadliest foe." [1] That was just the program Blaine intended to follow. He knew that the hope of victory lay in the still potent appeal to party loyalty as a synonym of loyalty to the Union; and in convincing enough voters in the doubtful Northern States that such bloody affrays as the "Hamburg massacre" of July 4 in South Carolina and the continual race riots in anarchical Louisiana were symptoms of the "shotgun rule" by which the unrepentant South was determined to wreak vengeance for its defeat and to wreck the reconstruction settlement. This, notwithstanding the fact that the Democratic platform declared: "For the Democrats of the whole country we do here reaffirm our faith in the permanence of the Federal Union, our devotion to the Constitution of the United States, with its amendments universally accepted as a final settlement of the controversies that engendered civil war." [2]

---

[1] Hayes to Blaine, Sept. 14, 1876.
[2] Edward Stanwood, *The History of the Presidency,* Vol. I, p. 375. Charles Nordoff of the New York *Herald,* one of the fairest and ablest of correspondents, wrote a series of letters to his paper in 1875 (later published in book form under the title, *The Cotton States*) in which he gave a very different picture of conditions in that section from the

It became evident as the campaign proceeded that the event hung in the balance. Not since the election of Lincoln in 1860 had there been a party struggle so fiercely contested. In addition to the weight of the scandals of the Grant régime (doubly magnified in the national pride of the centennial year) the Republicans had to bear the responsibility for a severe industrial panic, which is always charged upon the party in power. On the other hand, the Democrats were still paying the penalty for such past follies as their condemnation of the war as a "failure" in 1864, their espousal of the "Ohio idea" of rag money in 1868,[1] and their endorsement of Greeley's candidacy in 1872. They were still charged, however unjustly, with disloyalty to the Union. John Sherman called the Democratic Party "the left wing of the rebel army." As Professor Haworth remarks, "If confidence in the Democrats had been equal to disgust with the Republicans, Tilden would have had an easy victory." [2]

As for the candidates themselves, there was not much to choose between them. Both were honest public servants; both were pledged to the reform of the civil service and the elimination of corruption in the departments of the government; both were opposed to the continuance of bayonet rule in the South; both set the welfare of the country above narrow partisan ends. If Hayes had the advantage of a fine record in the Civil War,[3] Tilden, as the polling was to show, had the confidence of a majority of the people. It was only the excitable and gullible part of the electorate that could be persuaded by the "spellbinders" either that Hayes would be a tool in the hands of unscrupulous party bosses or that Tilden was a "rebel sympathizer," who had not only made his un-

---

one painted by the Republican orators. In a letter of December 27 he says: "I have the word of Northern missionaries laboring entirely among the colored people that the period of violence is past. It is easy to make a list of crimes in any Southern State, as in any Northern State. Certainly there is no more lawlessness in Georgia . . . than in Pennsylvania. . . . In a journey through six Southern States last spring and summer, I saw with one exception not a single respectable Republican who did not freely tell me that there was no need of a Force bill . . . that what the party needed in those States was purification from the control of rogues and plunderers."

[1] Hendricks was a soft money man, and it required no little ingenuity to handle the currency question in the campaign in such a way as to satisfy the hard money followers of Tilden without alienating the Hendricks supporters. Thomas Nast's cartoons in *Harper's Weekly* represented the Democratic "monstrosity" as a Tammany tiger with a Tilden head at one end of its body and a Hendricks head at the other, trying to keep from being pulled apart in the middle.

[2] Paul L. Haworth, *The Hayes-Tilden Disputed Presidential Election of 1876*, p. 328.

[3] It is noteworthy that, with the exception of Grover Cleveland, every elected President from the close of the Civil War to the end of the nineteenth century had been an officer (all but one a general) in the Union army.

holy millions while his country was going through the agony of war, but had also cheated the government out of thousands of dollars by filing fraudulent income tax returns.

At midnight of election day, November 7, it seemed certain that Tilden had won. He had carried the pivotal State of New York, by over 30,000, as well as the doubtful States of Connecticut, New Jersey and Indiana. The 65 electoral votes from these four States, added to the 138 from the States south of Mason and Dixon's line, would give him a total of 203, or 18 more than the necessary majority in the electoral college. It was a gloomy night for the Republicans, who had held the reins of government for fifteen years and fattened on its offices. To those imbued with the idea that all the virtue and loyalty of the country dwelt in their party, a Democratic victory seemed like the ruin of the Republic. Stanley Matthews of Ohio wrote: "I seemed all day to walk through the valley of the shadow of death. I felt as if a great conspiracy of ignorance, superstition and brutality had succeeded in overthrowing the hopes of Christian civilization represented and embodied in the Republican Party." [1]

Almost every Republican newspaper, including the rock-ribbed New York *Tribune*, conceded the election of Tilden. The Republican headquarters at the Fifth Avenue Hotel had closed, and the National Chairman, Zachariah Chandler, had gone to bed to drown his woe in sleep. Not so, however, a little group in the editorial sanctum of the New York *Times*, which had been the bitterest of Tilden's slanderers.[2] John C. Reid, the managing editor, insisted that Hayes must and should be the next President of the United States. There were three Southern States still under the control of the Federal government, namely, South Carolina, Louisiana and Florida. If the nineteen electoral votes of these States were counted for Hayes, he would have 185 votes to Tilden's 184 in the electoral column. Before dawn on the morning of November 8, Reid hastened from the office of the *Times* to the Fifth Avenue Hotel, where he found William E. Chandler, Secretary of the National Republican Committee, sunk in an armchair of the lobby, disconsolately reading the news of Tilden's victory in the early edition of the New York *Tribune*. The two men went up to Chandler's room and tabu-

---

[1] H. J. Eckenrode, *Rutherford B. Hayes, Statesman of Reunion*, p. 195.
[2] See, for example, the list of Tilden's alleged villainies published in a special supplement of the *Times* for May 18, 1876.

lated the votes as Reid had computed them. Then they routed Zachariah Chandler from his bed and secured his dazed consent to act as they wished in the matter. Then they hastened to the Western Union Telegraph office and sent dispatches to the Republican managers in the three Southern States: "Hayes is elected if we have carried South Carolina, Florida and Louisiana. Can you hold your State? Answer immediately." It was virtually an order to the Republican canvassing boards in these States to return majorities for the Hayes electors—and it was obeyed.

Zachariah Chandler, now thoroughly awake, sent out the official announcement from the Republican headquarters on the morning of November 8: "Rutherford B. Hayes has 185 votes and is elected." On the tenth President Grant ordered the General of the Army, W. T. Sherman, to instruct the commanders of the Federal troops in Louisiana and Florida "to preserve peace and good order and see that the proper and legal boards of canvassers are unmolested in the performance of their duties." It was at Grant's request also that a number of "visiting statesmen" from the Northern States, representing both parties, went down to Louisiana and Florida to observe the canvass. But they might as well have stayed at home and saved the carfare, for the Republicans quite naturally reported the violence which had kept the Negroes from the polls, while the Democrats charged the canvassing boards with rejecting Tilden ballots wholesale.

The upshot of all the confusion and wrangling was that two sets of returns, certified as "official" by conflicting authorities, were sent up to Washington from the States in question.[1] There was no legal provision for determining which set should be accepted as valid. Conflicting certificates were not anticipated by the framers of the Constitution. "The President of the Senate shall, in the presence of the Senate and the House of Representatives, open all the certificates and the vote shall then be counted," is the curt direction given (Amendment XII). If the President of the Senate, T. W. Ferry of Michigan, a strict Republican, were allowed to choose which set of returns were to be counted, the Hayes electors would be accepted. If the matter were

[1] There was also a double set of returns from Oregon, not because there was any doubt that Hayes had carried the State, but because the Democratic Governor, discovering that one of the three electors was technically disqualified by holding a postoffice job (Constitution, Art. II, sect. I, par. 2) had arbitrarily replaced him by the highest elector on the Tilden list. The Republicans had rightfully insisted that an eligible Republican should be chosen to fill the vacancy, and their contention was upheld by the electoral commission.

referred to the Democratic House or to the whole Congress, which was Democratic on a joint ballot, the Tilden votes would put a Democratic President in the White House. There had been instances before in which the counting of the vote of this or that State had been contested, but never before had the result of the election depended upon the contested vote. In 1865, when there was a question of accepting the votes of the States of Tennessee and Louisiana, which had been "reconstructed" under President Lincoln's ten per cent plan, Congress had adopted a joint rule providing that "no vote objected to shall be counted except by the concurrent vote of the two houses." This rule was not binding on future Congresses, and of course it could not be readopted by the Republican Senate of 1877, because then the refusal of the Democratic House to have any of the votes from any one of the disputed States counted would give Tilden the Presidency.

Some of the Republican leaders, like Morton and Blaine, believed that the President of the Senate should assume the responsibility of counting the votes (which would have been cast for Hayes), depending on the authority of President Grant and the intervention of the military, if necessary, to quell any resistance by the Democrats. Others, like Conkling, who really believed that Tilden had been elected, favored the creation of some extraordinary tribunal to decide the issue. There were suggestions that the decision be left to the Supreme Court or even to a jury drawn by lot—to which Tilden replied with just scorn that he "would not raffle" for the Presidency.

On motion of George W. McCrary (Rep.) of Iowa, a committee of fourteen, including Roscoe Conkling and Abram S. Hewitt, the chairman of the Democratic National Committee, was appointed from the Senate and the House to devise a plan for the solution of the deadlock. It reported a bill on January 19, 1877, providing for an Electoral Commission of fifteen members, five from the Senate, five from the House, and four designated Supreme Court Justices, who should themselves choose a fifth. All disputed returns were to be referred to this commission, to be decided by a majority vote, and the decision was to stand unless rejected by both Houses of Congress. The Republican Senate chose three Republicans and two Democrats to the Commission, the Democratic House three Democrats and two Republicans, and the designated justices were two Republicans and two Democrats. This left the deciding voice to the fifth justice. It was understood at the time that the bill was passed that the fifth member from the Supreme Court would be Justice David Davis, an Independent from Illinois, who had voted for Tilden. But on the day after the electoral bill was passed by the Senate (Jan. 25) Justice Davis was elected to the Senate by a fusion vote of the Democrats and Greenbackers in the Illinois legislature. Davis used his proximate retirement from the Supreme Court as an excuse for declining a place on the commission, doubtless glad to escape the responsibility of determining who the next President of the United States should be. Justice Joseph P. Bradley of New Jersey, a Republican, was chosen in his stead.

Blaine opposed the electoral bill in the Senate on January 24. "Looking at it with every desire to coöperate with those who are so strongly advocating it," he said, "I am compelled to withhold the support of my vote. . . . I do not believe that the Congress itself has the power which it proposes to confer on these fifteen gentlemen." [1] Still, he had no alternative to propose to meet the emergency. He advocated a constitutional amendment conferring on the Supreme Court the power "to peacefully and promptly settle all the troubles growing out of disputed electoral votes." [2] It was Conkling's powerful speech of January 23–24 that won for the bill the majority of the Republican Senate, which passed it on the morning of the twenty-fifth by a vote of 47 (26 Dem., 21 Rep.) to 17 (1 Dem., 16 Rep.).[3] The next day the House passed it by the overwhelming majority of 191 (158 Dem., 33 Rep.) to 86 (18 Dem., 68 Rep.). Thus it was the Democrats who put the bill through Congress, casting ten votes in favor of it to one against.

Why did they do this? First, because they feared that unless some such tribunal were set up the Republican President of the Senate would count the Hayes votes from the disputed States, and President Grant would, if necessary, use the Federal troops which were being gathered about Washington to uphold the decision; then, because they believed (as Hewitt assured Tilden) that Justice Davis would be the fifteenth

---

[1] The following day H. C. Bowen of the New York *Independent* wrote Blaine: "Thanks for your courage in opposing the 'arbitration' bill. The Democrats here are jubilant, while the Republicans wear long faces. . . . The news boys are flying about the streets crying, 'Great news from Washington. Tilden next President.' I believe that a large proportion of the Republican Party are opposed to the 'national raffle.' But if we are to arbitrate, why not take an impartial arbitrator like the Czar of Russia, or Dom Pedro, or Queen Victoria or the Pope of Rome!" Bowen to Blaine, Jan. 25, 1877.

[2] *Cong. Record,* 44th Cong., 2d sess., p. 898.

[3] *Ibid.,* pp. 825–831, 869–878.

member of the tribunal, ensuring a Tilden victory. Even the substitution of Bradley for Davis did not dismay Hewitt. He thought, as did the two Democratic justices on the commission, Clifford and Field, that Bradley would not allow political bias to becloud his impartial decision as a judge; and furthermore, Justice Bradley had shown himself favorable to the conservatives in the South by opposing the constitutionality of the Enforcement Acts and by various decisions which he had made when holding court in Louisiana.[1] The very evening before the first test case came on the counting of the Florida vote, a friend of Hewitt's called on Justice Bradley at his house and reported to Hewitt shortly before midnight that Bradley had read to him his decision (prepared for the next day) favoring the Tilden electors. After Hewitt's friend had left Bradley two prominent Republicans visited him and, together with Mrs. Bradley, persuaded him to change his mind. To Hewitt's astonishment and dismay, he voted for the Hayes electors. If this story (based on a "confidential source") be true, Justice Bradley is more to be blamed for revealing his opinion before the commission met than for changing his mind.

The entire month of February was taken up with the settlement of the disputed count. The counsel for the Democrats argued that it was the duty of the electoral commission to go behind the returns of the State boards and determine whether the votes had been fairly cast and counted. Otherwise, they said, the commission would have no reason for existing, being merely a registering body like the electoral college. The Republican counsel, on the other hand, declared that it was impossible for a national commission to investigate the conduct of the election in the States, its only function being to determine which set of returns sent up to Washington was the one properly certified by the State board. In this dilemma the traditional policy of the two parties was exactly reversed, the Democratic Party of States rights now pleading for the exercise of the Federal power, and the Republicans insisting (except in the case of Oregon) on respecting the full authority of the State boards. The decision of the commission in each case was in favor of the Republican returns by a strict party vote of eight to seven; and in each case the Democratic House rejected and the Republican Sen-

[1] See James Monroe, "The Hayes-Tilden Electoral Commission," in the *Atlantic Monthly*, Oct., 1893, pp. 529–530.

ate upheld the findings of the commission.[1] It was four o'clock in the morning of March 2, only two days before the date of the inauguration, that the canvass was finished and President Ferry of the Senate announced that Hayes and Wheeler were elected by a vote of 185 to 184.

During all the excitement the candidates themselves had refrained from taking the least part in the struggle. Hayes remained calmly at work in the Governor's room at the capitol at Columbus, and Tilden spent his time compiling a treatise on *The Presidential Count*. There were threats from the Democrats in some quarters that they would resort to force rather than see the election "stolen" from them, and the impetuous Henry Watterson of the Louisville *Courier-Journal* talked of marching on Washington with 100,000 men to seat Tilden. But in the region where the contest originated there was no disposition to challenge the result. The South had had enough of war. Besides, they were not so much interested in having a Democratic President in the White House as they were in getting rid of the last remnants of bayonet rule in their own States. And this deliverance they believed that they would be as likely to obtain from Hayes as from Tilden. Conferences had been held during the month of February between prominent Hayes spokesmen, like Stanley Matthews, Charles Foster, John Sherman, James A. Garfield and ex-Governor Dennison of Ohio and such Southern representatives as Senator J. B. Gordon of Georgia, Major E. A. Barker of Louisiana and L. Q. C. Lamar of Mississippi, in which pledges were given, doubtless with the candidate's knowledge, that "if Governor Hayes was inaugurated he would restore home rule in the States of Louisiana and South Carolina, and that the people of those States should control their own affairs in their own way, as free from any intervention of the Federal authority as the State of Ohio." [2] It was in reliance upon these pledges that the Southern Democrats refused to support any filibuster in Congress against the decision of the commission or to countenance any appeal to the Northern Democrats to seat Tilden by force.

Every Democrat in the country was convinced in 1877 (and, for that matter, is today) that Tilden was entitled to the presidential chair. Many a Republican, too, less frank than Conkling, believed that

---

[1] When the decision awarding the Florida votes to Hayes and Wheeler was submitted to the Senate, Roscoe Conkling ostentatiously walked out of the chamber rather than cast his vote for what he considered a miscarriage of justice.

[2] H. J. Eckenrode, *Rutherford B. Hayes, Statesman of Reunion*, p. 220.

the claims of the Hayes electors could not be substantiated by a careful examination of the behavior of the canvassing boards in two of the disputed States. John Bigelow, the biographer of Tilden, says that Blaine told him some months after the election that "if the Democrats had been firm the Republicans would have backed down." [1] While it is easier to believe that Mr. Bigelow misconstrued the conversation than that the aggressive, confident Blaine made so uncharacteristic a concession, it is nevertheless rather significant that, in the account of the disputed election in his *Twenty Years of Congress*, Blaine pronounces no judgment upon the merits of the decision, but states simply that "in the end the work of the Commission was confirmed and Mr. Hayes was declared to have been elected by the precise vote which Mr. Chandler, on behalf of the Republican National Committee, claimed the day after the polls closed in November—185 Republican electors, 184 Democratic electors." [2] "The Democratic dissatisfaction," he adds, "was instinctive and inevitable," [3] but he does not say either that it was baseless or that it was justified.

Volumes have been written on the disputed election of 1876, and historians are perhaps no nearer to a consensus of opinion on the subject today than were the politicians a half century ago. That Hayes was entitled to the three electoral votes of Oregon is beyond a doubt. He carried the State by a majority of over one thousand in a perfectly free and fair election. That he was entitled to the vote of South Carolina is almost equally certain. Enough of the large Negro population had gone to the polls [4] to make it unnecessary for the returning board to throw out Democratic votes in order to leave a Republican majority. The case of Louisiana was extremely complicated. The State had been in a deplorable condition of anarchy for a decade. Rival governors and legislatures had fought for power like the armed faction in one of the turbulent Latin-American republics, where elections precipitate rather than settle political strife. Fraud was countered by fraud in Louisiana. Whether the Democrats suffered more by having their votes thrown out by the canvassing board or the Republicans by having theirs excluded from the ballot boxes is impossible to say.

---

[1] John Bigelow, *Life of Samuel J. Tilden,* Vol. II, p. 74 note.
[2] James G. Blaine, *Twenty Years of Congress,* Vol. II, pp. 581–589.
[3] *Ibid.,* p. 589.
[4] The census of 1870 gave the population of South Carolina in 1870 as 289,667 whites and 415,814 Negroes.

James Ford Rhodes believed that Tilden carried Louisiana. "If Hayes had envisaged the facts as I do now (1906)," he writes, "he would have refused to accept the Presidency from the Louisiana return-ing board. On November 27 Hayes wrote to Sherman at New Orleans: 'A fair election would have given us about forty electoral votes at the South—at least that many. But we are not to allow our friends to defeat one outrage and fraud by another. There must be nothing crooked on our part. Let Mr. Tilden have the place by violence, intimidation and fraud rather than undertake to prevent it by means that will not bear the severest scrutiny.' " [1] On the other hand, the Southerner Eckenrode, while rightly accusing the Louisiana returning board of "the most fla-grant manipulation," says: "Yet, in an absolutely free election it appears that the State would have gone Republican; so it cannot be said that an actual injustice was done when the canvassing board, venal as it was, gave Louisiana to Hayes" [2]—as Mr. Eckenrode himself does in casting up the table of electoral votes.

It was the Florida election, however, that was the real crux of the situation. When it became certain in the early morning of November 8 that Tilden had carried New Jersey, Florida as well as Louisiana (both of which States the Republicans had been ready to concede to Tilden during the campaign) had to be put in the Hayes column to secure his election by a single vote. The whites outnumbered the Negroes in Florida and the Democratic Party was well organized. Professor W. W. Davis has conclusively shown in his exhaustive study of the Florida election of 1876 that, in spite of hundreds of ballots cast by Negro repeaters, the Tilden ticket still had a majority, and that the State can-vassing board at Tallahassee (two Republicans and one Democrat), under pressure from Senator W. E. Chandler, threw out over 1500 Democratic votes in order to manufacture a Hayes majority.[3] Samuel B. McLin, the chairman of the board, confessed later, after he had been rewarded with a judgeship in New Mexico, that at the time of the canvass "there was a combination of influences which must have operated most powerfully in blinding my judgment and swaying my

---

[1] J. F. Rhodes, *History of the United States from the Compromise of 1850,* Vol. VII, p. 236. The New York *Nation* of December 14, 1876 said: "We do not ourselves see how Mr. Hayes can, if he be the man he has been represented, take the place under the cir-cumstances. But that is a matter between himself and his conscience." The *Nation* lost some 3000 subscribers by this stand. Rhodes, *ibid.,* p. 245.
[2] H. J. Eckenrode, *Rutherford B. Hayes, Statesman of Reunion,* p. 191.
[3] W. W. Davis, *Civil War and Reconstruction in Florida,* pp. 687–738.

action. The conclusion is irresistible that Mr. Tilden was entitled to the electoral vote of Florida and not Mr. Hayes." [1] The canvassing board was ordered by the Supreme Court of Florida to reassemble, and on a recanvass it declared the Democratic State ticket elected. Whereupon a set of Tilden electors was sent up to Washington, certified by the new Democratic Governor, G. B. Drew. The Florida case was the first to be passed upon by the electoral commission. Because of its momentous decision then not to go behind the returns, the certificate of the Hayes electors, whose vote was cast on the day prescribed by the Federal law, was accepted by the fateful vote of eight to seven. This was a presage of the procedure followed in the case of the other disputed States which came farther down in the alphabetical list. It sealed Tilden's fate.

Nevertheless, it would have been folly for the Democrats to have done aught but acquiesce peaceably in the decision, as their leader advised. They were responsible for the passage of the Electoral Commission Act. The commission chosen consisted of able and honorable men who acted in accordance with a conscientious interpretation of their legal obligation. To have attempted to investigate all the charges of fraud and violence attending the election, in scores of precincts, parishes, and counties in the disputed States, would have been a Herculean task, as impossible from a practical, as it was questionable from a constitutional standpoint. And even if it could and should have been attempted, it would have taken not the few weeks that remained before inauguration day, but many long months, to finish. The United States would then have been without a recognized government—perhaps, like Louisiana itself, the anarchic arena for the conflict of desperate factions. The better way of order, even at the expense of exact justice, was followed when Hayes was quietly sworn into office on the evening of Saturday, March third,[2] and on Monday the fifth delivered his public inaugural as President of the United States.

[1] W. W. Davis, *op. cit.*, p. 732.
[2] The 4th of March falling on Sunday, the oath of office was administered to Hayes after a dinner given to him by Grant at the White House on Saturday evening. So from then to Monday there were two Presidents of the United States.

LEAVING his family in Augusta for the winter, Blaine went to Washington early in December, 1876, to be sworn in as United States Senator for the closing session of the Forty-fourth Congress. Occasionally he had a visit from his oldest son Walker, who was finishing his course at Yale; and when he could take a vacation from his political duties, as at the Christmas recess, he would go down to Augusta for the rest and joy which he always found in the companionship of his family circle, entering with zest into the simple conviviality of the Maine capital, taking his favorite walk (often just as dinner was announced) to the brow of the hill above the Kennebec where his remains now rest beside his wife's, or watching the younger children slide down the long slope from the north front of the capitol toward the river. Between him and Walker the bond of sympathy and affection was growing stronger every year. The young man was developing a character and industry which foretold the invaluable help that he was to render to his father later in the State Department. To a charming nature he added a sound judgment and an intense devotion to politics and law. He had accompanied his father on a western speaking tour in the campaign of 1876, and his letters to the family at home show that same eager comprehension of political issues which we find in his father's youthful letters from Kentucky a quarter of a century before. It must have been a delight for the new Senator to have his son down for a weekend from New Haven to share the emptiness of the Fifteenth Street house and a pride to take him to dinner with a few congenial spirits at Wormley's.

Though the transfer from the lower House to the Senate is generally coveted by members of Congress and always regarded as a promotion in dignity and influence, it is doubtful whether, in Blaine's case, this was true. There is a striking contrast between the man who stood at the Speaker's desk for six years, wielding the gavel as the acknowledged master of the House, and the man who took his modest place in one of the three seats in a little supplementary row at the rear of the Senate chamber. It is true that Blaine could never be kept in a

"back seat" in any assembly, and with the opening of the Forty-fifth
Congress, in March, 1877, he moved up into the arena—only two seats
away from Roscoe Conkling in the same aisle. In addition to his original sole committee assignment (Appropriations), he was then put on
the Naval Committee and made chairman of the committee on Civil
Service and Retrenchments. Nevertheless, Blaine never became the
leader in the Senate that he had been in the House. Nor is he today
thought or spoken of as a United States Senator with anything like
the interest that attaches to his career in the House or in the Department of State. For this there are several causes. In the first place, he
did not complete even his first elective term in that body, where length
of service is the hallmark of distinction. He hardly had time to become
adjusted (if indeed his temperament would have allowed adjustment)
to the more formal and jealous procedure of the upper House. He was
accustomed to the running fire of debate, to the interruptions and in-
terpolations which characterized the sessions of the Representatives;
and when his alert, rapidly moving mind led him to break in rather
impatiently upon a set senatorial speech, his colleagues lifted their eye-
brows and treated him to a sarcastic rebuke. Senator Carpenter of Wisconsin, after repeated interruptions from Blaine, turned to Vice President Wheeler to ask quietly who was recognized by the Chair. "The
Senator from Wisconsin is entitled to the floor," was the reply. "Oh,"
said Carpenter, "I was getting so much in doubt of it that I thought
probably that I was intruding upon the Senator from Maine." [1] Blaine
joined in the laugh at his expense, but he was not cured of the habit.[2]

Furthermore, Senator Blaine found himself in a political situation in
which he could not freely utilize his superb talents either for the defense or for the denunciation of the Administration. For reasons which
we shall notice presently, he became hostile to the policies of President Hayes at the beginning of his term, and at the end of the term
wrote to a friend that he had not stepped inside the White House for
thirty-seven months. Had he been in sympathy with the Administration he might have played a brilliant rôle as the champion of Hayes.
At the same time, it was impossible for him to play the leading rôle in

[1] Gail Hamilton, *Biography of James G. Blaine*, p. 459.
[2] Senator Whyte of Maryland once became so exasperated over Blaine's provocative
interruptions that he cried out: "We had peace and good order in this body before he
was transplanted from the other side of the Capitol. No place is big enough for him and
anybody else. . . . If he desires to keep the country in a ferment, he will return to the
other branch of Congress." *Cong. Record*, 45th Cong., 3d sess., p. 239.

opposition to Hayes. He found the parts there taken by the members of the "Senatorial oligarchy": Conkling, first of all, with Morton, Cameron, Wade, Chandler, Boutelle and Carpenter. Blaine did not belong to this group, and he had no intention of attaching himself to them as a neophyte. The very thought of becoming an ally of Conkling's in any cause whatever was enough to nauseate him. He was between two fires, therefore, unable to support Hayes heartily, unwilling to serve apprenticeship to the "oligarchy." Leadership under these conditions was impossible. Blaine made some remarkable speeches in the Senate, to be sure. His varied and exact knowledge of facts, his forensic skill, his genial persuasiveness made their due impression. But, after all, there was something missing of the Dantonesque audacity with which he had confronted Stevens, Cox or Butler in the House. He was at his best facing an antagonist. It is probable that during his senatorial years Blaine exerted more influence by his correspondence and his addresses in various parts of the country than he did by his speeches on the floor.

If Blaine knew of the "bargain" between the Hayes managers and the Southern politicians he said nothing of it during the weeks when the electoral commission was making its momentous decisions. But on March 6, 1877, he rose to defend the claim of William P. Kellogg of Louisiana to a seat in the Senate. Kellogg, he maintained, had been duly elected by a legislature which derived its legitimacy from the same returning board that had declared the electoral vote of the State for Hayes and Wheeler, and his commission bore the great seal of the State certified to by Governor S. B. Packard, who had received a thousand more votes than the Hayes electors. "You discredit Packard and you discredit Hayes," argued Blaine. "You hold that Packard is not the legal Governor of Louisiana, and Hayes has no title, and the honored Vice President who presides over our deliberations has no title to his chair. . . . I know that there has been a great deal said here and there, in the corridors of the Capitol, around and about, in by places and in high places of late, that some arrangement had been made by which Packard was not to be recognized and upheld. . . . I want to know who had the authority to make such an arrangement. I wish to know if any Senator on this floor will state that any person, speaking for the Administration that was coming in or the one that was going out, had any right to make such an arrangement. I deny it. I deny it without being authorized to speak for the Administration that now exists. But I deny it on the simple broad ground that it is an impossibility that the Administration of President Hayes could do it. I deny it on the broad ground that President Hayes possesses character, common sense, self-respect, patriotism. . . . I deny it for him, and shall find myself grievously disappointed, wounded and humiliated if my denial is not vindicated in the policies of the Administration . . . and I hope a Republican Senate will say that on this point there shall be no authority in this land large enough or adventurous enough to compromise the honor of the National Administration or the good name of the great Republican Party that called that Administration into existence." [1]

The next day Senator Bayard of Delaware blocked the seating of Kellogg by a motion to lay his credentials on the table pending the appointment of a special committee to which they should be referred. In language reminiscent of Jefferson's dismay at the outbreak of the Missouri controversy nearly sixty years before, Bayard rebuked Blaine for his narrow partisanship: "I recognized in the utterances of the Senator from Maine yesterday the same cry for sectional aggression we have heard here for years past. It falls upon my ear like the fire-bell at midnight, and fills me with apprehension. I earnestly hope it will not be heeded by the President and his constitutional advisers. This is no party appeal. It is an appeal to my country which cannot any longer bear and will not any longer bear the continuance of a policy of sectional aggression and interference based upon misunderstanding and injustice." [2]

Stung by Bayard's remarks, Blaine returned to the charge. He did not deny that he was "a little of a partisan, differing in that respect from the Senator from Delaware." He, for one, was not willing "to abandon the remnant that is left of the Republican Party between the Potomac and the Rio Grande." "I do not propose, either at the beck of Mr. Stanley Matthews or Mr. Evarts,[3] to say that the public good

---

[1] *Cong. Record,* 45th Cong., Special sess. of Senate, p. 16.
[2] *Ibid.,* p. 20.
[3] Blaine had just read a telegram from D. H. Chamberlain, the carpetbag Governor of South Carolina, saying that letters had been brought to him from Matthews and Evarts, advising him to resign the Governorship to the Democratic claimant, Wade Hampton, "for the good of the country." Matthews had been one of the chief Hayes managers in arranging the "bargain" for the abandonment of Federal support for the Republican governments in the South, and Evarts (who disclaimed any part in the advice given to Chamberlain) was Hayes' Secretary of State.

requires that the remnant of the brave men who have borne the flag
and the brunt of the battle in the Southern States against persecution
unparalleled in this country shall retire for the public good. . . . I
propose for myself, as long as I may be entrusted with a seat on this
floor, that, whoever else shall halt or grow weak, I will stand for the
Southern Union men of both colors; and when I cease to do that, before
any presence North or South, in official bodies or before public assemblies, may my tongue cleave to the roof of my mouth and my right
hand forget its cunning." [1] The applause which broke out in the galleries was silenced by the sharp rap of the president's gavel; but the
Senators were not stampeded by Blaine's oratory. They voted by more
than two to one (43 to 21) for Bayard's motion. It meant that the Republican Senate as well as the Democratic House was to approve the
President's policy of allowing the States of South Carolina and Louisiana to revert to home rule and white rule—even though it would be
Democratic rule.

When, in the course of the next month, President Hayes withdrew
the Federal soldiers from Columbia (April 10) and New Orleans [2]
(April 24) in fulfilment of his implied or explicit promise,[3] leaving no
alternative to Governors Chamberlain and Packard but to turn over
their authority to their Democratic rivals, Blaine found himself indeed
"grievously disappointed, wounded and humiliated"—more so even
than the Conklings, Chandlers and Camerons, because he had dared
to prophesy in the Senate that this was just what it would be impossible for the self-respecting and patriotic President to do. It meant the
end of the cordial relations that had existed between the two men during
the campaign of but a few months past [4] and the beginning of Blaine's

[1] *Cong. Record,* 45th Cong., Special sess. of Senate, p. 21.
[2] The capital of Louisiana was shifted from New Orleans to Baton Rouge in 1849; then
back again to New Orleans in 1864; then back again to Baton Rouge in 1882.
[3] There is in the Hayes papers a letter from Senator L. Q. C. Lamar of Mississippi,
dated March 3, 1877, which reads as follows: "It was understood that you meant to
withdraw all the troops from South Carolina and Louisiana. . . . Upon that subject we
thought that you had made up your mind, and indeed you so declared to me. The
Packard and Chamberlain governments in those States exist only so long as they are
supported by you. . . . Your declaration of what you would do prevented a fearful
crisis at the South, but the tension is too severe. If you would achieve what you have
begun, you must do as you said you would do." Quoted in Eckenrode, pp. 222–3. Did
Hayes perhaps need a bit of "bracing" after the favorable decision of the electoral
commission?
[4] There are several instances of the expression of mutual admiration between Blaine and
Hayes before the latter's accession to the presidency, such as Blaine's hearty congratulations to Hayes on his victory for sound money in the Ohio State campaign of 1875
and Hayes' effusive telegram of sympathy to Blaine in June, 1876, when the latter

self-imposed exile from the White House. It was Blaine himself who coined the phrase "Stalwart Republicans" to designate the group who would not sanction the President's policy of "abandoning the remnant" of the party in the South. The truth is that he and Hayes were miles apart on the party issue in the South. Hayes in his inaugural address declared that we were "in a situation in which we ought not to be, in a partisan sense, either Republicans or Democrats, but fellow citizens and fellow men to whom the interests of a common humanity are dear. . . . The President of necessity owes his election to the suffrages and zealous labor of a political party, but he should strive to be always mindful of the fact that he serves his party best who serves his country best." [1] The epigram (rare for Hayes) in the last phrase, Blaine would exactly reverse. "He serves his country best who serves the Republican Party best," was his motto. Honorable and able Democrats there were, to be sure, whose talents he recognized and whose friendship he prized; but the Democratic Party was wrong—wrong in everything: tainted with rebellion, unsound on the tariff, imbued with financial heresy, hostile to the war amendments and the national laws for their enforcement. The health and salvation of the country depended, in his eyes, on the continuance of the rule of the Republican Party. With this intense political conviction Blaine lost sight of the social and economic forces in the South which made the return to white rule inevitable. He was primarily concerned to preserve the colored vote in the South as a guarantee of the perpetuation of Republican success, however much he might rationalize this partisan desire as zeal for the defense of the Constitution and laws of the United States.

Some students of the epoch have maintained that Blaine's breach with Hayes was due to resentment at not having received sufficient

suffered the sunstroke on the church steps at Washington; "I have not been so affected since the death of Lincoln; all good men will pray as I do for your immediate and complete recovery." Not only had Blaine spoken effectively for Hayes in the campaign of 1876, but Hayes had come to Blaine's help in the State campaign in Maine. He wrote to Robert G. Ingersoll from Fremont, Ohio, on August 8, 1876: "I hear from Mr. Blaine that he feels somewhat solicitous and horribly doubtful as to the result in his State. He feels as I do that you could do great good there, as Maine is the first contested State to hold an election and it is very important that we should do well there. I therefore have taken the liberty to write to you to say that if it is possible for you to make a few speeches in Maine, you will do the cause much service by doing so, and greatly gratify

Sincerely yours

R. B. HAYES."

(For this letter I am indebted to Mr. Ingersoll's granddaughter, Mrs. Eva Ingersoll Wakefield.)

[1] James D. Richardson, *Messages and Papers of the Presidents*, Vol. VII, p. 445.

consideration at the hands of the incoming President. Blaine did ask in vain for a Cabinet position for William P. Frye, his late colleague and defender in the House and his staunch supporter in the Cincinnati convention. But there is no evidence that Hayes' refusal here was taken as an offense, especially as the President-elect offered a place in the Cabinet to Eugene Hale, Blaine's chief manager at Cincinnati and followed Blaine's advice in the selection of his Attorney-General, Charles Devens of Massachusetts. There was undoubtedly some talk of Blaine's having a place in the Administration. His old college chum, Tom Searight, wrote him from Denver, on June 19, 1876, to express regret that he had failed to get the nomination, adding: "Of course, you can have the first place in the Cabinet in case of Hay's (*sic!*) success." But Blaine himself entertained no such desire or expectation. The custom which Presidents generally follow of inviting the man who makes their nomination possible to become Secretary of State could not be invoked in this case. The Blaine delegates had not gone over to Hayes when the break came at Cincinnati, but had stood firmly by their candidate, even gaining forty-three votes which might have gone to Hayes on the final ballot. And since Hayes owed his nomination to the reform element in the party, aided by the bosses like Conkling and Cameron, who would take anybody to beat Blaine, he obviously could not hope to exercise any leadership of the party if he chose as his first Cabinet adviser the man who was anathema to both the reformers and the bosses. From the latter Hayes probably expected as little support in the Presidency as he actually got; but with the reformers he could hope to work in unison. For, while he had supported Grant in 1872 against the nominee of the Liberal Republicans, he now accepted the main principles of those same liberals as his platform—amnesty for the South and reform in the civil service. Blaine would have been uncomfortable, to say the least, sitting at the right hand of a chief with these views. It was no personal grievance for slighted ambitions that turned Blaine against the President. He was above such petty behavior. It was the conviction that Hayes had betrayed the party by abandoning the Republican remnant at the South and was injuring it by weak concessions to the "visionary" and "Pharisaical" civil service reformers.[1]

[1] A series of letters written by Gail Hamilton to the New York *Tribune* during the spring and summer months of 1877 contain vitriolic attacks on the Administration for its Southern policy and its efforts to reform the civil service.

On the other hand, when Blaine believed the President to be right he gave him hearty support in the Senate, notably on the currency issue, on which Hayes had won his victory in Ohio in 1875. That issue came to a head in the first year of the Administration, with the attempt to pass a bill through Congress for the free and unlimited coinage of silver at the ratio of 16 to 1 with gold. From the days of Alexander Hamilton gold and silver jointly had been the legal basis of the currency of the United States. We had the double standard. By the act of Congress of April 2, 1792, the standard gold eagle ($10) was to contain 247.5 grains of gold and the standard silver dollar 371.25 grains of silver. Dividing the number of grains of silver in a silver dollar by the number of grains of gold in a gold dollar (24.75), we get a quotient of 15. That is, the ratio of gold to silver was set at 15 to 1. Now if gold and silver were used exclusively for money (either actually coined or in bullion against which paper notes were issued), there would be no difficulty in maintaining any ratio between the two metals which Congress chose to fix. But gold and silver are also commodities, like leather, cotton, copper or wool, which are bought and sold in the operations of industry and commerce. They are used, especially silver, in the manufacture of a great variety of ornaments and luxuries. They therefore have a market value which depends not upon acts of Congress but upon the economic conditions of supply and demand. That the law of 1792 put too high a value on silver became evident as the years passed. Fifteen grains of silver were not worth a grain of gold in the market. And because the government thus "overvalued" silver, the producers of the metal, eager, like all producers, to get the best price for their commodity, brought it to the mint, with the result that gold tended to disappear from the coinage. In order to restore the "parity" of the metals, Congress by an act of January 18, 1837, altered the ratio to 16 to 1. But the new ratio in turn was found to "undervalue" silver at the mint, the silver in a dollar being actually worth $1.02 in the market. So it was profitable for the mine owners to sell their silver to the jewelers and for the bullion brokers to melt down the silver dollars, each of which would yield them a dollar's worth of silver and two cents besides. Silver then disappeared from the coinage, as gold had done under the earlier ratio. The whole process illustrated the law formulated by Thomas Gresham, one of Queen Elizabeth's treasury officials, that when two precious metals are used for money the cheaper will drive the more valuable out of circulation. Since, then, silver ceased to compete with gold at the mint, Congress, instead of trying again to redress the balance by changing the ratio, passed a law on February 21, 1853, for the coinage of "subsidiary" half dollars, quarters and dimes containing an amount of silver considerably less than the value stamped on the coins, and making such coins legal tender only to the amount of five dollars. Thus Congress abandoned the attempt of sixty years to keep the two metals on a parity, being now no more concerned to put fifty cents' worth of silver into a half dollar than to put five cents' worth of nickel into a nickel or a cent's worth of copper into a penny. Twenty years later, in revising the coinage list, it omitted the silver dollar altogether.[1]

Soon after this "Crime of '73," as the inflationists called the dropping of the silver dollar from the coinage list, large amounts of silver began to be thrown upon the market from the exploitation of newly opened veins of the precious metal, especially the rich Comstock lode in Virginia City, Nevada.[2] The value of silver dropped to less than a sixteenth of that of gold, and the mine owners were again eager to derive the profit of having the government take their product at the old ratio of 16 to 1. They were supported by the western farmers, who saw the prices of their wheat and live stock falling in panic years from 1873 on, and who, as debtors, wanted a cheaper dollar with which to pay the interest and principal of their mortgages. The line of cleavage between the "soft" (cheap) money men and the "hard" (dear) money men was not political but economic—not Republican against Democrat, but East versus West, banker versus farmer, creditor versus debtor. The latter classes would have preferred the continued issue of unsecured paper money (greenbacks) by the government, eliminating all control of the currency by the banking interests, domestic and foreign; but after repeated efforts to defeat or repeal the Resumption Act of 1875, which provided for the redemption of the greenbacks in coin, they fell back on their second line of defense. If they could not have paper instead of coin, they were determined to have silver coin

---

[1] That is, from domestic circulation. The mints were authorized, however, to coin a "trade dollar" of 420 grains for export to silver standard countries like Mexico and China.

[2] In the year 1877, at the peak of its production, this famous lode yielded $22,000,000 of silver. The adoption of the gold standard by the new German Empire in 1871, followed by Holland, Spain and Sweden, and the limitation of silver coinage in 1873 by the countries of the Latin Monetary Union (France, Belgium, Italy, Switzerland and Greece) increased the glut of silver in the world market.

on a parity with gold.

Early in 1878 Richard P. ("Silver Dick") Bland of Missouri, Chairman of the House Committee on Mines and Mining, got a bill for the unlimited coinage of silver at the ratio of 16 to 1 through the House by the huge majority of 163 to 34. Only six votes were cast against it from the States west of the Alleghenies and south of Mason and Dixon's line; only nine were cast for it by the representatives of New England and the Middle Atlantic States. In the Senate the bill was amended by Allison of Iowa to limit the purchase of silver for coinage to not more than $4,000,000 and not less than $2,000,000 a month. The Allison compromise was accepted by the House with great reluctance, Bland himself declaring, "Let us take what we have and supplement it immediately in appropriation bills,[1] and if we cannot do that I am in favor of issuing paper money enough to stuff down the bond-holders until they are sick. I protest this bill while I vote for it under protest."[2] In February, 1878, the Bland-Allison Bill passed the Senate by 48 votes to 21 and the House by 203 to 72.

In spite of the more than two-thirds majority for the bill in both Houses, and of the pressure brought upon the President by his Ohio friends (including his Secretary of the Treasury, John Sherman) to sign it, Hayes did not hesitate to send in his veto. He had warned the inflationists in his annual message three months earlier that, while he "would not disparage silver as one of the two precious metals which furnish the coinage of the world," he held that the bonded debt of the government, amounting to some $1,700,000,000, must be paid, interest and principal, in money as good as gold. For "the bonds were issued at a time when the gold dollar was the only coin in circulation or contemplated by either the government or the holders of the bonds as the coin in which they were to be paid."[3] In his veto message he repeated the warning. The market value of the silver in the proposed dollar of 412.5 grains was only 90 to 92 cents. It would be "a grave breach of the public faith" to pay the national creditors in this debased medium. "National promises should be kept with unflinching fidelity. There is no power to compel a nation to pay its just debts. Its credit depends on its honor. The nation owes what it has led or allowed its creditor to

[1] That is, by attaching amendments for the free coinage of silver as riders to the bills appropriating the money for the necessary expenses of the government.
[2] *Cong. Record,* 45th Cong., 2d sess., p. 1251.
[3] Richardson, *Messages and Papers of the Presidents,* Vol. VII, pp. 462-3.

expect. I cannot approve a bill which in my judgment authorizes the violation of sacred obligations." [1] Both Houses immediately passed the Bland-Allison Bill over the veto.

On this question Blaine saw eye to eye with the President. He had been a "hard money" man in his fight against the greenbacks in the House, ridiculing a currency that could be multiplied "as long as rags and lamp-black held out," and pertinently adding: "You may get rid of the five-twenties (bonds) by issuing the greenback; but how are you to get rid of the greenback except by paying coin?" [2] He now became an ardent "honest money" man in his fight against a 90 cent dollar. On February 7, 1878, he denounced the Bland Bill in the Senate.

He began by stating that he was in favor of the remonetization of silver, declaring that "Congress had no power to demonetize either gold or silver." This was a bit of sophistry, which could have had no other motive than to conciliate the soft money men. But after this initial sop, with the fallacious statement that the demonetization of silver in Germany was more responsible for its fall in price than its overproduction in America, Blaine gave no further comfort to the inflationists. If we should coin a silver dollar of full legal tender value obviously below the value of the gold dollar, we should be simply opening our doors and inviting Europe to take our gold. We should be forced to a single silver standard and our relation with the leading commercial countries of the world would be "crippled and embarrassed." He believed that we could "force Europe to the full recognition of the value of silver" by the size of our indebtedness to her, thus securing the use of the two metals on both sides of the Atlantic and saving the huge mining enterprises of the West, which could not be carried on "simply to provide backs for mirrors and to manufacture cream pitchers and sugar bowls." But he insisted on a silver dollar worth 100 cents in gold. Not 412.5 grains of silver, but 425 grains must go into the new legal tender dollars. "We hear it proclaimed in the halls of Congress," he concluded, "that the people demand cheap money. I deny it. . . . The people do not demand cheap money; they demand an abundance of good money. . . . They do not want a single gold standard that will exclude silver and benefit those already rich. They do not want an inferior silver standard that will drive out gold and not help those

[1] Richardson, *Messages and Papers of the Presidents*, Vol. VII, p. 488.
[2] See above, p. 56.

already poor." [1]

If this statement is not so forthright as the President's veto message of three weeks later, it is in substantial agreement with it. Blaine voted against the Bland-Allison Bill on the day of its passage, and also to sustain the veto which came from the White House. More than that, he made a tour of the West during the campaign of 1878, devoting his speeches almost entirely to the advocacy of honest money against the greenback heresy, which reached the peak of its strength in the congressional and State elections of that year.[2]

There was one other policy of the Administration that had the unwavering support of Senator Blaine. That was the President's fight against a hostile majority in the House (and after the elections of 1878 in the Senate also) who, having control of both branches of Congress for the first time in nearly twenty years, were determined, in the words of a Democratic Senator, to "wipe out every vestige of every war measure." Their particular point of attack was the legislation beginning with the Act of February 28, 1865, authorizing the use of "troops or armed men at the places where any general or special election is held in any State, if necessary to repel the armed enemies of the United States or to keep peace at the polls," [3] and repeated in the Acts of 1870 and 1871 for the enforcement of the reconstruction legislation and the Fifteenth Amendment. Their method of attack was to hold up appropriation bills necessary for the maintenance of the army and the payment of United States marshals and deputies, by attaching as "riders" to such bills amendments prohibiting the use of Federal troops to "keep peace at the polls." They justified their attack by the plea that "free" elections at the South were hampered by the Federal authority.

President Hayes, whose conciliatory attitude to the South had been proved by his withdrawal of the troops from Columbia and New Orleans, resisted the demand for the repeal of the election laws on constitutional grounds. If a bare majority of the legislature could stop the wheels of government, it would itself become the government, with

[1] *Cong. Record,* 45th Cong., 2d sess., pp. 820–822.

[2] Ellis P. Oberholtzer's statement (*History of the United States Since the Civil War,* Vol. IV, p. 30), repeating the strictures of the New York *Nation* for Jan. 31 and Feb. 14, 1878, that "Blaine voted against the Allison bill after having tried to follow a temporizing course in order to win favor, if he could, with the silver men" is hardly just. Blaine's course was no more "temporizing" than that of Hayes, who also approved the use of both gold and silver as currency. The important point, on which Blaine and the President were in perfect agreement, was that only a silver dollar worth 100 cents in gold must be coined.

[3] *Revised Statutes of the United States,* 2002.

"unchecked and despotic power in the House of Representatives." He urged the House to "return to the wise and wholesome usage of earlier days, which excluded from appropriation bills all irrelevant legislation." [1] But he urged in vain. Again and again he was obliged to send in his vetoes (a half dozen in all) of the rider-ridden appropriation bills, to summon Congress in special session to try to get the funds necessary to run the government, and even to ask the marshals and deputies to continue to work without the assurance of their salaries, before he succeeded in defeating these obstructive tactics and vindicating the constitutional theory of a "balanced government" against the Congress which boasted openly of its determination of "Johnsonize" him.

Blaine's support of the President in this long contest, however, was probably prompted by political motives as much as by constitutional scruples. It was the "abandonment of the brave remnant of the Republican Party between the Potomac and the Rio Grande" against which he fought. He was constantly receiving memorials and petitions from Southern Republicans complaining of violence and intimidation at the polls. On the opening day of the third session of the Forty-fifth Congress (Dec. 2, 1878) he had introduced a resolution into the Senate instructing the Committee on the Judiciary to "inquire and report to the Senate whether at the recent elections the constitutional rights of American citizens were violated in any of the States of the Union." [2] Nine days later, in supporting this resolution, he denounced the "frauds and outrages by which some recent elections were carried by the Democratic Party in the Southern States." [3] Southern newspapers were exulting in the Democratic victory of 1878, and were sending the ironic "greetings of a solid South to a divided North." [4] That had the effect on Blaine of waving a red rag before a bull. "I tell the men of the South (not the 'honorable Senators') here on this floor," he thundered, "that even if they could strip the Negro of his constitutional rights, they can never permanently maintain the inequality of white men in this nation. They can never make a white man's vote in the South doubly as powerful in the administration of the Government as a white man's vote in the North. . . . Let me now remind you that the government under whose

[1] Richardson, *Messages and Papers of the Presidents,* Vol. VII, p. 532.
[2] *Cong. Record,* 45th Cong., 3rd sess., p. 2.
[3] *Ibid.,* p. 84.
[4] From the Nashville *Banner* of Dec. 21, 1878, quoted in Gail Hamilton, *Biography of James G. Blaine,* p. 444. This is, so far as I know, the earliest use of the phrase "the solid South."

protecting flag we sit today sacrificed myriads of lives and expended thousands of millions of treasure that our countrymen of the South should remain citizens of the United States, having equal personal rights and equal political privileges with all other citizens. And I venture here and now to warn the men of the South that we will never suffer them to be more." [1]

As for the apprehension lest the South be ground under the heel of a military despotism, Blaine scouted the idea with statistics and ridicule in a speech of April 14, 1879. Two Democrats could not meet in the cloak room of the Senate, he thought, without smiling (or blushing) in the presence of this "prodigious farce," like Cicero's Roman augurs. There were only 1155 Federal soldiers in the entire South, most of them guarding the Mexican frontier [2] or the approaches to harbors and navy yards. These 1155 soldiers on 850,000 square miles of territory numbered one to every 1200 counties in the South. They were fewer than the police force of New York City. And they threatened to "intimidate, overrun, oppress and destroy the liberties of fifteen million people and rob them of their freedom at the polls!" Why, New England, with 120 Federal troops to a million inhabitants, was "far more overrun by the Federal soldiery" than was the whole South. The alleged fear of military coercion was a mere pretext, camouflaging the real issue, which was "simply to get rid of the Federal presence at Federal elections." "I do not profess to know," concluded Blaine, "what the President will do when these bills are presented to him. I certainly should never speak a word of disrespect of the gentleman holding that exalted position. . . . But, as there has been a speculation here and there, on both sides, as to what he would do, I should expect that the dead heroes of the Union would rise from their graves sooner than he should consent to be intimidated and outraged in his proper constitutional power by threats like these. . . . When you present these bills with threats like these to the living President who bore the commission of Abraham Lincoln and served with honor in the Army of the Union which Lincoln restored and preserved, I can think of only one appropriate response from his lips or his pen: 'Is thy servant a dog that he

[1] *Cong. Record,* 45th Cong., 3d sess., p. 86.
[2] In August 1877 there had been a serious threat of trouble on the Mexican border, following a jail-breaking murder and depredations on American property which led to apprehensions of a repetition of Juan Cortina's famous raids of 1859. See debates in the *Cong. Record,* 45th Cong., 1st sess., p. 388 f.

should do this thing?' " [1] The Senator from Maine could have spared this note of veiled uncertainty in his confidence in the President. Hayes was no Hazael to need the Prophet Elisha's warning. The election laws were not repealed until the second Administration of Grover Cleveland, when Blaine and Hayes were both in their graves.

On many occasions when he might have upheld the President's hands Blaine was silent. We look in vain through the *Congressional Record* for any sign of support of the Administration in its courageous handling of the great railroad strike in the summer of 1877, or for a sympathetic comprehension of the problem which confronted Hayes on the Mexican border in the same autumn. When the Democratic House appointed a committee, headed by Clarkson Potter of New York, in May, 1878, to investigate the title to the Presidency of the man whom the vitriolic Dana of the New York *Sun* persisted in calling "Rutherfraud B. Hayes" or "Returning Board Hayes," Blaine showed no such eagerness to defend the President as he had shown to defend Packard's title to the Governorship of Louisiana. "You discredit Packard and you discredit Hayes," had been his argument then. Now that Packard was discredited and the Democrat Nicholls installed in his place, he did not spring to the vindication of the President whom he held responsible for that substitution. To be sure he could not countenance the attempt to oust a Republican from the White House. He "stood first and last for the complete integrity of the title of the President." He could not say less—but he did not say more. [2] The Potter Committee was "hoist on its own petard." In the course of its investigation it subpoenaed some three thousand telegrams from the Western Union Company, which were thought to relate to the activities of the returning boards in the disputed States. These telegrams were in cipher, and the committee, unable to decode them, returned them all, as it supposed, to the company. But about seven hundred of them had been purloined, and after weeks of patient study two men on the staff of the New York *Tribune* discovered the key and translated and published the dispatches. They revealed the most shameless attempts on the part of some leading Democrats, like Manton Marble, Smith M. Weed, and Tilden's nephew W. T. Pelton (though without Tilden's knowledge) to bribe members of the re-

<hr>

[1] *Cong. Record,* 46th Cong., 1st sess., pp. 417–19.

[2] Blaine remarked to friends in private, as his daughter Mrs. Walter Damrosch recollects, that the difference between him and the President was that he always believed that Hayes had been elected, while Hayes himself did not!

turning boards in South Carolina and Florida to deliver votes for the Tilden ticket. After these disclosures the attacks on Hayes' title ceased.

Again, the Senator from Maine might have been a tower of strength to the Administration if he had brought his extraordinary powers of debate to Hayes' major policy of the reform of the civil service. He was chairman of the Senate Committee on Civil Service and Retrenchment, but he seemed strangely indifferent to the splendid work that Secretary Carl Schurz was doing for the purification of the Department of the Interior,[1] or the reforms of the New York post office under the Postmaster General, Thomas L. James, or the contest between Hayes and the Conkling machine for the reorganization of the New York Custom House on a basis of efficiency and honesty. President Grant had signed a bill on March 3, 1871, establishing a Civil Service Commission "to ascertain the fitness of candidates in the civil service as to age, health, character, knowledge and ability by examination," and had appointed the ardent reformer George William Curtis chairman of the commission. But in 1875 Congress failed to make any further appropriation for the commission. President Grant did not urge the matter, and the commission, while not formally dissolved, lapsed for want of legislative support. President Hayes, in his first message to Congress, recommended "a suitable appropriation to enable the Civil Service Commission to continue its work." [2] He continued to urge such an appropriation in each succeeding message of his Administration, but in vain. He was obliged to rely upon executive orders and to fight a hostile Senate for the confirmation of his appointees.

It is no part of our story to describe the bitter battle between President Hayes and Roscoe Conkling, which resulted in the ouster of Conkling's henchmen Chester A. Arthur and Alonzo B. Cornell from the positions of Collector and Naval Officer of the Port of New York, and the purification of the Custom House, through which two thirds of the imports of the country passed, from its pestiferous gang of placemen, profiteers, pensioners and machine politicians.[3] The point we note here is that Blaine allowed Conkling to carry his venomous diatribes against the Administration from the New York convention of the autumn of

---

[1] Claude M. Fuess, *Carl Schurz, Reformer,* pp. 248–250, 252–270.

[2] Richardson, *Messages and Papers of the Presidents,* Vol. VII, p. 465.

[3] See H. J. Eckenrode, *Rutherford B. Hayes, Statesman of Reunion,* pp. 267–280 and George F. Howe, "The New York Custom House Controversy, 1877–1879," in the *Mississippi Historical Review,* December, 1931, pp. 350–363.

1877 to the floor of the Senate, and sat quiet while that "becurled and perfumed grandee gazed at by the gallery-gapers," [1] strode up and down the aisle, pouring out his sarcastic invective against the President and the "political Pecksniffs and tricksters" who were leagued with him in an assault upon the Republican Party in the name of reform. Blaine may have refrained from participating in the debate because he felt that the quarrel was between the New York machine and the Administration, and hence outside his bailiwick; or possibly because he was loath to enter into any personal altercation with Conkling—since the two men had shown no recognition of each other on becoming colleagues in the Senate. But his silence may also be explained by the fact that he was never much interested in the reform of the civil service. [2] He was wont to complain in later years that it had taken away some of his best workers and left him only "dummies who could pass an examination." However, after the tragedy of Guiteau's pistol shot had shocked Congress into passing the Pendleton Civil Service Act, Blaine wrote a rather halting endorsement of the principle in his *Twenty Years of Congress*. [3] His hearty support of Hayes in the effort to purify the civil service would have brought credit upon himself and strength to the Administration; but his deep disagreement with the President on the treatment of the Republican claimants to the Governorship in Louisiana and South Carolina alienated him from the Administration at the start. For the greater part of Hayes' term Blaine did not set foot in the White House. [4]

---

[1] The phrase is Eckenrode's, *loc. cit.*, p. 280.

[2] James A. Garfield noted in his *Journal*, under the date of Dec. 1, 1872: "He (Blaine) is vigorous and intelligent, but cares a good deal more for the machinery of politics than I do. He believes the Civil Service Reform a humbug. I should favor (it) if for no other reason than that of getting partially rid of the enormous pressure for office." T. C. Smith, *Life and Letters of James Abram Garfield*, Vol. I, p. 529. Still, Blaine signed a Senate Report (No. 837, 46th Congress) on Feb. 4, 1881, recommending the adoption of a measure "which will be the first step toward a sound civil service reform," and in the presidential campaign of 1884 he frequently endorsed the clause in the Republican platform declaring that "reform of the civil service, auspiciously begun under Republican administration, should be completed by the further extension of the reform system already established by law to all the grades of the service to which it is applicable." *The Blaine and Logan Campaign of 1884*, compiled by T. B. Boyd, Chicago, 1884, p. 16.

[3] James G. Blaine, *Twenty Years of Congress*, Vol. II, pp. 648–651.

[4] Blaine made a tardy acknowledgment of the excellence of the Administration when he visited Ohio on his campaign tour of 1884. He was escorted to the platform at Frémont by ex-President Hayes and devoted most of his brief speech to the praise of that gentleman: "I am glad to have the opportunity to say here that it was the enviable fortune of your distinguished fellow-citizen to leave the people of the country in a far more prosperous condition at the close of his administration than that in which he found them on the day of his inauguration, and that he steadily gained in esteem throughout the whole term of his office." *The Blaine and Logan Campaign*, p. 79.

After his transfer to the Senate, Blaine, in spite of what he had suffered in the House from the charges of shady railroad transactions, showed no hesitation in entering upon a controversy over the Pacific lines.

On November 13, 1877, Senator Jerome B. Chaffee of Colorado made a powerful speech indicting the Union Pacific, the Central Pacific and three of the lesser Pacific railroads for flagrant violation of the acts of Congress which had subsidized them to the amount of over $60,000,000. They had neglected to pay the government out of their large profits the five per cent of net income required by the law as a sinking fund for the redemption of the bonds, and employed a shameless lobby at Washington to prevent the government, as Collis P. Huntington of the Central Pacific put it, from "robbing them of their property." [1] When Senator Thurman of Ohio introduced a bill in October, 1877, for the recapture of the money due to the government from these roads, Blaine opposed it so assiduously on the floor and in the lobbies that he earned the name of "Jay Gould's errand boy." The gist of his persistent argument against Thurman, Bayard, Edmunds and other Senators who were for holding the roads to their legal and moral obligations was incorporated in an amendment to the Judiciary bill forbidding Congress to "alter, amend or repeal" the charters of the roads as specified in the acts of July 1, 1862, and July 2, 1864. He wanted the "perpetual agitation against the Union Pacific" to end. The railroads could be trusted to take care of the sinking fund on the terms of his amendment and to pay their full debt to the government when their bonds became due. There was no danger from these corporations. The "exaggerated notion" that pressure had been brought to bear by them on Congress was "a pure work of the imagination." The retention by Congress of the power to interfere with their charters meant "punching and knocking and worrying and harrowing" the roads and "proposing to make capital of the agitation for twenty years." [2] We may dismiss the unfounded ac-

---

[1] Charles E. Russell comments: "As the 'property' of which Congress sought to 'rob' Huntington and his associates was money which they owed to the United States and had repeatedly refused to pay, the remark seems rather a rare flight in cynical humor." C. E. Russell, *Blaine of Maine*, p. 353, note. Of the behavior of the owner of the Union Pacific, Huntington wrote as follows on Dec. 17, 1877: "Jay Gould went to Washington about two weeks since . . . since which time money has been used very freely . . . Gould has large amounts of cash and he pays it without stint to carry his points." *Ibid.*, p. 353.

[2] For the long debates on the subject see the *Cong. Record*, 45th Cong., 2d sess., pp. 2195–98, 2270–73, 2331–38, 2362–67, 2371–83.

cusation of some of Blaine's critics that he was a beneficiary of any of the "large amounts of cash" which Jay Gould was lavishing at Washington "to carry his points." It is enough to note that he argued and labored for the renunciation by Congress of the legislative safeguards with which it had deemed it wise to surround its grants to the Pacific Railroad companies in the previous decade. His amendment was rejected on April 9, 1878, by a vote of 23 to 35, eighteen Senators being absent.[1]

The development of an American merchant marine was in Blaine's opinion a policy absolutely indispensable for our national prosperity. Our prestige would be gone if we "calmly resigned the scepter of the ocean to Great Britain"; our protectionist system would fall unless we found trade connections over seas, and especially in Latin-America, for the favorable exchange of our products of factories, farms and mines for the commodities which we had to import; and our navy would languish without the constant recruitment of sailors trained in the school of maritime experience. In the decade before the Civil War our merchant marine had equaled that of Great Britain. Our flag was seen in every part of the world. More than seventy per cent of our foreign trade was carried in American ships, in addition to the total volume of our coastwise and Great Lake trade, which had always been limited to vessels of American registry by our navigation laws. But the picture had sadly altered in the twenty years from Buchanan to Hayes. The British, by the adoption of steam and iron ships, had forged ahead of us even before the Civil War put an end to our mercantile expansion. Since the war our erstwhile rivals had completely outstripped us by paying generous mail subsidies to merchant lines, while we had, "with a few pitiful exceptions," refused to adopt the policy. As a result, by 1877 the tonnage of Great Britain's merchant marine exceeded ours in the proportion of eight to three, and less than thirty per cent of our foreign trade was being carried under the American flag.

On June 5, 1878, Blaine made an earnest plea in the Senate for a subsidy for a proposed line of steamers to ply between New York and Rio de Janeiro. Our trade with Brazil presented a striking example of the lack of reciprocity which Blaine deplored. While we took nearly fifty per cent of Brazil's exports, brought to us in foreign bottoms, we furnished her only about eight per cent of her imports during the years

[1] *Cong. Record*, 45th Cong., 2d sess., p. 2383.

1870–1877. "They do not know in Brazil," said Blaine, "what we have to sell, what we are able to manufacture and really offer them." [1] They were buying their butter and cheese, their boots and shoes, their locomotives and agricultural implements in Europe with the money which we were paying for their coffee, rubber, dyes and woods. We must get them into our store if we would sell them our goods. Dom Pedro, the Emperor of Brazil, had recently visited the United States and had been impressed with the opportunities for reciprocal trade with us. A New York shipbuilder, John Roach, dispatched an agent to Rio on the Emperor's return, and secured Dom Pedro's promise to contribute $125,000 a year toward a direct steamship line to New York, provided the American Congress would appropriate a like sum. On the basis of this promise Roach set to work to build the ships. But Congress was obdurate, in spite of Blaine's impassioned plea. If Brazil wanted the steamers she might build them. Roach, having made financial commitments, struggled on for a while. He wrote Blaine in August, 1879: "The English are doing everything to break up my line. We are now shipping goods from Europe to Rio, then bringing coffee from Rio to New York for 20 cents per bag, or $3.40 per ton. . . . The lowest price paid for coffee to New York before my line was started was from $8.50 to $10 per ton. I am going to stick it out for another year." [2] But in the end he had to abandon his project, and an English company took over the line.

Sincere as Blaine's convictions were that a subsidized merchant marine would be both a boon to the protective tariff and a nursery for the American navy,[3] his main motive was doubtless the desire to recover our due share of the carrying trade of the world, which was being drawn into a British monopoly. His speech begins and ends on this note. The question, he declared, was a much wider one than "the simple granting of a subsidy to Mr. John Roach." It was whether we should become

[1] *Cong. Record,* 45th Cong., 2d sess., p. 4131.
[2] John Roach to Blaine, Aug. 29, 1879.
[3] In 1885 Blaine wrote: "If the government of the United States had, since the close of the war, expended annually upon the mercantile marine one fifth of the amount that has been expended upon the navy, our ships would have covered every sea and the navy would have grown of itself. . . . If Congress had given a tithe of the encouragement to the building and sailing of ships that it has wisely given to manufactures, to the construction of railroads and to every industrial pursuit in the land, our flag would . . . have stood relatively upon the ocean as strong and as permanent as it stood before steam was applied to the carrying trade of the world. . . . The government (under Presidents Johnson, Grant and Hayes) expended more than $300,000,000 for the navy. It expended scarcely $3,000,000 to aid in building up its merchant marine, and much of that unwisely." *Twenty Years of Congress,* Vol. II, pp. 613–14.

"tributary to Great Britain." And he closed with the words, "I am sure you could get an unanimous vote in the British House of Commons against the grant of this aid by the American Congress. I am sure that a policy for which the British House of Commons would vote unanimously it is not for the interest of the American Government to uphold." [1]

In short, Blaine's position on the subsidy bill was consonant with his general attitude of thinly veiled hostility to Great Britain. He believed that England was trying to bully us into free trade and bluff us out of our just share in commercial enterprises. He harped on the unfriendly disposition of the English upper classes toward the Union during the Civil War, compiling from Hansard's *Debates* a list of over thirty disparaging or insulting references to the United States in Parliament, "without rebuke from the ministerial benches," and declaring that "the most distant generation of Americans" would "never be able to read the Parliamentary reports of 1861–1865 without indignation." [2] He once told Sir Edward Thornton, the British Minister at Washington, that "England as against the United States was always wrong"—adding by way of courtesy that she was always right as against the rest of the world.[3] Perhaps his wary anti-British bias came to him as an inheritance from his Scotch-Irish forebears. At any rate, he had ample chance to vindicate it in the case of the Halifax arbitration of the controversy over the Canadian fisheries.

From the moment of our separation from Great Britain, American fishing rights off the coasts of Newfoundland and Canada had been a topic of perennial dispute. As Stanley Matthews put it, there was "not a codfish on the banks that had not been subject to arbitration"; and James Russell Lowell, our genial Minister to the Court of St. James in the early 1880's, whimsically wrote to Lord Granville of the Foreign Office: "I fear I shall always present myself to your fancy like the young Tobit in the picture, trailing a fish which certainly is not growing fresher in the process." In the peace treaty of 1783 the Americans had secured full rights to share in the fisheries of the Grand Banks and the Gulf of St. Lawrence, in return for the British privilege of the free navigation of the Mississippi, which was supposed at the time to have its

[1] *Cong. Record,* 45th Cong., 2d sess., p. 4134.
[2] James G. Blaine, *Twenty Years of Congress,* Vol. II, pp. 478–482.
[3] Quoted by Gail Hamilton, *Biography of James G. Blaine,* p. 434.

source in Canada. The discovery of the true source of the river in Minnesota and the purchase of the mouth and the western basin of the river from France in 1803 made the Mississippi an exclusively American stream. The British, deprived of their *quid pro quo,* then regretted their concession to the American fishermen. Their commissioners at the Treaty of Ghent in 1814 contended that the War of 1812 had cancelled the fisheries clause in the treaty of 1783. This action was not only contrary to international law (for the British could have as plausibly maintained that the articles recognizing our independence or our boundaries had been "abrogated" by the War of 1812), but it reversed a decision of the law officers of the British Crown themselves (1768) to the effect that the fact of a subsequent war had not impaired the rights of the French, by a treaty of 1696, to share in the Canadian fisheries.

No agreement could be reached on the subject at Ghent, and from then on the fisheries were a constantly recurring object of dispute and inconclusive negotiations between Great Britain and the United States. A reciprocity treaty of 1854 gave us the right to take fish within the three-mile limit, in return for opening our markets free to Canadian grain, animals, furs, fish, lumber, coal and metals. This one-sided treaty was revoked, on American notice, in 1866, Blaine attacking it vigorously in the House. But our fishermen continued to take mackerel within the three-mile limit. By the comprehensive Treaty of Washington in 1871 a joint high commission was set up, to determine what, if any, compensation was due to England for our continued use of the Canadian fisheries. The tribunal sat at Halifax, Nova Scotia, from June to November, 1877, and awarded $5,500,000 in gold as damages against the United States, for the use of the inshore fisheries during the dozen years since the lapse of the reciprocity treaty. The American government protested, but paid the money.[1]

Every step of the Halifax negotiations met with bitter opposition from Senator Blaine. He regarded the whole procedure as a piece of high-handed injustice on the part of Great Britain. In the first place, that government virtually forced upon us the acceptance of M. Maurice Delfosse, the Belgian Minister at Washington, as the third, and presumably neutral, member of the arbitration tribunal. Secretary of State

[1] *The Halifax Commission, Documents and Proceedings, House Executive Document,* 45th Cong., 2d sess., No. 89.

Hamilton Fish had objected to M. Delfosse for the obvious reasons that the minister of a state which owed its very existence to Great Britain and whose sovereign was the first cousin of Queen Victoria and brother of the unfortunate "Empress" Carlotta, whose husband Maximilian had come to the end of his reign and his life through the intervention of the United States in Mexico, could hardly be an impartial arbiter. Indeed, Earl de Grey, during the negotiation of the Treaty of Washington, had confessed the "impropriety" of appointing a representative from Belgium or Portugal on the tribunal. Secretary Fish suggested the names of half a dozen truly neutral ministers resident in Washington, but Earl Granville, the British Foreign Secretary, succeeded by some rather devious diplomacy in getting Delfosse appointed. In the second place, the decision at Halifax, in order to be binding, should have had the unanimous approval of the arbiters, unless it was otherwise stated in the treaty. It was not so stated, and the American member of the tribunal, Mr. E. H. Kellogg, had refused to sign the decision. Finally, the award itself was grossly unfair. The American catch from the inshore fisheries was "not much over $300,000 a year," while the remission of our import duties on the products of the Canadian fisheries amounted to nearly $500,000 a year, or between $5,000,000 and $6,000,000 for the period in question. Add to this the damages of $5,500,000 asked from the United States, and it meant that we were being mulcted of "a million dollars a year for the privilege of catching less than $400,000 of fish." "If we should follow what I believe would be the inevitable course of Great Britain under similar circumstances," declared Blaine, "we should utterly refuse to pay a single penny, and ground our refusal both on the law and the equity of the case. . . . The treaty as it stands is a mockery of justice, and will mean the certain destruction of a great American interest. . . . When we were poor and weak as a nation, we so highly esteemed the value of the fisheries that we encouraged their development by rewards and bounties. These were abandoned some years ago, but we still preserved to our fishermen a preference in our own markets. Even that is given away by this treaty. By the Halifax Award we pay to Great Britain $1,000,000 per annum for destroying a school of commerce which, properly nourished, will be her great rival in the future. Against such a policy I enter my protest, if I stand alone. . . . If we cannot pay the American fisherman a bounty to encourage and sustain him, let us at least not pay a bounty to Great Britain to destroy him." [1]

On no subject during his senatorial career did Blaine speak with greater zeal or sharper challenge than on the question of vindicating the rights of American commerce against the designs of Great Britain to "seize the scepter of the ocean." He became thereby not only the leading advocate for the grant of government subsidies to merchant steamship lines, but also the statesman most conspicuous and responsible in the eyes of the British ministry for the Anglophobia which they so readily detected in their American cousins across the sea. The importance of this fact, in view of the transfer of Blaine from the Senate to the head of the State Department in March, 1881, will appear in a later chapter. In reality, Blaine was waging a losing fight for the encouragement of an American merchant marine, not against the jealous rivalry of Great Britain but against the irresistible trend of American economic interests since the Civil War. Our foreign shipping had gone to pieces during the war, and after the war domestic and foreign capital was absorbed in the more attractive and remunerative field of the development of our vast natural resources in the West, through mining operations, railroad building, bonanza farming and ranching, lumbering, and the exploitation of the great market offered by a rapidly growing population. Paradoxically enough, Blaine himself, by his ardent advocacy of a protective tariff, was contributing to the defeat of his no less ardent desire for the revival of our merchant marine. Yet he held tenaciously to the government subsidy as the solvent of the inconsistency.

In his last speech in the Senate, delivered only five days before he became Secretary of State, he returned to the protest of "a permanent dependence of the United States upon England for her ships." "Great Britain has always been our chief commercial rival. *Fas est ab hoste doceri.*" We can learn from her the value of the subsidy. We can take our rightful place in the race for world commerce "whenever we make up our minds that the instrumentality by which England conquered is the one which we must use . . . that a merchant marine and a naval establishment must go hand in hand, and that the Congress of the United States is derelict in its duty if it passes another naval appropriation bill without accompanying it in some form with . . . provisions

[1] Speech of Feb. 26, 1878. *Cong. Record*, 45th Cong., 2d sess., p. 1628. For Blaine's treatment of the fisheries question see also "The Halifax Award" in his *Political Discussions, Legislative, Diplomatic and Popular*, pp. 176–185, and *Twenty Years of Congress*, Vol. II, pp. 615–637.

looking also to the upbuilding of the American merchant marine." [1] But his words fell on deaf ears. And though his successor in the Senate, William P. Frye, continued for years to plead for the marine subsidy, it was only the exigencies of the World War that forced our government into the shipping business—from which it has been trying in vain to withdraw ever since.

During the Hayes Administration there came to a head a bitter controversy over the migration of the Chinese to the States of the Pacific coast. Chinese coolies had been imported by the thousands to do the rough work of grading on the Central Pacific Railroad. The Burlingame treaty of 1868 had permitted the free immigration of the Chinese to the United States (but not under contract). It was estimated that there were about 130,000 of them in the States of California, Nevada and Oregon in 1876, the largest settlement being the famous Chinese quarter of San Francisco. Although some ministers, philanthropists and publicists defended the Chinese as industrious, law-abiding residents, entitled both by treaty rights and by the tradition of our republic to hospitable reception here, the great majority of the whites hated them as cheap laborers with low standards of living and filthy habits, regarding them as an unassimilable element in our population, who came here on "an industrial predatory tour" to earn enough to return to the Celestial Empire or to have their bodies sent back on the "bone ships" to rest in its sacred soil. "Anti-Chinese Unions" and "Anti-Coolie Clubs" were formed in the cities of the coast, and the leather-lunged Irish orator of the sandlots, Denis Kearny, kept San Francisco in a turmoil of racial prejudice by his reiteration of the slogans, "The Chinese must go!" and "Four dollars a day and roast beef!" A petition with sixteen thousand signatures, sent to United States Senator Sargent of California, led to the appointment of a joint committee of Congress to visit California and investigate conditions. The report of the committee, decidedly hostile to the Chinese, was published in the summer of 1877, when the activities of Kearny and the anti-Chinese mobs in San Francisco were at their height. Senators Sargent of California and Mitchell of Oregon led the fight in Congress for the abrogation of the Burlingame Treaty.

The House passed a Chinese Exclusion Bill on January 28, 1879, by a vote of 155 to 72, and when the bill reached the Senate Blaine supported it heartily in speeches of February 14 and 15. He maintained that

[1] *Cong. Record*, 46th Cong., 3d sess., pp. 962–3.

the Chinese had violated the Burlingame Treaty from the beginning by failing to confine their subjects to "an entirely voluntary emigration," and that the United States were therefore both legally and morally justified in abrogating the treaty without giving notice to China. He pointed to the fact that "the incalculable hordes of China" were "much nearer to the Pacific coast in point of money and transit" than were our people of the Mississippi Valley; that it cost but thirty dollars to send an immigrant from Shanghai or Hong-Kong, as against fifty dollars to transport an American from Omaha to San Francisco. If we continued to allow the free immigration of "those who by overwhelming votes in both branches of Congress must forever remain political and social pariahs in a great free government," we should see our laborers of the Pacific coast reduced to the servile standards of the coolies and the white citizenry threatened with a social degradation worse than the South had ever feared under the rule of the Negro. Law and order in California could be maintained only by the intervention of the military arm five years hence if this immigration were allowed to continue. "Nowhere on earth," he concluded, "has free labor been brought into competition with any form of servile labor in which free labor did not come down to the level of servile labor. It has been tried against the African slave in the South; it has been tried against the peons in Mexico and Peru; it has been tried against the Chinaman in California. The universal result is the same. The lower strata pull down the upper, the upper never elevate the lower." [1]

Except for a few theorists like William Lloyd Garrison,[2] who believed that it was contrary to the principles of Christian brotherhood and American democracy to close our doors to any of the oppressed of the earth, everyone agreed that some effective restriction of Chinese immigration was necessary. The question was whether it should be done through the usual channels of negotiation with a friendly power, with whom we had a treaty on the subject, or whether we should take the matter into our own hands and exclude the Chinese by a defiant act of Congress.

Many of the leading Senators (including Blaine's colleague Hannibal Hamlin, Edmunds, Conkling, Hoar, Dawes, Matthews and Davis)

---

[1] *Cong. Record,* 45th Cong., 3d sess., pp. 1299, 1303.
[2] For Blaine's correspondence with Garrison defending his vote on Chinese exclusion see the New York *Tribune* of Feb. 17, 24, 27, 1879.

were in favor of notifying the Emperor of China of our desire to terminate the Burlingame Treaty on January 1, 1880, and inviting a joint consideration of a new agreement. But an amendment to this effect was lost, and the Senate passed the exclusion bill by a vote of 39 to 27. On March 1, 1879, President Hayes vetoed the bill. He was in sympathy, he said, with "the very grave discontent of the people of the Pacific States with the present workings of Chinese immigration and their still graver apprehensions therefrom in the future." But he was "convinced that . . . no reasons can require the immediate withdrawal of our treaty protection of the Chinese already in this country." Except for the abrogation of the French Treaty of 1778, there had been no instance in our history of the unilateral congressional termination of a treaty; and, "fortunately," he added, "the actual recession in the flow of emigration from China to the Pacific coast, shown by trustworthy statistics, relieves us from any apprehension that the treatment of the subject in the proper course of diplomatic negotiation will introduce any new features of discontent or disturbance among the communities directly affected." [1]

Though the President's insistence upon the "proper course of diplomatic negotiation" was resented by Blaine and the "exclusionist" majority in the Senate as indifference to the interests of American labor, nevertheless his course was right. He sent a commission to China, who negotiated a new treaty in the autumn of 1880, permitting the United States to "regulate, limit or suspend," but not absolutely to prohibit, Chinese immigration. And on the basis of this treaty, ratified by the Senate in May, 1881, a satisfactory restriction law was eventually passed and signed by President Arthur early in May, 1882.

It is simple enough to interpret a public man's utterances and policies according to a fixed conception of his character. To those for whom Blaine's every act was inspired by a consuming desire for the Presidency, his anti-Chinese speech only betrayed his willingness, as Garrison charged, "to barter his manhood for a prospective mess of pottage." And Blaine's reiteration of his concern for the American standard of living in his reply to Garrison was dismissed by the latter as "simply a repetition of the irrelevant allegations and empty fallacies contained in his senatorial rodomontade." [2] So Oberholtzer, a half century later, writes: "To gain friends on the Pacific coast he (Blaine) had ostenta-

---

[1] Richardson, *Messages and Papers of the Presidents*, Vol. VII, pp. 514–520.
[2] New York *Tribune*, Feb. 17 and 27, 1879.

tiously espoused the cause of the rabble in California against the China-man." [1] But a majority of his fellow Senators, who were not supposed to be suffering from what Zachariah Chandler called the "incurable disease of presidential fever," concurred with him in his Chinese policy; and it is doubtful if he gained more friends by it on the Pacific coast than he lost in other parts of the Union. His friend Garfield, who strongly advised Hayes to veto the Exclusion Bill, said, "I am satisfied that Blaine has made a great mistake in his advocacy of it." [2] The subsequent negotiations with China and the legislation of Congress based thereon prove that he was essentially right in his objective and wrong in his method of attaining it. There is no need to make him either a vulgar demagogue or an inspired prophet in the matter. There is no reason to believe that he was not both sincere and mistaken.

The most spectacular event of Blaine's senatorial years, however, occurred far from the halls of Congress. The Greenback or "soft money" movement, nurtured by five years of financial and industrial distress caused by the panic of 1873, reached its peak in the elections of 1878, when over a million votes were cast for the Greenback candidates. The party was especially strong in the agricultural West, but it also made headway in the Eastern States like New York and Maine in which frontier conditions still prevailed over large areas. In the September elections in Maine the Greenback "bloc" had prevented either the Republicans or the Democrats from polling the majority popular vote necessary for the choice of a Governor; and a fusion of Democrats and Greenbackers controlling the legislature had elected a Democratic Governor, Alonzo H. Garcelon. At the next annual election (Sept. 8, 1879) the Republicans regained a clear majority in the legislature, though the popular vote still showed no majority for Governor. The fusionists, with the official machinery of the State in their hands, aided and abetted by Governor Garcelon and his council, then set about to falsify the returns, throwing out the names of thirty-seven Republicans duly elected to the legislature. They were determined to retain control of the State House and reëlect Garcelon. When the rumors of this plan to "steal the State" were brought to Blaine in Boston by his son Emmons, he turned not to Washington to take his seat in the Senate, but to Augusta to fight for the installation of the Republican legislators. For

[1] E. P. Oberholtzer, *History of the United States Since the Civil War,* Vol. IV, p. 61.
[2] T. C. Smith, *Life and Letters of James Abram Garfield,* Vol. II, p. 677. See also the strictures on Blaine's Chinese policy in the New York *Nation,* Feb. 20 and 27, 1879.

more than twenty years he had been chairman of the Maine Republican Committee, accustomed to predict with uncanny accuracy the Republican majorities which his untiring political activities produced. Now he saw his dictatorship threatened, his party cheated out of its rightful victory, and worst of all his State likely, unless the fusionists were dislodged, to give its electors to the Democratic presidential candidate in the approaching campaign of 1880.

It was a tense and dangerous crisis that Augusta was passing through in the midwinter of 1879–1880. The usually quiet capital on the banks of the Kennebec seemed transformed into a Little Rock or a New Orleans in Reconstruction days. The fusionists filled the State House with armed men to repel any attempt of the Republican members-elect to take their seats, while, just across the street, the Blaine mansion, guarded by a band of armed volunteers, was the headquarters of the protesting Republicans, thronged day and night with lawyers, politicians and newspaper men, seeking the advice of their leader and laying plans for the peaceable capture of the capitol. Some advised force, but Blaine sternly vetoed that. Still there was imminent danger that a shot from either of the hostile factions would precipitate a bloody riot. Blaine himself was in no little danger of personal injury, as he walked in the grounds of his mansion, a fair target for a rifle shot from the cupola of the State House, or moved among the unrestricted crowd of visitors in the house, which might contain a fanatic bent on assassination.

The tension was relieved when Governor Garcelon, sensing the rising tide of popular indignation against the truculent attitude of the "defenders" of the bogus legislature, agreed to a legal settlement of the dispute. He was moved thereto by a courteous and conciliatory letter from ex-Senator Lot M. Morrill, then Collector of the Port of Portland, which enabled him to "save his face." The constitution of Maine gave the Governor permission "in important questions of the law" and "upon solemn occasions" to call upon the Supreme Court of the State for an "advisory opinion." "It is in the power of Your Excellency," wrote Morrill, "to restore peace, order, quiet and good feeling to the State and all its inhabitants, by asking the opinion of the judges on each law point involved." The case was submitted to the Court, the judges upheld the Republican claims, the excluded members took their seats and the legislature elected a Republican Governor.

When Blaine returned to his place in the Senate, he came wearing the laurels of the Maine victory. His reputation was greatly enhanced in the eyes of the "Blaine legion" throughout the country. The presidential year had opened. The Republican nominating convention at Chicago was but five months away. The party managers were counting the assets and the liabilities of the prospective candidates. Here was a magnificent new issue for Blaine's friends to stress, to obliterate the memory of Little Rock bonds and Mulligan letters. William P. Frye, in seconding Blaine's nomination at Chicago, was to rouse the convention to "tumultuous cheering" by his peroration on the great pilot who had safely brought to port the tempest-tossed ship "the State of Maine." "Freighted with the precious principles of this Republic, with the rights of American citizenship, with the privileges guaranteed by the Constitution, she was battling with the waves. The eyes of the whole nation were upon her. They beheld with intense anxiety the perils to which she was exposed. A true man was at the helm. Sagacious himself, he made even the foolish wise and courageous. He inspired the timid. Strong, he strengthened the weak. Calm, he restrained the impetuous and brought the imperiled ship with her precious cargo into the port of safety. . . . Take that man, wise, stout and brave, for your leader and he will surely bring you to safety and victory." [1] No mention was made of Blaine's senatorial record. That had been apparently eclipsed by the dramatic incident of the "State steal."

[1] *Proceedings of the Republican National Convention, held at Chicago, Illinois, June 2-8, 1880.* Reported by the official stenographer, Eugene Davis. Jno. B. Jeffrey Printing House, Chicago, 1881, pp. 178-9.

ONE OF the most persistent political legends, reiterated by historians and biographers, is that Blaine was consumed with ambition for the Presidency from the day he left the Speaker's chair to the end of his life. Even discounting his own oft-repeated assertions of indifference to the honor as the conventional concession to the popular maxim that the office should seek the man, there is abundant evidence from the letters of his family and his political friends to show that, except for the first of the five occasions on which his name figured prominently in Republican nominating conventions, his reluctance to engage in an active canvass was often a cause for anxious embarrassment among his backers. That he did ardently desire the nomination in 1876 we have already seen (p. 108). But after his narrow failure in the Cincinnati convention, he seemed to yield to a fatalistic, almost mystic, mood in regard to the Presidency. His was too penetrating a mind to be deceived as to the damage which the investigation of 1876 did to his reputation, however confidently he bore himself in the trial and whatever consolation he received from the plaudits of his friends and the implicit trust of his family. They remembered only the cheers which swept through the House and were echoed in the Republican press for his "vindication" from the slurs of "rebel persecutors"; but he carried the burden of the ordeal on his shoulders, like Sindbad's Old Man of the Sea.

But if Blaine showed some degree of apathy toward entering the presidential race again, his friends and backers only redoubled their efforts to secure his nomination. Conkling, Cameron and Logan were powerful anti-Hayes men, controlling the Republican machine in the three great States of New York, Pennsylvania and Illinois; but none of these ultra-Stalwarts had the popular following of Blaine. When he turned West in the summer of 1878 to combat the rising tide of Greenbackism, he was hailed everywhere as the indispensable leader of the Republican Party. Letters came to him by the hundreds in Washington and Augusta, assuring him of nation-wide support. He was the man to put an end to the "tomfoolery" of the Hayes régime, with its menace to "the fruits of the war" by complacency toward "rebels," and its threat to the solidarity of the party by the crusade for civil service reform. "It is better for the Republican Party" (and consequently for the country), wrote D. H. Chamberlain, the ousted carpetbag Governor of South Carolina, "that Hayes should be driven over neck, heels and boots, to the Democracy than that he should remain where he is nominally, while really serving Gordon, Hill and Company. The first necessity is to drive out traitors." [1] And at the same moment a Baltimore Republican was writing to the Secretary of the National Committee: "I do not think I am far out of the way when I affirm that out of the 22,000 Republicans in this city who voted for Hays (*sic*) not 500 approve his course. Should not this be a warning? In the future let us nominate no more candidates for expediency, but in 1880 nail our colors to the mast with a Blane (*sic*) or some other tried and true exponent of Republicanism . . . and go into the fight relying on the patriotism and good sense of the American people not to place our country in the hands of those who seek to destroy it." [2]

Indeed, it seemed to the Stalwarts that the party had fallen on evil days under President Hayes, although it is generally recognized now that the conciliatory and conscientious course of "his Honesty, the President" did more to rehabilitate it in the eyes of the American people than all the intransigent braggadocio of the Chandlers, Conklings, Logans and Camerons. Pennsylvania went Democratic in 1877, and the Republicans lost the President's own State of Ohio by 27,000 votes. Blaine, who certainly held no brief for the policies of the White House, had hard work to prevent the State convention of Maine, in August 1877, from passing a resolution of censure upon the President.

The political confusion in the party seeking to recover from the blow which it had received in 1876 and to reabsorb the reform element which was still fermenting with the leaven of 1872, was still worse confounded by the distressing economic situation. The severe panic which had broken upon the country in 1873 showed no signs of abatement when Hayes took the oath of office. "No general revival of business," says J. F. Rhodes, "took place until 1878. . . . These five years are a long dismal tale of declining markets, exhaustion of capital, a lowering in value of all kinds of property including real estate, constant bankruptcies, close economy in business and grinding frugality in living, idle

---

[1] Chamberlain to W. E. Chandler, Dec. 28, 1877. *Chandler Papers, Library of Congress.*
[2] W. F. Ancy to Chandler, *ibid.*

mills, furnaces and factories . . . laborers out of employment, reductions of wages, strikes and lockouts . . . depression and despair." [1] Four months after his entrance into the White House, Hayes had to call out Federal troops to quell the most serious strike in our history, which affected the railroads in fourteen States from Pennsylvania to Kansas, caused the destruction of $10,000,000 of property, and offered the disheartening spectacle of soldiers firing on American citizens in the cities of Pittsburgh, Baltimore, Reading and Chicago.

Finally, the steady growth of the inflationist sentiment, aided by the distress of the panic years, was making alarming inroads on the party strength in those Western States which had been its dependable strongholds since the Civil War. The midterm elections of 1878 gave the Democrats, who had been in control of the House since 1875, a narrow margin in the Senate as well; and for the first time since the Southern legislators had left Washington to join the ranks of the Confederacy a Republican President found himself confronted with a hostile majority in both Houses of Congress. It was high time that something drastic should be done if the Grand Old Party was not to go on the rocks.

The remedy of the Stalwarts was drastic enough. Their program was the return to the radicalism of Thaddeus Stevens and Charles Sumner, with no quarter shown to unrepentant rebels or their allies among the Northern Democrats or their new recruits from the muddle-headed, mushy-hearted "liberals" in the Republican fold. Their instrument was the machine, well oiled with patronage, turning out rewards for the regulars and punishments for the recalcitrants, manned by reliable manipulators who knew which side their bread was buttered on and wanted no interference from that "man milliner Curtis" or any other visionary "snivel service" reformers. The candidate must be no goody-goody like "Granny Hayes," but a strong, red-blooded man who identified patriotism with Republicanism and would stand no nonsense from "traitors" to the country or to the party. That man they found in General Grant—not the generous Grant of Appomattox, but the "tawdry Caesar" of the Enforcement Acts.

On May 17, 1877, Grant had sailed from Philadelphia with his wife and his nineteen year old son Jesse for an indefinite tour abroad, to recuperate from the strain of sixteen years of military and civil office. He

[1] J. F. Rhodes, *History of the United States from the Compromise of 1850,* Vol. VII, pp. 52–53.

had twenty-five thousand dollars to spend and was going as far as that sum would take him. It wouldn't have lasted long in his round of expensive receptions by crowned heads and potentates, but it was supplemented by more than double that amount realized from fortunate investments at home, so that eventually the tour occupied nearly two and a half years and carried the General and his party around the world. It was a triumphal progress which proved not a little embarrassing to Grant's natural democratic simplicity; for this plain American citizen was everywhere received with honors usually paid to visiting sovereigns, while United States vessels were put at his disposal when convenient and our ministers and consuls were instructed to show him every courtesy possible. He crossed and recrossed Europe, zigzaging from Edinburgh to Constantinople and from Lisbon to St. Petersburg, visited the pyramids of Egypt, the temples of India, the crowded marts of China and Japan, and landed at San Francisco on September 20, 1879, amid demonstrations of welcome-home as colorful and noisy as those which had bidden him godspeed at Philadelphia twenty-eight months before. All the details of which may be read in the pages of the garrulous Consul-General Adam Badeau's *Grant in Peace* or the two gargantuan volumes of *Around the World with General Grant,* by John Russell Young of the New York *Herald.*

Grant was undoubtedly the most popular man in America, if not in the world, when he again set foot upon his native soil. The shortcomings of his presidential years were forgotten by the people whose political memory is short and whose criterion of greatness is more often determined by the aclaim which reputation elicits than by the appreciation which intellect and character merit. Here was a man whom kings and princes had received in state, whom the people of Europe and Asia had thronged the streets to see pass by. Was it perhaps a case of a prophet's being not without honor save in his own country? "Had we wronged this noble soul; we would make it up to him." It pleased the Conklings and Camerons, who were already planning to return Grant to the White House, to dwell upon his enhanced fitness for the Presidency. Travel had broadened his views; he had studied the political systems of Europe and met the greatest of her statesmen in personal intercourse. If there had been any mistakes due to inexperience in the years of the Presidency, there was little danger that they would be repeated now. Of course, these politicians knew that the Grant who landed at San Francisco in 1879 was the same Grant who had sailed from Philadelphia in 1877. *Coelum non animum mutant qui trans mare currunt.* There is not the least indication that his trip had added a cubit to his mental or moral stature. He had met statesmen of whose policies his lack of historical or economic knowledge precluded any real understanding; he had been lionized by authors whose books he had never read or had the slightest intention of reading; he had hurried through museums, bored by canvases and sculptures which woke no response in his unfurnished mind. The pyramids had impressed him because they were so huge. The crowds had interested him. The banquets had satisfied him. In the enforced leisure of the deck chair he had read Mark Twain's *Innocents Abroad.*

Indeed, it was just because they knew that it was the same hebetudinous and manipulable Grant who came home as had gone abroad that the ultra-Stalwarts welcomed him. Nothing would have disconcerted them more than to have seen him return transformed into the paragon of independent and enlightened statesmanship which they declared him to be. It was his popularity, not his competency, which they intended to capitalize. With him again in the White House, they looked forward to the return of the good old days of the "senatorial oligarchy" and the complete repair of the somewhat crippled party machine. Roscoe Conkling, the master machinist, would be the grand vizier. To be sure, the General had come back a little too soon, but with skillful management and unremitting adulation his popularity need not evaporate in the nine months before the meeting of the nominating convention. As to the objections to a third term, those applied, of course, only to a consecutive third term.

Grant himself, apparently, did not cherish any ambition for the Presidency on his return to America. He wrote to Badeau from Japan in August that he was "not a candidate for any office." "I shall go to my quiet little home in Galena and remain there till the cold drives me away. Then I will probably go south—possibly to Havana and Mexico —to remain till April." [1] In December he replied to a friend in Philadelphia who asked him if he would not be disappointed, after such an ovation as he had received, not to be elected President, "Not at all, but Mrs. Grant would." [2] As the spring of 1880 advanced, however, the sap

[1] Adam Badeau, *Grant in Peace*, p. 518.
[2] Quoted in Rhodes, *History of the United States from the Compromise of 1850*, Vol. VII, p. 112.

of ambition mounted in the General's veins. Early in February the Pennsylvania Republican State convention, under the domination of Don Cameron, had, in spite of the strong sentiment for Blaine in his native State, instructed the delegates to the approaching Chicago convention to give Grant unanimous support. Conkling, a few weeks later, secured the pledge of the New York convention for Grant. And in May, the third member of the "triumvirate," General John A. Logan, by rather high-handed methods, got a solid Grant delegation from Illinois. Whether it was the assurance of his backers that his nomination was certain, or the challenge to his fighting instincts in the noisy opposition to a third term,[1] or the pressure brought to bear by his family, who had no more relish than he himself had for life in "the quiet little home in Galena," Grant finally became extremely anxious to receive the nomination.

Charles Edward Russell, who was then a young reporter, tells of being in Little Rock, Arkansas, one day in April, 1880, when Grant visited that city. "After dinner," he says, "Grant was in the parlor of the hotel reading dispatches. Something called him from the room, leaving the dispatches, it was said, on the table. In some way their contents became known in Little Rock. They left no chance to doubt that, whether Grant desired the nomination or not, he was keeping in perfect touch with every effort made to win it for him."[2] And Badeau gives us even more convincing proof of the General's conversion from passive receptivity to active canvassing for the nomination. "In May," he writes, "I went to visit him at the home of his son, Colonel (Fred D.) Grant. At Chicago I saw him constantly, either at Colonel Grant's house, or more frequently at General Sheridan's headquarters; for his son was on Sheridan's staff. . . . It was now only a few weeks before the convention, and Grant manifested as much anxiety as I ever saw him display on his own account. He calculated the chances, he counted

[1] The National Republican Anti-Third Term Committee, with ex-Senator John B. Henderson of Missouri as chairman, called a convention at St. Louis for May 6, to protest against the nomination of Grant. Henderson wrote to Blaine a few days before the convention met, soliciting active support for the anti-Grant movement: "It is not expected that you and Sherman and Edmunds will speak or write to the convention in person. But your friends should be on hand. The nomination of Grant means the defeat of the Republican Party in the coming canvass, if not its permanent overthrow. In such emergency, it is suicidal for you gentlemen to stand quiet while this thing is being accomplished. We want delegations from Iowa, Michigan, Illinois, Indiana and other States. Your friends can send them, and must do so. Action should be prompt." J. B. Henderson to Blaine, April 27, 1880.

[2] Charles Edward Russell, *Blaine of Maine*, p. 364.

the delegates, considered how every movement would affect the result, and was pleased or indignant at the conversion of enemies or the defection of friends." [1]

Meanwhile the leaders of the "Blaine legion" were chafing with impatience at the apparent apathy of the only man whose popularity was sufficient to stem the tide toward Grant. He was absorbed in a petty contest in the northeastern corner of the country (see pp. 155–157), while a great national crisis was impending. Senator W. E. Chandler of New Hampshire, the thin, nervous, witty tireless manipulator whom an ungracious critic described as "a man who never drew an honest political breath," was bombarding the Blaines with notes in his crabbed chirography, begging them to "take the leash off their friends and let them go to work." "Frye and I are fighting the battle without our chieftain," he wrote to Mrs. Blaine on Dec. 13, 1879. "Do you know, I think the beloved one does not like to fight as once he did. But we cannot fight third term and all who beat us before (1876) unless he pitches in. . . . Are we to fight or to wilt?" [2]

Mrs. Blaine was far less given to wilting than her more mercurial husband. Yet even she seemed to have lost her zest for battle in the confusion of factional discord which cursed the Republican Party in the Hayes Administration. On August 18, 1879, she wrote to her son Walker, who was soon to be admitted to the bar at St. Paul, Minnesota: "I am so deeply disgusted with American politics, our whole system of popular government, with its fever, its passions, excitement, disappointment and bitter reaction, that any sphere, however humble, which gives a man to his family seems to me better than the fever of high place." [3] And again to her cousin Miss Dodge, on November 9: "Mr. Blaine is in the best of health and spirits, while Grant is booming along, and welcome, if I were the only one to be consulted." [4] Even Walker, most faithful of armor-bearers, was ready to quit the fray. "I think Grant will be nominated," he wrote to his mother, November 20. "Father can afford to wait. . . . But have you observed that he is more popular than ever throughout the country, and I think we can content ourselves with that and let Grant be President."

But the Chandlers, Hales and Fryes had no such ideas. Chandler

[1] Adam Badeau, *Grant in Peace*, pp. 319–20.
[2] Quoted in Gail Hamilton's *Biography of James G. Blaine*, p. 478.
[3] *Letters of Mrs. Blaine*, edited by Mrs. Harriet Blaine Beale, Vol. I, p. 162.
[4] Gail Hamilton, *Biography of James G. Blaine*, p. 477.

wrote to Mrs. Blaine again on April 6, 1880: "As I now look at the situation generally, (1) Grant is to be beaten. (2) If the anti-Blaine men concentrate on Edmunds, B. will be nominated. (3) They cannot concentrate on either Washburne or Sherman, and if they could neither can beat B. . . . So I think B.'s chances are right good. I am glad he lies abed till noon. I don't want him to get sick (irony!). But more men are slaving and exerting themselves for him all over this country than they ever did for a man before." Joe Manley, the old family friend of Augusta, added his plea for action, on May 22: "It is now too late for Mr. B. to retreat. . . . He must be nominated at Chicago in June. . . . I think he owes it to himself and to his friends all over this country who are ready to sacrifice everything for his success to do all that lies in his power to win at Chicago. There is more involved than Mr. Blaine's success. The nomination of Grant is the inevitable defeat of the party, and the triumph of Democracy with all its attendant evils. I beg of you to have Mr. Blaine think of this matter and go himself to Chicago. If he is on the ground to lead his own fight he will be nominated. . . . He is a candidate and it is right and just that he should use all honorable means to secure his nomination. . . . It is impossible for Mr. Blaine to have any man at Chicago who could represent him as Conkling represents Grant, for no man does stand as Mr. Blaine's mouthpiece. . . . We have only to fear superior management. We have the people with us."

Blaine, however, had no intention of going to Chicago. He walked in the cool of the evening with Don Cameron, who had secured the Pennsylvania delegation for Grant, trying to persuade him of the folly of nominating the General for a third term.[1] James A. Garfield noted in his diary for May 23, 1880: "Called on Blaine and took a long walk. Blaine said he did not much expect the nomination at Chicago and would not have become a candidate but for the belief that he could more effectually prevent the nomination of Grant than anyone else. On the whole, he thought the nomination of Grant quite probable." [2] This, although only a month before he had told Garfield that he thought "Grant's nomination impossible." [3] It is this characteristic mixture of confidence and

---

[1] The Camerons and the Blaines were intimate friends. No names appear more frequently on the guest lists of the Blaine dinners in Washington than "Senator and Mrs. Cameron." The Camerons also visited the Blaines in Maine, and the Senator gave a pony to the youngest daughter, Harriet. See *Letters of Mrs. Blaine,* Vol. I, pp. 164, 172.
[2] James A. Garfield, Manuscript *Journal,* Library of Congress, Vol. II, p. 957.
[3] *Ibid.,* p. 956.

apprehension in Blaine that has baffled his biographers. It explains his fear of neither Morton nor Bristow nor Conkling in 1876, but only of "the Great Unknown." It accounts for the fatalistic intimations of his own defeat expressed to more than one of his intimates during the closing days of the campaign of 1884. He was a gladiator in debate and a spellbinder on the hustings. No one was his superior in divining and defining the trends of public opinion, but Colonel Ingersoll's famous appellation at Cincinnati was far from appropriate. Blaine was no "plumed knight" riding confidently in the van of his cohorts.

So, in the spring of 1880, instead of an aggressive leader marshaling his forces like a Jackson or a Roosevelt, we see a hesitant Blaine, importuned by his followers to don his armor and enter the battle. "The Republican voters are nine tenths of them for 'Jim' Blaine," writes one from Minnesota. Another from Illinois, "The State is ten to one for Blaine against the field, but he has no leader . . . plenty of soldiers and captains, but no general." From San Francisco Robert Gardner wires, "Will send a solid California delegation for Blaine." From Denver L. C. Carpenter writes to Chandler, "Public sentiment set very strongly toward Grant when he first landed, and if the convention had been held a month or two ago he would have had no opposition. Now, however, there is a strong current of feeling throughout the State for Blaine, and it seems to be increasing every day."

Even from lifelong Democrats came the appeal to Blaine to head the fight against Grant and his "political devils" Conkling, Cameron and Logan. Chauncey F. Black of York, Pennsylvania, wrote to Blaine on Jan. 29, 1880: "I shall do the little that lies in my power to elect the Democratic candidate this fall. But if we are to have a Republican President I trust his name will be Blaine. Along with other Democrats, I have promoted the Blaine boom in this State. Perhaps from the party policy standpoint we have overdone our work, for against Grant our success would be clear, while against you it is doubtful. But, be that as it will, the harvest is ready now for your sickle."

Whether or not Blaine could have garnered the harvest of victory in 1880 if he had thrust in his sickle with more vigor, assuming direction and issuing orders instead of receiving reports and appeals, is a question that cannot be answered. But if he was really "consumed with ambition" for the Presidency, one might say that "ambition should be made of sterner stuff."

The Republican convention met at Chicago on Wednesday, June 2, in the huge "amphitheater" constructed on the lake side. The hall was gayly decorated with flags and streamers, while from the railings of the balcony hung pictures of Republican worthies from the martyred Lincoln to Zachariah Chandler, whose grave was still fresh. The floor was crowded with 756 delegates and an equal number of alternates. A throng of more than ten thousand excited claquers filled the galleries. Seldom if ever in our history has a convention furnished a more complete exhibit of what David Lawrence has aptly called "barbecue politics." For four days the delegates wrangled over organization, credentials, resolutions and rules, while the spectators, heedless of the tattoo of the chairman's gavel, shouted, stamped and waved scarves and umbrellas. The daily morning prayers for divine guidance were but momentary, incongruous interruptions of the hubbub. "There have been times in the convention," wrote Garfield to his wife, "when it seemed that it could not be in America, but in the sections of Paris in the ecstasy of the Revolution." [1]

The Grant forces were early on the scene, marshaled by the aggressive Conkling and confident of victory. Their plan was to "rush" the convention by the selection of a Stalwart presiding officer who would recognize the Grant delegates in contests and uphold the unit rule, i.e., the casting of the total vote of a State for the candidate preferred by a majority of its delegation. It was not Blaine's lieutenants, Hale and Frye, who nipped this plan in the bud. They had not arrived at Chicago when it was started. The credit for blocking the manoeuvres of the Stalwarts, which would in all likelihood have resulted in the nomination of Grant on an early ballot, belongs to James A. Garfield, delegate at large from Ohio and manager of the Sherman forces. He obliged Senator Cameron, Chairman of the National Committee, to respect the opinion of the majority of the committee in selecting an anti-Grant man, Senator George F. Hoar of Massachusetts, as temporary (later made permanent) chairman of the convention. He thwarted Conkling in his arrogant pretensions to treat the delegates like the obsequious vassals of his own machine. When the New York leader moved to expel from the convention three West Virginia delegates who had dared to vote against his resolution pledging every delegate to the support of the nominee, Garfield defended the West Virginians in a magnificent

[1] T. C. Smith, *Life and Letters of James Abram Garfield*, Vol. II, p. 977.

plea for freedom of expression, which so obviously won the approval of the delegates that Conkling withdrew his motion.[1] But not graciously. Incapable of understanding how any man could act in politics from a disinterested motive, he tore a strip from the margin of his newspaper on which he scribbled, "I congratulate you on being the dark horse," and passed it on to Garfield.

That was not the end of Conkling's discomfiture, however. He suffered the worst blow of all in the defeat (449 to 306) of the unit rule and the report of the Rules Committee (Garfield chairman) to the effect that "in case the vote of any State, Territory or the District of Columbia shall be divided, the Chair shall announce the number of votes cast for any candidate." The States of New York, Pennsylvania and Illinois, controlled by the Grant triumvirate, had 170 of the 756 delegates. Had these 170 votes been cast solidly for the victor of Appomattox, they would, combined with the 176 sure votes from the Southern and border States, have brought him so near the nomination on the first ballot that a second roll call would have probably put him over. But with the defeat of the unit rule, the sixty-three anti-Grant delegates from New York, Pennsylvania and Illinois were free to cast their ballots for other candidates. Blaine received fifty of these votes, which brought his total to only twenty less than Grant's, and so established the deadlock which was to be finally resolved by the stampede to Garfield. A final rebuff to Conkling was the addition to the platform, at the instigation of two Edmunds delegates from Massachusetts, of a resolution endorsing civil service reform.[2] In short, it was evident from the action of the convention, before the name of a single candidate had been presented, that Grant's nomination would not be the easy triumph predicted by Conkling and Cameron, but would be won, if at all, in a hard fight against the field.

It was not till Saturday evening that the tired convention was ready, after wrangling all day over credentials and rules, to listen to the nominating speeches. Blaine's name was the first to be presented. It

---

[1] *Proceedings of the Republican National Convention* . . . reported by Eugene Davis, official stenographer. J. B. Jeffrey Printing and Publishing House. Chicago, 1881, pp. 49–50.

[2] It was this resolution which brought Webster Flanagan, a delegate from Texas, to his feet with the brutally frank confession of the Stalwart creed of the loaves and fishes: "We are not here, Sir, for the purpose of providing offices for the Democracy. There is one plank in the Democratic platform that I have ever admired, and that is, 'To the victors belong the spoils.' After we have won the race, as we will, we will give those who are entitled to positions office. What are we up here for?" (*Proceedings*, p. 164.) Uproarious laughter greeted Flanagan's remarks.

had already aroused a tumult of cheers whenever it had been mentioned casually in the convention, and here was the opportunity to capitalize that enthusiasm by a ringing speech like Colonel Ingersoll's at
Cincinnati four years before. But Ingersoll's rôle at Chicago was reduced to waving a red shawl in the antics of ballyhoo, while the important honor of presenting the candidate was entrusted to an insignificant millionaire from Detroit by the name of James F. Joy. A duller,
flatter performance than Mr. Joy's could hardly be imagined. He began
by regretting that circumstances had imposed on him the duty of making the nomination! He had been out of the country until just before
the meeting of the convention. Therefore he feared that his words
would "benefit the candidate but little," but he would bring him before the convention "in as brief a manner as possible . . . because we
are all now impatient for the voting." He then went on to state, erroneously, that his candidate had entered the House of Representatives in
1860 and that he had "traversed the country from Maine to the Mississippi" campaigning for Grant in 1868 and 1872 and for Hayes in
1876. He even, in a moment of inadvertence, spoke of his candidate
as James F. Blaine. He said in closing his remarks ("which have been
longer than I intended") that Michigan was not a doubtful State and
would put vigor and energy into the contest whether Mr. Blaine were
nominated or not.[1] The "long and continued applause" which followed
this asinine speech must have been largely due to relief that it was
over. Its maladroitness was partially redeemed by an enthusiastic seconding speech by E. M. Pixley of California and Senator Frye's par-
able of the pilot who had brought the good old ship "The State of
Maine" through the tempest of the past winter.

After a perfunctory speech by a Minnesota delegate presenting the
name of Senator William Windom, the State of New York was reached
on the roll call and Roscoe Conkling sprang upon a reporters' table
in front of the platform to deliver one of the most eloquent and sophis-
tical pleas ever heard in a nominating convention. He pictured Grant
as a paragon of wisdom and virtue, whose name was "the most illustrious borne by living men," a name that "will glitter, a bright and
imperishable star in the diadem of the Republic, when those who have
tried to tarnish it have moldered in forgotten graves." With him as
leader, the party would "grandly win"; for it would have "no defensive

[1] *Proceedings*, pp. 175–6.

campaign to wage, no apologies to make, nothing to explain away" (a slap at Blaine). As for the "third term bogy," it was mere rubbish, disquieting only to "those hopelessly longing for a first term and their dupes and coadjutors." What a stultifying fallacy to argue that because a man had been twice tried and found faithful (!), he must not, even after an interval of years in which his fitness had been still further enhanced by a wealth of knowledge and experience (!), be trusted again. "Without patronage, without emissaries, without committees, without bureaus, without telegraph wires running from his house or from the seats of influence to this convention, without electioneering contrivances"— Oh, docile, disinterested Triumvirate!— Grant's name was "on his country's lips." [1]

When the tumult and the shouting for the hero of Appomattox had died down, Garfield rose to nominate John Sherman of Ohio in by far the best speech of the convention. In an introduction reminiscent of Daniel Webster's simile of the storm-tossed mariner in his great reply to Hayne, Garfield reminded the convention that it was not from the billow crests but from the calm level of the sea that all heights and depths were measured. Not at Chicago in the heat of June, but at the ballot boxes of the Republic in the quiet of November would the deliberate judgment of the American people be registered. John Sherman was never a popular hero like Grant or Blaine, but his solid qualities of character and substantial services to his country were set forth by his spokesman with a sincerity which was the more eloquent for its restraint. If the speech actually did more to enhance the popularity of Garfield himself than of the stern-visaged Secretary of the Treasury who had not been able to win a solid delegation even in his own State of Ohio, it was not so much the fault of Garfield as the misfortune of Sherman.

Two more names were presented to the convention. Senator George F. Edmunds of Vermont, like Bristow in 1876, was the candidate of that group in the party who carried on the traditions of the Liberal Republicans of 1872 and who furnished the nucleus of the Mugwump revolt in 1884. And Elihu B. Washburne of Illinois, formerly a member of the Cabinet and Minister to France in the Grant regime, foolishly allowed himself to be put up in weak rivalry to his old chief. It was a few minutes before midnight of Saturday, June 6, when the

[1] *Proceedings,* pp. 179–182.

nominating speeches for the six candidates were finished and the wearied delegates and spectators went out into a raging storm of wind and rain to seek their lodgings.

On Monday the balloting began. Grant led with 304 votes, closely followed by Blaine with 284. The votes of Sherman (93), Edmunds (34), Washburne (30) and Windom (10) combined represented only twenty-two per cent of the entire convention. It was clear that the battle was between Grant and Blaine, and that as long as their forces remained faithful only Sherman votes could give either of them the majority (379) necessary for the nomination. Twenty-eight ballots were taken on Monday, and five more on Tuesday morning, without any essential change. Grant's strength fluctuated between 302 and 309, and Blaine's between 275 and 285. On the thirtieth ballot Sherman's count rose to 120 by the accession of Edmunds delegates from New England, and the Sherman backers jubilantly predicted the stampede of the anti-Grant delegates to their candidate. But it was a false alarm. The Secretary's vote quickly declined again to the proportions of a make-weight. The stampede was about to come, but not to Sherman. On the second ballot a Pennsylvania delegate had cast a vote for James A. Garfield, and on almost every succeeding ballot the Senator-elect from Ohio had received one or two votes, just to keep his name before the convention. He was not at all a "dark horse." Long before the convention met his name had been suggested from various quarters, and a group of devotees, like Wharton Barker of Pennsylvania, Streight of Indiana, Sheldon of Ohio, and especially Governor T. L. Pound of Wisconsin, were only waiting for the psychological moment to put him over.[1] Governor Pound told him early in February that neither Grant, Blaine nor Sherman would be chosen, and begged him not to "commit himself too irrevocably" to the latter. Two weeks later Sherman himself, in securing Garfield's rather reluctant consent to go to Chicago as a delegate at large from Ohio in support of his candidacy, told Garfield that he preferred him to any other candidate and would transfer his own strength to him if and when his own cause became hopeless.[2] On

---

[1] W. H. Mason of Atlanta, Illinois, wrote to Sherman, February 2, 1880: "In case there should be a struggle over the nomination, wouldn't General Garfield or Governor Foster or the Honorable E. B. Washburne be a possibility? I think Garfield would make a splendid President and I would like to vote for him. . . . If your Honor and Senator Blaine should fail to secure the nomination, I hope Garfield will win." *Sherman Papers*, Library of Congress, No. 44, 675.

[2] See Garfield's *Journal*, Library of Congress, under date of Feb. 18, 1880.

the thirty-fourth ballot Governor Pound threw the sixteen votes of the Wisconsin delegation to Garfield. On the thirty-fifth, Indiana gave him twenty-seven more, which, with scattering votes from Maryland, Mississippi and North Carolina, raised his total to fifty. On the thirty-sixth, the anti-Grant delegates from State after State flocked to Garfield's banner, nominating him by 399 votes. Grant's "old guard" of 306 remained faithful to the end.[1] Blaine had forty-two votes, Washburne five and Sherman three. Conkling moved to make the nomination unanimous, seconded by Hale of Maine and Foster of Ohio. The ticket was completed by the nomination of Chester A. Arthur of New York for Vice President on the first ballot—a sop to the Stalwarts.

Sherman's supporters believed that Garfield had betrayed the man who had secured his nomination to the United States Senate, and whose banner he should have held aloft until it went down in defeat. When the Wisconsin delegation cast its vote for him on the thirty-fourth ballot, Garfield did rise to a point of order, protesting that he had not authorized the use of his name. But at a word from Chairman Hoar, he meekly resumed his seat and let the convention have its way. George A. Fitch of Chicago wrote to Sherman on the day of the final ballot: "If defeated, thank the ambition of Garfield, the defection of Foster and the imbecility of the Ohio delegation." [2] Blaine himself thought that Garfield would probably lose the election on account of his behavior at Chicago. M. P. Curran, a reporter, in his *Life of Patrick Collins* (p. 82) tells of meeting Blaine on his return from White Sulphur Springs and riding from Boston to Portland with him on the train. "I should much prefer to see the party defeated with Garfield or some other candidate," Blaine is reported as saying, "to winning with Grant. . . . Garfield will be beaten. The Stalwarts will not vote for him and Sherman will never forgive him for his apparent treachery in the convention. Garfield was spokesman for Sherman, and Garfield's friends went to Chicago with a deliberate purpose to place their own man in nomination. Whether he was a party to this scheme or not, the friends of Sherman will hold him responsible." But Governor Dennison of Ohio telegraphed Sherman on June 8 that Garfield's con-

---

[1] A medal was struck by Chauncy I. Filley of St. Louis commemorating the fidelity of the 306, and as many of them as could met for an annual dinner in New York. See Thomas A. Platt's *Autobiography*, p. 608. When Platt wrote, in 1910, there were six of the group surviving, including B. F. Tracy, L. P. Morton and A. B. Cornell.

[2] *Sherman Papers*, Library of Congress, No. 49,379.

duct had been "frank and manly"; and Sherman sent a message from Washington the same day, instructing his delegates to vote for Garfield as soon as that gentleman's nomination should "appear to be reasonably certain." Many years later, in writing his *Memoirs,* Sherman completely exonerated his manager from any double dealing (Vol. II, p. 778).

Charles Emory Smith, President McKinley's Postmaster General, wrote in the *Saturday Evening Post* of June 8, 1901, that he left Chicago the morning after the convention on the same train with Senator Conkling and spent most of the day with him. "Senator Conkling," he says, "spoke with great freedom and unreservedly said that he would have far rather had Blaine nominated than Garfield," whom he described as an "angle-worm." But while Conkling despised Garfield as a canting hypocrite, his hatred for Blaine was the stronger emotion. Senator Jones of Nevada, who was favorably disposed to both Blaine and Grant, and believed that there was no antagonism of policy or purpose between them but only "the rival enthusiasm of equally strong and earnest followers," labored with his friend Conkling in the convention. "The country wants either Grant or Blaine," he said. "It does not want a dark horse. If Grant can't be nominated, take Blaine, and if Blaine can't be nominated, take Grant; but don't let them kill each other off and so nominate a candidate whom nobody wants." And while the stampede to Garfield was under way on the thirty-sixth ballot, Jones hurried to Conkling and besought him to cast the large New York vote for Blaine. Whether such a dramatic *coup* would have turned the tide and rallied the deserting forces of Blaine for victory we cannot tell; but it was too great a sacrifice of pride and prejudice to expect from the implacable Conkling. He cast the New York vote again for Grant, and the nomination of the "angle-worm" was assured. Blaine, content with having spiked Grant's guns in the convention, immediately sent a cordial message of congratulation to Garfield, with a pledge to work as hard for his election in November as he would have for his own. Grant, on the other hand, deeply chagrined by his defeat, not only failed in the elementary courtesy of felicitating his successful rival, but even scolded his backers for having allowed him to run for the nomination with the assurance that his success was beyond question.

Instead of Grant in the White House, then, with Conkling as "grand vizier," it was to be Garfield, with Blaine as the dominating personality and directing force of the Administration. Between the latter pair there was apparently not only the most complete political agreement, but also a personal affection like that of Damon and Pythias. Yet, there is something not altogether convincing in their mutual expressions of devotion. It is doubtful whether Blaine really considered Garfield the courageous and competent leader he found it desirable to represent him for the party's (and perhaps his own) interests; while Garfield, beneath equally profuse protestations of confidence, probably never overcame a lingering suspicion of Blaine's integrity. There was a trace of unction in Garfield, inherited from the days when he frequently exhorted the Christian Brethren and acquired the easy habit of puritanical censoriousness. There are many passages in his *Journal* and his letters to intimate friends showing that, while he admired Blaine's brilliant intellectual gifts during the dozen years in which the two men were associates in the House of Representatives, he had misgivings about his political morals.[1] It was perhaps his own distressing experience of having to defend his honor against the suspicions cast upon it in the Crédit Mobilier investigation that later made him more charitable in his judgment of the man who stood by him staunchly then. At any rate, after Blaine's prostration on the steps of the Washington church, the relations between the two men and their families became increasingly intimate.

But quite apart from any personal attachment, Garfield's obligation to Blaine was compelling. For it was the nearly two hundred and fifty Blaine delegates who had gone over to him on the final ballot that had made his nomination at Chicago possible. This obligation Garfield recognized to the full. On June 29 he wrote to Blaine, who had gone to White Sulphur Springs for relief from his gout, asking him virtually to draft the letter of acceptance, by indicating what should be said on the topics of the currency, Chinese immigration, the South, civil service reform, "and anything else that is close to your heart." Blaine replied on July 4, shrewdly declining to furnish "copy" for the letter, with the flattering assurance that Garfield himself was better qualified to deal with these subjects than he was.[2]

The letter of acceptance, however, was a poor performance. The New York *Nation* called it "a cruel disappointment to those Independ-

---

[1] T. C. Smith, *Life and Letters of James Abram Garfield*, Vol. I, pp. 466, 473.
[2] Correspondence in Gail Hamilton, *Biography of James G. Blaine*, pp. 486 ff.

ents who had hoped to find in it a trumpet call," and Horace White characterized it as "a surrender to the machine." Anxious to conciliate both factions of the party Garfield emphasized the Southern issue to win the Stalwarts and gave so equivocal an endorsement to civil service reform as to draw from Carl Schurz a public rebuke in a speech at Indianapolis. Garfield countered with an indignant letter in which he declared that anyone who thought he would surrender to congressional dictation on the subject would "find himself greatly mistaken when the trial came." [1] Yet he continued to sue for Stalwart support. Early in August, on the advice of W. E. Chandler and S. W. Dorsey, and greatly to the distress of Schurz and the reformers, he went to New York to attend a meeting of the Republican Committee at the Fifth Avenue Hotel. Blaine, whose very presence was a challenge to the New York leaders, was conspicuous at the meeting; but Conkling, for whose sake the candidate had traveled in the summer's heat from Mentor, refused to attend. Obviously, Garfield was not making much of a success in his attempt to carry water on both shoulders.

The prospects for a Republican victory in November were anything but rosy. The Democrats, by nominating General W. S. Hancock, the hero of Gettysburg, had deprived their opponents of the perennial issue of loyalty to the Union. Hancock's war record was as unimpeachable as Garfield's. With a Union major general in the White House there would be little to fear from the sinister designs of Confederate brigadiers in Congress. Moreover, the Democrats, mindful of their popular majority in 1876 and determined, as in the days of Andrew Jackson, to redress the "fraud" which had kept their candidate out of the Presidency, presented an energetic and united front, while the Republicans were split into the hostile factions of Stalwarts and Halfbreeds. The September elections in Maine, long regarded as prophetic of the result of the national poll in November, seemed to confirm the pessimistic auguries. For the first time since the formation of the Republican Party in 1854, the Democrats elected their candidate for Governor, H. M. Plaisted, albeit by the narrow majority of 164 votes. They were confidently claiming Indiana and, less confidently, Garfield's own State of Ohio. They hoped that Pennsylvania might give a majority for her distinguished son, General Hancock. They would surely carry New York if the Conkling machine should knife Garfield

[1] Bancroft and Dunning, *The Writings of Carl Schurz*, Vol. IV, p. 45.

(as Blaine in his conversation with Mr. Curran, above cited, thought it would). And, finally the former States of the secession, now freed from the coercion of Federal bayonets and the presence of political carpetbaggers for the first national election since the Civil War, were certain to cast their 138 electoral votes as a unit for the Democratic candidate. The "solid South" had been finally welded in the fires of hatred and revenge kindled by Thaddeus Stevens and his kind. For more than half a century (from 1876 to 1928) not a single Southern State that had been subjected to the military regime of the Reconstruction Acts cast its vote for a Republican candidate for the Presidency.

It was the ominous news from Maine that, like the death of Patroclus, brought the sulking Achilles from his tent. Garfield might be an "angle-worm" and an "artful dodger," but, after all, he was a Republican. If the Democrats should carry New York, and therewith the election, Roscoe Conkling and his "bread and butter brigade" would face worse starvation than could possibly come under the malevolent dispensation of James G. Blaine. The New York Republicans had evidently been pleading with their chief not to expose them to the danger of the executive guillotine, for soon after his August visit Garfield received word from Whitelaw Reid that Conkling had "announced his willingness to go to work" and would speak for the ticket in New York, Indiana and Ohio.[1] General Grant, whose opinion of Garfield was no higher than Conkling's, joined in the plea to the New York Senator to sink his disappointment over the nomination and lend his powerful aid to the success of the Republican ticket. So Conkling laid aside his lucrative law practice, canceling retainers to the amount of over twenty-five thousand dollars, and entered the campaign. On the evening of September 17 he spoke for over three hours in New York City to a crowd which packed the Madison Square Garden to the doors, pleading for the maintenance of the Republican Party in power as the only guarantee of the prosperity and safety of the country. There was no encomium of Garfield.

From New York Conkling went with General Grant to help win the October State of Ohio. They spoke to large audiences at Warren and Cleveland, and, at Garfield's insistence, stopped at Mentor on September 28, with Morton, Logan and others, to pay their respects to

[1] T. C. Smith, *Life and Letters of James Abram Garfield*, Vol. II, p. 1018.

the candidate. According to Conkling's biographer, Garfield rushed out of the house hatless in the rain to embrace the New York Senator and exclaim, "Conkling, you have saved me. Whatever man can do for man I will do for you." Conkling's lieutenant, Thomas C. Platt, in his *Autobiography* (p. 135), makes the assertion that on this visit Conkling "exacted a pledge" from Garfield (often referred to by the Stalwarts as "the Treaty of Mentor") that if he were elected he would make no Federal appointments in New York without consulting and securing the approval of the Republican machine in that State.[1] The Republicans carried Ohio in both the State and the national elections. Altogether Conkling made more than twenty speeches in the later weeks of the campaign, and it is highly probable that his aid was the determining factor in the narrow victory of the Republican ticket.[2] If Blaine nominated Garfield, says A. R. Conkling, Conkling elected him.[3]

It was inevitable that Blaine should play an important part in the new Administration. The President-elect made a brief visit to Washington at the end of November, to pack up the furniture of his house on I Street. He called at Blaine's house on the morning of the twenty-seventh and breakfasted with him alone. According to his *Journal* for that day, he told Blaine that he "had not made a single final decision" in regard to his Cabinet, and would not do so until February. Nevertheless, he virtually offered Blaine a place in it by asking him what would be his probable response if the invitation came, and whether he intended to be a candidate for the Presidency in 1884. "Because," he added, "I do not propose to allow myself or anyone else to use the next four years as a camping-ground for fighting the next presidential battle." To the latter query Blaine replied that he "would not again seek the

---

[1] In refutation of this persistent legend of a "bargain" between Garfield and the Stalwarts at Mentor, we have Garfield's own testimony in his *Journal* for Sept. 28: "I had no private conversation with the party but the call was a pleasant and cordial one all around." J. Stanley Brown, Garfield's private secretary, wrote to Professor T. C. Smith in 1924: "I was present during the entire period of the meeting, and there was never a moment when the Conkling group were closeted with the General, nor was there ever presented any opportunity for such a bargain. It was a deliberate lie." Professor Smith also quotes from Mr. Brown's letter in regard to the alleged precipitous greeting of Conkling by Garfield: "I was on that carriage, came with the visitors, and was present every moment of their stay. No such incident occurred." T. C. Smith, *op. cit.*, Vol. II, pp. 1032–34.
[2] The electoral vote was 214 to 155, but the popular vote, according to Edward Stanwood's figures (*The History of the Presidency*, Vol. I, p. 417) was 4,454,416 to 4,444,952, giving Garfield a plurality of less than 10,000 over Hancock.
[3] A. R. Conkling, *The Life of Roscoe Conkling*, p. 614.

nomination." And when, in answer to the former query, he began to speak of the reluctance with which he would leave his seat in the Senate, Garfield still further committed himself by pointing out the opportunities afforded by an executive career and concurring in the judgment that "only the Treasury or the State Departments would be desirable" for Blaine. They agreed to correspond freely on the subject.

Evidently, despite Garfield's remark about not making any final decision until February, both men regarded the breakfast conversation of November 27 as a definite offer of a Cabinet position. For on December 20 Blaine wrote to Garfield: "Your generous invitation to enter your cabinet as Secretary of State has been under consideration for more than three weeks. . . . I have waited only long enough to make up my mind definitely and conclusively. I therefore say to you, in the same cordial spirit in which you invited me, that I accept the position. . . . In accepting this important post I shall give all that I am and all that I can hope to be freely and joyfully to your service. You need no pledge of my loyalty both in heart and in act. . . . Your Administration must be made brilliant, successful and strong in the confidence and pride of the people; not obviously directing its energies to reëlection, but compelling that result by the logic of events. . . . To that most desirable consummation I feel that, next to yourself, I can contribute more influence than any other man. I say this not from egotism or vain-glory, but merely as a deduction from an analysis of the political forces which have been at work in the country for five years past and which will be operative for many more years to come. I hail it as one of the happiest circumstances connected with this important affair that, in allying my political fortune with yours—or rather merging mine in yours—my heart goes with my head, and that I carry to you not only political support but personal and devoted friendship. It is this fact that has led me to the momentous conclusion embodied in this letter—for, however much I might admire you as a statesman, I would not enter your Cabinet if I did not believe in you as a man and love you as a friend." To this rather sentimental effusion Garfield replied briefly, expressing his "great satisfaction" with the decision, and declaring that it would be better for Blaine and indispensably necessary for himself that the decision should be "known to nobody but ourselves and our wives." [1]

However, the news that Blaine was to be Secretary of State in the new Administration leaked out immediately. It was reported in the New York and Chicago papers the very day that Garfield was writing of the necessity for keeping it secret. The news, once out, could not, of course, be denied. It threw the New York Stalwarts into a rage, not because Blaine was to be in the Cabinet, which they fully expected, but because his prompt appointment, before any provision had been made for them, and weeks before any other Cabinet officer was chosen, seemed to confirm their fear that he was to dominate the Administration. They immediately demanded the Treasury Department as an offset to Blaine's influence. Levi P. Morton of New York was their candidate. Some of them, including Morton himself, claimed that Garfield had virtually promised the Treasury to the New York banker. He had done nothing of the sort, but he had assured the Stalwarts that they would not be excluded from the Administration.

His position was a difficult one in the midst of the factions which rent the party. The reformers like Schurz and Curtis, with little encouragement from his record, were trying to "galvanize" him into an independent executive of the Hayes type. The Stalwarts, not trusting "this man Garfield," were alternately attempting to coerce or cajole him into giving them their due share of recognition. Ever since his nomination, he had been sincerely desirous of reconciling the factions. June 29 might have been called "reconciliation day" in his *Journal,* for on that date he wrote no less than four letters of good-will. To Whitelaw Reid of the New York *Tribune* he said: "I have made all reasonable personal advances for harmonious action. The Grant and Blaine men will have no grounds of complaint about my letter of acceptance if I can help it. . . . I should cordially welcome suggestions about the letter from Conkling and Blaine. The latter I will write to; I cannot now open correspondence with the former. He must do that and will find me cordial." [2] In the letter to Blaine already mentioned (p. 174) Garfield also sounded the note of optimism: "The feeling among the Republicans generally is hopeful and good. Your friends, partaking of your own spirit, are generous and helpful, because they love a com-

---

[1] The correspondence is in Gail Hamilton, *Biography of James G. Blaine,* pp. 494–5.
[2] T. C. Smith, *Life and Letters of James Abram Garfield,* Vol. II, p. 998.

mon cause and because you and they are responsible for my nomination. In one quarter alone are the oracles dumb and seem not yet to have determined whether it shall be peace or war." [1] To Governor Foster of Ohio, Republican national committeeman, he wrote a long letter discussing the prospects of the campaign: "I shall be glad if the committee can secure the services of Thomas C. Platt (!) as Secretary. His acquaintance with the political elements in the State of New York would make his services of great value." And, finally, to the vice presidential candidate, Arthur, like Platt a Conkling man, he wrote to ask him to coöperate with Foster in the discussion of measures calculated to bring harmony into the party. [2] In a word, Garfield's position was summed up in a sentence written to Joseph Medill of the Chicago *Tribune* just after the election: "I want all Republicans, including the '306,' to consider themselves in full fellowship." [3]

Now Blaine had not even waited until his acceptance of the Cabinet position before submitting views on the conduct of the Administration which contrasted sharply with those of his chief. On December 10, 1880, he wrote a portentous letter to Garfield, "in strict confidence," which, had it come under the eyes of Conkling or Schurz, would have at once killed any remotest hope of harmony. He divided the Republican Party into three sections. Far from expecting them to coalesce, he set them off against one another with merciless discrimination. The first group he called, "for convenience of designation," the "Blaine section." They represented the great majority of the normal Republican districts of the country, Grant's delegates at Chicago being "almost wholly from States and districts hopelessly Democratic." This Blaine section was now all Garfield's "without rebate or reserve," thanks to the Blaine delegates at Chicago; and in it alone were his true friends to be found. "The second section," he continued, "is the Grant section, taking all the South practically, with the machine in New York, Pennsylvania and Illinois, and having the aid of the rule or ruin leaders. I think I am not wrong in saying that this section contains all the desperate bad men of the party, bent on loot and booty. . . . These men are to be handled with skill, always remembering that they are harmless when out of power and desperate when in possession of it." Of course, he said, it would be folly to wage open war upon them. "They

---

[1] Gail Hamilton, *Biography of James G. Blaine*, p. 486.
[2] T. C. Smith, *Life and Letters of James Abram Garfield*, Vol. II, pp. 999–1000.
[3] *Ibid.*, p. 1046.

must not be knocked down with bludgeons; they must have their throats cut with a feather." The third section, the "unco' guid" and the reformers by profession, were "upstarts, conceited, foolish, vain, without knowledge of measures, ignorant of men . . . noisy but not numerous, pharisaical but not practical, ambitious but not wise, pretentious but not powerful." They were the worst possible advisers, but were to be treated with respect (!). They never would coöperate with the Grant section, of course, but they could easily be won over to the Blaine section and "hitched to your Administration." [1]

Ominous as the tone of this Catilinarian classification was for the peace of the party, worse followed when Blaine began forthwith to put into effect his counsel of the gentle assassination of the Stalwarts. Garfield had but just finished reading Blaine's audacious letter and confided to his *Journal*: "On many accounts he would be a brilliant Secretary of State; other adjustments might be more difficult," when a delegation of three New York Conklingites arrived at Mentor, on the evening of December 13, to urge again the appointment of Levi P. Morton to the Treasury. They failed to move Garfield from his position that it would be both unwise and unconstitutional to choose a Wall Street banker for the position; but at the same time they secured a promise from the President-elect that he would not injure Morton's chances for the United States Senatorship by interfering in the New York elections, nor pick his Cabinet until after the senatorial election was over. But Blaine, whom Garfield, for obvious reasons, had not informed of his conference with the Stalwart emissaries, proceeded to do the very thing that Garfield had promised should not be done. He went to New York on December 30 to consult with the anti-Conkling men, and at a dinner at Whitelaw Reid's house the next evening persuaded Chauncey M. Depew to enter the State contest "for the purpose of securing the election of a Senator who would support the Administration." [2] Furthermore, he prepared an editorial for the *Tribune* of January 3, 1881, in which he stated "by authority" that, while the Garfield Administration would not foment any quarrels, it would "see to it that the men from New York or from the other States, who had the courage at Chicago to obey the wishes of their districts in the balloting for the President" should not "lose by it." This behavior strengthened the conviction of the

---

[1] Gail Hamilton, *Biography of James G. Blaine*, pp. 490–1.
[2] D. S. Alexander, *History of the State of New York*, Vol. III, p. 466.

Stalwarts that Blaine was to be permitted to dominate the Administration and "ride down under the wheels of his triumphal car" the men who had fought him in the convention. It was not enough to have spiked Grant's guns at Chicago: he was determined to sack the Stalwart camp.

Still, Garfield struggled to redeem his pledge of welcome to "full membership in the party" of all Republicans, and wrestled with the problem of finding a New Yorker for the Cabinet who would be both loyal to the Administration and acceptable to the Stalwarts. He invited Conkling to Mentor and "had a full conversation on the Cabinet and kindred subjects" with him (Feb. 16). But as Conkling still harped on the fitness of Morton for the Treasury, which was "the only post that would satisfy New York," the visit only served to increase the President-elect's perplexity and the New York Senator's scornful distrust.[1]

Garfield even went so far as to suggest inviting Conkling himself into the Cabinet. "What would you say," he wrote to Blaine on January 31, "to exchanging seats, you for the Treasury, he (Conkling) for State?" To this extraordinary proposition Blaine replied in no uncertain terms: "His appointment would act like strychnine upon your Administration—first bring contortions, and then be followed by death." [2]

Professor Smith had no difficulty in refuting the statement of T. C. Crawford that "Blaine made up the Cabinet.[3] The President-elect offered posts to five men to whom Blaine strenuously objected, and two of them, William L. Windom (Treasury) and Thomas L. James (Postmaster General) accepted, while a third, Levi P. Morton, after accepting the Navy portfolio, withdrew at the behest of the New York Stalwarts, who considered the position beneath the dignity of their claims. Furthermore, Garfield opposed Blaine's persistent recommendation of William B. Allison of Iowa for the Treasury until the eleventh hour

---

[1] J. L. Connery, "Secret History of the Garfield-Conkling Tragedy," *Cosmopolitan Magazine*, June, 1897, p. 150.

[2] T. C. Smith, *Life and Letters of James Abram Garfield*, Vol. II, p. 1078. This letter of Feb. 5, 1881, to Garfield, with its bitter denunciation of all the New York Stalwarts, does not appear in Gail Hamilton's volume. Nor is there any mention of Blaine's visit to New York and his intrigues with the anti-Conkling men. Her carefully selected extracts give the false impression that "General Garfield and Mr. Blaine were equally desirous of harmony in the interests of effectiveness, but neither was willing to sacrifice one faction to another." (p. 497).

[3] T. C. Crawford, *Life of James G. Blaine*, p. 494.

(when Allison also declined) and paid no attention whatever to Blaine's suggestions of Stephen B. Elkins and Walter Q. Gresham for Cabinet positions. Indeed, Blaine did not "pick out" a single one of his six colleagues at Garfield's council table.[1] Nevertheless, it was Blaine's influence, exerted through assiduous correspondence with his chief and political intrigue with the anti-Stalwart forces in New York, that defeated whatever hope there was of the realization of Garfield's good intentions to heal the rift in the party. Conciliation was no part of Blaine's program. Could he have foreseen the terrible tragedy in which the factional strife was to eventuate, he would have endured even the haughty mien of Conkling himself opposite him at the Cabinet table. After all, Garfield was to be the chief, and the Stalwarts could hardly have "run away" with the Administration.

---

[1] The war portfolio and the Attorney Generalship went to Robert T. Lincoln of Illinois and Wayne MacVeagh of Pennsylvania respectively, who were acceptable to the Grant "triumvirs," Logan and Cameron, in those States. Samuel J. Kirkwood of Iowa (Interior) and William H. Hunt of Louisiana (Navy) were insignificant nonpolitical appointments. It was not until the very day of Garfield's inauguration that the Cabinet was finally completed by Windom's acceptance of the Treasury.

A GRAYING man of fifty-one, growing a little slower of motion and heavier of tread, troubled with gout for which he sought relief from time to time at White Sulphur Springs, West Virginia, and becoming in general somewhat too apprehensive of the state of his health,[1] Blaine entered his spacious office at the southern end of the ponderous building which housed the departments of State, War and Navy, conscious of opening a new chapter in his career and filled with enthusiastic plans for the glory of the Garfield Administration, the Republican Party and his own reputation. He had no technical qualifications for the position of Secretary of State, no training in diplomacy or international law, no experience in the executive department of the government. As a member of legislative bodies for over twenty years, he had developed a wonderful proficiency in debate, into which he injected the pungent positiveness and eristic confidence of his journalistic pronouncements. "His talents," says a severe critic, "were oratorical and his tastes political in a personal and party sense." [2] But, for all that, Blaine was far from being merely the beneficiary of that deplorable custom in our American practice of bestowing cabinet positions, ambassadorships and other high offices upon persons conspicuous for their contributions to the success of the Party rather than for their qualifications for the particular office in question. His ability to grasp the essential points in a complicated problem, his wide knowledge of history and political science, his desire to see justice prevail in international relations and especially his zeal for making the influence of the United States a factor in world politics, all gave promise of an unwonted vigor in the policy of our State Department.

It is temptingly easy to assume a single clear-cut motive for the behavior of public men, though the poignant realization of the complexity of motives in any decision of importance in our own lives should warn

---

[1] "I write propped up on pillows, having been suffering horribly all the week with gout," wrote Blaine to Whitelaw Reid on Feb. 13, 1881. Conkling speaks of his having "risen from a sick bed" on March 21 to combat the New York appointments. Mrs. Blaine mentions a suspicion of Bright's disease in a letter of June 6, (Vol. I, p. 206) and on several occasions refers a bit teasingly to her husband's enjoyment of poor health.

[2] Ellis P. Oberholtzer, *History of the United States Since the Civil War*, Vol. IV, p. 100.

us against that assumption in the case of those whose responsibilities and commitments are more exigent than ours. For example, the Washington correspondent, T. C. Crawford, who wrote the best of the contemporary biographies of Blaine, states baldly that "he accepted the office (of Secretary of State) because he knew that with that acceptance he would have practically the control and direction of the national Administration. . . . The entire Cabinet was made up in accordance with the wishes of Mr. Blaine." [1] Conkling was sure that Blaine's sole motive in entering the Cabinet was to complete the discomfiture of the Stalwarts at Chicago by excluding them from any influential post in the new Administration. Edward Stanwood, perhaps interpreting Blaine's purpose too strictly in the light of his actual policy, emphasizes the opportunity which Blaine saw for making the United States the dominant factor in the political and commercial relations of the American republics. Gail Hamilton finds in the strong personal friendship and perfect political accord between the two men the motive which compelled Blaine to devote his talents to making Garfield's Administration glorious in our annals. And Garfield himself, in urging Blaine to enter the Cabinet, suggested that it might be a welcome change of duties for him and a "rest" after his long service in Congress. Doubtless, something of all these motives influenced Blaine's decision, and more besides. For example, the social prestige attaching to the intercourse of a man of Blaine's genial gifts with the representatives of the foreign powers at Washington was not to be overlooked. Mrs. Blaine wrote to her son Walker in St. Paul, after a big dinner party, on January 16, 1881: "All the world is paying court to the coming or expected Secretary of State. Socially you know it is about the best position. We shall sell the house (on 15th Street) at once. We intend to put up a very nice and expensive house." [2]

Finally, there was a political situation in Blaine's own State of Maine which may have counted for more than all the motives mentioned in his decision to leave the Senate for the State Department. For the first time since the organization of the Republican Party, the people of Maine had elected a Democratic Governor, and that in a presidential year. Did it mean that the power which Blaine had exer-

---

[1] Crawford, *Life of James G. Blaine*, pp. 485, 494. We have already seen how absurd the last statement was (see p. 182).
[2] *Letters of Mrs. James G. Blaine*, Vol. I, p. 191.

cised for twenty-two years as chairman of the Republican State Committee was slipping? Did it perhaps foreshadow the election of a Democratic legislature which would deprive him of his senatorial seat in 1882? Friendly hints were coming to him, even from Garfield himself, that it might be better for him to give up his long tenure of the Maine chairmanship in view of increasing complaints of his dictatorial and arbitrary management. And the situation was made more serious still by a threatened split in the Republican ranks in Maine. William P. Frye and Eugene Hale, both warm friends of Blaine, were rivals for the seat in the United States Senate to be vacated by Hannibal Hamlin on March 4, 1881. The former wrote to W. E. Chandler on December 22, 1880, describing the ugly feeling between the Frye and Hale factions and suggested that it could be ended by a "quiet word" announcing that Blaine would enter the Cabinet and thus leave two senatorial seats to be filled instead of one.[1] Chandler immediately passed the idea on to the President-elect, adding his own plea for the restitution of harmony in Maine: "Today I have letters from that State," he wrote, "showing a bitter fight about the Senatorship. Assaults upon Hale are being made with malignity and bad blood is getting up which it will be hard to allay. It may result in defeating both Hale and Frye. . . . The point is that if Mr. Blaine is to be invited into the Cabinet and is to accept and vacate his seat, it would promote peace and quietness and facilitate a settlement of the Maine problem to have it determined by both you and himself shortly. I can only say that if Mr. Blaine is asked into the Administration I shall be greatly pleased and shall urge him to accept." [2] Hale also wrote to Chandler, on January 2, 1881: "If Blaine is going into Garfield's Cabinet . . . it will help things greatly to let you know in season for Frye to act, *if he will,* so as to stop the contest here before next Friday evening. . . . I can see how the reasons for the Cabinet grow wider and deeper with Blaine. He would be the power in the Cabinet, and yet would get a kind of repose grateful to a battle-tired man." [3]

Every consideration of political precedent and personal friendship dictated the choice of Blaine for the first place in the Cabinet, and a

---

[1] *Chandler Papers* in the Library of Congress, Dec. 22, 1880.
[2] *Ibid.*
[3] Blaine, as we have seen, had already accepted the tender of the Cabinet position before this correspondence between Frye, Chandler and Garfield, and had been enjoined by the latter to keep the appointment secret. Was the immediate "leak" of the news connected with the tense situation in Maine?

flood of letters from his admirers to both Garfield and himself reinforced the popular demand for the choice. Yet there were misgivings, even to be found in Garfield's *Journal* (but not mentioned by the eulogistic biographers of Blaine) lest he should introduce embarrassing political animosities into the President's councils. John Sherman wrote to Garfield on January 21: "If you can only restrain his immense activity and keep him from meddling with the other departments, you will have a brilliant Secretary." [1] But it would have taken more force than a Garfield could ever have exerted to restrain the political activity of his Secretary, who "ate, drank and breathed politics." The Administration was hardly a fortnight old when the test came. On March 20 Conkling conferred with the President, at the latter's request, about appointments, and Garfield "adopted many of his suggestions," including nine Federal positions in New York. On parting, Conkling asked the President when he intended to make a change in the Collectorship of the Port, the most important appointment in the State,[2] and Garfield put him off with the amiable reply that that was a matter which could wait for a while. The next evening, Garfield's *Journal* records, "Blaine came in at dinner and expressed great distress at the New York appointments." He returned at ten-thirty and stayed till near midnight. We have no record of the conversation between the two men, but we may be certain that it was not confined to the policy of the State Department. On the twenty-second the President sent to the Senate a list of nominations which created a sensation in the country and consternation in the breasts of the Stalwarts. Judge William H. Robertson, the leader of the Blaine forces in the New York delegation at Chicago, was named to succeed Merritt as Collector of the Port, and a place was provided for Merritt by transferring Grant's intimate friend and biographer, Adam Badeau, from the lucrative position of Consul General at London to the post of Minister to Switzerland. Grant's brother-in-law Cramer was moved from Switzerland to Denmark to make room for Merritt.

It was all an ill-advised piece of factional strategy, a palpable hit at Grant's friends and a declaration of war against the New York Stalwarts. General Merritt was discharging his duties with an efficiency

---

[1] T. C. Smith, *Life and Letters of James Abram Garfield*, Vol. II, p. 1148.
[2] It will be remembered that Hayes had dismissed Conkling's adherent Chester A. Arthur from the position in 1878, and replaced him by General E. A. Merritt, who was acceptable to the reform element in the party.

and honesty which left no valid reason for his removal. If President Garfield wished to show his independence or his defiance of any dictation from Senator Conkling, he could have done so in no better way than by a firm refusal to dismiss Merritt. Undoubtedly, Judge Robertson deserved recognition, but he need not have been rewarded with the only position that the Stalwarts were unwilling for him to have. Conkling himself suggested that he might be given a prosecuting attorneyship, which, considering the fact that it was for Blaine and not for Garfield that Robertson had worked at Chicago, would seem to have been generous enough treatment at the President's hands. How apprehensive Blaine was lest Garfield should yield to the pressure from the Stalwarts to withdraw Robertson's nomination is shown by the frequent doses of tonic which he administered to the President in his characteristic notes filled with dashes and abbreviations. "Y^r work today creates a splendid impression," he wrote the day the nominations went in. And again, "You must be firm and resolute as if you were fighting Chickamauga over again." The reference to Chickamauga was a master stroke, an appeal to the proudest moment of Garfield's life when he stood with General Thomas, the "Rock of Chickamauga," holding back the fierce attacks of Bragg's infantry for four hours. Garfield held firm as a rock in this battle too, to Blaine's great satisfaction —and his own eventual undoing.

A senatorial committee on conciliation, headed by H. L. Dawes of Massachusetts, tried to heal the strife. But Conkling strode up and down before the committee, declaring that Garfield had promised not to make a change in the collectorship without consulting him, that Blaine had risen from a sick bed to make "a midnight visit" to persuade the President to break his word and "upset the *entente cordiale*," and that he had in his possession an autograph letter of Garfield's which he prayed God he might not have to reveal, but which, if he did, "would make this President bite the dust." [1] As the quarrel grew more embittered, the President, egged on by his Secretary of State and White-

---

[1] The letter was one from Garfield to Jay Hubbell, written during the campaign, asking "how the departments were doing" in the matter of securing contributions, and advising Hubbell to get the assistance of the Second Assistant Postmaster, Brady. It was not the kind of letter that a good civil service reformer would have written, but there was nothing disgraceful or incriminating in it. Senator Dawes, to whom the President showed a copy, advised him to publish it at once, but Blaine vetoed the suggestion, and Garfield, as usual, followed Blaine's counsel. When S. W. Dorsey gave the letter to the press a little later, it fell rather flat.

law Reid, grew more determined. He would have it known without delay, as he wrote to Dawes, "whether he was the registering clerk of the Senate or the Executive of the Government." [1] Not only did he not withdraw Judge Robertson's name, but, on May 5, he withdrew the five other unratified New York nominations, thus making the confirmation of Robertson a test case. When it became certain that the Senate would confirm the nomination, as it did on May 18, Conkling and Platt sent a joint letter to Governor Cornell, resigning their seats in the Senate. They were defeated in their appeal to the legislature at Albany for reëlection, in spite of the aid rendered to them by Vice President Arthur; and the victory remained with President Garfield—or rather with James G. Blaine.

It was a costly victory. Banquo-Conkling was in his political grave, to be sure, but it was for Banquo's issue, the Stalwart Arthur, that Macbeth-Blaine had "filed his mind" and "put rancours in the vessel of his peace." The passions stirred by the factional contest led to the murder of Garfield, the accession of the Stalwart Arthur, the relegation of Blaine to private life, and therewith the frustration of all the high hopes and ambitious plans with which he had entered the Cabinet. Driving past the State building a few months after his retirement, he remarked plaintively to his wife: "Here I fully expected to raise my Ebenezer for eight years." [2] His actual tenure of office was less than ten months.

The outcome of this conflict between the Stalwarts and the Half-breeds was of such tragic significance for Blaine's career that it is worth while to pause a moment before discussing his policies as Secretary of State, to consider his responsibility for the political feud which rendered them abortive. Professor Smith has argued at length to prove that it was Garfield and not Blaine who took the initiative and controlled the negotiations in the fight with the Stalwarts.[3] But his arguments, based on certain passages in Garfield's *Journal* and in Blaine's and Garfield's letters, seem to us unconvincing. He cites, for example, an entry of Garfield's on May 29: "No member of the Cabinet behaves with a more careful respect of the rights of his brother members than Blaine." But this statement is so palpably contradicted by the facts that one can

[1] H. L. Dawes, "Conkling and Garfield," in the *Century Magazine*, January, 1894, p. 344.
[2] *Letters of Mrs. James G. Blaine*, Vol. II, p. 31.
[3] T. C. Smith, *Life and Letters of James Abram Garfield*, Vol. II, pp. 1107–1142.

regard it only as a bit of "defense mechanism" on Garfield's part. For Blaine insisted upon the nomination of W. E. Chandler as Solicitor General in the Department of Justice, in spite of the hostility of Chandler to the Attorney General, and pressed the matter until MacVeagh threatened to resign from the Cabinet. He even drafted a letter to MacVeagh for the President to sign, setting forth Chandler's merits; but in the end gave way and still saved his face by getting Chandler to agree to decline the appointment if it was ratified by the Senate. This act of renunciation on the part of the New Hampshire Senator was rendered unnecessary, however, because the Senate rejected his name. Again, the appointment of Judge Robertson as Collector of the Port of New York, for which Blaine was so zealous, was a matter which did not concern his own Department of State but Secretary Windom's Department of the Treasury.

Professor Smith finds further proof of the independence of Garfield in a letter which he wrote to his friend Hinsdale on April 4, 1881, declaring that he had determined to present Robertson's name for the collectorship, in order to balance his concessions to Conkling by "recognizing the other side in a conspicuous manner" and rewarding "those Independent Republicans who followed me at Chicago in resisting the unit rule." [1] But there is not the slightest evidence in this language that the idea of appointing Robertson was not suggested by Blaine, whose advice and counsel had been sought by Garfield from the moment of his nomination at Chicago. There was no particular reason why Garfield, with his professed purpose of conciliating the Stalwarts, should have singled out Judge Robertson for preferment; while there was every reason why Blaine, who was both indebted to Robertson and determined to "cut the throats of the Stalwarts with a feather," should do so. The whole logic of the situation points to Robertson as Blaine's not Garfield's candidate.

Again, Professor Smith cites Blaine's note of congratulation to Garfield on the appointments of March 22 (see p. 188) as evidence of the President's autonomous action: "Your work of today creates a splendid impression." The phrase "your work" would never have been employed by Blaine, says Professor Smith, "if it was his own plan that Garfield was carrying out." But that is precisely the language that Blaine or any other astute politician *would* have used to a President

[1] T. C. Smith, *Life and Letters of James Abram Garfield*, Vol. II, p. 1109.

carrying out his own plan. Does Professor Smith believe for a moment that Blaine would have been naïve enough to write to his titular chief: "Your execution of *my* plan creates a splendid impression."

Finally, Professor Smith adduces certain passages from Blaine's famous eulogy on Garfield delivered before both Houses of Congress, the Supreme Court, the diplomatic corps and distinguished guests on February 27, 1882, lauding the far-sighted courage and firmness of the martyred President. It takes no expert in historical criticism or psychological analysis, however, to detect the frailty of a set funeral oration as a source of sober truth. Blaine himself in his oration on Zachariah Chandler two years before had spoken of "the generous indulgence conceded to eulogy." Indeed, the pious exaggerations of eulogy are apt to be no less misleading than the deliberate misrepresentations of slander. Garfield was a man of conspicuous talents, powerful in the arena of debate, learned, industrious, clear-headed, fair-minded and gifted with an exceptionally sympathetic and attractive nature. But firmness of decision was exactly the trait which was missing from his mental and moral make-up. We need not depend on the "angle-worm" characterization of his hostile critics, like Conkling and Grant, for confirmation of this judgment. His own Ohio friends, like John Sherman, John Hay and President Hayes, set down in passages not intended for the eye of the public their misgivings on this point. John Hay, whom he urged to become his private secretary, admonished him to be firm: "One thing thou lackest yet, and that is a slight ossification of the heart. I woefully fear you will try too hard to make everybody happy—an office which is outside of your constitutional powers. Confine your efforts in that direction to Mrs. Garfield and the children. As for other matters, do as you think right, and it will be right nine times in ten and not far wrong the tenth time, though the heathen rage and the people imagine a vain thing." [1] Hayes recorded in his diary that Garfield had "large faculties—memory, analysis, fluency and the debating faculty," but that he was "not original, not firm, not a moral force. His course at times when trouble came betrayed weakness." [2] And Sherman wrote in his *Recollections* in 1895: "His will power was not equal to his personal magnetism. He easily changed his mind and veered honestly

[1] W. R. Thayer, *The Life and Letters of John Hay,* Vol. I, p. 447.
[2] C. R. Williams, *Life of Rutherford B. Hayes,* Vol. II, p. 364.

from one opinion to another." [1] Rhodes,[2] Sparks,[3] Cullom,[4] and Andrews,[5] concur in the judgment that Garfield was deficient in political initiative and courage. Judge Peters of Maine wrote to Blaine in December, 1880: "I have my fears of Garfield. I know him so well. He is too much on the pow-wow, and under compromise will put his camp in possession of the enemy." [6]

The most damaging evidence against Professor Smith's assertion of Garfield's "complete independence of Blaine in the whole (Robertson) affair" [7] is the fact that from the day of his nomination Garfield showed his dependence upon Blaine's counsel again and again. It was always Garfield who sought advice and Blaine who gave it—often unasked. Nor did the President-elect, as Rhodes remarks, "seem to feel the slightest irritation at words wherein the future Secretary seemed to assume that he would be the dominating head of the Administration." There is no parallel in our history, not even in Clay's correspondence with the elder Harrison, to the patronizing deference of Blaine's letter of December 10, 1880, to the President-elect, outlining the policy of the coming Administration, or to the editorial pronouncement in the New York *Tribune* of January 3, 1881. On the same day that the editorial appeared, Walker Blaine wrote to his father from St. Paul: "Your taking that position (in the Cabinet) will mean—and the country will so understand it—that you are the head of the Administration . . . and the chief counsellor of its policy." [8] Nor did the almost pathetic dependence of the President upon his Secretary of State cease until he finally succumbed to the wound inflicted by Guiteau's bullet. "Crump (one of the physicians attending Garfield) has often told me," writes George W. Crook, for many years the major domo of the White House, "how the President begged him to get Blaine to his bedside." [9] "I had myself observed," he says on another page, "that on Cabinet days Secretary Blaine would arrive early and be closeted with the President for some time before the rest of the Cabinet officers arrived.

[1] John Sherman, *Recollections*, Vol. II, p. 807.
[2] J. F. Rhodes, *History of the United States from the Compromise of 1850*, Vol. VIII, p. 146.
[3] E. E. Sparks, *National Development*, pp. 182, 191.
[4] S. M. Cullom, *Fifty Years of Service*, p. 127.
[5] E. B. Andrews, *The United States in Our Own Time*, p. 334.
[6] Peters to Blaine, Dec. 13, 1880.
[7] T. C. Smith, *Life and Letters of James Abram Garfield*, Vol. II, p. 1156.
[8] Gail Hamilton, *Biography of James G. Blaine*, p. 530.
[9] George W. Crook, *Through Five Administrations*, p. 273.

When the meeting was called the Secretary of State, instead of going into the room with the President, would come in through the door leading from the main entrance as though he had just entered the White House." [1] And this was the Cabinet officer than whom none "behaved with more careful respect of the rights of his brother members!"

But if Blaine cannot be absolved, in view of this cumulative evidence, from responsibility for the rift in the Party, it does not prove that a different course of action would have ensured peace and harmony. In extenuation of Blaine's attack on the Stalwarts, it is only fair to say that a conciliatory policy might have reduced him and Garfield to impotence. They were between the devil and the deep sea. In Roscoe Conkling they had an implacable enemy who boasted that he would "make this President bite the dust." They believed that they had to fight fire with fire; and they were urged to the fight by a chorus of supporters. The President's conference with Conkling on the New York appointments, on March 20, which so "greatly distressed" Blaine, was deplored by papers like the New York *Times,* the Philadelphia *Inquirer* and the Boston *Herald* as "the complete surrender of the Administration to the dictation of Senator Conkling." Whitelaw Reid exhorted the President not to waver. "You are absolute master of the situation," he wrote. "Conkling will every month become more and more powerless. I really believe you have him where there is a chance to make an end of him and of the corrupt, insolent and bullying elements which he has carried into our politics." [2] And a Federal officer of Buffalo sent the Secretary of State the supererogatory warning that the President might as well "attempt to placate a volcano in eruption" as to satisfy Senator Conkling." [3] It is not just to Blaine to ascribe his policy to a desire for "personal vengeance" against Conkling. He believed that the success of the Garfield Administration depended first of all on the elimination of the Stalwart faction from the party counsels. He had his way. But could he have foreseen that a consequence of his triumph would be the defeat of his own cherished program, he would probably have chosen rather to endure the opposition of a dozen Conklings.

For, after all, the specific tasks to which Blaine was called as Secretary of State lay pretty much outside the sphere of factional politics,

[1] George W. Crook, *Through Five Administrations,* pp. 262–3.
[2] Royal Cortissoz, *Life of Whitelaw Reid,* Vol. II, p. 63.
[3] Sherman Rogers to Blaine, "personal," May 16, 1881.

and need not have been interrupted by the perpetuation of the Chicago feud. Conkling was not interested in the diplomatic service. He had suggested to the President that the Halfbreeds might be rewarded with foreign missions. He would "hold his nose" while they were sent out of the country. With the support of a President who sympathized fully with his policy, Secretary Blaine, in eight years or even in four, might have accomplished the major part of a foreign program which would have anticipated in many features the work of Roosevelt, Root and Hay twenty years later, and which, in the judgment of his most hostile critics, constitutes his chief claim to statesmanship.

Our Secretaries of State, with a few exceptions like John Quincy Adams, Daniel Webster and William H. Seward, had followed the Jeffersonian precedent of abstention from voluntary participation in foreign affairs. During the first few decades of the Republic, to be sure, a considerable amount of diplomatic negotiation had been necessitated by the logic of the situation. The new nation, its gristle not yet hardened into bone, had to contend for the complete recognition of its autonomy by the European powers which still persisted in regarding it as a makeweight in their political rivalries. Dissension with Great Britain over the fulfilment of the terms of the peace treaty of 1783; embarrassments leading to actual war in the efforts to get rid of the obligations implied by the treaty of alliance with France in 1778; the designs of Spain to close the Mississippi to our commerce and so detach the lower western country from the Union; the proscription of our flourishing foreign trade and the seizure of our vessels and sailors by the arbitrary Orders in Council and Decrees of England and France, engaged in their mighty duel for world power—these and many other vexations from the European powers kept our ministers and special envoys to the courts of London, Paris and Madrid busy during the Administrations from Washington to Madison.

But with the full recognition of the political independence and territorial integrity of the United States, and the lure of the lands along the "western waters," Europe grew more and more remote and diplomacy declined to the point of desuetude. If questions arose now and then touching our interests or honor, they were dealt with *ad hoc,* as rather annoying interruptions of our serious business of political rivalry and economic expansion at home. Diplomacy came to be looked on as a slippery game, fit for beribboned, aristocratic prevaricators like a Talleyrand or a Metternich, but unsuited to the forthright honesty of the American character. Foreign legations were parceled out as political rewards, with little regard to the linguistic, legal or social qualifications of the incumbents. There was no continuity in our foreign policy, because, strictly speaking, we had no foreign policy—only the negative purpose, as expressed in the Monroe Doctrine, of keeping Europe from interfering with the affairs of this continent. There were no professional diplomatic careers, no schools for diplomatic training. We were proud of the tradition of political isolation.

It was impossible for a man of Blaine's versatile activities and ambitions to play the rôle of a Micawber in the State Department. Eager to make the Garfield Administration glorious in our annals, he would do his part by securing for the United States a prestige in world politics and a share in world commerce commensurate with the statistics of their increasing population and wealth, which he never tired of reviewing in his congressional speeches and public addresses. The persecution of the Jews in Russia, the imprisonment in Irish jails of alleged seditionists claiming American naturalization papers, the vindication of an exclusively American control over any canal to be cut through Nicaragua or the Isthmus of Panama, the extension of the Monroe Doctrine to the distant Hawaiian Islands, the friendly interposition of the United States to end war between the republics of Latin-America and so lay the basis, in a Pan-American conference, for the arbitration of political quarrels and the expansion of commercial intercourse—all entered into the plans of the State Department during the busy ten months of Blaine's Secretaryship. Not that he initiated all these policies. The files of the department already contained a routine correspondence on many of them, extending over a number of years. The distinctive marks of Blaine's handling of these diplomatic problems were the vigorous directness with which he attacked them, the confidence with which he asserted the American point of view, and the presumption, always conveyed in unexceptionable language, that, having heard the American point of view presented clearly and forcibly, no foreign Minister of intelligence and probity could fail to acknowledge its justice.

It was quite natural that Great Britain, with her far-flung empire, her supremacy on the seas and her commercial and political interests in the Western Hemisphere, should offer the most serious challenge to Blaine's ambitions for American prestige. We have already seen how, as the representative in Congress of a State vitally interested in the shipbuilding and fishing industries, he had fought against the relinquishment of "the scepter of the ocean" to England. He never was reconciled to the injustice of the Halifax award of 1877, and he resented the continued infraction by Canadian fishermen of the shore rights guaranteed to the Americans by the Washington treaty of 1871. Even after the tardy settlement by Great Britain of claims for depredations committed against our fishermen in Fortune Bay in 1878, the outrages did not cease. "In one case," wrote Blaine to James Russell Lowell, our Minister to London, on August 19, 1881, "a large and angry mob of these Newfoundland fishermen took possession of an American fishing vessel, cut her anchor and set her sails for the avowed purpose of causing her to drift on the rocks. And the universal testimony of our fishermen is that they are absolutely forbidden both by the show and use of force from taking bait on the coasts of Newfoundland. . . . If at any time fishing vessels of the United States should resolve to meet force with force, it would raise an issue equally unpleasant to both governments."

Our Senate passed an indignant resolution in 1879 urging that measures be taken to "remedy the intolerable situation," but satisfactory negotiation on the vexed subject was hampered by the fact that we had to deal with the chancellery at London, while the provincial authorities of Canada and Newfoundland, relieved from direct diplomatic responsibility because they had no foreign office, seemed to feel free to disregard the imperial instructions. Nor was there a sufficient police force at the Canadian fishing stations to protect the Americans in their treaty rights. Several clauses of the Treaty of Washington were subject to a twelve year limit on notice by either party. Thoroughly dissatisfied with both their terms and their operation, Blaine was eagerly looking forward to the time when they could be supplanted by a more equitable agreement. He had written to Garfield in December, 1880, a week before his acceptance of the portfolio of State: "The concessions and guarantees contained in XVIII to XXV and in articles XXVIII, XXIX and XXX have a ten year limit for notice and two years after notice. This throws the whole subject open for fresh and I hope more lasting adjustment during your 'first term' . . . and gives a splendid opportunity to achieve some things of which we have already spoken. . . . Can't you quietly drop a note to Hayes suggesting that the whole question of a readjustment of Canadian matters should be left without embarrassment to your Administration?" [1] In the dispatch of August 19, 1881, to Lowell, just quoted, Blaine notes with satisfaction that "the time is approaching when the present treaty provisions will expire." But already his "splendid opportunity" for a settlement of the Canadian questions was blasted. President Garfield was on his deathbed, and in another four months Blaine was to be out of public life for the first time in twenty-three years.

The tragedy of Garfield's assassination frustrated other diplomatic negotiations undertaken by Secretary Blaine, and in some important instances resulted in the reversal of his policies at the hands of his successor. One such instance was his attempt to secure Great Britain's consent to a modification of the Clayton-Bulwer Treaty of 1850, which provided for a joint Anglo-American guarantee of the neutrality of a Nicaraguan canal. As in the case of the fisheries dispute, Blaine did not originate the discussion. Since the French had secured a concession from the Republic of Colombia in 1878 to build a canal across the Isthmus of Panama (a province of Colombia), and Ferdinand de Lesseps, the builder of the Suez Canal, had organized a company for the construction of the Panama Canal, public opinion in the United States had been growing keener on the subject. A special committee of the House had been appointed in December, 1879, to investigate the possibility of building an American canal. President Hayes, in a special message of March 8, 1880, had declared that an isthmian canal would be "virtually a part of the coast-line of the United States" and must therefore be under American control.[2] And the next month the House resolved that the President be authorized to "take immediate steps for the formal and final abrogation" of the Clayton-Bulwer Treaty. Again, less than three weeks before Blaine took office, both Houses of Congress protested against a canal built by foreign capital or controlled by foreign regulations, and on March 2, 1881, the special committee of the House appointed in 1879 reported, urging "prompt and energetic action to protect the interests of this country." [3]

Blaine's action was both prompt and energetic. Disturbed by rumors that several European countries were to be invited by Colombia to share in the guarantee of an isthmian canal, he dispatched a strong

[1] Quoted in Alice Felt Tyler, *The Foreign Policy of James G. Blaine*, pp. 19–20.
[2] J. D. Richardson, *Messages and Papers of the Presidents*, Vol. VIII, p. 585.
[3] *House Document No. 390*, 46th Cong., 3d sess.

note to Lowell on June 24, 1881, with copies to our Ministers to the foreign countries concerned. While the Clayton-Bulwer Treaty was not mentioned in this note, Blaine's dissatisfaction with it was clearly manifested. He dwelt on our treaty of 1846 with Colombia (then called New Granada), pledging the United States to protect the transit by railroad or canal across the isthmus and to defend the sovereignty of Colombia over the province of Panama. He insisted that the United States were both competent and determined to remain the sole guarantors of the canal, and that "any attempt to supersede that guarantee by an agreement between European powers which maintain strong armies and patrol the sea with large fleets, and whose interest in the canal and its operation can never be so supreme and vital as ours, would partake of the nature of an alliance against the United States and would be regarded by this Government as an indication of unfriendly feeling." [1] He based his argument on the "paramount interest" of the United States, an interpretation of the Monroe Doctrine already put forward by our expansionists of the mid-century, like Douglas, Clay and Polk; and he instructed the Ministers to whom the note was sent to communicate it to the governments to which they were accredited as "nothing more than the pronounced adherence of the United States to principles long since enunciated by the highest authority of the government." [1]

The Continental powers either ignored the note or expressed their lack of interest in its contents. Earl Granville, the British Foreign Secretary, waited nearly five months before replying (Nov. 10), and then dismissed the note with the curt observation that the question of the guarantee of a canal "had already been settled by the engagements of the Clayton-Bulwer Treaty and that Her Majesty's Government relied with confidence upon the observation of all the obligations of that treaty."

Before his lordship's complacent admonition reached Washington, Blaine had sent a second note to Lowell (Nov. 19) setting forth a number of reasons why the Clayton-Bulwer Treaty should be "essentially modified." It had been negotiated over thirty years before, under exceptional circumstances, which had long ceased to exist. It

---

[1] The entire "Correspondence Relating to the Interoceanic Canal" from 1840 to the close of the century may be found in *Senate Documents, Nos. 161* and *237* (Serial number 3853), 56th Congress, 1st session. The apposite extracts are in *Foreign Relations for 1881*, and Blaine's three notes to Lowell are reprinted in his *Political Discussions*, pp. 311–335.

was "a menace to the fulfilment of the new duties and responsibilities which the rapid development of the States of the Pacific coast had enjoined upon the American Government." Moreover, by putting an isthmian canal virtually at the mercy of a British or a French fleet, while the United States were prohibited from using any military force force for its protection, the treaty offended the spirit of the Monroe Doctrine, and "impeached our rightful and long-established claims to priority on the American continent." The British government must in all fairness see that, just as it controls the inner route to India and forces an enemy to strike at its Eastern possessions only by doubling the Cape of Good Hope, so the United States should be allowed to make a potential European enemy sail around Cape Horn in order to reach our Pacific coast. Again, it was most fitting that the United States should have the political and military control of the canal, since we were the great power most likely to be at peace. Only in a single instance in a hundred years had the United States exchanged a hostile shot with any European power, and it was in the highest degree improbable that for a hundred years to come that experience would be repeated (!).

In view of these facts and of the readiness of the United States to build the canal now without the aid of British capital, it seemed just to ask for certain changes in the treaty, the most important of which were the permission to the United States of fortifying the canal, of acquiring the military and naval stations necessary to its protection and of closing it to belligerent vessels in time of war. The United States would seek "no exclusive or narrow commercial advantage" from the canal, but would declare by public proclamation that "the same tolls and obligations for the use of the canal shall apply with absolute impartiality to the merchant marine of every nation on the globe." Blaine expressed the President's earnest hope that the modifications of the treaty suggested would be conceded by Her Majesty's Government in the same friendly spirit in which they were asked, and that in them would be found "additional evidence of the desire of this Government to remove all possible grounds of controversy between the two nations, which have so many interests in common and so many reasons for honorable and lasting peace." Mr. Lowell was instructed to furnish Lord Granville a copy of this note if he requested it.

After receiving Lord Granville's note of November 10 pointing to the finality of the Clayton-Bulwer Treaty, Blaine sent a third dispatch

to Lowell (Nov. 29), in which he reviewed at length the misunderstand-
ings and vexations to which the treaty had given rise in the first decade
of its existence, and declared that the present proposal of our government was to "free it from those embarrassments and leave it, as its
framers intended it should be, a full and perfect settlement for all time
of all possible issues between the United States and Great Britain with
regard to Central America."

Blaine's isthmian policy is often cited as an outstanding example of
his "jingoistic" diplomacy. It is true that some of his contentions were
better calculated to stimulate the patriotic pride of his fellow Americans than to satisfy the impartial judgment of the historian. For example, the appeal to the Monroe Doctrine (always a sure way to rouse
popular support) was hardly justified: for a multilateral guarantee of
an isthmian canal was neither a project of European colonization in the
Western Hemisphere nor a threat to the republican systems of government there. The language too of an agreement of the nations to guarantee the neutrality of the canal as "partaking of the nature of an alliance against the United States" was provocative, and was resented by
the London press. That is just what the nations had done, by the Treaty
of Constantinople, in regard to the Suez Canal—so that Blaine's illus-
tration of Great Britain's exclusive control of the route to India broke
down. But in spite of these flaws, Blaine's notes were diplomatically
correct. They did not go beyond the proposal to secure Great Britain's
free consent to the modification of the Clayton-Bulwer Treaty. They
contained no threat of reprisals or of a unilateral annulment of the
treaty. They were more moderate than the House resolution which
called upon the President to "take immediate steps for the formal and
final abrogation of the convention of 1850." George William Curtis,
who was anything but an admirer of Blaine, characterized the note of
June 24, in *Harper's Weekly*, as "a temperate and dignified document,
stating our position with blended spirit, courtesy and decision. . . .
He has what may be called the American instinct, an essential quality
in our Foreign Secretary, yet restrained in its expression by an equally
American tact and good sense." Which was high praise from Mr. Curtis.

When Lord Granville's notes of January 7 and 14, 1882, reiterating
his government's stand on the finality of the treaty, reached Washington, Blaine had already been out of office for more than a month. His
successor, Frederick T. Frelinghuysen, carried on the correspondence

in a desultory fashion for nearly two years; but in the end gave up the contention for the modification of the treaty.[1] It remained in force until 1901, when it was replaced by the Hay-Pauncefote treaty, which secured for the United States the very privileges and advantages in an isthmian canal for which Blaine had contended twenty years before. Much that was "jingoism" in 1881 had become "manifest destiny" by the close of the century.

Another subject of diplomatic correspondence with Great Britain, of less intrinsic importance than the canal, but with a far greater repercussion on American politics was the imprisonment of certain Irishmen who claimed American citizenship, on the suspicion of stirring sedition against the British government. Ever since the Act of Union of 1801 had put an end to the legislature at Dublin and brought the Irish peers and commoners into the Parliament at Westminster, there had been agitation for the restoration of home rule for Ireland. Under the leadership of the great Daniel O'Connell, the movement had been peaceable and law-abiding. But O'Connell's eloquent appeals for Irish freedom in a series of monster mass meetings conjured up a spirit of revolt which he could not lay, and with his passing in 1847 the control fell into the hands of the Young Ireland leaders, who advocated the violent measures which culminated in the Phoenix Park murders in the spring of 1882. Parliament had attempted to crush the spirit of Irish revolt, which had vexed the English government for six centuries, under Plantagenets, Tudors, Stuarts and Hanoverians, by a series of coercive acts. The most severe of these measures, entitled "An Act for the Better Protection of Persons and Property in Ireland," was passed on March 2, 1881, two days before Blaine became Secretary of State. It gave the Lord Lieutenant of Ireland power to arrest and imprison, without jury trial or bail, any person declared in the warrant to be "reasonably suspected" of inciting to violence or intimidation.

Early in March, Michael P. Boynton was arrested under the Protection Act and thrown into Kilmainham jail. He appealed to Minister Lowell for redress, claiming American citizenship on the ground both

---

[1] Instead of pursuing Blaine's policy of an amicable arrangement with Great Britain, Frelinghuysen went over Granville's head and negotiated a treaty directly with Nicaragua, giving the United States the exclusive right to build and control a canal across that country. The Frelinghuysen-Zavala treaty was sent to the Senate in December, 1884, but when Cleveland came into the Presidency the next year, he very properly withdrew it as "a contravention of our existing obligations." J. D. Richardson, *Messages and Papers of the Presidents*, Vol. VIII, p. 327.

of his father's naturalization and of his own service in the United States Navy during the Civil War. He also had received a passport signed by Secretary Seward in 1866. After a careful examination of the case, Mr. Lowell was not satisfied with the evidences of Boynton's American citizenship and consequently refused to press for his release; and Blaine approved our Minister's course. However, the case of Joseph B. Walsh, who was arrested at about the same time as Boynton, was clearly one which called for American intervention. Walsh had been duly admitted to citizenship by the Superior Court of New York City on October 16, 1875; and in calling the attention of Lord Granville to that fact Lowell wrote that while the President was "anxious not to embarrass in any way the action of a friendly government in dealing with a very difficult and delicate question of domestic policy," he could not but "feel solicitous not to ignore any just claim of American citizens to his intervention in their behalf." Granville insisted in his reply of June 28, 1881, that his government could not recognize a distinction between British and foreign subjects "in respect to unlawful acts committed within the limits of the British Empire," and that the law had been impartially applied to all suspects. Nevertheless, the order for Walsh's release was given in October, ostensibly on the ground of his illness, but perhaps not without the influence upon Lord Granville of a number of articles on the Irish question from American newspapers, sent to him by Lowell at his own request.

In the midst of the excitement raised by the press in some urban centers where the Irish element was strong, Blaine maintained a judicious attitude toward the coercive policy of the British government. He disavowed any claim "that the fact of American citizenship could of itself operate to exempt anyone from the penalties of a law which he had violated." Our government would not attempt to shield its citizens within British jurisdiction from the legal consequences of their acts. But at the same time he insisted that we could never consent to see American citizens deprived of "the common principles of criminal jurisprudence" which constituted the safeguard to personal liberty. He therefore instructed Mr. Lowell in the Walsh case to "make such temperate but earnest representations" to Lord Granville as would, in his judgment, "conduce to his speedy trial, or, in case there is no specific charge against him, his prompt release from imprisonment." [1]

---

[1] Blaine to Lowell, June 26, July 2, 1881. *United States Foreign Relations*, 1881, pp. 530–532.

In spite of this very proper procedure, Blaine was savagely attacked for his "criminal neglect to protect American citizens against English despotism." The New York *Irish World* of December 10, 1881, contained the following screed: "Broken in health and threatened with blindness, Mr. Boynton has at length been released from Kilmainham. He passes from the prison to the hospital, there perhaps to end his life, the latest victim of British tyranny. There is no more shameful chapter in the history of our international relations than the one which records how this Union soldier has been allowed to pine away in his prison cell week after week without the government for which he risked his life interfering to secure for him even so much as a trial by jury. The Boynton case will ever remain a blot on our history. The man who has been guilty of allowing this Union soldier to be imprisoned without trial in a foreign country on a vague suspicion ought to be driven from public life. In his flunkeyism to the English government, James G. Blaine . . . has no conception of what is due to the honor of the United States, and should never again be placed in a position where he can disgrace our government."

The question descended into an issue of party politics. The cases of Boynton, Walsh and McSweeney were exploited by the Democrats in an effort to detach from Blaine's support the large number of Irish-Americans who were drawn to him by his own Irish descent, his Catholic relatives, and his general defense of American interests against the political and commercial rivalry of England. But in the end Blaine's Irish policy in 1881 gained rather than lost friends for him. When the excitement died down, thinking men recognized the justice of his course and agreed with Mr. Lowell that it was a misconception of the privileges of naturalization for those who came to our shores from the Emerald Isle to regard themselves "as Irishmen who have acquired the right to American protection rather than as Americans who have renounced a claim to Irish nationality." [1] Even the *Irish World* supported Blaine in the campaign of 1884.

Seventeen years before the United States annexed the Hawaiian Islands, Blaine, who would have welcomed that event in his day,[2] helped to pave the way for its consummation by his insistence on retaining the islands as a "part of the American system." Here again he

---

[1] Lowell to Frelinghuysen, March 14, 1882. *United States Foreign Relations,* 1882, p. 206.
[2] Edward Stanwood, *James G. Blaine,* pp. 301, 359.

came into controversy with Great Britain. We had negotiated a reciprocity treaty with King Kalakaua in 1875 which, in addition to providing for virtual free trade between the islands and the United States,
had pledged the Hawaiian government not to lease or otherwise dispose
of any territory to a foreign power, or to grant to any other nation the
commercial privileges guaranteed to the United States. The British
government protested that the latter provision violated the "most favored nation" clause of its treaty of 1852 with Hawaii; and furthermore, the British commissioner in the islands, while warning the
Hawaiians against the imperialistic designs of the United States, was
trying to secure the right to import into the islands coolie labor from
the British colonies in the Far East and to exercise a kind of political
protectorate over these immigrants. In notes to Lowell dated April 23
and December 10, 1881, and to J. M. Comley, our minister to Hawaii,
dated June 30, November 19, and December 1, 1881, Blaine set forth
his Hawaiian policy.[1] The islands, he said, were the "key to the maritime dominion of the Pacific States," and closely related to our productive and commercial system. The reciprocity treaty of 1875 made them
"practically members of an American Zollverein in an outlying district
of the State of California." Ministers Lowell and Comley were to make
it clear in London and Honolulu that the islands were not a field for
economic exploitation or political penetration by any nation of the
world—except the United States. If the Hawaiian government itself
should find it impracticable to maintain an independent position of
neutrality, then "this government would unhesitatingly meet the situation by seeking an avowedly American solution for the grave issues
presented." Such language, of course, meant annexation or, at least,
an undisguised American protectorate. Blaine's Hawaiian correspondence was vitiated by special pleading and by arguments based upon
American pride of prestige rather than upon strict regard for international law. He dismissed the "most favored nation" clause of the
British-Hawaiian treaty of 1852, which conflicted with our reciprocity
treaty of 1875, as cavalierly as he had pressed for the abrogation of
certain sections of the Clayton-Bulwer Treaty. Furthermore, the Monroe Doctrine had no application to a group of islands in the mid-Pacific.
Exitus probat acta. As in the case of the Isthmian canal, the country

[1] This correspondence is to be found in a volume on *United States Foreign Relations,*
1894, which deals exclusively with our diplomatic relations with the Hawaiian Islands.

came in a score of years to set the seal of its approval on Blaine's Hawaiian policy.

In the midst of his altercation with England it must have been a gratification to Blaine to be able to show that country a courtesy which cost him no diplomatic concessions, but elicited from the Queen's government an expression of lively appreciation. The centennial anniversary of Cornwallis' surrender at Yorktown occurred in October, 1881. The arrangements for welcoming the guests of honor, among whom were descendants of Von Steuben, Lafayette, and ten of the French military and naval officers who had served in the American Revolution, were entrusted to Robert R. Hitt, the First Assistant Secretary of State, and Walker Blaine, whose commission as Third Assistant Secretary was the last document to be signed by President Garfield (July 1, 1881). Blaine's accomplished son won high plaudits for his graceful speech of welcome to the French delegation at the banquet given to them by Governor Cornell at the Fifth Avenue Hotel in New York on the evening of October 5, and for his personal conduct of the Von Steuben party on their visits to New York, Washington, Richmond, Chicago, St. Louis and Boston. The celebration at Yorktown filled the week of October 13–21 with speeches, dinners, regattas, balls, fireworks, and military and naval reviews. President Arthur's speech at the laying of the cornerstone of the Yorktown monument on October 19, the day of Cornwallis' surrender, sounded the note of friendship and good-will toward Great Britain. "No such unworthy sentiment as exultation or rancor," said the President, "could find harbor in our hearts, so profoundly thrilled with the expressions of sorrow and sympathy which our national bereavement has evoked." For during the long period of Garfield's agony, which had ended just a month before the celebration at Yorktown, the people of England, from Queen Victoria down, had hung with interest on every bulletin of the President's condition, and at the end the Queen had written a widow's message of sympathy to the newly-made widow.

The great multitude at Yorktown, therefore, greeted with enthusiasm the following executive order read by the Secretary of State: "In recognition of the friendly relations so long and so happily existing between Great Britain and the United States; in the trust and confidence of peace and good-will between the two. countries for all the centuries to come; and especially as a mark of the profound respect entertained by the American people for the illustrious sovereign and gracious lady who sits upon the British throne—it is hereby ordered that at the close of the ceremonies commemorative of the valor and success of our forefathers in their patriotic struggle for Independence, the British flag shall be saluted by the forces of the Army and Navy of the United States now at Yorktown." This order, with its equally courteous note of transmission from Secretary Blaine, was received with deep appreciation by the British government. "For one hundred years," wrote Earl Granville to Mr. Lowell from Walmer Castle, on October 25, "the relations of the two countries which have so much to connect them have never been so cordial and so friendly. May they long continue to be so."

The dearest ambition of Secretary Blaine was to draw the republics of Latin-America into a voluntary recognition of a sort of benevolent protectorate on the part of the great republic of the North. The Monroe Doctrine prohibited the invasion of their territory for European colonial enterprises and the subversion of their republican systems of government. But beyond these negative and defensive aims it did not go. The cultural and commercial ties of the Latin-American countries with Europe were much stronger than those with the United States, and naturally these intimate relations had their influence upon the political currents in Latin-America. Blaine's persistent efforts in Congress to build up a direct line of steamship communication between New York and Rio de Janeiro envisaged a wider policy than the mere improvement of our trade with the South American republics. That was to be but the entering wedge for the penetration of American influence in those countries, to wean them from their traditional orientation toward Europe.

When Blaine came into the State Department, with the opportunity to supplement his congressional pleas by direct diplomatic action, he immediately set to work to extend the good offices and strengthen the prestige of the United States in the countries south of the Rio Grande. Indeed, one might gather from his own words that this was not only his chief concern but his only concern as Secretary of State; for in an article on "The Foreign Policy of the Garfield Administration," published in the Chicago *Weekly Magazine* of September 16, 1881, he dealt only with Latin-American affairs. The objects of the policy, he said, were: "First, to bring about peace and prevent futile wars in North and South America; second, to cultivate such friendly commercial ties with all American countries as would lead to a large increase in the export trade of the United States, by supplying those fabrics in which we are abundantly able to compete with the manufacturing nations of Europe." To attain the second object was Blaine's chief aim. He was an early advocate of what came to be known as the "dollar diplomacy" of Secretary Knox in the Taft Administration: namely, the utilization of our foreign agencies for the increase of American commercial and financial prestige. But in order to accomplish this in Latin-America, it was necessary first to discourage the "resort to arms" which in no part of the world was "so prompt as in the Spanish-American Republics," and to establish the peace which was "essential to commerce, the very life of trade and the solid basis of international prosperity." [1]

When Blaine came into office there were several situations in Latin-America which offered opportunities for more vigorous action on the part of our State Department. Boundary disputes (a perennial source of discord among the Latin republics, because of the indeterminate limits of the old provinces and viceroyalties under the former Spanish rule) were threatening war between Argentina and Chili, Costa Rica and Colombia, Mexico and Guatemala. President Barrios of the latter country was attempting to bring the five republics of Central America into a political union under his domination. European creditors were pressing Venezuela for the payment of various loans and claims incurred during a half century past. And the War of the Pacific, started by Chili against Bolivia and Peru in 1879, for the control of the nitrate beds in Bolivian territory, was still in progress. Most of these questions had received diplomatic attention by Blaine's predecessor, William M. Evarts. He had encouraged our ministers to Chili and the Argentine to use their good offices to avert a war between those countries by the proposal of a compromise boundary line; he had sent Mr. C. A. Logan as a special minister to the Central-American republics to promise our support of any plan to put an end to the interminable quarrels between them; he had agreed, after a correspondence of two years on the subject with our Minister at Caracas, to have an American agent receive and disburse the amounts due from Venezuela to her foreign creditors, if they would approve the arrangement; and he had extended his good offices in the War of the Pacific to the point of inviting representatives from the belligerent countries to meet with our Ministers, Osborn (Chili), Christiancy (Peru) and Adams (Bolivia) on board the United

[1] James G. Blaine, *Political Discussions, Legislative, Diplomatic and Popular*, p. 411.

States vessel *Lackawanna* in Arica harbor, in October 1880, to discuss, vainly as it proved, the possibility of American mediation.

The charge by Blaine's enemies, assiduously spread for political reasons, that he plunged recklessly into Latin-American affairs, like a bull in a china shop, creating discord among the republics south of the Rio Grande and exposing the United States to the danger of war, to say nothing of his attempting to "put the nitrate beds of Peru in his own pocket," is not supported by the facts. Both the substance and the tone of his correspondence with our representatives in Latin-America were in essential agreement with the policy of Mr. Evarts, though his activity was more pronounced and his hope of bringing about the harmony necessary for the expansion of our trade with Central and South America were more lively than his predecessor's. While approving a Central-American union, as Evarts had done, and, in fact, as our government has always done,[1] Blaine refused to abet the plans of the Guatemalan President to force a union under his own dictatorship. At the same time he pressed upon Minister Morgan the idea that Mexico should accept the good offices of the United States to deter her from absorbing the weaker republic of Guatemala, declaring that such an act would not be "in harmony with the friendly relations existing between us and Mexico, but injurious to the best interests of all the republics on this continent."[2] The Mexican publicist Matias Romero, at one time Minister at Washington, justified Mexico's refusal to arbitrate the dispute, on the ground of Blaine's partiality for Guatemala, but admitted that Blaine's "serious mistake" was due to his "very earnest desire to have arbitration take the place of war to end international disputes."[3] Blaine had shown no partiality to Guatemala, however, and had even become convinced that she must relinquish her claim to the territory in dispute —as she did in the final settlement of the case in 1883. If his language to Mexico was somewhat peremptory, it was because peace or war hung

[1] A partial realization of this plan came in the Administration of Theodore Roosevelt, when a Central-American Court of Justice was established at Cartago, Costa Rica, on May 25, 1908, with jurisdiction over all cases in dispute between the five republics, and an international bureau was opened to promote their common interests in trade, industry, agriculture, education, and legal reform. But this promising experiment lasted only a decade. The court was wrecked in 1918 by the refusal of Nicaragua (backed by the United States) to accept its decision condemning the Bryan-Chamorro Treaty of 1916. Secretary Hughes made an abortive attempt to revive the Central-American union in 1921.

[2] Blaine to Morgan, November 28, 1881. *United States Foreign Relations*, 1881, p. 816.
[3] American Geographical Society, *Journal*, Vol. XXIX, p. 308.

on the decision of that country. Morgan had informed him that Mexican troops had been sent to the border and that the Mexican President had sent a belligerent message to his Congress. Blaine was not willing to see the Guatemalan republic crushed by its northern neighbor and perhaps the independence of all Central America threatened, without protest from the United States. And the best testimony to the wisdom of that protest is the resentment which it aroused in the Mexican government.

Something more than a general concern for the preservation of peace in Latin-America, as the condition for the expansion of our commerce, prompted Blaine's intervention in the boundary dispute between Colombia and Costa Rica. There the question of American treaty rights was involved. The two countries had agreed in December, 1880, to resort to arbitration, designating the King of Belgium, the King of Spain and the President of the Argentine Republic as the order of their choice of arbitrators. Before this arrangement had been ratified by the Colombian Congress, Blaine came into office, and on May 26, 1881, he notified both Minister Dickman at Bogotá and Minister Logan in Central America of the objections of our government. He approved the principle of arbitration and dismissed the obvious slight to this country, in not being invited to act in the matter, with the remark that "the United States of America does not expect or claim the position of necessary arbitrator in differences between these two republics." Nevertheless, he added in his note to Dickman, "it cannot but seem strange that Colombia has not communicated to this government its intention to submit to arbitration the boundaries of the state of Panama, the territorial integrity of which the United States of America have guaranteed by a treaty the provisions of which they have been more than once called upon to execute." Our opinion should have been consulted, he contended, both as to the nature of the arbitration and the choice of the arbiters; and he warned both the countries that the United States would not "hold itself bound, where its rights, obligations or interests may be concerned, by the decision of any arbitrator in whose appointment it has not been consulted and in whose selection it has not concurred." [1]

Moreover, Blaine moved effectively to block any interference by the European powers in the dispute. He instructed our Ministers at Brussels

---

[1] Blaine to Dickman and Logan, May 31, 1881. *United States Foreign Relations,* 1881, pp. 106, 356.

and Madrid to notify the governments of Belgium and Spain, in case
their sovereigns should be asked to act as arbitrators, that we would
not consent to be bound by their decision.[1] As in the case of his identic
note of June 24, 1881, to Lowell and other American Ministers at European courts, he based his *non possumus* upon the Treaty of 1846 with
Colombia, which gave the United States the right and duty to protect
the sovereignty of Colombia over the province of Panama and to guarantee the neutrality of transit by rail or canal across the isthmus. Costa
Rica resented Blaine's action as an "insult," declaring that she had not
only not been a party to the Treaty of 1846 but had not even been notified of it, and contending that the United States, on account of its obvious interest in the region under dispute, would not be a proper or impartial arbitrator. Colombia, too, though less vehement in protest, was
no better satisfied with Blaine's course. That republic was, as we have
already seen,[2] only too ready to be rid of the obligations of the Treaty
of 1846. Fearing that the protection offered by the United States was
turning into tutelage and dictation, she had herself proposed admitting
European powers to a share in the guarantee of the isthmus. Blaine's
insistence, therefore, upon our privileges under the Treaty of 1846
brought anything but improvement in our relations with both Colombia
and Costa Rica. But he was willing to pay the price of their temporary
resentment in order to secure the main object of his intervention:
namely, the prevention of European arbitrators, selected without reference to the United States, from deciding a Latin-American controversy in which, to use a phrase made familiar in resent days, "the
United States has or claims an interest."

The third boundary dispute, that between Chili and the Argentine,
was well on its way to settlement before Blaine came into office. He
furthered the negotiations begun by Evarts, however, instructing our
Minister to the Argentine of our readiness to act as an impartial arbitrator if asked to do so. The two republics adjusted their boundary line
without calling in outside aid, and Blaine was the recipient of a cordial
letter from the Argentine Minister in Washington, expressing the
"grateful sentiments" which his country entertained "toward this great
republic and its worthy representatives who have just furnished evidence of the feeling of genuine friendship which is cherished by the

[1] Blaine to Putnam, May 31, and to Fairchild, June 25, 1881. *Ibid.*, pp. 70, 1057.
[2] See above, p. 197.

United States for the South American republics." [1]

It was Blaine's diplomacy in the War of the Pacific, however, which brought down upon his head not only the severest criticism of "meddling and muddling" in Latin-America, but also the accusations of personal corruption. Let us review the situation briefly. Chili held the trump cards. Her arms had been steadily victorious. The coveted guano and nitrate beds were in her hands, and, in the opinion of our Minister, Mr. Osborn, she intended to keep them. She had been ready in the summer of 1880 to accept the proffered mediation of England, France and Italy, on the basis of the transfer of the province of Tarapaca to her; but Bolivia and Peru looked rather to our government, which was known to be opposed to the cession of any territory as a *sine qua non* of peace negotiations. The attempted mediation of the United States at the meeting on board the *Lackawanna* in Arica harbor had been a failure. Just as Blaine came into office the situation was complicated by a revolution in Peru, which drove President Piérola from his capital to the mountains, where he still maintained a guerilla government.

With utter anarchy impending in Peru, Chili consented to the establishment of a provisional government under Dr. Calderón, a prominent lawyer of Lima; and Blaine, seeing in the new government an instrument with which Chili might deal for the arrangement of terms of peace, and the withdrawal of her troops from the soil of Peru, instructed our Minister at Lima, Isaac P. Christiancy, to recognize Calderón (April 9, 1881). The following September Admiral Lynch, the Chilean commander occupying Lima, suspecting that Calderón was intriguing with the United States, dissolved the new government and sent Calderón as a prisoner to Chili. Anarchy and civil war again threatened in Peru. Calderón's Vice President, Montero, now took to the mountains of the interior and replaced Piérola as the leader of the patriots, determined not to surrender an inch of their territory. It was not until the autumn of 1883 that the Monterists were subdued and the Treaty of Ancón was concluded, by which the province of Tarapaca was ceded outright to Chili, and Tacna and Arica were to be held by Chili for ten years, after which a plebiscite was to be taken in those provinces to determine to which country they should permanently belong. [2]

[1] Carrié to Blaine, June 28, 1881. *United States Foreign Relations,* 1881. p. 15.
[2] The Tacna-Arica question vexed South American politics for nearly fifty years. After the World War the United States again intervened, and in the Harding and Coolidge Administrations Generals John J. Pershing and William Lassiter endeavored vainly

Blaine's every step in the negotiations to clear up the mess of the War of the Pacific was dogged by misfortune. This was due, doubtless, in part to his own lack of patience in dealing with peoples with whose peculiar temperament he had little sympathy. The pride and punctilio of the Latin mind irked him. His nervous vigor would have swept away the web of obstruction woven by the factious and dilatory diplomacy of the belligerents. He could not see why Chileans and Peruvians should not hasten to accept as beneficial to them what he assured them was beneficial. But that Blaine's misfortune was not due wholly to his own ineptitude, as his critics charged,[1] is shown by the similar failure of both his predecessor and his successor in the State Department to bring order out of chaos on the western coast of South America. The crux of the matter was that victorious Chili wanted no intervention, mediation or arbitration by the United States. Her commercial and financial interests bound her closely to England. Indeed, Blaine asserted in 1882 before a congressional committee on the investigation of his negotiations with the belligerent powers that the War of the Pacific was "an English war on Peru with Chili as the instrument." If this statement was an exaggeration, there was enough truth in it to make any attempt to arrive at a fair settlement look like undue partisanship for Peru.

Moreover, Blaine was unfortunate in his choice of Ministers. He replaced Osborn and Christiancy, who were continually at loggerheads with each other, by two envoys whose only claim to office seems to have been their services as generals in the Civil War. General Judson Kilpatrick was sent to Chili and General Stephen A. Hurlburt to Peru. On both Blaine urged moderation and impartiality. He hoped that Chili would consent to treat on the basis of a war indemnity instead of the cession of territory from Peru, and that Peru would accept "any reasonable conditions and limitations" in order to hasten the peace. But Kilpatrick and Hurlburt proved to be even less satisfactory envoys than their predecessors. They became violent partisans, quarreled with each other, and each accused the other of incompetence and insubordination.

---

to arrange for the long-delayed plebiscite. It was never taken. In February, 1929, Chili and Peru finally came to terms by the allotment of Arica to the former and Tacna to the latter country.

[1] See especially Wm. H. Hurlburt's *Meddling and Muddling: Mr. Blaine's Foreign Policy* and W. H. Hall's *Mr. Blaine and His Foreign Policy,* published in a series of campaign pamphlets in 1884, which, with the hostile attacks in the New York *Nation* of December 15, 1881, and February 2 and 5 and August 13, 1882, constitute the severest criticism of Blaine's policy.

Kilpatrick, married to the niece of a Chilean prelate, fell completely under the influence of the "court society" at Santiago, and spent the last days of his life (he died before the year was out) as an advocate for Chili rather than as a Minister of the United States. While Hurlburt's indiscretions in communicating directly with the Chilean Admiral Lynch and the fugitive Piérola to the effect that the United States would intervene if necessary to support the Calderón government, and in negotiating with Peru for the cession of a coaling station and a railroad running from the coal mines to the coast, to be turned over later to American capitalists, drew from Blaine a scathing rebuke that he should have so far "violated every rule of prudence and propriety that should govern the conduct of a representative of this country." [1] Blaine finally decided to replace both Ministers by a special envoy, who was instructed to eschew all partisanship.

The man chosen for this important mission was William H. Trescot of South Carolina, one of the most accomplished diplomats in our history. He had been secretary of our legation at London before the Civil War, and at the close of the war had been sent to Washington to defend the interests of his State in questions arising under the Reconstruction Acts. He had served as counsel for the United States on the Commission of 1877 which determined the Halifax fisheries award, and had been one of the three envoys sent by President Hayes to China in the spring of 1880, to revise the immigration treaty. In February, 1881, Secretary Evarts had chosen him to negotiate a protocol with Colombia in respect to our rights and obligations on the Isthmus of Panama. This experienced diplomat was accompanied by Walker Blaine. The new envoys were received with effusive hospitality. Walker wrote to his father from Callao, Peru, on Christmas day: "I really think that they look upon us as a sort of saviors, and Trescot says that it will be necessary to send a fleet to rescue us at the end of the mission, so little will the performance that we hope to succeed in correspond with Peruvian expectations." [2] From Santiago de Chili he wrote the next month of the enthusi-

---

[1] Blaine to Hurlburt, November 11, 1881. *Senate Executive Documents,* 47th Congress, 1st session, No. 79, p. 565. The Minister's brother, Wm. H. Hurlburt, says in *Meddling and Muddling* (p. 55): "My brother gave me distinctly to understand that he was going out to Peru commissioned to support the Calderón government, if he found it possible to bring about peace on the basis of a war indemnity for Chili. . . . He was instructed to support Peru against Chili, who relied on England." The author of *Meddling and Muddling* charges Blaine with mendacity and ingratitude, and with making a scapegoat of his brother.

[2] Gail Hamilton, *Biography of James G. Blaine,* p. 551.

asm of the people and the good augury of the conversations already held between Trescot and the Chilean Foreign Minister, Balmaceda. "It really would not do for me to say how great lions the members of the commission are. Peru was at our feet, and everyone in Chili is devotion itself. If we come out successfully, I expect to have a statue erected both in Lima and in Santiago at public expense. You have no idea how well Father is known down here . . . better than anybody, I think: nor have you any idea how they hate Hurlburt. But they say that they gave Kilpatrick the grandest funeral ever seen in Chili, the government paying every bill, at a cost of more than $10,000." [1]

But even before Trescot and Walker Blaine had landed in Peru, from the same *Lackawanna* on whose deck the futile conference of Arica had been held a year before, events in Washington had already decreed the failure of their mission, and made it certain that Lima and Santiago would be spared the expense of erecting statues to them. On December 19 Blaine turned the State Department over to Frederick T. Frelinghuysen of New Jersey, who proceeded forthwith to reverse his predecessor's Latin-American policy. He so modified the instructions to Trescot, in a note of January 9, 1882, as to estop him from making any representations to Chili regarding the cession of territory from Peru, or indeed from urging any terms of peace at all; and in the same note he withdrew the invitation issued by President Arthur, at Blaine's request, the previous November, for a Pan-American Congress to be held at Washington in the late autumn of 1882.[2]

To the latter subject we shall turn in a moment, noting here the effect of the change in Trescot's instructions. The unfortunate thing was that before these new instructions reached Trescot, and while he was still writing to Frelinghuysen of the progress of his negotiations with Balmaceda, the change of front at Washington had become known to the Chilean government. The United States Senate had called for the entire correspondence on the diplomacy of the War of the Pacific, and made public not only the quarrels of our Ministers in Bolivia, Peru and Chili with each other and with the State Department, but also the note of January 9. The Chilean Minister at Washington had promptly informed his government of the situation; and when Trescot sought an audience with Balmaceda for the purpose of presenting an invitation to the con-

[1] Gail Hamilton, *Biography of James G. Blaine,* p. 553. On Kilpatrick's death President Arthur made Walker acting minister to Chili.
[2] Frelinghuysen to Trescot, January 9, 1882. *United States Foreign Relations,* 1882, p. 57.

ference, he was informed by Balmaceda that not only was the invitation withdrawn but that his own new instructions were coming soon! Trescot's amazement and indignation at receiving the first knowledge of his diplomatic duty from the Foreign Minister of the country to which he was accredited was expressed in his dispatch to Frelinghuysen of February 3, 1882: "I could not suppose that such an instruction would be made public while I was endeavoring to secure, and not without some hope of success, the amicable solution of this delicate and difficult question. Still less could I believe that if my original instructions had been seriously modified, any communication of such change would have been made public, or even confidentially to the Chilean government, before I could possibly have received it. I could not admit what the Secretary (Balmaceda) clearly implied, that I did not represent the wishes or intentions of my government, and that he was better instructed than myself as to the progress of my mission." [1]

Balmaceda naturally refused to go on with the conversations on the terms of peace, and there was nothing left for Trescot to do but to resign his post and return to the United States. He made no public protest, but his feelings were probably in accord with the vehement criticism of our State Department contained in Walker Blaine's letters to his father. On February 4 he wrote: "Our position here is at the present moment most cruelly awkward. I expect nothing now but mortification to the country and to all of us personally as citizens of the country. . . . I don't believe that in my time the United States will ever get back influence worth considering with any one of these South American countries, and if the Department had stood firm we could, I honestly believe, have settled the question to the satisfaction of all and to our own advancement. . . . Of course, we can't move a foot just now." [2] And again, on April 9: "I cannot tell you how disgusted, mortified and humiliated I feel by the action of our government in Washington. It is disgraceful to our nation that men should be trusted with great office who will so misuse the power thus given them. . . . For the love of Heaven and my own self-respect, get me ordered home and let me resign!" [3]

Disappointing as the interruption of Trescot's mission was to Blaine,[4]

---

[1] *Senate Executive Documents,* 47th Cong., 1st sess., No. 181.
[2] Gail Hamilton, *Biography of James G. Blaine,* p. 554.
[3] *Ibid.,* p. 562.
[4] See his article in the *Washington Post* of March 23, 1882, on the revocation of his instructions to Trescot.

the revocation of the invitation to the Latin-American republics to send delegates to a conference at Washington was the severest blow to his diplomatic policies. The project did not originate with Blaine. As early as 1820 Henry Clay had advocated "a human freedom league in America," to embrace "all nations from Hudson's Bay to Cape Horn." [1] And a generation later, another great expansionist, Stephen A. Douglas, proposed "a general union for commercial purposes of all the various political communities on the American coast and the adjacent islands, from the frozen ocean to the Isthmus of Panama . . . without molesting or necessarily changing their political relations, national affinities and forms of government." [2] Meanwhile, various suggestions looking toward a league or union for the encouragement of peace, the furtherance of commerce and a common defense against possible European aggression, had come from the South American republics themselves. The most notable of these suggestions had resulted in Simon Bolivar's Congress of Panama, in the summer of 1826, at which Mexico, the Central-American states, Colombia and Peru were represented, and which drew up an abortive treaty of "union and perpetual confederation."

Owing to the caution of President John Quincy Adams and the dilatory action of our Congress, the envoys selected by Henry Clay to represent the United States failed to reach Panama in time to attend the Congress. The project of a Latin-American union was not abandoned, however. Again and again, from individual states or groups of states came the call for a congress; and in 1847 and 1856 such congresses, representing a half dozen or so of the republics, met at Lima and Santiago and adopted resolutions of union "as members of the great American family." In September, 1880, Colombia and Chili signed a treaty providing that in case they could not agree on an arbitrator in any dispute they would submit the question to the President of the United States; and the next month Colombia addressed a circular letter to all the South American republics, asking them to attend a congress at Panama the following September, to give their adherence to the Colombia-Chili convention of 1880. Fourteen nations accepted this invitation; but on account of the unexpected prolongation of the War of the Pacific the congress did not meet.

Blaine was therefore only following a policy long cherished on both

[1] H. Von Holst, *Constitutional and Political History of the United States,* Vol. I, p. 413.
[2] Stephen A. Douglas, "An American Commercial Union and Alliance," *Washington,* 1889, p. 36.

sides of the Rio Grande when he secured the consent of the Administration to issue an invitation on November 29, 1881, to all the Latin-American countries to meet at Washington on November 22, 1882, to "seek a way of permanently averting the horrors of cruel and bloody combat between countries oftenest of one blood and speech, or the even worse calamity of internal commotion and civil strife." "The President," Blaine continued, "is especially desirous to have it understood that, in putting forth this invitation, the United States does not assume the position of counseling or attempting, through the voice of the Congress, to counsel any determinate solution of existing questions which may now divide any of the countries of America. Such questions cannot properly come before the Congress. Its mission is higher. It is to provide for the interests of all in the future, not to settle individual differences of the present. For this reason the President has indicated a day for the assembling of the Congress so far in the future (a full year) as to have good ground for the hope that by the time named the situation in the South Pacific countries will be happily terminated. . . . It is far from the intention of this government to appear before the Congress as in any sense the protector of its neighbors or the predestined and necessary arbitrator of their disputes. The United States will enter the Congress on the same footing as the other powers represented, and with the loyal determination to approach any proposed solution, not merely in its own interest or with a view to asserting its own power, but as a single member among many coördinate and co-equal states." [1]

On January 7, President Blanco of Venezuela accepted the invitation, expressing his congratulations to our government for inaugurating a policy "so transcendental, elevating, far-seeing and practical," and adding, "the future of South America may be looked upon as assured under the safeguard of the great republic, which is at once our teacher and our model." Acceptances from Guatemala, Brazil, Salvador, Nicaragua, Honduras, Bolivia, Costa Rica, and Mexico followed in the next few weeks. Then further replies were shut off by the reversal of Blaine's policy at Washington. "The United States," wrote Frelinghuysen, "is at peace with all the nations of the world, and the President wishes hereafter (note that the invitation to the Congress had been sent more than six weeks before!) to determine whether it will conduce to that general peace for this government to enter into negotiations and consulta-

---

[1] *United States Foreign Relations,* 1881, pp. 13–15.

tions . . . with selected friendly nationalities (the Latin-American republics) without extending a like confidence to other people with whom
the United States is on equally friendly terms. . . . The principles
controlling the relations of the republics of this hemisphere with other
nationalities (the Monroe Doctrine) may on investigation be found to
be so well established that little would be gained at this time by reopening a subject which is not novel." [1]

This note, with its bland repudiation of the commitments which we
had already made, roused Blaine to write an open letter of remonstrance
to President Arthur on February 3, 1882. After reminding the President
of the cordiality with which he had endorsed the invitations of the
previous November, Blaine turned to Frelinghuysen's misgivings lest
we should offend other friendly powers by asking the Latin-American
nations to a Congress.

"This," he wrote, "is certainly a new position for the United States,
and one which I earnestly beg you will not allow this government to
assume. European powers assemble in Congress whenever an object
seems to them of sufficient gravity to justify it. I have never heard of
their consulting the government of the United States in regard to the
propriety of their so assembling, nor have I ever known of their inviting
an American representative to be present. . . . If (the proposed Congress) is now to be arrested for fear it may give offense in Europe, the
voluntary humiliation of the United States could not be more complete,
unless we should petition European governments for the privilege of
holding the Congress. . . . Nor can I see, Mr. President, how European governments should feel 'jealousy and ill-will' toward the United
States because of an effort on its part to assure lasting peace between
the nations of America, unless, indeed, it be the interest of the European
powers that the American nations should at intervals fall into war and
bring reproach on republican institutions." Though we were at peace
with all the world, as Mr. Frelinghuysen said, the American republics
were not at peace among themselves. "It was the existence or menace of
these wars," Blaine continued, "that influenced President Garfield and,
as I supposed, influenced yourself, to desire a friendly conference of
all the nations of America to devise means of permanent peace and consequent prosperity for all. . . . The invitation was not mine. It was
yours. I performed only the part of Secretary of State to advise and

[1] Freylinghuysen to Trescot, January 9, 1882. *Ibid.*, 1882, p. 57.

draft. You spoke in the name of the United States to each of the independent nations of America. To revoke that invitation for any cause would be embarrassing; to revoke it for avowed fear of 'jealousy and ill-will' on the part of European powers would appeal as little to American pride as to American hospitality. . . . I do not say, Mr. President, that the holding of a peace congress will necessarily change the currents of trade, but it will bring us into kindly relations with all the American nations. It will promote the reign of law and order. It will increase production and consumption. It will stimulate the demand for articles which American manufacturers can furnish with profit. It will, at all events, be a friendly and auspicious beginning in the direction of American influence and American trade in a large field which we have hitherto neglected and which has been practically monopolized by our commercial rivals in Europe." [1]

This temperate and cogent remonstrance (which the New York *Nation* of February 9 was pleased to call "a political manifesto, if not a declaration of war against the Administration") may have influenced President Arthur to send a special message to Congress on April 18, 1882, referring to the discretion of that body the question of proceeding with plans for the Pan-American assembly. The message reflected little credit upon the President's intellect or courage. "In giving this invitation," he said, "I was not aware (!) that there existed differences between several of the republics of South America which would militate against the happy results which otherwise might be expected from such an assemblage. . . . It was hoped that these differences (of which he was 'not aware') would disappear before the time fixed for the meeting of the Congress. This hope has not been realized." But the President neglected to say that less than two months of the year allowed for the realization of that hope had elapsed before Secretary Frelinghuysen's note to Trescot had made such a realization impossible. "I am glad to have it in my power," the President concluded, "to refer to the Congress of the United States, as I do now, the propriety of convening the suggested international Congress, that I may be thus informed of its views, which it will be my pleasure to carry out." [2]

This extraordinary exhibition of what is vulgarly called "passing the buck" drew no immediate rejoinder from Blaine himself, but a letter

[1] New York *Tribune*, February 4, 1882.
[2] J. D. Richardson, *Messages and Papers of the Presidents*, Vol. VIII, pp. 97–98.

to the New York *Tribune* of May 15, signed "Hickory" and probably written by Gail Hamilton, exposed the President's inconsistency with withering sarcasm: "What has frozen the genial current of the President's soul that gushed so peacefully last fall? What blight has fallen on the executive heart, that the hope which, in November 1881, was strong enough to bud and bloom into a full-blown invitation to distant countries, has now in this green-growing April wilted into a petition to an unconcerned Congress at home? . . . But, great heavens, Mr. President, the deed is done! What sort of home manners is this which invites people thousands of miles away, and four months after appeals to a Congress, which confessedly has nothing to do with the matter, to know whether it is proper or not! . . . What remains for the United States to do? Congress must either say yes or no. If yes, will the President issue another invitation, affirming that the first was a 'feeler'? And how are the republics to know that four months hence the President may not be seized with another qualm and appeal, say, to the Supreme Court for its opinion on the propriety of the measure? . . . And suppose Congress says no. Will we write to the republics, 'You shall not come. I had a perfect right to invite you, and I did invite you. But Congress, which had no finger in the pie till I took and jabbed it in, now pronounces against the pie, and so do I. I gave the invitation without thinking much about it, and never dreaming that you would accept. But seeing you stir in the matter, I bestirred myself also, and take it all back.' "

That there was widespread sentiment in the country in favor of the proposed congress is beyond doubt. Eight or ten bills were introduced in both Houses of Congress during the spring and summer months of 1882, and from June 5 to August 7 no fewer than twenty-three petitions were received from a dozen States praying for the convocation of the peace conference. But men of Stalwart sympathies were now in the seats of power, determined to cast discredit on Blaine's policies, whatever their merit.[1] "Congress is in session," wrote Mrs. Blaine to her daughter Margaret in Paris, on December 7, 1881, "so we are daily expecting your Father's head to roll in the basket." [2] And again on December 16:

---

[1] That the policies were really Blaine's is evident, in spite of his assertions in his letter to Arthur and in his article on the Foreign Policy of the Garfield Administration, that he was only carrying out the President's wishes. There is nothing in Garfield's public or private writings to show that he had any interest in Latin-American affairs; and it is clear from Arthur's behavior, as noted above, that he had merely concurred in his enthusiastic secretary's plan for a Latin-American congress, without giving the matter serious consideration.

[2] *Letters of Mrs. James G. Blaine,* Vol. I, p. 258.

"All the Stalwarts are going in, and although the mills of Arthur may seem to grind slow, yet they grind exceeding fine." [1]

Three days later Blaine left office, and within three weeks his South American policy was sabotaged. Once more Mrs. Blaine wrote to her daughter, on February 2, 1882 (the day before Blaine sent his open letter of remonstrance to the President), "Jacky (Walker) was very wise when he foresaw that the Frelinghuysen dynasty might not settle itself into the saddle without an impulse to ride down your Father. Undoubtedly, the State Department intended to take the life of your Father, which they expected to take with all due regard for the convenances. . . . They revoked his instructions, though they were Arthur's as well; they kept back his papers; they sent to Congress garbled dispatches of Trescot; they permitted garbled letters of Christiancy to be sent to Congress. . . . Your Father will be vindicated in every particular. His policy is a patriotic one, and the people are going to so recognize it. Not a selfish thought is in it, but it is in all its ramifications American." [2]

Congress having failed to take action on Arthur's message of April 18, Secretary Frelinghuysen sent a circular letter to our Ministers in the Latin-American countries formally canceling the invitation to the proposed conference at Washington, but at the same time expressing the President's belief that the fact of such a conference having been called had "not been without benefit" as directing attention to "the importance of having a more defined policy . . . governing the international relations of the republics." [3] With these "weasel words," and with the general hope expressed in President Arthur's annual message of December 4, 1882, that the time might be near when international differences should be settled "without resort to arms, by the beneficent processes of arbitration," [4] the interest of the Administration in Latin-America came to an end. Several of the republics, in their reply to the cancellation of the invitation, voiced their regret that the project should be abandoned and their hope that it would be revived at no distant date.

And Blaine published a final justification of his action in his letter of September 16, 1882, to the Chicago *Weekly Magazine*. "The assembling of the Peace Congress," he wrote, "was not in derogation of any right or prerogative of the Senate or the House. The money necessary

[1] *Letters of Mrs. James G. Blaine,* Vol. I, p. 269.
[2] *Ibid.,* pp. 295–297.
[3] *United States Foreign Relations,* 1882, p. 4.
[4] J. D. Richardson, *Messages and Papers of the Presidents,* Vol. VIII, p. 131.

for the expenses of the conference (which would not have exceeded $10,000) could not with propriety or reason have been refused by Congress. If it had been, patriotism and philanthropy would have promptly supplied it. . . . In no event could harm have resulted from the assembling of the Peace Congress. Failure was next to impossible. Success might be regarded as certain. . . . The labors of the Congress would have probably resulted in a well-digested system of arbitration. Such a consummation was within our grasp. It would have been a signal victory of philanthropy over the selfishness of human ambition, a complete triumph of Christian principles as applied to the affairs of nations. It would have reflected enduring honor on our country and would have imparted a new spirit and a new brotherhood to all America. . . . The example of seventeen independent nations solemnly agreeing to abolish the arbitrament of the sword and to settle every dispute by the peaceful methods of adjudication, would have exerted an influence to the utmost confines of civilization and upon the generations of men yet to come." [1]

Blaine was writing with the ardor of an apologist. His confidence in the efficacy of a peace congress to avert the perennial conflicts, internal and external, of the Latin-American countries looks optimistic to us in the light of a half dozen of such congresses held in the last fifty years. But it was not Blaine's extravagant hopes that his opponents attacked. They nourished and spread abroad the idea that he had entered upon his Latin-American policy in a temper of amateurish rashness and with the purpose of selfish aggrandizement. They pictured the rather dull and ponderous Frelinghuysen, with his Dutch solidity of mien, as a rescuer, "likely," in the words of the New York *Nation* of December 12, 1881, "to take us safely through the muddles in which we have recently been involved." The Springfield *Republican* said on the same day: "Mr. Frelinghuysen is understood to hold that the American Eagle should not strain his naturally fine voice by shrill and prolonged screamings on small occasions." The implacable New York *Nation* repeatedly accused Blaine of supporting fraudulent claims against the Peruvian government for his own pecuniary profit; [2] and W. H. Hurlburt, the brother of the deceased Peruvian Minister, went so far as to charge Blaine with attempting to foment a war with Chili in order to force

---

[1] J. G. Blaine, *Political Discussions, Legislative, Diplomatic and Popular*, pp. 413, 419.
[2] See especially the issues for December 15, 1881, February 2, May 5, September 15 and 18, 1882, and October 2, 1884.

President Arthur to retain him in the Cabinet.[1]

To the congressional investigation of Blaine's complicity in the Peruvian claims we shall turn presently. To the charges of ineptitude, rashness, "meddling and muddling," and eagle-screaming, the language of his own diplomatic correspondence quoted above and a fair comparison of his policies with those of his predecessor and his successor furnish the best answer. The simple truth is that the whole matter was drawn into the maelstrom of factional politics for the purpose of discrediting the most prominent figure in the Republican Party and the most conspicuous contestant for the next presidential nomination. Blaine's policy was reversed not from the fear that it would prove disastrous so much as from the fear that it might prove successful. As an early biographer says: "Mr. Blaine was left in the unfortunate position of having proposed and entered upon a course of action which was so suddenly abandoned as to leave it without fair trial. He was judged by the ragged ends of his policy." [2] Historians and statesmen of the present day, far removed from the political feuds of Halfbreeds and Stalwarts, are well-nigh unanimous in the judgment that Blaine's Latin-American policy was his most notable contribution to American public life. In it he showed himself far in advance of his age, and on it have been based all our subsequent efforts to secure the coöperation of the republics of the Western Hemisphere for the maintenance of peace, the reciprocal benefits of commerce, the mutual respect for diverse customs and cultures, and a common adherence to the principles of justice. Even so severe a critic of Blaine as his latest biographer, Charles Edward Russell, in speaking of Blaine's Latin-American policy, rather grudgingly concedes that "nothing else in his official career is so likely to draw the thoughtful heed of future investigators." [3]

For all that, Blaine cannot be absolved from all responsibility for the political turn which resulted in the reversal of his policy and in his own return to private life. It will not do simply to attribute this misfortune to the assassination of Garfield, and to say with Gail Hamilton that therewith "all this wide-reaching beneficence (of Blaine's policies) came to a crazy and calamitous end." [4] For that ending itself, as we have seen, Blain had unwittingly helped to prepare the way by his un-

[1] W. H. Hurlburt, *Meddling and Muddling, Mr. Blaine's Foreign Policy*, p. 68.
[2] C. W. Balestier, *Life of James G. Blaine*, p. 178.
[3] C. E. Russell, *Blaine of Maine*, p. 382.
[4] Gail Hamilton, *Biography of James G. Blaine*, p. 514.

relenting persecution of the Stalwarts. He showed no quarter when he was in power, and acting under a President who was in sympathy with his views. And when the change in the Administration came, his enemies showed no quarter to their defenseless foe. He had helped forge the weapon of partisan proscription and hatred which returned to smite him at the moment of his apparent triumph—a political boomerang.

WITH his retirement from the Secretaryship of State and his almost simultaneous resignation of the Chairmanship of the Republican State Committee of Maine, at the close of the year 1881, Blaine found himself for the first time in more than a score of years free from political responsibility of any sort. It would be misleading to say that he had retired to "private" life; for, though out of office, he continued to remain very much in the public eye. He had no business to return to, no profession to resume. His brief experience as a journalist in the early Maine days had been completely obliterated by politics, which remained to the end of his life his one absorbing pursuit. It is true that in correspondence and conversation with his friends he often spoke as a man glad to be relieved of the burden of public office, but the whole tenor of his life belied these protestations of renunciation. Clear and sharp as his perception was when dealing with a specific situation, skillfully as he marshaled the data and urged the argument to make good his case, he seemed subject to considerable vacillation, and even self-deception, in the consistent ordering of his total career and his ultimate ambitions. To attribute his oft-repeated expressions of indifference to political preferment, however, to sheer hypocrisy, as those historians and biographers are obliged to do who interpret his whole life purpose as an unremitting drive for the Presidency, is to ignore the psychological fact of the alternation of confidence and disillusionment in persons of a mercurial temper. Blaine was decidedly a man of ups and downs. It was not hypocrisy, but a congenital disposition to discount the fears of personal discomfiture too heavily, as well as to be unduly elated over the prospects of success, that best explains Blaine's political variableness.

To this psychological factor must be added the physical. The state of Blaine's health (and, even more, what he apprehended to be the state of his health) entered constantly into his calculations. The many references to the subject in Mrs. Blaine's letters to her absent children, even in the reassuring passages like "Your Father is in the best of health and spirits," show how likely his health and spirits were to be less than the best. Evidently during the whole of the burdensome year of 1881 he was subject to attacks of gout, for the relief of which he had gone to White Sulphur Springs in West Virginia the previous summer. President Garfield recorded in his *Journal* for March 19, 1881: "Finding that Secretary Blaine was confined to his home by illness, I drove over to see him in reference to the part we should take in the Czar's funeral"; and again on March 25: "Cabinet meeting at noon. Blaine ill and absent"; and the next day: "I called on Blaine, who is in bed with inflammatory rheumatism." [1] Emmons Blaine wrote from Chicago on February 3: "I'm sorry Dr. Barker is coming on, for I can already see Father furtively putting new prescriptions in his pocket and preparing himself for another conflict with modern drugs. Don't let them be alone together for a moment." [2] On November 30 Mrs. Blaine wrote to her daughter in Paris: "Your Father gains constantly. He is now regaining his flesh, which does not give him apparently the satisfaction it ought." There are passages also in Mrs. Blaine's letters, sometimes in a vein of pleasantry which may conceal a bit of annoyance, testifying to the demands which her husband's apprehensions made upon her. He was more like one of the children than the head of the house when one of these moods came upon him. He must have her by his side. "I almost wish your Father did not want me so constantly," she wrote to her daughter on July 25,[3] and the next March, when her youngest son "Jamie" was in bed with a fever which threatened diphtheria, she sighed: "With the care and nursing, I have had your Father to sustain, who, regularly as the hour when twilight lets its curtain down and pins it with a star, lets down his spirits and pins them with his woe-begone countenance." [4] Seven years later she was writing to her son James at Waterville: "Do not get depressed. It is a family tendency which must be put down with a strong hand." [5] These passages from intimate family letters by no means justify Gamaliel Bradford's picture of Blaine as a chronic weakling, leaning on his wife for support.[6] On the contrary, he was an exceptionally vigorous man, looked up to by his adoring wife and children as a paragon of wisdom and strength. But these lapses into valetudinarianism furnish a clue to the inconsistency often noted in his personal reac-

[1] Garfield's *Journal*, Library of Congress, sub dates.
[2] Gail Hamilton, *Biography of James G. Blaine*, p. 532.
[3] *Letters of Mrs. James G. Blaine*, Vol. I, p. 223.
[4] *Ibid.*, Vol. II, p. 4.
[5] *Ibid.*, p. 235.
[6] Gamaliel Bradford, *Wives*, pp. 252, 256.

tion to the lure of political office.

Even had Blaine been determined to quit politics altogether, and decided to accept any of the urgent invitations that poured in upon him to enter a business career or newspaper work or the lecture field, his enthusiastic host of followers would not have released him. He was the one, the indispensable party leader, kept to the front by the irresistible pressure of the onward urging cohorts. Every attack on his public policy or his private character brought to his banner new recruits who were jubilant over the skill and audacity with which he confounded his enemies. Every political setback that he received redoubled the zeal of his supporters for a triumphant come-back. When he failed to get the nomination in 1876 he was deluged with letters not so much consoling him for missing the prize as commiserating the country for not knowing where to bestow it. When he proved not strong enough to reach the goal himself in 1880, but furnished the "interference" for Garfield to penetrate the stubborn Grant defense, his followers hailed it as the earnest of success four or eight years hence. He was their perpetual and only candidate, and their faith and numbers grew with every move in his political strategy. For them he had triumphantly routed the "arch-rebel" Jefferson Davis, the mendacious Mulligan and the dictatorial Conkling. Colonel Robert G. Ingersoll expressed their devotion in a characteristic outburst: "Before leaving this world I want to see a man of genius in the White House, and you are the only chance I know." [1]

So Blaine continued to reside in Washington and to keep in close touch with political life. His wife's letters are filled with accounts of dinners and receptions, at which they met the important personages of the capital. Always eager to defend his Latin-American policy, Blaine kept his name before the public by his open letter to President Arthur and in articles and interviews. He appeared before Congress to deliver the eulogy on Garfield, and before the investigating committee of the House to justify his conduct in the negotiations with Peru and Chili. He had no sooner left the Cabinet than plans were afoot to induce him to return to public life. His old friend Joseph Manley was urging him to go back to the Senate; but he could not, of course, displace either of his devoted followers Hale and Frye, for whom seats in the upper house had been provided simultaneously by his own resignation and Hannibal Hamlin's retirement from the Senate in 1881. The next spring the Re-

[1] Ingersoll to Blaine, November 25, 1878.

publicans of Maine were appealing to him through a widely circulated petition to enter the campaign of 1882 as candidate for Congressman at large. Their efforts were in vain, however. "Nothing would as yet induce him to go back to public life," wrote Mrs. Blaine to her daughter on May 8: "to put the energy and time and temper into the House which it would require to secure and hold its control, he told me this morning, would lose him a fortune, which the same effort otherwise applied would make for him." [1] This was but one of the recurring protestations of Blaine's final abjurations of politics, in the midst of the constant speculation of the public on his future political fortunes. "Your Father says he is not even thinking of public affairs, while every issue of the press contains at least one résumé of his intentions and ambitions, the upshot of all being the Presidency in 1884. I am just becoming content with the situation. As soon as people cease asking me if I am going to leave Washington, I shall be entirely so." [2]

Next to his failure to win the nomination in 1876, the greatest disappointment in Blaine's public life was the sudden interruption of his activities in the State Department in 1881. He had rightly regarded the victory of Garfield as his own, and he needed only the mere presence of Garfield at the head of the government as the aegis under which he could plan and execute his plans for the orientation of the Administration and the pursuit of a vigorous "American" policy in dealing with foreign powers. His personal sympathy and solicitude for the stricken President during the anxious weeks of the summer, when hope alternated with despair, was none the less genuine if with it was mingled the thought that his own fate hung upon his chief's. There is a phrase in Mrs. Blaine's letter to her daughter of July 30, when the hopes for Garfield's recovery were highest, which contains in seven words of jubilant relief the whole story of the summer's anguish: "Because he lives we shall live also." [3] But Garfield died, and with him passed more of his Secretary's hopes and ambitions than were ever told. When the murderer Guiteau was hanged on June 30, 1882, Mrs. Blaine sighed in her letter to Paris: "Oh, if he only could have died one little year earlier, the difference to me! Your Father said the other day, as he drove by the State Department, 'Here I fully expected to raise my Ebenezer for eight years.' But you must not imagine that he suffers from one regret for

[1] *Letters of Mrs. James G. Blaine*, Vol. II, p. 16.
[2] *Ibid.*, Vol. I, pp. 277–8.
[3] *Ibid.*, p. 228.

public life; quite the contrary, you could not at present drive him back. The love will revive, I doubt not, but now he is bound to try other paths." [1]

It was not only his Ebenezer that Blaine was intent on raising in the summer of 1881. He was building a mansion more adequate than the modest house on 15th Street for the functions which would devolve upon him as the head of the State Department. At first he had purchased a lot on 16th Street and had already begun the grading, when his eye fell upon a more desirable site just beyond Dupont Circle at Massachusetts Avenue and 20th Street, free from "the vicinage of stables" on 16th Street. He determined that he must have the Dupont Circle lot at any price. To his great delight he found that it was owned by his devoted friend William Walter Phelps of New Jersey, whom Garfield had appointed Minister to Austria. A hurried exchange of cablegrams with Phelps secured the property on advantageous terms, with the only proviso that Blaine should build a commodious dining room in his new house. Senator George Pendleton of Ohio took the 16th Street lot off Blaine's hands, and by midsummer the walls of the new mansion were rising. It was a constant source of delight and relief to the Secretary during the trying months of labor and suspense to run out to watch the progress of the building. Nor did his liberal conception of the proper kind of home for the man who was to be the "premier" of the Administration for eight years fail of encouragement by the members of the family.[2] In July there were "daily drives" out to the house, which was "steadily pushing itself above ground"; in August, Blaine's agility was causing his wife "great anxiety, as he now mounts the ladders and overlooks the second story floor." In January, 1882, the rooms for the various members of the family were beginning to take assignable shape. "I went into your room," wrote Mrs. Blaine to Margaret in Paris, "and echoed Duchess Mary's prayer as she crossed the threshold of Lintergen." [3] But it was to be another year before the new home was ready for occupancy.

---

[1] *Letters of Mrs. James G. Blaine,* Vol. II, p. 31.

[2] We intend to put up a very nice and expensive house." (Mrs. Blaine to Walker, January 16.) "I am delighted that we are going to build, but I am awfully afraid that Father will build a cheap house . . . I don't want him to ruin himself on such an investment, but cheap houses are not going to pay in Washington." (Emmons to Mrs. Blaine, January 12.) "We have plans for the house, and they are so huge and expensive that we are now engaged in striking out every pretty thing to reduce the expenditure to the limits of your Father's purse." (Mrs. Blaine to Margaret, March 24.)

[3] *Letters of Mrs. James G. Blaine,* Vol. I, p. 284.

230   JAMES G. BLAINE

From the end of June to the middle of November, 1882, the family was at Augusta, and Blaine was busy with the composition of the first volume of his *Twenty Years of Congress*.[1] Little progress seems to have been made on the new house during the summer; but an offer of $20,000 for the 15th Street residence by General McClellan early in November spurred Mrs. Blaine to persuade her husband to give up the old house and let her "go on and get a few rooms ready in the new domain for immediate occupancy." The family returned to Washington, and on November 29 Mrs. Blaine dated her last letter from the 15th Street house, which was sold to William R. Travers of New York.

Blaine was "full of tender regrets· for the old place." To it the family had returned winter after winter from Augusta for more than a decade, to have the door flung open by "the faithful Robert." In it the older sons and daughter, Walker ("Jacky"), Emmons ("Mons") and Alice, had grown from school days to manhood and womanhood; and the younger trio, James ("J'aime"), Margaret and Harriet, from childhood to youth. Gathered about the breakfast table the family had read the eagerly awaited letters from Walker in Paris or St. Paul or Santiago, from Emmons in Chicago, or from the daughters in school in Paris or Farmington. In the library Blaine had spent many an evening in conference with his political associates or working over his papers and speeches with his dependable secretary "Tom" Sherman at his side. The house had its sad memories as well—the hours of suspense when its master lay unconscious, prostrated by the sunstroke on the steps of the church that June Sunday in 1876, and the dismay and confusion brought by the news that the President had been shot down at Blaine's side in the Pennsylvania Railroad Station, the President who only the evening before had called at the house, in happy anticipation of his trip to Williamstown, and who had walked back to the White House arm in arm with Blaine, the assassin dogging their steps, but not daring to shoot for fear that his bullet might hit the wrong man. Mrs. Blaine shared something of her husband's nostalgia in breaking up the old home, but felt "assured" that the new one would be "far, far sweeter than this has been." [2] Early in December the family moved to Wormley's, "a per-

[1] "Yesterday was set for our hegeira (from Augusta), but the weather continuing warm and Indian-summer like . . . we are staying on and on. Your Father thinks he is better off here, and as he has commenced writing his *Twenty Years of Congress*, we shall very likely stay on a fortnight longer." Mrs. Blaine to Margaret, November 1, 1882. *Letters of Mrs. James G. Blaine*, Vol. II, p. 59.
[2] *Letters of Mrs. James G. Blaine*, Vol. II, p. 64.

fectly horrid little hotel," until the shopping in New York could be completed for the occupancy of the new mansion at least "in Bohemian fashion."

It was not furniture, carpets, India rugs and hangings alone that comprised the list of purchases. There was also a trousseau to be bought. The eldest daughter, Alice, on a visit to Kansas in the spring of 1882, had met Colonel John J. Coppinger of the United States infantry, stationed at Fort Leavenworth. He was an Irishman by birth and a Roman Catholic in religion, who had served as captain in the Roman army and received the decoration of Chevalier for gallant conduct at La Roca in 1860. His engagement to Alice Blaine was announced at Christmas. "Don't you think this an astounding event to drop into the midst of my curtains and carpets and paper-hangings with which I thought my whole soul was filled?" wrote her mother to Margaret in Paris.[1] The marriage was celebrated in the new house on the morning of February 7, with all the family present except the daughter in France, to whom Mrs. Blaine sent a lively account of the festivities:

At half past eight we had breakfast, so that the caterer might have the dining-room in season. Then came Lizzie to dress heads, and when mine was done I at once dressed so that I might be at the service of others. Your Father, however, did not need me, as he emerged from his room in full morning dress. A perfect array of attendants appeared to wait on Alice. . . . Emmons took charge of the reception, assisted by Jamie, Tom Sherman and Mr. Phelps, who came and went from the top of the house to the bottom 100 times in his anxiety lest anything unforeseen and unprovided should mar the occasion. Father Chappelle was also with us. Alice looked and appeared beautifully. Her dress was a marvelous success, and Col. Coppinger walked around and about her, picking up her train and admiring her in the most unconcealed manner. Presently up flew Emmons breathless, to say that in ten minutes Jamie would come up for Father Chappelle. Accordingly, at the appointed time that youth came up and solemnly escorted the Padre from our sight, and at the same moment Col. Coppinger and Mr. Emmet disappeared down the back stairs into the dining-room, where they were to await the signal from Emmons. Another moment and W. W. P(helps) came in view to say that the stairway was cleared for the family. So down we went. I had just time to take Mr. Bancroft (George Bancroft, the historian) and the President within the ribbons, when Col. C. and Mr. Emmet came in, and now Alice, looking like a perfect beauty, was coming down the stairway with your Father, and as she came up Col. Coppinger stepped forward and the simple ceremony commenced. . . .

---

[1] *Letters of Mrs. James G. Blaine*, Vol. II, p. 65.

The service was all in English and was very brief, but impressive, and as soon as it was over the ribbons were dropped and the congratulations commenced. Everybody said it was the prettiest wedding Washington had ever seen. . . . The breakfast was ample and very handsome, and I had no end of compliments on myself, my children, the house, and unlimited praise of the bride, who deserved all that could be said of her. . . . At four Alice and her husband left for New York, where they are now and where they are staying for a week before going to Kansas.[1] The presents are perfectly splendid. . . . Father Murphy even sent what Walker profanely describes as a very poor likeness of Christ and a very good one of himself. I ought to send you some newspaper accounts of the wedding, but the one luxury which I cannot command is time.[2]

The Blaines lived only the one winter of 1882–3 in the new mansion at Dupont Circle, a happy winter during which the head of the house was busy on his first volume, taking his recreation in long walks in the neighboring woods and fields which were then the outskirts of the city. But the house was large and expensive and not now needed for the official entertainments for which it had been planned. In 1883 it was leased to the Leiters at a handsome rental, and that winter Blaine rented the Marcy house on the west side of Lafayette Square. The abandonment of the mansion on which so much money and care had been spent was scarcely ever referred to by the family. Gail Hamilton dismisses the transaction with the brief statement that "the house had recommended itself to larger purses than Mr. Blaine's."

We know little of Blaine's private finances. His political opponents were assiduous in spreading the story of improper sources of revenue to furnish the substantial income necessary to support a large family in the comfortable style in which they lived. For besides the establishment at Augusta, in which Mrs. Blaine casually mentions six servants, there were the Washington homes, and later a charming villa, "Stanwood," at Bar Harbor on the Maine coast. The children enjoyed expensive schooling both at home and in Europe. Mrs. Blaine was a generous shopper, fond of the best things for home and personal equipment. The family was given to genial hospitality, serving dinners to their guests which were a delight even more from the "flow of soul" than from the excellence of

---

[1] Late in October, 1883, Mrs. Blaine visited the Coppingers at Fort Leavenworth, to be present at the birth of her daughter's son James G. Blaine Coppinger on November 11. At the same time Colonel Coppinger was transferred to Fort Assiniboine. His wife and baby spent the ensuing winter in Washington, and in the spring of 1884 Mrs. Coppinger went out to join her husband, leaving little "Blainey" with his grandparents for the first three years of his life.

[2] *Letters of Mrs. James G. Blaine,* Vol. II, pp. 83–86.

the viands. There was a good deal of traveling between Maine and Washington, with trips to White Sulphur Springs or the West or Europe, and there was a continual coming and going of various members of the family. Mrs. Blaine apparently managed the budget, sending V's or X's to the children at school and writing about the pile of accumulated bills for which checks were being sent out. We hear much of outgo, but almost nothing of income. Because Blaine's modest salary as Congressman, Senator and Secretary of State could not go far to meet the current expenses of the family, color was given to the accusation of his enemies that he "wallowed in spoils." But the one definite case that was pressed to investigation, namely, the charge that he had profited handsomely by using his position as Speaker of the House to secure favors for the Little Rock and Fort Smith Railroad, revealed the fact that, however much the complicated transactions with Fisher, Scott and others may have injured his moral standing or his political career, they had resulted not in a financial profit for the defendant, but in a "severe loss."

Blaine made early investments in coal and iron lands and in real estate (he even owned town lots in Denver, Colorado) which, with the rapid rise in values during the years of industrial boom after the Civil War, netted him a considerable income. He speculated freely in the stock market.[1] He had wealthy friends, like Andrew Carnegie, W. W. Phelps, Jay Cooke and Stephen B. Elkins, who were able to put him in the way of profitable ventures. Elkins was his most constant financial adviser. This "son of the middle border," who developed into a multi-millionaire baron of industry and spent the last sixteen years of his life (1895–1911) in the United States Senate, had gone out from Missouri to New Mexico in a prairie schooner in 1864 and amassed a fortune in mining, real estate and banking. He was the territorial delegate in Congress during the last sessions of Blaine's Speakership, and the two men formed a friendship which grew more intimate with every year that passed. Elkins supported Blaine for the presidential nomination in 1876 and 1880, and was his chief lieutenant in the campaign of 1884. He spent many an evening closeted with Blaine in his library, and perhaps the colloquies were equally divided between politics and investments.

One form of speculation that laid hold on Blaine with compelling power was the promotion of Western railroad building, in which enthu-

[1] "Tell Father I shall send him some stock points in the spring," wrote Emmons from Chicago, February 2, 1881. "Stocks have gone up tremendously, and we shall put the last inch into the house," wrote Mrs. Blaine to her daughter on May 22.

siastic visions of the country's development were mixed with glittering financial profits for the entrepreneurs. As a private citizen his participation in these schemes, judged by the rather low ethical standards in business in the years following the Civil War, would not have brought opprobrium upon him; but the charge of the use of his influence in Congress, as Speaker of the House, to secure legislation favorable to the projected roads convinced many that he was prostituting his high office for the sake of personal gain.[1] We have some further light on Blaine's activity in railroad promotion from the Jay Cooke collection of letters in the Pennsylvania Historical Society Library. From them we learn that Blaine tried to interest Cooke in the autumn of 1869 in the Little Rock and Fort Smith Railroad, which was to run, with its southern extension via the El Paso route, through "the richest land of the Southwest" in cotton and corn. The land grant of 1,600,000 acres would be worth $1,800,000 and traffic would be "good from the start." [2] A few days later Henry D. Cooke, the head of the Washington branch of the firm, wrote to his brother Jay: "Speaker Blaine has been talking to me about taking an interest in the L. and F. S. Railroad. He says this proposition is made more liberal to us than to any other parties because they want us connected with the enterprise. Blaine says he is very sure we could realize an advance without much delay by the sale of $52,000 land-grant bonds and $65,000 first mortgage bonds, leaving us the common and preferred stock clear or nearly so." [3] In a later letter of Blaine to Jay Cooke, the proposition was summed up in the following terms: "You agree to pay in the aggregate $91,500 cash and receive in exchange therefore (1) $50,-000 common stock, (2) $50,000 preferred stock, (3)$70,000 land bonds, (4) $82,500 first mortgage bonds."

Henry D. Cooke saw Blaine on several occasions in October, 1869, and was assured that "material assistance could be got from Congress, probably $8,000 to $10,000 a mile in United States bonds, which should be issued as the road progressed," Blaine urging that the legislation should precede the signing of the contract.[4] But Jay Cooke replied that while he would be glad to aid Blaine, he could not "take hold of the offer now." [5] Blaine, however, refused to let the matter drop. He wanted the

[1] See above, pp. 83–99.
[2] Blaine to Jay Cooke, October 14, 1869.
[3] H. D. Cooke to Jay Cooke, October 18, 1869.
[4] E. P. Oberholtzer, *Jay Cooke*, Vol. II, p. 152.
[5] Jay Cooke to H. D. Cooke, October 21, 1869.

backing of the great Philadelphia banker for the Little Rock and Fort Smith road, and with that object in mind he was ready to aid Cooke in his own pet enterprise, the Northern Pacific. "Blaine is in the city," wrote Henry Cooke to his brother on October 16; "he has valuable suggestions on the Pacific Railroads and legislation. He says that if we manage our case with discretion we can get a handsome money subsidy from Congress." And again on November 1, "You must see and satisfy Blaine. I have been working up the idea of a government subsidy with him and others—think it can be carried through with good management." But neither Blaine's work for the Northern Pacific bill (which passed the House on May 26, 1870, by the narrow margin of 107 to 85), nor his personal conference with Jay Cooke at the Fifth Avenue Hotel in New York, early in November, 1869, could win the financier over to the support of the Little Rock and Fort Smith enterprise.

Our interest here is not in the appeal to Cooke's cupidity and vanity which Blaine made in the long letter of November 10, 1869, offering him $252,500 in stock and bonds of the Little Rock in return for $91,500 cash, and assuring him that he would out-Napoleon in strategy by accepting this opportunity.[1] It is the closing paragraphs of this remarkable letter that reveal Blaine's financial stake in the matter: "And now, in conclusion, a few words personal and special to the great enterprises which are before you. I may say without egotism that my position will enable me to render you services of vital importance and value—services for which I cannot desire or accept profit or gain for myself. . . . But you can greatly aid me by accepting the offer made in this letter. I would certainly not ask you to aid me at your own expense, but in view of the fact that the offer is one from which you could in no event run the hazard of loss(!), . . . I have no hesitation in urging it upon you. I am willing to serve you where I am absolutely debarred from any participation in profits. Are you not willing to aid me when you can do so with profit

---

[1] "Bonaparte, you remember, lost his great and final battle by carelessly neglecting to secure the advanced position of Quatre Bras. What I now want to offer you is the Quatre Bras of the Southern Continental Railroad. That secured, the field of Waterloo is yours. Yours without a struggle! That neglected, the enemy may carry off the prize. Your house can and ought to be the leading railroad power of the world, and the scepter is within your grasp. The field which I open to you is second only, if indeed second, to the great northern enterprise (the Northern Pacific) which you are so carefully considering. By controlling both, you double the profits of each, and you prevent the collisions and strife which injudicious rivalry would surely engender. And to have control of two continental lines is an object, allow me to say, worthy of the highest ambition of any man!" Certainly, Blaine was doing his best not to be a "deadhead" in the Little Rock and Fort Smith promotion.

to yourself at the same time? Just how your subscription to the enterprise will aid me, I need not explain. Sufficient that it is so. Your participation in the future, even if practicable for you, would be of no benefit to me. What I desire is for you to make the contract now. Please give me a decided answer by the 17th, Wednesday of next week." [1]

Why this repeated protestation, in a letter marked "strictly private," of the absolute debarment from "any profit or gain for myself"? Why the reluctance to explain why Cooke's subscription to the Little Rock enterprise would aid the writer, or why the contract must be signed immediately to be of benefit to him? With just what purpose and what results did Blaine succeed in involving his major financial transaction in a web of mysterious complications and contradictions? Perhaps an ampler number of Blaine's letters than we possess would help to answer these questions—and perhaps they would only serve to deepen the confusion.

Whatever the size and source of his income, however, we know that Blaine was at times in financial embarrassment. He apparently suffered serious losses in the period immediately following his retirement from the State Department. "All that fine Fortunatus' purse which once we held the strings of and in which we had only to insert the finger to pay therewith for the house, has melted from the grasp which too carelessly held it, and we must look about for new investments, the comfort of which I find is that there is still enough left to spare for investments," wrote Mrs. Blaine to her daughter at the close of the year.[2] There are other passages at about the same time, like "First and foremost your Father will try to retrieve his fortunes," or "It is not so much the money that I care for as the time in which it has taken to itself wings," or Walker's half-serious little note from Chili, on January 28, 1882: "I would telegraph congratulations (to his father on his birthday), but it would still further bankrupt the family." [3]

The embarrassment was due to a brief but rather severe depression which followed the prosperous years 1879 to 1881. The poor harvests both at home and in Europe in the autumn of 1881 resulted in high food prices, diminished exports (except for gold), a scarcity of money and high interests rates. The revenue of the railroads fell off sharply and the

[1] Blaine to Jay Cooke, November 10, 1869.
[2] Mrs. Blaine to Margaret, December 29, 1881. *Letters of Mrs. James G. Blaine*, Vol. I, p. 277.
[3] Gail Hamilton, *Biography of James G. Blaine*, p. 553.

fall of their securities on the stock market carried down the general list and wiped out the margins of the speculators. It was very likely this financial stringency which prevented the family from carrying out the plan of a European trip in the summer of 1882, a plan several times referred to in Mrs. Blaine's letters and evidently communicated to friends. For we find Andrew Carnegie writing to Blaine early in the year to congratulate him on his correspondence with Lord Granville on the Clayton-Bulwer Treaty: "I have decided to run down and see you. Want to talk a little over what had been thought of for next summer. . . . You are exactly right about Clayton Treaty. America is going to control anything and everything on this Continent. . . . No *joint* arrangements, no entangling alliances with monarchical, warlike Europe. America will take this Continent in hand alone. But your personal intercourse with certain people over there will do much good. Never fear your reception. It will be grand. The highest authority, the *Spectator,* has agreed with your claim. No American party could take ground against it." [1] More than five years were to pass, however, before the European trip was realized, the most delightful part of which were the days spent as Mr. Carnegie's guests at Kilgraston and Cluny Castle in the Scotch Highlands.

A little known activity of Blaine's during his brief tenure of office under President Garfield was his contribution to America's participation in the most famous of international organizations for relief. During our Civil War, the Reverend Henry W. Bellows of New York had been the founder of the United States Sanitary Commission, whose care for the sick and wounded soldiers in the camps and hospitals had won the gratitude of President Lincoln and the admiration of the civilized world. The memory of Florence Nightingale's work of mercy in the Crimean War was still fresh, and at the very moment when Dr. Bellows and his associates were organizing the Sanitary Commission, a young Frenchman named Henri Dunant stirred the sympathies of all Europe in a pamphlet describing the horrors of the slaughter at Solferino—horrors which so nauseated the Emperor Napoleon III that he refused to continue the Italian war. As a result of the barbarisms revealed by Dunant, an international conference was held at Geneva, in August 1864, and the International Red Cross Convention (or Treaty of Geneva) was organized under the symbol of the reversed colors of the Swiss flag, a red cross on

---

[1] Carnegie to Blaine, January 14, 1882.

a white field. The representatives of a dozen European countries pledged the adherence of their governments to the new society. Two delegates from the United States were present at the conference, George G. Fogg, our Minister to Switzerland, and Charles S. P. Bowers, the European agent of our Sanitary Commission. The latter's story of the work which the Commission was doing in the war that was still being waged in America had a profound influence on the delegates. But Secretary Seward had instructed Mr. Fogg, in accordance with our traditional policy of avoiding "entangling alliances" with Europe, not to commit the United States to any agreement or treaty. "You are authorized," he wrote, "to attend the meeting in an informal manner, for the purpose of giving or receiving such suggestions as you may think likely to promote the humane ends which have prompted it."

When the Civil War was over, Dr. Bellows, in letters to Seward of April 27 and May 12, 1866, urged that the United States "join the civilized world in putting under the protection of international law the servants of mercy who represent the universal good-will of the Gospel, even upon the horrid field of war," and that our government "show itself as humane and Christian as the whole circle of European governments, Austria and Turkey excepted, have proved themselves." [1] But Seward, while courteously acknowledging the letters and documents which Dr. Bellows had sent him, only referred them to the War Department, which returned them with a formal note of declination. The attempt of the French Minister at Washington two years later to interest our State Department in the Geneva Convention met with no better results. There the matter rested until an energetic woman took it up and pressed it to fruition. Miss Clara Barton, an employee in the Treasury Department during the Civil War, had done noble service as a voluntary nurse, caring for the soldiers wounded in the battles in the neighborhood of Washington. On a visit to Europe for her health in 1869, she visited Geneva and became deeply interested in the work of the Red Cross, gaining a practical knowledge of its operations by nursing in the Franco-Prussian War of 1870. She returned to America in 1873 to devote herself to the enlistment of our country in the cause. Appointed as American representative by the Red Cross Commission in 1877, she approached President Hayes on the subject with a letter from M. G. Moynier, the President of the Red Cross Commission, urgently inviting the United States

[1] *The Red Cross Courier,* May 15, 1931, p. 310.

to adhere to the Geneva Treaty. But the influence of the Seward tradition (Seward's son Frederick being Under Secretary of State in the Grant and Hayes Administrations) continued to prevail at Washington, and no reply was made to M. Moynier's letter.

As soon as Garfield was installed in the White House, Miss Barton renewed her efforts. There is in the archives of the State Department a translation of the Moynier letter, with a marginal notation in Garfield's handwriting, March 30, 1881: "Will the Secretary of State please hear Miss Barton on the subject herein referred to?" Blaine's reply to Miss Barton on May 20 was cordial: "Will you be pleased to say to M. Moynier, in reply to his letter, that the President of the United States and the officers of this government are in full sympathy with any wise measures tending toward the amelioration of the suffering incidental to warfare. The Constitution of the United States has, however, lodged the entire war-making power in the Congress of the United States; and as the participation of the United States in an international convention of this character is consequent upon and auxiliary to the war-making power of the nation, legislation by Congress is needful to accomplish the humane end that your society has in view. It gives me, however, great pleasure to state that I shall be happy to give any measures which you may propose careful attention and consideration, and should the President, as I doubt not he will, approve of the matter, the Administration will recommend to Congress the adoption of the international treaty which you desire." [1] The next evening a group of distinguished residents of Washington, including the Swiss Consul General, John Hitz, who seventeen years before had requested the United States to send delegates to the Geneva Conference, met at Miss Barton's home and inaugurated the American Association of the Red Cross. The organization was completed on June 9, with the signature of the constitution, the election of Miss Barton as president, and the draft of articles of incorporation, which were filed on July 1, 1881. The assassination of President Garfield the next day postponed the ratification of the convention for the moment. But Miss Barton, encouraged by the "almost unspeakable gratification which Mr. Blaine's response had given her," went on with the organization of local Red Cross units.

Meanwhile, pursuant to a resolution of the Senate, Blaine, on December 10, laid before President Arthur a report, with appropriate

[1] *The Red Cross Courier,* May 15, 1931, p. 311.

papers, "touching the Geneva Convention for the relief of the wounded in war," adding that he deemed it unnecessary "to enlarge upon the advisability of the adhesion of the United States to an international compact at once so humane in its character and so universal in its application as to commend itself to the adoption of nearly all the civilized powers." On December 12, Arthur submitted the report to the Senate in a special message,[1] and upon favorable action by that body, he affixed his signature to the Treaty of Geneva on March 16, 1882. It was not until Miss Barton had resigned in 1904, at the age of eighty-two, that the American National Red Cross in its present form, with its widely extended peace activities and its official status,[2] was reorganized by the congressional charter of 1905. The organization which Blaine so effectively helped to bring into being has grown from a membership of a little over three thousand at the end of 1905 to more than four million today, with an additional enrollment of over seven million Junior Red Cross members in our schools. The aid which it has furnished not only to the sick and wounded in time of war, but also to millions of sufferers from fires, floods, famines, cyclones, epidemics and other catastrophes has been the noblest testimony to the sympathy and generosity of the American people.

Two days after Blaine had surrendered the portfolio of State he was invited by Congress to deliver the memorial address on the martyred President. At first he was minded to decline the honor, in the fear (shared by his wife) that his emotions would get the better of his voice. But William McKinley of Garfield's State of Ohio, Chairman of the House committee on the exercises, insisted that he was the one man fully qualified to do justice to the occasion. Yielding at last, Blaine sat down to prepare his Eulogy on Garfield with a painstaking assiduity such as he had devoted to no other composition in his career. Eleven times he revised the manuscript, reading it over and over again to the members of the family, weighing every phrase and word for justness of judgment, clarity of statement and beauty of style.

The Eulogy was delivered on February 2, 1882, in the hall of the Representatives, before the President and his Cabinet, the Supreme Court Justices, the members of the House and Senate, and the diplomatic corps, while the galleries were packed with the families of officials and

---

[1] J. D. Richardson, *Messages and Papers of the Presidents,* Vol. VIII, p. 66.
[2] Since Taft's day the President of the United States has been president of the National Red Cross.

with guests who were fortunate enough to obtain cards of admission.

Blaine rose to the occasion in splendid form, avoiding any hint of partisan animosity or political controversy, and appraising Garfield's services in the army, in Congress and in the White House with an enthusiasm which must have moved many in his audience to believe that he was dealing with a man of superlative wisdom, tact and courage. Of course, the Eulogy, as befitted the occasion, was an encomium rather than a dispassionate estimate. To have weighed Garfield's character in the scales which the impartial historical scholar uses would have seemed to him as inappropriate as Wordsworth's pedant "botanizing on his mother's grave." He loved Garfield. He, too, had known the bitterness of having to defend his official record against the accusation of shady financial dealings. And perhaps there was a reminiscence of personal justification in the passage in which, for once departing from the restraint of faultless taste, he dwelt on the "prolonged agony" for a sensitive nature of enduring a storm of detraction and vituperation:

> No might nor greatness in mortality
> Can censure 'scape; back-biting calumny
> The whitest virtue strikes. What king so strong
> Can tie the gall up in the slanderous tongue? [1]

"The great mass of these unjust imputations," said Blaine, "passed unnoticed, and with the general debris of the campaign (of 1880) fell into oblivion. But in a few instances the iron entered his soul and he died with the injury unforgotten, if not unforgiven." Perhaps the credit for forgiving, if not forgetting, the Crédit Mobilier investigation should go rather to Garfield's fellow citizens.

But whatever reservations we may have as to the historical statements in the Eulogy, in form and spirit it deserved the great praise that was showered upon it by the press of the country and by the scores of letters of appreciation received by the orator, including as the most prized of all a pathetic note of gratitude from the inconsolable widow. Especially in the closing paragraphs, where he spoke of the martyred President's resignation to the witless and wanton ruin which the assassin's bullet had brought to all his plans, sundering the warm friendships of a lifetime and rending sweet family ties, Blaine blended eloquence, poetry and pathos in a marvelous tribute. There is no finer passage in

---

[1] Shakespere, *Measure for Measure*, Act I, Scene 2, lines 19–22.

the literature of eulogy than the prose poem with which Blaine closed his oration: "As the end drew near, his early craving for the sea returned. The stately mansion of power had been to him a wearisome hospital of pain, and he begged to be taken from its prison walls, from its oppressive stifling air, from its homelessness and hopelessness. Gently, silently, the love of a great people bore the pale sufferer to the longed-for healing of the sea, to live or die, as God should will, within sight of its healing billows, within sound of its manifold voices. With wan, fevered face tenderly lifted to the cooling breeze, he looked out wistfully upon the ocean's changing wonders; on its far sails whitening in the morning light; on its restless waves rolling shoreward to break and die beneath the noonday sun; on the red clouds of evening arching low to the horizon; on the serene and shining pathway of the stars. Let us think that his dying eyes read a mystic meaning which only the rapt and parting soul may know. Let us believe that in the silence of the receding world he heard the great waves breaking on a farther shore, and already felt upon his wasted brow the breath of the eternal morning." [1]

Not many weeks after this auspicious appearance before Congress, Blaine was again called to the Capitol on a far different errand. On February 24, 1882, the House of Representatives adopted the following resolution:

WHEREAS, it is alleged in the Chili-Peruvian correspondence recently and officially published on the call of the two Houses of Congress, that one or more of the ministers plenipotentiary of the United States were either personally interested in or improperly connected with business transactions in which the intervention of this government was requested or expected, and

WHEREAS, it is further alleged that certain papers in relation to the same subjects have been improperly lost or removed from the files of the State Department, therefore:

RESOLVED, that the Committee on Foreign Affairs (C. G. Williams chairman) be, and are hereby instructed to inquire into the said allegations and accusations, and ascertain the facts relating thereto, and report the same, with such recommendations as they may deem proper.[2]

Into the complicated investigations following this resolution, which lasted from March to August, 1882, and fill more than four hundred pages of closely printed type, we cannot go in detail. The alleged "im-

---

[1] J. G. Blaine, *Political Discussion, Legislative, Diplomatic and Popular*, pp. 503–525.
[2] *House Report*, 47th Cong., 1st sess., No. 1790, p. 1.

proper" conduct of the Ministers concerned their connection with certain companies or individuals pressing claims against the Peruvian government for discoveries and services pertaining to the rich guano and nitrate deposits of that country. The claims had been dormant for many years, but were revived now with the hope that our government, to which the Peruvians were looking (not without encouragement) to protect them from a "Carthaginian peace" imposed by Chili, would make the recognition of the claims a part of the settlement.

These claims were as extravagant in their demands as they were flimsy in their foundations. One of them derived from a Frenchman named Alexander Cochet, who pretended to have made the scientific discovery, in 1840, of the fertilizing properties of guano, and to have become thereby entitled to a third of the value of the Peruvian guano, which amounted to "at least $500,000,000." The basis of Cochet's claim was a Peruvian law passed in 1833 to elicit hidden property in the movement for the suppression of the convents! "Anyone," read the law, "who shall discover property belonging to any suppressed convent, *or other property belonging to the state,* shall have a right to a third part of such property." Cochet died in a poorhouse in Paris in 1864, bequeathing his irrelevant claim to an illegitimate son in Peru, who, in turn, made it over to the "Peruvian Company" in the United States, represented by a New York lawyer named Jacob R. Shipherd. Shipherd made several calls on Secretary Blaine in the endeavor to secure his backing for the Peruvian Company, and tampered with the Minister designate to Peru, General Hurlburt, holding out to him the bait of a $250,000 interest in the company. When Hurlburt reached Lima and looked into the claim, he had no hesitation in reporting to the State Department (February 27), the utter worthlessness of the goldbrick which the Peruvian Company had bought. Cochet had lived and died in France; his son had never been legitimized, and therefore had no right to the inheritance; the law of 1833 had no application to guano deposits; and, finally, a mixed commission of Peruvians and Frenchmen had sat upon the case in Paris and judged the claim null and void. This evidence was sufficient for Blaine, who, in spite of Shipherd's importunities, never gave the slightest countenance to the Peruvian Company.

In his testimony before the committee Shipherd not only made no apology for his offer of $250,000 to Hurlburt, but constantly sought to represent Hurlburt and Blaine as hospitable to his claims. He quoted

Senator W. H. Blair of New Hampshire, who had been present at one or more of his interviews with Blaine, as saying to him: "Now, Shipherd, let me tell you something. Don't you hesitate to quote the Secretary, and quote him strongly. Quote him a great deal more strongly than anything the Secretary ever said to you, and you will be inside the facts." [1] He also asserted that he had sent Blaine a copy of the letter to Hurlburt, and that neither Blaine nor "any other of the respectable and eminent gentlemen to whom it was shown suggested any impropriety in it." [2] When Blaine first heard of Shipherd's approaches to Hurlburt (in the correspondence which Hurlburt sent up from Peru), he wrote Shipherd a scathing letter (December 3, 1881), declaring that he had promised no more than that Minister Hurlburt should carefully examine the Cochet claim (with the result which we have seen) and adding, "Beyond this you had no right to demand or expect any aid from the State Department, and your holding a private correspondence with General Hurlburt is a gross infraction of every rule of propriety." [3] In his anger at Blaine for this "betrayal of the interests of American citizens in Peru," Shipherd made the outrageous charge that General Hurlburt, from the day of his arrival in Lima, had been in the pay of the Crédit Industriel, a French rival company which held $72,000 of Peruvian bonds for European creditors; and that he had entered into an agreement with the Peruvian government for a monopoly of shipments of guano and nitrate, a royalty of $10 a ton to be paid to the government and an equal sum to be reserved for the payment of the bonds. Blaine's dispatch to Hurlburt was, "The influence of your position must not be used in favor of the Crédit Industriel or any other speculative interest," and Hurlburt's reply was, "It has not been and will not be." [4]

Shipherd's testimony was a mass of prevarications, contradictions and evasions. He refused at times pointblank to answer questions put to him by the committee, and escaped punishment for contempt only by his clever sophistry. His attempt to implicate Blaine in the endorsement of the Cochet claim ("in as cordial and coöperative relations with me, I may say, as any stockholder in my company") [5] was an utter failure.

There was another claim against the government of Peru, however,

---

[1] *House Report*, 47th Cong., 1st. sess., No. 1790, p. 106.
[2] *Ibid.*, p. ix.
[3] *Ibid.*, p. 106.
[4] *Ibid.*, p. 93.
[5] *Ibid.*, p. 132.

in which Blaine did take an active part. About the same time that Cochet was working in Peru, another French citizen, Theophile Landreau by name, made discoveries of nitrate and guano deposits which he rated at the value of several hundred million dollars, and he too claimed remuneration under the Peruvian law of 1833. He made an agreement with the government in 1865 for certain royalties on the sale of guano, which contract the government repudiated the next year. Landreau was prohibited by the terms of his contract from seeking redress by diplomatic intervention, and when he brought suit in Peru, the court refused to assume jurisdiction. His brother, J. C. Landreau, who claimed American citizenship,[1] and who asserted that he was in partnership with Theophile, pressed the claim on our State Department so successfully that Secretary Fish in 1874 instructed our Minister to Peru to use his good offices "unofficially" for the settlement of the claim; and Secretary Evarts in 1879, on the advice of the law officer of the department, referred it to President Hayes as "entitled to the consideration of the American Government." Furthermore, the House of Representatives unanimously adopted a resolution (not concurred in by the Senate) in February, 1880, to the effect that "the President be requested to take such steps as in his opinion may be proper to secure to said J. C. Landreau a formal settlement and adjustment of his claim against the government of Peru."

With the executive and legislative encouragement thus given to the Landreau claim, Blaine believed that it should not be ignored. His position was stated in instructions in Hurlburt under date of August 4, 1881:

In regard to the Landreau claim, I see no reason to differ from the conclusions to which my predecessors seem to have arrived. John C. Landreau was an American citizen, apparently entitled under a lawful contract to reasonable compensation for important services rendered to the Peruvian government. In conformity with the established practice of our government, while you cannot in such a case make an official demand for the settlement of this claim, you will employ your good offices to procure its prompt and just consideration. . . . While this government will not, as at present informed, undertake to construe the contract or to decide upon the extent of the compensation due Landreau, you are instructed to call the attention of the Peruvian government to this injustice, and say that the government of the United States will

[1] He had a certificate of naturalization and had served as consul at Santiago, Cuba, a position which a foreigner could not hold. Still, no record of his naturalization was found in the Louisiana court which he claimed had granted him the certificate.

expect some adequate and proper means to be provided by which Landreau can obtain a judicial decision upon his rights. . . . Peru is bound in duty and honor to do one of three things: namely, supply an impartial tribunal, extend the jurisdiction of the present courts, or submit the case of Landreau to arbitration. I desire also to call your attention to the fact that in the anticipated treaty which is to adjust the relations of Chili and Peru, the latter may possibly be compelled to submit to a loss of territory. If the territory to be surrendered should include the guano deposits which were discovered by Landreau, and for the discovery of which Peru contracted to pay him a royalty upon the tonnage removed, then the Peruvian government should in the treaty stipulate with Chili for the preservation and payment to Landreau of the amount due under his contract. If the transfer be made to Chili, it should be understood that this claim of an American citizen, if fairly adjudicated in his favor, shall be treated as a proper lien on the property to which it attaches, and that Chili accepts the cession with that condition annexed. . . . You will take special care to notify both the Chilean and Peruvian authorities of the character and status of the claim, in order that no definitive treaty of peace shall be made in disregard of the rights which Landreau may be found to possess.[1]

It will be noted that in this dispatch Blaine went far beyond his "predecessors" in the endorsement of the Landreau claim. And his ill-advised policy herein brought its deserved condemnation. In the first place, the claim was based upon exactly the same misinterpretation of the old Peruvian law concerning "concealed property" as was the Cochet claim which Blaine dismissed as worthless. In the second place, the alleged "partnership" of Theophile and John Landreau was as questionable as the right of Cochet's illegitimate son to inherit property. And in the third place, even if the American citizenship of J. C. Landreau were above suspicion, it is difficult to see how he had the right to invoke the intervention of our government in a case which originated in the poor claim of an alien, and which had been voided by the executive authorities of Peru with the tacit approval of the courts. The language of the House Report was not extravagant when it spoke of "the obvious impropriety of our intermeddling with this bad claim of a French adventurer."[2]

Moreover, by insisting upon the recognition of this claim by Chili as a lien upon any of the guano territory ceded to her by Peru, Blaine still further embroiled the relations between the two republics and

[1] *House Report,* 47th Cong., 1st sess., No. 1790, p. xii.
[2] *Ibid.,* p. xxiv.

prejudiced the prospects of peace. The Chilean government, convinced that our State Department was backing Minister Hurlburt in his obvious partiality for Peru, overthrew the Calderón government which they had helped to establish for the sake of concluding a peace, and occupied Lima with their military forces. They were wrong in attributing to Blaine the responsibility for Hurlburt's unauthorized behavior. For, as we have seen, the Secretary in his dispatches of November 22 and December 3, 1881, had rebuked the Minister for his conduct,[1] and had notified him that a special mission was being sent to Chili and Peru to deal with the whole complicated situation. Nevertheless, the mischief had been done before the arrival of the Trescot Mission. And the root of the mischief lay in Blaine's defense of the Landreau claim.

Not that there was anything dishonest in his conduct. The accusations brought by his political opponents in the campaign of 1884 that he was financially interested in the Peruvian claims and was "trying to put the guano beds into his pocket," have no justification. The House investigating committee reported that "there has not been the slightest intimation or even hinted suspicion that any officer in the Department of State has at any time had any personal or pecuniary interest, real or contingent, attained or sought, in any of these transactions." [2] Neither is the charge that Blaine deliberately baited Chili with the Landreau claim in order to goad her into further hostility to Peru and perhaps also to the United States—so as to force Arthur to retain him in office to meet the crisis,—worthy of notice. Blaine's unfortunate policy in the Chili-Peru imbroglio was due, I believe, to his conception of the dramatic rôle which the United States should play in the affairs of this continent. It was of a part with his aggressive diplomacy in the demand for the revision of the Clayton-Bulwer Treaty and the defense of American fishing rights on the Newfoundland shores. Having accepted the validity of John Landreau's claim to American citizenship, he was ready to press his claims to guano royalties even to the point of obstructing his own professed purpose of bringing about peace between Chili and Peru. His policy encouraged the latter country to believe that the United States would not permit her dismemberment, and led the former country to suspect that we were scheming to deprive her of the fruits of victory. When, as a consequence, the Chilean commander at

[1] See above, p. 244.
[2] *House Report,* 47th Cong., 1st sess., No. 1790, p. vi.

Lima seized Calderón as a tool of the United States and carried him off
to Santiago, Blaine took it as an insult to our government. "You will
say to the Chilean government," he wrote in his instructions to Trescot,
December 1, 1881, "that the President considers such a proceeding as an
intentional and unwarranted offense . . . of such unfriendly import
as to require the immediate suspension of all diplomatic intercourse."
The government of the United States must be "treated with the respect-
ful consideration to which its disinterested purpose, its legitimate influence and its established position entitle it." [1]

Although Blaine's veiled threat to Chili was accompanied with the
usual diplomatic expressions of good-feeling and the disavowal of any
desire to dictate to a sister republic (as in the case of Wilson's dealing with Mexico a generation later), its real meaning was not lost on
the Chilean government. Blaine's insistence on the vindication of the
Landreau claim as a matter of American principle had converted the
mediatory proffer of good offices on our part into a demand upon Chili
which, if persisted in on one side and resisted on the other, could not
but render any negotiations for peace nugatory. "If our good offices
are rejected," ran the instructions to Trescot, "and this policy of the
absorption of an independent state (Peru) be persisted in, this government will consider itself discharged from any further obligation to be
influenced in its action by the position which Chili has assumed, and
will hold itself free to appeal to the other republics of this continent
to join in an effort to avert consequences which cannot be confined to Chili and Peru, but which threaten with extreme danger the political institutions, the peaceful progress and the liberal civilization of
all America." [2] This was dangerously near to the language of an ultimatum, which would leave the Administration confronted with the
dilemma of maintaining the Monroe Doctrine in South America only at
the expense of imposing our will upon victorious Chili by force. The
relief with which the Chilean authorities greeted the change of front at
Washington and the consequent annulment of the Trescot mission, was
voiced in a letter of Signor Martinez, the Chilean Minister to the United
States, to his chief in Santiago: "The passing of Blaine means the

[1] Blaine's most important dispatches containing instructions to our Ministers in Peru
and Chili are printed in his *Political Discussions, Legislative, Diplomatic and Popular*, pp.
343–372.
[2] *Senate Executive Documents*, 47th Cong., 1st sess., No. 79, p. 178.

dawning of a new era." [1]

The congressional investigation was not directed against Blaine or any member of the State Department. Still, Blaine's name was inevitably drawn into it, both by reason of his instructions to our Ministers and by the testimony of Shipherd. Moreover, the interest of the country at large was almost wholly concentrated on its effects upon the political fortunes of the leading figure in the Republican Party. Representative J. A. Kasson, a member of the committee, wrote Blaine toward the close of the investigation, "I have regretted the significance which your attention has given to statements which, if not challenged by a man of your importance, would have hardly been known to one person in 10,000 in the country." [2]

Blaine followed the reports of Shipherd's invidious testimony as long as his patience could stand it, and then wrote to Chairman Williams, on April 14, 1882, that he desired "to be heard in reference to the Peru-Chili matters now under investigation." On the twenty-fourth he was duly sworn as a witness, and appeared before the committee for three days to present his version of the matter, with a great number of letters and documents.[3] Having come before the committee at his own request, he conceived his rôle as that of volunteering corrective information rather than being grilled by cross-examination. Both of the Ministers had died, Kilpatrick in December, 1881, at his post in Santiago, and Hurlburt, the chief witness for the defense, just as he was leaving Peru to return to this country, early in April, 1882. Blaine had little difficulty in riddling the testimony of "old Mulberry Shipherd," as ex-Senator Whyte of Maryland called him, but in the course of the examination a most unseemly incident occurred.

Perry Belmont, a young New York Democrat, just turned thirty, was serving his first term as a member of the House and was on the important Committee on Foreign Affairs. Belmont, in contrast to the older members of the committee, took a censorious and aggressive attitude toward Blaine, which the latter regarded as an insult to a man of his years and standing—an insult, moreover, deliberately planned by his political enemies. "I am not here as a witness in a police court to be badgered," declared Blaine. "I am here to answer questions, if you

[1] Quoted in Henry Clay Evans, *Chili and the United States*, p. 114.
[2] Kasson to Blaine, July 26, 1882.
[3] *House Report*, 47th Cong., 1st sess., No. 1790, pp. 188–242.

will permit me to answer them as I desire. But don't you attempt to correct me on my answers." [1] Belmont was not satisfied with Blaine's version of his action on the Landreau claim, however, and continued to "badger" him until the examination descended into offensive personalities. Blaine declared that Belmont was only the tool of "the dirty Democratic press throughout the United States," which had been spreading false reports of his instructions to Trescot, and Belmont retorted: "I think you are a bully and a coward." [2]

After this personal encounter before the committee, Belmont made a long speech in the House on July 5, in which he portrayed Blaine as the marplot who had brought us to the verge of war with Chili. "I do not state," he concluded, "that there was a deliberate purpose to bring things to such a pass in our relations with the belligerent states in the Pacific, but I have stated and have endeavored to sum up the results of this diplomacy; and I leave it to this House and to the country to decide what verdict shall be rendered upon such stewardship of such a trust." [3]

Whether or not the "dirty Democratic press" stood "as prompter and mentor behind Mr. Belmont," the charge of incompetent stewardship which Belmont pressed so acrimoniously was another arrow in the quiver of the Democrats and the anti-Blaine Republicans. "Meddling and muddling" in South America was one of the counts against Blaine in the campaign of 1884, exploited by the Democrats in much the same way as Woodrow Wilson's Mexican policy was exploited by the Republicans in the campaign of 1916. On the other hand, Blaine's supporters hailed his testimony before the committee as another triumph over his political detractors. "You have not lost a tittle of your snap and vitality," wrote the Democratic ex-Senator from Maryland, Wm. P. Whyte; [4] and the Reverend De Witt Talmage, inviting him to lecture at the Brooklyn Tabernacle, said: "I have thought many a time to write you congratulatory letters over your Garfield oration, as over your demolition of Shipherd and Belmont, as over the fact that when anyone attacks you he gets cut clean through, with one stroke of the battle-axe, from scalp to heel." [5]

Blaine himself closed his testimony on the hectic afternoon of April

[1] *House Report*, 47th Cong., 1st sess., No. 1790, p. 211.
[2] *Ibid.*, pp. 238–9.
[3] *Cong. Record*, 47th Cong., 1st sess., p. 5647.
[4] Whyte to Blaine, April 24, 1882.
[5] Talmage to Blaine, June 19, 1882.

27 with the defiant challenge: "I have nothing to withhold. I court the most careful and searching investigation into these matters . . . If there is only one chapter in my life of which I am proud, and of the complete and absolute justification of which in history I feel sure, it is that in connection with the policy laid down by the Administration of President Garfield with respect to the South American states." [1] Further interesting light is thrown on the matter by the letters of Mrs. Blaine to her daughter in Paris: "I do not know with what particularity the text of the Chili-Peruvian papers may be cabled to Europe, but as there is a great deal of talk on this side concerning them, I hasten to say, 'Let not your heart be troubled, neither let it be afraid' . . . What he, the Pater, may do hereafter, I do not know, but at present he has decided on the patient dignity of a perfect silence. He says he never wrote papers of which a man or his children ought to be more proud, and that there is not a single word in them he would have changed" (January 28); "There was nothing which our beloved wanted so much as to get his South American policy before the world, and a great deal of it is now where everybody can read it. Moreover, all the diplomats evidently regard the late Secretary of State as the one formidable American. In Europe, of course, your Father's policy, which is decidedly American, you will see very much criticized. And you must remember that this is really greatly to his credit. A policy which European countries would applaud could not be very American" (May 1); "I am persuaded that ultimately every tongue will cease to wag against this South American policy" (August 2).[2]

Toward the end of June, 1882, the family left Washington for Augusta, Walker (who had just returned from South America) accompanying them as far as Baltimore, and Emmons meeting them at Boston to negotiate the transfer of the baggage across the city. Blaine himself saw them as far as New York, and joined them a few days later in Augusta. Here they remained until the middle of November. The summer and autumn months offered Blaine a welcome rest from the strenuous duties and anxieties of the previous year. There were walks, drives, visits from friends, picnics and yachting parties, with every now and then a brief business trip to Boston or New York. Early in September Blaine reluctantly redeemed a promise to Senator Plumb of Kansas to

[1] *House Report*, 47th Cong., 1st sess., No. 1790, p. 242.
[2] *Letters of Mrs. James G. Blaine*, Vol. I, pp. 293–5; Vol. II, pp. 12–14, 39.

journey to Topeka to address the State Fair. Politics could never be wholly in abeyance with Blaine; and the approach of the Maine elections in September found him again "in the newspapers, after quite a lull," and "waking up large audiences" in the campaign to oust the Democratic Governor Plaisted. Walker, who had declined the invitation of Secretary Frelinghuysen to remain in the State Department, and had been appointed assistant counsel to J. A. J. Creswell on behalf of the United States before the court of commissioners of the Alabama Claims, came on from Washington to contribute by his effective speeches to the Republican victory of over four thousand on September 11. The return of the Blaines to Washington was accompanied, as we have seen with the excitement of getting into the new mansion and the wedding of the eldest daughter Alice to Captain Coppinger, early in February, 1883.

Meanwhile Blaine, having declined many tempting offers of a business career, had made up his mind to devote himself to the writing of history, which had always been one of his passions. He had spoken casually to friends of his intention, when the days of his "carefree old age" should arrive, of writing a critical history of Caesar's campaigns in Gaul, and more seriously of reinterpreting the War of 1812, whose causes and effects he believed had never been given their due importance by American historians. He finally chose, however, a more congenial subject, which combined history with personal reminiscence: namely, "the story of the United States Congress from the beginning of Lincoln's Administration to the end of Hayes'." "Your Father is writing a book, his own *Twenty Years of Congress*," wrote Mrs. Blaine to her daughter on March 19, 1883. "It will probably not be interesting to you and me (!), but think of the many, many who will want to read and own it." [1] By mid-April he had "written about 200 pages," and Miss Dodge (Gail Hamilton) was "going over it critically to see if it is all right for the printers' hands." [2] During the summer at Augusta he was "writing assiduously," and in the spring of 1884 the first volume of *Twenty Years of Congress* was published by the Henry Bill Company of Norwich, Conn. Work on the second volume was interrupted by the presidential campaign of 1884, but resumed the following winter, and

[1] Gail Hamilton, *Biography of James G. Blaine*, p. 619.
[2] *Letters of Mrs. James G. Blaine*, Vol. II, p. 97.

completed in time for publication in January, 1886.[1]

The two ponderous tomes of more than 1200 pages, encumbered rather than relieved at intervals by the insertion of full-page engravings of medallion groups of politicians, are narrowly political in scope and devoid of the "human" interest (often a pretext for a meretricious superficiality) which seems to be a necessary ingredient for a popular piece of historical writing in our generation. They belong to the era which built houses like Jay Cooke's "Ogonz" and adorned the grounds with iron deer and dogs. Though their mottled page-tops gather dust on the library-shelves today, the volumes were hailed as a *chef d'œuvre* at the time of their publication. "The book puts you easily and securely in the front rank of American men of letters," wrote John Hay, after reading the first volume.[2] The London *Times* was impressed with its dignity of style and moderation of judgment: "Mr. Blaine has expressed a decided opinion on all the issues of the Civil War," it said, "but he is able to appreciate the arguments and respect the motives of those whom he holds to be most widely mistaken." Benjamin Harrison called the book "a most valuable and enduring contribution to our political literature." Senator Anthony of Rhode Island found it "fair in its statements, calm in narrative, elegant and polished in its style. It will give you a name as an historian not unworthy of your fame as a statesman."[3] The latest biographer of Blaine, Charles Edward Russell, is extravagant in his praise, considering the *Twenty Years of Congress* "the greatest book ever written by an American on a political subject, and one of the most fascinating books in the language."[4] We shall have a word to say later on Blaine as a historian. Here we are interested in him as an author, in the circumstances rather than in the contents of his work.

That the work was something entirely different from the disinterested composition of a "carefree old age" was evident when the first volume appeared on the eve of the campaign of 1884. If the early volumes of Bancroft's *History of the United States* "voted for Jackson," Blaine's first volume voted for Lincoln. Its 602 pages were devoted to a long review of the slavery struggle from the days of the Missouri Com-

[1] Blaine wrote *propria manu* at the rate of about a thousand words a day, says his biographer, T. C. Crawford. Until Louis A. Dent joined him at Augusta in May, 1885, he employed no secretarial help in his work; and he never learned to dictate.
[2] John Hay to Blaine, June 21, 1884.
[3] Henry B. Anthony to Blaine, July 25, 1884.
[4] C. E. Russell, *Blaine of Maine*, p. 391.

promise and to the four years of Congress during the Civil War. It was, in spite of the judgment of the London *Times*, a "political manifesto." And, in spite of the courteous language with which it handled the Democratic statesmen, it was a confident apologia for the wisdom, the patriotism and the providential beneficence of the policies of the Republican Party. Frequent references were made in the press to the forthcoming volume, and the anti-Blaine organs, like the New York *Nation*, regarded the advance publication of extracts from the book as campaign material, designed to "fix attention upon Blaine's person and name."[1] The publishers were anxious to have the volume appear before the campaign should get under way. Mr. Haskell of the Henry Bill Company wrote to Blaine in the autumn of 1883, to report the success which the agents were having in placing subscription orders for the work, and to urge him to set a definite date when the completed manuscript could be delivered: "If we can have the book for the holidays, it will scotch the report that has been going the rounds of the Western papers that the first volume will not be ready until after the election of 1884."[2] The volume as a matter of fact did not appear in time for the holiday sales, but it did come out in ample time for the presidential campaign.

The financial returns from *Twenty Years of Congress* must have been highly gratifying. The Joseph Medills of Chicago, writing to thank Blaine for the gift of the set, hoped that the books would not only add to his fame, but would bring him "silver and gold galore."[3] I have found no reference in Blaine's correspondence or in the family letters to the income which he received from the *Twenty Years of Congress;*[4] but the fact that the financial embarrassment of 1882–1883 did not recur and that the villa at Bar Harbor was built immediately after the second volume was published, would show that Blaine was now entirely relieved from financial worry. More explicit evidence is furnished in B. J. Hendrick's recent *Life of Andrew Carnegie*, in a letter which the little ironmaster wrote to William E. Gladstone, urging him to the profitable venture of publishing his memoirs, as Grant and Blaine had done:

---

[1] See especially the issues of February 7, 28, and April 3, 1884.
[2] C. C. Haskell to Blaine, October 31, 1883.
[3] Katherine Medill to Blaine, March 11, 1886.
[4] T. C. Crawford tells us that the royalties for the first few months were in excess of $100,000. (*James G. Blaine*, p. 547.)

Kilgraston House
June 29, 1887

Dear Mr. Gladstone,

Don't buy Mr. Blaine's book, as he will be so glad to be permitted to send you a copy with the author's regards. He is your sincere admirer, and when you and he are next in power I expect a treaty to be made between the two countries agreeing to *arbitration*. What a service for you to make war impossible between English speaking men. *It is coming.*

Such books as General Grant's and Mr. Blaine's "Thirty (*sic!*) Years of Congress" are sold by subscription. The former, it is expected, will reach a sale of about 700,000 copies. Blaine has already 200,000 subscribers, and may reach 400,000. He nets about 75 cents (3s.) per copy—say £60,000 or $300,000.

I only give you Blaine's from hearsay, although I remember he once told me that his publishers assured him . . . that he might count upon fifty to sixty thousand pounds. He has already received more than half that sum.

Mr. Blaine and I talked, as we walked home, of your proposed book, "Gladstone's Fifty Years in Parliament." No doubt, if properly managed, you would net a large sum for it. We thought £40,000 ($200,000) was a sure estimate, while it might be double.

To secure copyright in America, part of it must actually be written there. One page is enough . . . but in these days seven pleasant days' sail to New York is nothing.

I have written Mr. Blaine that you would be pleased to accept a copy of his book, and if you want to talk further to him do not hesitate. *You can trust him.*

Yours always,
Andrew Carnegie.[1]

After this excursus into the activities of Blaine during the interlude between his retirement from the State Department and his nomination for the Presidency, let us return to the political scene.

[1] Burton J. Hendrick, *Life of Andrew Carnegie,* Vol. I, pp. 284–5.

THE transformation of "Chet" Arthur, New York machine politician and henchman of Roscoe Conkling, into Chester Alan Arthur, dignified and admirable twenty-first President of the United States, is a striking example of the power of a solemn responsibility to elicit excellencies of character hitherto latent. Arthur's nomination to the Vice Presidency in 1880 by a nerve-frayed, expiring convention, as a sop to the Stalwart wing of the party, had awakened a disgust among the reformers which was tempered only by the reflection that as presiding officer of the Senate he would have little opportunity for harm. But when Guiteau's bullet struck down President Garfield, the thought of Arthur's succession brought consternation to the hearts of the men who hoped that a new era of reform had been inaugurated with President Hayes. The ex-President himself confided to his *Diary* that the accession of Arthur would be "a national calamity," and that his regime would be a Conkling Administration, "without the moral support of any of the best elements of the country." [1] Senator Thomas F. Bayard of Delaware wrote to Schurz, when the hope for Garfield's recovery was still strong, "May Heaven avert the contingency of Arthur's promotion!" [2] The fact that at the very moment of the tragedy in the Pennsylvania Station the Vice President was in Albany, lobbying for the reëlection of Conkling and Platt to the United States Senate, was a sinister omen.

Nevertheless, when he was called upon to take the oath of office as President, eleven weeks later, Arthur rose to the responsibilities of his high position with a dignity and fidelity which dismayed his old cronies and disarmed his apprehensive critics. The caustic New York *Nation* was compelled to acknowledge before his term had expired: "Arthur's Administration will not suffer by comparison with any of its predecessors since Lincoln's; indeed, it is above the average of post-bellum Administrations in point of respectability." [3] The new President invited all the members of Garfield's Cabinet to retain their portfolios

---

[1] Rutherford B. Hayes, *Diary and Letters,* Vol. IV, pp. 23–4.
[2] Bayard to Schurz, July 7, 1881. Frederic Bancroft, ed. *The Speeches, Correspondence, and Political Papers of Carl Schurz,* Vol. IV, p. 147.
[3] New York *Nation,* April 24, 1884.

until after the meeting of Congress in December. Secretaries Hunt of the Navy and Kirkwood of the Interior remained until April, 1882, and Robert T. Lincoln was kept in the War Department to the end of the Administration. Nor were the men who eventually replaced the Garfield appointees of the extreme Stalwart type (with the exception of William E. Chandler in the Navy Department), though the Blaineites raised the cry of "the Stalwarts coming in everywhere," and prophesied that "Conkling and Grant will come to the front, the friends of Garfield and yourself (Blaine) be proscribed and compelled to take back seats, and the Republican Party divided and demoralized and perhaps destroyed." [1] Conkling was, to be sure, offered a seat on the Supreme Court bench, which he rather scornfully declined. Platt was offered nothing. And, to the disgust of both, Blaine's nominee, W. H. Robertson, whose appointment by Garfield had been the cause of their resignation from the Senate, was retained in the office of Collector of the Port of New York.

Arthur's policies, too, left little to be desired in the eyes of the friends of good government. His message to Congress in December, 1881, was the first annual message since the Civil War to refrain from the perpetuation of sectional animosities by reference to the South, which had been the stock in trade of Republican politicians and orators for fifteen years. His sincerity in the cause of civil service reform was proved by his cordial signature of the Pendleton Act of 1883, creating the Civil Service Commission, his appointment of Dorman B. Eaton as its chairman, and his transfer of some fourteen thousand offices to the classified list—though he himself had been ousted from the New York custom house five years before by President Hayes, in pursuance of the same principle of reform. He approved the project for the downward revision of the tariff, which came to naught because the protectionist interests in Congress were strong enough to thwart even the moderate reform recommended by the Republican fact-finding commission. He insisted upon a fair treatment of the Chinese, by vetoing an exclusion act which he deemed inconsistent with the convention which President Hayes had negotiated with the Chinese Government. His veto of the outrageous "pork-barrel" River and Harbor bill of 1883 (which was immediately repassed by both houses of Congress over the veto) was commended by State conventions of both parties and praised by the liberal press in all

[1] Joseph A. Homan to Blaine, February 28, 1882.

parts of the country.

In spite of this meritorious record, Arthur did not escape the fate of his predecessors John Tyler and Andrew Johnson, who, having been given the second place on the ticket in order to placate a section or faction of the party, had been elevated to the Presidency by the accident of their chief's demise. The fundamental cause of his discomfiture was the fact that he could satisfy neither wing of his party. He fell between two stools. Stalwarts like Platt and Conkling accused him of ingratitude for not making a clean sweep of the Halfbreeds and restoring the party to the control of the machine which had dominated it in the days of President Grant. On the other hand, no exhibition of wisdom or moderation could make him acceptable to the Garfield-Blaine group, whose brief day of power had been ended by the assassin who boasted that the motive of his dastardly deed was to bring Arthur into the Presidency.

Nor could the erstwhile member of the "big four" of the New York Republican machine expect to find permanent favor in the eyes of reformers like Schurz and Curtis, whatever concessions he might make on this or that point to the rising demand for the purification of public life. They felt that his policies were dictated by expediency rather than by principle. There was too much of the old leaven of Stalwartism in him for the making of a genuine Independent. Had he not offered the arch-enemy of civil service reform a place on the Supreme Bench and invited that prince of political manipulators, William E. Chandler, into the Cabinet? Was he not still the friend of spoilsmen like the Dorseys and Dudleys and Bradys, who set party above principle and were faithful to no common interests except the "communion of pelf"? And so, scorned by the Stalwarts as an apostate, endured by the Halfbreeds as a nemesis, and suspected by the Independents as a trimmer, Arthur was almost a man without a party, dependent for such support as he had upon the following which a President is always able to build up by the bestowal of patronage.

Handicapped as the President was by these embarrassments, his Administration was still further discredited by the exposure of the Star Route frauds, as malodorous a scandal as had ever disgraced the Grant regime. The Star Routes, so called because they were marked with an asterisk on the lists of the Post Office Department, were some nine thousand routes of postal delivery by riders or stagecoach drivers, situated mostly in the sparsely populated territories of the far West.

Suspicion was aroused during the closing months of Hayes' term by the increase in the cost of running ninety-three of these routes (some of which carried only a half a dozen letters a week) from $763,000 to over $2,700,-000. And when Thomas L. James, the efficient Postmaster of New York, became Postmaster General in the Garfield Administration, he undertook, with the coöperation of Attorney General MacVeagh, a vigorous examination of the Star Route service. Though warned by the investigators that the trail of suspicion was leading to men of prominence in the party, Garfield stood by his Cabinet officials. "Cut the cancer out," he ordered, "no matter whom it hurts." [1] Arthur, too, forwarded the investigation by appointing as Attorney General Benjamin H. Brewster, who had been working on the case with MacVeagh. The investigation revealed what the special agent of the Department of Justice called "an amazing boldness" on the part of "the men who conspired to defraud the government." Contracts carrying exorbitant compensation had been allotted without competitive bidding, by corrupt post-office officials and their congressional allies, who pocketed the graft. In a single year the contract for a route in Nevada had been raised from $2,982 to $49,000, and for one in Dakota and Montana from $2,350 to $70,000; while $50,000 was appropriated from the Treasury to recompense a contractor "who carried over the mountains the entire mail in the leg of his boot." [2]

Indictments against Thomas J. Brady, an Assistant Postmaster General, Stephen W. Dorsey, United States Senator from Arkansas and Secretary of the National Republican Committee, Dorsey's brother and brother-in-law, and a number of lesser fry involved in the conspiracy were brought before the grand jury of the District of Columbia early in 1882. The trial, which lasted from March to September, was a travesty of justice. Clever lawyers for the defense, including Robert G. Ingersoll (who, to his credit, later repented of his part) obfuscated the issue by dwelling on legal technicalities, until the jurymen were so confused that they lost sight of the pertinent facts. Only two men, mere satellites, were convicted. The jury disagreed in the case of the major conspirators like Brady and Dorsey. Brought to a second trial by the persistence of the Attorney General, they were all acquitted in June, 1883, amid cheers in the courtroom. Colonel Ingersoll entertained Dorsey at his home that evening, and a crowd of Negroes serenaded the

[1] *House Miscellaneous Documents,* 48th Cong., 1st sess., pt. 2, p. 335.
[2] *House Report, No. 2165,* 48th Cong., 1st sess., p. 5.

acquitted conspirator, who flattered their historical comprehension, if not their partisan zeal, by a speech in which he compared himself to the blameless Warren Hastings pursued by the vindictive slanders of Edmund Burke.[1] Brady had already been dismissed from the Post Office Department by President Arthur, and Dorsey, "the originator and inspiring genius" of the Star Route frauds, resigned his position on the national committee and disappeared from public life after the trial. But the President had to remain in the White House to bear the obloquy brought upon his Administration by the acquittal and escape of what the Attorney General called "the worst band of organized scoundrels that ever existed since the commencement of the government." [2]

The American people, however, have generally shown so deplorable a tendency to allow their indignation over frauds committed on the Treasury to evaporate in a brief ebullition of cynicism, that even the Star Route scandal might have passed (as did the oil scandal revealed in the Harding-Coolidge regime) without serious damage to the Administration. A worse blow to Arthur's chances of winning popular support was the business depression which hit the country soon after his inauguration. The upbound from the panic years of 1873–1878, in the eternal seesaw of glut and liquidation which characterized our uncoordinated competitive economic system, was marked during the latter half of the Hayes Administration. Custom duties, under the essentially unchanged tariffs of the Civil War, were creating a mounting surplus in the Treasury, which offered Congress the temptation to increased pensions, internal improvements, and general departmental extravagances. The exports of foodstuffs and raw materials rose sharply, to stimulate and balance the importation of European capital for the development of American industries and railroads. Mills and factories, starved by five years of idleness, began to turn out goods faster than they could be absorbed by the buying power of the people. Reaction set in with crop failures in 1881, which started a train of economic misfortunes— diminished exports, reduced railroad revenues, falling prices on the stock exchange, the unloading of speculative securities, wage cuts resulting from strikes and lockouts, industrial plants shut down, taxes and public expenditures mounting.

It was in the midst of such conditions, easily visualized by the Amer-

---

[1] New York *Nation*, June 21, 1883.
[2] *Appleton's Annual Cyclopaedia*, 1882, p. 766.

icans of the early 1930's, that the mid-term elections of 1882 were held. Naturally enough they resulted in a rebuke to the party in power, which is always held responsible for economic distress. The Democrats regained control of the House in a tidal wave which engulfed 71 congressmen, including 34 chairmen of committees. The state elections were equally disheartening for the Administration. In Maine, as we have seen, the Republicans, by virtue of a strenuous campaign in which Blaine and his son Walker did yeoman's service, defeated the Democratic Governor by a narrow margin. But in only two (New Hampshire and Nebraska) of the other dozen States which chose Governors in 1882 were the Republicans successful; while in such important States as Ohio, Indiana and Illinois, where there was no Governor elected, the Democrats carried the truncated State ticket and returned increased delegations to Congress. In the States of the North Atlantic seaboard, where the Irish element was strong, much capital was made out of Mr. Lowell's remissness in securing the release of alleged American citizens imprisoned in Irish jails under the Coercion Acts; and a mass meeting at Cooper Union, New York, on April 3, after listening to speeches by Mayor Grace and several Democratic Congressmen and to letters from Governor Curtin of Pennsylvania, Samuel J. Tilden and Roscoe Conkling (!) denouncing the Administration, passed a resolution condemning Lowell's "sycophancy" to Great Britain and demanding his recall. Furthermore, the influence of the reformers and Independents was a strong factor in the defeat of the Republicans in the great States of Pennsylvania and New York. The citizens of Philadelphia, in their fight against the infamous "gas ring," had elected a courageous young Democrat, Robert E. Pattison, as City Comptroller in 1877 and reëlected him in 1880. The Democratic State convention nominated him for the Governorship in 1882, and, with the support of the Republicans who were disgusted with the Cameron machine, which had dominated the State since the Civil War, elected him, together with five additional Congressmen, in November.

Most important of all was the Democratic victory in New York. The politics of the Empire State were in a sad tangle in 1882. Three years before, the Conkling machine, then at the height of its power, had put Alonzo B. Cornell into the Governor's chair, in spite of the defection of the Independents, or "Young Scratchers," led by Horace Deming and R. R. Bowker. But Cornell, though he was a Stalwart and a member of the "big four," developed an unsuspected vigor of independence in his high office. He offended Conkling by refusing to use his influence with the legislature for the reëlection of Conkling and Platt to the United States Senate after their petulant resignation, and still further by vetoing tax legislation favorable to Jay Gould's interest in the New York elevated railroad, for which Conkling had become counsel on his relegation to private life.[1] For this "ingratitude" Conkling and Gould were determined to prevent the renomination of Cornell, who had the support of the Halfbreed wing of the party. President Arthur, hoping to build up support in the Empire State, foolishly lent himself to this conspiracy of avarice and revenge, by allowing the Stalwarts to draft his Secretary of the Treasury, Charles J. Folger, as their candidate. Folger's nomination was forced through the Republican State Convention at Saratoga, September 20, with the help of votes from "rotten boroughs" and of a forged proxy; but it created a disgust among the liberals of the party that augured a wide defection from the ticket in the November election.

Meanwhile, the Democrats were apparently in no more harmonious state. The Tildenites, led by Daniel Manning, the able proprietor of the Albany *Argus,* were supporting General H. W. Slocum, who had commanded a wing of Sherman's army on the famous "March to the Sea." A wealthy financier and ex-Congressman from Watertown, Roswell P. Flower, was appealing to the anti-Tilden forces in all parts of the State by the promise of ample campaign largesses. In the Democratic stronghold of New York City a new anti-Tammany organization had been formed in April, 1881, under the sponsorship of Abram S. Hewitt, Tilden's campaign manager in 1876. This "County Democracy," as it was called, rapidly attracted tens of thousands of the solid business and professional men of the city, and won so surprising a victory in the local elections of 1881 that it was allotted a number of delegates in the State convention of 1882 larger than those of the two older organizations, Tammany Hall and Irving Hall, combined. The Democratic leaders in the western part of the State (which had heretofore been quite ignored in the selections for gubernatorial or senatorial candidates) were beginning to take notice of the remarkable Administration of the Mayor of Buffalo, Grover Cleveland, an industrious, inflexible executive, honest to the core, whose courageous vetoes were wrecking

[1] D. S. Alexander, *Political History of the State of New York,* Vol. III, p. 493.

the schemes of the "ring" for plundering the city on contracts for sewers, paving, street cleaning, water supply, and other public utilities. Cleveland wanted the nomination for Governor, but refused to make the slightest commitment either to Manning or to Tammany Hall. His backers could muster only 66 votes on the first ballot in the convention at Syracuse, to 98 for Slocum and 97 for Flower. But he gained five votes on the second ballot, while his two rivals were tied at 123. Then the County Democracy, at the bidding of Hewitt and William C. Whitney, threw its 38 votes to Cleveland. The great majority of the Flower delegates joined them, John Kelly belatedly swung into line with the Tammany vote, and the Mayor of Buffalo was nominated with 211 ballots to 156 for Slocum. In the election which followed six weeks later, Secretary Folger proved to be a veritable man of straw. His candidacy was tainted with fraud, his campaign was listlessly apologetic, and his support by half the Republican press was lukewarm. On the other hand, the Democrats rallied to Cleveland in a body. Tammany Hall and the County Democracy stood shoulder to shoulder in New York City, and the original Cleveland men in Buffalo and the western counties were staunchly supported by the up-State Tildenites, led by Manning. Cleveland's plurality in the election of November 8, was 192,854 in a total vote of a little over 900,000, the largest plurality ever given up to that time for any candidate for Governor in any State of the Union.

The Republicans regained in 1883 a little of the ground lost, their most notable victory being the ouster of that "old mountebank" Benjamin F. Butler (whom Harvard College had refused to honor with the customary degree of LL.D. conferred upon the chief magistrate of the State) from the Governorship of Massachusetts. But the Administration had received a serious blow in the fiasco of Arthur's excursus into the politics of New York, and the party morale was weaker than it had been in 1880. The benefits of the Hayes régime had been largely dissipated by the factional wrangles of the Garfield and Arthur Administrations.

Meanwhile, what of Blaine's attitude? He was out of politics and could not be "dragged back" into them. He was busy safeguarding his threatened finances, building his new house, marrying his eldest daughter, writing his book. If he cast a wistful glance at his shattered Ebenezer as he drove past the State building, or wrote an article to defend his South American policy, or left his desk to repel the insults of young Perry Belmont before the House committee, or gave some time of his summer in Augusta to help eject the only Democratic Governor who had sat in the capitol of Maine since the formation of the Republican Party—these were only sporadic manifestations of the political leaven which had been working steadily in his life for a quarter of a century. The most obvious fact, of course, was the change in his relationship to the Administration when Arthur came into power. He had been the "alter ego" of President Garfield, the ally "in shining armor," shaping the policies domestic and foreign for an anticipated glorious regime of eight years. He had been as much at home in the White House as in the State Department. He gave a formal dinner, "much dreaded" by Mrs. Blaine, to the President in November, 1881, and dined at the White House on March 9, 1882. But there was no cordiality on either side.[1] Ten months later Mrs. Blaine was writing to her daughter in Paris: "This is the third day that I have dined out in succession, and now your Father has the Marquis of Lorne's [2] dinner tomorrow at the Legation, and Sunday, General Sherman. But the President omits him from the State dinner on Saturday, which I think is stupid of him, as probably the one man whom Lorne wants to see is our Beloved." [3]

Indeed, it is from the letters of Mrs. Blaine, who was the faithful barometer of her husband's political feelings, that we get the attitude of the family toward the new incumbent of the White House. There is a tone of depreciation in these letters. The President had a knack of "seeming to do things, while never putting his hands or his mind near them." [4] "All his ambition seems to center in the social aspect of the situation. Flowers and wine and food and slow passing with a lady on his arm and a quotation from Thackeray or Dickens, or an old Joe Miller told with an uninterfered-with particularity—for who would interrupt or refuse to laugh at a President's joke?—make up his book of life, whose leaves are certainly not for the healing of the nations." [5] "I do not think he knows anything. He can quote a verse of poetry or a page from Thackeray or Dickens, but these are only leaves springing from a root out of dry ground. His vital forces are not fed, and very

---

[1] "The dinner was extremely elegant—the flowers, the damask, the silver, the attendants. . . . But this is all there is of it." *Letters of Mrs. James G. Blaine*, Vol. II, p. 5.
[2] Governor General of Canada, and daughter-in-law of Queen Victoria.
[3] *Letters of Mrs. James G. Blaine*, Vol. II, pp. 78–9.
[4] *Ibid.*, Vol. I, p. 294.
[5] *Ibid.*, Vol. II, p. 8.

soon he has given out his all. I hardly know whether we are on terms with him . . . The last time he was here, he spoke to me of his chagrin that we had not been invited to the White House, but time wears on and the invitation lingers, and I do not think a perfectly well-bred President would make such an apology. He certainly commands his own house and table." [1] "I think this Administration is doomed. I do not believe anything will seize it but perdition, and I do not love it." [2] "You must not suppose that I cherish any antagonism toward Arthur. I do not in the least. He is light-weight, and I do not propose to sink the scale with a lie to the contrary—that is all." [3] Arthur was invited to Alice Blaine's wedding, of course, but in her long letter describing the happy event (see p. 231) Mrs. Blaine hardly mentions his presence. And when she called a few weeks later on the President's sister, Mrs. Haynesworth, she had only to report that the White House was "an abode of gloom." [4]

Yet Arthur and Blaine were not ill-disposed toward each other. The President remembered that Blaine had defended him in the Senate when Hayes was investigating his conduct of the New York custom house.[5] But the public relations between the two men were naturally terminated when Blaine left the State Department and shortly afterward wrote his open letter protesting against the reversal of his South American policy. Outwardly Blaine and Arthur remained on terms of cold and correct civility, greeting each other with punctilious hat raising when they passed on the street, and meeting from time to time at social functions. In the late summer of 1882, hearing that the President contemplated a trip to Mount Desert, Blaine invited him to visit the family at Augusta, and received "a very nice letter" in reply, leaving the invitation in abeyance until the presidential plans should be made "a little more definitely." [6] In spite of all these personal amenities, however, Blaine remained as indifferent, not to say hostile, to the Arthur Administration as he had been to that of President Hayes. If he regretted

[1] *Letters of Mrs. James G. Blaine*, Vol. I, pp. 309–10.
[2] *Ibid.*, p. 305.
[3] Gail Hamilton, *Biography of James G. Blaine*, pp. 613–4.
[4] *Letters of Mrs. James G. Blaine*, Vol. II, p. 93.
[5] Walker Blaine wrote to his father from New York in 1878: "I met Collector Arthur, who was very cordial, inviting me to his house . . . and telling me that he would be very glad to do anything for me in his power. 'Your father has laid me under a debt of gratitude,' he said. 'Of course I heard of his speech only in confidence, but he made a magnificent defense for me in Executive Session!' " Quoted in Gail Hamilton's *Biography of James G. Blaine*, p. 517.
[6] *Letters of Mrs. James G. Blaine*, Vol. II, p. 42.

the injurious effects of the Star Route trials, the business depression and the reverses of 1882 upon the fortunes of the party, there was perhaps a compensating satisfaction in the thought that these misfortunes were occurring under the regime of that wing of the party whose "perdition" was the wishful prophecy of his wife.

However, Blaine could not remain indifferent to the vicissitudes of the Administration if he wished to regain his political heritage. Such questions as civil service reform, tariff revision, Chinese exclusion, governmental extravagance, prohibition, and the growth of an insurgent movement could not be ignored. If he had yielded to the importunities of his friends to reënter the Senate or House after his resignation from the State Department, he would have undoubtedly discussed these questions with his usual vigor on the floor of Congress. How far he did discuss them in his private correspondence we cannot tell, because so few of his letters have been preserved. We do know, however, that he was in close touch with Demarest Lloyd, the Washington correspondent of the New York *Tribune,* through whom he was warning Whitelaw Reid of the danger of a Democratic tariff, which would be an entering wedge for free trade. "The attitude into which tariff legislation is drifting," he wrote to Reid on February 19, 1883, a fortnight before the mutilated bill of the Hayes tariff commission was passed by Congress, "promises the most serious discomfiture to the Republicans and immense advantage to the Democrats. Practically it amounts to this, that the Republicans, being held responsible by the country for all that is done,[1] are yet being driven to submit to such tariff adjustments as the Democrats dictate. . . . We need one of your old-fashioned bugle blasts in the *Tribune* for the protection interest, strong, aggressive, cogent, such as you know how to write."[2] And in November he submitted a scheme to Charles Emory Smith of the Philadelphia *Press* for maintaining the tariff and at the same time reducing the Treasury surplus, which had risen to $511,000,000 in the two preceding fiscal years. Blaine's plan, which was essentially a revival of Henry Clay's nearly half a century before, was to keep the high custom duties and the excise taxes (a sop to the prohibitionists), and to relieve the Treasury by distributing the excise revenue to the

---

[1] At the time Blaine wrote this letter all the branches of the government were in the hands of the Republicans, as the Democratic House elected in November, 1882, would not come in until March 4, 1883.

[2] Royal Cortissoz, *Life of Whitelaw Reid,* Vol. II, pp. 81–2.

States in the ratio of their population. This distribution scheme would free almost every State in the Union from the need to levy a State tax. It was extravagantly praised by the *Tribune* as "the most statesmanlike suggestion of a generation." [1]

The reform of the civil service was another subject of which Blaine was compelled to take notice by the events of the Arthur Administration. After the assassination of Garfield, the formation of the National Civil Service League at Newport in August, 1881, the decisive Republican defeat in November, 1882, and the hasty passage of the Pendleton Act in the "lame duck" session of Congress in the winter of 1882–1883,[2] Blaine could no longer speak of the civil service reformers in the scornful language of his letter of December 10, 1880, to Garfield, as the "unco' guid," "upstarts, conceited, foolish, vain . . . noisy but not numerous, pharisaical but not practical, ambitious but not wise, pretentious but not powerful." [3] He had, as we have seen, looked coldly upon the efforts of President Hayes to purify the service, and had defended Arthur in his administration of the New York custom house. Insisting that the Republican Party had always been the party of reform, he had seen in the critics of our "much maligned" civil service two types of agitators: the Democrats, who would endanger the reconstruction settlement by restoring the political power of the South; and the Independents, who would sacrifice the wholesome ascendency of the Republican Party to impracticable nostrums, conceived in the realm of fancy or borrowed from the practices of Great Britain. But in his Eulogy on Garfield he had already begun to recognize the public demand for civil service reform, by declaring that the martyred President, from the time of his inauguration, had been "earnestly seeking some practical way of correcting the evils arising from the distribution of overgrown and unwieldy patronage," and that "had he lived, a comprehensive improvement in the mode of appointment and the terms of office would have been proposed by him and, with the aid of Congress, no doubt perfected." [4]

As the campaign of 1882 progressed, Blaine committed himself further to the cause of civil service reform. He would have no permanent

---

[1] See editorial, "Free Homes or Free Whisky," New York *Tribune*, November 29, 1883.
[2] The Democrats claimed that the sole object of the Republicans in passing the act was to fix the tenure of offices before they had to yield the House to their opponents on March 4, 1883.
[3] Gail Hamilton, *Biography of James G. Blaine*, p. 491.
[4] James G. Blaine, *Political Discussions, Legislative, Diplomatic and Popular*, pp. 518–9.

tenure after the "royalist" fashion, but he would favor appointments to office for a term of seven years (thus "breaking joints" with the presidential terms) and would have the incumbents protected against removal except on duly specified and proved charges. However, these and subsequent signs of a change of heart were interpreted by Blaine's opponents as a bid for the support of the Independents in the approaching presidential campaign.[1] In the midst of that campaign, the New York Times dismissed Blaine's professions of devotion to civil service reform as "the traditional tribute paid by vice to virtue." [2]

All considerations of the sincerity or opportunism of Blaine's professions aside, the contention that he needed to keep himself before the public by such puerile devices as publishing extracts from his forthcoming volume is nonsense. There was not the slightest danger of his becoming obscure or forgotten, even if he had chosen to retire to Robinson Crusoe's island. He was by far the most popular figure in the Republican Party, and his popularity grew steadily during the Arthur Administration. Wherever the fortunes of the party were threatened he was in demand, and he was kept busy declining invitations like William B. Allison's to "come and rally the hosts in Iowa with one blast from your horn." [3] His opinion on all the major questions of the day was eagerly welcomed by the leaders and the rank and file of the party. Alan Johnstone wrote him from England, in June, 1883, enclosing the report of John Bright's speech on the American tariff, and asking what response we should make in the campaign of 1884. Far from there being any need to "boom" him for the Presidency, the chief anxiety among his followers like Whitelaw Reid and W. W. Phelps was lest he should be put forward too early and too prominently. Evidently, there had been some talk of his being appointed Minister to England to succeed Lowell when Arthur came in.[4] But if the new President was contemplating following Conkling's advice to Garfield to send the Halfbreeds out of the country on foreign missions, Blaine had no intention of accepting such a mission. He was in thorough accord with the program outlined by Whitelaw Reid in a letter from London, October 28, 1881: "To take the mission to England would be to confess your fall and accept a pension from your conqueror. It would be to

1 New York Nation, September 14, 1882.
2 New York Times, July 21, 1884.
3 Allison to Blaine, July 25, 1883.
4 See the letter from Andrew Carnegie, January 14, 1882. Above, p. 237.

become a dependent of Chester Arthur, instead of the greatest independent political force in the country. To go quietly to Augusta, take care of your health, have a good time and take your fair share in political campaigns as they come along, is to garner and increase that force. You are the residuary legatee of Garfield's popularity. You ought to be and can be chosen at the next election as his successor. To that end Augusta is worth a thousand Londons." [1] Even as late as March of the presidential year Reid was afraid that the time was not yet ripe for an open advance toward the nomination. "I've been a little scared of late," he wrote Blaine, "over what some of us persist in calling your boom. It began to look too booming for March." [2]

A year before, the Philadelphia *Press* had put Blaine's name at the head of its columns as the inevitable candidate for 1884. The iron and steel interests of Pennsylvania, represented by men like J. M. Swank, Joseph Wharton, and the latter's nephew Wharton Barker, together with the textile interests, were waging a spirited campaign for the maintenance of the protective system against the "British" doctrine of free trade, which would sap the prosperity of our factories and reduce our laborers to the level of the "paupers" of Europe.

Meanwhile, the reform element in the party had been gaining in numbers and influence. We have already noted the overthrow of the Cameron machine in Pennsylvania and the disintegration of the Conkling machine in New York. The year 1881 saw the entrance into public life of two young Republicans recently graduated from college, Seth Low being elected Mayor of Brooklyn and Theodore Roosevelt going to Albany for his first term as Assemblyman. Both were ardent reformers, and their appearance on the political scene was prophetic of the part which the younger generation was to play in the campaign of 1884. The Independents were wholly right in concentrating their opposition upon Blaine and ignoring Arthur, who was but the figurehead of the party. Carl Schurz was the animating spirit of the Independents. Retiring from the Secretaryship of the Interior in Hayes' Cabinet on March 4, 1881 (the last public office he was to fill), he was invited by Henry Villard to become the editor-in-chief of the New York *Evening Post*. With him was associated Edwin L. Godkin, editor of the New York *Nation,* the incomparable journalist whose brilliant and unsparing attacks on every form of venality, hypocrisy and corruption in

[1] Royal Cortissoz, *Life of Whitelaw Reid,* Vol. II, p. 77.
[2] *Ibid.,* p. 93.

public life for a decade and a half had made him the most hated and the most admired publicist in America. A third partner on the paper was Horace White, who had been editor of the Chicago *Tribune* for ten years (1864–1874) prior to the acquisition of that journal by Joseph Medill. The *Evening Post* was a daily, and as such offered its brilliant trio of editors the opportunity for a more sustained and cumulative criticism than the weekly *Nation,* which still remained under Godkin's direction and became virtually a weekly edition of the *Post.*

Schurz began his work on the *Evening Post* on May 26, 1881, with a "long and serious article on civil service reform," and continued hammering at corruption in high places until the summer of 1883, when he resigned from the editorship because of an inability to work harmoniously with the equally zealous but temperamental and dictatorial Godkin.[1] On August 8, 1882, Schurz came out in the *Post* with a savage attack on Blaine as a man unworthy of the presidential nomination and unfit for the presidential office; and when Blaine made his tardy concessions to the principle of civil service reform the next month, Godkin followed Schurz with a still more savage attack on him as a spoilsman and a friend of spoilsmen from the beginning of his career: he "had wallowed in spoils like a rhinoceros in an African pool." [2]

On taking charge of the *Evening Post,* Schurz had moved his residence from Saint Louis to New York, where he was to spend the remaining quarter of a century of his busy life. His immediate concern was to prevent the nomination of Blaine for the Presidency, and it was largely through his influence that George William Curtis was persuaded to turn *Harper's Weekly,* with its telling cartoons by Nast, against the Maine statesman. On February 12, 1884, Schurz spoke at a dinner of the Young Men's Republican Club of Brooklyn on the duty of preserving the ideals of George Washington. He called upon the youth of the nation to purge our politics of corruption, and sounded the tocsin of revolt against Blaine by declaring that his record showed him to be unfit for high office. The next day he helped organize the "Conference Committee of Independents," and persuaded the conference to address an appeal to the Republican voters to support only candidates who could

---

[1] Claude M. Fuess, *Carl Schurz, Reformer,* p. 273. Allan Nevins, *The Evening Post: a Century of Journalism,* pp. 438 ff.

[2] Blaine, believing Schurz to be the author of this scathing article, retorted in a letter to the Chicago *Tribune,* September 12, in which he accused the former Secretary of the Interior of having failed to accomplish reforms which he announced "with a ringing flourish of trumpets."

command the confidence of genuine reformers. Auxiliary committees were formed in Chicago, Cincinnati and other cities.[1] That Schurz was the chief lion in Blaine's path was evident; and it is equally evident that Blaine cherished a resentment against Schurz. Blaine's comments on his political opponents, and even upon the "rebels" from Jefferson Davis down, are singularly free from bitterness in the pages of the *Twenty Years of Congress;* but he dipped his pen in gall to portray Schurz as a political renegade "of uncertain and erratic tendencies," an Ishmaelite whose hand was against every man. "He has not become rooted and grounded anywhere, has never established a home, is not identified with any community. . . . The part he upheld yesterday met with his bitterest denunciations the day before, and tomorrow he will support the political organization of whose measures he is the most merciless censor today. He boasts himself incapable of attachment to party. . . . He cannot even comprehend that exalted sentiment of honorable association in public life which holds together successive generations of men—a sentiment which in the United States causes the Democrat to reverence the memory of Jefferson, Jackson and Douglas, which causes his opponent to glory in the achievements of Hamilton, Clay and Lincoln. . . . He aspires to the title of 'Independent,' and has described his own position as that of a man sitting on a fence with clean boots, watching carefully which way he may leap to keep out of the mud. . . . Nor is Mr. Schurz's independence of party more complete than his independence of true American feeling. He has taken no pride in appearing under the simple but lofty title of a citizen of the United States (!). . . . To Mr. Schurz the Republic is not great. 'This country,' he said in his Centennial lecture, 'is materially great, but morally small.' "[2] This uncharitable, and in the main unjust, characterization, embalmed for posterity in his book, was Blaine's rejoinder to the man who, "with the possible exception of a stupid clergyman," was most responsible for keeping him out of the White House.

Meantime, if we may attach credit to his statements both before and after the campaign, Blaine was not looking toward the White House. Gail Hamilton had "a long talk with him" in May, 1882, in which he said that there was only one place that he coveted in the future: "The Presidency might go, but he would like to carry out his views of statecraft

[1] *Appleton's Annual Cyclopaedia*, 1884, p. 767.
[2] J. G. Blaine, *Twenty Years of Congress,* Vol. II, pp. 439–41.

272   JAMES G. BLAINE

in 1885 as Secretary of State." [1] The following November he told Whitelaw Reid that he "did not wish to pose for an hour as a presidential
candidate." [2] A month later Mrs. Blaine wrote to her daughter: "Your
Father said yesterday that the Presidency came no more into his calculations. . . . He is so anxious to have a retirement in which he can
write"; [3] and again, on March 12, 1883: "I know the nomination of
1884 is not a *sujet défendu* exactly, for we all say what is in our minds.
But it is a *sujet* never there (!). Your Father is as little a candidate as
though he had succeeded in '76 and '80. The one thing he perhaps does
desire is to be once more Secretary of State." [4]

These disclaimers, however, which could be multiplied many fold,
did not prevent his friends from laboring for his nomination, even as
they have not convinced most of the historians of the period that he
was not an eager candidate for it. W. W. Phelps wrote jubilantly to Mrs.
Blaine on July 22, 1883, after a visit to Elberon, that both Grant and
Cornell were confident that Blaine would be the next President. The
same day John J. Ingalls wrote from Atchison, Kansas, with some dismay, that there were rumors that Blaine would not run in 1884. [5] And on
October 15 Walker Blaine wrote to his sister: "General Beale told me
that he regarded Father as the only candidate for the Republicans.
That's pretty strong for such a Grant man. But I doubt much whether
the Republicans can elect anybody." [6] Perhaps this last sentence is the
key to the position of Blaine, who knew full well what efforts his supporters were making for him, and yet could not stifle the misgivings
that he would be beaten at the polls. It was not the nomination but the
election that worried him. With his aptitude for discounting future failure with present forebodings, he endeavored to put the nomination out
of his calculations, refusing to busy himself to secure delegates, writing
to his "volunteer campaign manager" Stephen B. Elkins to allow no
pledges to be made or money spent in his behalf, [7] and remarking a few
weeks before the convention, with a curious combination of diffidence
and power: "I do not think I shall be nominated, but I am disturbing
the calculations of others at an astonishing rate." [8] "If he cannot himself

[1] Gail Hamilton, *Biography of James G. Blaine*, p. 564.
[2] Royal Cortissoz, *Life of Whitelaw Reid*, Vol. II, p. 91.
[3] Gail Hamilton, *op. cit.*, p. 618.
[4] *Letters of Mrs. James G. Blaine*, Vol. II, p. 90.
[5] Ingalls to Blaine, July 22, 1883.
[6] Gail Hamilton, *Biography of James G. Blaine*, p. 622.
[7] James Ford Rhodes, *From Hayes to McKinley*, p. 208.
[8] Gail Hamilton, *op. cit.*, p. 624.

be President," wrote Mrs. Blaine to Margaret, "neither can any other Republican without his consent." [1]

Blaine did not come out for any other candidate. He could not, of course, as the "residuary legatee of Garfield's popularity," support President Arthur.[2] His old rivals were rapidly passing out of the picture. Hayes, who had abjured a renomination in 1880, would not even run for Governor of Ohio three years later to save the state from a Democratic victory under George Hoadly. Grant had allowed a group of rascals in Wall Street, led by Ferdinand Ward, to capitalize his great reputation and his thirst for riches by drawing him as a "silent partner" into a swindling scheme, of whose operations he knew nothing and cared nothing so long as he drew the handsome dividends paid him; until the "firm" of Grant and Ward crashed in May, 1884, leaving him penniless. He died the following year, fighting bravely against the cancer in his throat for time to finish the *Memoirs* which were to pay his debts. Conkling's political career was over, and his machine in ruins. John Sherman, running true to form, was demonstrating his inability to get more than a scattering support outside of his own State of Ohio. It looked for a moment as though Senator Benjamin Harrison of Indiana might loom large as a candidate. He visited Maine to aid in the Republican redemption campaign of 1882, and was entertained by Blaine at Augusta. "There was Ben Harrison," wrote Mrs. Blaine to her daughter, on September 3, "who is very likely to be the next presidential nominee— did I hear you sigh?—and your Father would not but have him entertained in this house for all the world." [3] Nevertheless, when Blaine went west a few days later to redeem his promise to speak for Senator Plumb in Kansas, he ignored Harrison's pressing invitation to "make some speeches in Indiana," where "we very much need you and shall be much disappointed if you do not come." [4] Blaine probably did not need the warning conveyed in one of the few letters of Mrs. Blaine to her husband that have survived: "I see that you are reported as taking part in a political conference yesterday at which Harrison was present. I am sure you did not; but I venture to say, Don't. All I ask you is to stay dumb." [5]

[1] *Letters of Mrs. James G. Blaine*, Vol. II, p. 91.
[2] "I do not desire or expect the nomination," wrote Blaine to Ingalls, on February 22, 1884, "but I don't intend that man in the White House shall have it." Rhodes, *op. cit.*, p. 208.
[3] *Letters of Mrs. James G. Blaine*, Vol. II, pp. 48–9.
[4] Harrison to Blaine, September 9, 1882.
[5] *Letters of Mrs. James G. Blaine*, Vol. II, p. 52.

JAMES G. BLAINE

Blaine had no intention of "grooming" Harrison for the Presidency in
1884.[1]

Only nine days before the meeting of the convention, however, Blaine
wrote a letter, marked "Confidential and strictly and absolutely so," to
General William T. Sherman, which deserves a place among the curiosi-
ties of political literature. It ran:

Washington, D.C.
May 25, 1884.

My dear General:

This letter requires no answer. After reading it file it away in your most
secret drawer or give it to the flames. At the approaching convention at Chicago
it is more than possible . . . that you may be nominated for the Presidency.
If so you must stand your hand, accept the responsibility and assume the
duties of the place to which you will surely be chosen if a candidate. You must
not look upon it as the work of the politicians. . . . If it comes to you, it
will come as the ground-swell of popular demand—and you can no more refuse than you could have refused to obey an order when you were a lieutenant
in the army. If it comes to you at all it will come as a call of patriotism. It
would, in such an event, injure your great fame as much to decline it as it
would for you to seek it. Your historical record, full as it is, would be rendered
still more glorious by such an administration as you would be able to give
the country. Do not say a word in advance of the convention, no matter who
may ask you. You are with your friends, who will jealously guard your honor.
Do not answer this.

One can imagine how the grizzled old soldier rubbed his eyes on the
receipt of this amazing letter. He answered it promptly in no uncertain terms. He had chosen his career and fulfilled his destiny. He was
now in a good home, "with reasonable provision for old age, surrounded
by kind and admiring friends, in a community where Catholicism is
held in respect (Mrs. Sherman was a Roman Catholic), and where my
children will naturally grow up in contact with an industrious and frugal
people." He would in no event entertain or accept a nomination for the
Presidency, nor could "patriotism" be construed to make such a claim
on him. Any Senator could "step from his chair into the White House
and fulfill the office of President with more skill and success than a
Grant, Sherman or Sheridan, who were soldiers by education and nature,

[1] The Harrison supporters fought fiercely in the state convention in the spring of 1884
to have his name presented to the national convention as the choice of Indiana. But the
Blaine managers, combining with the backers of Walter Q. Gresham, blocked the Harrison
boom, and the Indiana delegation gave 18 of its 40 votes to Blaine, and 9 to Arthur,
on the first ballot.

but not schooled in the practices by which civil communities are and should be governed." He would account himself "a fool and a madman and an ass to embark anew, at sixty-five years of age, in a career that may at any moment become tempest-tossed by the perfidy, the defalcation, the dishonesty or neglect of any one of a hundred thousand subordinates utterly unknown to the President of the United States." "I remember well," he concluded, "the experience of Generals Jackson, Harrison, Taylor, Grant, Hayes and Garfield, all elected because of their military services, and am warned, not encouraged, by their sad experiences. No, count me out. The civilians of the United States should and must buffet with this thankless office, and leave us old soldiers the peace we fought for and think we earned." [1]

This straightforward and sensible reply apparently satisfied Blaine of the futility of attempting to "draft" General Sherman, for we hear nothing further from him on the subject. There is evidence, however, that there was a considerable demand for "Sherman for President." The General himself, in his reply to Blaine said that he "had a great many letters from all points of the compass to a similar effect." John Sherman seemed to think that his brother might be drafted by popular demand. He wrote to the General just a month before the convention: "It is certain that if Blaine is not named in the early ballots a movement will be made for your nomination, and if entered upon you will go like wildfire. Someone should be authorized to make a definite and positive refusal if you have concluded to decline the nomination, if tendered. My own opinion is still that, while you ought not to seek, or even beforehand consent to accept the nomination, yet if it comes unsought and with cordial unanimity you ought to acquiesce. I believe it would be best for the country, honorable to you and your children, and far less irksome than you have thought." [2] General Sherman lost no time in making his "definite and positive refusal." To J. B. Henderson, who was chosen permanent chairman of the convention, he telegraphed that if his name were presented, the honor should be "declined with emphasis." An attempt was made by Senator Hoar and George W. Curtis to swing the convention to General Sherman, but when a large number of delegates voiced objections to have "a father confessor in the White House"

---

[1] The letters of Blaine and Sherman are printed in Gail Hamilton's *Biography of James G. Blaine*, pp. 624–5. Sherman did not commit Blaine's letter to the flames, but published it in the *North American Review* for December, 1888.

[2] *The Sherman Letters*, p. 357.

it was abandoned.[1] The General received only two votes (from Michigan) on the first ballot.[2]

As the opposition to Blaine increased in the spring months of 1884, his supporters redoubled their zeal, dismissing the Independents as holier-than-thou prigs or as renegades seduced by the British doctrine of free trade—"a squad of men who were attempting to bully the party."[3] But a "squad of men" containing figures like Schurz, Curtis, Lodge, Hoar, White, Eliot and Godkin could not be disposed of quite so cavalierly. Ex-President Hayes, who was neither a renegade nor a free trader, confided an extremely unfavorable opinion of Blaine to his *Diary* on April 19, 1884: "He lacks the confidence of thoughtful, high-minded and patriotic people. They doubt his personal integrity; they think he is a demagogue."[4] Curtis declared that if Blaine were nominated the campaign would be "a prolonged explanation" and a "practical abdication of Republican character and purpose."[5]

A more spectacular attack was made by the cartoonists Nast and Gillam. The latter, in a wantonly coarse cartoon in *Puck* for April 16, which was exploited with telling effect during the campaign, portrayed Blaine as "Phryne before the Chicago Tribunal." Blaine stands, clad in a loin cloth, a "magnetic pad" on his chest, his averted eyes hidden by his upstretched arm, before the jury seated like Roman Senators on their marble benches. The cloak has just been removed from his shoulders, revealing his body all tattooed with the legends "Mulligan Letters," "Bribery," "Anti-Chinese Demagogism," "Northern Pacific Bonds," "Little Rock," "Jingoism," "Bluster"; while the judges, among whom one sees the faces of Curtis, Evarts, Schurz, Beecher, Jewell, Edmunds and even Logan, are gazing on the scene with various expressions of horror, sadness, disgust or cynical amusement. The Blaine papers

---

[1] George F. Hoar, *Autobiography of Seventy Years*, Vol. I, p. 407.

[2] General Sherman's attitude toward the nomination is made hopelessly enigmatic by two events which are at variance with the professions quoted above. In the first place, the permanent chairman, to whom he telegraphed his emphatic refusal to run, lauded "the grand old hero of Kenesaw Mountain and Atlanta" in his speech on taking the chair, as one who, if patriotism called, would "not be silent, but would grasp the banner and march to a civic victory no less renowned than those of war." And, in the second place, General Sherman himself, writing to Blaine on the day of the nomination, said: "I am told that the proper thing to do is for rival candidates to shake hands, and for the defeated to congratulate the victor. I will now admit that I was a candidate before the Chicago convention (!), but am nevertheless willing to congratulate you on your brilliant success before that august body, and I honestly wish you success at the election next November." (Gail Hamilton, *Biography of James G. Blaine*, p. 626.)

[3] New York *Tribune*, May 5, 1884.

[4] C. R. Williams ed., *The Diary and Letters of Rutherford B. Hayes*, Vol. IV, p. 146.

[5] E. P. Oberholtzer, *History of the United States Since the Civil War*, Vol. IV, p. 169.

promptly called attention to the fact that Gillam was an Englishman, but that did not erase the shameless cartoon. The circulation of *Puck* ran into the millions, and the "Tattooed Man" became the picture of Blaine in the minds of masses of people who were incapable of examining his record. With the exception of Nast's famous drawing of the Tammany Ring, "Who Stole the People's Money," at the time of the exposure of Boss Tweed's colossal plundering of New York City in 1871, it is doubtful if any cartoon in our history ever had the vogue and influence of Gillam's Tattooed Man.

Blaine's friends came to his defense manfully. Whitelaw Reid in the *Tribune* reiterated daily the faith of the people in the "ability, integrity and sturdy Americanism" of the ex-Secretary of State. The aspersions of his opponents, "false, malignant and unsustained by evidence," were only the camouflage to hide their hostility to the American protectionist system. The tariff was the real issue, on which Blaine bade Reid to "agonize more and more." W. W. Phelps prepared an elaborate article, which appeared in the *Evening Post* for April 26, 1884, examining in detail the charges made against Blaine in his railroad dealings, tearing the alleged damaging testimony of the Mulligan Letters "to shreds" (in the opinion of the *Tribune*) and generally refuting the "stale slanders" that were being resuscitated by the Democrats and the Independents on the eve of the convention. The Blaineites were confident of success. They were already beginning to divide the spoils of victory. If some of them were apprehensive of defection in the ranks, most of them believed that the disgruntled Independents would rally to the support of their brilliant leader (as, indeed, many of them did) after he had demonstrated his hold on the party by distancing his rivals in the race for the nomination.

The eighth national convention of the Republican Party met at Chicago on June 3, 1884, in the same Exposition Building which had been the scene of Garfield's nomination four years before. The Reverend F. M. Bristol, in the opening invocation, thanked God for the splendid history of the Republican Party and besought (vainly, as it proved) that "the coming political campaign may be conducted with that decency, intelligence, patriotism and dignity of temper which become a free and intelligent people." [1]

---

[1] *Official Proceedings of the Convention*, Rand McNally and Company, Chicago, 1884, pp. 3, 4.

The first test of sentiment among the 820 delegates revealed an opposition to Blaine which, had it been concentrated on any other single candidate, would have spelled his defeat. The Blaine forces, which controlled the national committee, had selected for temporary chairman ex-Governor Powell Clayton of Alabama, a recent recruit from the Arthur camp. When Clayton's nomination was made, Henry Cabot Lodge of Massachusetts immediately moved that the name of John R. Lynch, a colored delegate from Mississippi and a supporter of President Arthur, be substituted. His motion was seconded by "an active, nervous, light-haired, gray-eyed young man who had just thrown off a straw hat and scrambled to his perch on a chair with juvenile agility, and was greeted with a burst of rousing applause." [1] It was the first appearance of Theodore Roosevelt, delegate at large from New York, on the national stage. He was twenty-five years old. Defending the freedom of the convention to reject the recommendation of the national committee, he urged that the vote on the temporary chairman be taken by an individual poll of the delegates: "Let each man stand accountable to those whom he represents for his vote. Let no man be able to shelter himself behind the shield of his State. . . . One of the cardinal doctrines of the American political government is the accountability of each man to his people; and let each man stand up here and cast his vote, and then go home and abide by what he has done." [2] In spite of the plea of the Powell-Blaine men that there should be "no division with respect to so simple a question" as choosing a temporary chairman, "when we are proposing to start with unanimity and courage to lay the foundations of a campaign that shall lead to victory," [3] the roll call resulted in the choice of Lynch by a vote of 424 to 384. But the anti-Blaine forces were mistaken in interpreting this vote as a presage of the ex-Secretary's defeat. It was the only check he received in the convention.

The various committees on credentials, permanent organization, rules and platform were chosen with harmony and dispatch. The usual number of memorials and petitions were presented—from the Woman's Christian Temperance Union, representing twenty-eight States and Ter-

---

[1] New York *Times*, June 4, 1884.
[2] *Proceedings*, p. 10. Except for a few words on the third day in regard to the apportionment of delegates in the next convention, Roosevelt took no further part in the proceedings. He continued to cast his vote steadily for Senator Edmunds, but refused to join the revolt of the Mugwumps when Blaine was nominated.
[3] *Ibid.*, p. 7.

ritories, asking for a prohibition amendment to the Constitution; from the Irish National League of America, asking that "American land should belong alone to those willing to assume the duties and responsibilities of American citizenship; from the Delaware delegation, recommending the limitation of the Presidency to a single term of six years; from a California delegate, asking that "the great and fundamental industry of our country" be recognized by the addition of a Secretary of Agriculture to the President's Cabinet; from Senator Hoar of Massachusetts, advocating nation-wide woman suffrage.[1]

All of these propositions were duly referred to the Committee on Resolutions, and there died. The only resolution that provoked a lively discussion on the floor was the revival of Roscoe Conkling's motion in the convention of 1880 that no delegate should be entitled to hold his seat who would not pledge himself to support the nominee of the convention. George Knight of California, speaking in behalf of the resolution, virtually acknowledged that its purpose was to bind the members to support Blaine. "There are already whispers in the air," he said, "of men high in the Republican Party, or that once stood high in the party, openly and avowedly declaring that they will not support one man if he be nominated by this convention. . . . That kind of men we want to know, and the sooner they are out of the Republican Party the better." Stung by this insult, the more pointed because Knight had specified "editors of newspapers or great periodical journals" as among those deserving to be "branded," George William Curtis was on his feet in an instant, protesting: "A Republican and a free man I came into this convention. By the grace of God, a Republican and a free man I will go out of this convention. Twenty-four years ago I was here in Chicago and took part with the men who nominated the man who bears the most illustrious name in the Republican Party. The gentleman last upon the floor says that he dares any man on this floor to vote against his resolution. I say to him in reply that the presentation of such a resolution in such a convention as this is a stigma, is an insult to every honorable member who sits here."[2] Curtis' spirited challenge, like Campbell's of West Virginia in 1880, as a "Republican who carries his sovereignty under his own hat," won the instant applause of the convention; and Hawkins of Tennessee, who had moved the resolution, hastened to

[1] *Proceedings*, pp. 31, 36, 44, 45.
[2] *Ibid.*, pp. 37–8.

withdraw it.

On the third day William McKinley, Chairman of the Committee on Resolutions, read the platform. Running true to the traditions from which national conventions have not departed since their inception a century ago, it "pointed with pride" to the accomplishments of the party in power, and "viewed with alarm" the disasters which the triumph of the opposing party would bring upon the country. It commended the "wise, conservative and patriotic policy" of President Arthur, whose "eminent services are entitled to and will receive the hearty approval of every citizen." Conspicuous among its score of planks were: the maintenance of our customs duties "to afford security to our diversified industries and protection to the rights and wages of our laborers"; a sound currency, based, if possible, on an international agreement fixing the relative value of gold and silver coinage; the public regulation of railway corporations; the exclusion of contract labor; the further reform of the civil service, "auspiciously begun under a Republican Administration"; generous pensions; the upbuilding of the navy and the encouragement of foreign commerce; abstinence from entangling political alliances; and a denunciation of the "fraud and violence" by which the Southern Democracy was defeating "a free ballot, an honest count and correct returns" in our national elections. The platform was unanimously adopted; the members of the national committee for the ensuing four years were named; and, the formal business of organization thus completed, the convention adjourned until 7.30 in the evening for the nomination of candidates.

Connecticut was the first State reached in the alphabetical roll call to bring a response, when Augustus Brandegee made his way to the platform and, in a flamboyant oration, placed the name of Joseph R. Hawley before the convention. In his effusive panegyric there was one passage whose pointed reference to Blaine could not be missed: "General Hawly believes in the morality of practical politics. He is a reformer. . . . His public record is without a flaw. There is nothing to apologize for; there is nothing to conceal; there is nothing to extenuate and naught to defend. The fierce light which beats against the presidential candidate will explore his record in vain. He will come out brighter for the blaze." [1] It was a note which was to be sounded more than once again in the presentation speeches; but its effect was rather to fan than to dampen

[1] *Proceedings*, p. 100.

the ardor of the devotion of the "Blaine legion" to their chief. Unquestioned innocence commanded respect, to be sure, but the triumphant refutation of foul slanders aroused enthusiasm.

When the State of Illinois was reached, Senator Shelby M. Cullom nominated the popular major general of volunteers, John A. Logan, who "never lost a battle" and who stood "closer to the great mass of people in this country than almost any other man now engaged in public affairs." [1] The "Black Eagle," as General Logan was called, might be the idol of the soldiers of the Grand Army of the Republic (for he had been three times elected commander of the organization and had been active in Congress in pushing pension bills), but for the intelligentsia and the reformers in the party he was only the uncouth member of the triumvirate of Conkling, Cameron and Logan, who had secured a solid Grant delegation in the Illinois State convention of 880 by methods so shameless as to rouse the better citizens of Chicago to call a mass meeting of protest and to send anti-Grant delegates to the national convention to contest the credentials of the Logan appointees on the floor.

Indiana, Iowa, Kansas, Kentucky and Louisiana were called without reply. Then came the turn of Maine, and pandemonium broke loose. "There was an instant, clear, loud shout, the cheer rattling through the hall like a volley of infantry, then deepening as it grew in force like the roar of a cannon, then swelling like the crash of a thunderbolt. With a common impulse the audience, delegates and spectators, sprang to their feet. From the stage to the end of the hall, a distance of an eighth of a mile, the cheering became a wild tumult of applause. When Judge West, the blind orator of Ohio, was helped to the platform by two young men, the applause again rolled through the hall, and as the orator, lifting his right hand above his head, compelled silence, ten minutes of uproar was followed by a silence in which a whisper could be heard." [2]

The nominating speech of Judge West was no such perfunctory performance as James F. Joy's in the same hall four years earlier. It had all the fiery enthusiasm of Ingersoll's at Cincinnati in 1876. There were many men worthy to bear the banner of the party, he said, but only one "grand civic hero" who would kindle the ardor of Republicans young and old all over the nation, to "sweep onward to certain victory." He was the Ajax Telamon of the party. "Through all its conflicts, from the bap-

<hr>

[1] *Proceedings*, p. 102.
[2] Quoted from an eye-witness by Gail Hamilton, *Biography of James G. Blaine*, pp. 572–3.

tism of blood on the plains of Kansas to the fall of the immortal Garfield, wherever humanity needed succor or freedom needed protection or the country a champion, wherever blows fell thickest and fastest, there in the forefront of the battle was seen to wave the white plume of James G. Blaine, our Henry of Navarre. Nominate him, and the shouts of September victory in Maine will be reëchoed back by the thunder of October victory in Ohio. Nominate him, and the camp fires and beacon lights will illuminate the continent from the Golden Gate to Cleopatra's Needle. Nominate him, and the millions who are now in waiting will rally to swell the column of victory that is sweeping on. In the name of a majority of the delegates from the Republican States and their glorious constituencies who must fight this battle, I nominate James G. Blaine of Maine." [1]

The magic name was no sooner uttered than pandemonium broke loose again. "Whole delegations mounted their chairs and led the cheering, which instantly spread to the stage and deepened into a roar fully as deafening as the voice of Niagara. The scene was indescribable. The air quivered, the gas lights trembled and the walls fairly shook." [2] The delegates stripped the flags, shields and banners from the stage and the galleries and paraded up and down the aisles. A helmet decorated with a snow-white plume was raised on a color staff and borne to the platform. Men tore off their coats and waved them wildly, while hats and umbrellas were tossed in the air, and the bands vied in vain with the babel of shouting. Even women in the galleries "jumped up and down, disheveled and hysterical." The whole scene, wrote President Andrew D. White of Cornell, a delegate at large from New York, was "absolutely unworthy of a convention of any party, a disgrace to decency and a blot upon the reputation of our country." [3] The New York *Nation* called it "a mass meeting of maniacs." [4] When order had been finally restored, Blaine's name was seconded by Cushman K. Davis of Minnesota, Colonel W. C. Goodloe of Kentucky, Thomas C. Platt of New York and Galusha A. Grow of Pennsylvania. Their words added nothing of significance to the speech of Judge West, but there was plenty of significance in the fact that Conkling's former colleague, who but three years before had resigned with him from the Senate in protest against Blaine's

[1] *Proceedings*, pp. 104–106.
[2] New York *Tribune*, June 6, 1884.
[3] Andrew D. White, *Autobiography*, Vol. I, p. 206.
[4] New York *Nation*, June 12, 1884.

defiance of the Stalwarts in the Robertson appointment, now "rose with pleasure" to second Blaine's nomination—"believing as I do that his turn has come." [1]

President Arthur, who was eager for the nomination, had no mean support in the convention. The "mercenary brigade" of Federal office-holders in the Southern States, which would not contribute a single electoral vote to the Republican column, sent delegations to Chicago pledged to the President, and to their 195 votes were added 31 of the 72 from New York, where many of the big business interests backed Arthur as a "safe" candidate. One of their representatives, Martin I. Townsend of Troy, presented Arthur's name in a sane and forceful speech. He pertinently asked how, after having declared in their platform that the President's "wise, conservative and patriotic policy" was entitled to the "hearty approval of every citizen," they could consistently refuse him the endorsement of a renomination. The fact that Conkling and Platt were opposed to Arthur was enough in itself to recommend him. And what will the Democrats say if we repudiate this "good and faithful servant"? "You have been prating ten years about the reform of the civil service, about having a nonfactional Administration. You found one, as you say yourselves. And yet for the purpose of picking up somebody else you have struck down and cast into oblivion, as far as you had the power to do it, the very man who has done the work that you set him to do." [2] Bingham of Pennsylvania, Winston of North Carolina, Lynch of Mississippi and Pinchback of Louisiana (the last two colored delegates) seconded the nomination. But Arthur's name failed to arouse the delegates. Everything that came after the wild demonstration for Blaine was in the nature of an anticlimax. Arthur was, after all, only a "President by accident," who had alienated the Stalwarts without conciliating the Halfbreeds. The only credit that the latter would give him was that he had "done less mischief than he

---

[1] In his *Autobiography* (p. 181) Platt says: "Just before departing for the Chicago convention of 1884, I called on Senator Conkling. I astonished him by announcing, 'I am going to Chicago to fight for the nomination of James G. Blaine. What do you think of that?' Conkling was struck speechless. When he found his breath, he exclaimed, 'Well, Senator Platt, you are about to do what I could not bring myself to do. You know what Blaine did to us.' 'Yes, but Arthur has deserted us, Edmunds is the choice of the most offensive of our New York foes. Blaine is to be preferred to either of them.' Conkling warned me that I was committing an egregious blunder. But I went to Chicago, secured the nomination of Blaine (!), and returned with at least the satisfaction of having compassed the defeat of Arthur and Edmunds." Platt even did his utmost "to induce Senator Conkling to take the stump for Blaine." (p. 183.)

[2] *Proceedings*, pp. 110–114.

was expected to do." "All in the world that we want of him," wrote Reid to W. W. Phelps a few months before the convention, "is to die with reasonable decency when the necessity of his political death at last dawns on his vision." [1]

It was now drawing near midnight, but the convention voted down a motion to adjourn, and the roll call continued. J. B. Foraker of Ohio rose to nominate John Sherman, deprecating the "noise and demonstration" in which the delegates had indulged a little while before, but the only response that he got was another outburst of cheering when he incidentally mentioned his "admiration for that brilliant genius from Maine." If he hoped to dampen the ardor for Blaine by concluding his speech with the demand for a candidate who had a record "so clear, so bright as not only to defy criticism, but at the same time to make him the representative of all the highest and purest ambitions of the great Republican Party," [2] he had only his pains for his reward.

Vermont was the last of the States to present a candidate, in the person of Senator George F. Edmunds, on whom the Independents—like Schurz, Curtis, White and Roosevelt in New York, and Pierce, Codman, Hoar, Lodge, Crapo and Long of Massachusetts—had pinned their hopes of defeating Blaine. Edmunds was the most distinguished member of the Senate, in which he had served continuously since 1866 and of which he had been elected president *pro tempore* when Arthur went into the White House. His name had stood next after Grant's, Blaine's and Sherman's on the first ballot in 1880. All that ex-Governor Long claimed for him in the finely tempered speech in which he put his name in nomination before the delegates was true: the "tested service," the "tried incorruptibility," the "unscathed walk through the storms and fires of public life." The country had confidence in the Republican Party and demanded as its standard bearer a man who represented no wing or faction of the party. Senator Edmunds was the man to meet this need. Against no other candidate could less be said than against him; for no other candidate could more be said.[3] Curtis sec-

[1] Royal Cortissoz, *Life of Whitelaw Reid*, Vol. II, p. 92. Grant wrote to Adam Badeau on April 8, 1884, that the Arthur Administration was an "ad interim" one which had "fewer positively hearty friends than any except Hayes possibly. But Arthur will probably go into the convention second in the number of supporters, when he would not probably have a single vote if it was not for his army of officials and the vacancies he has to fill." Adam Badeau, *Grant in Peace*, p. 558.
[2] *Proceedings*, p. 123.
[3] *Ibid.*, p. 125.

onded the nomination by a glowing tribute to Edmunds as "a man identified with every great measure of the Republican past and a pioneer in every measure of its future reform." His name would be a pledge of the utter destruction of "whatever disgraces the public service, whatever defiles the Republican name and whatever defeats the just expectations of the country and of the Republican Party." [1]

It was long past midnight when the "tide of eloquence," as one weary delegate put it, at length subsided. The convention had listened for more than five hours to sixteen nominating speeches, and when Foraker of Ohio moved that it proceed to ballot, an acrimonius debate over the question of adjournment followed. In the midst of the confusion and wrangling, when it became impossible at times for the delegates to hear the Chair put the motions, adjournment was finally approved by a viva voce vote at a quarter past two on the morning of June 6, and the balloting postponed till eleven o'clock the same morning.

Blaine's strength was shown on the first ballot, when he received 334½ votes from 38 States and Territories, even taking 21 of the 46 delegates of Ohio from John Sherman. Except for the solid delegation from Maine, however, he had but a single vote from the New England States. Arthur's name came next (as Grant had prophesied) with 278 votes, all but 52 from New York and the States south of Mason and Dixon's line. Then the figures dropped sharply to 93 for Edmunds, 63½ for Logan, 30 for John Sherman, 13 for Hawley, and 4 and 2 respectively for Robert T. Lincoln and General Sherman, who had not been formally nominated. The only possible chance of defeating the Maine statesman lay in a merger of the Arthur and Edmunds votes, which would have brought the President's total up to 371, or only 40 short of the necessary majority. But Arthur was as unacceptable as Blaine to the Massachusetts delegation, which cast 25 of its 28 votes for Edmunds. Thus, paradoxically enough, it was the Massachusetts Independents who made Blaine's nomination inevitable.[2] The second and third ballots showed a steady gain for Blaine (334½ to 375), while Arthur virtually

[1] *Proceedings*, p. 127.
[2] George F. Hoar states in his *Autobiography of Seventy Years* (Vol. I, p. 406) that it was the replacement of Alanson W. Beard, the efficient Collector of the Port of Boston by a satellite of Ben Butler's that alienated the Massachusetts Republicans from the President. But for this offense to "the best people" of the Bay State, he says, all but three of their delegates to the Chicago convention would have supported Arthur. "There would have been no movement for Edmunds, and but for that movement Mr. Arthur would have received the nomination." Both the clauses of this last sentence seem to me highly debatable, to say the least.

286 JAMES G. BLAINE

held his own (278 to 274), and Edmunds, Logan and Sherman lost ground. On the completion of the third ballot a motion for a recess was lost by a vote of 364 to 450. It was clear that the tide toward Blaine could not be stemmed.

Then Judge Foraker, John Sherman's spokesman, moved that the rules be suspended and that "James G. Blaine be nominated by acclamation." Angry shouts of "No! No!" mingled with the cheers that greeted this motion; and Foraker withdrew it to allow the call for the fourth ballot to proceed. When Illinois was reached, Cullom withdrew the name of General Logan and cast 34 of the 44 votes of the State for Blaine. A few moments later Foraker withdrew Sherman's name and announced the solid vote of Ohio's 46 delegates for Blaine. These not unexpected shifts [1] carried Blaine's vote far above the required majority. At the end of the ballot the vote stood 541 for Blaine, 207 for Arthur, 41 for Edmunds, 15 for Hawley, 7 for Logan, and 2 for Lincoln. When the frantic demonstrations of rejoicing which had accompanied the clerk's announcement had calmed down, the nomination was made unanimous. Logan was named for the Vice Presidency on the first ballot, with only 7 dissenting votes. A telegram was read from President Arthur, pledging "Earnest and Cordial Support" to the candidate. Platt's prophecy was fulfilled. Blaine's turn had come.

[1] Logan, who was utterly unfit for the Presidency, entered the lists only for the sake of "making a trade," according to the New York *Nation* (Apr. 3, 1884). And Reid had written to Blaine in the same month: "Elkins tells me that General Tom Ewing says he has assurances from John Sherman that at the proper time you will get his strength in Ohio." (Royal Cortissoz, *Life of Whitelaw Reid*, Vol. II, pp. 93–4.)

Chapter XII   *The Mugwump Campaign*

A MAN of far less political sagacity than James G. Blaine could not but be aware of the protest against venality and corruption in high places which was gathering strength in the second decade after the Civil War. The Liberal Republican movement of 1872, though securing the acceptance of its "preposterous" candidate, Horace Greeley, by the Democratic convention, was unable to stem the tide of popular enthusiasm for the reëlection of the North's great military hero; but the cumulative effect of the revelations of such scandals as the Crédit Mobilier, the Sanborn contracts, the Tweed Ring, the whisky frauds, and the Belknap graft, was to weaken the claims to support by the party which had held the reins of government since the Charleston batteries had turned Major Anderson out of Fort Sumter. The Republican Party of Lincoln had preserved the Union and abolished slavery. These were great accomplishments, gratefully recognized by the allegiance of the majority of the citizens north of Mason and Dixon's line. But the Republican Party of Grant had degenerated into an association of spoilsmen (with honorable exceptions), pandering to wealth, avid of power, vexed by faction, and covering their obvious derelictions of present duty with the emotional appeal to the electorate to "vote as they shot" and preserve "the fruits of the war." It was living on past capital, and its resources dwindled as the political currency of "treason," "copperheadism," "Southern outrages," and general Democratic diabolism contracted. In 1876 a clear majority of the votes of the country had been cast for the Democratic candidate, Tilden, who had been kept out of the White House only by a strictly partisan, eight to seven vote of the special electoral commission chosen to determine between rival sets of election returns from South Carolina, Louisiana, Florida and Oregon. President Hayes' honest Administration had done much to redeem the prestige of the party, but Hayes himself had been flouted by the Stalwart wing of the party, while factional strife and the insolence of powerful bosses raged with fresh violence during the Administrations of Garfield and Arthur.

As Arthur's term progressed, there were evidences enough that the reform spirit which had flared up in 1872, 1876 and 1880 was not dead. The anti-Grant men of 1880 had formed an association at Chicago, with Wayne MacVeagh at its head, to organize nation-wide meetings of protest in case the military hero were nominated for a third term. When that danger passed and MacVeagh went into Garfield's Cabinet, the movement naturally fell into abeyance; but, nevertheless, such incidents as the revolt of Pattison against the Cameron machine, the election of Seth Low as Mayor of Brooklyn and of Grover Cleveland as Governor of New York, the formation of reform clubs in various cities, and the Democratic victories of 1882 in Michigan, Illinois, Kansas, Colorado and other supposedly safe Republican States, all showed how strongly the current of discontent was running—a current which was still further reinforced by the general business depression of the early '80's. The New York *Nation* in the late autumn of 1883 estimated that there were 80,000 independent voters in the Empire State.[1] Blaine himself doubted whether "any Republican could be elected in 1884."

However, the collapse of the Edmunds movement and the general weakness of the opposition to Blaine's nomination at Chicago confirmed the standpat Republican leaders in their attitude of contempt for the Independents, as a negligible group of disgruntled, conceited Pharisees, posing as "holier-than-thou" virtuosos in politics. The enthusiasm for Blaine swept the convention with a force which carried the Edmunds men off their feet. Lodge left Chicago for the East with the announcement that he would support the Blaine and Logan ticket. Roosevelt departed for the West, dissatisfied with the nomination, but apparently undecided whether to bolt the ticket or not.[2] George William

---

[1] New York *Nation*, November 29, 1883.

[2] Roosevelt gave out the noncommittal statement: "To say that I am satisfied with the nomination of Mr. Blaine would be false. I have participated in a Republican convention, and by all the usages of the party I would be expected to support the nominee." (New York *Times*, June 7, 1884.) Rumors were circulated that he intended to remain in the Republican fold, but when the New York *Evening Post* telegraphed him for confirmation of the report, he replied (June 12) that he had "nothing for publication." On the other hand, when the campaign was near its close and Roosevelt was working for Blaine and Logan, Horace White published a letter in the New York *Times* (Oct. 23, 1884) telling how Roosevelt had come to his hotel room late in the night following Blaine's nomination and, reading a dispatch which White was sending to the *Post*, predicting a revolt among the Republicans, had declared that the wording was not strong enough: "If I were writing it, I would say that any proper Democratic nominee will have our hearty support." This alleged remark Roosevelt promptly repudiated, as he had denied the report in June that he would support Blaine. "I utterly fail to recognize my own words," he said in the Boston *Globe* of October 24. He had "felt bitterly angry," he confessed, at the result of the convention's work, and had so expressed himself

Curtis, who had spoken in the most glowing terms of his devotion to the Republican Party, hesitated for a month after the nomination of Blaine, and then came out for the Democratic candidate.[1]

That the Blaine supporters were sadly mistaken in their estimate of the strength of the opposition became evident immediately after the convention adjourned. On June 7, a meeting of the Massachusetts Reform Club was held at the Parker House in Boston, which repudiated Blaine and Logan and organized to defeat their election by the appointment of a committee including such outstanding citizens as Charles Francis Adams, jr., Josiah Quincy, Morefield Storey, William Everett, James Freeman Clarke, and Thomas Wentworth Higginson. The New York *Times* the next day published a batch of letters filling three columns, from Republican voters who were bolting the ticket. On the thirteenth a second meeting was held in Boston, attended by over five hundred Independents, representing "the best brains" in the city, "united to rebuke corrupt men and corrupt methods in politics." Higginson, Clarke, Everett and President Eliot of Harvard made addresses. An executive committee of one hundred was appointed to conduct the independent campaign, and delegates were chosen to attend a conference to be held in New York four days later. The meeting censured the Massachusetts delegates to the Chicago convention for not opposing Blaine's nomination "unanimously and to the end," though as a matter of fact only one of the twenty-eight Massachusetts men had voted for Blaine on the first three ballots and only three on the final ballot.[2]

"in private conversation, to two or three gentlemen," but in the excitement of the moment he had not wished to commit himself, and had therefore "positively refused to say anything in public." Which does not, of course, preclude the possibility that Mr. White was one of the two or three gentlemen to whom Roosevelt expressed his "bitter anger" in private conversation. Henry Cabot Lodge says that he and Roosevelt had agreed *before the convention* to support the nominee, whoever he might be (H. C. Lodge, *Correspondence with Theodore Roosevelt*, Vol. I, pp. 13–14); but evidently it took some effort on the part of Lodge in mid-July to bring Roosevelt to a final decision to take the stump for Blaine. (See especially, Henry F. Pringle, *Theodore Roosevelt*, pp. 85–88, and M. A. De Wolfe Howe, *The Portrait of an Independent, Morefield Storey*, pp. 154–159.)

[1] E. A. Rollins, a bank president of Philadelphia, wrote Blaine on the day of the nomination; "A brother-in-law of George William Curtis told me this morning that Curtis said that if you were nominated he should support you, although he should do it reluctantly." Rollins to Blaine, June 7, 1884.

[2] One reason for the opposition to Blaine in Massachusetts dated from an unforgotten incident of 1878. In speaking on the resolution to place a statue of William King of Maine in the old hall of the House of Representatives, Senator Blaine had needlessly brought into his eulogy of King disparaging remarks about the "thoroughly unpatriotic, if not treasonable" attitude of Massachusetts in the War of 1812, and had provoked the protest of the Massachusetts Senators, Dawes and Hoar, for "raking open the embers of a buried political animosity which Massachusetts as well as Maine regrets." (*Cong. Record*, 45th Congress, 2d session, pp. 456–460.) Nevertheless, on election day Massachusetts gave

The New York meeting of the Independents, which was held at the house of Joseph H. Harper on June 17, was presided over by George W. Curtis. Schurz took the lead, which he was to maintain with vigor during the whole campaign, by denouncing the nomination of Blaine and Logan as "in absolute disregard of the reform sentiment of the nation," and inviting the Democrats to name a candidate whom the Independents could conscientiously support.

Meanwhile letters of congratulation were pouring in upon Blaine from all parts of the country, thanking God for the nomination and predicting a triumphant election. The chairman of the Republican Executive Committee of New York addressed him as "My dear Mr. President." [1] A judge of the Supreme Court of Indiana wrote: "The nomination was made in response to the almost unanimous voice of the masses of the Republican Party." [2] The Reverend Robert Collier, just returned from a trip to Europe, wrote: "You must be elected. This holier-than-thou so-called independent bolt is contemptible." [3] Andrew Carnegie, receiving the news of the nomination while on a coaching trip in England, rushed to the nearest telegraph office and cabled to Blaine the prophetic lines of Lady Macbeth:

> Glamis thou art and Cawdor; and shall be
> What thou art promised—

a not particularly felicitous quotation, as Hendrick has suggested, "in view of the fate that befell Macbeth." [4] On June 20 the notification committee, headed by chairman J. B. Henderson, waited upon Blaine at his home in Augusta (the entire California delegation accompanying the committee from Chicago), and after the formal interchange of courtesies, remained for a reception on the lawn and a buffet supper.

Three weeks later Blaine published his letter of acceptance. [5] A full half of the fifteen printed pages of the letter were devoted to a defense of the protective tariff, which Blaine was determined to make the sole issue of the campaign. With a great array of figures he discussed the growth of manufacturing and agricultural wealth since the

---

Blaine a majority of 20,000 (as against 53,000 for Garfield in 1880), and all the other New England States except Connecticut chose Republican electors.

[1] J. B. Chaffee to Blaine, June 10, 1884.
[2] W. G. Colerich to Blaine, June 14, 1884.
[3] Robert Collier to Blaine, June 12, 1884.
[4] Burton J. Hendrick, *The Life of Andrew Carnegie*, Vol. I, p. 251.
[5] J. G. Blaine, *Political Discussions, Legislative, Diplomatic and Popular*, pp. 420–434.

Civil War, attributing it to the protective policy of the Republican Party. "Nothing stands in our way," he said, "but the dread of a change in the industrial system which has wrought such wonders in the last twenty years, and which, with the power of increased capital, will work still greater wonders of prosperity in the twenty years to come." He recalled his efforts as Secretary of State to further peace, friendship and closer commercial ties with the republics of South America, and declared that this policy should be renewed, since the $100,000,000 or more which we owed annually on our unfavorable trade balance with Latin-America was a tribute paid in coin or its equivalent to the European nations which supplied the manufactures which we could easily send to the Southern Hemisphere. While the great powers of Europe were steadily enlarging their colonial domination in Asia and Africa, it was our special province to improve and expand our trade with the nations of America. No field had been cultivated so little. None promised so much. He would enlarge the original political, protective, unilateral scope of the Monroe Doctrine into one of mutual guarantees of peace and reciprocal advantages of commerce.

The brief paragraphs on the "hopes of our common country" mirrored the anticipation expressed in some of the letters of his supporters that the Republicans would carry States in the South.[1] Speaking in a new language of conciliation, to end the "age of hate," Blaine now found that prejudices had yielded and that "a growing cordiality warmed the Southern and Northern heart alike." The mutual confidence and esteem of the two sections were "more marked than at any period in the sixty years preceding the election of President Lincoln," and this was due partly to time and partly to the "application of Republican principles"(!). If there were occasional violent outbreaks still in the South, the public opinion of the country regarded them as exceptional and hopefully trusted that each would be the last. The South needed capital, not controversy. It had already entered on a career of industrial development and prosperity. It should not lend its electoral votes to destroy its own future.

But the old reconstructionists were not lured by this appeal for Southern votes. Representative C. A. Boutelle of Maine, whose criti-

---

[1] "With proper efforts I believe you can carry West Virginia, Virginia, North Carolina, and Florida. This would break the solid South and would be the breaking of a glorious day after a long and dark night for Southern Republicans." Thomas Settle of Greensboro', N. C. to Blaine, July 19, 1884.

cism of the letter was invited by Blaine, replied: "You are the best judge of what is politic, but if I were speaking on national issues I should assign more prominence and importance to the overthrow of popular government in the South. Your view of the improvement there is more optimistic than mine. . . . I would have preferred not to have had the settled policy of Southern proscription referred to as 'exceptional' and 'occasional.' I should also place the establishment of political and civil rights and the vindication of the ballot as the paramount issue, taking precedence over merely material and economic questions (the tariff). But I suppose I am behind the times, and at any rate I admit that I am a radical. P.S. I have an impression that you have written a very trenchant paragraph that you read to me in the first draft, setting forth the menace of the composition of the Senate from the South without regard to the popular will." [1] Blaine had begun his letter with a hearty endorsement of the Chicago platform, but Boutelle slyly hinted that he had overlooked the concluding paragraphs of that platform, which denounced "the fraud and violence practiced by the Democrats in the Southern States," and pledged to the Republicans of the South the passage of such laws as would "secure to every citizen, of whatever race or color, the full and complete recognition, possession, and exercise of all civil and political rights." [2]

Remarks on the civil service, religious liberty, a sound currency, the conservation of the public domain as a "sacred trust for the benefit of those seeking homes," the restoration of our merchant marine, and the sacredness of a free ballot completed the letter. The New York *Tribune* declared that it had "elevated the standard of public discussion for coming generations." [3] But for the anti-Blaine men, inside the party and outside, it was only a tissue of sophistries and hypocrisies. The claim that the prosperity of the country since the Civil War was due to a high protective tariff was a clear case of *post hoc ergo propter hoc*. Why select one factor, and that a very dubious one, to the exclusion of such important elements in our growth as the wealth of our natural resources, the opening of the West by the transcontinental railroads, the lure of free homesteads, and the enterprising spirit of the American people! The passages on the South and on civil service reform were represented by the New York *Nation* as the belated and insincere

[1] C. A. Boutelle to Blaine, July 1, 1884.
[2] *Proceedings of the Convention*, p. 94.
[3] New York *Tribune*, July 17, 1884.

professions of an astute politician out for votes. For the rest, the letter was "a collection of platitudes drawn out to the utmost limit of verbosity." [1]

The Independents, or "Mugwumps," [2] having invited the Democrats to put up a candidate whom they could "conscientiously support," were meanwhile watching with eagerness the outcome of the Democratic convention, which met at Chicago on July 8. Carl Schurz wrote to Senator Thomas F. Bayard of Delaware on June 28: "We are together against Blaine and for honest government. I should be glad to see you in the presidential chair on the 4th of March, 1885. If my vote could put you there, I should not hesitate a moment. . . . I have no right to meddle with the business of the Democratic Party, but I know you will not consider it an intrusion if I give you my views of the situation. The revolt in the Republican Party is at this moment very strong. But it would be a mistake to consider Blaine a weak candidate. He is weak in his own party, but he will have the support of the Irish dynamite faction, and the speculators and rascals will flock to him without distinction of previous condition. He will have a large campaign fund at his disposal. The Democratic candidate in order to beat him will therefore need the support of the independent Republican vote. There are only two possible Democratic candidates for whom that vote can be counted upon—you and Cleveland. The nomination of either of you would make success reasonably sure. . . . I am sure it is as clear to you as it is to me what a terrible calamity for the country Blaine's election would be." In order to avert that calamity, Schurz begged that there might be an understanding between the friends of Bayard and Cleveland in the convention to the effect that "as soon as it becomes clear that the one cannot be nominated, his forces go over to the other . . . so that in any event the success of the common cause be safe." [3]

Cleveland was nominated on the second ballot, with 683 votes to 81½ for Bayard and 45½ for Hendricks, in spite of the noisy opposition of the Tammany orators Thomas F. Grady, John Kelly and Bourke Cockran, who insisted that the independent Governor who had

---

[1] New York *Nation,* July 24, 1884.

[2] "Mugwump" was an Algonquin Indian word meaning "big chief." It was appropriated from Eliot's Indian Bible by the Indianapolis *Sentinel* at the time of the Liberal Republican movement of 1872, to designate the Independents who thought they were bigger than their party. Charles A. Dana revived the term in the New York *Sun* in March, 1884, and it was used throughout the campaign (and after) as a derisive epithet for the "holier-than-thou Pharisees" who bolted the Blaine ticket.

[3] Bancroft and Dunning, *The Writings of Carl Schurz,* Vol. IV, pp. 205–8.

vetoed the five-cent fare on the New York elevated railroad and had signed the Roosevelt measures for the more efficient and honest administration of the city's government could never carry the indispensable State of New York. Their real hostility to Cleveland, which they camouflaged under the pretext of his unpopularity with the laborers and the Roman Catholics, was due to the knowledge that under the administration of a man to whom Tammany Hall had always been anathema, their opportunities for patronage and plunder would be curtailed. The Tammany Braves had come to Chicago, 700 strong, in white plug hats, determined to head off Cleveland's nomination at any cost. But their attempt was as futile as Alfred E. Smith's "stop Roosevelt" movement in the Democratic convention of 1932. Daniel Manning, proprietor of the Albany *Argus* and chairman of the New York State Committee, had thrown his powerful support to Cleveland, when Samuel A. Tilden declined to run.[1] Abram S. Hewitt and William C. Whitney of the County Democracy were for Cleveland, and the brilliant E. K. Apgar of the Albany *Evening Journal* was winning thousands of waverers to the Cleveland banner by his editorials and his personal canvass in all parts of the State. When the defeat of Grady's motion to release the delegates from the unit rule allowed Manning to cast the 72 votes of New York solidly for Cleveland, the victory was won. And when General Edward S. Bragg of Wisconsin, in seconding the nomination of Cleveland, looked defiantly into the glowering faces of the Tammany Braves and thundered, "We love him for the enemies he has made!" he brought the convention to its feet in a tumult of applause.

For weeks the Tammany leaders sulked in their tents. The unspeakable Grady, whose ambition for a seat in the United States Senate had been thwarted by Governor Cleveland's direct interposition, went over to the support of Ben Butler, who was running on an independent ticket, with the backing of Dana's New York *Sun*.[2] But early in September

---

[1] There had been a good deal of enthusiasm for the "old ticket" of Tilden and Hendricks, which had been counted out by the "fraud" of 1876; but Tilden in 1884 was a man of seventy, whose broken health would not allow him to undertake the labors of a presidential campaign.

[2] Butler had been nominated on May 14 by a convention of the Anti-Monopoly Party, demanding in their platform an interstate commerce act, the direct election of Senators, a graduated income tax, a tariff favorable to labor rather than to capital, the cessation of land grants to corporations and speculators, and the fostering care of the government for the greatest of American industries, agriculture. Two weeks later Butler was nominated by the National Greenback Party at Indianapolis. He had delayed his acceptance of these nominations in the hope that he might also capture the great Democratic convention at Chicago with the help of the anti-Cleveland men—as Bryan did twelve

John Kelly, realizing that, however badly the organization might fare at the hands of Cleveland, it had still less to expect under a Republican Administration, called a meeting of the Tammany general committee and secured a grudging endorsement of the Cleveland and Hendricks ticket.

At first the regular Republicans professed to be as well pleased as the Mugwumps with the nomination of Cleveland. The Democrats had done them a great service, they said, in putting up a candidate who was utterly inexperienced in national politics and little known beyond the limits of his own State of New York—which, for the rest, many leading Democrats, like "Marse Henry" Watterson of the Louisville *Courier-Journal,* feared that he could not carry against the hostility of Tammany Hall, the Catholic Church and organized labor. Titus Sheard, the Speaker of the Assembly at Albany, wrote to Blaine on July 22: "Cleveland is the weakest candidate the Democrats could have nominated"; and a few days later the organizer of the Blaine and Logan Stock Exchange Club wrote enthusiastically of "the remarkable rise in the market due to the belief that we shall carry the State," and assured Blaine that he need have no fear.[1] Thomas V. Cooper, the chairman of the Republican Committee of Pennsylvania, "red-headed and hopeful," was bombarding Blaine with bulletins of certain victory. He was canvassing all the owners of vessels (including the oyster boats!) on the Jersey shore at his own expense, organizing Blaine clubs among the Irish, sending out 450,000 pieces of campaign literature, and ready to "let loose the dogs of war" in the shape of 20,000 "thoroughly organized workers."[2]

On the other hand, there were disquieting omens for the Republicans. Influential newspapers were going over to Cleveland's support. The New York *Times, Herald* and *Telegram* joined the *Nation,* the *Evening Post* and *Harper's Weekly* in the fight against Blaine, leaving the *Tribune* and the *Commercial Advertiser* as his only powerful organs in the great metropolis. In Philadelphia, the *Times* and the *Record* turned Mugwump. So did the Boston *Advertiser,* the *Transcript,* the *Herald,* and Samuel Bowles' Springfield *Republican.* But Joseph Medill of the

---

years later. But Butler was no Bryan. He made considerable noise at the convention, but when he failed even to find a spokesman to put his name before the delegates, he quitted the Democratic party as he had quitted the Republicans before.

[1] Charles T. Collins to Blaine, July 31, 1884.
[2] T. V. Cooper to Blaine, June 14, July 17, 26, 29, August 8, 1884.

Chicago *Tribune* and Murat Halstead of the Cincinnati *Commercial,* who had been opposed to Blaine in 1880, now joined his side. Though many of the anti-Blaine men of the pre-convention days, like Roosevelt, Lodge, Andrew D. White, Hamilton Fish, Edmunds, George F. Hoar and his brother Rockwell, gave more or less grudging support to the ticket,[1] the list of determined Mugwumps grew longer and more imposing every week. There was a strange confusion of public opinion on the question of Blaine's political morality, cutting across lines of party and profession. Men of unimpeachable ethical probity, like Senator Hoar, Gerritt Smith, General O. O. Howard, and William M. Evarts, defended him against the "stale slanders" circulated by his detractors. College presidents and ex-presidents, like Cyrus Hamlin of Middlebury, Vermont, John H. Ewing of Washington, Pennsylvania, Theodore Woolsey of Yale and Mark Hopkins of Williams, were as convinced of his righteousness as Eliot of Harvard and Seelye of Amherst were of his crookedness. Clergymen like De Witt Tallmage, Robert Collier and Egbert Smythe thanked God for his splendid character and achievements. The poet Whittier was "pained" by the rumor that he disapproved of Blaine, and Mrs. Harriet Beecher Stowe "held up both hands" for him—while her brother Henry Ward Beecher, who had himself passed through the ordeal of a trial for moral transgression, denounced him as a corrupt charlatan.

Blaine himself was not insensible to the strength of the Mugwump movement. He had used the occasion of the visit of the notification committee to Augusta for a conference with John B. Henderson on the threatening situation. Henderson wrote his friend and erstwhile fellow St. Louisan, Carl Schurz, a few days later (July 1): "In Augusta I saw Mr. Blaine and had a conversation with him in which he expressed regret—much regret—that you were indisposed to support him. Indeed, your rumored (!) opposition gives him more concern than that of any and all others. . . . You know I am no stickler for regular nominations. I have not said and shall not say one word against that independence in politics that condemns bad conduct or bad methods in political action; but I do believe that if Blaine be elected he will give us a good Administration. He can afford to rise above the shackles of party, and he will do it. If he has been a Prince Hal in days

---

[1] Edmunds, for example, made a single speech toward the end of the campaign, in which he commended the party, but sedulously avoided any praise of the candidates.

gone by, when responsibility comes he will be a Henry V. The Falstaffs who have followed him that thrift might follow fawning, will not be recognized in shaping his policies nor be suffered to bring odium upon his Administration. I expect to be in New York before the 25th (of July) and I hope that you may be able to suspend all further movements on the political chessboard till I can see you. . . . Tomorrow I will write frankly to Blaine on the methods to be adhered to should he be elected, and when I see you I hope to be able to satisfy you in reference to his policy. I am so confident myself that I am anxious to have my personal friends feel as I do." [1]

The Mugwump leader was not moved by this deferential appeal, however. He replied in a friendly spirit to Henderson's letter, disabusing him of the hope of any change in his attitude toward Blaine's candidacy. He could not "look upon Mr. Blaine as a mere jolly Prince Hal, who has lived through his years of indiscretion and of whom the Presidency will make a new man." Nor would such a change, even if possible, "lessen the evil effect which the mere fact of his election would inevitably produce." [2] What that effect would be, in his opinion, Schurz had declared bluntly in a letter to ex-President Hayes a week before: "I oppose Blaine because I believe that the election to the Presidency of the United States of the man who wrote the Mulligan letters and who stands before the country as the representative of the practices which they disclose would be a precedent fraught with incalculable evil. . . . It would be a terrible thing to teach our young people that such a record does not disqualify a man for the highest honors and trusts of the Republic. . . . Nothing a Democratic Administration may bring with it can possibly be as bad in its general and permanent consequences as the mere fact of Mr. Blaine's election." [3]

Schurz set to work with redoubled vigor after the nomination of Cleveland to defeat the Blaine and Logan ticket. He wrote at length to Lodge (whose "regularity" was doubtless strengthened by the fact that he was a candidate for a seat in Congress in the autumn of 1884), endeavoring to persuade him to sacrifice his immediate ambition and "obey his best impulses" by joining the Mugwumps. He was the moving spirit in arranging for a national conference of anti-Blaine Republicans, which was attended by several hundred delegates in the University

[1] Bancroft and Dunning, *The Writings of Carl Schurz*, Vol. IV, pp. 212–3.
[2] *Ibid.*, pp. 214–5.
[3] Quoted from the Hayes manuscripts by Claude M. Fuess, *Carl Schurz, Reformer*, p. 287.

Club Theater in New York, July 22; and he was made chairman of a national committee, which opened modest headquarters in Nassau Street, New York, and devoted itself to securing speakers and circulating literature in support of the Democratic candidate.

At the very moment of the conference, however, an event occurred which struck dismay into the hearts of the Mugwumps and seemed to put an end to Cleveland's chances for election. As the delegates were emerging from the University Club, they had put into their hands copies of an obscure Buffalo paper, the *Evening Telegraph,* containing a sensational account of a liaison between Cleveland and a disreputable widow named Maria Halpin a dozen years before, which had resulted in the birth of an illegitimate son. The story of the consternation of a little group of Mugwumps gathered at dinner at the University Club that evening has frequently been told—how Schurz sat at the head of the table, enveloped in gloom, while Storey, Godkin and others reflected his anxiety in their own woe-begone faces; how Curtis, Codman, Lyman Beecher and others entered as the coffee was being served, to add a Greek chorus of despair; how the tension was relieved by the humorous logic of an anonymous guest from Chicago, who spoke up saying: "Well, from what I hear, I gather that Mr. Cleveland has shown high character and great capacity in public office, but that in private life his conduct has been open to question; while, on the other hand Mr. Blaine has been weak and dishonest in public life, while he seems to have been an admirable husband and father. The conclusion I draw from these facts is that we should elect Mr. Cleveland to the public office which he is so admirably qualified to fill, and remand Mr. Blaine to the private life which he is so eminently fitted to adorn." [1]

However, the matter was far too serious to be dismissed with a witticism. The Mugwumps, ignoring the issues of the tariff, the currency, labor, prohibition, the South, and foreign policy, had based their campaign wholly on the lack of moral character in the Republican candidate; and here was the revelation of a lapse in the moral character of the Democratic candidate, a lapse which the great middle class of the country, with its religious conviction of the sanctity of the home and family, would condone far less easily than the alleged prostitution of public office for

[1] Extract from Morefield Storey's *Autobiography,* in M. A. De Wolfe Howe's *Portrait of an Independent,* pp. 150–1. Before Mr. Storey had released the mss. of his *Autobiography* for publication, he had communicated this incident to J. F. Rhodes, who printed it in his *From Hayes to McKinley* (1919), pp. 221–3.

private gain. It looked as if all the labor of the Mugwumps had gone for nothing. How could they continue, cried Curtis in despair, to support Grover Cleveland? Henry Ward Beecher wrote to Schurz begging him to put off his Brooklyn speech against Blaine, scheduled for August 5, until they could be sure of their ground. Beecher had heard from the Reverend Dr. Ball and other "eminent clergymen" of Buffalo that Cleveland was a grossly dissipated man, whose "debaucheries continue to this hour," and that it was these ministers of the Gospel who had advised the publication of the Maria Halpin story in the *Evening Telegraph*.[1]

We do not know who was responsible for injecting this scandalous incident into the campaign. Nearly a year later the Democratic New York *World* published the story that on the day after Cleveland's nomination Colonel Z. A. Smith, editor of the Boston *Journal* (a Blaine paper) and a former secretary of the Maine Republican Committee, visited Augusta and conferred with Blaine; that Smith had sent a reporter to Buffalo to investigate Cleveland's past private life; that the *Telegraph* article appeared the day after the reporter left Buffalo; and that the next day the Boston *Journal* "printed all its scandalous story on its first page, with glaring headlines."[2] The obvious insinuation of the *World* that Blaine was the instigator of this attack on Cleveland's character is too monstrous to be believed.[3] Nevertheless, Cleveland, in a letter to his friend Bissell, declared that he could "never forget nor forgive" his political opponent for not publicly expressing his disgust with the introduction of such an element into the campaign.

When a more outrageous counter attack was launched against Blaine by some unscrupulous Democratic papers, in the preposterous story that his marriage in Kentucky had been invalid and that his eldest son Stanwood had been born out of wedlock,[4] Cleveland to be sure refused to countenance any exploitation of the scandal, sharply ordering his secretary to lock and keep in the safe the "proofs of Blaine's guilt" which had been put into his hands. But neither man made a public protest against the defamation of the other's character. Probably, if

[1] Bancroft and Dunning, *Writings of Carl Schurz*, Vol. IV, p. 222.
[2] New York *World*, May 19, 1885.
[3] A. K. McClure in *Our Presidents* (p. 322) asserts, without proof, that "Blaine furnished the Cleveland scandal to the National Committee."
[4] It was only by the law of 1852, two years after Blaine's marriage, that a license was required by the State of Kentucky. The marriage, though lacking this formality, was perfectly valid. See Boston *Herald*, Sept. 27, 1884.

the story of Cleveland's indiscretion had been made public in the spring, it would have prevented his nomination; certainly, if it had been revealed in the late autumn, it would have cost him the election. But, coming as it did in the middle of the campaign, it afforded ample time for the investigation of the actual facts of Cleveland's character and conduct as contrasted with the exaggerated charges, and it gradually fell into the insignificant place which it deserved. There is no indication that it affected the vote on election day.

Schurz went on with his Brooklyn address as scheduled. His subject was, "Why James G. Blaine should not be elected President," and the argument, which fills forty-nine pages in his *Writings* (Vol. IV, pp. 224–272), presented the case against Blaine with a completeness unequaled in any other campaign document. Avoiding on the one hand the scurrilous personal abuse which degraded the campaign "to the level of a brawl on the backstairs of a tenement house," and on the other hand the emotional rhetoric which obscured the issues under a cloud of verbiage, Schurz examined the record of Blaine's transactions with Warren J. Fisher and pronounced it damning. He rejected the contention that Blaine was merely a victim of political abuse, as Washington and Lincoln had been, showing that these men had never had to resort to such desperate methods to vindicate their honesty as Blaine had employed. The very nomination of Blaine, he declared, had already had the effect of "taking the moral backbone out of many men" (read Lodge, Roosevelt and Hoar) who had been "aggressively honest before." What then would his election mean? It was not a time to be stampeded by the cry of party loyalty. The welfare of the nation was far more important than the continuance in power of any political organization. "If the great party which had abolished slavery and saved the Republic" was to serve as an instrument to poison the life of the same Republic, then the truly proud Republicans would "wash their hands of it." There was but one issue before the American people. The honor of the nation was at stake, and it was the duty of every good citizen to do his part to render forever hopeless the attempt of any party, old or new, "to win success without respecting that vital condition of our greatness and glory, which is honest government."

Schurz's speech was printed in English and German and distributed throughout the land. A young German from Milwaukee, named Paul

Bechtner essayed a reply in an open letter, which Schurz acknowledged courteously and promised to discuss in his coming campaign tour through the West. Senator Hoar also published an answer to Schurz, in which he declared that Blaine had been "triumphantly acquitted," not only by his own defense in the House of Representatives, but also by his unanimous election to the Senate by the Maine legislature, his appointment as Secretary of State, and his nomination for the Presidency. Hoar deplored the effect upon the young men of the nation of continually harping on the theme of corruption in high places.[1] But Senator Hoar himself in 1876 had pronounced one of the most scathing philippics against the corruption of the Grant regime (see above, p. 70); and as to Blaine's vindication by subsequent political honors, Schurz, in a long letter of remonstrance to Hoar, on August 22, pointedly asked the Senator if the election of Benjamin F. Butler as Governor of Massachusetts in 1882 and his nomination for President by the Anti-Monopoly and Greenback Parties had changed his unfavorable opinion of Butler or constituted a "triumphal acquittal" of the charges against his political integrity.

In September the Mugwumps found another arrow for their quiver. Not all of the Blaine-Fisher correspondence on the Little Rock and Fort Smith securities had been included in the package of letters which Mulligan brought to Washington in June, 1876, and which Blaine had permanently "borrowed" from him in Mr. Atkins' parlor in the Riggs House. There were in the safe of the law office of Sohier and Welch in Boston several more of the Blaine letters, which Mulligan had refrained from making public after Blaine had missed the nomination in 1876 and again in 1880, but which he now thought of releasing. The firm of Sohier and Welch wrote to Schurz on September 3, 1884: "Mr. Mullikan (*sic!*) is a client of ours, and has shown us various letters of Mr. Blaine's which would probably be of use to you in a political point of view, especially if explained by him. We think and feel certain that if you would come on here he would show them all to you. He is some-

---

[1] Hoar had attacked President Eliot a few weeks earlier as representing a little body of men about Cambridge whose influence "tended to degrade the public life of the Commonwealth by teaching our educated youth to be ashamed of their history." There was hardly a man in public life, he said, who had not been "compelled to undergo the contemptuous criticism of these gentle hermits of Cambridge." New York *Tribune*, July 16, 1884. A poll of the students at Harvard College, managed by an enthusiastic young Blaineite named Rowland B. Mahany, resulted in a narrow majority for the Republican candidate.

what unwilling to go to New York." [1]

This was a godsend for the Mugwump headquarters in Nassau Street. Horace Deming, a prominent Brooklyn lawyer, was sent to Boston to follow up the trail. He met Mulligan, who, after a conference with More-field Storey, agreed to hand the letters over to the Boston Committee of One Hundred, if such action met the approval of his friend the Reverend James Freeman Clarke. Mulligan met a small group of Mugwumps at Young's Hotel, where they sat "from eight o'clock in the evening until about two A. M.," examining the letters and discussing the best use to be made of them. "Mulligan," says Storey, "wished to make a statement of the facts, using the letters as evidence that his statement was true. I opposed this on the ground that, if Mulligan made a statement, Blaine would attack it and him, and that the letters would be lost sight of; while if we printed only the letters it was Blaine himself who made the statements and he must be believed by his own friends. As a result, the letters were printed in the Boston *Journal* (September 15), prefaced by a statement that the originals were in the hands of Sohier and Welch, leading Boston lawyers, and if their authenticity was denied they would be shown to any person who had the right to inquire." [2]

Blaine promptly acknowledged the genuineness of the letters, declaring in an interview, published in his old paper the Kennebec *Journal,* that there was not a word in them that was not "entirely consistent with the most scrupulous integrity and honor." He hoped that every Republican newspaper in the country would republish them in full. Many of them did so rather reluctantly, seeking by editorial comments to make them appear innocuous. The new letters did not, in fact, add much of importance to the old ones, but the very fact of their publication served to revive and intensify the interest of the public in the "stale slander" of the Little Rock affair. There was one letter, however, in the new batch, marked "confidential," which was more damaging to Blaine's case than any that had appeared before. It was written from Washington, on April 16, 1876, eight days before Blaine made his first defense on the floor of the House (see above, p. 84). To prevent the possibility of the letter being opened by a third person, it was not sent to Fisher's address in Boston, but to the Parker House, where

[1] *The Schurz Papers,* Library of Congress, quoted by M. A. De Wolfe Howe in *The Portrait of an Independent,* p. 152.
[2] M. A. De Wolfe Howe, *The Portrait of an Independent,* p. 152.

Fisher was instructed by telegraph to call for it and to answer it by return mail. The letter ran:

My dear Mr. Fisher.

You can do me a very great favor, and I know it will give you pleasure to do so—just as I would do for you under similar circumstances. Certain persons and papers are trying to throw mud at me to injure my candidacy before the Cincinnati convention, and you may observe they are trying it in connection with the Little Rock and Fort Smith matter. I want you to send me a letter such as the enclosed draft. You will receive this tomorrow (Monday) evening, and it will be a favor I shall never forget if you will at once write me the letter and mail the same evening. The letter is strictly true, is honorable to you and to me, and will stop the mouths of slanderers at once. Regard this letter as strictly confidential. . . . Kind regards to Mrs. Fisher.

Sincerely,
(Burn this letter)   J. G. Blaine

The draft which Blaine enclosed and asked Fisher to copy and mail by return post read as follows:

The Hon. James G. Blaine, Washington, D.C.

Dear sir: I observe that certain newspapers are making or rather insinuating the absurd charge that you own or had owned $150,000 of Little Rock and Fort Smith Railroad bonds, and that you had in some way obtained them as a gratuity.

The enterprise of building the Little Rock and Fort Smith Railroad was undertaken in 1869 by a company of Boston gentlemen, of whom I was myself one. The bonds of the road were put upon the market in this city on what was deemed very advantageous terms to the purchaser. They were sold largely through myself. You became the purchaser of about $30,000 of the bonds on precisely the same terms that every other buyer received, paying for them in instalments running over a considerable period, just as others did. The transaction was perfectly open, and there was no more secrecy in regard to it than if you had been buying flour or sugar. I am sure that you never owned a bond of the road that you did not pay for at the market rate. Indeed, I am sure that no one received bonds on any other terms.

When the road got into financial difficulties and loss fell upon you, you still retained your bonds, and you held them clear through to the reorganization of the company in 1874, exchanging them for stocks and bonds of the new company. . . .

Concealment of the investment and everything connected with it would have been very easy had concealment been desirable; but your action was as open and fair as the day. When the original enterprise failed, I knew with what severity the pecuniary loss fell upon you, and with what integrity and nerve you met it. Years having elapsed, it seems rather hard at this late date to be compelled to meet a slander in a matter where your conduct was in the highest degree honorable and straightforward. You may use this letter in any way that will be of service to you.

Very sincerely yours,

Warren Fisher, Jr.[1]

Fisher did not comply with Blaine's extraordinary request nor did he burn the letter and its enclosure. It would have been well for Blaine had he done so; for nothing else that the Republican leader had written or said returned to plague him more than this secret attempt to get a vicarious vindication, dictated by his own pen. When the Cleveland parade moved up Fifth Avenue a few days before the close of the campaign, a detachment of men carried sticks topped with sheets of writing paper, which they lighted with matches as they marched, chanting monotonously

Burn this letter, Burn this letter,
Kind regards to Mrs. Fisher.

Though the question of Blaine's political morality was constantly kept to the fore by the Mugwumps, there were other issues in the campaign which gave the Republican managers cause for anxiety. They had encouraged the independent candidacy of Ben Butler, believing that he would draw a large number of Democratic votes from the laboring class, the soft money men and the immigrant elements.[2] Patrick Collins tells how W. E. Chandler and a few other ardent Blaine supporters met Butler on board a warship at Portsmouth, New Hampshire, late in July and agreed to furnish funds for him to stump New York, New Jersey and Connecticut. He was to have a share of the Massachusetts patronage in case Blaine was elected. He traveled in a luxurious private car, well stocked with liquors, and Wayne MacVeagh told Curran that the National Republican Committee owed Butler $7,000 at the close of the campaign.[3] General Joseph Hawley of the

---

[1] *Mr. Blaine's Railroad Transactions*—a pamphlet published by the New York *Evening Post*, containing articles appearing in the *Post* on Blaine's candidacy and a reprint of all the Mulligan letters. Page 24.

[2] The New York *Tribune*, for example, affected a preference for Butler over Cleveland during the whole campaign. See issues of August 19, 20, 25, 30, 31, 1884.

[3] M. P. Curran, *The Life of Patrick Collins*, pp. 92–93. Butler himself indignantly denied that he had been subsidized by the Republicans. *Butler's Book*, pp. 982–3.

Hartford *Courant* wrote Blaine that he was sure that if Butler ran he would take 300,000 votes from the Democrats.[1]

At first the Democrats were so apprehensive of Butler that they sent Samuel J. Randall of Pennsylvania to attempt to get him to withdraw his candidacy. Butler was courting John Kelly and Thomas F. Grady (the latter eventually supported him), and had he been able to bring the disaffected Tammany Hall to a revolt, Cleveland's chances of carrying New York would have been ruined. The whole situation was changed, however, when Tammany came out openly for Cleveland in September. Butler then became a liability rather than an asset for the Republicans. Whether or not any of the 17,000 votes cast for him in New York were counted for Cleveland, as the Republican managers claimed, the many times 17,000 votes which the Republicans believed he would take from Cleveland were cast for the Democratic candidate. Two days after the election Chandler wrote Blaine, complaining bitterly that the New York managers had flouted his "experience and well-known coolness and carefulness of judgment in emergencies" by not working harder for Butler, whose total strength could have been raised to 30,000 in the State, since it was "easier to get five Irish votes for Butler than one for Blaine and Logan." "But some of our people," he concluded acidly, "acted as if they preferred to have Cleveland elected rather than save our ticket through the exertions of Butler and Dana. I am afraid their obstinacy has lost us the election." [2]

Another untoward factor for the Republicans was the attitude of the prohibitionists. Since Kansas had put an amendment into her constitution in 1880, forbidding the manufacture or sale of alcoholic liquor except for scientific or medicinal purposes, the temperance question had become an important issue in several Middle Western States, like Michigan, Indiana, Illinois and Ohio. John P. St. John, the Republican Governor of Kansas at the time the amendment was ratified, became an ardent advocate of enforcement and was defeated for a second reëlection in 1882. He then devoted himself entirely to the temperance cause, hoping to persuade the Republican convention of

---

[1] Hawley to Blaine, July (no day), 1884. Blaine, however, did not share the opinion of Chandler and Hawley that Butler's candidacy would help the Republicans. He wrote to Elkins on July 27: "If Butler runs he will get 250,000 votes, more or less—less probably (he actually got 175,370). If he does not run who will get a majority of these votes. I think I would, and hence would gain by his staying out." Edward Stanwood, *Life of Blaine*, p. 285.

[2] W. E. Chandler to Blaine, November 6, 1884.

1884 to adopt a prohibition plank. But the platform committee refused to listen to Miss Frances E. Willard of the W.C.T.U. when she presented a petition signed by 20,000 names, and kicked the petition under the table. Indignant at this treatment, the prohibition forces united in persuading ex-Governor St. John, who was a dynamo of energy and a speaker of rare eloquence, to accept a nomination for President at their national convention at Pittsburgh, on July 23. They condemned the Republican Party for having done nothing to further the cause of temperance during its long tenure of power. Such alarming reports of the inroads of the prohibitionists upon the Republican prospects in the Middle West reached New York that an attempt was made to get St. John to withdraw from the race; and when he indignantly refused, the attacks on him by the Republican press as a "renegade," a "hypocrite," and a "crypto-Democrat" provoked the fiery crusader to come to New York and open headquarters "in an attic under the roof of the Fifth Avenue Hotel," to devote himself wholly to the defeat of Blaine (which he later boasted of having accomplished) in the pivotal Empire State. The Republicans treated him with scorn, but they were rudely awakened when he polled over 25,000 votes in New York on election day— one sixth of his entire strength in the country. Ex-Governor Cornell, in reviewing the causes of Blaine's defeat, emphasized the temperance movement, "which was neglected and allowed to assume undue magnitude" by the state managers.[1] And Cyrus Field attributed to the movement the first place in the varied list of reasons for the Republican failure.[2]

Nor were the relations between Blaine and Logan such as to inspire confidence in party harmony. The "Black Eagle" of Illinois had been a thick and thin supporter of Grant in 1880. He was now put on the ticket to attract the soldier vote, Blaine being the first Republican nominee since the Civil War who had not worn the general's stars in the Union army. But it is doubtful whether Logan added any strength to the ticket. He was rough and cantankerous where Blaine was suave and conciliatory. He baited the South and frantically waved the bloody shirt, when Blaine was trying by honeyed words to win support in Virginia, North Carolina and Tennessee, to offset the possible loss of doubtful States in the North. He quarreled with the party leaders in

---

[1] A. B. Cornell to Blaine, November 15, 1884.
[2] Cyrus Field to Blaine, November 18, 1884.

Illinois till we find the Speaker of the State Assembly writing to Blaine to beg him to reconcile Logan and Congressman Farwell.[1] Elkins, Reid and other high priests of the party hoped that Blaine would keep on good terms with his running mate; for various rumors of incompatibility of temper were current, and the political rhymesters had lampooned "Black Jack's" grammar and grouch at once in the couplet:

> We never speak as we pass by,
> Me to Jim Blaine nor him to I.

If politics made these uncongenial candidates bedfellows, preference kept each of them on the extreme edge of his own side of the bed.

Then there was Roscoe Conkling, now out of public life, but ready to deal a final stoke of vengeance on the man who had compared him to a turkey-gobbler and a singed cat on the floor of the House eighteen years before. Conkling had taken the stump for Garfield in 1880, only to be rewarded with the "base ingratitude" which had driven him to resign his senatorial seat. It was too much to expect him now to support the man whom he considered responsible for his political Waterloo. When asked to enter the campaign for Blaine, his laconic reply was, "No, thank you, I don't engage in criminal practice."[2] But there is good evidence to show that Conkling was not content to play the passive rôle of sulking in his tent. Anonymous letters signed "A Stalwart Republican" appeared in the New York *World* for May 29, and August 12, attacking Blaine's record ferociously. Conkling was counsel for the *World*. "One night," says Charles Edward Russell, "in the proof room of the New York *World* a proofreader slipped into his pocket the manuscript of one of these letters and took it home. Two years afterwards he quietly submitted it to a handwriting expert together with a specimen of Conkling's acknowledged writing. The expert declared both specimens to have been written by the same hand."[3] It was no secret that Conkling was working for Blaine's defeat. Warner Miller reported him as "ugly,"[4] and John A. Stewart, reporting to Blaine on the New York situation, wrote: "Roscoe Conkling thinks the Demo-

---

[1] L. C. Collins to Blaine, July 1, 1884.

[2] Blaine himself wrote to Elkins on July 27: "Can Conkling be induced to speak for us? It would be an immense thing for us. How can he be induced to do so?" Edward Stanwood, *James G. Blaine*, p. 285.

[3] Charles Edward Russell, *Blaine of Maine*, p. 403.

[4] Miller to Blaine, September 9, 1884.

crats will carry New York, but with him the wish is father to the thought." [1] Finally, Conkling gave his "continuous assistance and advice" to a group of Democrats and Mugwumps, including William G. Rice, William C. Whitney, Curtis and Schurz, who for ten days following the election devoted themselves to securing a fair count of the Cleveland ballots throughout the State.[2] That Conkling's enmity was the decisive factor in Blaine's defeat, as Platt and Dana maintained, is hardly credible.[3] Still, it is significant that Conkling's home county of Oneida which had given Garfield a plurality of 1946 votes in 1880, was carried by Cleveland by a margin of 100 in 1884. That defection alone cost Blaine nearly double the number of votes necessary to offset Cleveland's plurality in the State.

Unremitting efforts were made by each party to win the support of the two important groups of the "hyphenated" voters of the time, the German-Americans and the Irish-Americans. The former had generally been Republicans, owing to their sympathy with the Northern cause in the Civil War; whereas the latter, ever since the days of their heavy migration to the cities of the Atlantic seaboard, had been absorbed largely into Democratic organizations like Tammany Hall. But in 1884 social and political cross-currents were undermining these traditional allegiances. The temperance movement was agitating the Middle West, and the Germans loved their beer. They were sedulously taught by Democratic editors and orators that the Republicans were responsible for the prohibition propaganda (was not Governor St. John a Republican?), and articles from Blaine's pen in the Kennebec *Journal* of thirty years before were quoted to show that the Republican candidate was a friend of prohibition. Moreover, thousands of them were won over to Cleveland by the German speeches of their idol, Carl Schurz, who appealed to their ingrained sense of civic righteousness in his diatribes against Blaine and his unscrupulous supporters. On the other hand, the Republicans were confident of winning thousands of recruits from the ranks of the Irish-Americans. Blaine was played up as the great champion of the Irishmen claiming American citizenship who were imprisoned under the Coercion Acts, whereas he had given the support

[1] Stewart to Blaine, October 18, 1884.
[2] F. L. Stetson and Wm. G. Rice, "Was New York's Vote Stolen?" *North American Review*, January, 1885, p. 85.
[3] "But for his passage at arms with Conkling when both were members of the lower house of Congress, Blaine would have unquestionably been elected President in 1884." T. C. Platt, *Autobiography*, p. 186. New York *Sun*, November 8, 1884.

of the State Department to the cautious and dilatory policy of Minister Lowell. John Devoy of the New York *Irish Nation* and Patrick Ford of the *Irish World* were enthusiastic supporters of Blaine in the State which numbered some 500,000 Irish-born citizens. A great Irish-American rally for Blaine was held in Chickering Hall, July 28, and a few weeks later the convention of the Irish Land League at Boston declared that, if Blaine were elected, "Ireland would be free in thirty days." John C. Fremont, "the Pathfinder," was for importing O'Phelan of the Land League to campaign for Blaine. O'Phelan "was endorsed by Mr. Parnell," and "would certainly create among Irishmen here great enthusiasm for you." [1] "I guess your Donegal and Londonderry blood will carry you through," was the prophecy of one of Blaine's devoted followers.[2]

But aside from his inheritance from the Galbraiths, the Lyons and the Gillespies, and the connections of his cousin (Sister Angela) and other relatives with the Roman Catholic Church, Blaine made a strong appeal to the Irish through his record in Congress and in the State Department as a champion of American interests against the alleged encroachments and pretensions of Great Britain. His speeches denouncing the Halifax Award, the Fortune Bay outrage and the Canadian reciprocity treaty, his efforts to restore the pre-war American merchant marine to contest the commercial supremacy of the world with England, his attempt to eliminate the British from the joint control of an isthmian canal, and especially his constant insistence on the protective tariff as an "American" policy for the defense of our industry and labor against the disastrous competition of British free trade— were all dwelt on by the Republican press as evidences of what would today be called "100 per cent Americanism." Cleveland was the "British candidate." John Bright in the House of Commons was prophesying the accession of the United States to the principles of the repeal of the corn laws.[3] The Mugwumps were at heart free traders, camouflaging their economic heresy under the pretense of moral indignation at Blaine's public record. They were dancing to the tune called by the

[1] Frémont to Blaine, September 19, 1884.
[2] Thomas Ewing to Blaine, August 23, 1884.
[3] "I believe that the question in the United States between a high protective tariff and a merely revenue tariff is nearing its solution . . . and that when that great people are brought to the issue whether, having struck off the chains from the Negro, they are to leave the fetters of protection upon the industry of all their countrymen, they will declare it to be the inalienable right of every American . . . to spend his money in the cheapest market in the world (loud cheers)." Speech of John Bright in Parliament, June 6, 1883.

English, "who feared to lose their South American trade if Blaine were elected." [1]

During the summer months Blaine remained at his home in Augusta, keeping in close touch with the Republican canvass in a score of States, and deluged with letters of premature congratulation and anxious inquiry. Some asked for advice; more offered it. He had to listen to complaints of the ineptitude of campaign managers, the scarcity of good speakers, the difficulties of raising funds. "The crying need of this campaign," wrote a New York worker, "is a cheap paper that reaches every day the masses. The *Tribune*, the *Commercial Advertiser* and the *Mail and Express* do not reach the men on whose votes this contest will largely turn." [2] Moreover, the *Tribune's* boycott of Typographical Union Number 6 was injuring the Republican cause among the laborers. Disquieting reports were coming out of the West. The Butler movement was gaining in Michigan. The Prohibitionists were developing unexpected strength in Iowa and Wisconsin. Indignation was rife in Indiana over the shameless conduct of Commissioner W. W. Dudley of the Pension Bureau, who doubled his field force in September and October, to make sure of the soldier vote, by the lavish encouragement of reratings and new applications for pensions. Governor Grosvenor of Ohio was distressed over the rumor that Blaine was a large holder of stock in the Hocking Valley iron and coal syndicate, which was fighting the demands of the miners and exasperating organized labor all through the State. [3]

A steady stream of tracts and pamphlets was pouring from the Democratic and Mugwump headquarters, representing Blaine as "a friend of the railroads, musket in hand, firing from behind the breastworks of Jay Gould's lobby": a Know-Nothing and a persecutor of foreign-born citizens and Roman Catholics; a "Jingo" who pursued "an atrocious foreign policy" in the State Department; a "corrupt

---

[1] John Roach to Blaine, June 12, 1884. Roach was the wealthy but illiterate shipbuilder whose plans for a merchant line between New York and Rio de Janeiro, Brazil, Blaine had so heartily supported in the Senate six years before (see above, p. 146). A specimen of Mr. Roach's orthography is found in a penciled note to Blaine, just after the Republican victory in Maine: "Dear Mr. Blain, What is the Mater with Main? Where is the independent mud throwers? Now for oHio. our Friends must not Slack up Because we had a victore in Main we must keep the Raskells on the run." John Roach to Blaine, September 10, 1884.
[2] A. M. Gibson to Blaine, July 19, 1884.
[3] Grosvenor to Blaine, July 10, 1884. The fact was that Blaine, who was interested in mining properties in many States, had once had an option on some shares in the Hocking Valley Company, but had not bought them.

jobber" who first tried to conceal, and then to pervert the evidence which convicted him of prostituting his high office for personal gain. As the campaign wore on, it degenerated into a contest in vilification. Cleveland was a "lecherous beast," a "hangman," an "obese nincompoop," a "drunken sot." Blaine was a "liar," a "crook." "You may search the records of political controversy of the Anglo-Saxon race from the Heptarchy to this bitter day," wrote James O. Putnam of Buffalo, "and you shall look in vain for a parallel to that lowest deep in which this campaign is wallowing." And Henry Adams wrote his friend Gaskell in England: "The public is angry and abusive. We are all swearing at each other like demons." [1]

Meanwhile the Republicans were failing to use their greatest asset in the canvass, namely, the magnetic presence and persuasive arguments of their candidate. Blaine was sitting on the side lines. Appeals began to come from New York, Connecticut, Pennsylvania, the border States and the West for the inspiration of his "personal power." He could win thousands of votes in Kentucky; he would compose the quarrels in Illinois; he would ensure victory in the doubtful State of Connecticut; he would stem the tide of Butlerism and fusion in Michigan; he would rescue New York from the "apathy and bungling" for which the State committee was being freely criticized. Early in September Warner Miller, who had been elected to Conkling's place in the Senate, replied to Blaine's query as to whether he should go to New York: "I see no reason against it; it would inspire the party with zeal." Furthermore, he would have Blaine go on a speaking tour "through Pennsylvania and Southern Ohio to Chicago, and return through Northern Ohio and Central New York." [2] Blaine had apparently considered the question early in the campaign, for we find Murat Halstead writing to him on June 17: "I do not think well of your taking the stump; it is a killing business for a presidential candidate."

There had been instances of candidates campaigning in their own behalf, like Greeley in 1872 and Weaver in 1880, but the custom, inaugurated on a grand scale by Bryan and continued by practically every candidate since, of touring the country and appealing for the support of the ticket, to large audiences, extended in these days to tens

[1] *Letters of Henry Adams*, p. 360.
[2] Miller to Blaine, September 9, 1884.

of millions by the radio broadcast, had not yet become established. It was still looked upon as rather below the dignity of the candidate, to whom the honor of election was supposed to come unsought. As the pressure increased, however, Blaine reluctantly yielded. The September 8 election in Maine returned a Republican majority of 20,000. It was indispensable, in view of the ticklish situation in New York, to win the October election in Ohio. West Virginia was also an October State, and victory there would be a good augury for "wresting Virginia, North Carolina, and possibly other Southern States from the control of the Bourbons." [1]

Carl Schurz had left New York early in September for the middle West, and began a strenuous anti-Blaine campaign with a speech before six thousand German-Americans at Milwaukee, which he followed with more than a score of addresses in English and German in Indianapolis, Detroit, Cleveland, Cincinnati, Columbus and other cities. On September 12 Tammany Hall came out in support of Cleveland and Hendricks. On the fifteenth the new Mulligan letters appeared in the Boston *Journal* and the Springfield *Republican*. The moment had come for Blaine to throw off his blanket, quit the side lines and take his place in the line-up.

He left Augusta on September 17 for a tour which was to carry him into Massachusetts, New York, Pennsylvania, West Virginia, Ohio, Michigan, Indiana, and Illinois, and to end only when he returned to his home on the morning of Election Day, November 4. He was accompanied by his son Walker, Senator Hale and his old friend Joe Manley; and his party of politicians and reporters was joined at various places for longer or shorter portions of the trip by prominent men like Reed, Hawley, Cullom, Foraker, Hanna (who spelled his name "Blain"), Plumb, Logan, Medill, Frémont and Lew Wallace. Republican Governors and ex-Governors escorted him to the platform and introduced him to cheering audiences. Grant called at a public reception at New York to shake his hand and predict success.[2] Hayes, oblivious of Blaine's thirty-seven months of avoidance of the White House during his own Presidency and of Gail Hamilton's scathing articles of 1877 in the *Tribune,* introduced him at Frémont with expressions of satisfaction at the opportunity to do him honor, and received in reply from

[1] Miller to Blaine, September 9, 1884.
[2] T. B. Boyd, *The Blaine and Logan Campaign of 1884*, p. 52.

Blaine an acknowledgment of "the enviable fortune" which the country had enjoyed in having had in Hayes a President who "from the day of his inauguration steadily gained in public esteem throughout his whole term of office (!)." [1] A remarkable spirit of harmony characterized the whole trip. The candidate rode in processions escorted by uniformed Blaine and Logan marchers, reviewed parades of torchbearers and cavalcades of women in brilliant scarlet jackets with waving snowy plumes on their hats, and received the innocent homage of schoolgirls in white dresses, carrying nosegays and banners.

Blaine rose to the occasion of the trip with his customary geniality and tact. Whether he was addressing twenty thousand people in a set speech in a great metropolitan auditorium or giving a moment's greeting to the crowd that gathered around the rear platform of his train as it passed through a rustic village, he had just the right thing to say in just the right way. He was always vigorous, lucid, sympathetic, persuasive. He never descended to personal abuse of his opponent or noticed the abuse which was being heaped on himself. Only once did he pause to defend himself against a personal charge, when he assured the people of Ohio that he had never owned a share in the Hocking Valley mines. The constant theme of his speeches was the laudation of the protective tariff as the guarantee of American prosperity and the symbol of American patriotism. So long as there was a hope of carrying West Virginia he refrained from any discussion of the sectional issue. At Grafton, West Virginia, on October 6, he said: "I am addressing a slave State no longer. I am appealing to the new South. I am appealing to West Virginia not to vote upon a tradition or a prejudice, not to keep her eyes to the rear but to look to the front. . . . I leave you as a State that stands in the van of the new South, inviting the whole South to join in a great national movement which shall make us a people with one aim, one Constitution, one destiny." [2] But when West Virginia eight days later went Democratic, Blaine dropped this conciliatory language to the South which was bringing upon him criticism from the Stalwarts and the Grand Army men. [3]

[1] Boyd, *op. cit.*, p. 79.
[2] Boyd, *op. cit.*, p. 104.
[3] M. Woodhull of New York, writing to W. E. Chandler on September 29 and October 7, thought it was a grave mistake for Blaine to "spread a genial feast of taffy before the South," as he was doing in his speeches and as he had done in his book. He had "deliberately excluded the Southern issue from the campaign," and the result was "languor." "Do you suppose Mr. Blaine would himself have taken the stump if he had not felt

Blaine left Ohio immediately after the gratifying Republican victory of 11,000 in the State election of October 14, and in his rapid tour of Michigan, Indiana, Illinois and Wisconsin during the next fortnight, he mingled with his defense of the tariff language reminiscent of his former attack on the "rebels." For example, at Fort Wayne, Indiana, he said: "The elections in Ohio and West Virginia have put a new phase on the national contest, or rather they have reproduced the old phase. The Democratic Party, as of old, consider now they have the solid South again; they believe that they will surely get one hundred and fifty-three electoral votes from the sixteen Southern States, and they expect, or they hope, or they dream that they may secure New York and Indiana (cries of 'Never! Never!') . . . and will seize the government of the nation. I do not believe that the men who added luster and renown to your State through four years of bloody war can be used to call to the administration of the Government the men who organized the great Rebellion ('No! No! Never!') . . . That would mean that the constitutional amendments to which they are so bitterly opposed shall be enforced only so far as they believe in them. . . . To give them control of the government would mean a change the like of which has not been known in modern times. It would be as if the dead Stuarts were recalled to the throne of England, as if the Bourbons should be invited to administer the government of the French Republic, as though the Florentine Dukes should be called back and empowered to govern the great Kingdom of Italy." [1] Here spoke the Blaine of 1876.

While Blaine was rousing the enthusiasm of the middle West, a cloud of gloom and defeatism was spreading over the great pivotal State of New York. In mid-October Blaine received letter after letter weighted with anxiety and appeals for the aid of his presence. The State committee was at loggerheads over policies; the "despicable" local nominations in New York City were a handicap; St. John was recruiting four fifths of his strength from the Republican ranks; Conkling was

a chill coming down upon him from the North and the West? . . . The *Tribune* tells us that we have Blaine and should not want anything more. . . . But the issue is much greater than Mr. Blaine. That is the danger of allowing the Democrats, dominated by the solid South, to come again into power. And, after all, is it not base cowardice on the part of the Republican Party, as well as false politics, to abandon this issue? Do we not almost deserve defeat if we do not meet the issue which the solid South persists in making?" *W. E. Chandler Papers*, Library of Congress.

[1] Boyd, *op. cit.*, pp. 137–8.

predicting a Democratic victory; Whitelaw Reid could "find hardly a man in the clubs who was going to vote for Blaine." [1] "I think it would be well if you could reach here the latter part of next week and have interviews with some of our leading men," wrote John A. Stewart the day Blaine entered Indiana at South Bend.[2] Already, a week before, James D. Warren, chairman of the state committee, had not only urged Blaine to visit New York, but had planned his itinerary. "It is of the highest importance," he wrote Blaine at Detroit, "that we should be advised very soon of the time of your return to this State, and the number of days that you will be with us. . . . The contest promises to be more severe here than anywhere else. . . . Your presence will greatly help and we should have it for a week. . . . It is of course understood that there will be a mammoth demonstration while you are here. It would be of incalculable help if, during the last week of the campaign, you could go from here up through the heart of the State, through our northern tier of counties to Plattsburg. You could return to Maine over the mountains, if it be your purpose to reach home before Election Day. The calls upon us for your presence are very numerous and urgent." [3]

It was not a snap decision, therefore, that Blaine had to make when he reached Jamestown, Sunday, October 19, on his homeward trip, as to whether he should return immediately to Augusta or heed the Macedonian cry from New York. Andrew S. Draper, chairman of the executive committee of the State, met him at Jamestown and urged the former course. "Go up the line of the New York Central to Syracuse, stump the northern counties—they need it. Then go home to Portland (*sic!*)." [4] Blaine hesitated "as he stood at the window watching the falling rain." The six weeks of continuous campaigning had wearied him, as was to become evident from certain incidents of the closing days of the canvass. On the other hand, there was the elation of recalling the events of these six strenuous weeks—the marching clubs, the enthusiastic receptions, the glorious victory in Ohio, the instant response of great audiences to his magnetic appeal. The middle West he believed was safe for the Republican ticket. Had he the right to refuse

---

[1] Royal Cortissoz, *Life of Whitelaw Reid,* Vol. II, p. 96.
[2] October 18, 1884.
[3] J. D. Warren to Blaine, October 11, 1884.
[4] Quoted from a conversation with E. L. Murlin of Albany, by Allan Nevins, *Grover Cleveland,* p. 181.

to make the same contribution to its success in New York as he had made in Ohio? He did not need to be told what an inspiration his presence would be to the anxious Republicans of the metropolis. On the morning of the twentieth he set his face toward New York City. He could not know that this momentous decision would cost him the Presidency of the United States.

Blaine followed the first half of the itinerary proposed by Chairman Warren, speaking at several towns on Monday, the twentieth, and addressing a great meeting at Elmira in the evening. Thomas C. Platt was on the platform with him, and the next day introduced him to the crowd that had gathered in the driving rain to welcome him to the ex-Senator's home town of Owego. There were speeches at Binghamton, Deposit, Port Jervis, and Middletown, New York, and when the train reached Paterson, New Jersey, W. W. Phelps was waiting to present Blaine to the forty thousand enthusiasts who were there to greet him with cannon and fireworks. A little before seven o'clock in the evening of October 28, the special bearing Blaine and his party drew into the Erie depot at Jersey City, and the candidate was escorted to his suite at the Fifth Avenue Hotel, where Mrs. Blaine and her daughter Margaret had arrived the night before.

Wednesday, October 29, was the day of ill omen. It began with the gathering of several hundred Protestant clergymen of various denominations in the parlor of the hotel at ten o'clock in the morning. After adopting resolutions expressing their confidence in "the purity of the personal character" of the Republican standard bearers and condemning the "coronation of conceded personal impurity as represented by the head of the Democratic ticket," the reverend gentlemen went out into the corridor and grouped themselves at the foot of the broad staircase down which Blaine came to meet them, leaning on the arm of Dr. James King of the Methodist Church.

Dr. Armitage of the Fifth Avenue Baptist Church had been selected as spokesman for the clergy, but when he failed to return from Philadelphia in time to attend the meeting, a dull-witted Presbyterian minister named Samuel D. Burchard, who was described by the New York *Sun* as "a Silurian or early Paleozoic bigot," and by Blaine later as "an ass in the shape of a preacher," was hastily chosen to fill Dr. Armitage's place. Standing beside Blaine near the bottom of the stairway, Dr. Burchard addressed him in a brief speech of congratulation, in which he said: "We are your friends, Mr. Blaine, and notwithstanding all the calumnies that have been urged in the papers against you, we stand by your side (shouts of 'Amen!'). We expect to vote for you next Tuesday. . . . We are Republicans, and don't propose to leave our party and identify ourselves with the party whose antecedents have been rum, Romanism and rebellion. We are loyal to our flag. We are loyal to you."

Several other ministers followed Dr. Burchard. Blaine, absorbed in the preoccupation of his reply, or chatting with a bystander, failed to hear, or at least to realize the importance of the phrase, "rum, Romanism and rebellion." He took no notice of it in his response, which was chiefly devoted to showing that the protective tariff was an adjunct to Christian charity. One of the reporters present, however, did realize the significance of Burchard's abusive alliteration, and hastened to Senator A. P. Gorman at Democratic headquarters with the story. The astute Gorman at once saw the political capital that could be made out of the phrase. The next Sunday morning handbills were distributed at the doors of thousands of Catholic churches all over the country quoting the insulting words. By some of the more unscrupulous Democratic publicity agencies the remark was attributed to Blaine himself.

When he at last realized the havoc which Dr. Burchard's alliteration was creating, Blaine made the disclaimer which he should have made on the stairway of the hotel. Speaking at New Haven on the evening of November 1, he said that he had received a letter asking him why he had "charged the Democratic Party with being inspired with rum, Romanism and rebellion." "My answer is," he went on, "first that an unfortunate and ill-considered expression of another man was falsely attributed to me; and, in the next place, it gives me an opportunity to say at the close of the national campaign that in the public speeches which I have made I have refrained carefully and instinctively from any disrespectful allusion to the Democratic Party. . . . I am the last man in the United States who would make a disrespectful allusion to another man's religion . . . and though a Protestant by conviction myself, I should esteem myself most degraded if . . . I could in any presence make a disrespectful allusion to that ancient faith in which my mother lived and died." [1] Blaine's friends assured him that this "felicitous" apology entirely "offset the damage" done by Burchard's

[1] J. G. Blaine, *Political Discussions, Legislative, Diplomatic and Popular*, pp. 461–2.

remark.[1] But even as they were writing, Gorman's flyers were being thrust into the hands of the thousands of worshipers flocking to the Catholic churches. How many Catholic votes Blaine lost in New York alone by Burchard's bigoted blunder it is impossible to say, but no one can doubt that it was many times the number of Cleveland's eventual plurality in the State.[2]

On Wednesday afternoon Blaine reviewed a parade of the business men of the city who marched from Bowling Green up Broadway to Madison Square in the driving rain. The *Tribune* said that there were twenty-five thousand men in line, but the *World* allowed only half that number. Wearing high silk hats and carrying canes, section after section of drenched enthusiasts marched past the reviewing stand chanting:

> Blaine, Blaine, James G. Blaine.
> O-O-O-hi-O.
> No-No-No Free Trade.

But the day was not over when the last bedraggled parader had got home to put on dry socks. While he was stumping in the West, Blaine had received an invitation from a group of wealthy New Yorkers to dine with them at Delmonico's some evening during the last week of the campaign. He replied from Evansville, Indiana, October 24, to "the honorable Wm. M. Evarts, John Jacob Astor and others," accepting with much pleasure and indicating Wednesday the twenty-ninth as a convenient date.[3] When he entered the elaborately decorated ballroom of Delmonico's that evening and was escorted to the seat of honor by Evarts and Cyrus W. Field, he faced a company of some two hundred of the "money kings" of the metropolis. Jay Gould was there, and Russell Sage, Levi P. Morton, Whitelaw Reid, Cornelius Bliss, D. O. Mills, Jesse Seligman, Henry Clews, B. F. Jones, Augustus Kountze, and so on through a long list of millionaires, mitigated here and there

---

[1] Thomas Ewing to Blaine, November 2, 1884.

[2] The ill-starred Burchard, too, tried to "explain" his perfectly clear remark about the three antecedents of the Democratic Party, in a letter to the New York *Sun,* in which he said that he had been "greatly misunderstood." Naturally, the letter only aggravated the offense. Incidentally, Burchard's phrase did not even have the merit of originality. On November 9, 1876, two days after the election which seemed to him to have made Tilden President, Garfield wrote: "The future of our country no one can tell. It now appears that we were defeated by the combined power of rebellion, Catholicism and whisky, a trinity very hard to conquer." T. C. Smith, *Life and Letters of James Abram Garfield,* Vol. I, p. 613.

[3] It has been overlooked by Blaine's biographers that this acceptance pledged Blaine to go to New York City several days before the decision at Jamestown.

by the name of a clergyman or a judge. The flowers were the rarest, the wine the choicest, the food the daintiest that money could buy. Reporters were excluded, except for one representative of Jay Gould's Associated Press, who was allowed to stay through the speech-making but not to attend the parlor meeting of the magnates after the banquet, where the important business of raising funds for the last drive of the campaign was discussed.

Blaine's speech at the dinner was a fervid encomium of the prosperity which Republican rule had brought to the country in general and to New York in particular. There had never been in all the history of the world, he said, a parallel to the financial progress which had raised the wealth of the Empire City from $1,800,000,000 to $6,300,000,000 in a period of twenty years, and the Republican Party was not "arrogant" when it claimed the credit for organizing and maintaining the industrial system "which has enabled you to make this marvelous progress." The paramount issue of the campaign was the preservation of the protective tariff, a sound banking and currency system and the constitutional amendments which followed the Civil War. If these policies should be reversed (as they would be by a Democratic victory) "then you will have to recast your accounts and review your ledgers and prepare for a new, and I may say, a dangerous departure." The Republican Party was not "on trial." In its twenty-three years of power "it had advanced the interest of the country as none of its predecessors had been able to do. It had elevated the standard of America and increased its wealth in a ratio . . . never before dreamed of." [1]

This glorification of wealth before a group of millionaires, when the country was suffering from the effects of a depression which had thrown thousands of men out of work and reduced their families to dire poverty, was seized upon by the anti-Blaine press the next morning under captions like "Belshazzar's Feast" and "The Boodle Banquet." McDougall's cartoon in the *World* depicted "Belshazzar Blaine and the Money Kings," with blazing diamonds in their shirt fronts, seated at the sumptuous feast, while a poor fellow with a shivering wife and a starving skeleton of a child begged for the crumbs which fell from the table. There is no doubt that the millionaires' dinner, which Stephen B. Elkins had tried to persuade Blaine not to attend and which he had refused to attend himself, alienated great numbers of the laboring class.

[1] T. B. Boyd, *The Blaine and Logan Campaign of 1884*, pp. 186–188.

J. C. F. Beyland, editor of *Der New Yorker Republicaner,* who was valiantly combating Schurz and the Mugwumps, had declared the week before that "the Irish, the working people and the plain people" were for Blaine, and that the Irish and German-American mass meeting at Chickering Hall on the night of Tuesday the twenty-eighth would "knock the stuffing out of the Ottendorfer-Schurz-Salomon-Siegel combination of renegades and deserters and Judas Iscariots." [1] But the events of October 29 knocked the stuffing out of Beyland's prophecy. "Burchard lost us thousands, the Delmonico dinner hundreds of voters," wrote ex-Governor Cornell, in summing up the causes of the Republican defeat.[2]

The remainder of the week was crowded with engagements—on Thursday a reception by the ladies at the Brooklyn Academy of Music; a dinner party, with Mayor Low and Senator Sherman among the guests; and speeches in the evening at the Brooklyn Opera House and at an open air meeting at Williamsburg, where, in spite of the incessant rain, thousands of people waited for two hours to hear Blaine speak for five minutes. On Friday a rally at Chickering Hall in the afternoon, with speeches by Blaine, Sherman, Evarts and Frémont, and in the evening the review of a torchlight procession of thirty thousand members of Blaine and Logan clubs (still marching in the rain) from towns and cities within a radius of a hundred and fifty miles from New York. On Saturday a dash into Connecticut to address large audiences at New Haven, Hartford and South Norwalk, and a great farewell rally at the Academy of Music in the evening, under the auspices of the Columbia College Blaine and Logan Club.

Meanwhile Cleveland had been quietly attending to his duties in Albany. Except for a visit to Buffalo on the evening of October 2, to review a parade of Democratic organization from the western part of the State, he had refused to engage in any campaign activities until the closing week of the canvass, when he spoke at Bridgeport, Connecticut, and Newark, New Jersey. On the first of November he came to New York to witness the great Democratic parade which was to outdo the torchlight procession in Blaine's honor the evening before. The city was all Cleveland's that Saturday afternoon, while Blaine was absent on his excursion into Connecticut. He was spared at any rate the sight and

---

1 Beyland to Blaine, October 23, 1884.
2 Cornell to Blaine, November 15, 1884.

sound of the cheering host of forty thousand Cleveland men, many of them former Republicans, who marched up Broadway and Fifth Avenue, filling the wide streets from curb to curb, and saluting their robust chief as he stood under the slate-cold sky on the flag-draped reviewing stand at Madison Square. "We could see ahead of us," wrote a participant in the parade, "as far as the eye could reach the divisions which had preceded us, with their banners waving, and we could hear constantly repeated the war cry of

> Blaine, Blaine, James G. Blaine,
> Continental liar from the State of Maine! [1]

In the evening, when the Blaine rally at the Academy of Music was going on, the "younger set" of the Democrats paraded, repeating the insulting slogans and performing their "Burn this letter!" stunt.

On Monday morning, November 3, the Blaine family left New York for their home in Augusta. They stopped for receptions and speeches at Springfield, Worcester and Newton before reaching Boston for a final banquet at the Hotel Brunswick. The strenuous days in New York had wearied Blaine, but even the hostile comments provoked by Burchard's blunder and the Delmonico dinner had not shaken his judgment that the chances of victory favored the Republicans. If he apprehended defeat, he gave no sign of misgiving in his public utterances. He concluded his speech at the Brunswick with a note of calm assurance: "I have returned somewhat weary, somewhat broken in voice, as your ears have already detected, but I have returned with even a more profound belief than I had in the judgment . . . of the great mass of American citizens; and I go to my home tomorrow not without a strong confidence in the result of the ballot, but with a heart that shall not in the least degree be troubled by any verdict that may be returned by the great American people." [2] After reviewing a torchlight procession from the balcony of the hotel, he waved a farewell to the crowd which filled Boylston Street and the Public Garden opposite, insistent in their cries for a speech, with a hearty, "Good-night, good-bye, good fortune on the morrow!" [3]

---

[1] W. B. Hornblower, in the *Cleveland Papers*. Quoted by Allan Nevins, in *Grover Cleveland, a Study in Courage*, p. 180.

[2] T. B. Boyd, *The Blaine and Logan Campaign*, p. 213.

[3] As a little boy, holding my father's hand in that dense crowd, I remember the thrill I got from my glimpse of the tall gray figure who filled so conspicuous a place in the public eye fifty years ago.

Blaine sat in the parlor of his home in Augusta on election night, surrounded his family and friends who were more anxious than himself over the returns which were slowly coming in, indicating a close battle in the doubtful States which would decide the election. Soon after ten o'clock he left the room saying, "Good-night, gentlemen, I'm going to bed. Don't disturb me unless something decisive comes in." But his secretary Tom Sherman and William H. Bigelow sat by the wire in the library until morning. "By midnight," says Sherman, "we knew the result, but I let Mr. Blaine and the family sleep on. Late in the morning, when I could find him alone, I went to his room with a bunch of 'demnition totals.' He was in bed, apparently as unconcerned as if he had never been a candidate." To his secretary's tearful announcement he replied: "Bless you, it doesn't make the difference of a pulse-beat to me personally. I'm sorry for my friends and that the party loses. To me it is more of a relief than a cross."[1] And to a friend he wrote a few days later: "I feel quite serene over the result. As the Lord sent upon us an ass in the shape of a preacher and a rainstorm to lessen our vote in New York, I am disposed to feel resigned to the dispensation of defeat which flowed directly from these agencies. In missing a great honor I escaped a great and oppressive responsibility. You know how much I didn't want the nomination.[2]

Cleveland's unquestioned victory in Connecticut, Indiana, New Jersey, Delaware and the States of the solid South gave him 183 of the 401 electoral votes. New York's 36 would send him over the necessary majority of 201 by an ample margin. From the returns which came in slowly Tuesday evening, Cleveland's friends Apgar, Lamont, Rice, Thatcher and others, who were gathered with him at the Executive Mansion at Albany, were confident that he had carried the State by a substantial majority. But when the strong Tammany wards of New York City showed large gains for Blaine, and some of the up-State counties began to look dubious, Colonel Rice became convinced that Cleveland's margin would be slim, "perhaps not over two hundred."

[1] Thomas H. Sherman, *Twenty Years with James G. Blaine*, pp. 94–5.
[2] Blaine to Murat Halstead, November 16, 1884. Blaine's equanimity was not shared by his family. Mrs. Blaine wrote to her daughter Mrs. Coppinger at Fort Hays on November 30: "You need not feel envious of anyone who was here during those trying days (of the canvass). It is all a horror to me. I was absolutely sure of the election, as I had a right to be from Mr. Elkins' assertions. . . . It is easy to bear now, but the click-click of the telegraph, the shouting through telephone in response to its never-to-be-satisfied demand, and the increasing murmur of men's voices coming up through the night to my room will never go out of my memory." *Letters of Mrs. Blaine*, Vol. II, pp. 120–1.

In the name of Chairman Manning, Rice, Apgar and Lamont sent telegrams to representative Democrats in every county of the State, requesting them to keep an eye on the count of the ballots and to send to Albany certified copies of the returns as they were filed in the county clerk's office. Excitement ran high in New York and other large cities. Cheering and jeering crowds packed the streets in front of the bulletin boards. When the rumor was spread that Jay Gould's Western Union Telegraph Company was holding back returns or tampering with them in Blaine's favor, a mob of men threatened to march to Dey Street and sack the Western Union building and "hang Jay Gould." [1] The Republicans made the charge that in the Democratic precincts thousands of Butler votes were counted for Cleveland. The Democrats, in response to an appeal from the national chairman Gorman, formed a committee of fifty New York lawyers, including F. L. Stetson, James C. Carter, William C. Whitney, and Carl Schurz ("with the continuous assistance and advice of Roscoe Conkling"), who devoted themselves for ten days to a searching scrutiny of the returns throughout the State.

Senator George F. Hoar and Edward Stanwood both asserted many years later that Blaine had been deprived of New York's electoral vote, and thereby of the election, through fraud.[2] When Stanwood repeated his charge in an article on "Election Superstitions and Fallacies" in the *Atlantic Monthly* for October, 1912, Colonel Rice and F. L. Stetson replied with convincing facts out of their own intimate experience in the canvass of the votes, to show that the Republicans had had equal representation with the Democrats on the returning boards, that the

[1] Jay Gould himself sent Cleveland the following telegram on Friday, November 7: "Governor Cleveland: I heartily congratulate you on your election. All concede that your Administration as Governor has been wise and conservative, and in the larger field of President I feel that you will do still better, and that the vast business interests of the country will be entirely safe in your hands." The original telegram is in the possession of Cleveland's former secretary, the Honorable William G. Rice of Albany.

[2] "I suppose it would hardly be denied now by persons acquainted with the details of the management of the Democratic campaign, at any rate I have heard the fact admitted by several very distinguished members of the Senate of the United States, that the plurality of the votes of New York was really for Mr. Blaine, and that he was unjustly deprived of the election by the frauds at Long Island City, by which votes cast for the Butler electoral ticket were counted for Cleveland." G. F. Hoar, *Autobiography of Seventy Years* (1903), Vol. I, p. 408.

"New York was counted for Cleveland, but there were then and there are now few Republicans cognizant of the facts who doubt that a plurality of the votes was actually cast for Mr. Blaine. It was openly claimed at the time and commonly believed by Republicans, though the Democrats warmly denied it, that in many precincts of New York City the votes for Butler were cast for Cleveland. The conviction, a few years later, of the unscrupulous boss of a town near New York (John Y. McKane of Gravesend) of falsifying returns confirmed in their opinion those who held the view that Blaine was really elected." Edward Stanwood, *Life of James G. Blaine* (1905), p. 291.

count had been more scrupulously supervised and checked than at any previous presidential election, and that "no responsible person or paper" in November, 1884, "adhered to the charge" that Blaine was defeated by fraud.[1] The Republican National Committee announced on November 9 that "the most careful and thorough measures were being taken" to ascertain whether any errors or frauds had been committed in the New York count, and the chief Blaine organ, the *Tribune,* conceded on November 16 that the canvass just completed had not established the existence of any such errors or frauds. That canvass resulted in a plurality of 1149 for Cleveland, out of a total vote of 1,167,169 in the State, of which St. John polled 25,016 and Butler 16,994. "If we had only had a thousand more votes in New York," sighed Blaine's old friend William E. Chandler to Mr. Stetson, at the close of Cleveland's inaugural parade. "It was a lack of votes, not a theft of votes, that lost the State to Blaine." [2]

In the scores of letters of condolence and confidence that came to Blaine from all parts of the country there were outbursts of dismay and disgust over the election of the Democratic candidate,[3] but there was no suggestion that his election was tainted with fraud. There was plenty of discussion of the causes for Blaine's defeat in New York— the Mugwump defection; the failure to push Butler; the ineptitude of the State committee, "who seemed to think that brass bands and coal-oil were more valuable than the work of thinkers"; the temperance movement; the treachery of the "malignant Conkling"; the idiotic alliteration of Burchard's; the Delmonico dinner; the weather up-State [4]—but nowhere in these contemporary letters is there a hint that New York's vote was "stolen" from the Republicans.

Finally, there is no substantial evidence that Blaine himself believed that he was cheated out of the election and that he refrained from making an issue of the case only because he remembered the tension at the time of the disputed election of 1876 and feared that the country could not stand a repetition of the crisis eight years later. During the

[1] W. G. Rice and F. L. Stetson, "Was New York's Vote Stolen?" *North American Review,* January, 1914.
[2] *Ibid.,* p. 88.
[3] "The lecherous beast goes into the White House, with the venomous Copperheads." E. F. Webb to Blaine, November 11, 1884. "After 20 years of contest the rebel flag is unfurled on the capitol and the flag of our Fathers and Union and Liberty is struck," Cassius M. Clay to Blaine, November 6, 1884.
[4] W. E. Chandler, Alonzo B. Cornell, Cyrus W. Field, Albion W. Tourgee to Blaine, November 6, 11, 15, 1884.

canvass conducted by the New York lawyers, he never claimed to have carried the State or made the least effort to have the Republican committee press such a claim. To the correspondent of the Boston *Journal*, who asked him on November 16 what he thought about the result of the count, he replied that "he had no more means of knowing than an unborn child." [1] Two evenings later he addressed his friends and neighbors of Augusta, who had come to his house to serenade him, thanking them for their support and deploring as a great national misfortune "the transfer of the political power of the Government to the South," which "furnished nearly three fourths of the electoral votes that defeated the Republican Party," and which would now "step into command of the Democratic Party." But he did not question the result of the poll. "The national contest is over," he said, "and by the narrowest margin we have lost." The cities of New York and Brooklyn had thrown their strength with the solid South and "were the decisive element in the election." "The contest just closed," he concluded, "utterly dwarfs the fortunes of candidates, whether successful or unsuccessful . . . I have discussed the issues and consequences of that contest without reference to my own defeat, without the remotest reference to the gentleman who is elevated to the Presidency. Toward him personally I have no cause for the slightest ill will; and with entire cordiality I may express the wish that his official career will prove gratifying to himself and beneficial to the country, and that his administration may overcome the embarrassment which the peculiar source of its power imposes on it from the hour of its birth." [2]

[1] Rice and Stetson, *op. cit.*, p. 92.
[2] J. G. Blaine, *Political Discussions, Legislative, Diplomatic and Popular*, pp. 466–471.

Chapter XIII *Letters and Travel (1884–1888)*

EARLY IN December, 1884, the Blaine family returned to Washington for the winter, which they spent in the Windom house on Scott Circle, and Blaine set to work diligently on the second volume of his *Twenty Years of Congress*. In spite of his stoical, or even "relieved" acceptance of the result of the campaign, a note of regret appears in his correspondence immediately after the election. "The whole campaign was a disaster to me," he wrote to a friend, "personally, politically, pecuniarily. I ought to have obeyed what was really a strong instinct against running. My regrets do not in the least take the form of mourning over defeat in the election, but over my blunder in ever consenting to run. It was the wrong year, and gave my enemies their coveted opportunity." [1] He had, in fact, expressed his doubts in private whether any Republican could be elected in 1884. Three fourths of the States which had voted for Garfield in 1880 had chosen Democratic Governors since. Moreover, the spectacular failure of the firm of Grant and Ward in the spring of 1884 had cast a shadow upon the party of which the General had been the titular head for eight years, and strengthened the demand of the reformers for a candidate against whom no charge of questionable public conduct could be brought.

Yet Blaine had every reason, as hundreds of letters from his admirers assured him, to feel proud of his part in the campaign. His speeches had been models of vigor and eloquence. His tact and patience had been unfailing. Not a single false or weak note had crept into his appeals for the support of Republican principles. No other Republican candidate could have carried Ohio; no other, certainly not Arthur or Edmunds, could have contested New York on practically even terms with Grover Cleveland. "You have done your share of the work necessary to your election," wrote W. E. Chandler, when the result was hanging in the balance, "and you can rest serene even if the fates place you in history with Henry Clay." [2] And his old friend Dr. Lincoln wrote from Washington: "I have been watching with increasing

---

[1] Edward Stanwood, *Life of James G. Blaine*, pp. 292–3.
[2] W. E. Chandler to Blaine, November 6, 1884.

wonder and admiration your unprecedented and brilliant canvass, fond of trusting that I should enjoy the extreme pleasure of sending you my warmest congratulations on the issue. But now I can only express to you my unfeigned sorrow for a result so unfortunate for the country and so painful to your friends in Washington. It seems the fate of the great men of this country to merit, but of the insignificant to attain, the highest political preferment. . . . You have demonstrated to all the world your unsurpassed fitness for the high position for which you contended, but the judges were incompetent, imbecile." [1] There was no repining, however. The next election would tell a different story. The Blaine and Logan clubs were already inscribing 1888 on their standards. "I praised the Lord when I read your speech last night," wrote Murat Halstead on November 19; "we go toward the future with that banner flying." [2]

Comforting as these testimonials must have been to Blaine, the anticipatory interest which his friends took in the literary work to which he now returned was probably an even greater satisfaction, for he believed that he was through with active politics and that the time had come when he could realize his early dream of devoting his declining years to the writing of history—even if not the history of Caesar's campaigns in Gaul or of the War of 1812. Dr. Lincoln, in the letter just quoted, waxed quite eloquent over the prospect; "now may we not express our jealousy for the time you have given up to the turmoil of political life, which might be so much better devoted to the delight of letters and the good of mankind? What do we care for the political life of Tully, proud as he was of it, in comparison with those books which in his enforced leisure he produced for the delectation of all time. . . . In this temporary disappointment I delight to presage a life still happier and if possible more brilliant than the past, and hope (here falling into Tully's Latin) *ut haec studia, quae secundas res ornant, adversis perfugium ac solatium praebeant."* Others expressed their satisfaction in terms no less sincere, if less effusive. "Tell Blaine," wrote General Sherman to his daughter, "that as a matter of course I have read his first volume with greedy interest, and that I await with more for his second volume, which must treat of the Reconstruction wherein lies the germ of his own failure to be President (!) . . . It will be simply

[1] N. S. Lincoln to Blaine, November 16, 1884.
[2] Murat Halstead to Blaine, November 19, 1884. The speech referred to was Blaine's response to the serenade of his neighbors at Augusta on the seventeenth.

immortal if he is equally frank and illuminating." [1]

Whatever "temporary disappointment" the family may have had in seeing Blaine enter his study instead of the White House was offset by the joy in his absorption in his work. "I can really look back happily in many ways upon the outcome of the election of 1884," wrote Walker to his father after the volume was completed, "for I feel that with the responsibilities of the Presidency added to the necessity of finishing your book, the work would have been too great. At it was, the book took more than a year of hard work in the quiet of the country and of Washington, and it will prove as valuable a memorial of your fame as a successful administration. But for the future I have great hopes and great ambitions, centered not upon the Presidency, but upon your going back into public life. It seems to be an era of indifference and incompetency just now, but I am sure better things must come in the future." [2]

Blaine sat down to write his second volume of *Twenty Years of Congress*, not only relieved of his personal preoccupations with the Presidency, but also with certain other favorable omens. The reception of the first volume had been most encouraging. As early as the spring of 1883, J. W. Harper, learning from W. W. Phelps that Blaine "was engaged upon a history of his, or our, times," had asked Phelps to get the publishing contract for Harper and Brothers. "I am sure," he wrote, "that Mr. Blaine's narrative will hold the American people, because it will be human—real flesh and blood—the record not of a Machiavellian observer, but of an active participant, a brave fighter and a gallant leader in the most critical events of our nation's history. So, when it comes quite convenient to you, I wish you would give Mr. Blaine to understand that while the doors of Franklin Square always stand open to 'them literary fellers,' such as scholars and poets and novelists and essayists and travelers, the proprietors generally go down to the sidewalk to welcome the historian of his own time, and with uncovered heads reverently help him to unload the manuscript from his triumphal car on the elevated railroad." [3] Mr. Harper and his partners were spared the danger of contracting pneumonia by standing bare-headed on the pavement to welcome Blaine with his manuscript, for the author had arranged for its publication on a subscription basis with the Henry

[1] From a fragment of an undated letter in the Blaine collection, evidently passed on by Rachel Sherman to the family.
[2] Walker Blaine to Blaine, February 3, 1887.
[3] J. W. Harper to W. W. Phelps, March 13, 1883 (in the Blaine letters).

Bill Company, of Norwich, Connecticut. But Mr. Harper had been right in his estimate of the popularity of the volume. Just how large the sales were in 1884 and 1885 we do not know, but the royalties were sufficient to relieve Blaine of the financial embarrassment under which he had been laboring since he left the State Department (see above, p. 236); and the coincidence of his royalty receipts with the better returns from his coal and iron properties put him in easy, if not affluent circumstances for the rest of his life. He was able to build a handsome villa at Bar Harbor, and, when he returned to public life, to purchase a new residence in Washington.

Furthermore, the second volume of *Twenty Years of Congress* was bound to be more interesting than the first, because it would treat of the period of Blaine's own influential participation in national affairs, and would contain his estimates of the personalities and policies of the statesmen with whom he was associated. Only two (1863–1865) of his own eighteen years as Congressman and Senator had found a place in the first volume, a large part of which was taken up with a "Review of the events which led to the political revolution of 1860." And while this summary of our history down to the Civil War was presented in a lively and popular style, it was devoted almost exclusively to a rehearsal of the well-known efforts of the North to check the extension of territory and the increase of power of the slaveholding section of the country.

Finally, though we may believe that Blaine wished to write with the impartiality and objectivity which should characterize the work of a historian, the very fact that the first volume was composed during the months when the author was the most prominent candidate for the Republican nomination, and was published early in the presidential year, invested it with the character of a campaign document in the eyes of many critics. For instance, the studious moderation and even courtesy with which Blaine treated the Southern statesmen in his book, as compared with the virulence with which he had attacked them on the floor of Congress,[1] led to the accusation that he was trying to be all

---

[1] Compare, for example, the speech of January 10, 1876, arraigning Jefferson Davis for the "murders" at Andersonville, with the kindly and almost apologetic reproach administered to Mr. Davis for his decision to "engage in the secession movement." "This decision," says Blaine, "was a great surprise to Northern Democrats, among whom Mr. Davis had many friends. For several years he had been growing in favor with a powerful element in the Democracy of the free States, and, but for the exasperating quarrel of 1860, he might have been selected as the presidential candidate of his party."

things to all men in order that he might win votes. "Read Mr. Blaine's book!" exclaimed a Stalwart New York Republican to W. E. Chandler in a letter written a few weeks before the close of the 1884 campaign. "Aside from the genial feast of taffy which he spreads before everyone, the richest taffy of all is for the South. I really think, if the book should be put in the hands of anyone who had never heard of our war and knew nothing of the antecedent history of our country, he would come to the conclusion that . . . the South had been greatly outraged in some occult way not fully explained by the author. It would be ill-natured to say that Blaine was bidding for a possible future Democratic-Southern nomination for the Presidency when he wrote the book, but it certainly looks as if he thought it might be good policy to placate Southern hostility and possibly win Southern support." [1] Of course, the entertainment of the idea of Blaine's seeking a "Democratic-Southern nomination" would convict a man of imbecility rather than of "ill-nature." At any rate, if Blaine did yield in any degree to the temptation to "soft-pedal" the offenses of the South in his first volume, that temptation was removed when the election- of 1884 was over and the result was accepted with equanimity.

The work on Volume II proceeded rapidly. When Louis A. Dent, Blaine's new secretary, joined him at Augusta in the early spring of 1885, he found Blaine working on chapter five, which dealt with the Black Codes of the Johnson governments in the Southern States. The labor of the summer was interrupted only by the occasional entertainment of friends or by trips to Bar Harbor to look over sites for the new cottage. When the winter of 1885–6 (which the family spent at Augusta) set in, the volume was nearing completion. "Your Father is doing a prodigious work on his book," wrote Mrs. Blaine to Walker in Washington, December 4, 1885. "Last night he read us his chapter on the Fisheries." [2] The volume came from the press in February, 1886,

No man gave up more than Mr. Davis in joining the revolt against the Union. In his farewell words to the Senate there was a tone of moderation and dignity, not unmixed with regretful and tender emotions. There was also a spirit of confidence and defiance. He evidently had full faith that he was going forth to victory and power." (*Twenty Years of Congress* Vol. I, pp. 245–6.) See also the remarks on Chief Justice Taney and the Dred Scott Decision, "viewed after the lapse of years which curbs the passions and tempers the judgment." (*Ibid.* p. 134.)

[1] M. Woodhull to W. E. Chandler, October 7, 1884. *Chandler Papers*, Library of Congress. We have noticed above (p. 313, note 3) Mr. Woodhull's complaint of Blaine's subordination of the Southern issue in the campaign of 1884.

[2] *Letters of Mrs. James G. Blaine*, Vol. II, p. 126. This chapter (xxvii) was the second from the last. For Senator Blaine's part in the fisheries dispute and the Halifax Award, see above, pp. 148–150.

as we learn from a letter of the twenty-sixth of that month from Robert R. Hitt, who had been Assistant Secretary of State under Blaine in 1881, acknowledging "the quick and thoughtful kindness that sent the primeur at the first hour," and praising the work as having "a more varied interest than the first volume—coming nearer the living moment and living men—the very age and body of the time, its form and pressure." [1]

The second volume of the *Twenty Years of Congress* covers the period from the accession of Johnson in 1865 to the election of Garfield in 1880. But the subject matter is very unevenly distributed over these years. The first sixteen chapters, or 421 of the 676 pages, are devoted to the slightly less than four years of Johnson's Administration. The next nine chapters (pages 422 to 594) deal with the Grant regime. And the Administration of President Hayes, on which Blaine had congratulated the country so heartily in his campaign speech at Frémont, Ohio, is disposed of in the remaining 82 pages. Thus, instead of an increasing richness of detail as we "come nearer the living moment and living men," we find a sharp decline of interest. And the utterly disproportionate emphasis on the strife between President Johnson and the radicals of Congress over the Reconstruction policies betrays the real purpose of the volume. It is essentially an apology for the congressional dictatorship which forced the Reconstruction measures upon the defeated South. As such, despite the merits of clarity and vigor of style, of sustained movement in the narrative, of skillful synthesis of public events and of felicity in the characterization of public men which at times reminds one of Macaulay's vignettes, it cannot rank with the impartial and objective treatments of the period by scholars like Rhodes and Oberholtzer. Blaine was too much of a partisan to view dispassionately, even after a score of years, the events in which he had played so conspicuous a rôle. He was first, last and always for his party, thoroughly convinced not only that it had a monopoly of the men who were fit to run the government, but also that, contrary to the famous motto of President Hayes, he served his country best who served his party best.[2] Every judgment, therefore, of Blaine's writings must take its departure from this fundamental tenet of his

---

[1] R. R. Hitt to Blaine, February 26, 1886.

[2] "What I liked about him," said Thomas C. Platt, "was his bold and consistent contention that the citizen who best loved his party and was loyal to it, was loyal to and best loved his country." *Autobiography*, p. 185.

political philosophy.

It would be impossible here to review in detail the *Twenty Years of Congress,* but a few characteristic passages may be noticed in confirmation of the opinion of the work just advanced. Because the radical Reconstruction measures were approved by a majority of the Republican Party, they were, in Blaine's eyes, not only just in themselves, but also necessary for the salvation of the country. Hence the subtle rationalization by which he converts President Johnson's resistance to the unconstitutionality and cruelty of those measures into treason against the Union. "The people," he says, "discerned with keen precision the absolute facts of the case. They saw that the policy of the President was at war with the creed and spirit of the Republican Party, and that, if carried into effect, the legitimate fruits of the bloody struggle which had afflicted the Nation would be lost to posterity, the laws of humanity would be violated, and a fresh rebellion against national authority would be invited." [1] Now, whatever Johnson's faults (and they were many), a disposition to encourage a new "rebellion" or to sacrifice the fruits of the war in the abolition of slavery and the preservation of the Union was certainly not among them. No stauncher Union man than Andrew Johnson, from the day when he alone of all the Southern Senators refused to join the secession until the day of his death, could be found in the United States. And Blaine knew it. It was not the keen discernment of the people of the North that detected treason in Johnson's policies, but the bitter hostility of the radicals, who imputed treason to him as a pretext for compassing his political ruin. Blaine's argument comes to this, that because the radicals had got control of Congress, Johnson should have endorsed their policy, however repugnant it was to his sense of justice and of his own constitutional prerogatives. "The President," says Blaine (p. 82), "seemed to have no comprehension of the fact that with inconspicuous exceptions the entire Republican Party was composed of Radicals, men who in aim and sympathy were hostile to the purposes indicated by his policy." On the contrary, the President had the most vivid comprehension of the strength and the enmity of the radicals, and it was his refusal to bend to their will that exasperated them to the point of impeaching him. Nor were his supporters among the Republicans either few or "inconspicuous." The latter adjective cannot justly be applied

[1] Volume II, p. 126.

to men like Seward, Welles, McCulloch, Stanbery, Evarts, Doolittle, Grimes, Fessenden and Henderson. Congress had upheld Johnson's first veto of the Freedman's Bureau bill early in 1866, and had the President possessed the qualities of patience, tact and conciliation, he might have consolidated the moderate sentiment in Congress and the country behind his policy.

For that policy was essentially the one bequeathed to him by Abraham Lincoln. Here we cannot absolve Blaine from misrepresenting the position of the great leader of the Republican Party. Blaine's admiration for Lincoln was so intense that he naturally wished to have the weight of the martyred President's name on the side of the radical reconstructionists. "It is scarcely conceivable," he writes (p. 123), "that had Mr. Lincoln lived any serious difficulty could have arisen between himself and Congress respecting the policy of reconstruction." But serious difficulty *had already* arisen between Mr. Lincoln and the radicals in Congress over just the issue on which they fought Johnson— namely, the executive policy of moderation in dealing with the South. Lincoln's pocket veto in the summer of 1864 of the Wade-Davis bill, which set aside his "10 per cent" plan, and required a majority of all the voters in a seceded State to take the oath of allegiance to the Constitution and the Union before that State's reconstruction could begin, had provoked a fiery attack on him by the authors of the bill. The Wade-Davis Manifesto charged the President with a "studied outrage on the legislative authority of the people," and warned him that "if he wishes our support, he must confine himself to his executive duties, to obey and execute and not to make the laws . . . and leave political reorganization to Congress." What would have happened "if Booth had missed," how successful the wise and patient Lincoln would have been, where Johnson failed, in winning the support of Congress for his program of the restoration of the South to the Union "with malice toward none and with charity for all," it is impossible to say. But it is to impugn Lincoln's character as well as to ignore his actions, to suggest that he would for a moment have acquiesced in the punitive policy of congressional reconstruction.

Nor can we agree with Blaine when he uses Lincoln's name in justification of the policy of wholesale Negro suffrage imposed on the South by the Reconstruction Acts and the Fifteenth Amendment. It is true that in the spring of 1864 Lincoln had written to Michael Hahn, the newly elected Governor of Louisiana as reconstructed under the 10 per cent plan, "barely suggesting" for Hahn's "private consideration" whether, in the approaching State convention, the franchise might not be extended "to some of the colored people . . . as for instance the very intelligent and especially those who have fought gallantly in our ranks." [1] This cautious private, limited and tentative suggestion is converted by Blaine into a manifesto in support of Negro suffrage. "Lincoln's meaning," he says (p. 40) "was one of deep and almost prophetic significance. It was perhaps the earliest proposition from any authentic source to endow the Negro with the right of suffrage, and was an indirect but most effective answer to those who subsequently attempted to use Mr. Lincoln's name in support of policies which his intimate friends instinctively knew would be abhorrent to his inerrant sense of justice." It would be difficult to compress more misrepresentation into a single sentence. Mr. Lincoln's "intimate friends" (who were certainly not the radicals) knew that nothing would have been more abhorrent to his sense of justice than the policy of general Negro suffrage forced upon the South at the point of the bayonet, and that if he had suspected that his suggestion to Governor Hahn was "prophetic" of such a policy he would have been appalled. What he had actually proposed was that a convention of white men, acting by the authority of the State of Louisiana might consider conferring the suffrage upon a very limited number of Negroes. What Congress did was suddenly to enfranchise the whole mass of adult male Negroes in the South by national action, not only making them eligible to participate in the State conventions to frame new constitutions, but even prescribing that such constitutions must embody the grant of universal Negro suffrage.

Between these two types of procedure there is no resemblance, and it is hard to understand how Blaine could in the above passage claim Lincoln as a supporter of the radical policy, "had he lived," while some pages earlier he had more accurately defined the issue between the President and the radicals: "It must frankly be admitted that Mr. Lincoln's course was in some of its aspects extraordinary. It met with . . . violent opposition from the more radical members of both Houses. If Congress had been in session at the time (of the Wade-Davis Manifesto), a very rancorous hostility would have been developed against the President." (p. 43.) Precisely so. But what reason

[1] Nicolay and Hay, *Abraham Lincoln, A History,* Vol. VIII, p. 434.

is there to think that had Mr. Lincoln lived a few months more "no serious difficulty could have arisen between himself and Congress respecting the policy of reconstruction"?

Furthermore, Blaine makes it clear that his sympathies in this matter were, after a lapse of twenty years, still with the radicals of Congress and not with the President. "It is to the eminent credit of the Republican members of Congress," he writes (p. 147), "that they stood in a crisis of this magnitude true to principle, and firm against all the power and patronage of the Administration. No unmanly efforts to compromise, no weak shrinking from duty, sullied the fame of the great body of Senators and Representatives." But was it not inconsistent for a man who entertained such an opinion to deplore the fact that so few of the Southerners who stood for the Union in 1860 [1] joined the Republicans after the war? "The men who had the courage to stand for the Union in time of war," he writes (p. 473), "should not have separated from its friends in time of peace. . . . Every day affords fresh proof of the disasters which have resulted to the Republican party of the South from the loss of so large a proportion of the original Union men." True enough. But it was exactly the radical congressional reconstruction policy, which Blaine endorses so heartily, that condemned the Republican Party in the South to become an organization of ignorant Negroes, led by unscrupulous carpetbaggers and scalawags—an organization sure to disintegrate as rapidly as home rule was restored to the Southern whites. And it was only the policy of Lincoln and Johnson, which Blaine denounces, that could have established an enduring Republican Party south of Mason and Dixon's line. The political misfortune that has made one large section of our country solid (with trifling exceptions) in the support of one party, whatever the merits or faults of that party's platform or candidate, might have been averted if the wise policy of Lincoln had not been frustrated by the radicals. It ill behooves one who praises the mischief done by the latter to indulge in vain regrets over the failure of the former.[2]

[1] In the election of 1860 the ten States which eventually joined South Carolina in secession cast 418,003 votes for Douglas and Bell, both Union candidates, as against 436,772 for Breckinridge, who represented the Calhoun-Davis doctrine of States rights, even if it led to the dissolution of the Union.

[2] General Sherman, who had lived many years in the South before the war, wrote to his daughter shortly after the election of 1884: "In 1865 the Republicans could have taken into their party four-fifths of the young men who had fought and were mad with Jeff Davis, Toombs, etc., etc., who had betrayed them into Rebellion—but the party

For one of the foolish and vengeful acts of the radicals Blaine does make honest amends. Despite his persistent animus against President Johnson, he confesses that the impeachment proceedings "were not justifiable in the charges made," and that their success would have resulted in "greater injury to free institutions than Andrew Johnson in his utmost endeavor was able to inflict." (p. 376.) For the Tenure-of-Office Act, the violation of which by Johnson was made the basis of the impeachment, "was an extreme proposition, a new departure from the established usage of the Federal government and personally degrading to the incumbent of the presidential office." It had "grown out of abnormal excitement," and was "a blunder, all the more considerable because the act was not needed to uphold the Republican policy of Congress in aid of which it was devised." (p. 273.) [1]

Blaine also acknowledges that some of the Southern States under carpetbagger rule "had wretched governments, officered by bad men who misled the Negro and engaged in riotous corruption." Yet he contends that a majority of the so-called carpetbaggers and scalawags were honorable and unobtrusive men, whose merits were obscured by the transgressions of a few scoundrels and who therefore "did not obtain a fair hearing at the bar of public opinion." (p. 472.) He asserts that if these men had been allowed to establish as good governments in the South as they had been reared under in the North, "they would have conferred upon all the reconstructed States a blessing which, as prejudice wore away, would have caused their names to be respected and honored." We doubt whether the records of the reconstruction period would support this favorable view of the character of the majority of the carpetbaggers in the South, or whether even the best of them, operating with the ludicrous electorates which Congress had forced upon them, could have built up governments which would have been a blessing to the South. In one prophetic sentence Blaine sums up his apology for the regime of military reconstruction imposed by the radical Congress upon the Southern States: "History and the just judgment of mankind will vindicate the wisdom and the righteousness of the Republican policies, and that vindication will al-

rejected them with disdain and insult—put over them forcibly adventurers and illiterate negroes—sure to produce reaction. Now in 1884 we pay the penalty."

[1] Blaine had voted against impeachment in the House in December, 1867, but two months later he joined with every other Republican member in an affirmative vote. He frequently spoke, in later years, of his regret for this change of vote. For a fuller analysis of Blaine's condemnation of the impeachment proceedings see above, Chapter III, pp. 57, 58.

ways carry with it the condemnation of Andrew Johnson." (p. 304.)
Blaine was a poor prophet here. Historians are virtually unanimous in
their vindication of the policy of Andrew Johnson and their condemnation of the congressional policy of reconstruction.

The chapters (xvii to xxv) on the Grant regime are, as we might
expect them to be, highly laudatory. Blaine not only pays deserved
tribute to Grant as the General of the Union Army, but endorses the
extravagant opinions of Grant's qualifications for the Presidency expressed by the Republican leaders at the time of his first nomination
in 1868. Congressman George S. Boutelle, the prime mover in the
impeachment of Johnson, had stood at Grant's side, when a crowd had
gathered before the door of his house in Washington on the evening
after the nomination, and speaking in the name of the serenaders had
assured the General that the American people would elect him by an
overwhelming majority and would support his Administration, because
they were convinced that it would be "characterized by firmness, by
integrity, by patriotism, by good sense—all the manly qualities."
Schuyler Colfax, the vice presidential candidate, set the same crowd to
cheering by comparing Grant to Washington, as "first in war, first in
peace and first in the hearts of his countrymen." [1] Charles A. Dana,
newly come to the editorship of the New York *Sun,* drew on the inexhaustible reservoir of his rhetoric in a campaign biography of Grant,
whom he had come to know and admire in the days when he had
visited the front as Assistant Secretary of War, lauding the General
as a man who "possessed abilities and attainments which entitle him
to a place among the wise and prudent statesmen of the country." [2]
The press generally held the nomination to be the best and wisest possible, and an earnest of a return to the "simplicity and virtues of the
early hours of the Republic." [3]

No hint of the ghastly failure of Grant's Administration to realize
these prophecies appears in Blaine's pages. The exposures of the
scandals which, in Professor Dunning's phrase, brought us to "the
nadir of national disgrace,"—the Crédit Mobilier, the whisky frauds,
the Sanborn contracts, Secretary Robeson's extravagant maladministration of the Navy Department, Secretary Belknap's plunder of the
Western army posts, and the general hostility of the Administration to

[1] The Philadelphia *Inquirer,* May 23, 1868.
[2] Charles A. Dana, *Life of Ulysses S. Grant,* p. 424.
[3] E. P. Oberholtzer, *History of the United States Since the Civil War,* Vol. II, p. 158.

reform which forced Attorney General Rockwood Hoar and Secretary of the Interior Jacob D. Cox to resign from the Cabinet—are not men-tioned. The Liberal Republican movement, which protested against abuses in the civil service and the continuance of military coercion in the South, is dismissed by Blaine as a manifestation of peevish faction-alism, an "effort of dissatisfied partisans," representing "in some degree a difference of policy" with the Administration, but "more largely a clashing of personal interests and ambitions." (p. 516.) He blames Secretary Bristow for allowing his name to be associated "with the growing cry for reform." (p. 568), but he has no word of censure for the officials or congressmen, like Belknap, Butler, Ames and Colfax, whose names were smirched with proved charges of public misconduct. One searches these pages in vain for any corroboration of the scathing, yet just, indictment of the Administration which Senator Hoar brought in its closing year.[1]

That Blaine should have been loath to dwell upon these shortcom-ings of President Grant's Administration we can understand when we recall the circumstances under which the second volume of *Twenty Years of Congress* was written, for even as Blaine was working on the book, Grant, ruined in fortune and suffering from the ravages of a cancer at the base of his tongue, was valiantly fighting off death in his cottage at Mount McGregor, until he could complete the *Memoirs* which were to provide a settlement for his creditors and comfort for his family. The closing sentences of the *Memoirs* were written on July 19, and four days later the General's eyes were closed. The sympathy of the country for the hero of Donelson, Vicksburg, Chattanooga and Petersburg was unbounded. It was no time to speak of the shadows which the clouds of the presidential years had cast over his brilliant services for the preservation of the Union. The first act of President Cleveland, on March 4, 1885, had been to sign the bill restoring Grant to his full rank as General of the Army. It was symbolic. It meant the emergence of Grant the victorious soldier from the partial eclipse of Grant the baffled and betrayed politician.

On August 8 the funeral obsequies were celebrated at New York, and at the same hour memorial services were held in many cities and towns of the Union. Blaine was the speaker at the Augusta meeting. "For more than twenty years," he said, "General Grant was the most

[1] See above, p. 70.

conspicuous man in America—one to whom leaders looked for leadership, upon whom partisans built their hopes of victory, to whom personal friends by tens of thousands offered the incense of sincere devotion. It was according to the weakness and the strength of human nature that General Grant's primacy should be challenged, that his party should be resisted, that his devoted friends should be confronted by jealous men in his own ranks and by bitter enemies in the ranks of his opponents. But all these passions, all these resentments are buried in the grave which today receives his remains. . . . Controversy over his civil administration closes, as Democrats and Republicans alike unite in pronouncing him to have been in every act and in every aspiration an American patriot." [1]

Distasteful as it might have been for Blaine, after speaking such words, to return to his library to write the history of what actually happened in Congress during the Grant Administration, it was plainly incumbent on him to do so. The material was at hand in the *Congressional Globe* and *Record*. He himself had been a member of one or the other House during the whole period. A man of his eminence, writing a volume which was certain to be read by tens of thousands of his fellow citizens who had not read a page of the congressional debates, had the responsibility of handing down to posterity as faithful and complete a picture of the time which he described as the limitations of his space would allow. Yet, by selecting only those measures which were creditable to the Republican Party, and passing over in silence the evils which called forth such indictments as Senator Hoar's speech and James R. Lowell's centennial poem, "The World's Fair," [2] Blaine

---

[1] J. G. Blaine, *Political Discussions, Legislative, Diplomatic and Popular*, pp. 475–6.

[2] In Lowell's satirical poem Brother Jonathan advises
> Columbia, puzzled what she should display
> Of true home make on her Centennial day,

to exhibit her civil service scandals, her financial heresies, her corrupt tribunals, her rings and grafters,
> And challenge Europe to produce such things. . . .
> She'll find it hard to hide her spiteful tears
> At such advance in one poor hundred years.

(J. F. Rhodes, *History of the United States from the Compromise of 1850*, Vol. VIII, p. 192.) In the spring of 1870 Lowell saw President Grant in Washington and was "struck with the pathos of his face; a puzzled pathos as of a man with a problem before him of which he does not understand the terms." (*Ibid.*, Vol. VI, p. 384.) Grant's old comrade in arms, General W. T. Sherman, wrote in October of the same year to his brother, Senator Sherman: "I have observed with great concern that General Grant is moved by the urgent demands of remonstrances of men who care no more for him, and who would gladly sacrifice him. . . . Ben Butler, Logan and men of that stripe. . . . I saw him yesterday and he seems to be unconscious that he is losing the confidence of some of the best men of the country. Still, I want to stand by him, for as his term draws

sacrificed the impartiality of the historian to the propaganda of the partisan. Page after page of clever thumb-nail sketches of the new members of Congress might better have been filled with an impartial account of the proceedings of Congress.

The two large volumes of *Twenty Years of Congress* are, in truth, not so much a history as a political manifesto, proclaiming the unblemished record of the Republican Party, and warning the country of the political and financial evils which were sure to attend the return of the Democrats to power. Blaine's contemporaries, who read the volumes with such eagerness and lavished such deserved praise on their erudition, their cogency of argument and their clarity of style, were deeply interested in the thesis which the author was seeking to establish. Many of them had been participants in the scenes described. Coming as it did at the close of a long period of Republican ascendancy, the work appealed strongly both to those who rejoiced in the vindication of the party's policies and those who condemned those policies as ample justification for turning the party out of power. The Democrats were now entrusted with the conduct of the government for the first time since the Civil War, and the book was a challenge to them to prove the falsity of Blaine's theory of their unworthiness. Grover Cleveland's judicious Administration did much to dull the effect of Blaine's manifesto, and a later generation, accustomed to the alternation of Republican and Democratic Administrations in the decade following the publication of Blaine's work, naturally turned to the more objective and dispassionate histories of years from Lincoln to Garfield, written by scholars like Dunning, Dewey, Rhodes and Oberholtzer. Few critics could be found today, we surmise, who would agree with the extravagant praise bestowed upon Blaine's work by Charles Edward Russell, the most severely unsympathetic of Blaine's biographers: "But when every defect has been summoned and considered, *Twenty Years of Congress* remains the greatest book ever written by an American on a political subject and one of the most fascinating books in the language." [1]

The success of *Twenty Years of Congress* made it easy for Blaine, while his hand was in, to yield to the importunities of his friends (and

to a close he will have a hard time, and I don't want you to abandon him, unless self-respect compels you, and then the more outspoken you are the better." (*W. T. Sherman's Letter Book*, quoted in Lloyd Lewis, *Sherman, Fighting Prophet*, p. 606.)

[1] Charles Edward Russell, *Blaine of Maine*, p. 391.

his publishers) to gather some of the most important of his fugitive pieces into a volume which he published in 1887, under the title, *Political Discussions, Legislative, Diplomatic and Popular.* The fifty-three items in the collection include addresses in Congress, at public dinners and at Republican rallies; communications to newspapers and magazines; dispatches from the State Department; extracts from campaign speeches of 1884; the open letter to President Arthur on the reversal of his Latin-American policy; and eulogies of Senator Zachariah Chandler, President Garfield and General Grant. The documents are published without notes or comments, and there is no index. Yet, even as a "scissors and paste" production, the volume is useful for the student who wishes to understand the main lines of Blaine's political thought and diplomatic policies without the trouble of consulting the *Congressional Record* and the archives of the State Department.

Blaine's literary labor at Augusta, however, did not occupy all his time in the two years following his defeat for the Presidency. Though he continued to speak of his retirement from politics, he was still, and up to the last year of his life, the peerless leader of the Republican Party, which began to prepare for his triumph in 1888 as soon as the ballots of November 4, 1884, had been counted; [1] while for the Democrats and the Mugwumps he was the one man whose "come-back" was feared. During the whole of Cleveland's first term he was regarded as the leader of the opposition. Requests came to him continually to appear at social and political functions. In March, 1885, he was invited to attend a dinner at Oliver Ames' palatial home in Boston, to meet Governor Robinson and the State officials of Massachusetts.[2] In October he was urged to speak in Virginia in behalf of John S. Wise, who was running for Governor against Fitzhugh Lee, and who had deserted the party of his illustrious father, Governor Henry A. Wise, to join the Republicans as an advocate of William Mahone's "readjustment" policy of the conditional repudiation of the State debt.[3] Except for occasional addresses, such as his eulogy of Grant, Blaine refused these invitations; but when the second volume of his book was

---

[1] "The true Republicans of Indiana keenly feel their disappointment, but the result has not entirely cast them down. Already they are beginning to buckle on their armor for conflicts to come and are donning the Blaine badge for 1888—trusting and believing that the people of the United States will yet elevate you to the place they have so long desired you to fill." J. A. Dynes of the Indianapolis *Gazette,* Dec. 1, 1884.

[2] Oliver Ames to Blaine, March 16, 1885.

[3] Hiram Shaw of Kentucky to Blaine, October 13, 1885.

off the press, he was free to obey the impulse to political activity which no avocation could ever quite absorb.

The Republican prophecies of the disasters which would come upon the country if Cleveland were elected failed to materialize. Business improved. Surpluses accrued in the Treasury. There was no attempt either to repudiate the national debt or to assume the Confederate debt, to pension Confederate veterans or to abolish pensions for Union veterans.[1] The war amendments stood undisturbed and the Negroes were not remanded to slavery. Cleveland stood firm in his opposition to currency inflation, advocating the repeal of the Bland-Allison Act. Even the tariff, in spite of the President's reiterated pleas for revision, remained unchanged, enough Democrats in the House joining with the Republicans to defeat the Morrison bill for horizontal reduction in 1886, and the Republican Senate refusing to act on the Mills bill which, under the spur of Cleveland's insistence, had passed the House in July, 1888, a month after the Republican national convention had met at Chicago.

It is true that Cleveland gave due recognition to the South in his appointments to diplomatic and consular posts, and that he invited into his Cabinet as Attorney General ex-Governor Augustus H. Garland of Arkansas, a former member of both branches of the Confederate Congress, and as Secretary of the Interior Senator L. Q. C. Lamar of Mississippi, who had drawn up the ordinance of secession for his State in 1861. But there was no disposition on the part of the President or any of his advisers to deliver the government into the hands of "Confederate brigadier generals." [2] Nor did Cleveland's removals from office in the first year of his Administration equal those made by Grant in 1869. Blaine himself called at the White House in the spring of 1885, before going down to Maine, and at his request President Cleveland retained his old friend Joseph Manley as postmaster of Augusta. Indeed, were it not for the fact that partisan animosity is always able to live like the chameleon "on the air promise-crammed" (with the plums of office), it would have had scant nourishment during the years of Cleveland's wisely conservative Administration, conducted, as he

[1] Though Cleveland vetoed more than two hundred private pension bills, as well as the General Dependent Pension bill which put on the rolls all needy veterans who had seen three months' service, the fact that pension appropriations increased from $60,000,000 to over $80,000,000 during his term shows that the deserving soldiers were not forgotten.
[2] See Blaine's sharp criticism of the appointment of Thomas F. Bayard of Delaware (a disunionist in 1861) as Secretary of State. Vol. II, pp. 443–6.

himself phrased it, "in the spirit of strict constitutional government."

It was during this Administration that James Bryce, who had been a frequent visitor to our country and a keen observer of our institutions, published the first edition of his *The American Commonwealth*. He wrote: "There are now two great and several minor parties in the United States. The great parties are the Republicans and the Democrats. What are their principles, their distinctive tenets, their tendencies? Which of them is for tariff reform, for a spirited foreign policy, for the regulation of railroads and telegraphs by legislation, for changes in the currency, or for any other of the twenty issues which one hears discussed in the country as seriously involving its welfare? This is what a European is always asking intelligent Republicans and intelligent Democrats. He is always asking because he never gets an answer. The replies leave him in deeper perplexity. After some months the truth begins to dawn upon him. Neither party has, as a party, anything definite to say on these issues; neither party has any clean-cut principles, any distinctive tenets. Both have traditions. Both have certainly war-cries, organizations, interests enlisted in their support. But those interests are in the main those of getting or keeping the patronage of the government." [1] And again: "Men talk of one party as being 'in power,' meaning thereby the party to which the President belongs. But they do so because that party enjoys the spoils of office, in which to so many politicians the value of power consists." [2]

The truth of Bryce's caustic remarks was never better illustrated than it was in Cleveland's first term, when Democrats like Vance of North Carolina, Pugh of Alabama and Voorhees of Indiana antagonized his on civil service reform, while Republicans like Curtis and Roosevelt came to his defense; when a group of Democratic high protectionists, led by Samuel J. Randall of Pennsylvania, joined with the Republicans to defeat proposals for tariff reduction; when the country was regaled by the comedy of two prominent Republican Senators, Edmunds and Cullom, wrangling over the ratification of a Democratic appointee to the Chief Justiceship of the United States; when a bill for the free and unlimited coinage of silver was supported by a majority of twenty-six on the Democratic side of the House, and defeated only by the votes of the Republican minority cast against it; and when the only measures that

[1] James Bryce, *The American Commonwealth*, Vol. II, p. 21.
[2] *Ibid.*, Vol. I, p. 292.

could get through Congress were nonpartisan bills, such as those
regulating the presidential succession and the electoral count, bestowing citizenship on Indians who renounced their tribal allegiance, stiffening the penalties against polygamous Mormons, and creating the
Interstate Commerce Commission to protect shippers against the
extortionate rates and discriminatory practices of the railroads. And
all of these measures originated not in the Democratic House as part
of a legislative program to realize the Administration's policy, but in
the Republican Senate, which had opened fire on Cleveland the moment his first Congress had met.[1]

The mid-term congressional and State elections are always regarded
as a sort of referendum on the endorsement of the Administration. If
there were no clear-cut political issues to contest in 1886, nevertheless
a series of industrial disturbances of exceptional violence occurred in
many parts of the country. The number of strikes increased from 645
in 1885 to over 1400 in 1886; the number of companies affected from
2284 to 9861. Traffic on 6000 miles of the Gould railroad lines of the
Southwest was tied up in March by a strike which involved the poorly
organized Knights of Labor and was conducted by agitators like the
ruffianly Martin Irons of St. Louis. Riots and bloodshed occurred in
several counties of Kentucky and Missouri before the strike was put
down. On May 4, a meeting of anarchists was held in the old Haymarket of Chicago to protest against the rough handling by the police
of strikers for the eight hour day in the McCormick Reaper Works.
When a squad of 170 policemen advanced to disperse the meeting, a
fatal bomb was thrown into their midst, precipitating a fusillade of
shots which resulted in the death or serious injury of more than a score
of men on each side. A clash between the social revolutionists and the
militia in Milwaukee in September was also attended with fatalities.
And while these scenes of violence were being enacted in the West, the
Eastern States were vexed with strikes of 20,000 men in the bituminous
coal fields of Pennsylvania and West Virginia, of 10,000 workers in
the textile and the boot and shoe industries of New England, and of

---

[1] These bills were the work of prominent Republican Senators like Hoar, Dawes,
Edmunds, Sherman, Ingalls and Cullom. The last named, the sponsor of the Interstate
Commerce Act, says in his *Fifty Years of Public Service*, p. 229: "The Democrats had a
majority of something like forty in the House, and elected John G. Carlisle Speaker. This
is practically the same situation that had prevailed during the previous Congress, except
this time the Democrats, in addition to a majority, had the Chief Executive as well. But
they were just as powerless to enact legislation as they had been before."

the car drivers and conductors on the street railways of New York and Brooklyn. The situation all over the country was so serious as to elicit from Cleveland the first presidential message on the subject of labor, recommending the establishment of a Federal Industrial Commission to investigate the relations between workers and employers and to coöperate with the head of the new Bureau of Labor, Carroll D. Wright, in the improvement of those relations.

Besides taking advantage, by clever appeals to the large labor vote, of the embarrassment which the industrial unrest caused for the Administration, the Republicans found, or pretended to find, in Cleveland's record good cause for waving the bloody shirt. The President had shown himself a friend of the "rebels" by his Cabinet appointments, and had "insulted" the veterans of the G.A.R. by his pension vetoes and his "sneery and flippant language" in exposing the flimsy claims on which many of the private pension bills were based. He was no true patriot. The Democratic Party, in Senator Sherman's bitter phrase, was only "the left wing of the Confederate army." Elihu Root, chairman of the New York state convention, brought rounds of applause from the delegates when he declared: "The Republican Party is the party which has freed the slave and saved the nation's life." Jefferson Davis furnished more ammunition for the Republicans, and provoked an acrimonious correspondence with young Theodore Roosevelt, by making a speech at Montgomery, Alabama, in the spring of 1886, in which he extolled the cause for which the South fought as "one of the holiest that had ever inspired man."

A third main point of attack against the Administration was its alleged subserviency to British interests. The President was denounced as a free trader, ready to sacrifice the prosperity of American industry and labor to the fatal competition of European standards. Secretary of State Bayard was accused of "truckling" to Great Britain in the negotiations over the rights of American fishermen in Canadian waters. The termination of the Treaty of Washington on July 1, 1885, had automatically restored the fisheries to their status under the treaty of 1818, which had been a source of constant wrangling for more than half a century. Its vexatious provisions were now enforced by the Canadian authorities with "churlish and inhospitable" severity, in revenge for the closing of the free American market to the salted, pickled and cured fish of Canada by the abrogation of the Treaty of

Washington. The masters of over a hundred American fishing craft which had put into Canadian ports in the summer of 1886 were involved in quarrels with the authorities, and the schooner *David J. Adams* of Gloucester was seized by a British patrolling cruiser when she entered Digby Gut for bait. These indignities revived the bitter memories of the Halifax Award of 1877 and the Fortune Bay incident of 1878, and united the maritime States from Maine to Maryland in protest.

President Cleveland tried to reach an agreement with England. He arranged for a temporary extension of the provisions of the Washington Treaty through the summer of 1885, and in December recommended to Congress the establishment of a mixed commission to settle the conflicting claims. But the Senate, led by New England zealots on the question, like Frye of Maine and Edmunds of Vermont, would have no more parleys. We had been "duped" by the British long enough. We wanted protection. A warship or two in the waters about Nova Scotia would be a more convincing argument for our rights than any remonstrances at the foreign office in London. Our quarrel was with the Canadians, and unless the Canadian officials ceased to hide behind the skirts of an imperial authority three thousand miles away, which absolved them from responsibility for their conduct by denying them the competency to negotiate with us directly, we ought to retaliate by barring their products entirely from our markets. Both Houses of Congress finally passed resolutions early in 1887, empowering the President to impose such a boycott if the Canadians persisted in their "unwarranted and unfriendly" treatment of American fishermen.[1]

Blaine entered the mid-term campaign of 1886, to make his contribution to the restoration of a Republican Administration two years later. His first concern was to secure a decisive victory for the State ticket in the Maine elections of September. In a speech on "The Political Issues of 1886" at Sebago Lake, on August 24, he bracketed all the main complaints against the Administration in the formula of protection *versus* free trade. His thesis was diametrically opposed to the one which James Bryce was elaborating at the same moment. The differences between the Republican and the Democratic organizations, he said, had not been "adjusted," but had grown "more palpable and pronounced" since the fourth of March, 1885. The American people

[1] *Appleton's Annual Cyclopaedia,* 1887, p. 181.

must wake to a "new and more earnest struggle over policies that are irreconcilable, over measures that are inherently and inevitably in conflict." For on the outcome of this conflict depended the very welfare of the country. If there was turmoil in the labor world, it was because both the prosperity of the employers and the wages of the workers were threatened by the uncertainty in which the industrial system was kept by the constant attempts of the Democrats to undermine the protective tariff. If there was danger from the South, it was not the danger that the Negro would be reënslaved but rather that he would tend to enslave the white labor of the North by dragging wages down to the level which he was ready to accept in the industries into which he was entering in increasing numbers. It was not so much a "rebel" South as a Democratic "free trade" South that was the menace now.

Even the fisheries dispute, which Blaine reviewed again in his Sebago Lake speech, came down in the end to the question of the tariff. For what else were the British contending than for the advantages which had been secured for Canadian products in our markets by the reciprocity treaty of 1854 (abrogated in 1866) and had been too largely recovered by the Treaty of Washington in 1871? Blaine stood for the protection of the American laborer on the fishing smack as well as in the shoe factory. The President (of whom he "wished to speak at all times with respect") had done an unprecedented thing in giving a pledge to the British foreign office to recommend to Congress the establishment of a mixed commission to deal with the fisheries question, in return for the British agreement to extend the provisions of the Treaty of Washington for six months after its termination. If the President of the United States had been so injudicious as to hamper his executive freedom in such fashion six months before the meeting of Congress, the Senate was a better defender of American interests and American honor by refusing to endorse his bargain—especially as a new treaty for the arbitration of the fisheries question by a mixed commission would "probably be filled in the end with provisions as odious and burdensome to the American fishing interests as those from which they had just escaped." [1]

Blaine's courteously severe indictment of the political, economic and diplomatic policies of the Administration in the Sebago Lake

[1] J. G. Blaine, *Political Discussions, Legislative, Diplomatic and Popular*, pp. 468–502.

speech was a strong factor in the success of the Republicans in Maine. They elected their candidate for Governor, Joseph R. Bodley, and won all four of the congressional districts. Nevertheless, the victory in Maine was no harbinger of a Republican landslide in the November elections. The Democrats, to be sure, lost Indiana by a narrow margin, but they elected Governors in New Jersey, Colorado and California and came within a few votes of winning Minnesota and New Hampshire. Their representation in the House was cut down from 184 to 160, but at the same time the Republican majority in the Senate was reduced from eight to two. On the whole, there was little to indicate that the country was dissatisfied with the Administration of Grover Cleveland. He had been faithful enough to the principle of civil service reform to win the commendation of George William Curtis,[1] and to incur the condemnation of Democratic spoilsmen like Senators Vance and Gorman, Boss Kelly of Tammany Hall, David B. Hill, Adlai E. Stephenson and "Marse Henry" Watterson. He had vindicated the prerogatives of the presidential office against the partisan attack of hostile Senators. He had stood firmly against the inflationist schemes of the majority of the Democratic members of the House, recommending the repeal of the Bland-Allison Act of 1878 and rejoicing in the defeat by Republican votes of a bill for the free coinage of silver. In spite of the diatribes of certain Republican newspapers and of officers of the G.A.R. against his "insults" to Union veterans in vetoing pension bills, his policy was supported by public opinion and even upheld by the veterans themselves at their encampment at St. Louis in 1887, when they refused by a vote of 173 to 318 to condemn him for the veto of the general Dependent Pension bill. It was apparent in the autumn of 1886 that it would be no easy job for the Republicans to oust from the White House this President, whose moderation, courage and disinterested devotion to the public weal were every month winning a larger measure of approbation from his fellow countrymen.

After the Maine elections Blaine was invited to speak in Ohio, Pennsylvania, New Jersey, Tennessee and Michigan. Governor Foraker of Ohio wrote to him on September 16, seconding the request of

---

[1] Curtis, in his presidential address before the National Civil Service Reform League in August, 1885, said: "Since the spoils system was first generally introduced into our national administrations, no President has given such conclusive evidence of his reform conviction and his courage in enforcing his convictions as President Cleveland." G. W. Curtis, *Orations and Addresses*, Vol. II, p. 300.

the Republicans of Chattanooga, Tennessee, for an address "some time next month," and on the following day wrote him again in behalf of the "four or five hundred members of the Young Men's Blaine Club of Cincinnati," who wanted him to open their new headquarters on September 30, when they would be hosts to all the other Republican clubs of southern Ohio.[1] Some historians have assumed, quite gratuitously, that Blaine was animated by personal ambition alone in his participation in the campaign of 1886. Oberholtzer, for example, writes: "Blaine was on the stump defending his title to party leadership. . . . It was universally understood and acknowledged that his position with reference to a renomination in 1888 depended on the outcome of the campaign." [2] But if Blaine's title to party leadership stood in need of any defense, it is strange that he declined so many opportunities to vindicate it in various parts of the country.

One invitation he did accept in October, when he went to Pennsylvania with his sons Emmons and James for the threefold purpose of aiding the Republican candidate for Governor, General Beaver, of inspecting his "savings bank," as he called the coal deposits on his land in Elizabeth, and of visiting the college at Washington from which he had graduated nearly forty years before. The reception which the people of western Pennsylvania gave to their distinguished native son was as enthusiastic as that which had welcomed Lafayette at Bunker Hill fifty years after the outbreak of the American Revolution. At Pittsburgh and Alleghany the crowds of cheering citizens blocked the passage of his carriage, drawn by four white horses and flanked by a mounted escort, as they pressed closer to shake his hand or to get a word of personal reminiscence from him. When he approached his native town of Brownsville, "the entire population locked up stores and houses and went across the bridge that spans the Monongahela to the railroad station to meet its distinguished son. The quiet little streets never saw such a commotion before. Flags waved from every window. Every square inch of the narrow sidewalk was filled with the moving inhabitants, who overflowed the roadway . . . and had the impulse not been resisted by some of the more decorous citizens, the horses would have been unhitched and Mr. Blaine's carriage would have been dragged by eager hands." [3]

[1] J. B. Foraker to Blaine, September 17, 1886.
[2] E. P. Oberholtzer, *History of the United States Since the Civil War,* Vol. IV, p. 43.
[3] Quoted from an eye-witness by Gail Hamilton, *Biography of James G. Blaine,* p. 596.

Blaine drove over the familiar old National Road from Brownsville to Washington, recalling the days when he had walked out as a boy to meet the "June Bug" and had been taken up beside the driver to rumble down over the new bridge into the town. At the college he was amused to scan the records of the Literary Society and see his name entered as "fined for non-performance in debate." He sat at the right of the president on the platform of the college, while his proud uncle, John H. Ewing, now past ninety, sat on the left, and the two were introduced as "the most illustrious graduate" and "the oldest living graduate" of Washington and Jefferson College. His address to the students offered no suggestions that could be called contributions to modern methods of pedagogy, but it was full of humerous reminiscences and homely advice to master the elementary subjects of spelling, grammar and geography.

The year 1886 saw the fulfilment of another of Blaine's cherished projects besides the completion of his *Twenty Years of Congress*. He loved the sea. How profoundly its mystery and majesty impressed his sensitive nature is shown in the concluding paragraph of his *Eulogy on Garfield*. We have seen how strongly he was tempted, when he became editor of the Portland *Advertiser* in 1857, to leave the Stanwood homestead in the little inland city of Augusta and established a new home in the "very beautiful city" of Portland, "situated directly on the ocean." [1] During the hectic campaign of 1884 he had spent some weeks with his family in the Ash cottage at Bar Harbor on Mount Desert Island, to escape the interminable procession of politicians and delegations that came to Augusta. The beauty of the island on the rugged Maine coast captivated the Blaines. Their dear friends Senator Eugene and Minnie Hale lived at Ellsworth, only eighteen miles away. Another devoted friend, Elinor Medill, daughter of Joseph Medill of the Chicago *Tribune*, was spending the summer at Bar Harbor.

Blaine returned to Augusta and to the strenuous campaign trip of the autumn of 1884 with the picture of the beautiful waters and the wooded drives of Mount Desert indelibly impressed upon his mind. The next summer, in the midst of the work on his book, he made a brief visit to the island as the guest of the Medills. Mrs. Blaine wrote to Walker on August 19, 1885: "Your Father came at four yesterday, pleased with his visit, with his host, with their menage, most pleased

[1] See above, p. 30.

with Elinor, and full of a delightful enthusiasm for Bar Harbor and a house there, which he thinks would build up his health—an argument with him irresistible. There are two lots with a bay front of 175 feet. . . . The situation would please me, but the price knocks all my little castle into pieces." [1]

Though the price of lots on the bay front was prohibitive, a charming piece of ground was found, sloping from the woods to the "lower road," with a superb view of Frenchman's Bay, and on September 24 we find Mrs. Blaine writing to her daughter Margaret at Yarmouthport: "I am just back from Bar Harbor. Walker and I came over this afternoon, your Father having left us there yesterday to sign the contract, as he had promised to be in Lewiston today to attend the fair. . . . Ground is to be broken today on the lot, and by Monday the whole thing will be started. . . . We spent all our first afternoon on the lot, having with us the architect, Mr. How, the builder, the stone mason and all the Blaines. We decided on the site, ran out tape measures the length of the house and L, drove in stakes for the corners, pointed out the curve of the driveway, and when the shades of night began to fall, left the hillside for the hospitality of the Belmont." [2]

Blaine was as keenly interested in the progress of the summer cottage at Bar Harbor as he had been in the construction of the mansion on Dupont Circle five years before, but the length of the journey from Augusta to Bar Harbor prevented him from watching the details of the masons', the carpenters' and the plasterers' work from day to day, climbing ladders to the second story and picking his way among tool kits and shavings as he had done at Washington. He couldn't resist the holiday impulse, however, to get a glimpse of his new toy on Christmas day. "In the afternoon your Father and I suddenly decided to try Bar Harbor," wrote Mrs. Blaine to Walker on December 27, "but very fortunately the train was very late, so we only persevered to the station, and such a night and following days as settled on this coast! Had we reached there we could not have got away, and there we should now be, for it is too cold to think for a moment we could have driven to Ellsworth, and this furious gale would not even let you look out to sea." [3]

Early in April the Blaines were in Boston, shopping for rugs, carpets,

[1] *Letters of Mrs. James G. Blaine,* Vol. II, p. 121.
[2] *Ibid.,* pp. 123–4.
[3] *Ibid.,* Vol. II, p. 128.

glass, china and hangings for the new house, which was ready for occupancy in the summer. It was christened "Stanwood." Spacious enough to provide modest entertainment for guests and for the sons, daughters and grandchildren who have returned to it in various groups for the last half century, it made no pretense to vie with the elaborate palace-cottages which the ultra rich have erected along the fashionable Maine coast. A loop driveway led in from the heavily wooded upper road to the hospitable front portico and the hall with living room (now enlarged into a charming music room) on the right and dining room on the left. The feature of the house was a broad veranda running the whole length of the east side, high above the lawn that sloped to the lower road, and commanding a marvelous view of the blue water, studded with gemlike islands, beyond. Though Blaine himself had but a few years, and those years of uncertain health, to enjoy the summer repose of Bar Harbor, the gracious hospitality of the family made "Stanwood" a Mecca for a host of friends and a synonym for warm and informal welcome.

Blaine was busy at Augusta in the winter of 1886–1887 compiling the material for his *Political Discussions*. He planned to go by the first of March with his youngest daughter Harriet to visit the oldest daughter Alice, who was stationed with her husband Colonel Coppinger at Fort Gibson on the Arkansas River, in the eastern part of the present State of Oklahoma. But it was past the middle of the month before Mrs. Blaine could write to Walker: "The proof is all out and the author and H. hope to start Tuesday week. I am crazy to get your Father out of that hot library and from over that old writing table." [1]

At the moment when Blaine was finishing up his proofs and getting ready for tthe Western trip, his mind was much occupied with the question of the Canadian fisheries. It was just before the expiration of Congress in March, 1887, that both Houses had authorized the President to retaliate by a boycott of Canadian trade if our fishermen continued to be "unjustly vexed and harrassed" in the lawful pursuit of their industry. Though such a proclamation might well bring a crisis in our relations with Great Britain, petitions and addresses came to the President, urging him to take the step, and the Republican press in the Eastern States accused him of a cowardly surrender of American rights. Blaine's opinion on the controversy was eagerly sought. His

[1] *Letters of Mrs. James G. Blaine*, Vol. II, p. 149.

chapter on the fisheries was being read by thousands of his fellow citizens. W. J. Longley, the Queen's Attorney General of Nova Scotia, and the political editor of the leading liberal Halifax daily, wrote Blaine a long letter on October 4, 1886, begging him to work for harmony: "Let us in North America pull together. As you are so much larger, richer and more powerful than we are, you can afford to be magnanimous. A little more wisdom on the part of American states-men would give immense aid to those of us who are laboring to bring about a more rational condition of affairs between the two countries." The Attorney General cited the incidents of the past few years to show how prejudices were yielding to the truth of the old adage that "blood is thicker than water"—the sympathy of the whole British nation when "poor Garfield was stricken down," Arthur's gracious gesture in order-ing the British flag to be saluted at Yorktown, the public funeral for General Grant in London, the honors paid to Minister Lowell, the cordial reception of English celebrities in America. The Tory Party, which, unfortunately, had been in power in Canada almost ever since the Confederation of 1867, had developed a "sort of Canadian jingo-ism"; but the Tory party must not be confused with the Canadian people. The Liberals stood for cordial relations and mutually beneficent trade with the United States. They advocated even the right of Canada to negotiate her own commercial union with the United States, "with a common tariff against the rest of the world." And the Attorney General had "every reason to believe that within the next six or eight months the Liberals will get into power." [1] From the American side also Blaine was besought to restrain the jingoes. An anxious correspondent from Andover, Massachusetts, wanted to be assured that "war with Great Britain would not result from the fisheries." For, he added, "anything is possible to a passionate people under Democratic rule." [2]

Toward the close of his Sebago Lake speech Blaine had dismissed the question with a suspensive judgment: "We await the publication of Mr. Bayard's [3] correspondence with Great Britain on the seizure of American fishing vessels with deep interest, and with the hope, if not the expectation, that he will leave his country in a better position at the close of the negotiations than he has thus far maintained." [4] He

[1] W. J. Longley to Blaine, October 4, 1886.
[2] Austin Phelps to Blaine, February 7, 1887.
[3] Thomas F. Bayard of Delaware, Secretary of State in Cleveland's first term.
[4] J. G. Blaine, *Political Discussions, Legislative, Diplomatic and Popular,* p. 500.

now refrained from antagonizing the Administration further on the subject. He probably approved President Cleveland's refusal to proclaim the retaliatory measures authorized by Congress, for, in spite of his alleged "Anglophobia," he had no desire to exacerbate the controversy to a point which would threaten a peaceful settlement. Such a settlement was reached through the work of a joint commission of three American and three British members in the autumn of 1887, and on the fifteenth of the following February a treaty was concluded which President Cleveland submitted to the Senate on the twentieth with a message declaring that the treaty had been framed "in a spirit of liberal equity and reciprocal benefits," furnishing "a satisfactory, practical and final adjustment of a long standing controversy." [1] On March 5, 1888, Secretary Bayard transmitted the papers to the Senate, with a note to the effect that now for the first time since 1818 American fishermen were guaranteed "the full measure of their rights on the Canadian and Newfoundland coasts.[2] The treaty of February 15 was rejected by the Republican Senate, solely to embarrass Cleveland in a presidential year. But an executive agreement (always the resource- of Presidents against senatorial treaty wrecking) was arranged by the plenipotentiaries, by which American fishermen were allowed to procure licenses for a period of two years, "pending the ratification of the treaty." This protected them against the depredations from which they had suffered, and under this system, renewed by statute and extended to the year 1924, fairly satisfactory conditions prevailed in the Canadian fisheries until well into the twentieth century.[3]

Blaine was abroad when this concluding chapter of the controversy which had troubled the Cleveland Administration from its beginning was being written. On June 7, 1887, he sailed from New York on the North German Lloyd steamer *Ems* for Southampton, with Mrs. Blaine and their daughters Margaret and Harriet, for an indefinite stay in Europe. The three sons, Walker, Emmons and James, were at the pier to see them off, and General Sherman sent a "memorandum for Mr. Blaine" of the important persons whom he should meet in Scotland. But Blaine needed no introductions in the British Isles. As soon as the family reached the Metropole Hotel in London invitations

[1] J. D. Richardson, *Messages and Papers of the Presidents,* Vol. VIII, p. 603.
[2] *Senate Executive Documents,* 50th Cong., 1st sess., No. 113, p. 2.
[3] H. L. Keenleyside, *Canada and the United States,* pp. 270–1.

poured in upon them. On June 29 they attended the Queen's garden party at Buckingham Palace, which, in spite of the magnificent gowns and jewels and uniforms, Mrs. Blaine found "gloomy, frigid and totally unimaginative." [1] The next night Blaine dined with Lord Rosebery, and receptions and dinners followed at the Duke of St. Albans', Lady Margaret Beaumont's, Lady Ardilawn's and the Baroness Burdett-Coutts'.[2]

After three weeks of London society, keyed to unusual activity in the summer of Queen Victoria's Jubilee year, the Blaines went up to Scotland to visit Andrew Carnegie and his bride at Kilgraston Castle in the valley of the Earn, near Perth.[3] "Here we are at a country seat," wrote Mrs. Blaine to Emmons on July 15, "such as this island alone I imagine can show—a gillie in tartans to wake us every morning with his pipes, a coach and four to take us daily withersoever we will, two cooks to spread a table before us in this garden of the Lord, and twenty servants to wait on us at bed and board. Andrew Carnegie may be little, but his hoard and his heart are great, and he is a happy bridegroom and rejoiceth as a bridegroom. . . . Your Father is getting so much benefit from the open air, in which he spends the entire day. . . . He has discarded woolen socks and gaiters and one overcoat, and is getting really a color. Also he has danced the Haymarket, which is our Virginia reel, on the lawn and has played skittles." [4] There were coaching parties to Edinburgh, Abbotsford, and Carnegie's birthplace Dumfermline. Guests came and went—the Hales, the Hays, the Courtland Palmers and others. Mrs. Carnegie poured coffee for sixteen one morning.

[1] *Letters of Mrs. James G. Blaine,* Vol. II, p. 154.
[2] At the same time, Blaine declined to meet Lord Hartington for political reasons and refused an invitation to the Foreign Office because, as he said, he could not with propriety be the guest of Lord Salisbury, after the way he had written about him in his *Twenty Years of Congress.*
[3] Carnegie at the age of fifty-one had married Miss Louise Whitfield of New York, in April, 1887, and had sailed with his bride to spend the summer in Scotland, as was his custom. His income at this time was estimated at $1,800,000 a year. He had long been a friend and admirer of Blaine, confidently predicting his election to the Presidency in 1884 (see p. 290). At almost the moment Blaine's second volume appeared Carnegie had published his *Triumphant Democracy,* a book of 500 and more pages of unmitigated laudation of the political, industrial and cultural achievements of the American Republic, and aptly described by Carnegie's latest biographer as "a fervent and rollicking exhibition of statistics, a mighty paean based upon the census of 1880, a kind of literary coaching party through America's wheat fields, corn prairies, coal and iron mines, railways, manufacturing plants, not omitting aspects of more spiritual import such as the American common school, the American home, even American art and literature." B. J. Hendrick, *The Life of Andrew Carnegie,* Vol. I, p. 274.
[4] *Letters of Mrs. James G. Blaine,* Vol. II, pp. 156–7.

A week before the Blaines left, a young man of twenty-five arrived at Kilgraston who was destined to play an important rôle in the history of the family. He was Walter Damrosch, conductor at the Metropolitan Opera House, the New York Symphony Society and the New York Oratorio Society, who had by chance crossed the Atlantic on the same steamer with the Carnegies and had been invited to visit them in Scotland when he had finished his summer's study of the Beethoven symphonies with his father's lifelong friend Hans von Buelow, at Frankfort. Mr. Damrosch, whose "life had been spent among musicians," was immediately attracted to the "great statesman" and his devoted wife and daughters. He got only "a glimpse" of them on that visit, he writes in his autobiography; "but," he adds, "there were delightful rumors of a four weeks' coaching trip from London to Scotland which Mr. Carnegie was planning for the following summer and for which we were all to be invited." [1]

From Kilgraston the Blaines crossed to Ireland for a visit to Colonel Coppinger's family in Cork. Blaine found the people of Ireland "a discouraged or even a heartbroken race," but thought that "their cause" (home rule) was progressing. "They wished to give me a great banquet at Dublin," he wrote Walker, "but I felt that to accept would simply be eating and drinking the substance of the poor. One must come to Europe to see how much we have at home. I have lost sight of politics." [2]

The last week of August found the family at Homburg, Germany, with the Fricks, the Hales and the Depews. Blaine drank the waters dutifully for the prescribed duration of the "cure." It is difficult to know just what was the state of his health at this time. His wife makes frequent allusions to it, sometimes expressing real anxiety, as in her letter of February 14 from Florence to Margaret in Rome,[3] but oftener treating her husband's "constant speculations on his own physical condition" as an obsession to be humored.[4] That there was a genuine con-

---

[1] Walter Damrosch, *My Musical Life*, p. 92.

[2] Gail Hamilton, *Biography of James G. Blaine*, p. 644.

[3] "Dr. Baldwin has this morning told his patient that he is confident that he is at the bottom of his trouble, which is not paralysis at all, but uric acid, which is the acid of gout. There is no paralysis, and from this time we can say goodbye to all our nervous fears. If his leg is stiff and his side numb, it is not the brain which is at fault, but this acid working in the system and to be dislodged slowly and with perseverance." *Letters of Mrs. James G. Blaine*, Vol. II, p. 174.

[4] For example, "Your Father is getting thoroughly tired of Florence, though his doctors grow dearer and dearer day by day. Himself is surely improving, and were he other than the child of genius would probably not know that there was anything the matter with him" (*Ibid.*, p. 183). "Your Father is I think well; whether he can be made to be-

cern for Blaine's health beneath these bantering allusions we cannot doubt. Mrs. Blaine was a woman who combined with her intellectual gifts and her intense devotion to her husband and children a courageous, pragmatic spirit which could never brook repining or despair.[1]

By the first of November, 1887, the Blaines were back in Paris, after a trip to Vienna and Budapest. It was while he was at the French capital in the closing weeks of the year that Blaine suddenly broke into American politics again, with a message which kept his name prominently before the Republican managers and the country at large during the remaining eight months of his stay in Europe. That political story we shall tell in the next chapter. Here let us complete the narrative of his trip on its social side.

In December, 1887, Miss Abigail Dodge (Gail Hamilton) joined the family in Europe, and the opening of the new year found them at the Hotel Cavour in Milan, after crossing the Alps by the St. Gothard Pass. They stayed a fortnight at Milan, then moved on to Florence, whence further interesting political communications came from Blaine. With the advent of spring the party visited Sorrento, Naples and Rome, and made their way northward leisurely, often traveling by carriage, via Savona, San Remo, Monte Carlo (where the "gaming tables were crowded with all the odds and ends of continental life" and "gold was like the sands on the seashore") and Lyons to Paris again. Early in June they were back at the Hotel Metropole in London, waiting the arrival of the Carnegies from New York.

Mr. Damrosch again came over on the same steamer with the Carnegies, and the coaching party—consisting of the four Blaines, Miss Dodge, Henry Phipps (a partner of Carnegie's) and his wife, Dr. Charles Eaton (pastor of the Universalist church to which Mrs. Carnegie belonged) and Mr. Damrosch—left the hotel on June 8 in a gay new coach. John Morley and Lord Rosebery were among the friends to see the party off, when the horn sounded and the four high-stepping horses drew away from the door of the Metropole and the men on the coach raised their gray top-hats in a farewell salute. They drove up the

lieve it himself is another question. . . . He wakes every morning thinking he has taken a cold, but he comes to breakfast hale and hearty" (*Ibid.*, p. 206). "There is no trouble save in his feelings. He loves the confessional and the lay sister (me)—why I do not know, as I always shrive him out of hand." (*Ibid.*, p. 218.)

[1] Mrs. Blaine wrote to her youngest son, on January 24, 1889: "Your letter which came this morning was a little blue. . . . Do not get depressed. It is a family tendency which must be put down with a strong hand." (*Ibid.*, p. 235.)

east coast of England, visiting the cathedral towns of Cambridge, Ely, Peterborough, York and Durham. At night they stopped at comfortable inns, and "at noontime halted at some picturesque nook by the bank of a river or on some grassy meadow in the shade of the trees" to eat the luncheon which they carried in hampers.

"The discussions between Mr. Blaine and Mr. Carnegie at these picnic luncheons," wrote Mr. Damrosch, "were certainly fascinating to listen to, and especially illuminating to an American musician whose horizon had perhaps been bounded too exclusively by his own ambitions and the problems of his own art. Mr. Blaine knew England, its history and its great families, far more intimately than any Englishman I have ever met. It is well known that he never forgot anything, and whenever we stopped either for luncheon or at an inn for the night, he would immediately proceed to add to his immense store of knowledge by questioning the local farmers, field workers or innkeepers regarding the economic or political conditions of that part of the country." [1]

On July 3 the long coaching trip came to an end, when the party caught sight of the towers of Cluny Castle with the American flag floating from the highest turret. Cluny, the summer home of the Carnegies for the decade 1888–1898, was a beautiful estate of eleven thousand acres in the Grampian Hills, close by the little hamlet of Kingussie, where "Bonnie Prince Charlie" had bidden his followers farewell after their disastrous defeat on Culloden Moor. The castle was an imposing structure of white granite, situated in a dense Highland forest of firs, beeches and larches, with "the heather-covered, snow-capped mountains" in the rear, and in front "the river Spey, in view for several miles, winding in and out of the hills . . . and the country for miles around a glistening stretch of lochs, mountain streams, angry white cascades, arcaded woods and by-paths." [2]

In this paradise the Blaines spent three happy weeks of July. Mrs. Blaine wrote to Walker on the tenth, describing "the immense hospitality" of Cluny, the drives and walks in the bracing mountain air, the long days "which reduce candle-light to a minimum." "We leave the dinner table at nine and . . . only Damrosch, who plays Wagner music every evening, needs candles to make out his operas. . . . We had expected to leave tomorrow, to spend one day in Edinburgh and from

[1] Walter Damrosch, *My Musical Life,* p. 96.
[2] B. J. Hendrick, *The Life of Andrew Carnegie,* Vol. I, 325.

Saturday to Thursday in London, sailing from Southampton on the 19th; but the Inman Line has invited us to sail on the *City of New York* on the 1st of August. Your Father is perfectly well and in the best of spirits. Think of it! Today he has driven in a soaking rain in an open carriage sixteen miles. The convention made no ruffle and has left none on the bosom of his content. Not for the world would he have the campaign on his hands." [1]

For all that, Blaine, as he confessed in a letter to John Hay a week later, was "anxious to reach home, to see how the political currents are drifting. Newspapers here give little information when you are beyond touch with the inside and real movements. It has seemed to me that Harrison has many elements, besides the one of geography, for a good canvass. It seems truly awful to contemplate the possibility of the Democrats securing another lease. I am longing for one good talk with an American who knows something. You are one of that kind, but as a man grows older, the number grows less." [2] Blaine had decidedly not "lost sight of politics." He never did and he never could.

The welcome which Blaine received when the *City of New York* came up the bay on August 10 was surpassed only by that which had been given to Grant when he had landed in San Francisco nine years before, after his trip around the world. Delegations from Republican clubs in various parts of the country were waiting to present their addresses. New York City was bedecked with flags and bunting. From craft of every sort in the harbor a din of whistles and horns greeted the tender to which the Blaines had been transferred at quarantine, as she moved up to the pier. Bands played "Home Again," while the president of the New York Blaine Club made the speech of welcome in the crowded cabin of the tender. Blaine had returned, as Murat Halstead reported, "erect, bright, quick, alert, crisp and sparkling," refuting "in a most satisfactory way the sinister stories that have been industriously circulated about his health." [3] He was ready to throw himself into the campaign for the return of the Republican Party to the control of the government. But the public reception was of little account as compared

---

[1] The Republican nominating convention had been held at Chicago the previous month, and Blaine was relieved from the annoyance of the reporters who had dogged his steps during the coaching tour, with the hope of getting "inside information" of a change of heart on his part, under the urgent pleas of Elkins, Reid, Manley and other determined Blaineites at the convention, on the matter of accepting a nomination.

[2] Gail Hamilton, *Biography of James G. Blaine,* p. 647.

[3] *Ibid.,* p. 608.

with the joy and gratitude over the reunion with the sons and brothers from whom the travelers had been parted for upward of a year. "We will never be separated again!" exclaimed Blaine. Nor were they—until the grim reaper began, all too soon, to wield his sickle.

No MORE courageous paper ever came from the hands of a President of the United States than Grover Cleveland's third annual message to Congress, on December 6, 1887. In his two previous messages he had asked Congress in vain to revise the tariff, which was steadily rolling up a surplus in the Treasury, imposing an unjustified burden of taxation upon the people and taking tens of millions of dollars from their legitimate employment in the channels of trade. Cleveland had been studying the tariff ever since his inauguration,[1] and had become convinced that it was a "ruthless extortion" of the people's money and "a violation of the fundamental principles of a free government." At the same time he made it clear that it was the revision and not the abolition of the tariff which he advocated. "It has been the policy of the government," he wrote, "to collect the principal part of its revenues by a tax upon imports, and no change in this policy is desirable. But the present condition of affairs constrains our people to demand that by a revision of our revenue laws the receipts of the Government shall be reduced to the necessary expenses of its economical administration. . . . A reasonable and timely submission to such a demand should certainly be possible without disastrous shock to any interest." [2]

When, therefore, Congress expired on March 4, 1887, without having reduced the tariff, Cleveland took counsel with several Democratic leaders as to the best method of bringing the matter more conspicuously to the attention of the public, and decided to devote the whole of his message the following December to an exposition of the iniquity of high protection. Some of his advisers, like Secretary Carlisle, Abram Hewitt, Representative Mills of Texas, and Henry Watterson of the Louisville *Courier-Journal,* were heartily in sympathy with this bold departure; but most of the party politicians regarded it with dismay. Such a manifesto, they said, would alienate the high protectionist Democrats (led by Randall of Pennsylvania), would lose the Irish vote by being interpreted as a plea for British free trade, and, published on the eve

---

[1] R. M. McElroy, *Grover Cleveland, The Man and The Statesman,* Vol. I, p. 268.
[2] J. D. Richardson, *Messages and Papers of the Presidents,* Vol. VIII, pp. 509–10.

of a presidential year, would certainly result in the defeat of the party. But Cleveland was adamant. It was far more important, he said, for the American people to hear his views on the leading issue of the day than for him to be returned to the White House. "What is the use of being elected," he replied to one timorous objector, "unless you stand for something?" [1] So the message went to Congress.

It was a long, carefully prepared indictment of the protective system, which had stood virtually unmodified since the Civil War. The surplus in the Treasury had grown from $17,839,000 in 1885 to $55,367,000 in 1887, and would reach $140,000,000 by the end of the fiscal year, June 30, 1888. Such a condition "multiplied a brood of evil consequences." The public Treasury, which should exist only as a conduit carrying the people's tribute to its legitimate objects of expenditure, becomes a hoarding place for money needlessly withdrawn from trade and the people's use, thus crippling our national energies, suspending our country's development, preventing investment in productive enterprise, threatening financial disturbance and inviting schemes of public plunder. The President examined the various suggestions for the reduction of the surplus without disturbing the protective system, and found them all unsatisfactory. To go into the market to buy government bonds which had not reached maturity would both encourage speculation and cost the government millions of dollars in premiums; [2] to abolish the internal revenue duties on tobacco, whisky and beer would offend the moral sense of the community; to keep the surplus on deposit in the banks would be "exceedingly objectionable in principle, as establishing too close a relationship between the operations of the Government Treasury and the business of the country." There was no sound remedy except the revision of "our present tariff laws, the vicious and inequitable and illogical source of unnecessary taxation."

To the contention of the protectionists that the high tariff rates were necessary to guarantee the wages of the American workmen against competition from the pauper labor of Europe, the President replied that only 2,623,000 out of the 17,392,000 of our population gainfully employed were "in such manufacturing industries as were claimed to be

---

[1] R. M. McElroy, *Grover Cleveland, The Man and The Statesman*, p. 271.

[2] John Sherman (*Recollections*, Vol. II, p. 1007) thought that the surplus should be devoted to the purchase of bonds, though the government 4's were selling at 123 to 129, and the 4½'s at 106 to 109 in the market. It cost the Treasury $45,000,000 for bonds purchased in 1889–90 (A. D. Noyes, *Forty Years of American Finance*, p. 125).

benefited by a high tariff," and even that small percentage of our workers, who were also consumers, had to pay back all the premium they received as wages in the enhanced price of the articles which they had to buy.

Against the argument that competition would always prevent prices from becoming monopolistic, he asserted that it was notorious that such competition was "too often strangled by combinations quite prevalent at this time, and frequently called trusts, which have for their object the regulation of the supply and price of the commodities made and sold by the members of the combination," and that the people could "hardly hope for any consideration in the operation of these selfish schemes." He saw no injury resulting either to the laborers or to the manufacturers in the "radical reduction" of duties, while the public would be immensely benefited and our merchants would have a "far better opportunity of extending their sales beyond the limits of home consumption, saving them from the depression, interruption in business and loss caused by a glutted domestic market, and affording their employees more certain and steady labor with its resulting quiet and contentment."

The question, he concluded, should be approached in a spirit higher than partisanship. Both the great parties had repeatedly condemned the laws which permitted the collection of unnecessary revenues from the people, and had promised their correction. "Our progress toward a wise conclusion will not be improved by dwelling upon the theories of protection and free trade. This savors too much of bandying epithets. It is a condition which confronts us, not a theory. The question of free trade is absolutely irrelevant, and the persistent claim made in certain quarters that all the efforts to relieve the people from unjust and unnecessary taxation are schemes of so-called free traders is mischievous and far removed from any consideration of the public good." [1]

Nevertheless, persistence in the assertion that Cleveland's message was a free trade manifesto was precisely the course which, for obvious political reasons, his opponents took. "Free trade cant and humbug," was the Chicago *Journal's* characterization of the message. "Simpleton," "ignoramus," "idiot," "fire-bug in public finance," were some of the epithets hurled at the President by the protectionist papers. "A thousand thanks to President Cleveland," was the sarcastic comment

[1] J. D. Richardson, *Messages and Papers of the Presidents,* Vol. VIII, pp. 580–91.

of the Philadelphia *Press,* "for the bold, manly and unequivocal avowal of his extreme free trade purposes (!)." Senator Sawyer of Wisconsin called the message "a week, flabby document—free trade rot of the worst description." [1]

Indeed, the message was a godsend to the Republican politicians, who were embarrassed by the lack of a definite issue for the coming campaign. Their prophecies of the disasters which would attend a Democratic Administration of the government had proved quite futile. The country was more prosperous than it had been in Arthur's term. Cleveland stood firm in support of a sound currency. He had increased the number of government employees under the civil service laws from 14,000 to 28,000. He had withstood the spoilsmen in his own party to a degree which made most of them his bitter foes. He had even been applauded at a Republican banquet given to Theodore Roosevelt in New York, in May, 1887, when the guest of honor mentioned his name and gave him "credit for all the good he has done." [2] It was undeniable that President Cleveland was gaining the confidence of the people steadily. Unless some issue could be found on which to rally the opposition, his reëlection seemed assured. That issue Cleveland had now furnished himself in his bold challenge of the protective tariff.

Blaine was at the Hotel Binda at Paris when the abstract of the President's message was published in the European newspapers on the morning of December 7. He was immediately solicited by George W. Smalley, the veteran reporter of the New York *Tribune* in London, to give his views on the message either by letter or in the form of an interview. He chose the latter and dictated answers to a series of questions put to him by a stenographer. The interview was cabled to the *Tribune* in full for publication on the morning of the eighth, and was widely copied by the Republican papers of the country.

The "Blaine Letter," or "Paris Letter," as this interview was called, was a severe indictment of the message. In his opening sentences Blaine struck the note which he knew would be most certain to raise hostility to the message, namely, its approval by Great Britain. He had been "especially interested in the comments of the London papers," all of which assumed that the message was a free trade manifesto and anticipated "an enlarged market for English fabrics as a consequence of the Presi-

[1] For comments of the press and of business men on the message see Allan Nevins, *Grover Cleveland, A Study in Courage,* pp. 383–88.

[2] Nevins, *loc. cit.,* p. 367.

dent's recommendations." The President, to be sure, did not advocate "absolute" free trade. Nevertheless, by cutting down the tariff to a strictly revenue basis, he would bring disaster upon the manufacturer, the wage earner and the farmer alike. For the American manufacturer, even with free raw material, could not compete with the finished European goods produced by cheap labor, without reducing the wages of his own workers below the point necessary to maintain the high American standard of living. Our farmers would suffer, too, because their chief dependence was upon a growing and prosperous population in the United States to furnish the home market for the consumption of their grain, livestock and fruit. The abolition of the tariff might result in an increase of export trade, but that would be a meager compensation for the influx of cheap foreign-made goods which would inundate our markets. The President's expectation of increasing our foreign trade by the removal of the protective duties reminded Blaine of the farmer who, wishing to drain his swamp, made a channel from it to the river, only to find that the level of the river was higher than that of the swamp— with consequences "that need not be told."

"But do you not think it is important to increase our export trade?" asked the reporter. "Undoubtedly," replied Blaine, "but it is vastly more important not to lose our own great market for our own people. . . . It is not our foreign trade that has caused the wonderful growth and expansion of the Republic. It is the vast domestic trade between thirty-eight States and eight Territories with their population of perhaps 62,000,000 today. The whole amount of our export and import trade together has never, I think, reached $1,900,000,000 in any one year. Our internal home trade on 130,000 miles of railway, along 15,000 miles of ocean coast, over the five Great Lakes and along 20,000 miles of navigable rivers, reaches the enormous annual aggregate of more than $40,000,000,000. . . . It is into this illimitable trade, even now in its infancy, and destined to attain a magnitude not dreamed of twenty years ago, that the Europeans are struggling to enter. It is the heritage of the American people, of their children and of their children's children. It gives an absolutely free trade over an area nearly as large as all Europe. . . . President Cleveland now plainly proposes a policy that will admit Europe to a share of this trade."

Just how the American farmers, who were seething with discontent at the very moment when Blaine dictated these words, were to dispose of their increasing surpluses of products if our doors were closed to the payment for them by the admission of foreign manufactures does not appear. Nor is Blaine's panegyric on our self-containedness quite consistent with his efforts under Republican Administrations before and after Cleveland's to encourage our foreign trade both by shipping subsidies and by reciprocity agreements. Nevertheless, Blaine was undoubtedly as sincere in his Paris interview in supporting the protective tariff as Cleveland was in opposing it. That his political acumen sensed the opportunity for a party victory on the issue confirmed but did not create this conviction.

Blaine readily conceded that the Treasury surpluses ought to be reduced. But that could be easily accomplished without interfering with the beneficent system of protection. For example, the internal revenue tax on tobacco should be repealed immediately. Tobacco was the poor man's necessity, as much so as tea and coffee. The tax was imposed upon it only by the necessity of the government to seek extraordinary revenues during the Civil War, and to remove it now would not only reduce the surplus by many millions but also enhance the prosperity of the tobacco growing States. The tax on whisky should remain, but the revenues from it need not go to swell the Treasury surplus. "Whisky has done a vast deal of harm in the United States," he said; "I would try to make it do some good. I would use the tax to fortify our cities on the seaboard. In view of the powerful letter addressed to the Democratic Party on the subject of fortifications by the late Samuel J. Tilden in 1885, I am amazed that no attention has been paid to the subject by the Democratic Administration." In short, the question was not primarily that of overtaxation, as the President insisted. There were plenty of ways of getting rid of the surplus, even to the distribution of it among the States in order to lighten the burden of the excessive taxes paid on real estate. As to the free admission of raw materials, Blaine thought that while "some greedy manufacturers" might approve, no wise protectionist would favor it. For if the home trade in raw materials were seriously injured the railroads would be the first to feel it; and if that vast interest were crippled the whole financial fabric of the country would be shaken.

Finally, Blaine was asked, "What must be the marked and general effect of the President's message?" "It will bring the country where it ought to be brought," he answered, "to a full and fair contest on the question of protection. The President himself makes it the one issue by presenting no other in his message. I think it well to have the question settled. The Democratic Party in power is a standing menace to the prosperity of the country. That menace should be removed or the policy it foreshadows should be made certain. Nothing is so mischievous to business as uncertainty, nothing so paralyzing as doubt." [1]

The significance of the Paris Letter was not in its contents, which were but the reiteration of the protectionist arguments advanced by Blaine in many a former speech or article. Its significance lay in the very fact of its publication. By stepping thus promptly and voluntarily into the political arena with his challenge to the President, Blaine created the impression among his followers at home that he was announcing his candidacy for the approaching presidential nomination. John Hay wrote him jubilantly from Washington, "I must thank you for my share of the enjoyment of your counterblast published in the *Tribune* today. We were all lost in disgust at the message and not knowing just what to do with it, when, as we might have expected, but did not, came from over the sea the clear blast of the trumpet, declaring battle and bringing the fighting men into well-ordered ranks. You have given us our platform for next year." [2] Blaine himself realized, as he confessed in an interview with T. C. Crawford at Florence a few weeks later, that his Paris Letter was "generally regarded as his formal appearance in the campaign as a candidate"; yet he said that when he gave his interview to the *Tribune* reporter he had already become "fully decided" not to allow his name to go before the convention. He had acted only for the party. He was "fresh from reading the message," and saw in it the opportunity for Republican victory. He would strike while the iron was hot.

Of course, the demand for Blaine would have been strong even if he had really remained "entirely out of politics" during his European vacation. Still, that demand was so suddenly stimulated by the Paris Letter,[3] so many messages of anticipation came to him from his followers at home, that he felt obliged to define his position. On January 25, 1888, he wrote from his hotel in Florence to B. F. Jones, chairman

[1] New York *Tribune,* December 8, 1887.
[2] John Hay to Blaine, December 8, 1887.
[3] "It is doubtless safe to say that had the delegates to the convention been elected in December, 1887, there would not have been chosen a dozen in all the country who would have preferred any other candidate to Mr. Blaine." Edward Stanwood, *History of the Presidency,* Vol. I, p. 459.

of the Republican National Committee: "I wish you to state to the members of the Republican Party that my name will not be presented to the National Convention called to assemble in Chicago in June next for the nomination of President and Vice President of the United States. I am constrained to this decision by considerations entirely personal to myself, of which you were advised more than a year ago. But I cannot make this announcement without giving expression to my deep sense of gratitude to the thousands of my countrymen who have sustained me so long and so cordially that their feeling has seemed to go beyond the ordinary political adherence of fellow partisans and to partake somewhat of the nature of personal attachment. For this most generous, loyal friendship I can make no adequate return, and shall carry the memory of it while life lasts."

That Blaine had been of two minds in regard to running again for the nomination is shown by his note to his old friend Patrick Ford, the leader of the Blaine-Irish forces, a few days before he sent his Florence letter: "I am going to withdraw my name from the list of candidates. Ever since the result of 1884 I had made my mind up to run again if called upon by an undivided and unanimous party, but not to run if a contest were required to secure my nomination. I did not take this position from any pique or pride, but because I thought unanimity was required to give me the prestige and power for a successful canvass. I cannot say that I ever expected unanimity, and therefore it is that I withdraw without surprise and certainly without regret. I feel indeed a certain sense of relief that my party does not decide to devolve the task on me. Sherman is a determined candidate from Ohio. Harrison will be equally so from Indiana, and Hawley will have the delegates from Connecticut. . . . Having once been nominated and defeated, I cannot consent to be a *claimant* appealing to the party to *try me again.* . . . All this, of course, is confidential. I shall certainly not put any explanation in my letter of withdrawal, save that the reasons are *personal to myself.*" [1]

Perhaps Blaine underestimated the degree of unanimity in the party for his nomination, which was comparable only to the determination of the followers of Andrew Jackson, after his defeat in 1824, to seat him in the White House at the next election. How could Blaine know five months before the convention met that his party had decided not to

[1] Gail Hamilton, *Biography of James G. Blaine,* pp. 603–4.

devolve the task of running for the Presidency upon him? Perhaps, too, and more likely, the state of his health in the early weeks of 1888 was responsible for his letter to Chairman Jones. He had taken a severe cold, standing on the rear platform of the train while crossing the Alps, and had been under the constant care of the doctors at Milan and Florence. Apprehensiveness lest he might be really worse than he was troubled his mind, and made the very thought of enduring the turmoil of another campaign irksome to him. Mrs. Blaine too, who was his constant mentor, had misgivings, as we have seen, lest his symptoms of numbness in the side and limbs might portend paralysis. She approved her husband's course. "The letter of declination goes off in a day or two," she wrote to her daughter in Paris. "Do not cry. It has to go, and we shall all be the happier for being spared a summer of suspense with the chances of defeat in the autumn." [1]

An interesting side light on the situation is furnished by a cable dispatch to the New York *World* on February 25, from T. C. Crawford (later Blaine's biographer), who was one of the few callers received at the Hotel Florence and Washington. He "found Mr. and Mrs. Blaine in the large red and gold parlor of their suite, which directly overlooks the river (Arno) . . . Mr. Blaine's hair and beard are longer than he usually wears them. This to a slight extent changes his appearance. He was dressed in a rough tweed suit. His eyes looked bright and clear, his color good, and he displayed the same alacrity in moving about as in years past. In no way do his movements indicate illness. . . . The bright and pleasant weather here has made his recovery a rapid one, and he is now going about as he did in Paris and London. He drives in the afternoon and takes long walks in the morning. His most intimate friends see no sign of regret at his withdrawal from politics."

Asked whether he would ever again permit his name to go before a convention, Blaine replied "in a most emphatic negative." His letter of declination, he said, was not "a hap-hazard, offhand affair," but the result of careful deliberation. It had been prepared some weeks before it was sent, and "had been withheld from publication only out of regard for the appeals in letters and dispatches from personal friends in the United States," who had urged upon him that "the prospects of the party were now much brighter than they were in 1884," and that he could be elected "without raising a finger in the campaign." To which

---

[1] *Letters of Mrs. James G. Blaine,* Vol. II, p. 172.

he replied that he could not accept a nomination without working as hard for the success of the ticket as he had done four years earlier. He could not go through another such contest, he said, even with the certainty of the Presidency at the end of it. The struggle was too great; there was nothing in life worth it. He was sorry to learn that the unfriendly press regarded his letter of withdrawal as "a mere strategem for again calling public attention to himself as a candidate." Nothing could be farther from the truth. "You have no idea," he concluded, "what a relief it is to me to think that when I come back to New York in the summer, I shall not be going back there to face reception after reception and to enter into the turmoil and excitement of a political canvass. I can now come back quietly, after the convention has once decided the result, and enjoy my own life in my own way, free, I hope, from further criticism or comment." [1] *Dis aliter visum!*

Meanwhile the Florence letter was causing a great flurry in the political dovecotes at home. It was the chief topic of conversation in Wall Street and at the Capitol, and the newspapers printed columns of comments upon it from the politicians of both parties. Opinion was sharply divided on the sincerity and finality of Blaine's declination. On the one side were those who rejoiced that a candidate so formidable to the prospects of their own favorites had been removed, and who used every argument to prove that the letter was definitive. On the other hand, the men who would have no other candidate but Blaine declared that the letter would neither prevent Blaine's friends from nominating him nor himself from accepting the nomination. The demands of the Party rose superior to individual preference. Blaine was too good a patriot to refuse the call if it came.

An editorial of February 13, 1888, in Blaine's old paper, the Kennebec *Journal,* expresses best, perhaps, the hopes of his backers: "We know not all the reasons which have caused Mr. Blaine to send his declination to the National Committee and are authorized in no way to speak for him or to interpret his course of action. We know that he has strong personal reasons for not wishing to accept the Republican candidacy, and for avoiding the great responsibilities which the Presidency would impose upon hm. But the needs of the country and the demands of the great national party with which his name and fame are so closely identified should and must override all personal considerations.

[1] New York *World,* February 26, 1888.

To make absolutely sure Republican victory over the opponents of American protection the voice of the Republican masses calls James G. Blaine to lead them. This expression of sentiment comes spontaneously from all sections of the Union. . . . Believing that thoughtful patriotism, sound policy and the hopes of the surest victory call for Mr. Blaine's unanimous nomination, we cherish confidently the hope that he will obey the popular will when he sees how necessary it is that private feelings should yield to the loyal devotion of his heart to the great party."

On the other hand, the Chicago *News* of February 14 congratulated Blaine on "doing a service to his party" by withdrawing, and congratulated the party on "being once more free of an influence that first distracted it with a quarrel over spoils and then led it to defeat. And should the Republican Party take advantage of Mr. Blaine's withdrawal and nominate a man worthy of the party's early record—strong, able, honest and patriotic—it will go into the election of 1888 with better prospects than seemed possible a week ago."

Opinion on Capitol hill was equally divided. Most of the Senators and Representatives believed that Blaine's declination was sincere, but they differed as to its effect. Some believed that it cleared the way for a free contest at Chicago between the "favorite sons" of the various States; others thought that it would mean Blaine's nomination by acclamation. The Democrats quite generally interpreted it as a gesture of despair, when, as Representative O'Neill of Missouri said, "the strongest man in the Republican Party throws up the sponge." The Republicans declared that it assured victory through Blaine's powerful support of whatever candidate should be nominated. All the while the thick-and-thin Blaine men were clamoring for his nomination, letter or no letter. Representative Milliken, from Blaine's old congressional district in Maine, said: "I do not think Mr. Blaine's candidacy is a matter which he can settle for himself. I consider his letter entirely sincere, but it will take some stronger declaration than that to induce his friends to let him retire from the field. . . . As a candidate he can do more now than any other man to put the party back in power. For this reason his friends will not accept his refusal as final. I have received dispatches from various parts of the country today which show this." [1] The New York *Tribune* printed a score of letters, and "could have printed thou-

[1] The Washington *Star*, February 14, 1888.

sands," from Republicans, asserting that they had no second choice, and so long as Blaine lived would have no second choice, for President of the United States.

The conflicting interpretations of his Florence letter and the continued importunities of his friends at home led Blaine to define his position more clearly in a letter from Paris, on May 17, to Whitelaw Reid, editor of the New York *Tribune:* "Since my return to Paris from southern Italy on the 10th inst., I have learned (what I did not believe) that my name may yet be presented to the National Convention as a candidate for the Presidential nomination of the Republican Party." Since some of his friends, construing the Florence letter as an "unconditional withdrawal" (as it should be construed), had given their support to "eminent gentlemen who are candidates for the Chicago nomination," he would incur the reproach of being uncandid with those who had always been candid with him if he should now, "by speech or silence, by commission or omission," permit his name to be used. "I am not willing," he said, "to be the cause of misleading a single man among the millions who have given me their suffrage and their confidence. . . . Assuming that the Presidential nomination could by any possible chance be offered to me, I could not accept it without leaving in the minds of thousands of these men the impression that I had not been free from indirection, and therefore I could not accept it at all. The misrepresentations of malice have no weight, but the just displeasure of my friends I could not patiently endure." [1] Even this explicit refusal, however, did not put an end to the hope and belief of Blaine's backers that he would accept the nomination if "drafted" by the convention.

On June 5 the Democrats met at St. Louis and renominated President Cleveland by acclamation—the first time that a roll call had been dispensed with in their conventions since the renomination of Van Buren in 1840. Their brief platform was devoted chiefly to the tariff, commending Cleveland's December message and calling for a "fair and careful revision of the tax laws, with due allowance for the difference between the wages of American and foreign labor." It invited an "exacting scrutiny of the faithful, able and prudent administration of Grover Cleveland." Supplementary resolutions endorsed the Mills bill, then pending in Congress, recommended the immediate admission into the Union of the Territories of Washington, Dakota, Montana and New

---

[1] Gail Hamilton, *Biography of James G. Blaine,* p. 606.

Mexico, and declared the sympathy of the party with the efforts of Gladstone and Parnell to secure home rule for Ireland.[1]

The Republican convention assembled at Chicago on June 19, when Blaine was approaching the border of Scotland on the coaching trip. What went on under his "gray top-hat" we do not know, but we may be certain that the political situation at home was not crowded out of his mind by the beauties of the English landscape. Arthur Brisbane, Stephen Bonsal and other reporters were following his trail, to pick up at first or second hand any scrap of his intentions that they could cable to America. "Our host," wrote Mrs. Blaine to her son James, "is not a man to turn a deaf ear to a reporter's appeal, and I observe that at all our stopping places some one from the post-office sends in a card." [2] Indeed, Carnegie was as eager as the "Blaine legion" at Chicago to have the convention draft his political idol, and there is evidence that without Blaine's knowledge he was encouraging the efforts for his nomination. For example, on the second day of the convention, Mr. Smalley, on Blaine's instructions, cabled to the New York *Tribune* from London: "Mr. Blaine asks me to say that all rumors in the United States pretending to give letters or dispatches from him or any of his party touching political topics of any kind may be promptly discredited unless signed by Mr. Blaine himself. He has sent nothing whatever on the presidential question except his Florence and Paris letters, and has had no correspondence of any kind with any gentleman named in connection with the Republican nomination." [3]

On the same day, however, a cable from Bellingham, England, where the coaching party had spent the previous night, was published in the New York *Sun* and the Philadelphia *Press,* as follows: "Mr. Blaine does not speak of political matters in any way, but Mr. Carnegie, who is, of course, well able to express the feelings of his guest, said: 'If Mr. Blaine is nominated he will not refuse.' Then Mr. Carnegie wrote the following for publication: 'If the Republican Party finds that it cannot agree on a leader, and then calls upon its former leader to lead it again, it goes without saying that it would be his duty to do so (and Mr. Blaine has never failed to do his duty), more especially since it is now clear that the campaign is to be fought on the issue of protection *versus* free trade, the former of which Mr. Blaine feels to be essential to his coun-

[1] Edward Stanwood, *History of the Presidency,* Vol. I, pp. 469–71.
[2] *Letters of Mrs. James G. Blaine,* Vol. II, p. 207
[3] New York *Tribune,* June 21, 1888.

try's prosperity.' " Moreover, Mr. Carnegie had in his pocket at the moment a cypher code of the names of the important aspirants for the Republican nomination, which he had received from Stephen B. Elkins before sailing from New York, and which he was to use as a guarantee of the authenticity of his cable dispatches from Great Britain. What use he made of this code we shall see presently. We now return to the scene in Chicago.

The platform adopted by the Republican convention on June 21, after paying tribute to leaders of the party who had recently passed on,[1] and declaring that the Democrats were in power only "by the suppression of the ballot in the South by a criminal nullification of the Constitution and laws of the United States," devoted most of its attention to the tariff. It denounced the Mills bill as the measure of a party "serving the interests of Europe," and for the first time committed the Republicans to a "stand pat" position on the subject, by a plank declaring: "We favor the entire repeal of the internal taxes rather than the surrender of any part of our protective system." [2] It spoke for bimetallism, condemning Cleveland for his efforts to "demonetize silver" in his recommendation of the repeal of the Bland-Allison Act of 1878.[3] And finally it accused the Administration of "inefficiency and cowardice" in its conduct of foreign affairs, especially in its negotiations with Great Britain over the fisheries, which showed an "unpatriotic tendency to destroy a valuable national industry and an indispensable resource of defense against a foreign enemy." [4]

The interest of the convention, however, was not in the platform, but in the contest for the nomination. Never before or since in our history has a presidential convention distributed its votes among so many aspirants. Blaine's reiterated declination had thrown the field open to all comers. Fourteen names were voted for on the first ballot, and five more received scattering votes before the contest was decided. But the most astonishing thing was the extent to which the convention was dominated by a man three thousand miles away and apparently indifferent to the result. It was said that a month before the convention met nearly four hundred of the delegates had expressed their preference for

---

[1] Grant had died on July 23, 1885, Arthur on November 18, 1886, Logan on December 28, 1886, and Conkling on April 18, 1888.
[2] Edward Stanwood, *History of the Presidency,* Vol. I, p. 474.
[3] *Ibid.,* p. 475.
[4] *Ibid.,* pp. 476–7.

Blaine. "The Republican Party," said the New York *Nation* of May 3, "wants Blaine for the candidate and means to have him." His portrait was carried in a big procession the evening before the convention met, and his name called out wild enthusiasm, particularly in the galleries. The apprehension of a stampede to Blaine permeated the atmosphere and entered into the manoeuvres of all the managers. Walker and Emmons Blaine were at Chicago, as Gail Hamilton remarks, "to defend their father's wishes, which, it hardly need be said, were not their own." [1] But the contemporary dispatches show that, with whatever intention they may have come to the convention, they remained to work with Elkins, Manley, Boutelle and other determined Blaine supporters for their father's nomination. A. M. Jones telegraphed to Sherman on the twenty-first, "No danger of Gresham. Look out for Blaine. Walker has been showing me how his father will be nominated tomorrow forenoon." And G. B. Raum wrote to Sherman on the evening of the twenty-third: "As I telegraphed you, the Blaine movement has been steadily pushed. Elkins has been aided by various persons, and two of Mr. Blaine's sons have been on the ground all the while. They have claimed a majority of the convention and that Blaine could and would be nominated." [2]

Senator John Sherman of Ohio was the most prominent of the avowed contestants at Chicago. It was the fourth Republican convention in which he had striven for the nomination, and he had the backing of a strong group of men, including Governor Foraker, Charles Foster, J. E. Bateman, G. B. Raum, William McKinley and Marcus A. Hanna. Sherman had assured Blaine in 1887 that he would not stand in his way, if Blaine desired the nomination, and in an interview reported in the Washington *Star* of February 13, 1888 (after the publication of Blaine's Florence letter), he said: "Mr. Blaine is one of the foremost Americans, whom every Republican would have delighted to honor, and it is a source of regret that he has concluded not to make the race again." Sherman announced that he was out for the Ohio delegation, now that Blaine's name was withdrawn. It was only on that hypothesis that he had "entered the lists." That this announcement was for public consumption, however, and by no means represented Sherman's real conviction, is clear from his telegram to Mark Hanna on the opening day of the con-

---

[1] *Biography of James G. Blaine,* p. 607.
[2] *Sherman Papers,* Library of Congress, Vol. 450, No. 29314.

vention: "My theory is that Blaine is a candidate, has been from the beginning and will be until defeated. The telegrams of yesterday are but the announcement of it. . . . We cannot run from a battle. My withdrawal is his nomination. We cannot transfer my vote to anyone without producing that result. I hope Quay and you will stand firmly together. Keep my vote steady if possible, and all will be right." [1] A passage in Mrs. Blaine's letter of February 22 to her daughter is significant: "I had a sweet letter from Mr. [Levi P.] Morton calling your Father's [Florence] letter a masterpiece and not seeing how it could be accepted. You can trust John Sherman for seeing, however." [2]

On the first ballot, taken Friday, June 21, Sherman led with 229 votes, more than twice the number (111) of his nearest competitor, Walter Q. Gresham of Indiana, but hardly more than half the 416 votes necessary for the nomination. Chauncey M. Depew was third, with 99 votes largely made up of the 72 of the New York delegation cast for their "favorite son" by way of a complimentary ballot. [3] Then followed ex-Governor Russell A. Alger of Michigan (84), [4] Benjamin Harrison of Indiana (80), Senator Wm. B. Allison of Iowa (72), James G. Blaine of Maine (35), [5] and so on down the long list. The next two ballots showed little change, but on the fourth ballot Depew dropped out and fifty-eight of New York's votes went to Harrison, who jumped from 94 to 217, only eighteen votes behind Sherman. It was evident when the convention recessed on Saturday, the twenty-third, after the fifth ballot, that Sherman could not be nominated. As usual, he had failed to gather strength as the balloting proceeded. He was five points below his initial

---

[1] *Sherman Papers, Library of Congress,* Vol. 449, No. 29212.

[2] *Letters of Mrs. James G. Blaine,* Vol. II, p. 185.

[3] Depew had declared in the spring of 1887 that he was "absolutely in favor of Mr. Blaine for the next Republican nomination and that the presidency of the New York Central Railroad was the only presidency he desired to hold." The Depew boom was launched, however, at a dinner of the Brooklyn Republican League on February 13, 1888, when Stuart L. Woodford announced that "now Blaine is out of the field," the party must follow the standard of "the one man who can certainly carry New York against any Democrat who can be nominated." New York *Herald,* February 15, 1888.

[4] As Secretary of War in the first years of the McKinley Administration, Alger was to obtain a brief notoriety from the charge of having furnished "embalmed beef" to our soldiers in the Spanish-American War.

[5] Blaine's small vote is explained by a dispatch of A. M. Jones to Sherman on June 21: "Blaine's personal friends hope either to adjourn the convention or to stampede it after the third ballot to Blaine. Leaders are urging no votes for Blaine on the first few ballots, scattering their strength among Alger and Harrison, so as to make them close to you. I have talked with the Blaine leaders and found the above to be correct." (*Sherman Papers,* Library of Congress.)

vote, while Harrison and Alger had gained 137 and 51 respectively.

Then the wires between Washington and Chicago were kept hot with telegrams between Sherman and his managers. Blaine was the man they feared. Though he had but forty-eight votes, his shadow was looming over the convention. His managers had approached Governor Foraker (who had put Sherman in nomination) with the offer of second place on the Blaine ticket; and, although the Governor, in his reminiscences, declared that he would not have accepted the offer without Sherman's consent,[1] suspicions of his defection were rife. "The Ohio delegation is already broken," wired Murat Halstead to Sherman; "the Governor goes next ballot for Blaine. He thinks you have no chance left. . . . The friends of Blaine claim the Alger vote solid and the indications are that the Blaine movement will succeed. They are claiming everything and holding that the support they have given you (!) calls for support in return. Blaine will certainly be nominated, unless the movement can be checked by placing McKinley in nomination and concentrating the anti-Blaine forces. Can we afford to lose this opportunity of securing a nomination for the State? Give us a word and we believe we can pull McKinley through. In my judgment the question is coming on the next ballot between Blaine and McKinley." [2]

Other Sherman supporters joined in the plea that he would withdraw in favor of McKinley. George F. Hoar, who had supported Blaine in 1884, wired to Sherman: "Your nomination now seems impossible. If you promptly telegraph Ohio delegation authorizing them to present McKinley he will probably be nominated. Otherwise it looks like Blaine." [3] Mark Hanna, who had assured Sherman on May 30 that his sole ambition was to make him President of the United States, now gave up hope for the Ohio Senator, and begged him to "save the party from the Blaine lunatics" by declaring for McKinley. Everything was "in a mess." New York was "in the Blaine movement." Its vote for Harrison was "only a cover." "I do not give up till the last hour, but want your definite instructions what to do. Answer quickly." [4] M. D. Leggett telegraphed Sherman on Sunday morning: "Your case looks hopeless, made so by the Blaine tricksters. Blaine must be defeated or we are

---

[1] Joseph B. Foraker, *Notes of a Busy Life*, Vol. I, p. 368.
[2] *Sherman Papers*, Vol. 450, No. 29405.
[3] *Ibid.*, No. 29411.
[4] *Ibid.*, Vol. 450, No. 29332.

ruined. Believe a majority would unite on McKinley if he were free.[1] Don't delay final action too long. I believe you have power to defeat Blaine." [2]

But Sherman was cold to all these suggestions of withdrawal. Twice on Saturday he wired to Hanna: "Let my name stand. I prefer defeat to retreat. I have no right to say that Foraker should not vote for McKinley as against Blaine. Each delegate should act as he deems best for his country. . . . I like McKinley, but such a movement would be unjust to others, and as I view it, a breach of implicit faith. . . . I will be true and frank. Stand to our position and fall, if need be, with honor. I understand Foraker thinks I am under obligation to support Blaine. This is totally unfounded. I am grateful to Foraker and the rest, but not to Blaine. His course has been deceptive and I think dishonorable." [3]

The "dishonor" referred to was nothing more than Sherman's fear that his withdrawal would mean Blaine's nomination. For, in spite of the fact that Joseph H. Manley had written to Sherman on May 30 that he "would do all in his power to secure his nomination," [4] and that Charles Foster had told him a week before the convention met that he had assurances from the "Blaine people" that they were not going to Chicago to push Blaine's candidacy,[5] it was evident to him that such statements deserved little faith. Manley was working as hard as Elkins and Blaine's sons to swing the convention to the Maine statesman. Green B. Raum, in whose dispatches from Chicago Sherman placed the fullest confidence, wired on Friday the twenty-second: "The consultations of the night were kept up till four this morning. . . . The Blaine movement is open and aggressive. We think that if you cannot be nominated, Blaine will be." Come what might. Sherman was

[1] McKinley absolutely refused to profit by Sherman's weakness, as Garfield had done in 1880. When a few votes were cast for him, he rose to say that he was present as a supporter of John Sherman and forbade anyone who was his friend to vote for his nomination.

[2] *Sherman Papers*, Vol. 450, No. 29542. As an example of the popular clamor for Blaine, we may quote a letter written to Sherman on Sunday the 24th by Stuck and Jones, dealers in dry goods, groceries and crockery, at Central Station, West Virginia: "We have scanned the situation all over and find that nine tenths of the people are for James G. Blaine. Not but what they believe you are a good man, *but you cannot be elected*. . . . For the sake of the Republican Party and good government, telegraph your withdrawal and support the man that the people wants, that illustrious leader of leaders and champion of Republican principles, James G. Blaine. Your own people prefer Blaine, and West Virginia would be certain for the Democracy were you the candidate." *Sherman Papers*, Vol. 450, No. 29543.

[3] *Ibid.*, No. 29387.

[4] *Ibid.*, Vol. 446, No. 28555.

[5] *Ibid.*, Vol. 448, No. 28932.

determined not to contribute to such an outcome by retiring from the field and releasing his more than two hundred delegates.

Meanwhile Blaine's friends were not confining themselves to manoeuvres at Chicago, but were urging him to reconsider his refusal to allow his name to be formally presented for the nomination. He read the reports of the convention in the London papers, and doubtless read much more between the lines than was contained in their meager information. He cabled twice from Edinburgh on Saturday, the twenty-third, in response to the importunities of Manley and Boutelle: "Earnestly request my friends to respect my Paris letter" and "I think I have a right to ask my friends to respect my wishes and refrain from voting for me. Please make this and former dispatch public." [1] Finally they appealed to Carnegie, whose eagerness to have his distinguished guest nominated was as keen as their own. But Carnegie was equally unable to break down Blaine's resolution, and reluctantly cabled to Elkins in the secret code they had agreed upon: "Too late. Victor (Blaine) immovable. Take Trump (Harrison) and Star (Phelps)." [2]

On Monday Harrison's vote jumped from 231 on the sixth ballot to 544 on the eighth, while Sherman's dropped from 244 to 118. Alger, who was charged by the Sherman men with the wholesale purchase of Southern delegates, had a hundred votes. Gresham, extolled as the farmers' friend, had fifty-nine. Five delegates persisted in voting for Blaine and four for McKinley. It may well have been that the deadlock of Saturday would have been resolved eventually in Harrison's favor, even without the cables from Blaine and Carnegie, for Harrison was the only contestant who had gained on every ballot, and Raum had wired to Sherman on Saturday evening that the movement for Harrison was "genuine and really dangerous." It may have been also that, even if Blaine had consented at the eleventh hour to be a candidate, he would not have been able to find the 461 votes necessary for the nomination; for delegates who would have voted for him enthusiastically at the start had made other commitments, and certainly he was the last man for whom Sherman would have been willing to release his delegates. For all that, Blaine was in truth the "Warwick of 1888," the man who put Harrison on the throne: not so much because of his eleventh hour cable to the convention, as because, by his Florence and Paris letters of declination, he had

---

[1] Gail Hamilton, *Biography of James G. Blaine*, p. 607.
[2] B. J. Hendrick, *Life of Andrew Carnegie*, Vol. I, p. 328.

prevented at the start a united, irresistible movement in his own behalf.[1]

Harrison promptly and cordially acknowledged his indebtedness. In response to a cable of congratulation from Blaine (which he gave to the press) he wrote, on June 30: "From your most intimate and trusted friends I had the assurance that in a possible contingency you and they might regard my nomination with favor. It was only such assurances that made my Indiana friends hopeful of success, and only the help of your friends made success possible. It will give me pleasure always to show my high appreciation of the efficient and conclusive support your very close friends gave to me in the convention. I am now looking forward with great interest to the time when you shall return and give to the campaign the impetus that only your voice can give to it. If it suits your plans, I would like to have an early visit from you, and Mrs. Harrison requests that you will bring Mrs. Blaine with you." [2] Harrison also wrote on the same date to Walker Blaine in Chicago, thanking him for the assurance that the nomination would be agreeable to his father.[3]

Benjamin Harrison was without doubt the most available candidate the convention could have chosen. Born on an Ohio farm in 1833, in comparative poverty, he had made his way through Miami University, studied in the law office of Bellamy Storer in Cincinnati, and at the age of twenty-one had taken his bride to Indianapolis to establish his home and his profession. He was serving as reporter of the Supreme Court of Indiana when the Civil War broke out. On the advice of Governor Oliver P. Morton, he promptly raised a volunteer regiment, which he led with such conspicuous gallantry, especially during Sherman's great Atlanta campaign, that he was brevetted in March, 1865, as Brigadier General. Resuming his legal career after the war, he advanced steadily to the leadership of the Indiana bar. He had joined the Republican Party at its inception, casting his first vote for Frémont in 1856 and giving valuable service in every subsequent Republican campaign. In 1876 he was

---

[1] The resentment of the Sherman men at Blaine's presumption to dictate names to the convention was expressed in a letter of A. Melford to Sherman two days after the nomination of Harrison. Melford hoped that Harrison would be defeated. "It is better," he wrote, "to be right than to elect a President at the brisk dictation of the autocratic ruler of the Republican Party as he goes coaching over the Highlands. . . . One more Blaine defeat, I think, will bring the party back to the days of Lincoln and Grant." *Sherman Papers*, Vol. 451, No. 29720.

[2] Gail Hamilton, *Biography of James G. Blaine*, p. 646.

[3] Not knowing the address of Blaine in Scotland, Harrison was enclosing his letters of thanks to him and Carnegie in the one to Walker to be forwarded, when Stephen B. Elkins arrived at Harrison's house in Indianapolis (a significantly early visit) and furnished him with the addresses.

narrowly defeated for the Governorship of Indiana by "Blue Jeans" (James D.) Williams, but four years later he was elected to the United States Senate, where he served a single term, declining Garfield's offer of a Cabinet position. As chairman of the Indiana delegation in the Republican conventions of 1880 and 1884 he had supported "that matchless statesman, James G. Blaine." And in 1880 he had fully earned the support which the matchless statesman was now to give him, when he announced the vote of the Indiana delegation for Blaine on thirty-four successive ballots, resisting the lure of Conkling's bid for a third term for the "hero of Appomattox" in the suggestion of a Grant-Harrison ticket.

Aside from his consistently fine record on the battlefield and at the bar, Harrison's availability was enhanced by certain fortunate circumstances. Grandson of General William Henry Harrison, the hero of Tippecanoe, and great-grandson of Benjamin Harrison of Virginia, a signer of the Declaration of Independence, he bore an illustrious name. But that name, as he sometimes reminded his audiences, was the only capital left to him by his ancestors. He was a self-made man in the best sense of the American tradition. His devout religious faith (he was an elder in the Presbyterian Church and taught an adult Bible class for many years) was another point in his favor with the great mass of the American people, though the less reverential would have their joke about the oysters and eggs being "opened with prayer" at the White House during the Harrison régime. From the political point of view his candidacy was still further strengthened by the fact that he came from the pivotal State of Indiana,[1] and that, as a Western man favoring bimetallism, he was free from any obnoxious connections with the "gold bugs" of Wall Street and not unacceptable to the growing sentiment of agrarian discontent in the granger States.

Against these assets, however, must be set certain liabilities. Harrison was not an ingratiating person. He was ignorant of the arts by which the politician appeals to the emotions and prejudices of the masses— flattery, sophistry, clever misrepresentation, dogmatic exaggeration, and the like. He had a puritanical austerity of manner which repelled

---

[1] It is interesting to note that New York and Indiana were the only States that shifted their electoral vote from the Democratic to the Republican column in 1888. Cleveland carried both states in 1884 and was elected; in 1888 he lost both and was defeated. It was sound judgment that led the convention of 1888 to reject Blaine's advice to take W. W. Phelps of New Jersey for the vice-presidential candidate, and to substitute for him Levi P. Morton of New York.

any attempts at back-slapping familiarity. Though courteous to all, and genial in the company of his intimate friends, his formal dignity with strangers or casual acquaintances gave the impression of cold indifference, if not superciliousness. One contemporary was ungracious enough to say that Harrison "distilled poison like an adder." His tastes and temperament were those of a high-grade lawyer, not of a politician. He detested the logrolling, the bargaining, the patronage mongering which seemed inseparable from "practical politics." He spoke seldom and cultivated few friendships in the Senate, and it was said that most of his Republican colleagues in that body were opposed to his nomination for the Presidency. To a man of his self-sufficiency it must have been uncomfortable, however courteous his acknowledgments, to be beholden to another, and a vastly more popular, member of the party for his nomination; for, while he was officially designated as the leader of the party by virtue of that nomination, he knew that Blaine was the idol of the party, standing in somewhat the same relation to him as Henry Clay had stood to his grandfather, William Henry Harrison, half a century before. On the August day when Blaine landed from his European trip the eyes of the country were turned not to Indianapolis but to New York; and the Indiana delegation joined the throng that went down the harbor to greet the returning idol with the song:

> Welcome, with one acclaim,
> Plumed Knight of loyal fame,
> Great son of Maine!
> Welcome to thee we bring,
> "Welcome!" our forests ring,
> "Welcome!" the prairies sing,
> Welcome to Blaine! [1]

Harrison sent a letter of greeting, regretting that the meeting of the State convention would prevent several of the prominent Republicans of Indiana from going to New York for the auspicious event.

With Blaine's return the Republican campaign really began. Harrison, ever since the nomination (except for a fortnight's vacation on Middle Bass Island on Lake Erie, as the guest of ex-Governor Foster of Ohio) had remained at his home in Indianapolis, receiving almost daily delegations, ranging from a few score to several thousand in num-

---

[1] The first of a number of stanzas of fulsome doggerel written for the occasion by Mr. William H. Hamilton of Hagerstown, Maryland.

bers, who came to present their congratulations and pledge their support. Comrades of the Grand Army of the Republic, survivors of his old regiment, political clubs, State delegations, farmers, railroad workers, colored men, German Americans, commercial travelers—a motley lot trod on one another's heels as they swarmed up to his door, some of them rolling log cabins or cider barrels, or bringing coons, eagles and other emblems of the campaign of 1840; and for each group he had a brief and appropriate word of greeting. These impromptu "front porch" speeches, nearly a hundred in number, were models of good taste; and, while they offered no opportunity for an extended discussion of issues they made clear the candidate's fidelity to the main points of the party platform—the protective tariff, liberal pensions for Civil War veterans, a free ballot in the South, an honest civil service and the cultivation of closer diplomatic and commercial relations with the Latin-American countries. Most admirable of all was the candidate's exhortation to keep the campaign from degenerating into the contest of mud slinging which had disgraced the election of 1884. "Let the American people," he said at the beginning of the canvass, "encamp on the high plains of principle and not in the low swamps of personal defamation or detraction." [1] But impeccable as they were, Harrison's front porch speeches were hardly more than a curtain-raiser for the play.

It was Blaine whom the people wanted to see and hear. On the day that he was expected to land in New York (August 8), Harrison, addressing the Republican State convention at Indianapolis, announced the entrance of the hero upon the stage: "Today, at the chief seaport of our country, that great Republican, that great American, James G. Blaine, returns to his home. We shall not be disappointed, I hope, in hearing his powerful voice in Indiana before the campaign is old." [2] It was not till the campaign was near its end, however, that Blaine came to Indianapolis as Harrison's guest (October 11); and when he came he was welcomed by throngs which made Harrison's delegations of the summer look like knots of farmers gathered around a village store. Fifty thousand citizens greeted him on his arrival in the city and twenty-five thousand paraded in his honor. He spoke to an audience of thirty thousand at the Exposition Grounds in the afternoon and in the evening the largest hall in the city was packed to the doors to hear his brilliant

[1] Charles Hedges, *The Speeches of Benjamin Harrison*, p. 31.
[2] *Ibid.*, p. 82.

speech on the issues of the campaign.

From the day he landed, Blaine threw himself into the fray with a zest and vigor which belied the persistently circulated reports of his shattered health. Until the September election had returned a satisfactory Republican majority in Maine, he confined his efforts to that State, attacking the Democratic Administration especially on the issues of the tariff and foreign policy. On August 23 President Cleveland sent a special message to Congress, asking for "immediate legislation conferring upon the Executive the power to suspend by proclamation the operation of all laws and regulations permitting the transit of goods, wares and merchandise in bond across or over the territory of the United States to or from Canada." [1] This was by way of retaliation against Great Britain for her refusal to let our fishermen in Canadian waters send their catch across Canada in bond, duty free. It will be recalled that Congress had given such retaliatory powers to the President in the law of March 3, 1887, but that Cleveland had preferred to negotiate a treaty on the subject with Great Britain, and that the treaty of February 15, 1888, which he submitted to the Senate as a "satisfactory, practical and final adjustment of a long standing controversy" had been rejected by the Republican majority in that body.[2]

Blaine now regarded Cleveland's reversion to the retaliatory policy and his threatening language about a government "doing but half its duty when it protects its citizens at home and permits them to be imposed upon and humiliated by the unfair and overreaching disposition of other nations," [3] as nothing but a desperate, jingoistic appeal to save himself from impending defeat in November.

On September 1, Blaine wrote a long letter to Congressmen W. W. Phelps and R. R. Hitt, begging the Republican members of the Committee on Foreign Affairs not to support Cleveland's request for retaliatory powers against Great Britain. "Pray look at the situation," he said; "the popular tide is at present running heavily against him (Cleveland) and the uprising in behalf of protection threatens to distance him in the race. He seeks for a new issue. He is ashamed to use the powers of retaliation (the law of March 3, 1887) which he has neglected for a year and a half. He wishes to discredit them . . . to convince the people that the Republicans have been humbugging on the

---

[1] J. D. Richardson, *Messages and Papers of the Presidents,* Vol. VIII, p. 623.
[2] See above, p. 354.
[3] Richardson, *op. cit.,* p. 627.

fisheries question and have only given him the semblance and not the substance of a retaliation measure. Moreover, it is not to be doubted that if he gets the power in his hands which this new retaliation will give him, he will use it to the extent of stirring up an apparent row with Canada and with England, just enough to unsettle the entire Irish vote, certainly enough to enable the Democratic Irish to reclaim a large proportion of the 80,000 Irish who voted the Republican ticket in New York in 1884. In his present position the President is open to the keenest of political weapons, ridicule. I have been on the stump continually since his message and can testify that the disapprobation of his position by large audiences is absolutely unanimous, so far as I can judge. . . . I think immeasurably the strongest ground is to treat the President's message as the campaign dodge of a candidate, hard pressed on an issue on which he has been beaten before the country, and all the more disastrously beaten because he forced the issue himself. I think we have all the weapons in our hands for pushing him over the precipice, if we steadily hold to the ground that the main issue is protection *versus* free trade, and that he has shown himself incompetent to deal with the fisheries question." [1]

This letter is quoted at some length because it illustrates Blaine's campaign methods. Harrison could make a hundred graceful speeches expressing his faith in Republican policies and Republican success, without reference to President Cleveland. But Blaine must be aggressive, concrete, combative, emphasizing political strategy rather than general principles. He sought out the weak points in his opponent's armor, and, like the Homeric heroes of old, fought to bring down his foe in personal encounter, advancing upon him with the bold spear thrusts of assertion, the shock of statistics, and the shafts of sarcasm. People in general love a fight. They acclaim an aggressive leader. The qualities in Blaine which made him a "matchless statesman" in the eyes of the multitude were the very qualities which made him a matchless politician—an extraordinary factual equipment, imperturbable confidence, alert vigor of attack and consummate adroitness in defense.

During the last weeks of the campaign Blaine toured the West and wound up with speeches in Connecticut and New York. He stressed the blessings of the protective tariff for the American manufacturer, farmer and laborer, stimulating American patriotism by a comparison of our

[1] Gail Hamilton, *Biography of James G. Blaine,* pp. 609–610.

prosperity with the hard conditions in the less favored countries of Europe which he had visited, and by harping on the danger of allowing the British heresy of free trade, with which the Democratic Party was infected, to demoralize our industries and impoverish our people. He charged the Cleveland Administration with an ineptitude and vacillation in its diplomatic negotiations with England which sacrificed the clear rights of American fishermen under the Twenty-ninth Article of the Treaty of Washington. And he reiterated the condemnation of the Democratic Party for encouraging (and profiting by) the infraction of the Constitution and laws of the country in the suppression of a free ballot in the Southern States. The throngs of tens of thousands who greeted him at the Exposition Grounds in Indianapolis or the Polo Grounds in New York went wild with enthusiasm over his excoriation of the Democrats as unfit to be entrusted with the government of the country.

Early in September a clever but shabby bit of strategy of which Blaine had no knowledge was staged in order to give color to the charge that President Cleveland was the "British candidate." A certain Mr. Osgoodby of Pomona, California, wrote to Sir Lionel Sackville-West, the British Minister at Washington representing himself as a naturalized Englishman by the name of Charles F. Murchison, and asking how he should vote in the coming election. The extraordinarily stupid Minister fell into the trap and replied in terms unmistakably favorable to Cleveland. Osgoodby gave Sir Lionel's letter to the press and it was circulated as a campaign document, winning one knows not how many Irish votes for the Republicans. President Cleveland immediately asked for the recall of the blundering Minister, and when Lord Salisbury demurred, Secretary Bayard was instructed to hand Sir Lionel his passports.[1]

The Republicans bent their efforts to regain the doubtful States of Indiana and New York, which had assured Cleveland's election in 1884. In the former State Blaine did his most strenuous stumping, speaking

---

[1] The correspondence between E. J. Phelps, our Minister to London, and Lord Salisbury on the subject of Sackville-West's recall is in the *Letter Books* of the American Embassy at London, under the dates Oct. 31, Nov. 1, 2, Dec. 4, 24, 1888. From this correspondence it appears that while Sir Lionel's letter of Sept. 15 to "Murchison" entered into the reasons for his recall, his chief offense was "the published imputation to the President and Senate of discreditable motives in their action touching the subject of the Canadian fisheries." (Phelps to Salisbury, Nov. 2, 1888. See the New York *Times* of Oct. 23.) A facsimile of Sir Lionel's letter was printed in the New York *Tribune* three days before the election.

to large audiences at Indianapolis, Green Castle, Evansville, Lafayette, Jeffersonville and the battlefield of Tippecanoe. With generous expenditures of campaign funds and the assiduous muster of the "floaters" in "blocks of five" by W. W. Dudley, the treasurer of the Republican National Committee, Harrison came through in Indiana with a slim margin of 2,300 votes. He also carried New York by a majority of 12,000 in a total vote of over 1,300,000, under conditions which gave rise to the charge of a "corrupt bargain." David B. Hill, the Democratic candidate for reëlection as Governor, was unfriendly to Cleveland, and Hill's Republican opponent for the Governorship was Warner Miller, who, it will be recalled, had been elected by the New York legislature, together with E. G. Latham, to replace Conkling and Platt when they resigned from the United States Senate in their quarrel with Garfield in the summer of 1881. Moreover, Platt who was in complete control of the Stalwart organization in New York, and whose ambition to be Secretary of the Treasury was the consuming desire of his life, had brought the New York delegation to the support of Harrison in the convention of 1888 and worked hard for him during the campaign, evidently in the belief that he would be rewarded with the coveted Cabinet post.[1]

Now, because Hill defeated Miller while Cleveland lost to Harrison in New York, the cry was raised that Hill had bartered with Miller's enemy Platt, delivering Democratic votes for Harrison in return for Republican votes for Hill. Banners inscribed "Harrison and Hill" were actually displayed in many parts of the State. However, Cleveland himself many years later (1906) exonerated Hill from any treachery to the Democratic national ticket. Hill's victory over Miller was due to his favor with the liquor interests because of his veto of the high license Crosby bill; while Cleveland lost the State partly because of the dissatisfaction of the large manufacturers with his tariff policy and partly because of the disaffection of the Tildenites, who resented the President's neglect of their old hero. On election day (Nov. 7) Harrison car-

---

[1] In his *Autobiography* (p. 206) Platt wrote: "Immediately after the nomination of Harrison, friends suggested to him that I be given the Secretaryship of the Treasury in case he was elected. Indeed, a promise of this portfolio, which I and members of the National Committee regarded as binding, was made. . . . But when, notwithstanding a letter in President Harrison's own handwriting promising the appointment, I was suddenly informed that William Windom of Minnesota had been selected, I felt that there was little use of pinning my faith upon anybody or training myself for high office." Platt, however, does not print the alleged promissory letter of the President-elect.

ried all the States north of Mason and Dixon's line except Connecticut and New Jersey, with an electoral vote of 233 against 168 for Cleveland. But Cleveland's popular plurality of over 100,000 proved that Harrison's ancestry, Blaine's oratory and Osgoodby's trickery combined had not availed to convince a majority of the American voters that the welfare and honor of their country were unsafe in the hands of a Democratic Administration.

That Blaine would be rewarded by the highest post of honor in the Cabinet was taken for granted. Five days after the election his devoted friend Patrick Ford wrote to him: "The great victory won is above all men's your victory. You struck the keynote of the campaign in your Paris interview and you opened the campaign on the very day of your arrival. . . . You must be Secretary of State." [1] A few days later Senator Eugene Hale wrote in great anxiety, because he had heard from W. E. Chandler and Levi P. Morton that Blaine had expressed an unwillingness to accept any Cabinet portfolio: "In proper ways I have been trying to remove such impressions, but I do not know how far General Harrison shares them and whether I should write to him. What do you think about that? Let me know." [2] And the next month General Alger wrote: "I should look with alarm to the future of the party if you were passed by without being offered the State portfolio." [3] On the other hand, Blaine's enemies in the party were dismayed by the apprehension of his domination of the Administration. After Blaine's appointment to the Cabinet, ex-Secretary Benjamin H. Bristow wrote to Judge Gresham: "As you know, I kicked clean out in 1884 because I could not vote for Blaine. Have I now voted for him after all? It looks pretty much that way. Hereafter I shall insist on putting my ballot in the box with a string to it, or if I can't do that, will go fishing on election day. Blaine *per se* is bad enough, but Blaine as Secretary of State with Windom in the Treasury to do his bidding and a lot of nobodys in the other departments whom he can control without their knowing it is a situation far worse than any that has existed hitherto. . . . It is quite clear that Blaine and Steve Elkins have inveigled Harrison into the selection of Windom by artful means; but what hope is there of a President who can be caught at the outset by such fellows. . . . I should take a very gloomy view of the future if it had not already been demonstrated that

[1] Patrick Ford to Blaine, November 12, 1888.
[2] Hale to Blaine, November 21, 1888.
[3] R. A. Alger to Blaine, December 26, 1888.

we can stand more jobbery and bad administration than any government upon the earth." [1] This utterly inaccurate summary of the political situation must be set down to mere venom.

Harrison doubtless intended from the first to offer Blaine the position which custom and courtesy demanded that he should. At the same time, his self-sufficiency, his distaste for the manipulations and bargainings which characterized the conduct of party politics, and his strong sense of the dignity conferred upon him by the election to the chief magistracy made any thought of being coerced by public pressure into the recognition of the popular idol of the party irksome to him. He was determined not to tolerate a "power behind the throne" or an "uncrowned king" of the Administration. This was probably why he allowed week after week to pass after the election without a word to Blaine as to his Cabinet plans; and when he finally did offer Blaine the State portfolio, on January 17, 1889, it was in a letter of rather formal courtesy: "My dear Mr. Blaine, I beg to offer you the position of Secretary of State and very sincerely and cordially to request your acceptance of the office. Hoping to hear favorably from you at your early convenience, I am, Very respectfully and sincerely yours, Benjamin Harrison." This formal proffer was accompanied by a longer "private" letter, detailing "some further and more familiar things" which the President-elect wished to emphasize—first, the necessity of "a spirit of the most perfect cordiality and confidence" between the two men; second, the assurance of coöperation in the improvement of our relations with the Central and South American states; third, the hope that the problems pending with European governments and requiring "early and discreet attention" would be dealt with in a way to "bring about just and peaceful conclusions"; and finally, the need of preserving harmony in the party and of conducting the Administration "without any selfish thought or ambition," on such a high plane as would recommend it to the confidence of all the people. Four days later Blaine accepted the appointment in a letter to "My dear General," in which he expressed his "heartiest accord" with the points emphasized by the President-elect and his appreciation of the honor as well as the responsibilities of the position which he was invited to fill. "In becoming a member of your Cabinet," he said, "I can have no motive, near or remote, inconsistent with the greatest strength and highest interests of your Administration and of

[1] Bristow to Gresham, Feb. 21, 1889. *Gresham Papers*, Library of Congress, Box C.

yourself as its official and personal head."

It is necessary only to compare the conventional tone (less so, to be sure, on Blaine's part) of the scanty and belated correspondence between General Harrison and his future Secretary with the almost daily exchange of letters and notes between "My dear Blaine" and "My dear Garfield" eight years before, to realize the vastly different conditions under which Blaine was to assume his second incumbency of the State Department. The exuberant and rather sentimental Garfield had immediately appealed to Blaine as partner, mentor and confidant. He had asked Blaine to furnish him suggestions for various passages in his letter of acceptance. He had consulted him on the make-up of his Cabinet. He had welcomed his advice as to how to deal with Conkling, Cameron, Logan and the other party chieftains. He had gratefully received his analysis of the factions in the party and his outline of the policies necessary to make the Administration glorious and a reëlection inevitable. He had sought his counsel on the wisdom of attending a meeting in New York. He had humbly received his admonition not to let "instinctive generosity" interfere with the assertion of the "dignity and independence of the great office" which he was about to fill. And on the morning of inauguration day he had, in the name of "the love and comradeship of eighteen years," bidden Blaine to come to him at the White House the first moment that he was free. Not only were Blaine and Garfield intimate personal friends who had entered Congress at the same time and had "never for a single moment in eighteen years had a misunderstanding or a coolness," [1] but the mutual affection was shared by the wives and families.

Harrison, on the other hand, while he grudgingly admired Blaine's brilliant gifts, showed not the slightest disposition to lean upon him as a friend or to seek his political guidance. It was Harrison, not Blaine, who outlined the policy of the incoming Administration. There is no indication that he consulted Blaine in the choice of his Cabinet, notwithstanding Bristow's suspicion that Blaine and Elkins had "inveigled" him into the selection of Windom for the Treasury. In fact, Blaine later confessed, rather plaintively, to friends seeking appointments that he had little influence with the President in such matters. The plain truth is that, in spite of their outwardly courteous and cordial relations with each other, the two men were congenitally antipathetic—

---

[1] Blaine to Garfield, Dec. 20, 1880, in letter accepting the Cabinet post.

the one undemonstrative, severe, legal minded and concerned with principles rather than with personalities; the other genial, sympathetic, born with the power of rousing men's emotions of patriotism, partisanship and prejudice, of personal devotion and resentment.

On the Fourth of March, 1889, Harrison took the oath of office at the hands of the new Chief Justice of the Supreme Court, Melville W. Fuller, and delivered his inaugural address in a pouring rain driven by gusts of wind which made his words inaudible except to the front fringe of the shivering crowd that filled the plaza at the eastern side of the Capitol.[1] Grover Cleveland obligingly held a large umbrella over his successor's head during the ceremony. It would be interesting to know what thoughts were passing through Blaine's head as he listened to the protracted and rather commonplace inaugural address of his new chief. He was older now, much older in body than the addition of eight years of life would seem to warrant. His illness abroad, in spite of his apparently complete recovery, had left its mark upon him. Ex-Secretary Bayard, writing to Schurz a few days after the inauguration, said: "*Entre nous,* having seen Blaine for the first time in seven years, I am compelled to think him a very enfeebled man." That the phrase was exaggerated, Blaine's immense labor in the State Department for the next three years was to prove. Nevertheless, we can see from many an incident of those years how heavy a toll that work was taking from a spirit hampered by official formality and harassed by private sorrows.

[1] Old men whose memory went back a half a century could recall that Harrison's grandfather, on a similarly inclement inauguration day, had caught the chill which hastened his death a few weeks later. And the reader who is interested in coincidences, or inclined to the belief in omens, may be reminded that the three Republican Presidents since Lincoln who have failed to be reëlected after a renomination (Harrison in 1892, Taft in 1912 and Hoover in 1932) were all inaugurated in the midst of a storm.

Chapter XV   *"A Spirited Foreign Policy"* (*1889–1892*)

AMERICAN historians have generally signalized the Spanish-American War as the event which started our republic on what President McKinley called "the new and untried paths" of world power. Doubtless this judgment is justified in the main by such important consequences of the war as the acquisition of the Philippine Islands and Puerto Rico, the annexation of Hawaii, the quasi protectorate over Cuba, our participation in the first Hague Conference and our championship of the open door policy in China. The United States at the turn of the century became the predominant power in the Caribbean and a major power in the Pacific. Nevertheless, this expansion was neither so sudden nor so unheralded as it is often represented. It was less a transformation than an evolution. The very phrase "manifest destiny," which was commonly used to "rationalize" the new imperialism, implied the fulfilment of a process rather than the departure from a principle. A steady expansion across the Alleghenies, across the Mississippi, across the Rockies, had been the dominant theme of the "Epic of America" since the founding of the colonies. Even before the Western frontier had disappeared (as acknowledged in the census of 1890) or the natural products of the country had become so abundant as to demand distant markets for their overflow, prophetic minds like William H. Seward and James J. Hill were calculating the effects of the contact of the United States with the lands beyond the Pacific.

We have already seen how determined Blaine was during his first brief incumbency of the State Department to circumvent any designs of British intervention in the Sandwich Islands and to "make and keep Hawaii a part of the American system." [1] The cordiality with which the Continental European powers, and eventually Great Britain, recognized the supremacy of American interests in Hawaii and came to regard our reciprocity treaty of 1875 with the islands as a virtual protectorate removed any diplomatic obstacle to our annexation of Hawaii in case the sentiment there and in the United States should favor such a move. [2]

[1] See above, pp. 203–205.
[2] Professor John Bassett Moore writes: "H. A. P. Carter, for many years the highly esteemed Minister of Hawaii at Washington, more than once related to me the incidents

Indeed, the policy of the Harrison Administration pointed toward annexation. In June, 1889, the President appointed J. L. Stevens of Maine, an old friend of Blaine and a former editor of the Kennebec *Journal,* as Minister to Hawaii. Stevens encouraged the annexationist sentiment among the old missionary families and the sugar planters of the islands, and brought such pressure to bear as he could—with the aid of a United States war vessel in the harbor of Honolulu—upon the Hawaiian king and court.

The McKinley tariff of 1890, by admitting Cuban sugar to the United States free of duty and giving the American sugar growers a countervailing bounty of two cents a pound, threatened to ruin the Hawaiian planters. Moreover, in their zeal for the protection of the products of the American factories and farms, the framers of the McKinley Act had levied duties on commodities which were included in the reciprocity treaty with Hawaii, "without," as the President confessed in his message to Congress of December 1, 1890, "indicating the necessary exceptions in favor of that Kingdom." The President was "bound to assume" that such inconsistency was "wholly unintentional" and hoped that Congress would "repair what otherwise might seem to be a breach of good faith on the part of this Government." [1] Secretary Blaine also wrote to Mr. Carter, the Hawaiian Minister at Washington, on February 10, 1891, of the hope of relieving Hawaii from the injurious effects of the McKinley Act.

While dampening such sentiment as there was at the Hawaiian court in the autumn of 1889 for becoming a dependency of the United States, this incident of the tariff only spurred the American element in the islands to plot the more diligently for annexation. And when King Kalakaua died at San Francisco, on a visit to the United States in 1891, leaving the throne to his despotic anti-American sister Lilioukalani, events moved to a revolt in the islands, which overthrew the Queen in January, 1893, and established a provisional government under the protection of marines landed from the United States cruiser *Boston,* at the request of Minister Stevens.

Blaine's death came in the same month as the Hawaiian revolt. He

of a night which, while on a special mission to Berlin, he spent by invitation at Friedrichsruhe, where Bismarck, as he smoked his big pipe, assured him that Germany would not stand in the way of the closest relations between Hawaii and the United States." G. H. Ryden, *The Foreign Policy of the United States in Relation to Samoa,* Introduction, p. xiii.

[1] J. D. Richardson, *Messages and Papers of the Presidents,* Vol. IX, p. 110.

had been out of office since the previous summer, and consequently had no part in the events which followed—the annexation treaty submitted to the Senate by Harrison and withdrawn by Cleveland, the five year interim of the provisional government in Hawaii, and finally the quiet annexation of the islands by the United States during the Spanish-American War of 1898. Nevertheless, there is no doubt that this was a consummation which he had devoutly wished. He had upheld Stevens, had approved the presence of the marines at Honolulu, and had advised the President to "take" (the word reminds us of Theodore Roosevelt and Panama) Hawaii when the proper moment should come. "I think there are only three places that are of value enough to be taken," he wrote to the President from Bar Harbor on August 10, 1891; "one is Hawaii and the others are Cuba and Porto Rico. Cuba and Porto Rico are not imminent and will not be for a generation (!). Hawaii may come up for decision at any unexpected hour, and I hope we shall be prepared to decide it in the affirmative." [1] But the Hawaiian pear, to use Stevens' simile of February, 1893, was not fully ripe to pluck before Blaine left office.

Two other problems of the Pacific were among the unfinished business of the State Department when Blaine resumed his duties as Secretary, in March, 1889. The one arose out of our diplomatic relations with Great Britain and Germany concerning the little group of the Samoan Islands lying some twenty-two hundred miles to the southwest of Hawaii; the other was a controversy with Great Britain over the right of Canadian vessels to hunt seals in the waters of Bering Sea.

In the earliest decades of the nineteenth century American interests in the Samoan (or Navigators') Islands had been limited to securing from the native chieftains fair treatment and protection for the crews of our whaling vessels in the southern Pacific, when stress of weather or shortage of food or water might force them to enter inside the coral reefs which lined the shores of Upolu and Tutuila. We sent no missionaries to the islands, as the English did, nor did we establish any centers there for the South Sea trade, like the great Hamburg firm of Godeffroy and Sons of Apia, founded in 1857. With the completion of the transcontinental railroad, however, in 1869, and the establishment two years later of the Webb steamship line between San Francisco and Australia, *via* Hawaii, the Samoan Islands, lying midway of the five-

[1] Gail Hamilton, *Biography of James G. Blaine,* p. 692.

thousand mile run between Honolulu and Sydney, began to acquire importance in American eyes. In the midsummer of 1871 Mr. Webb sent an agent, Captain Wakeman, to the islands to ascertain what prospects there were for establishing a port of call and commercial relations. Wakeman's report was highly encouraging. He not only found at Pago-Pago on the island of Tutuila "the most perfectly land-locked harbor in the Pacific Ocean," and noted the large business which the Hamburg firm was doing with the natives at Apia (Upolu), but he even reported that the Europeans in Upolu seemed to be "all in favor of having American law established over the islands." [1] In this judgment Wakeman was wrong, for there is evidence that Theodore Weber, who was both German consul general and agent for the Godeffroy firm at Apia, was urging upon Berlin the idea of an eventual protectorate over the Samoan Islands.

Wakeman was followed in 1872 by Commander Richard W. Meade of the United States vessel *Narragansett,* who made a "treaty" with the Samoan chieftain at Pago-Pago, securing to the United States the exclusive privilege of establishing a naval station in the harbor, in return for "the friendship and protection of the great Government of the United States." [2] Commander Meade furthermore drew up a set of commercial regulations for the port of Pago-Pago and organized a "confederacy" of the chiefs of Tutuila, under an improvised Samoan flag, who pledged themselves to maintain peace with one another and obey the regulations. This extraordinary procedure of the Commander's was undertaken not only without any authorization from Washington, but even without the knowledge of his naval superior, Rear Admiral Winslow, who was in command of the Pacific fleet. It seems to have been dictated by Henry A. Pierce, our Minister in Hawaii, who wrote to Meade on January 19, 1872: "In view of the future domination of the United States in the North and South Pacific Ocean, it is very important that the Navigator Islands should be under American control, ruling through the native authorities. . . . You will no doubt take such action there for the protection of American interests as may seem to you just and proper." [3]

In spite of its irregularity Commander Meade's course had the approval not only of Secretary of the Navy Robeson and Secretary of

---

[1] G. H. Ryden, *The Foreign Policy of the United States in Relation to Samoa,* p. 51.
[2] *Ibid.,* pp. 6, 7.
[3] *Ibid.,* p. 60.

State Fish, but also of President Grant, who sent the treaty with the Samoan chieftains to the Senate on May 22, 1872, for ratification. The treaty was duly referred to the Committee on Foreign Relations and was never reported out to the Senate for a vote, but that did not hinder President Grant from encouraging the growth of American influence in Samoa. He sent an able adventurer, Colonel A. B. Steinberger, to the islands as a special agent, ostensibly to report on their physiography, their population, their products and their harbors. The Colonel was reminded that his mission was in no sense a diplomatic one and was instructed "to avoid conversations, official or otherwise, with any persons (i.e. the British or German consul) respecting the relations between this and any other country." [1] Steinberger, however, had no idea of playing the rôle of an "unofficial observer." He ingratiated himself with the native chiefs, promulgated a code of laws, won the support of most of the Europeans in the islands, became the "prime minister" of the new King Malietoa—in short, seemed to be well on his way to becoming a dictator in Samoa, when he was arrested by our consul at Apia and deported in a British ship to the Fiji Islands.

The Steinberger incident, added to the chronic warfare between the native chiefs and the rivalries between the British, German and American consuls (the *Furor consularis,* as Lord Salisbury called it), made necessary an official statement of the policy of the United States toward the islands. At the instigation of the American consul at Apia, King Malietoa's "Secretary of State," a giant chief who had been educated by the English missionaries, came to Washington in the autumn of 1877, was received by President Hayes at the White House, and negotiated a treaty between the Samoan Islands and the United States, which was ratified by the Senate the following February. We might have set up a protectorate over the islands, or even annexed them outright in 1878, because Bismarck was not yet interested in colonial expansion and Salisbury was indifferent to the pleas of the New Zealanders to take Samoa into the British sphere of influence. Or we might have refused to assume any responsibility for the political status of Samoa, confining the negotiations to the protection of the lives, the property and the commercial privileges of Americans residing there. But we took neither of these logical courses. We committed ourselves to responsibility without power, and in return for the confirmation of the concession at Pago-

[1] G. H. Ryden, *op. cit.,* p. 88.

Pago (already ours without dispute) we guaranteed the autonomy of the native Samoan government—a synonym for tribal anarchy. This commitment, to be sure, blocked any suspected project of Germany or Great Britain to annex the Samoan Islands, but it also prevented the United States from effective coöperation with those powers in imposing order upon the warring factions. As the confusion increased from year to year, with the wars of rival "kings" and "vice-kings," supported by rival consuls, commercial agents, land grabbers and concessionaries, an attempt was made at a conference of Secretary of State Bayard with the British and German Ministers at Washington, in the summer of 1877, to devise an efficient government for Samoa. Von Albersleben, arguing that political control should be given to the power with the largest landed and commercial interests in the islands, proposed a German protectorate. Sackville-West supported his German colleague. But Bayard, standing firm on the treaty of 1878, insisted on preserving the autonomy of the islands. The conference adjourned *sine die* on July 26.

The adjournment was with the understanding that the *status quo* in Samoa should not be disturbed, but soon afterward the German consul, Becker, entered on a course of unwarranted aggression. He deposed Malietoa and deported him to the Cameroons, setting up his rival Tamasese as king. He overthrew the tripartite government of the city of Apia, established in 1879, and raised the German flag over the government building. Civil war was revived. Tamasese was driven out by the rebel chief Mataafa, whose warriors inflicted a humiliating defeat, from ambush, upon the German marines (December 18, 1888). Whereupon Becker's successor, Dr. Knapp, ordered the shelling of the native villages, declared martial law and ordered Mataafa to turn over to him the administration of Samoa. These aggressive measures were not approved by Prince Bismarck. He thought it deplorable that "affairs in those remote and unimportant islands should disturb the relations between the United States and Germany which were elsewhere so friendly." And he informed our Minister, Pendleton, in Berlin that consul Knapp had been rebuked and that his proclamations would be withdrawn.[1]

Meanwhile the indiscriminate depredations of the civil war were exposing the lives and property of the Americans in the islands to the

[1] George H. Pendleton to Bayard, Feb. 2, 1889.

gravest danger. Our Senate and House passed resolutions requesting the President to submit the entire Samoan correspondence. One British, three German and three American war vessels were in the harbor of Apia in the early weeks of 1889, all watching one another with jealous tension, ready at a provocative gesture to clear their decks for action. On January 15, 1889, President Cleveland notified Congress of the "delicate and critical situation" in Samoa. Acting within the restraints which the Constitution placed on the executive power, he had "insisted that the autonomy and independence of Samoa should be scrupulously preserved"; but now he submitted the subject to "the wider discretion" of Congress.[1] Five days later a note was forwarded to the United States from the foreign office in Berlin, proposing a renewal of the Washington conference of 1887. On February 5, Secretary Bayard replied that the President fully shared in the desire expressed by the Prince Chancellor "to bring the blessings of peace and order to the remote and feeble community of semicivilized people inhabiting the islands of Samoa," and that the United States would "at once take steps to be represented at such a meeting in Berlin." [2]

A month later Harrison succeeded Cleveland in the White House, and it fell to Blaine, who had been assiduously studying the Samoan correspondence,[3] to take the diplomatic negotiations out of Bayard's hands, much to Bayard's chagrin, who wrote to Carl Schurz on February 28: *"Entre nous,* I have been crippled a good deal by poor Pendleton's invalid condition, and but for that I believe the Berlin conference *in re* Samoa would have been now progressing or even probably the matter settled. As it is, Harrison (Blaine! alas!) must appoint the American envoys; but I do not see how they can fail to follow the lines of the protocol as stated by me." [4]

There had been much criticism of Bayard's "weak-kneed" policy in regard to Samoa by the Republican press and orators in the presidential campaign of 1888—a criticism based upon a very imperfect knowledge

[1] J. D. Richardson, *Messages and Papers of the Presidents,* Vol. VIII, p. 804.

[2] G. H. Ryden, *The Foreign Policy of the United States in Relation to Samoa,* pp. 426–7.

[3] On Feb. 10, Mrs. Blaine wrote to her daughter Margaret: "Now your Father is reading aloud Samoa to Walker, and my thoughts diverge to Malietoa"; and the next day to her son James: "Your Father is now looking up Samoa on the map. It would be worth your while, if you have not already done so to read up on Samoa. I thrill when I think of the part which your Father may play in the future of this country." *The Letters of Mrs. James G. Blaine,* Vol. II, pp. 243, 245.

[4] *Correspondence and Political Papers of Carl Schurz,* ed. Frederic Bancroft, Vol. V, pp. 16, 17.

of his actual dispatches, and prompted, of course, by partisan politics. As a matter of fact, when Blaine gave his instructions to our delegates to the Berlin conference (John A. Kasson, W. W. Phelps and George H. Bates) on April 11, 1889, reviewing the action of the German consuls at Apia and insisting that no power should be allowed to "assume a position which might curtail the rights of the United States under the treaty of 1878," he acknowledged that this position had been defended by Secretary Bayard "with great acuteness and force," and that Bayard's remonstrances had "the entire approval of the President (Harrison)." [1]

Yet, there was a marked heightening of tone in Blaine's language: "Nor can the Government of the United States forget what we are satisfied the other treaty powers (we had no treaty with either Germany or Great Britain in regard to Samoa!) will cordially recognize—that our interest in the Pacific is steadily increasing, that our commerce with the East is developing rapidly (it was insignificant in 1889, as compared with Germany's and Great Britain's!), and that the certainty of an early opening of an isthmian transit from the Atlantic to the Pacific under American protection (it was twenty-five years before the Panama Canal was opened!) must create changes in which no power can be so directly or more directly interested than the United States; and that in any questions involving present or future relations in the Pacific this Government cannot accept even temporary subordination, and must regard it as inconsistent with that international consideration and dignity to which the United States by continental position and expanding interest must always be entitled." [2] The paragraph is an epitome of Blaine's foreign policy. The emphasis is shifted from concern for the autonomy and independence of Samoa to the proclamation of the growing power and prestige of the United States.

Two days after President Harrison had appointed the American delegates to the Berlin conference, an event happened in Samoa which helped to prepare the way for an amicable settlement between the three great powers by removing any possibility of a clash between their war vessels in the harbor of Apia. On March 16 a terrific hurricane struck the harbor, submerging or driving upon the reefs all the German and American ships. The British cruiser *Calliope* alone escaped destruction by crowding on steam until her boilers were red hot and battling her

---

[1] *Kasson Papers*, Department of State, p. 24.
[2] *Ibid.*, pp. 29–30.

way out to deep water amid cheers from the American sailors on the
deck of Admiral Kimberley's doomed and drifting *Trenton*. Forty-six
men and four officers (including Captain Schoonmaker of our *Vandalia*)
were drowned, and the casualty list would have been far longer but for
the heroic work of the natives in rescuing the exhausted men from the
angry waters.[1]

Under the sobering influence of this "act of God" the conference met
at Berlin on April 29, and, after six weeks' labor, devised a scheme for
the tripartite control of Samoa—the so-called Condominium. King
Malietoa was restored to the throne, but the administration of the government was complicated by the conflicting authorities of the consuls,
a council with a foreign president and a chief justice appointed by the
King of Norway and Sweden. The Condominium was a failure from the
start, and after ten years of constant wrangling it was terminated. The
Samoan Islands were then divided, Tutuila and the smaller islands to
the east going to the United States and Upolu and Savaii to Germany,
while Great Britain was satisfied with concessions in Africa.[2] By ratifying the Condominium of 1889, the United States departed from its traditional policy of shunning "entangling alliances" and entered into a
political pact with European powers for the first time since the termination in 1800 of the Franco-American Treaty of 1778. It was the small
beginning, the thin entering wedge of imperialism. "The significance of
the Samoan incident," wrote John Bassett Moore in 1912, "lies not in
the mere division of territory, but in the disposition shown by the
United States, long before the acquisition of the Philippines, to go to
any length in asserting a claim to take part in the determination of a
group of islands thousands of miles away, in which American commercial
interests were so slight as to be scarcely appreciable." [3]

Blaine's diplomacy in the Samoan affair is revealed in detail in the
Kasson Papers and treated exhaustively and objectively in Professor
G. H. Ryden's recent (1933) volume on *The Foreign Policy of the
United States in Relation to Samoa*. The official correspondence gives
no support to the story, started by Gail Hamilton and repeated by Harry

[1] For a vivid description of the hurricane see R. L. Stevenson's *A Footnote to History;
Eight Years of Trouble in Samoa*. Also Admiral L. A. Kimberley's "Samoa and the Hurri-
cane of March 1889" in the *Papers of the Military Historical Society of Massachusetts*,
Vol. XVI.

[2] We still hold American Samoa as a colony. German Samoa was made a mandate
of New Zealand by the Treaty of Versailles at the close of the World War.

[3] J. B. Moore, *Four Phases of American Development: Federalism, Democracy, Imperialism, Expansion,*" p. 187.

T. Peck, Charles Edward Russell and others, that Blaine reversed the weak and timid policy of Bayard, who had allowed Germany to "elbow the United States out of its rights and concessions" in Samoa, and that he inspired the American commissioners at Berlin to stand firm and united for our demands, inflicting a humiliating defeat on Prince Bismarck by compelling Germany to "back down" and concede us every point. Peck drew on his lively imagination to present a picture of the German Chancellor bullying the conference, "agitating his huge bulk, raging, frowning portentously," and so frightening the American envoys that they warned Blaine of the dangerous situation. Whereupon Blaine "stiffened their backbone" by "flashing back the terse reply: 'The Chancellor's irritability is no measure of American rights!' " [1] This is pure myth. It misrepresents Blaine's position entirely. The Chancellor took no part at all in the meetings of the conference. It was his son, Count Herbert Bismarck who was the presiding officer, and whose conduct at every point was so courteous and conciliatory as to elicit hearty thanks from Mr. Kasson and the other delegates at the closing session. Moreover, the Chancellor himself had proposed the Berlin conference six weeks before Blaine came into office, and had instructed the German Minister at Washington to say that the imperial government had no intention of putting in question the independence of the Samoan Islands, but wished only to create a condition there which should ensure the security of the lives and property of the foreign inhabitants. And two days before the conference opened Count Herbert *voluntarily* withdrew the German claim to a protectorate over the islands, which had been urged by Von Albersleben at Washington in 1887, thereby endorsing Bayard's opposition to the control of Samoa by any one of the interested powers. In short, it was Bayard's diplomacy that was crowned with success at Berlin; and none of the commissioners contributed more to that success than Count Bismarck.

There was far more friction between Kasson and his American colleagues than there was between the American and the German commissioners. In fact, Blaine had on more than one occasion to rebuke our envoys for their mutual jealousies and dissensions. He himself had little to suggest in the way of a positive program, but he frequently interposed objections which were prompted by the fixed idea that Germany and Great Britain were determined to outwit our commissioners and

---

[1] Harry Thurston Peck, *Twenty Years of the Republic,* p. 188.

impair our rights. On two occasions he "canceled" and "withdrew" instructions, at the request of Kasson, which, if insisted upon, would have prevented an amicable settlement. In spite of the praise heaped upon Blaine for his vigorous defense of American rights in the Samoan crisis, it is impossible to find in the General Act of Berlin any evidence of constructive diplomacy on his part or of any glorious victory over the "irritable" German Chancellor.[1]

The second, and more serious, problem of the Pacific which confronted Blaine when he reëntered the State Department was the controversy with Great Britain over the fur seal fisheries in Bering Sea. The large body of water lying between Alaska and Kamchatka and screened from the main Pacific to the south by the graceful curve of the Aleutian Islands was discovered for Russia by the Danish navigator Vitus Bering in the eighteenth century, and until the cession of Alaska to the United States in 1867 it remained a Russian lake, washing the shores of the Czar's dominions on every side. A great herd of fur bearing seals resorted each spring to the Pribilof Islands in Bering Sea to bear and rear their young; and in the autumn slipped through the passages of the Aleutian chain to the warmer waters of the Pacific. By a Ukase of 1821 the Czar warned all foreign vessels not to approach within one hundred Italian miles of the Russian shore of the north Pacific, so making Bering Sea a *mare clausum* and the taking of seals therein a Russian monopoly.

When the United States acquired Alaska "and the waters thereof" from Russia, Congress took over the monopoly, giving a twenty year lease to the Alaska Commercial Company for the sole privilege of hunting seals on the Pribilof Islands (July 1, 1870). Only the male "bachelor" seals between two and four years old were allowed to be taken, lest the herd be depleted. But the rapid advance in the price of

---

[1] The legend of Blaine's rebuke to the "irritable" Chancellor is doubtless based on the following facts. In early June, when the conference had finished its work except for a minor detail, the American commissioners asked permission to sign the Act in order that they might escape from the intolerable heat of the city. Blaine refused the request on the ground that the President had not been able to determine from the dispatches of our commissioners how far his instructions had been followed out. Whereupon, the commissioners cabled him that the delay was causing irritation among their German and English colleagues. Blaine's reply, containing some objections to the Act and a rebuke to the commissioners for not keeping him sufficiently informed of the "successive steps" in its formulation, closed with the sentence: "Irritability on the part of your English and German associates is not a determining factor with the Government of the United States." (G. H. Ryden, *The Foreign Policy of the United States in Relation to Samoa,* p. 508.) The irritability actually lay with the American commissioners.

sealskins (from \$2.50 in 1868 to \$30.00 in 1890) attracted the "boot-leggers," who sailed into Bering Sea to shoot the seals as they roamed the waters around the islands for food, or who hovered about the Aleutian exits to kill the seals as they swam through on their southern migration. This pelagic, or deep-sea, sealing threatened the extinction of the herd because no distinction could be made between male and female, old and young. Continued protests from the Alaska Commercial Company against the increasing number of Canadian vessels engaging in this prohibited industry finally led our government to take drastic measures. In August, 1886, our revenue cutter *Corwin,* under orders from Cleveland's Secretary of the Treasury, Daniel Manning, seized three Canadian schooners in Bering Sea and took them to Sitka, where Judge Dawson of the district court of Alaska found their masters guilty of breaking the laws of the United States and condemned the vessels to be sold. As the vessels were all operating outside the three mile limit, their seizure could not be justified in international law except on the ground that Bering Sea was a *mare clausum,* whose waters were as completely under the jurisdiction of the United States as were those of Chesapeake Bay.

The British Minister at Washington, Sir Lionel Sackville-West, straightway protested against the action of the American government, and a controversy was started which showed no signs of abatement during the remainder of Cleveland's term. Further seizures were made in 1887, and new protests entered by Sir Lionel. An attempt was made by Secretary Bayard to get a joint agreement to suspend seal hunting from April 1 to November 1, 1888, but Lord Salisbury reversed his first favorable attitude to the suggestion because of the pressure from the Canadian Tories, whom he was eager to keep in office and who were incensed at the rejection of the Canadian fisheries treaty of February 15, 1888, by the United States Senate.[1] Cleveland's Minister to London, E. J. Phelps, kept urging upon the Administration to "put an end to the pursuit of the seal by Canadian ships, which is unjustifiable and illegitimate," but Secretary Bayard still clung to the hope of settling the dispute by an international agreement. Finally, under pressure from the lobby of the Alaska Fur Company, Congress passed a bill, on March 2, 1889, defining our jurisdiction over Alaska to "include and apply to all the dominion of the United States in the

[1] See above, p. 354.

waters of Bering Sea," and authorized the President to issue an annual proclamation warning against the violation of the law and "to have said waters patrolled and infractors seized." Such was the situation when Blaine entered the State Department.

At first the new Secretary tried to arrange a plan with Baron Rosen, in charge of the Russian legation at Washington, for the joint policing of the seal fisheries by Russia and the United States, which were the only countries owning the breeding places of the herds. The two governments were to agree to apply to the vessels of all nations the same regulations which they imposed on their own for the protection of the seals, and they hoped that this humane course, quite irrespective of any claim to maritime jurisdiction in Bering Sea, would secure the recognition of all friendly nations. After the Samoan question had been adjusted at the Berlin conference, Blaine left Washington for his summer cottage at Bar Harbor, and his secretary Louis A. Dent followed a little later, bringing the final draft of the agreement with Baron Rosen.[1] A little later still the crestfallen Baron arrived at Bar Harbor with the news that his government refused to approve the pact. The Foreign Minister, de Giers, was having trouble with Great Britain over problems of the Near East and Central Asia, and was unwilling to complicate the situation by any hint of joint action with the United States to coerce or cajole Great Britain in the matter of the seal fisheries. Blaine was therefore left to deal directly with Lord Salisbury on the subject.

As ex-Secretary John W. Foster (Blaine's successor) pointed out in an article in the *North American Review* of December, 1895, there were three courses open to the Harrison Administration. The United States might drop the pretensions to jurisdiction over the "waters of Alaska," inherited either by treaty or by prescription from Russia, and allow pelagic sealing to continue undisturbed. This would have meant the rescinding of the Act of Congress of March 2, 1889, the abandonment of the claims sustained for three years by Secretary Bayard, and the repudiation of the action of our revenue cutters and our Alaskan court in the seizure and condemnation of the Canadian vessels—obviously a course of obsequiousness to Great Britain which Blaine would have been the last man in the country to endorse. Or we might

---

[1] Mrs. Alice Felt Tyler in her *The Foreign Policy of James G. Blaine,* Appendix II, published for the first time copies of the drafts of the Blaine-Rosen agreement from the *Baron Rosen Papers* in the archives of our State Department.

follow Mr. Phelps' advice to continue defiantly to seize and condemn vessels engaged in pelagic sealing, let the results be what they might. He was certain that "such a resolute stand" would "at once put an end to the mischief complained of." But Blaine was no more willing than Bayard to recommend a course which would have led inevitably to a crisis, and perhaps to armed conflict, with Great Britain. The third and sensible way out of the dispute was the way of arbitration. But, again, Blaine was unwilling to submit the matter to a tribunal until he had fought a diplomatic battle of over two years in the vain attempt to convince Lord Salisbury of the justice of the American claims.

On August 24, 1889, Edwardes, the British Chargé d'Affairs at Washington, notified Blaine that, contrary to Bayard's assurances the summer before, Canadian vessels were being molested in Bering Sea; and five weeks later, when the seizure of the *Black Diamond* and the *Triumph* was confirmed, Lord Salisbury entered a sharp protest. Sir Julian Pauncefote, the new British Minister at Washington, had a long conference with Blaine on November 1, which served only to bring out the latter's insistence that it was the right and duty of the United States, in the interest of "good morals" (*boni mores*), to put an end to the destructive pelagic sealing. The pressure of Sir John Mac-Donald's Tory government in Canada was being constantly exerted upon the foreign office in London to defend the rights of the Canadian sealers; and when Sir John was consulted by Lord Salisbury on the question of a commission to settle the dispute, he laid down several conditions as preliminary demands: the United States must forego any claims to Bering Sea as a *mare clausum;* Canada must be represented on the commission and must approve its findings; compensation must be made for the vessels seized. We have already had sufficient evidence of Blaine's inveterate hostility to Canada (on the Reciprocity Treaty of 1854, the Fortune Bay incident of 1877, the Halifax Award of 1878, and the general denial of American fishing rights under the Washington Treaty of 1871) to show how little Sir John's demands were likely to smooth the way for a peaceful settlement. Lord Salisbury wisely refused to uphold the extreme Canadian pretensions, and in his instructions of January 28, 1890, to Sir Julian, he approved of a tripartite negotiation between Great Britain, the United States and Russia at Washington, subject only to the conditions that no more vessels be seized and that the claims for those already seized should be settled by an agreement between Great Britain and the United States.

Meanwhile Blaine and Lord Salisbury had entered upon what proved to be a protracted and rather tedious diplomatic wrangle to vindicate their respective claims. In a long note of January 22, 1890, Blaine based his argument not on a legal claim to jurisdiction over Bering Sea as a *mare clausum,* but on the broader grounds of international good morals. Pelagic sealing was a practice *contra bonos mores,* no matter what the nationality of the vessels engaged in it might be, and was consequently detrimental to the interests of Great Britain as well as to those of the United States. The law of the sea might in theory confer the right to capture wild animals (*ferae naturae*) beyond the three mile limit, but the law of the sea was not lawlessness. Where it conflicted with obvious international good order, as notably in the case of piracy, it must yield to the higher law. Blaine then proceeded to the argument from prescriptive rights—a more uncertain ground. Under Russian control, until our purchase of Alaska in 1867, and thereafter under American control for a score of years, the sealing in Bering Sea had been conducted under regulations respected by the world at large. It had been profitable to all parties connected with it: to the American government, to the Alaskan Company, to the native Aleuts and even to "a large body of English laborers who had constant employment and received good wages." Why, he asked, was this satisfactory status suddenly disturbed. "Whence did the ships of Canada derive the right to do in 1886 that which they had refrained from doing for more than ninety years?" "By what reasoning did Her Majesty's Government conclude that an act may be committed with impunity against the rights of the United States which had never been attempted against the same rights when held by the Russian Empire?" And finally Blaine resorted to the *tu quoque* argument. Great Britain was not deterred by the three mile limit from exercising control over the pearl fisheries of Ceylon, which extended more than twenty miles from the shores of the island; nor would she, he was sure, permit destructive methods of fishing on the Grand Banks of Newfoundland, even though such "vicious acts" were committed more than three miles from the shore. In his outspoken zeal Blaine even came dangerously near to accusing the British Foreign Office of a blunted moral sense: "One step beyond that which Her Majesty's Government has taken in this controversy," he concluded, "and piracy finds its justification." [1]

Blaine's urgent argument had no more effect on Lord Salisbury than the plea of a brilliant prosecuting attorney on a staid judge. In language none the less forceful because of its impeccable diplomatic courtesy, the noble Lord, on May 22, contested every one of Blaine's arguments. No nation in times of peace could prescribe regulations under which it was lawful to seize the vessels of a friendly nation on the high seas. There was no property right in wild animals until they were actually reduced to possession, and hence no offense to good morals in capturing seals beyond the three mile limit. As to the contention that Russia had acquired and passed on to the United States a prescriptive right to control the Bering Sea fisheries, Salisbury not only cited numerous early protests on the part of the United States as well as Great Britain against the Russian assumption, but submitted a list of British vessels which had been engaged in pelagic sealing in Bering Sea ever since the acquisition of Alaska by the United States. He agreed with Blaine that the nations should concede to the United States the same rights in the lands and waters of Alaska that they had conceded to the Russian Empire; but denied that the nations, the United States included, had ever conceded to the Russian Empire "exclusive privileges in the non-territorial waters of Bering Sea." In a further note of June 14, in view of a confirmed report that the United States were about to send more revenue cutters to enforce the President's proclamation against pelagic sealing, Lord Salisbury instructed Sir Julian to protest against the disturbance of any British vessels operating beyond the territorial waters of the United States and to declare that "Her British Majesty's government must hold the government of the United States responsible for the consequences which may ensue from acts which are contrary to the established principles of international law." This was the language of an ultimatum.

We cannot consider in detail the series of notes in which Blaine again and again returned to the attack on Salisbury's unyielding position.[2] It came down in the end to the question of whether Bering Sea was considered a part of the "Pacific Ocean" as that phrase was used in

---

[1] *United States Foreign Relations,* 1890, pp. 366 ff.

[2] In his message to Congress of July 23, 1890, President Harrison submitted a list of thirty-one notes exchanged on the subject since August 24, 1889, between Blaine, Edwardes, Lord Salisbury and Sir Julian Pauncefote. *Senate Executive Document,* No. 450, 51st Cong., 1st sess.

the treaties of 1824 and 1825 between the United States and Russia and Great Britain and Russia respectively. Blaine brought all the resources of his dialectic skill and his historical equipment to the defense of the negative, furnishing a vast array of maps, charts, protocols, newspaper excerpts and records of the Alaska Fur Company to prove his contention; and convicting Lord Salisbury of garbling a dispatch sent by John Quincy Adams to our Minister in St. Petersburg in 1823, by omitting the very phrase which established the Russian claim to exclusive jurisdiction over Bering Sea. The words in question were: "which (jurisdictions) so far as Russia's rights are concerned, are confined to certain islands north of the 55th degree of latitude and have no existence on the continent of America." But, however indefensible Lord Salisbury's omission of those words was, it is doubtful whether they sustain Blaine's claims. They could do so only on the interpretation that the "certain Islands" (i.e. the Aleutian Islands) which run to the south of Bering Sea, really make that sea a separate body of water from the Pacific Ocean. That was exactly the point in dispute.

During the season of 1890 there were no more seizures of vessels; [1] and on June 15, 1891, a *modus vivendi* was agreed upon, by which both governments prohibited the killing of seals until the following May and sanctioned the seizure by either British or American naval officers of any vessel offending against this prohibition "in the said waters of Bering Sea outside of the territorial limits of the United States." Great Britain was also to be allowed to send commissioners to the Pribilof Islands to study the conditions of the sealing industry, with a view to presenting the British case before arbitrators. Blaine and Sir Julian eventually arrived at an agreement to submit the dispute to arbitration, and a treaty to that effect was signed at Washington on February 29, 1892, and ratified by the Senate a month later. The tribunal of seven members (two to be appointed by the President of the United States, two by Her Britannic Majesty, and one each by the President of the French Republic, the King of Italy and the King of

---

[1] Mr. Tupper, the high commissioner of Canada in London, claims in his *Recollections of Sixty Years* (p. 209) that he frightened Blaine into this concession. But Blaine's letter to Harrison of March 6, 1891, shows that he had no intention of provoking hostilities: "If we get up a war cry and send vessels to Bering Sea, it will reëlect Lord Salisbury . . . not a man in a million believes that we should ultimately have war." Quoted in Gail Hamilton, *Biography of James G. Blaine*, p. 671.

Norway and Sweden) was to meet in Paris. The important questions to be decided were as follows:

1. What exclusive jurisdiction did Russia assert and exercise in Bering Sea prior to the cession of Alaska?
2. How far were these claims as to the seal fisheries recognized and conceded by Great Britain?
3. Was Bering Sea included in the Pacific Ocean, as that term was used in the Treaty of 1825 between Russia and Great Britain?
4. Did not Russia's former right of jurisdiction in that part of Bering Sea within the Alaskan treaty line of 1867 pass unimpaired to the United States under that treaty?
5. Had, therefore, the United States the right to protect the seals frequenting the Pribilof Islands when such seals were found outside the ordinary three mile limit?

Blaine had no part in the work of the tribunal, for he had resigned from the Cabinet three months after the arbitration treaty was signed, and died two months before the tribunal met at Paris on March 23, 1893.

That tribunal rejected the claims of the United States on every count, and its decision was hailed by Blaine's enemies as a proof of the complete failure of his major diplomatic negotiation. The New York *Nation* remarked shortly after the award in August, 1893, that the arbitrators had "declared Mr. James G. Blaine's history to be fiction; his geography, fancy; his international law, a whim." But is this summary indictment of the dead statesman's diplomacy fair? Blaine did not precipitate the controversy with Great Britain over Bering Sea; he inherited it. It was in the Cleveland Administration that the seizures of Canadian sealing vessels began, and the judicial and legislative departments of our government supported the executive in its action; for the brief which the Federal judge at Sitka followed in condemning the vessels was prepared in Attorney General Garland's office at Washington, and the law of March 2, 1889, asserting the dominion of the United States in the waters of Bering Sea, was passed before Blaine came into office. Blaine himself did not wish to base his argument upon our exclusive jurisdiction over Bering Sea as a *mare clausum*. In a note to Sir Julian, December 17, 1890, he said: "The government has never claimed it; it expressly disavows it." [1] He sought

---

[1] *Foreign Relations of the United States*, 1890, p. 501.

rather to secure by international agreement the condemnation of the destructive pelagic sealing as *contra bonos mores*. When his efforts in this direction failed through the refusal of the Russian government to support Baron Rosen and the unwillingness of Lord Salisbury to offend the Tory government of Canada, there was nothing left for Blaine to do but to drop the matter entirely or fall back upon the position of Cleveland, Bayard and Garland. He may have urged this position in language at times more befitting the eristic editorial than the suave diplomatic note, but his method (which was inevitably *his* method) was, after all, less important than the cause in which it was employed. He fought for that cause with a vigor, a resourcefulness, a historical equipment and a logical astuteness which aroused the enthusiasm of his supporters and the reluctant admiration of his opponents.

Instead, therefore, of maintaining, as most of the historians of the Bering Sea incident do, that Blaine devoted his exceptional talents and knowledge to a bad cause, it would be more just to say that he was forced by public opinion and by circumstances over which he had no control to urge faulty arguments in behalf of a good cause. For it was the protection of the seal herds and not the dominion of the United States in Bering Sea that was the main concern of his diplomacy, and the tribunal, in spite of its rejection of his arguments, recognized the justice of his contention. It prescribed regulations for the protection of the seals, which were approved both by Act of Congress (April 15, 1894) and by British Orders in Council (April 18, 1894), to the effect that no seals were to be killed within a zone of sixty miles around the Pribilof Islands, there was to be a closed season against pelagic sealing from May 1 to November 1, the vessels were to operate under stringent licenses, and no explosives or firearms were to be used in hunting the seals.

These regulations by no means gave the full measure of protection to the seals which Blaine wished the United States to exercise under the fifth clause of the arbitration program: for neither was the sixty mile zone wide enough nor the three months of closed season long enough to remedy all the evils of pelagic sealing; but the regulations were as much of a concession as could be won in the face of the Canadian objections to any restraint at all upon the industry, and they were certainly a substantial vindication of Blaine's diplomacy. That the seal herd was not destroyed entirely, as it would have been if the indiscriminate killing begun in 1886 had been allowed to continue without hindrance, must be credited in large part to the vigor with which Blaine upheld the protests of Bayard and Phelps. With the handing of a treasury check for $473,151.26 to Sir Julian Pauncefote on June 16, 1898, in payment of the damages assessed against the United States for the seizures of British vessels in Bering Sea, the diplomatic incident was closed.

While Blaine was in the midst of his spirited correspondence with Lord Salisbury, an event occurred in New Orleans which seriously disturbed the relations between the United States and Italy. A desperate band of Italians, suspected of being affiliated with the Mafia, or "black hand," which flourished in Sicily and the fastnesses of the southern Apennines (until their banditry was crushed out by the strong hand of Mussolini in 1927), had organized a reign of terror in New Orleans. Their work of intimidation, extortion and assassination culminated in March, 1891, in the murder of D. C. Hennessy, the chief of police who had devoted himself with rare courage to hunting down the criminals. When the jury, either through threat or bribery, dealt gently with the accused, acquitting some and remanding others to a further trial, a group of several thousand indignant citizens broke into the jail in which eleven Italian prisoners were confined and lynched them all. The Italian Premier, Marquis Rudini, at once cabled to his Minister at Washington, Baron Fava, demanding the punishment of the ringleaders and an indemnity for the victims of the citizens mob.

Blaine was prompt with the assurance that our government would use all its power under the Constitution to protect foreign subjects residing in the United States. On March 15 he telegraphed Governor Nicholls of Louisiana (sending copies of his dispatches to Baron Fava and to our Minister, Horace Porter, at Rome), deploring the rash deed of the citizens who had dishonored their judicial tribunals by taking the law into their own hands, and urging the Governor to take steps to prevent any further mob violence and to see to it that the offenders were brought to a speedy trial.[1] Beyond this the government at Washington could not go: for the prosecution of crimes against persons or property fell within the jurisdiction of the State not the Federal courts.

Not content with what seemed to him, in his lack of knowledge of the dual character of sovereignty in the United States, an attempt to

[1] *Foreign Relations of the United States,* 1891, p. 667.

shift responsibility from the Federal government to the State of Louisiana, or thinking to strengthen his none too stable ministry by a display of patriotic firmness, Rudini pressed his demands to the point of a virtual ultimatum. On March 20 he cabled to Fava: "Necessary that United States give us official communication that the guilty of New Orleans massacres have been brought to justice." And four days later he insisted that if steps were not immediately taken to punish the murderers his government "would be under the painful necessity of recalling its Minister from a country where justice could not be obtained." The Marquis' ill-advised importunity drew from Blaine a sharp rebuke to the effect that the United States never had received and would not now receive orders from any foreign power, and that he could not change, much less violate, our institutions, whatever persons in Italy might think of them. Baron Fava was withdrawn from Washington on March 31 and Mr. Porter left Rome. The Italian press worked up a campaign of hostility to the United States, which found expression in heated mass meetings of denunciation and insults to American residents. There was even the absurd rumor of an Italian fleet being mobilized to descend upon New Orleans.

But Rudini, realizing that he had carried his bluff too far, altered his tone. Instead of demanding that the lynchers be "punished," he asked (as Blaine had) that they be "brought to trial." That was really what he had meant, he said, by the word "punished." Instead of demanding an immediate indemnity, he asked that the United States recognize in principle that an indemnity was due to the relatives of the slain men. It was not difficult to effect an adjustment on the basis of these more moderate demands, for Blaine himself was ready to admit that the treaty obligations of the United States warranted the eventual payment of an indemnity if it were shown that Italian nationals in this country had failed to receive the protection which they had a right to claim in our courts. He knew, as did Rudini, that the recall of Baron Fava was a grandstand play to impress the Italian people; and he refused to regard that bit of mock heroics as the serious crisis which the severance of diplomatic relations usually implies.

Instead, he continued calmly to reason with the secretary of the Italian legation, Marquis Imperiali, who had not been instructed to quit Washington with his chief. No government, Blaine informed the Marquis, however high its civilization or adequate its machinery of justice, could guarantee even its own citizens "against violence prompted by individual malice or by sudden popular tumult." The foreign resident must be content in such cases to share the same redress that is offered by the law to the citizens." [1] We shall see presently that this very sound judgment caused Blaine no little embarrassment when the question arose of the punishment of a mob for injuries done to American citizens in a foreign country. Incidentally, the grand jury which sat at New Orleans two months after the lynching failed to bring indictments against any of the citizens and no one was brought to trial.[2]

President Harrison, in his annual message of December 9, 1891, took a conciliatory attitude. The "most deplorable and discreditable incident" at New Orleans, he said, did not arise out of any animosity toward the Italian people or imply any disrespect to the government of Italy. The unfortunate manner in which the Italian claims had been pressed could be condoned by "the excitement and indignation which the crime naturally evoked." Though the Italian government had seen fit to recall its Minister, he had "no doubt that a friendly conclusion" of the controversy was attainable.[3] Congress responded to the President's suggestion of an indemnity, and on April 12, 1892, Blaine notified Marquis Imperiali that he was authorized by the President to offer $25,000 to the families of the victims of the "lamentable massacre" at New Orleans, with the hope that thereby "all memory of the unhappy tragedy" would be obliterated and enduring friendly relations between the two countries restored.[4] As investigation had brought out the fact that only three of the eleven victims were Italian subjects, the Italian government gratefully accepted the indemnity offered and full diplomatic relations were resumed.

Compared with the Samoan and Bering Sea controversies the Italian incident was only a tempest in a teapot. It boiled up suddenly and died down in a few weeks. There was no element in it involving a departure from traditional American policy or challenging the American interpretation of international law. No economic interests were in dispute, no commercial rivalries involved. To be at his best Blaine needed a case which gave opportunity for the exercise of subtle argument and the utilization of the vast fund of historical knowledge at his command.

---

[1] *Foreign Relations of the United States*, 1891, p. 685.
[2] J. B. Moore, *Digest of International Law*, Vol. VI, p. 839.
[3] J. D. Richardson, *Messages and Papers of the Presidents*, Vol. IX, p. 182.
[4] *Foreign Relations of the United States*, 1891, p. 728.

Instructing the Italian government in the elementary fact of our political system that criminal jurisdiction belongs to the State authorities offered little scope for either his dialectics or his erudition. Furthermore, Blaine needed a foeman worthy of his steel, and the awkward lunges of the Marquis Rudini were no such challenge as the expert rapier play of the Marquis of Salisbury.

The most serious of the international crises with which Blaine had to deal in the Harrison Administration was the imbroglio with the Republic of Chile. Don José M. Balmaceda had been elected president of that republic in 1886. He was an able, enlightened and progressive ruler, but he was also dictatorial in his assertion of the presidential prerogative. The Chilean congress repudiated his ministry, but he refused to bow to the majority in congress, as other executives had done, contending that the constitution of 1833 had established the presidential and not the parliamentary form of government. In this he was technically right, but he was violating a long established custom. When the congress refused to vote appropriation bills, Balmaceda issued a defiant proclamation on New Year's Day, 1891, and with Bismarckian audacity extended the budget by executive decree. The congressional faction immediately retorted with a declaration of war on the "usurping" president. Holding the rich nitrate regions in the northern provinces, controlling most of the Chilean navy, and supported by the strong British and German interests in the country, the congressionists had no difficulty in defeating the president's armies and occupying the capital of Santiago, where they set up a provisional government under the presidency of Jorge Montt. Balmaceda fled for refuge to the Argentine legation, and shortly afterward committed suicide in the vain hope that his sacrifice would induce the victorious congressionists to spare his followers from vengeance. The provisional government was recognized by the foreign powers, including the United States (September 5, 1891).

Why should this revolution, any more than a hundred others in Latin-America, have involved the United States? With its origins and objects, to adopt a Wilsonian phrase, we had nothing to do. And yet, within six weeks of the recognition of the Montt government we were engaged in a controversy with Chile which brought the two countries dangerously near to the brink of war. The reasons for this deplorable situation are to be found in a series of events which exasperated the

Chileans to a point where they committed an outrage upon our sailors which roused the wrath of our citizens from the Atlantic to the Pacific. Let us pass these incidents in brief review.

In the first place, the large and influential group of Chileans who were hostile to Balmaceda were offended by Blaine's choice of a minister to represent the United States at Santiago. Patrick Egan was a "Blaine Irishman," but lately naturalized in the United States, after escaping the imminent danger of imprisonment in Ireland for his activities in the Irish Land League. He was even accused of complicity in the Phoenix Park murders. Blaine himself was far from popular with the Chileans, who believed that in his conduct of the State Department in 1881 he had tried to deprive them of the fruits of their victory in the war against Peru and Bolivia.[1] They remembered his open charge that it was "England's war" and that the British interests were only using Chile as a cat's-paw to draw their chestnuts from the fire. And now the appointment of an Irishman as Minister to Santiago seemed like a slap in the face to the large group in Chile who were bound to England by such close economic ties that a former Minister had spoken of Chile as a "commercial dependency" of Great Britain.

Egan was an able and upright official, and his conduct was correct in supporting the Balmaceda government to which he had been accredited, so long as it stood. He was also correct (and humane) in giving asylum in the American legation to Balmacedist refugees, including three members of the fallen Cabinet, who would probably have been executed if they had been turned over to the Montt government for trial.[2] Nevertheless, the appointment of so obvious and active a partisan of Balmaceda to the Santiago mission, on the eve of the inevitable struggle of the factions in Chile, was, as Professor Hart has said, "unsuitable and impolitic."[3] The New York *Sun,* on September 30, printed an interview with a certain Mr. Foster, who was acting in Washington as "secretary" of the congressionist party: "Mr. Foster said that the people of Chile knew Mr. Egan and had no confidence in him or respect for him. They felt that he was largely responsible for the war (!)

[1] See above, pp. 211, ff.

[2] Egan was on less firm ground, however, when he demanded safe conduct for the refugees to leave the country. His frequent dispatches to our State Department show the annoyances and insults which he suffered from the agents of the Montt government, who charged him with harboring "spies" and encouraging "plots" in the American legation for the restoration of the Balmaceda government. *House Executive Documents,* 52d Cong., 1st sess., pp. 168–196.

[3] A. B. Hart, *Practical Essays in American Government,* p. 107.

because as a friend of Balmaceda he had encouraged him to acts of hostility and had assured him of the sympathy of the United States . . . and if there was a rupture between the two countries it would be entirely his fault. . . . I cannot understand why the Administration keeps him there to affront our people." [1]

Another cause of friction was the *Itata* incident. The congressionists were well supplied with money from their control of the nitrate beds, but they lacked arms and ammunition. They sent an agent named Trumbull to the United States to buy rifles. Balmaceda's Minister at Washington protested; but Blaine, however loath he was to see the insurgent cause helped, answered that the purchase of arms here and their shipment from the country was not an infringement of the laws of neutrality. Trumbull purchased five thousand rifles and sent them across the continent to San Francisco, where they were loaded on an American ship which he had hired. Meantime the Chilean vessel *Itata,* in the service of the congressionists, had put into the port of San Diego. She had Chilean marines aboard and cannon, too (which she concealed before giving her manifesto to the custom officials). She was at San Diego ostensibly for the purpose of taking on provisions, but her real purpose was to receive the shipment of rifles. Suspicious of her status as a merchant vessel, Attorney General W. H. H. Miller ordered her detention at San Diego and put a Federal deputy marshal aboard her. But on May 6, 1891, she left the port, carrying the marshal, and proceeded to the neighborhood of the Catalina Islands, where she took aboard the rifles and headed for Chile, setting the marshal ashore on the way.

The President, the Attorney General and Secretary Tracy of the Navy immediately concurred in dispatching the cruiser *Charleston* to chase and seize the *Itata.* The insurgent government at Iquique had also dispatched the cruiser *Esmeralda* to meet and convoy the *Itata.* The two equally matched cruisers put in at the port of Acapulco, Mexico, where they expected that the *Itata* would stop, and, as the captain of the *Charleston* was instructed to demand the surrender of the *Itata* if she were found in the convoy of a Chilean warship, there is no telling what might have happened if the ship which the two cruisers were looking for had suddenly appeared in the Mexican harbor. Fortunately, the *Itata* went straight to Iquique, where the con-

[1] *House Executive Documents,* 52d Cong., 1st sess., p. 231.

gressionist authorities, heeding the protest which had already reached them from Washington, delivered her over, with the rifles, to our Rear Admiral W. P. McCann to be taken back to San Diego. It made little difference that the suit brought in the Federal court in California to test the legality of the seizure resulted eventually in the judgment that there had been no violation of the neutrality laws. The damage was done to the congressionist cause when the cargo of rifles was surrendered at Iquique, and the demand for that surrender was proof enough to the insurgents of the hostility of the United States to their cause.

Still another incident added to the resentment of the congressionists against the great Republic of the North. Shortly after the overthrow of the Balmaceda government, a certain Señor Vergara published a series of newspaper articles in which he accused the American Rear Admiral George Brown of entering the harbor of Quinteros with the cruiser *San Francisco,* on the morning of August 20, of there discovering the intended movement of the congressionist forces upon Valparaiso, and of proceeding immediately to Valparaiso to give this valuable information to the Balmacedists. In a frank letter of September 8 to Minister Egan, Admiral Brown showed the utter falsity of this charge, telling how the landing of the congressionist forces at Quinteros was a matter of public knowledge when he went on shore there and how it was known to the Balmacedists in Valparaiso and telegraphed to other points long before he reached Valparaiso at five o'clock in the afternoon. It is not unlikely that Balmacedists themselves concocted this story of Admiral Brown's breach of etiquette and neutrality, in the hope of embroiling the congressionists in a quarrel with the United States. At any rate, the chief Balmacedist paper in Valparaiso stated that the "news" of the congressionists' movements was brought to the city by the *San Francisco.*

However, a "leakage" of military information had nothing to do with the decisive victory which the congressionists won on August 28, opening their way to the Chilean capital. That was due to the superiority of the arms which they had obtained from Germany. Coming as it did, however, in the midst of the controversy between Egan and Señor Matta over the Balmacedist refugees in the American legation, this new charge of unneutral conduct on the part of the United States still further increased the hostility of the congressionists toward the government at Washington.

The smoldering ill feeling burst into flame in a horrible scene enacted in the streets of Valparaiso in the evening of October 16. Captain W. S. Schley of the cruiser *Baltimore* had given shore leave on that day to more than a hundred sailors and petty officers. Two of the men were drinking in the True Blue saloon when a fight was started by a Chilean sailor spitting in the face of one of the Americans who promptly knocked him down. The Americans ran out into the street, where they and their fellow tars were set upon by the gathering mob and unmercifully kicked, beaten, stoned and stabbed. Boatswain's mate Riggin was shot dead and a coal heaver named Turnbull died a few hours later from eighteen knife wounds. Several sailors were taken to the hospital and more were dragged through the streets to the police station. The police, according to the testimony of a number of eyewitnesses of the brawl, instead of protecting the Americans, joined in the fray, using their pistols and bayonets. After an hour of fighting in the tenderloin district of the city the fury died down and the arrested sailors were allowed to return, with such of their wounded companions as were able, to the *Baltimore*.

The report of the *Intendente* of Valparaiso to the government at Santiago represented the affair as a brawl between drunken sailors, for which one side was no more responsible than the other. The police had done their best to protect the Americans by taking them to the station. Captain Schley had been very imprudent in allowing so large a number of his men to visit the city, where they would be certain, like all sailors on shore leave, to seek the low resorts where trouble was easily brewed. On the other hand, an investigation held on board the *Baltimore* the morning after the fray placed the blame wholly on the Chileans. The American sailors were unarmed. Captain Schley, who had been in the city himself until five in the afternoon, testified that the men were sober and quiet.[1] The attacks upon them, occurring simultaneously in several parts of the city, were a deliberate and unprovoked insult to the uni-

---

[1] Doubtless, Captain Schley was overcomplimentary to the sailors when he vouched for their sobriety. Commander Robley D. ("Fighting Bob") Evans, who arrived at Valparaiso with the gunboat *Yorktown* soon after the *Baltimore* had left, and who was himself subjected to no little annoyance from the Chilean war craft in the harbor, wrote in his *A Sailor's Log* (p. 259): "His (Schley's) men were probably drunk on shore, properly drunk. They went ashore, many of them, for the purpose of getting drunk, which they did on Chilean rum paid for with good American money. When in this condition, they were more entitled to protection than if they had been sober. . . . Instead of protecting, the Chileans foully murdered these men, and we believe with the connivance and assistance of armed policemen. That was the issue, not the question of whether they were drunk or sober."

form of the United States.

Blaine was in poor health at his summer home at Bar Harbor when the Valparaiso incident occurred, and did not return to Washington until the end of October. He fully accepted Captain Schley's report of the affair as an unprovoked attack on the uniform of the American sailors, but, profoundly interested as he was at the time in the establishment of friendly relations with the Latin-American republics and in the success of his reciprocity policy, he did not wish to see the Valparaiso affair magnified into a major diplomatic crisis. Therefore he did not wholly approve the peremptory tone of the note of October 23 dispatched to Egan by Acting Secretary of State, F. W. Wharton (of course with President Harrison's sanction), which complained of the Chilean government's delay in acknowledging responsibility for the outrage and promising full reparation.[1]

Señor Matta, the Chilean Foreign Minister, was stiff in his reply to Wharton's note. The affair was being investigated, he said, by the appropriate authorities under Chilean law, which alone was competent to deal with criminal cases in Chilean territory. When the *sumario,* or inquiry, of the investigating board should be ready, the Minister would have the honor to communicate its conclusions to Mr. Egan. Meanwhile, he could not accept the complaint that the delay was "an expression of unfriendliness toward the government of the United States which might put in peril the maintenance of amicable relations between the two countries." [2] The inquiry dragged along week after week, in spite of a polite request from Blaine on November 25 that it be expedited. The Chilean Minister at Washington blandly replied that, though the law of his country might be "slow in its processes," it was "exact in its conclusions." Blaine still remained patient, though the press of Santiago and Valparaiso continued to abuse him and Egan, and some of the Republican papers in our own country accused him of supineness. The Democratic press, on the other hand, quite generally charged him with trying to stir up a war with Chile.

President Harrison reviewed the Chilean situation briefly in his message of December 9, 1891. He regretted that the reply of Señor Matta to Wharton's note of October 23 had been "couched in an offensive tone," and he asserted the correctness of the conduct of our

[1] T. C. Crawford, *Life of James G. Blaine,* p. 617.
[2] Matta to Egan, October 27, 1891. *House Executive Documents,* 52d Cong., 1st sess., p. 210.

Minister and our naval commanders. He hoped that the investigation of
the court at Valparaiso would be completed soon and the result communicated to our government, "together with some adequate and
satisfactory response" to our protests. "If these just expectations should
be disappointed or further needless delay intervene," he concluded, "I
will by special message bring this matter again to the attention of Congress for such action as may be necessary." [1]

The President's message provoked the excitable Señor Matta to an
extraordinary breach of diplomatic conduct. He composed a telegram
on December 11, which he had read to the Chilean Senate, published in
the newspapers of Santiago, and sent to the Chilean Minister at Washington, not to be delivered to Blaine but to be given to the American
press. In this telegram he declared that the statements on which the
President's message and the report of Secretary of the Navy Tracy
were based were "erroneous or deliberately incorrect," that the Wharton
note was "aggressive in purpose and violent in language," that the delay
in the investigations at Valparaiso had been due to the non-appearance
of the officers summoned from the *Baltimore,* that there was "no exact-
ness or sincerity" in what was said at Washington by those who were
"interested in justifying their conduct," that the instructions (to Egan
and the naval officers) to maintain impartiality and friendship had "not
been complied with, neither now or before," and that "the right, the
dignity and the final success of Chile" would be vindicated "notwithstanding the intrigues which proceed from so low a source and the
threats which come from so high a source." [2]

The reaction of our government and people to this insulting dispatch
was one of extreme indignation. Minister Egan immediately suspended
relations with Señor Matta, and President Harrison would probably have
severed diplomatic relations with Chile had not Blaine counseled delay,
on the ground that the provisional regime at Santiago was shortly to be
superseded by a permanent government, in which a new Minister of
Foreign Affairs might be of a more friendly disposition toward the
United States. As it was, a squadron of eight cruisers was concentrated
in the Pacific and work was speeded up in the navy yards of Brooklyn
and San Francisco. Commander Evans noted in his diary for December 28 that he had seen a telegram from W. R. Grace, a friend of

[1] J. D. Richardson, *Messages and Papers of the Presidents,* Vol. IX, pp. 184–186.
[2] The telegram in the original Spanish and in the English translation is in the *House
Executive Documents,* 52d Cong, 1st sess., pp. 267–269.

Blaine's, stating that Harrison was for war, and the Navy Department as well, while Blaine could not "stem the tide" toward war unless Chile made immediate and ample apologies.[1] Congressman McCreary of Kentucky declared that talk of war was rife throughout the land, and that "a million men would respond to the call to arms."[2] The excitement reached such a height that the body of Riggin, the murdered sailor, lay in state for a short period in Independence Hall, Philadelphia —an honor given before only to the remains of Abraham Lincoln and Henry Clay.[3]

The permanent government inaugurated at Santiago just before Christmas did show a better disposition toward the United States. The new Minister of Foreign Affairs, Señor Luis Pereira, put an end to the annoying surveillance of the American legation and allowed the refugees to be put on board the *Yorktown* to be conveyed to a place of safety. However, on the subjects of the Matta telegram and the responsibility for the Valparaiso fray the new government failed to give us satisfaction, and on January 21 it asked for Egan's recall. Blaine could "stem the tide" no longer. On that same January 21 he sent an ultimatum to Chile: "I am now directed by the President to say that if the offensive parts of the dispatch of the 11th of December are not at once withdrawn and a suitable apology offered, with the same publicity that was given to the offensive expressions, he will have no other course open to him except to terminate diplomatic relations with the government of Chile." As to the demand for the recall of Egan, the President did not "deem it necessary to make any present response: it will be quite time to consider this suggestion after a reply to this note is received, as we shall then know whether any correspondence can be maintained with the government of Chile upon terms of mutual respect."[4]

President Harrison followed up this ultimatum with a special message to Congress on January 25, accompanied by a volume of 650 pages containing the correspondence, reports and testimony pertaining to the whole Chilean controversy. He commended Egan for his "dignity, discretion and courage." He stood firm in his judgment that the Valparaiso affair was an insult to our national honor, for which the Chilean communications had "not in any degree taken the form of a manly and

[1] Robley D. Evans, *A Sailor's Log*, p. 277.
[2] The New York *Nation*, January 14, 1892.
[3] Henry Clay Evans, *The Relations of the United States and Chile*, p. 152.
[4] *House Executive Documents*, 52d Cong., 1st sess., Vol. I, pp. 307–8.

satisfactory expression of regret, much less of apology"; and he declared that, while we desired to cultivate only friendly relations with all the governments of this hemisphere, we were bound to extend our protection to our citizens, even to the humblest sailor, "when made the victims of wantonness and cruelty." It was an invitation to Congress to authorize the President to use the army and navy of the United States to obtain satisfaction from Chile.[1]

On the very day that President Harrison sent this message to Congress, the Chilean Foreign Minister was composing his long note in reply to Blaine's ultimatum of January 21. He made the best defense he could (as he was bound to do) of the Chilean side of the case, but ended with a complete surrender to the demands of the United States. He accepted in principle a reconsideration of the verdict of the board of investigation of the Valparaiso affair, and suggested the submission to the Supreme Court of the United States or to an arbitration tribunal the question of determining "the reparation which Chile may have to make for that lamentable occurrence." He deplored the passages in the Matta dispatch which were offensive to our government, and absolutely withdrew such expressions, making this declaration "without reservations, in order that it may receive such publicity as your government may deem suitable." He assured the honorable Secretary of State that the Chilean government would take no step in regard to a change in personnel in the American legation at Santiago without the accord of the government of the United States, "with which it desired to maintain friendly relations."[2] This courteous note of Pereira left nothing to be desired in tone or content to satisfy our government. The war scare subsided as quickly as it had risen. Without resort to arbitration, but relying, as Blaine advised, on the "good sense" of Chile,[3] an agreement was reached by which the Chilean government paid $75,000 to the families of Riggin and Turnbull and the sailors who were injured in the street fight at Valparaiso.

Blaine made no direct claim to have restrained President Harrison from more drastic measures against Chile, but we have good evidence that he was exercising a moderating influence. For example, in his telegram of January 21 to Egan he said: "The President was disposed to

[1] J. D. Richardson, *Messages and Papers of the Presidents*, Vol. IX, pp. 215–226.
[2] *House Executive Documents*, 52d Cong., 1st sess., Vol. I, pp. 309–312.
[3] Blaine to Harrison, January 29, 1892. Cited in Gail Hamilton, *Biography of James G. Blaine*, p. 676.

regard the dispatch (of Matta's) as indicating a purpose to bring about a suspension of diplomatic relations, but, in view of the fact that Mr. Matta was acting provisionally . . . notice of this grave offense has been delayed." Again, on January 29, four days after President Harrison's special message had gone to Congress, Blaine wrote, in view of the apology from Pereira which had reached the State Department on the twenty-sixth: "My Dear Mr. President, I herewith send you a draft of a note to Chile. It may seem to you too cordial, but I believe it to be in the highest sense expedient. I have relied on Chile's good sense for reparation. . . . We can afford to be very generous in our language and thus make a friend of Chile, if that is possible." To which Harrison replied on the same day: "I had outlined what I thought would be a suitable response (to Pereira) and have now adapted it to your note, a good part of which you will see is incorporated. What I have said, I think you will agree, has rather enlarged than diminished the expressions of cordiality." [1]

The charge made by some of the Democratic newspapers that President Harrison encouraged the war spirit at the beginning of a presidential year, in order that he might unite the country behind him for a reëlection, is too base to deserve notice. Equally despicable is the innuendo that Blaine changed his tone and wrote his peremptory note of January 21 so as not to be outdone by the President in the bid for popular favor. The two men, in spite of a disharmony which we shall have to notice in later pages, were in substantial accord in the conviction that Chile must make suitable amends for the insult to the honor of our country. If Blaine put more emphasis on a conciliatory manner (*suaviter in modo*), while Harrison pressed more eagerly for a settlement (*fortiter in re*), it was chiefly because the former had more at heart the success of Pan-American coöperation, which would suffer enormously by the alienation of one of the richest and most powerful of the Latin-American republics.

We may pause at the close of this chapter on the four major diplomatic negotiations of the years (1889–1892) of Blaine's second administration of the State Department, to ask how far the phrase "a spirited foreign policy" fairly describe his aims and accomplishments. That phrase was used by his friends in anticipation, and by his enemies

---

[1] *House Executive Documents*, 52d Cong., 1st sess., Vol. I, p. 308. Gail Hamilton, *Biography of James G. Blaine*, pp. 676, 677.

in apprehension, of an aggressive, dictatorial conduct by a man who had risen to the leadership of his party and who, having been frustrated in his ambition to attain the Presidency, was determined to seek compensation by strutting in a grand manner on the international stage. But a study of his actual diplomatic policy in the last three years of his active political life gives little support to this theory. In the Samoan and Bering Sea cases he was not stirring up a controversy or precipitating a quarrel, but endeavoring to settle an inherited dispute along lines already laid down by acts of Congress and executive initiative of a previous Administration. The story of his dramatic defiance of Prince Bismarck is, as we have seen a pure myth; and if he used vigorous language in his notes to Lord Salisbury, his object was not so much to gain a special privilege for the United States at the expense of Great Britain as to persuade his lordship to agree to a humane pursuit of seal hunting which would eventually benefit Great Britain, the United States and the world at large. In the two controversies which arose in 1891, neither of them by any provocation on his part, he showed more patience than aggression. This was particularly true in the Chilean affair; but even in the case of the New Orleans lynchings it was the Italian Minister, press and populace that raged and threatened, while Blaine (not without some sharp words, to be sure) waited for them to come to their senses.

In short, despite the popular impression that Blaine utilized his last tenure of office to indulge a growing spirit of "jingoism," I believe that the facts bear witness to a moderation of such a spirit when compared with the policies of his earlier period in the State Department. In 1881 Blaine was alert, vigorous and filled with high emprise. Though twice disappointed in the race for the presidential nomination, he was the virtual head and directing force of an Administration which he expected to make glorious beyond compare in our annals. He spoke in a tone of conscious authority on questions of party policy at home and used the language of secure prestige in dealing with foreign countries. He was inaugurating a new era, laying the foundations of a lasting Ebenezer.

It was a different Blaine who accepted the belated invitation of General Harrison to resume charge of the State Department in 1889. The intervening years had chastened his ambition and somewhat dampened his ardor. They had seen the reversal of his cherished policy by a

Republican President and the assault upon his political doctrines by a Democratic President. They had witnessed his rejection by the American electorate in 1884 and the renunciation of his opportunity to appeal again to that electorate in 1888. They had taken their toll of physical strength, if not of mental vigor. The grandiose vision of 1881 was not recovered eight years later. The Blaine of 1889–1892 was not the herald of national policies, but the head of a department, performing the duties of that department with diligence and skill, but under the limitations of a due recognition of subordination to a not too sympathetic chief and the handicap of an increasing uncertainty of health. If his foreign policy in these latter years was "spirited," that adjective must be understood as meaning that it was inspired by the proper resolve to conserve the interests of the United States in the Pacific and in South America. It was more protective than provocative, more defensive than defiant, more conciliatory than coercive.[1]

---

[1] As early as 1884 we have an interesting side light on Blaine's attitude toward participation in European questions. On December 26 of that year Sir Lionel Sackville-West reported to Lord Grenville "a long and interesting conversation with Mr. Blaine," in the course of which Blaine criticized his successor Mr. Frelinghuysen for having taken part in the Congo conference at Berlin. "How can we maintain the Monroe Doctrine," said Blaine, "when we take part in conferences on the internal affairs of other continents? We shall either be told some day to mind our own business or else be forced to admit foreign governments to participation in the questions affecting America. This will be the result of the new departure in foreign policy." *Records of the British Foreign Office*, 115/745, No. 373, Confidential. This reference was kindly furnished by Professor George F. Howe of the University of Cincinnati.

BY COMMON consent, the outstanding public service of James G. Blaine was his encouragement of closer political and commercial relations between the United States and the republics of Latin-America and his advocacy of the peaceful principle of arbitration among the nations south of the Rio Grande. To understand his contribution to these admirable objects, it is necessary to consider briefly both the political situation of the Latin-American states in the nineteenth century and the attitude of the United States toward them.

When the Spanish colonies on the mainland of the New World (including Mexico, Central America and all of South America except Brazil and the Guianas) took advantage of Napoleon Bonaparte's overthrow of the Bourbon dynasty at Madrid to declare their independence of the mother country one after the other, it was natural that the consciousness of a common effort in a common cause should come to supplement their local and particular grievances. But they had no representative assemblies and none but the most rudimentary organs of self-government out of which to develop a political machinery of cooperation such as the confederation which the colonies of North America had formed half a century before in their struggle for independence from the British Crown. Consequently, such progress as was made toward solidarity was due to the zeal of the "liberators," the great military leaders like José de San Martin (Argentina) and Simon Bolivar (Colombia), who led their devoted armies from one state to another to deliver their compatriots from Spanish rule.

A further impetus to some sort of political union was furnished by the reactionary policy of the chief European nations following the overthrow of Napoleon. In 1815 the sovereigns of Russia, Prussia and Austria joined in a league (the Holy Alliance), a little later joined by France (the Quadruple Alliance), to restore the legitimate dynasties which had been ousted by Napoleon and to crush out the seeds of liberty and democracy which had been sown by the French Revolution. They held congresses at Aix-la-Chapelle (1818), Troppau (1820) and

Verona (1822), at which they sat as a committee of censors on the state of Europe, spying out every movement of rebellion against divinely commissioned rulers, and lending their armies to put down revolt or restore legitimacy wherever occasion offered (Naples, Piedmont, Spain). There were rumors even that the Alliance, after completing its reactionary program in Europe, would send an expedition across the Atlantic to restore the Latin-American colonies to the Spanish Crown. What better way to frustrate such an attempt than to organize an American league of freedom to counter the European league of despotism!

It was the Brazilian José S. Rebello who first proposed such a league, when he came to Washington in the spring of 1824 to negotiate for the recognition of the independence of Brazil from the Portuguese Crown, and, in his formal presentation to President Monroe, suggested "a concert of American powers to sustain the general system of American independence." [1] A few months later Rebello proposed to Secretary Adams an offensive and defensive alliance between Brazil and the United States, to which the other states of South America should be invited to adhere. But Henry Clay, who succeeded Adams in the State Department in March, 1825, though an ardent supporter of the independence of the Latin-American states, rejected the proposed alliance, both on the practical ground that the invasion of Brazil by a European army at the behest of Portugal was "an improbable contingency," and on the theoretical ground that an offensive and defensive alliance would be an infringement of the policy of neutrality which the United States had maintained in the wars of liberation of the South American continent.[2] Considering the unequivocal pledge which we had made in the Monroe Doctrine of 1823 to defend the Latin-American states against any attempt of European countries to overthrow their newly acquired liberty, Secretary Clay's citation of our "policy of neutrality" in the wars of the previous decade might seem a little outmoded and squeamish.

Meanwhile, the great liberator Simon Bolivar, "the Washington of South America," had laid the basis for Latin-American coöperation by issuing an invitation, on December 7, 1824, to the governments of Mexico, Central America, Brazil, Argentina, Chile, and Great Colom-

[1] John Quincy Adams, *Memoirs*, Vol. VI, p. 359.
[2] W. S. Robertson, "South America and the Monroe Doctrine, 1824–1828," in *Political Science Quarterly*, Vol. XXX, p. 96.

bia [1] to send delegates to a congress to be held on the Isthmus of Panama. The congress was to act as a great Amphictyonic Council, guarding the independence of the Latin-American republics, interpreting their treaties, settling their disputes and directing their mutual political and commercial policies. Only two of the states south of the Isthmus (Peru and Great Colombia) were represented, together with Mexico and Central America, at this Pan-American Congress which met in June, 1826, and Colombia was the only state to ratify its project of a perpetual union. Bolivar was profoundly discouraged by the failure of the congress, and when his federation of Great Colombia disintegrated into the independent and often mutually hostile republics of Colombia, Ecuador and Venezuela, he laid down his dictatorship and retired to the country, where he died in 1830, convinced that his life's labors had gone for naught and that he had "but plowed the sea."

Nevertheless, his idea of an international American conference did not die. It cropped up again and again in the next two generations, with partial realization in sporadic regional congresses, until at last it found fulfilment in the series of Pan-American Congresses which began at Washington in 1889 and of which the seventh was held at Montevideo, Uruguay, in December, 1933.[2]

The "Republic of North America" was not included in the original invitation to the congress at Panama. It was not a Pan-American congress, but a Pan-Latin-American congress, that Bolivar planned and that was advocated by the publicists and statesmen of South America who labored to revive his project. However, the ministers of Colombia and Mexico, on instructions from their governments, extended the invitation to the United States to send delegates to Panama, and President Adams accepted the invitation, on the urgent recommendation of Secretary Clay. The story of our hesitating and belated attempt to participate in the congress has been told in every textbook of American history: how Adams in a special message to Congress sent

---

[1] Bolivar was not only President of Great Colombia (Colombia, Ecuador, and Venezuela) but also dictator of Peru. He had freed five great provinces of South America from Spanish rule. As early as 1815, when in exile in Jamaica, he had written a letter expressing the hope that some day the countries of Latin-America might "constitute one great republic" with its "august congress of representatives . . . to treat and discuss important subjects of war and peace with the nations of the other three fourths of the world." W. S. Robertson, *The Rise of the Spanish American Republics*, p. 233.

[2] The second Pan-American Congress met at Mexico City in 1901–2, the third at Rio de Janeiro in 1906, the fourth at Buenos Aires in 1910, the fifth at Santiago de Chile in 1923, the sixth at Havana in 1928.

in the names of the two American delegates, Sergeant and Anderson; how Congress halted over the approval of the mission, lest it should lead us into "foreign entanglements" or commit us to a discussion of slavery which would be embarrassing for the South; how it was not until well into May, 1826, that Secretary Clay was finally able to give his instructions to the two delegates; how one of them (Anderson) died on his way to Panama and the other arrived at the Isthmus only after the congress had adjourned (July, 1826). Fifty-five years were to elapse after this fiasco before the attempt was again made to bring delegates from Latin-America and the United States together in an international American congress.

Meanwhile, there had been developing in the United States an attitude toward Latin-America which, though often carelessly confused with Pan-Americanism, was in reality quite in contrast, if not in conflict, with that policy. This was the Monroe Doctrine of 1823, by which the United States undertook by itself, unilaterally and *proprio vigore,* to guarantee the independence of the new republics. The Monroe Doctrine was *our* answer to the threats of the Holy Alliance, as the project of Bolivar was Latin-America's answer to those threats. But the announcement by President Monroe of our intention to protect and defend the Latin-American states under certain contingencies was a far different thing from the participation with those states as equal colleagues in measures looking toward their closer union or their common safety.

It was just this sharp dichotomy of the powerful guardian on the one side of the Rio Grande and the score or so of unfledged republics on the other that lent a tinge of patronage to the Monroe Doctrine in the United States and gave rise in Latin-America to the suspicion of a designed overlordship on the part of the "great colossus of the north." Indeed, three years before the Monroe Doctrine was formulated, Henry Clay, speaking in the House of Representatives, emphasized the advantages that would accrue to the United States by recognizing the independence of the new republics: "It is in our power," he said, "to create a system of which *we shall be the center* and in which all South America *will act with us.* In respect to commerce *we should be the most benefited. This country* would become the place of deposit of the commerce of the world. . . . *We should become the center* of a system which would constitute the rallying point of human wisdom against all the despotism of the Old World." [Italics mine.] [1] Evidently, the United States were to be the central jewel of the cluster, surrounded by the seed-pearls of the Latin-American republics, and in the middle years of the nineteenth century the spread-eagle oratory of the Websters, Bentons and Douglases, the filibusters of William Walker and the insolence of the Ostend Manifesto did nothing to disabuse the southern half of the American continent of the apprehension that the manifest destiny of the United States might not be considered attained until our possessions extended to the Isthmus of Panama and our dictates to the Strait of Magellan.

Now the peculiar merit of Blaine's Latin-American policy was its purpose to bring the Monroe Doctrine and Pan-Americanism into harmony. To that end he would modify the stark dualism of the Doctrine by having the delegates of the United States meet those from Latin-America on a footing of absolute equality, and would dissipate the suspicions of political encroachment on the part of the United States by devoting the meetings of the congresses to matters of obviously common advantage to all the states concerned. His attempts to convene such a Pan-American congress during his first brief period as Secretary of State was, as we have seen, frustrated by the assassination of President Garfield and the revocation by President Arthur of the invitation already sent out to the Latin-American republics. When Blaine left the State Department in December, 1881, and a few weeks later wrote his dignified letter of remonstrance to Arthur,[2] he doubtless felt, as Bolivar had half a century before, that he had but "plowed the sea." But the idea of a Pan-American congress had taken sufficient hold on the people and on Congress to survive. Resolutions favoring the project continued to be introduced into the House and Senate. Even President Arthur himself, in July, 1884, after the War of the Pacific was over, approved an act of Congress providing for a commission to visit Central and South America to study the sentiments of the people there on the subject of a congress.

The result of the favorable report of the commission was an act of Congress of March 24, 1888 (which President Cleveland allowed to become law without his signature), authorizing the President to invite delegates from all the independent countries of Latin-America to meet

[1] Speech of May 10, 1820. *Annals of Congress*, 16th Cong., 1st sess., p. 2226.
[2] See above, p. 218.

at Washington the following year. On July 13, 1888, Secretary Bayard sent out the invitations to Mexico, Haiti, Santo Domingo, and the fifteen republics of Central and South America. The date set for the congress was October 2, 1889, and the subjects proposed for discussion were the establishment of regular communications between ports of commerce, the formation of an American customs union, a uniform standard of weights and measures, uniform copyright and patent laws, the adoption of a common monetary (silver) unit, and, most important of all, the agreement on a general plan of arbitration for the settlement of all controversies in which the honor or independence of the several states was not involved. Each state was to send as many delegates as it pleased, but was to have only one vote in the congress. The deliberations were to be "consultative" merely, without prejudice to existing treaties.

Blaine was abroad when these preliminaries of the congress were being arranged (he landed in New York twenty-six days after Bayard had sent out the invitations) and consequently had no part in them. But it was a striking instance of "poetic justice" that when the delegates from thirteen Latin-American nations and the United States met in the diplomatic room of the State Department on October 2, 1889, they were received by the man who had proposed the congress eight years before. In his opening address Blaine welcomed the delegates to Washington and to every section and State of the Union in behalf of the government and people of the land. "Your presence here," he said, "is no ordinary event. It signifies much to the people of all America today. It may signify far more in the days to come. No conference of nations has ever assembled to consider the welfare of territories so vast and to contemplate the possibilities of a future so great, so inspiring. The nations here represented fall but little short of 12,000,000 square miles in their territorial extent—more than three times the area of all Europe —and but little less than a fourth part of the globe. . . . These great possessions today have a population approaching 120,000,000. The delegates whom I am addressing can do much to establish permanent relations of confidence, respect and friendship between the nations which they represent. They can show to the world an honorable and peaceful conference of eighteen [1] independent American powers, in

---

[1] Eventually, there were 17 states represented in the congress, Santo Domingo being the only one to decline Bayard's invitation. Chile's acceptance was conditioned on the assurance that political and military questions should be ruled out of the deliberations.

which all shall meet together on terms of absolute equality, a conference in which there can be no attempt to coerce a single delegate against his own conception of the interests of his nation, a conference which will permit no secret understanding on any subject but will frankly publish to the world all its conclusions, a conference which will tolerate no spirit of conquest but will aim to cultivate an American sympathy as broad as both continents, a conference which will form no selfish alliance against the older nations from which we are proud to claim inheritance, a conference, in fine, which will seek nothing, propose nothing, endure nothing that is not in the general sense of all the delegates timely, wise and peaceful."

There followed a brief credo of six articles, expressing faith in the voluntary coöperation of the American nations to preserve the Western Hemisphere from the burden of standing armies and the wars which had "cruelly afflicted the older nations of the world" and had "drenched Europe in blood." The anticipated results of the conference Blaine stated in a triple formula which seems like a reversal of the true order of importance: "It will be a great gain when we shall acquire that common confidence on which all international friendship must rest. It will be a greater gain when we shall be able to draw the people of all American nations into closer acquaintance with each other . . . by more frequent and more rapid intercommunication. It will be the greatest gain when the personal and commercial relations of the American states, North and South, shall be so regulated that each shall acquire the highest possible advantage from the enlightened and enlarged intercourse of all." [1]

At the close of his speech Blaine conveyed President Harrison's invitation to the delegates to be the guests of the nation on a tour of some of the principal cities of the East and the middle West, "with the double view of showing to our friends from abroad the condition of the United States and of giving to our people in their homes the privilege and pleasure of extending the warm welcome of Americans to Americans." W. E. Curtis of the State Department, former Secretary of President Arthur's South American commission, and municipal authorities, chambers of commerce and citizens' committees vied with one another in hospitality. Whether or not the six weeks "junket" made

---

[1] *International American Conference: Report of Committees and Discussion thereon.* 4 volumes, Washington, 1890, Vol. I, pp. 39 ff.

any contribution to the seasoned delegates' knowledge of American institutions or appreciation of American public sentiment, it was highly enjoyed by the "younger set" of secretaries and clerks.

An amusing incident occurred in connection with the delegates' visit to Philadelphia. John Wanamaker, Postmaster General in Harrison's Cabinet and proprietor of the largest department store in the city of brotherly love, shrewdly combined official welcome with private advertising. The delegates were conducted through his emporium with elaborate courtesy, and on leaving each was presented with a souvenir in the shape of a de-luxe volume describing the exceptional opportunities offered by the store, accompanied by a personal appeal which read: "Dear Sir, Confident of our commanding position in the mercantile world as leaders in retail commerce . . . we beg leave to ask your acceptance of this souvenir of your visit to our place of business, in the hope that it contains information sufficient to warrant its submission to your government as a portion of your report upon the honorable Congress to which you are accredited." [1] This unique gesture on the part of the merchant-prince-politician to "do his part" in the encouragement of closer trade relations between the United States and Latin-America provoked comments of mingled mirth and disgust in the press.

The conference reassembled in Washington on November 19 and settled down to the serious work of the agenda. Though Secretary Blaine was not a member of the United States delegation,[2] the congress fittingly elected him as its president, with authority to appoint the various committees. Blaine's many duties at the State Department made it impossible for him to preside regularly over the sessions, but he tried to be present on very important occasions, and even descended from the chair in the discussion on arbitration, to urge the adoption of a plan which he had himself drafted.

It would be impossible, within the limits of this chapter, to treat in detail the resolutions and recommendations which the conference adopted in its five months' deliberation, from November 19, 1889, to April 19, 1890. Both economic and political questions were discussed.

---

[1] H. T. Peck, *Twenty Years of the Republic,* p. 176.
[2] The ten delegates appointed by President Harrison included four manufacturers and two merchants. Senator J. B. Henderson was chairman, and Andrew Carnegie, Clement Studebaker and the veteran diplomat W. H. Trescot were among the members. Only one of the ten (Mr. Flint) could speak Spanish, though Trescot read the language.

Among the former the most important was the project for an American customs union, or *Zollverein,* which failed to win the support of the majority of the committee to which it was referred. Instead, they recommended the negotiation of separate reciprocity treaties. Other proposals of a social and economic nature were: the foundation of an international American bank; the construction of a Pan-American railroad to run from the Mexican border to the southern extremity of Chile; the improvement of lines of trade between the ports of the Atlantic and the Pacific and the Gulf of Mexico; a sanitary code for the protection of the public health; conventions to regulate trade marks, patents and copyrights; the establishment of a common monetary unit; and the adoption of the metric system of weights and measures by all the American republics. The political proposals included the recommendation of a treaty for the extradition of criminals and the project for a commission to prepare a common code of civil and commercial law.

By far the most absorbing subject of the conference, however, was the famous Article V of the Committee on General Well-being (*bienestar*), proposing the obligatory arbitration of all questions of diplomatic privileges, territorial limits, indemnification, rights of navigation, interpretation and implementation of treaties, and all other disputes of whatever nature, except only such matters as, in the exclusive judgment of any one of the nations involved, should compromise its independence. This comprehensive proposal met with lively opposition in the congress, led by the Chilean delegates, who saw in it the germ of a permanent court of arbitration dominated by the United States and interfering with the spoils of war—as they believed we had done in 1881. Blaine, for whom the arbitration agreement was the very capstone of the work of the congress, pleaded on the floor for the adoption of his plan, which declared that arbitration was accepted as "a principle of American international law." But the opposition was too strong to be overcome. The Chileans refused either to discuss or to vote upon the resolution, and the delegates of only seven (the United States, Argentina, Bolivia, Guatemala, Venezuela, Colombia and Brazil) of the seventeen republics signed the arbitration pact on April 9, 1890. This failure of a majority of the states to adopt the "new Magna Carta" was the bitterest disappointment of the congress for Secretary Blaine.

Nevertheless, the Washington Conference was not without its beneficial effects, both tangible and imponderable. Out of it came the organization of a permanent institution at Washington under the direction of a group composed of the resident Ministers of the Latin-American countries and our own Secretary of State, called the International Bureau of the American Republics. It has been the function of the Bureau to act as a sort of clearing house for Pan-American relations, disseminating information and encouraging coöperation in a great variety of interests, such as communications, cultural contacts, education, jurisdiction, commerce and arbitration; also to select the date and meeting place and to draw up the program for each subsequent Pan-American Congress. In 1908 Andrew Carnegie gave the money for a magnificent marble building at Washington to house the Pan-American Union, as the Bureau of the American Republics was re-christened at the Buenos Aires conference of 1910.

Fully as important as the establishment of the Bureau was the fact that for the first time delegates from nearly a score of republics "almost unknown to one another" had met and for twenty weeks discussed matters of common interest in "a spirit of mutual respect and consideration." [1] Some of them had come to Washington with a lurking suspicion that beneath its fair words our government harbored the design of establishing a meddlesome or coercive policy in Latin-America. It was even alleged in the opposition press that the delegates of Chile and the Argentine were the paid agents of Great Britain. But the obvious spirit of mutual deference, even when accord was not possible, dispelled any fear of imperialistic designs on the part of the United States. Undoubtedly, Blaine was overoptimistic when, in his farewell address to the delegates (April 19, 1890), he spoke of "the deliberate, confident, solemn dedication of two great continents to peace," and held up this "new Magna Carta which abolishes war and substitutes arbitration between the American Republics as the first and greatest fruit of the International American Conference." [2] For, apart from the fact that only seven of the nations signed the arbitration agreement, the history of the last half century has shown how unready the nations of Latin-America have been and still are to substitute arbitration for war. [3] The New York *Nation* of April 20, 1890, spoke in sarcastic language

[1] M. Romero, "The Pan-American Conference," *North American Review*, Vol. 151, p. 420.

[2] Gail Hamilton, *Biography of James G. Blaine*, p. 681.

[3] The failure of the seventh Pan-American Congress at Montevideo (December, 1933) to put an end to the long war between Bolivia and Paraguay for possession of the vast jungle area of the Gran Chaco in the heart of South America is a distressing example.

of the futility of the conference and ridiculed the "lachrymose senti-mentality" of Blaine's closing address. But the *Tribune* enthusiastically declared: "From this day the Monroe Doctrine passes by a process of diplomatic evolution into a stage of higher development."

Blaine's Pan-American policy naturally had its repercussions on our diplomacy with those European nations which, for commercial and cul-tural reasons, looked with a jealous eye upon every increase of the prestige of the United States in Latin-America. When, for example, the long standing dispute between Great Britain and Venezuela over the boundary line between Venezuela and British Guiana reached a criti-cal point at the close of the decade of the 1880's, with the severance of diplomatic relations between the two countries, Venezuela repeatedly solicited our good offices. A note of Señor Peraza, the Venezuelan Minister at Washington, to Blaine on February 17, 1890, is significant. The United States, he wrote, was the only nation that Venezuela could turn to for help, since "the European nations, irritated at the attitude which has been taken by the republics of Central and South America with the design of drawing closer their commercial relations with the United States, will not be willing to give any support to Venezuela." [1] There are indications that Blaine, if once the solidarity of the American states were assured, would have pressed his anti-British animus to the point of an ultimatum to Lord Salisbury. In a letter of October 28, 1891, to our Minister Scruggs at Caracas he spoke of "the continued and persistent advances of Great Britain upon the territory of Venezuela," of which we could not be a passive or disinterested spectator, and declared that we should "at an early date take an advanced and deci-sive step in support of the claims of Venezuela." Only Venezuela must do nothing to offend Great Britain and nothing without our knowledge and concurrence.

It is not unlikely that the contemporary controversy with Great Britain over the Bering Sea seal fisheries gave an added impetus to Blaine's championship of Venezuela, but even if he had been willing in 1891 to go as far as Secretary Olney did four years later in bidding defiance to Great Britain on the Venezuelan boundary question, he could have counted on no such support from President Harrison as Cleveland gave to Olney. Harrison went no further in his message of December, 1891, to Congress than to voice the hope that the Venezuelan

---

[1] *United States, Foreign Relations*, 1891, pp. 782.

question would be amicably settled, and the noncommittal assurance that the United States would "continue to express its concern at the appearance of foreign encroachment on territory long under the administrative control of American states." [1]

The committee on an American customs union had recommended to the Pan-American Congress the negotiation of separate reciprocity treaties between the republics. This project Blaine immediately embraced with ardor. On June 4, 1890, he wrote to President Harrison, submitting the report of the committee on the subject. The delegates of fifteen of the seventeen republics, he said, had indicated their desire to enter upon reciprocal commercial relations with the United States. "To escape the delay and uncertainty of treaties," he wrote, "it has been suggested that a practicable and prompt mode of testing the question was to submit an amendment of the pending tariff bill (the McKinley Bill of 1890) authorizing the President to declare the ports of the United States free to all the products of any nation of the American hemisphere upon which no export duties are imposed, whenever and so long as such nation shall admit to its ports free of all national, provincial, municipal and other taxes our flour, corn meal and other breadstuffs, preserved meats, fish, vegetables and fruits, cottonseed oil, rice and other provisions, including all articles of food, lumber, furniture and other articles of wood, agricultural implements and machinery, mining and mechanical machinery, structural steel and iron, steel rails, locomotives, railroad cars and supplies, street cars and refined petroleum. I mention these particular articles because they have been most frequently referred to as those with which a valuable exchange could be readily effected. The list could no doubt be profitably enlarged. . . . The opinion was general among the foreign delegates that the legislation herein referred to would lead to the opening of new and profitable markets for the produce of which we have so large a surplus and thus invigorate every branch of agricultural and mechanical industry." [2]

This letter President Harrison transmitted to Congress on June 19, with a brief message, calling attention to the fact that 87 per cent of the products now sent to our ports by the Latin-American nations were admitted free of duty. If sugar were placed on the free list, "practically

[1] J. D. Richardson, *Messages and Papers of the Presidents*, Vol. IX, p. 181.
[2] *Cong. Record*, 51st Cong., 1st sess., pp. 6256–9.

every important article exported from those states would be given untaxed access to our markets, except wool. "The real difficulty in the way of negotiating profitable reciprocity treaties," he said, was that "we have given freely so much that would have had value in the mutual concessions which such treaties imply." Still, he did not doubt that the present advantages which the Latin-American states enjoyed in our markets would dispose them favorably toward treaties or agreements tending to equalize and enlarge our mutual exchange. He thought that it would be time enough to consider the objection that we must cheapen labor in order to bring the cost of production down to a point where we could compete with the European nations in the trade of Latin-America, after we had fairly tried the effect of better lines of communication and more convenient methods of money exchange on that trade. The message hardly reflected the zeal of Blaine's letter, nor did it pass on to Congress the Secretary's recommendation of a reciprocity amendment to the pending tariff bill. Yet, the President expressed his readiness to act, if, after the passage of the bill, it should appear "that under the general treaty making power or under any special powers given by law our trade with the states represented in the conference can be enlarged upon a basis of mutual advantage." [1]

To appreciate the stubborn fight which Blaine put up for the inclusion of a reciprocity clause in the McKinley Bill, we must understand the background of the tariff situation in 1890. The Republican Party, when once the original objectives of its existence had been accomplished in the preservation of the Union and the abolition of slavery, underwent a great transformation. Although through the Reconstruction period and for years after it continued to appeal for the voters' support to such shibboleths as "vote as you shot" or John Sherman's "the Democratic Party is the left wing of the Confederate army," in reality the Republican Party became the stronghold of wealth and special privilege. It drew to itself the masters of the rising industries of the North and East which had been nurtured on the extraordinary demands of the army for food, clothing, blankets and munitions of every kind; the banking houses which had handled the government's large bond issues; the great railroad companies which had received princely subventions in land and credit from the government; the manufacturing plants which were flourishing under the protection afforded them by the

[1] J. D. Richardson, *Messages and Papers of the Presidents*, Vol. IX, p. 74.

high war tariffs. In the West, from the early 1870's on, there was a dawning realization that the economic interests of that section of the country did not coincide with those of the Eastern bankers who held the farmers' mortgages and controlled their credit, the railroad magnates who "charged all the traffic would bear," and the manufacturers who put into their own pockets the lion's share of the enhanced prices of the tariff-protected industries. Yet the West continued for a score of years, with only sporadic protests, to pay the piper while the Eastern capitalists called the tune. The West was faithful to the Republican Party because it had saved the Union and made generous donations of homestead lands.

The proverty-stricken post-war South hardly counted in the political councils of the nation. For more than a dozen years it lay under the reproach of rebellion, while Union generals (Grant, Hayes, Garfield) sat in the White House. Arthur was the first President after the Civil War to omit any reference to the "lost cause" in his inaugural address. The protests of the South, therefore, against the rising tide of the influence of the industrialists and bankers were ignored as the petulant complaints of an unreconciled section of the country. In a word, the stage was set for the triumph of the new protagonists of the Republican Party—the men who hung Abraham Lincoln's portrait on the walls of their convention halls but banished his spirit from their policies. They rode upon the wave of post-war prosperity, attributing each new increment of the country's wealth to their own wisdom and foresight, and utilizing such increments to reinforce their privileged status in the government.

The key policy of privilege was the high protective tariff, but it was not until the close of the 1880's that the political situation offered the Republican Party an opportunity to fix that policy upon the country in a definite and unequivocal fashion. The reviving Democrats had secured a majority in the House of Representatives in the election of 1874, and fifteen years of political deadlock followed, during which neither party had control of the executive power and both branches of Congress at the same time. Attempts of a Democratic House to reduce the tariff were futile against the opposition of a Republican President and Senate. The efforts of President Cleveland during his first term (1885–1889) to reform the "iniquitous" and "exorbitant" system which was enriching the few at the expense of the many, laying oppressive taxes on the necessities of life and piling up in the Treasury a surplus which should be flowing in the channels of trade, resulted in total failure.

Cleveland himself brought the matter to a head in his courageous message of December, 1887, which was devoted wholly to a denunciation of the protective tariff. The message, promptly attacked by Blaine in his Paris interview,[1] furnished the issue for the presidential campaign of 1888. The party lines were drawn with a distinctness unequaled since the election of 1860. The Democrats renominated Cleveland by acclamation, endorsing his message of the previous December and the abortive Mills bill framed on its principles. The Republicans stood firmly for high protection, declaring in their platform that they favored the repeal of all the internal (excise) taxes rather than the least breach in the walls of the protective tariff. The Republicans not only elected Benjamin Harrison President, but they secured a majority in both House and Senate. Thus, for the first time in a decade and a half a party controling all the branches of the government was in a position to break the long deadlock with a positive legislative program.

The Republicans, not without justification, interpreted their victory in a campaign devoted almost exclusively to the tariff issue as a mandate from the electors to continue the protective system. President Harrison was a staunch protectionist, and the Republican majority in Congress had behind them the manufacturers of the country, who had been welled into a more conscious solidarity of interests by the assaults of the previous Administration on their privileged position. When the Fifty-first Congress met in December, 1889, Speaker Thomas B. Reed of Maine appointed William McKinley, jr., of Ohio (whom he had defeated by a single vote in the choice of the caucus for the speakership) as chairman of the Ways and Means Committee. McKinley, who had entered Congress twelve years before, had devoted himself to the study of finance, and when Garfield was promoted to the Presidency the Ohio Congressman had taken his place as the leading authority on the subject in the House.

McKinley was the high priest of high protection. For him the system was not merely an economic blessing to the country, preserving our home market from invasion by a flood of foreign manufactures and protecting our laborers from the competition of the pauper wages of Europe, but it was almost a sacred institution, a guarantee of American

[1] See above, p. 364.

patriotism. "I believe in it," he said, "and thus warmly advocate it, because enveloped in it are my country's highest development and greatest prosperity, and out of it come the greatest gains to the people, the greatest comfort to the masses, the widest encouragement for manly aspirations. . . . It is our duty to protect as sacredly the labor and industry of the United States as we would protect her honor from taint or her territory from invasion." Here was no mere question of expediency, no dickering or logrolling, no sordid consideration of politics, privilege or profits. Others might descend to these low levels of argument, but McKinley lifted the subject to the empyrean heights of patriotic principle. And he boasted that his bill was "protective in every paragraph and American in every line and word."

The McKinley Bill passed the House on May 21, 1890, by a vote of 164 (all Republicans) to 142 (all Democrats but two). We cannot here analyze the measure in detail, but a few of its more important features must be noticed. First, it repudiated the Democratic doctrine of the free admission of raw materials and compensated for the duties charged on them by raising further the rates on the manufactured products, leaving for the free list only such necessary articles as did not compete with American production (tea, coffee, spices, drugs, and especially sugar). Again, it extended protection to the products of the farm as well as of the mill and factory. There had been some $250,000,000 of agricultural importations in 1889, subject to a meager tax, if any, as compared with manufactured articles. The farmer now was given adequate protection against the competition of Canadian eggs, wheat, butter and barley, Scotch potatoes and Dutch tobacco. The important provisions of the bill in regard to raw sugar we shall notice presently, but the most significant characteristic of the McKinley Bill was neither the incidence nor the amount of its rates. It was rather the new principle of tariff legislation contained in the bill as a whole.

In 1890 there was no demand for additional revenue for the Treasury. On the contrary, an embarrassing surplus had accumulated. The country was at peace with all the world and highly prosperous. There were no "infant industries" to be nurtured by government subsidy; they had all grown to lusty manhood. Our productive capacity was outgrowing the demands of the home market, and our cereals, meats and manufactures were seeking outlets through foreign trade to which prohibitive tariffs have always been an embarrassment. Yet, in the face of these facts, the Republican House passed the highest protective tariff hitherto known in our history. It was the unequivocal and unabashed proclamation of protection for protection's sake, relegating the fiscal (revenue) and commercial aspects of the question to an inconsequential place. And it has remained the pattern on which practically all subsequent tariff legislation in our country has been molded.

The accumulation of a surplus in the Treasury was, as we have seen, one of Cleveland's chief arguments for tariff reduction. The surplus, however, did not greatly disturb the Republicans. It was easier to deal with than a deficit, as Frederick D. Grant jauntily observed; and Congress set about spending it so successfully, on public buildings, soldiers' pensions, and naval construction, that by the end of Harrison's Administration it was completely wiped out. Nevertheless, in their platform of 1888 the Republicans took note of the embarrassing surplus, proposing to "effect all needed reduction of the national revenue by repealing the taxes upon tobacco . . . and the tax upon spirits used in the arts and for mechanical purposes," and by putting on the free list "those articles of foreign production, excluding luxuries, the like of which cannot be produced at home." [1] In fact, the title of the McKinley Bill was: "An act to reduce the revenue and equalize duties on imports and for other purposes." The method adopted in the bill, however, for reducing the surplus was not the repeal of the internal duties on tobacco and spirits, but the removal of the duty of two cents a pound on raw sugar. Sugar was a necessity of the rich and the poor alike. Nine tenths of the amount consumed in our country was imported, mostly from Cuba, Hawaii and the Latin-American republics. It was the largest revenue producer on the dutiable list, bringing into the Treasury between $50,000,000 and $60,000,000 annually. The loss of this income would go more than half way toward obliterating the surplus, and the payment of a compensating bounty of two cents a pound to the American producers of cane and beet sugar would extract about $7,000,000 more from the Treasury.

Now Blaine was placed in a trying position. He had always been, and still was, an ardent protectionist. He approved in general of the McKinley Bill. But a month before that bill passed the House he had spoken his farewell words to the Pan-American Congress, and he was all aflame with enthusiasm for putting into effect its recommendation

[1] Edward Stanwood, *The History of the Presidency*, Vol. I, p. 474.

for reciprocity agreements with the Latin-American countries. He was distressed by the one-sided character of our trade with those countries. Of our exports of approximately $850,000,000 for the year ending June 30, 1890, only $68,000,000, or eight per cent, went to Latin-America, whereas we imported thence goods to the value of $170,000,-000, leaving an unfavorable balance of $102,000,000 which we must pay as a virtual subsidy to the European trade with those countries.[1] Here was a market of 40,000,000 people on our own hemisphere, to which we had given hardly any consideration, and into which our food products, lumber, petroleum, furniture, machinery, steel rails, locomotives and a hundred other articles might find entrance through reciprocity agreements.

The chief asset in our hands for securing such agreements was the duty on raw sugar. With that we could bargain, offering its abolition in return for the free admission of our goods to Latin-American ports. But to remove the duty on sugar without exacting any *quid pro quo* from Cuba, Brazil or Venezuela was to throw away our one best chance of getting our due share of the Latin-American trade. The trouble was that the framers of the McKinley Bill, intent on protecting the home manufacturer and (to a less extent) the farmer, had slighted the importance of extending the foreign market. They had failed to realize that the days of Henry Clay had passed and that the home market could no longer absorb the products of our farms and factories. It was the opportunity in Latin-America that opened Blaine's eyes to that truth. McKinley's eyes were closed to it for another decade.[2]

Blaine began his battle for reciprocity before the McKinley Bill was introduced into the House, and even before it was completely framed in committee. On February 10, 1890, he had an interview with the eight Republican members of the Ways and Means Committee. "I endeavored," he wrote later, "to convince them that it would be expedient and wise to leave to the President as the treaty-making power an opportunity to see what advantageous arrangements of reciprocal trade could be affected. I was unable to persuade the committee to take my view. I mention this circumstance now because it has been charged

---

[1] *American Commerce* . . . 1821–1898. Treasury Department, Washington, 1899, pp. 3281–3314.

[2] In the last speech of his life, at the Pan-American Exposition at Buffalo, on September 5, 1901, the day before he was assassinated, McKinley laid off the high priest's robe of protectionism and pleaded for the principle of reciprocity, using language not unlike that of Blaine's in 1890.

in many quarters that the suggestion for reciprocity came too late." [1]
Commenting on this letter, the New York *Tribune* of July 27 remarked:
"He (Blaine) opposed in particular the imposition of a duty on hides
and the removal of the sugar duties. The House Committee made due
concession to him in keeping hides on the free list, but withheld the
other." On April 10, six days before the McKinley Bill came out of
committee and while the Pan-American Congress was still in session,
Blaine wrote to Chairman McKinley to protest again against taking
hides from the free list: "It is a slap in the face to the South Americans
with whom we are trying to enlarge our trade. It will benefit the farmer
by adding 5 to 8 per cent to the price of his children's shoes. It will yield
a profit to the butcher only—the last man that needs it. The movement
is injudicious from beginning to end. . . . Pray stop it before it sees
the light. Such movements as this for protection will protect the Republican Party into speedy retirement." [2] Hides did remain on the
free list, but the bill which passed the House on May 21 and went to
the Senate two days later made no provision for reciprocity.

Blaine now carried his battle to the Upper House. In spite of the
tradition of the "separation of powers," which keeps Cabinet officers
aloof from Congress, Blaine appeared before the Senate finance committee to plead with all his might for the sugar duty as a bargaining
weapon for reciprocity. The newspaper correspondent W. E. Curtis,
who had conducted the tour of the Pan-American delegates, was present
at the hearing and described it as follows: "Mr. Blaine, in the impetuous manner that is characteristic of him, declared that if sugar were
placed on the free list the greatest results sought for and expected from
the International Conference would be sacrificed. He declared that
it would be the most inexcusable piece of folly the Republican Party
was ever guilty of and that the leaders in Congress would realize it
before many months, and that if he were in the Senate he would fight
it to the best of his ability. He spoke with great earnestness and said
that he would give two years of his life for two hours on the floor
of the Senate when the sugar schedule was under consideration. Forty
millions of people had, he said, expressed their willingness (!) to admit
our food products free if we would take the duty off their sugar, and
in the face of that profession our Congress proposed to put sugar on the

[1] Blaine to W. P. Frye, July 22, 1890.
[2] Blaine to Wm. McKinley, April 10, 1890.

free list without asking any concession in return." [1] As a parting shot, Blaine launched the threat: "Pass this bill, and in 1892 there will not be a man in all the party so beggared as to accept your nomination for the Presidency." In the ardor of his plea he brought his fist down upon the table, where a copy of the bill lay, with such force that he knocked his silk hat to the floor, or, according to another version, smashed in its crown. Nation-wide publicity was given to the incident by the press, under such sensational headlines as, "Blaine Smashes His Hat on the McKinley Bill." Still, his zeal was unavailing with the committee. The bill was reported to the Senate on June 17 with many alterations but with sugar still on the free list and without any provision authorizing the President to manipulate the schedules in making reciprocity agreements or treaties with foreign nations. Two days later President Harrison transmitted to Congress Blaine's report of June 4 recommending the reciprocity amendment to the bill, and on July 7 the spirited debate on the subject, which was to accupy the Senate for the rest of the hot summer, began.

Unable to have even his modest two hours on the floor of the Senate, Blaine went to his summer home at Bar Harbor, not to rest but to follow with an eagle eye every word of the Senate debate and to urge the adoption of the reciprocity amendment (which his friend and neighbor Eugene Hale had introduced into the Senate on the same day that Harrison's message was received) in private correspondence, letters to the press, articles, pamphlets and speeches. "He appealed from the committee room," says Gail Hamilton, "to the court of the people." [2]

On July 11 he wrote an open letter to Wm. P. Frye of Maine, a member of the Senate Finance Committee: "I do not doubt," he said, "that in many respects the tariff bill pending in the Senate is a just measure and that most of its provisions are in accordance with the wise policy of protection. But there is not a paragraph or a line in the entire bill that will open the market for another bushel of wheat or another barrel of pork. If sugar is now placed on the free list without exacting important trade concessions in return, we shall close the door for a profitable reciprocity against ourselves. . . . Our free market for breadstuffs grows narrower. Great Britain is exerting every nerve to secure her bread supply from India, and the rapid expansion of the

---

[1] Quoted by John W. Foster in *Diplomatic Memoirs*, Vol. II, p. 4.
[2] Gail Hamilton, *Biography of James G. Blaine*, p. 686.

wheat area in Russia gives us a powerful competitor in the markets of Europe.[1] It becomes us, therefore, to use every opportunity for the extension of our market on both of the American continents. . . . The late conference of American republics proved the existence of a common desire for closer relations. Congress should take up the work where the International Conference left it. Our field of commercial development and progress lies south of us." [2]

Another open letter went to Senator Frye on July 25, again emphasizing the "absurdity" of our giving away our repeal of the sugar duty "for nothing," [3] and to the Mayor of Augusta Blaine wrote: "You are in error in supposing that I am opposed to sugar being admitted free of duty. My objection is not to free sugar but to the proposed method of making it free. If in the pending tariff sugar is placed on the free list, we give to certain countries a free market for $95,000,000 of their products, while they are not asked to open their markets to a single dollar of American products. . . . We ought to secure in return for free sugar a market for $60,000,000 or $70,000,000 of our own products. It will not require reciprocity treaties to secure this great boon. The tariff bill can contain all the necessary conditions." [4]

On August 29 Blaine made an important speech at Waterville, Maine, which was printed and circulated widely as a pamphlet. In this he undertook especially to refute the charge, frequently advanced in the Senate debates, that reciprocity was inimical to the principle of protection. "What I mean to speak of," he said, "is a system of reciprocity not in conflict with a protective tariff, but supplementary thereto, and presenting a field of enterprise that will richly repay the efforts and energy of the American people." [5] He believed, further, that we had

[1] In 1889 we exported $123,000,000 of breadstuffs, of which the British Isles took $73,800,000, or about 60 per cent. They also took nearly two thirds of our meat and dairy exports and more than two thirds of our cotton. These three items formed three fifths of our total exports. Edward Stanwood, *American Tariff Controversies in the Nineteenth Century*, Vol. II, p. 276.

[2] Gail Hamilton, *op. cit.*, pp. 686–7.

[3] Laughlin and Willis, *Reciprocity*, p. 188.

[4] Edward Stanwood, *American Tariff Controversies in the Nineteenth Century*, Vol. II, p. 279. Of course it was the prerogative of the President to negotiate reciprocity treaties at any time, but such treaties would have to be ratified by a two-thirds vote of the Senate. It was to avoid this hazard that Blaine wished to have incorporated in the tariff law itself an amendment authorizing the President to modify the rates in order to obtain reciprocal trade advantages.

[5] Laughlin and Willis, *op. cit.*, p. 186. Again and again Blaine had to defend himself against notices in the press of his hostility to the McKinley bill, inspired by the desire of the Democrats to detach the leading Republican of the country from the policy

missed a great opportunity by not using the abolition of certain duties (e. g. on coffee and tea) since the Civil War for securing equivalent concessions from foreign nations. It was time to alter this mistaken policy.

These repeated pleas of Blaine in behalf of a reciprocity amendment to the McKinley Bill had a tremendous effect on the people of the West, who saw in it the promise of enlarged markets for their produce. One of the Western members of the Ways and Means Committee, himself a bitter opponent of the amendment, complained that "Blaine's plan has run like a prairie fire all over my district." From boards of trade and produce exchanges in the West came petitions to Congress in favor of the amendment. President Harrison became more and more enthusiastic for the measure. He wrote to Blaine complimenting him on the Waterville speech and declaring that he thought that "the temper and disposition of our people both in Senate and House" was more favorable to reciprocity than it had been a few weeks ago. Indeed, the effect of the tariff bill on the West was a prime concern of the protectionist leaders. Only the die-hards among them could be blind to the agrarian unrest which was rapidly coming to a head in that section of the country, as witnessed by the growth of organizations like the Agricultural Wheel and the Farmers' Alliance, soon to be consolidated into the strong political opposition of Populism with its "curse upon both your houses" of Republicans and Democrats.

The Republicans had more to lose than the Democrats by the possible defection of the agrarian States. The time had obviously come when the high protectionists must do something to hold the West to the party, and something more than the sop thrown in the new duties on agricultural products; for these duties, after all, were illusory, since the West was looking rather for foreign markets for the export of its agricultural surplus than for the protection of the home market. Even the removal of the sugar duty would cheapen only one article of consumption of the farmer, whereas reciprocity held out to him the prospect of finding millions of customers for his barrels of flour and pork. The new schedules of the McKinley Bill would exact further tribute from him to the Eastern manufacturers in the increased price of his cloth-

of his party. He was even said to have exclaimed that he "spat" upon the bill. Of course, there was no truth in such representations.

ing, furniture, blankets, carpets, kitchen utensils, paint, fencing and tools. Something must be done to make these new duties palatable to the farmers, for already propaganda against the bill was being spread among them by Democratic emissaries who were frightening the farmers' wives by tales of the impending jump in the prices of their household necessities.

The upshot of the long and acrimonious debate in the Senate was the adoption on September 27, by a vote of 40 to 29 (15 members absent or not voting) of the reciprocity section, number 3, in the McKinley bill; and the amended bill, after consideration by the usual conference committee, was accepted by both Houses and signed by the President on October 1, 1890.[1] The reciprocity clause fell far short of embodying Blaine's ideas, as a comparison of that clause with the Hale Amendment shows.[2]

Section 3 of the McKinley Act of Oct. 1, 1890.

"That with a view to securing reciprocal trade *with countries producing the following articles,* and for this purpose, on and after the first day of January, 1892, whenever and so often as the President shall be satisfied that the government of any country producing and exporting sugars, molasses, coffee, tea, hides raw and uncured, or any of such articles, imposes duties or other exactions upon the agricultural or other products of the United States, which in view of the free introduction of such sugars, molasses, coffee, tea and hides into the United States he may deem to be reciprocally unequal and unreasonable, he shall have the power and it shall be his duty to suspend by proclamation to that effect the provisions of this act relating to

Senator Hale's Amendment of June 19, 1890.

"The President of the United States is authorized, *without further legislation,* to declare the ports of the United States free and *open to all the products of any nation of the American hemisphere* upon which no export duties are imposed, *whenever and as long as such nation shall admit to its ports free* of all national, provincial, municipal and other taxes, flour, corn meal, and other breadstuffs, preserved meats, fish, vegetables and fruits, cotton-seed oil, rice and other provisions, including all articles of food, lumber, furniture and all articles of wood, agricultural implements and machinery, mining and mechanical machinery, structural steel and iron, steel rails, locomotives, railway cars and supplies, street cars, refined petro-

---

[1] *Cong. Record,* 51st Cong., 1st sess., pp. 9943–10641.
[2] "Senator Hale . . . explicitly stated in a speech on January 24, 1894, that the reciprocity amendment to the McKinley Act, as introduced by him was drawn up by Mr. Blaine in the State Department." Laughlin and Willis, *Reciprocity,* p. 192.

the free introduction of such sugars, molasses, coffee, tea and hides, the product of such country, *for such time as he shall deem just,* and in such case and during such suspension *duties shall be levied, collected and paid* upon such sugars . . . as follows: (then follow the rates to be charged on the enumerated products).

leum, or such products of the United States as may be agreed upon."

Note the broader scope of the Hale (Blaine) Amendment as emphasized by the (writer's) italics. If that amendment had been adopted, it would have meant reciprocity with Canada and Mexico as well as with the countries of Central and South America. It would have included Argentine wool as well as Brazilian coffee and sugar in the list of duty-free commodities. It would not have limited the President to a temporary suspension of the free entry of certain specified articles in retaliation for "unequal or unreasonable" tariffs on our exports, but would have authorized him to declare our ports open to all the products of nations which admitted our agricultural and manufactured products free. In a word, it would have conferred upon the President the direct and extensive power of a blanket proclamation of something that looked dangerously like free trade in raw materials—for the other nations of this hemisphere did not pretend to compete with the United States in manufactured goods. The reciprocity actually adopted, on the other hand, was a kind of "back-handed" reciprocity, giving the President only the contingent and minatory power to proclaim punitive duties, carefully specified by Congress, against countries which, in his judgment, failed to reciprocate our generosity in admitting their sugar, molasses, coffee, tea and hides free. All these articles except sugar were, and had for many years been, on our free list. Were we as likely to win trade concessions from Latin-America by threatening to reimpose duties upon them as by offering to remit the duty on sugar in return for the free admission of our goods to Latin-American ports? Blaine believed not. But he was overborne by the stand-pat protectionists, like "the old-fashioned Senator" Platt of Connecticut and Senator Edmunds of Vermont, who were willing to relieve the Treasury surplus by removing the duty on raw sugar, because no harm to American manufacturing interests was threatened thereby, but who looked with suspicion upon reciprocity as the thin edge of the wedge which might rive the protective system.

Blaine combated this interpretation of his doctrine with vigor. Five days after the passage of the Senate bill (September 15) he published another open letter, addressed to Colonel W. W. Clapp of the Boston *Journal,* a staunch Blaine organ, in which he assured the New England manufacturers that their interests were amply protected in the bill, and that they stood, no less than the farmers of the West, to profit by the reciprocity policy. Did not the enlarged market in the Argentine Republic for the shoes of the Lynn factories compensate for the free admission of hides? And did not the rising tide of discontent in the West warn the party that if it wished to maintain its cherished policy of protection at all it must make substantial concessions to the agrarian sections? Far from being inimical to protection, reciprocity would be its salvation. "Every free trader in the Senate," he concluded, "voted against the reciprocity provision. The free trade papers throughout the country are showing a decided hostility to it. . . . They know and feel that with a system of reciprocity established and growing, their policy of free trade receives a severe blow. . . . The enactment of reciprocity is the safeguard of protection. The defeat of reciprocity is the opportunity of free trade." [1]

Further objections to the reciprocity clause of the McKinley Bill came from both branches of Congress on the score of its impairment of their prerogatives. The House had the constitutional privilege of originating money bills; but Section 3 of the present bill gave the President the authority to impose duties when in his discretion he deemed it necessary. It was the first time in our history that the levying of custom duties by executive proclamation was sanctioned. However, when cases were brought before the Supreme Court to test the constitutionality of Section 3, the decisions upheld the validity of that section on the ground that Congress itself had "prescribed in advance the duties to be levied, collected and paid on sugar, molasses, coffee, tea and hides," in the event of the President's proclamation of the suspension of the free entry of those commodities, and that therefore the President was not invested with the legislative power, but was "the mere agent of the law-making department to ascertain and declare the event upon which its expressed will was to take effect." [2]

[1] Laughlin and Willis, *Reciprocity,* p. 190, and New York *Tribune,* September 17, 1890.
[2] "Boyd v. United States" and "Sternback v. United States," *U. S. Reports,* 143, pp. 649 ff.

A more serious objection came from the Senate, which has always jealously guarded its executive power to participate in treaty making by ratification, modification or rejection. The embarrassments which our Presidents from Washington to Wilson have suffered from this "balance" of executive power is written on many a page of our history. The Senate naturally wants to have the obligations and privileges of our international relations embodied in formal treaties which are submitted to it for ratification; while the President, through "executive agreements," *"modi vivendi,"* "conventions," "special missions" and the like, often effectively directs our foreign relations without the intervention of the Senate. It is to be noted that Section 3 of the McKinley Act left to the President's sole discretion the suspension of the free entry of certain commodities to our ports in case of his failure, in his own judgment, to negotiate satisfactory commercial arrangements with the countries exporting such commodities. In other words, the bargains made with those countries, though often spoken of as reciprocity "treaties," were not in a strict sense treaties at all, but executive "agreements" signed by the President and proclaimed as in effect by him. If Section 3 was tainted with economic heresy in the eyes of the high protectionists, it was also apprehended by the jealous senators as a menace to their constitutional privilege.

The burden of our foreign diplomacy was so heavy upon Secretary Blaine, troubled as he was by indifferent health and domestic affliction, that, once the reciprocity section was incorporated into the McKinley Act, he left the negotiation of the agreements almost wholly in the hands of a man who, by long experience in the diplomatic service and by intimate acquaintance with Latin-American affairs, was eminently fitted for the task. This man was John W. Foster of Ohio, who, as chairman of the Republican state committee in the Grant campaign of 1872, had attracted the attention of Blaine and had received from him a cordial letter of congratulation upon "the wonderful thoroughness" with which he had done his work. "If you visit Washington the coming winter," the letter concluded, "I beg that you will do me the honor to call at my house—821 15th St.—where you will find the latch-string out and on pulling it will meet a Western welcome." [1] Foster was rewarded for his services by President Grant with the appointment as Minister to Mexico, and on visiting Washington to receive his instruc-

[1] Blaine to John W. Foster, November 10, 1872.

JAMES G. BLAINE

tions he was entertained by Speaker Blaine. The friendship thus begun between the two men remained unbroken until Blaine's death nineteen years later.

In 1880 Foster was transferred from Mexico City to St. Petersburg, where he remained until November, 1881. He then settled in Washington to resume his lucrative law practice, but early in 1883 he was persuaded by President Arthur to accept the Ministry to Madrid, in order to negotiate treaties of reciprocity between the United States and the Spanish colonies of Puerto Rico and Cuba. When he returned to Washington on December 8, 1884, with the treaties signed and ready to submit to the Senate, the elections of the previous month had broken the long tenure of power of the Republican Party. The short ("lame duck") session of Congress of the winter of 1884-5, therefore, under the adverse influence of the impending Democratic Administration, grew cool to Arthur's policies. Even Blaine himself, who was to become so ardent a champion of reciprocity a few years later, allowed his thinly veiled animus against Arthur to lead him to oppose the treatise. Though not in public office at the time, he frequently spoke to his friends in Washington of the inopportuneness of the commercial agreements negotiated with Mexico, Spain and the Dominican Republic, remarking for example to Congressman Robert R. Hitt, his former Assistant Secretary of State, that "there are too many treaties before the Senate just now." However much or little his influence contributed to the result, Blaine was not disappointed, therefore, when the Cuban treaty failed to come to a vote in the Senate and the Dominican treaty was withdrawn by President Cleveland soon after his inauguration. The Grant-Romero treaty of 1883 with Mexico, though not withdrawn by Cleveland, dragged on year after year in the Senate and was finally dropped. Reciprocity, therefore, seemed dead when Harrison came into office. Blaine revived it as a major instrumentality for strengthening the bonds of Pan-Americanism.

Now Foster was called again from his briefs and his law books to the service of the State Department. On the day after the McKinley Bill became law, he was invited to Blaine's house and asked to take charge of the reciprocity negotiations. He tells us in his *Memoirs* that Blaine's reasons for entrusting to him this important task were that his own duties were burdensome already, that his health was poor, that the negotiations would require much statistical work and embrace many governments, and that there was no one in his department to whom he chose to commit the task. "From that day," continues Foster, "the reciprocity negotiations under the law of October 1, 1890, were placed entirely in my hands, except so far as Secretary Blaine's signature was necessary. . . . For the next twelve months I was in constant personal intercourse with Mr. Blaine and often with the President, informing them of the progress of the negotiations and seeking their advice or direction on controversial or difficult matters." [1]

Foster believed that he could do the work in Washington, but he soon found it necessary to visit Cuba to confer with the leading sugar planters and the Governor General, and even to go to Madrid to overcome the resentment of the Spanish government for the failure of our Senate to ratify the treaties concluded in 1884. On his way back from his successful mission to Madrid, he stopped in London and was assured that the Colonial Office would allow the governors of the British West Indian possessions to make their own commercial agreements with the United States.

The first of the reciprocity agreements negotiated under Section 3 of the McKinley Act was with Brazil, signed on February 5 and proclaimed on April 1, 1891. By it Brazil continued to enjoy free entry into our ports of her sugar, hides and coffee, and we, in turn, secured the free admission into Brazil of a long list of agricultural and manufactured products and a reduction of 25 per cent of the duties on others. During the ensuing fifteen months, agreements of similar tenor were made with fourteen more governments, including Santo Domingo, the Central American states (except Costa Rica), the British West Indian possessions, British Guiana, Spain (for Cuba and Puerto Rico), Germany and Austro-Hungary.[2] Whether or not these reciprocity agreements, if they had operated over a long period of years, would have resulted in substantial relief to the American farmers and a great enlargement of our foreign commerce in general, it is impossible to say. The Republican national platform of 1892 pointed with pride to the success of the policy of reciprocity, "under which our export trade

---

[1] J. W. Foster, *Diplomatic Memoirs,* Vol. II, p. 6.

[2] The interesting reason why the last-mentioned European countries were eager to participate in the reciprocity pacts was that since the continental blockade of the Napoleonic wars had shut off their importation of sugar from tropical regions, they had encouraged the intensive cultivation of beet sugar at home, and wanted a share of our market for their surplus crop. The termination of the reciprocity agreements in 1894 caused no little hard feeling on the part of those countries toward the United States.

has vastly increased and new and enlarged markets have been opened for the products of our farms and workshops"; but the more sober analysis, by competent economists, of the statistics of our trade with those countries with which we had made reciprocity agreements resulted in the judgment that it was "difficult to recognize any particular effect directly traceable to our new treaty arrangements."[1]

It is true that Cuba must be exempted from this judgment. During the period from September 1, 1891, to August 27, 1894, when the reciprocity agreement was in force, our exports to the island doubled (from $12,224,888 to $24,157,698) and our imports rose from some $55,000,000 to $78,000,000, of which sugar alone represented more than $60,000,000. This trade fell off sharply in 1895, but it would be unjust to ascribe the decline wholly to the abrogation of the reciprocity agreement; for the serious revolutionary disturbances were already on foot which resulted in our armed intervention three years later to free Cuba from the Spanish yoke. With the great country of Brazil, from which conspicuously favorable results of the reciprocity agreement were expected, our trade showed hardly any improvement. The year before the agreement went into effect we sent merchandise to the value of $14,120,246 to Brazil, and the year following the agreement the figure increased only to $14,291,873. On the other hand, the year following the abrogation of the agreement showed exports of $15,165,079—a figure larger than that of any of the three years of reciprocity. Our exports to the British West Indies bear the same witness to the apparent ineffectiveness of the reciprocity pacts ($779,138 in 1891 and $7,764,178 in 1894).[2] "The truth of the matter seems to be," says Wm. S. Robertson, "that the reciprocity policy inaugurated by the McKinley Act was too short-lived to deflect greatly the currents of trade, while the retaliatory features of that act were scarcely calculated to produce good results upon the publicists of Hispanic America."[3]

Blaine's reciprocity clause had the misfortune of being attached to one of the most unpopular bills ever passed by Congress. Even before the first agreement had been concluded under its provisions, its doom was foreshadowed, for the congressional elections of November 6, 1890,

---

[1] Laughlin and Willis, *Reciprocity*, p. 217.
[2] *Ibid.*, p. 221.
[3] W. S. Robertson, *Hispanic American Relations*, p. 219. "Retaliatory" duties were actually proclaimed by President Harrison only against Colombia, Haiti and Venezuela, March 15, 1892. See Richardson, *Messages and Papers of the Presidents*, Vol. IX, pp. 265–270.

which were virtually a popular referendum on the McKinley Act, resulted in one of those sharp reversals of political power known as "land-slides." The Democrats returned 235 members to the House, where they had had but 159 in the Fifty-first Congress, while the Republican strength sank from 166 to 88. The futility of the attempt of the party of high protection to conciliate the West by the levy of duties on agricultural imports and the promise of enlarged markets through reciprocity agreements was evident when the States of Indiana, Illinois, Minnesota, Iowa, Kansas and Nebraska, which had sent 44 Republicans and 18 Democrats to the Fifty-first Congress, now returned 44 Democrats and 15 Republicans. The repudiation of McKinleyism was complete, and McKinley himself lost the seat which he had occupied in the House for seven consecutive terms. The Republicans still held the executive power and a slight majority in the Senate, enabling them to prevent for the two remaining years of the Administration any effective assault on the citadel of protection. But with the victory of Cleveland in 1892 the Democrats secured the Presidency and both branches of Congress for the first time since the Administration of James Buchanan. The days of the McKinley Act were numbered.

From the fiscal point of view, as well as the political, the reciprocity policy came at an inopportune moment; for, while the McKinley Bill was being debated in the summer of 1890, the Republicans, partly as a further bid for Western support for the high rates of that measure, passed the Sherman Silver Purchase bill, which obligated the government to buy 4,500,000 ounces of silver a month, which was added to the circulating medium in the form of silver certificates based on the bullion stored in the vaults of the Treasury. Since the silver certificates were redeemable in gold at the option of the holders, this inflation of the currency by annual increments of some $50,000,000 meant an increasing burden of support for the gold reserve. The silver, being legal tender, began to pour into the Treasury in payment of taxes and dues of various sorts, while gold had to be paid out for the settlement of foreign debit balances and, if demanded, for domestic redemption of the silver certificates. Thus there was set in motion what President Cleveland called the "endless chain," by which the gold reserve was drawn upon until it fell below the statutory minimum of $100,000,000, and when repleted by bond sales, was immediately drawn out again by the same silver magnet.

It is true that other events besides the passage of the ill-starred Silver Purchase Act conspired to bring embarrassment to the finances of the country in the "luckless years" of Cleveland's second Administration—the severe industrial panic of 1893, the failure of the great English banking firm of Baring Brothers, the closing of the mints of India to silver, the adoption of the gold standard by the empires of Germany and Austro-Hungary. The point we emphasize here is that the McKinley Act, with which the policy of reciprocity was bound up, deprived the Treasury of $56,000,000 of sugar duties and imposed on it a further burden of $7,000,000 for bounties to American sugar growers and threatened still further to embarrass it by such high rates on a variety of commodities as would restrict imports sharply. The act was passed in a prosperous year, when there was no apprehension that a surplus would soon be followed by a deficit in the Treasury. President Harrison in his final annual message (December 6, 1892), only a few months before the first omens of distress appeared, could "take great satisfaction in being able to say that the general conditions affecting the commercial and industrial interests of the United States" were "in the highest degree favorable."

The total value of our foreign trade had increased $128,283,604 over the figure of the previous year. Our exports of $1,030,278,148 had for the first time in our history passed the billion mark, and our imports, in spite of the McKinley rates, had exceeded the average annual value of the previous decade by $135,215,940. The value of imports on the free list also had touched a new high point of $457,999,658, and comprised 55.35 per cent of our total imports, as against 43.35 per cent in 1891. In the light of such figures the President deemed it "unnecessary to renew the argument in favor of a protective tariff" or to offer further justification of the efficacy of the new policy of reciprocity. The full benefit of the trade agreements would not be realized until better facilities of communication and exchange were found, but the President did not doubt that, if the trade agreements were "continued in force and aided by the establishment of American steamship lines," we should within a short period secure fully one third of the trade of the countries of Central and South America, instead of the meager eight per cent of that trade which we had enjoyed in the year 1885. The alarm which the reciprocity agreements had already inspired in our European competitors for the South American trade was the best testimony to the wisdom of our policy.[1]

Reciprocity, then, thanks to Blaine's enormous influence, had become an acknowledged tenet of party politics; and that fact alone would have militated against its retention by the victorious Democrats, even if the necessities of the Treasury had not been backed by the interest of certain Senators in having the duties on raw sugar restored. The new Ways and Means Committee of the Fifty-second Congress, under the chairmanship of William L. Wilson of West Virginia, moved directly to the attack in its report of December 19, 1893: "It is the purpose of the present (Wilson) bill to repeal in toto Section 3 of the tariff act of October 1, 1890, commonly, but most erroneously known as its reciprocity provision. . . . This section has brought no appreciable advantage to American exporters; it is not in intention or effect a provision for reciprocity, but for retaliation. It inflicts penalties upon the American people by making them pay higher prices for these articles, if the fiscal necessities of other nations [2] compel them to levy duties upon the products of the United States. . . . Moreover, we do not believe that Congress can rightly vest in the President of the United States any authority or power to impose or release taxes on our people by proclamation, or to suspend or dispense with the operation of a law of Congress." [3]

We have already seen that the Supreme Court eventually upheld the constitutionality of the delegation to the President of the power complained of in the last sentence quoted from the Wilson Committee's report.[4]

The Wilson tariff bill, which emerged from its mutilation in the Senate as the Wilson-Gorman Bill, to become a law without President Cleveland's signature on August 26, 1894, put an end to the brief experiment of reciprocity. Without expressly repealing the agreements already made, the bill made them waste paper by restoring raw sugar to the dutiable list, and prevented any further executive bargaining for reciprocal trade advantages by refusing to the President the power to suspend the free admission of any goods on the non-dutiable list. The flexible feature of the McKinley Act (to be revived in other forms

---

[1] J. D. Richardson, *Messages and Papers of the Presidents*, Vol. IX, pp. 306–313.
[2] Customs duties were almost the sole source of revenue for many of the Latin-American countries.
[3] *House Report* No. 234, 53d Cong., 2d sess., pp. 11–12.
[4] See above, p. 450.

and for other purposes in later tariff bills) was eliminated. The schedules returned to their rigid form. Congress vindicated its exclusive power to regulate foreign trade. Nevertheless, the leaven of a new theory of the uses of protection had entered into our economic thought, and that leaven has continued to work even to our own day—as witnessed by the revival of the reciprocity proposals in the discussions of the seventh Pan-American Congress at Montevideo in the closing month of 1933.

Blaine himself was spared the humiliation of seeing the repudiation of his cherished policy. A few weeks after President Harrison's annual message of December, 1892, had heralded the new adventure of protection tempered by reciprocity as "marching forward to conquer the trade of the world," and a few months before the harbingers of the "luckless years" began to appear, the wearied statesman passed away at his home in Washington.

HAVING IN the last two chapters studied the diplomatic activities of Blaine as Secretary of State in the Harrison Administration, we turn now to his personal and political fortunes, which were never allowed by his great body of devoted followers to become submerged in his official duties. After Blaine had rented his new Dupont Circle mansion to Mr. Joseph Leiter on a long time lease in 1883, the family had no fixed home in Washington for six years. The winters of 1883–1884 and 1884–1885 were spent in the Marcy house on Lafayette Square and the Windom house on Scott Circle respectively; those of 1885–1886 and 1886–1887 at Augusta; that of 1887–1888 in Italy. Early in January, 1889, Blaine returned to Washington after a long absence, and, with Mrs. Blaine and Walker, took rooms at the Hotel Normandie.

They were received with open arms by their large circle of friends at the capital. "My rooms are filled with flowers and my table is loaded with cards, invitations and notes of welcome," wrote Mrs. Blaine to her daughter Harriet at school at Farmington, Connecticut.[1] Walker was confined to his room for several weeks with a broken ankle in a plaster cast, but his father "dined out" evening after evening. It was good to be back among old friends like Robert R. Hitt, his former Assistant Secretary of State, and Senator Don Cameron; and it was especially good to be back on the eve of the return of the Republican Party to power, after four years of Grover Cleveland with his tariff heresies, his pension vetoes, and his Cabinet members from States south of Mason and Dixon's line. On January 20 came General Harrison's letter from Indianapolis "in his own handwriting, full of cordial words and good understanding," offering Blaine the State portfolio. "There is no doubt," wrote Mrs. Blaine to her son James at school at Waterville, Maine, "that your Father will accept this trust, and gladly."[2]

The acceptance of the first place in the new Cabinet made it necessary for Blaine to seek a suitable residence in Washington. At first there was some talk of building again on a vacant lot which Blaine still

---

[1] *Letters of Mrs. James G. Blaine*, Vol. II, p. 227.
[2] *Ibid.*, Vol. II, p. 231.

owned at Dupont Circle. Then the plan was entertained of selling this lot and buying land for a house on 16th Street. But Blaine's desire for building new houses seems to have been sated after the construction of "Stanwood" at Bar Harbor, and in the end he decided to take the old Seward house at 17 Madison Place, on the east side of Lafayette Square, but a few minutes' walk from the State Department building and the White House.

It was an old-fashioned colonial three-story red brick mansion, with garden and out-buildings in the rear. It had been built nearly sixty years earlier by Commodore John Rodgers. Many historic associations clung to the house. On its steps Philip Barton Key, son of the author of "The Star Spangled Banner," had been shot down in 1859 by Daniel E. Sickels for his criminal infatuation with Sickels' young and charming wife. In one of the upper chambers Secretary of State William H. Seward, lying ill on the night of Lincoln's assassination, had been attacked with a bowie knife by Louis Payne, the most desperate of the band of murderers, and had barely escaped with his life by rolling out of bed on the side away from the assassin. Secretary of War W. W. Belknap occupied the house for a time during the Grant Administration, and the Juno-like Mrs. Belknap died there, after leading a gay social life on the money which she and her husband stole from the government on contracts for supplies for the Indian forts in the West. Later the house was used for the storage of archives of the War Department, under whose weight the floors sagged so that when Blaine purchased and remodeled the property it was necessary to put in iron girders to strengthen the upper stories.

Blaine's energetic wife set to work with undiminished enthusiasm to plan with the architects and bargain with the furnishers for fitting out her new home—the fifth since the purchase of the State Street mansion at Augusta in 1862. "I have $20,000 for repairs and furniture," she wrote to her son. "If anyone had told me at your age, Jamie, that I should ever have $20,000 to handle at my own sweet will, I should have believed him or her, just as I believe in Aladdin's lamp, fascinating but supernatural." [1] She planned the rooms for the children, consulted them about the stuff for the curtains and the color of the wall papers, put in a new kitchen and six south windows, installed modern plumbing and heating. She brought some of the furniture from the old Augusta house,

[1] *Letters of Mrs. James G. Blaine*, Vol. II, p. 238.

and purchased new pieces in Boston and New York. On November 6, 1889, the family moved into "the sweet, sweet home." The eldest (bachelor) son Walker, Solicitor of the State Department, and the middle daughter, Margaret (engaged to Walter Damrosch), were the only children living with their parents. Alice lived at Governor's Island, New York, where her husband, Colonel Coppinger, was stationed. Emmons and his wife [1] were in Baltimore, where he was assistant to President Henry G. Davis of the West Virginia Central Railroad Company. The youngest son and daughter, James, jr., and Harriet, were away at school. On Sunday, November 10, there was a family "house-warming" party for luncheon. The Emmons Blaines came over from Baltimore, and Mr. Damrosch christened the new piano, "making it ring out melodiously."

Yet, the new "sweet" home was to be an abode of sorrow. Scarcely two months after the family moved in, the eldest son, his father's special pride and invaluable helper in the State Department, succumbed to pneumonia on January 15, 1890. His parents were still prostrated by this first break in the family circle since the death of the infant Stanwood nearly forty years before, when the eldest daughter Alice, who had come to Washington to attend her brother's funeral, followed him across the dark river (February 2). In June, 1892, a telegram came to the Blaines at Bar Harbor announcing the serious illness of the second son, Emmons, who had moved to Chicago as General Agent of the Baltimore and Ohio Railroad. Mr. and Mrs. Blaine and their daughters immediately got ready to go out to Chicago, but even as they were starting the news came of Emmons' death. Too late to bid good-by to the son on whom they had leaned especially for comfort since Walker's death, the Blaines made their dreary journey back from the grave, while the heart of the country went out in sympathy with them for the cruel fate which had bereft them of the three eldest of their six children within thirty months.

The youngest son (the "Jamie" or "J'aime" of his mother's letters) had made a secret marriage at the age of seventeen (in 1886), with Miss Marie Nevins of New York. The marriage was unhappy and ended in a divorce granted to Mrs. Blaine at Deadwood, South Dakota, on February 20, 1892, giving her the custody of their four-year-old son

[1] On September 26, 1888, Emmons Blaine had been married at Richfield Springs, New York, to Anita, the daughter of Cyrus H. McCormick, the reaper manufacturer of Chicago.

and granting her suit fees and alimony. Blaine was sorely distressed by the affair. A week after the divorce he gave a statement to the press, sharply criticizing Father Thomas Ducey, who had married the minor son without securing the consent of his parents.

In compensation for sorrows and vexations, however, the Blaines gained a charming, accomplished, and devoted son-in-law by the marriage of Walter Damrosch to their daughter Margaret in the new home at Washington, May 27, 1890. As the eldest daughter's wedding in the Dupont Circle mansion seven years before had been honored by the presence of President Arthur, so the second daughter's wedding found President Harrison among the guests.

The personal relations between President Harrison and his Secretary of State have never been clearly and authentically given to the public. A vast number of rumors, conjectures, suspicions and innuendos have been circulated to prove the jealous rivalry of the men beneath the punctilious courtesy of their official intercourse. In the private papers which Blaine preserved there is no letter or memorandum that throws light on his personal feelings toward the President. The private papers of Harrison, which have not been accessible to the present writer, will doubtless, when utilized by a scholar now at work on the biography of Harrison, furnish a satisfactory account of this vexed subject. Meanwhile, without trespassing upon the preserve of that biographer, we may point to a few of the indisputable facts and incidents which show that something more serious than mere "incompatibility of temper" underlay the failure of the President and his Secretary of State to work together with the same harmony as President Garfield and Secretary Blaine had done.

First of all, Blaine was kept waiting until five weeks before the inauguration of Harrison for the inevitable invitation to join the Cabinet, while the press was urging the appropriateness of the appointment with an insistence which might be interpreted as pressure brought to bear upon the President-elect. In an article published in the Portland *Sunday Telegram and Press-Herald* of February 9, 1930, Colonel Fred N. Dow, Collector of the Port of Portland and for many years a close friend of Blaine, tells of a meeting at Blaine's house in Augusta, about ten days after the election of Harrison, at which Senator Hale, Congressman Milliken of Blaine's old district, Governor Nelson Dingley and others were present. As soon as Colonel Dow was seated Blaine handed him a letter which he had received from the President-elect (probably the one in which Harrison thanked him for his aid in the campaign) and asked him what he thought of it. "I said," replied the Colonel, "he is to offer you the position of Secretary of State." "But he does not say so," replied Blaine. "What makes you think he is to invite me to be Secretary of State?" "Because," I insisted, "Mr. Harrison would never have written such a letter if he had not intended to invite you." Then the Colonel read the letter out loud "with the result of a general agreement among those present that the offer was to be made." Still, Blaine had to wait two months before the offer came. If Harrison had been balancing his name against others, it would have been a different matter. Was it a kind of perverse independence that prompted him to withhold the invitation just because the public was eagerly expecting it?

Again, at the very outset of the Administration Blaine was denied the favor he desired above all others at the President's hands, namely, the appointment of his son Walker as Assistant Secretary of State. There was no question of Walker Blaine's qualifications for the post. His association with William H. Trescot in the South American mission of 1881 and with J. A. J. Creswell as assistant counsel on the commission for the adjudication of the Alabama Claims the next year had given ample proof of his diplomatic discretion and his legal acumen. Besides, as a lawyer, he would have been of the greatest help to his father, who had had only the merest smattering of legal training. Harrison's objection to the appointment on the grounds of an aversion from the encouragement of nepotism came with strange irony from a President who found places in the government service for a number of his own and his wife's relatives. The real reason for the President's refusal is probably to be found in his determination that nothing resembling a "Blaine faction" should be built up on the patronage. Again and again Blaine had to confess sorrowfully to his friends that he was not in control of the patronage of his department and even that his known preference for an aspirant for a place was rather a liability than an asset with the Administration. Walker had to be content with the appointment as Solicitor—a post which he accepted graciously. The Assistant Secretaryship went to William F. Wharton, on the request of Representative Henry Cabot Lodge of Massachusetts. The request for the promotion of Colonel Coppinger met with no better reception.

Another untoward incident in the relations between the President and the Blaine family was told by George M. Pullman and reported in the Kansas City *Star* of March 14, 1901. According to this story, Mrs. Blaine called at the White House one morning in the spring of 1892 and reproached the President for his ungenerous treatment of her husband; the interview ending in Mrs. Blaine's curt dismissal. For this story, related nine years after the event, and so startlingly out of accord with Mrs. Blaine's character, I have found no contemporary evidence whatever. It probably grew out of the many rumors that circulated in the Washington "whispering gallery." However, there are many phrases scattered through Mrs. Blaine's letters that reveal her unfavorable estimate of the occupant of the White House. She spoke of Harrison soon after his election as "the oracle at Indianapolis," in whom Blaine had "little faith"; and two weeks after the inauguration she referred to Mrs. Harrison as "her American Majesty." She commented on the presentation of the diplomatic corps to the President by her husband on March 15, 1889, as "all interesting, though Harrison is of such a nature that you do not feel at liberty to enjoy yourself." She resented Harrison's coldness to her husband's recommendations for office: "All propositions are rejected. It is a most uncomfortable twist in the make-up of a man. The idea apparently is that, having given Blaine the head of the table, no distinctly personal friend shall also have a seat." Even when she recognized the dignity of the President's office, she could not refrain from a little dig at his person: "I found the President here going over the Samoan dispatches with your Father. He sat all crumpled up, his nose and his boots and his gloves almost meeting, but he was examining those dispatches with care and great intelligence, and although I am not drawn to him, I cannot refuse him the homage of respect." [1]

It was noticeable that President Harrison did not invite his Secretary of State to accompany him on any of his official trips to various parts of the country. For instance, when the President went to Cleveland on May 30, 1890, to dedicate the Garfield Memorial, he took Vice President Morton and Secretaries Windom, Miller, Wanamaker and Rusk, although Blaine was a trustee of the Garfield Memorial Association and by far the closest friend of the martyred President in all the officialdom of Washington. The following August the President invited

[1] *Letters of Mrs. James G. Blaine*, Vol. II, pp. 223, 244, 257–8, 262–3.

only Secretaries Rusk and Noble to go with him on the cruiser *Baltimore* to attend the Grand Army encampment at Boston; and when he went for a week's trip, early in October, to Indiana, Illinois, Iowa, Kansas and Missouri, he was accompanied by Secretary Tracy. There was undoubtedly good cause for not including Blaine in the presidential party which traveled to the Pacific coast in the spring of 1891, visiting eighteen States in its journey of more than nine thousand miles, for Blaine was overwhelmed with official duties then and his health was none too good. But when the President made his visit to Cleveland with four Cabinet members in May, 1890, there was no reason why Blaine should have been left behind. The Pan-American Congress had adjourned the previous month. The controversy with Great Britain over the Bering Sea seal fisheries had not reached an acute stage. The revolution in Chile had not yet broken out. The McKinley Bill had not come to its first vote in the House. And the time to begin the negotiation of reciprocity agreements was still six months off. One cannot avoid the suspicion that a President so jealous of his prerogative as Harrison was loath to appear in Garfield's territory of the Western Reserve accompanied by a Secretary of State whose very presence must suggest that Secretary's dominating position in the Garfield Administration of 1881. He had no intention of playing the rôle of the Merovingian King to his Secretary's Mayor of the Palace.

Finally, the manifest signs of Blaine's declining physical vigor would have strengthened the bonds of sympathy and understanding between the two men, had such bonds genuinely existed. In May, 1891, Blaine went to the Damrosch home in East 61st Street, New York, partly to see his new grandchild and partly to attend the opening festival of the New York Symphony and Oratorical Societies in the magnificent hall which Andrew Carnegie had built in West Fifty-seventh Street, largely as a testimony to his personal affection for Mr. Damrosch and his enthusiasm for the great contribution which Mr. Damrosch was making to the musical education of the metropolis. Professor John Bassett Moore, Counselor of the State Department, called on Blaine at the Damrosch house, at the President's request, and found him seated with his gouty foot propped up on a chair. Blaine insisted on rising, however, to bid Professor Moore good-by with the cheery innuendo, "You see I am not dead yet." [1]

[1] Conversation of the author with Professor Moore, June, 1931.

Still Blaine was taken ill at the concert in Carnegie hall. He was not in condition to go back to Washington, but went down to his cottage at Bar Harbor, where he remained until the end of October. During the summer much publicity was given to rumors and speculations on the seriousness of his illness. A prominent Democratic newspaper in New York came out in July with sensational headlines announcing, on the authority of "a friend of President Harrison's" that Blaine was suffering from an advanced stage of Bright's disease, and printed a detailed account of his symptoms, together with the opinions of a number of physicians in America and Europe on the inevitable doom of a patient suffering from the disease which the alleged chemical tests revealed. Blaine was justly indignant at this "infamous" publication, which he rebutted with a declaration of his physical soundness erring almost as far on the side of optimism as the offending journalist had erred on the side of pessimism. He wrote to his friend Charles A. Dana of the New York *Sun,* on July 29, that the reputed "results of analysis" which had been given to the public were "false and forged." "I have never had a single return which did not say, 'No sugar, no albumen, no casts,' and I have had them only from authority of the highest character. I have not the slightest touch of Bright's disease." [1]

Nevertheless, Dana sent his associate Edward P. Mitchell to Bar Harbor the next week, "not specially with regard to Blaine's health," [2] but to consult him on the political situation. "Mr. Blaine's interest in everything seemed unabated," reported Mitchell, "and his grasp of ideas unimpaired. I thought that he conversed with a little less verve than formerly, but there was no marked sign of enfeeblement. I thought, too, that his face was grayer and the familiar puffiness beneath the eyes much more pronounced than when I had seen him last. But he positively reiterated over and over again the assertion that he was getting better daily and that there had been no diagnosis showing Bright's disease." [3] Mitchell published an editorial in the *Sun* to this effect, and in 1924 stated in his *Memoirs* that he believed that the optimistic editorial was true when he wrote it. Yet, looking back over more than thirty years, he had come to the conclusion that the physicians had been practicing "a pious fraud of concealment" upon Blaine.

[1] Edward P. Mitchell, *Memoirs of an Editor,* p. 319.
[2] There were stories to the effect that President Harrison was sending emissaries to Bar Harbor to observe and to report upon the condition of Blaine's health.
[3] Mitchell, *op. cit.,* p. 320.

The prolonged absence of the Secretary of State from Washington at the time when the Bering Sea controversy with Great Britain was growing acute and the complications with the Chilean revolution were approaching a crisis,[1] inevitably devolved an additional burden of labor upon the President. That his rigid sense of justice and of the gratitude due for his pains tempered such sympathy as his rather cold nature might feel for his Secretary, we have evidence from several quarters. Murat Halstead in a penciled postscript to a letter to Mrs. Blaine, a few days before the family returned to Washington, wrote: "Please tell Mr. Blaine something I forgot. I happen to have heard in such a way *I know,* that the President would be gratified very much if there could be some expression made by Mr. Blaine of the credit due the President for his extra work in the State Department. I think the President takes some pride in it, and that perhaps what Mr. Blaine might be perfectly *willing* to say would be highly estimated and might smooth the ways of pleasantness." [2]

But Blaine, though always speaking of the President with respect, was not moved to make any gesture of gratitude to his chief. A few months later (May, 1892) Harrison complained bitterly to Senator S. M. Cullom of Illinois that he had been doing the work of the State Department for a year or more, that he had prepared every official document and had the originals in his own handwriting on the desk before him, and yet that the Secretary of State was giving out accounts of what was being done in the department and taking all the credit to himself. He expressed himself as "perfectly willing, to use a familiar figure, to carry a soldier's knapsack, when the soldier is sore of foot and tired, and all that he wanted in return was acknowledgment of the act and a show of appreciation." This was what he expected of Mr. Blaine, he said, and in closing the conversation he remarked that he intended some day to "disclose the true conditions of their relations." [3]

There was more behind the strained relations between the President and his Secretary of State than these words imply. It would have taken a duller man than Benjamin Harrison to be deceived as to the trend of public sentiment and party politics. Lacking the popular appeal to the masses which could have brought to heel the bosses who were dis-

---

[1] The attack on our sailors in the streets of Valparaiso occurred while Blaine was at Bar Harbor.

[2] Murat Halstead to Mrs. Blaine, October 24, 1891.

[3] Shelby M. Cullom, *Fifty Years of Public Service,* pp. 252-3.

appointed by his stern resistance to their demands on the patronage, he found himself deserted by the powerful guardians of the Republican State machines. Tom Platt of New York turned against him for his alleged breach of promise in regard to the Treasury portfolio.[1] Matthew Quay of Pennsylvania, who, as Chairman of the Republican National Committee, was credited with having carried New York for Harrison in 1888, resented the "cold shouldering" that he received from the President and Postmaster General Wanamaker, and went over bag and baggage to the support of Blaine for the nomination in 1892.[2] Don Cameron, the other Pennsylvania Stalwart, was one of Blaine's intimate social circle at Washington. Tom Reed of Maine, rising to prominence as Speaker of the House, while no friend of Blaine, was mortally offended at the President for the rejection of his candidate for the Collectorship of the Port of his native city of Portland. Mark Hanna, Treasurer of the National Committee, was requited for his zeal in collecting funds for the Harrison campaign of 1888 by having his candidate for a Federal office turned down without so much as a word of explanation to the applicant or to his sponsor. The disgust of the Old Guard politicians with the President's nepotism and frigid austerity found vent in a bit of malicious doggerel reflected in the "mirrors of Washington" of forty-odd years ago:

> The baby [3] runs the White House,
> Levi [4] runs the bar,
> Wanny [4] runs the Sunday School,
> And, damn it! here we are.[5]

[1] "I had for many years been very ambitious to conduct the Government finances. When I received what my friends and myself accepted as a positive pledge from President Harrison that he would gratify my aspirations I felt that I had nothing more in the world to seek. But when, notwithstanding a letter in President Harrison's own handwriting (which Platt does not publish) promising me the appointment, I was suddenly informed that William Windom of Minnesota had been selected, I felt that there was little use pinning my faith on anybody or training myself for high office(!)." *The Autobiography of Thomas Collier Platt,* pp. 206–7.

[2] Quay was especially bitter against Harrison for the readiness with which the latter had accepted his resignation from the National Committee in 1890, when Henry C. Lea of Philadelphia published some damning evidence of Quay's misappropriation of funds as State Treasurer of Pennsylvania.

[3] Referring to the President's grandson "Baby McKee," who, says William Allen White, "was forever crawling over the front page of the newspapers." (*Masks in a Pageant,* p. 87.)

[4] Vice President Levi P. Morton and Postmaster General John Wanamaker were both as solid pillars of the church as Harrison himself, though the former owned the Shoreham Hotel which dispensed choice drinks at its elaborate bar, and the latter was credited with a canny faculty of reconciling God and Mammon.

[5] "With few exceptions," wrote Platt in 1910, "those who did most to place Harrison

The President must have been aware, too, of the pressure which was being brought to bear on his Secretary to enter the lists for the nomination in 1892. Quay launched the Blaine boom in the Pennsylvania Republican convention at Harrisburg in August, 1891, by the following resolution: "It has been with especial gratification that the Republicans of this Commonwealth have observed the brilliant administration of the State Department by one of Pennsylvania's native sons, whose superb diplomacy has electrified the hearts of all Americans, extracted from foreign powers a degree of respect and admiration for the American flag hitherto unequaled, and opened wide to us in other lands commercial gates hitherto barred. In view of his magnificent achievement in diplomacy and statecraft, we earnestly express the hope that the Republican National Convention of 1892 may place in unanimous nomination for the Presidency (which nomination we feel sure will be followed by a triumphant election) the Honorable James G. Blaine of Pennsylvania and Maine." [1] The Pennsylvania delegates, however, were not willing to commit themselves to so definite a pledge nine months before the meeting of the national convention, and modified the last sentence of the resolution to read: "These magnificent achievements justify confidence and furnish new occasion for us now to reaffirm the loyalty and devotion of the Republicans of Pennsylvania to her most distinguished son, James G. Blaine." In the same week Felix Agnus of the Baltimore *American* wrote to Blaine at Bar Harbor: "To be brief, I want you to give me an inkling as to how to stand in the future. I hear you will run and I hear you will not. So what am I to do? Twenty years of discreet loyalty to you are certainly enough guarantee that whatever you may wish to say to me will be stored as you instruct." [2]

When Blaine returned to Washington in the autumn the solicitations multiplied. A long letter from Joseph Medill of the Chicago *Tribune* declared that the Republicans throughout the Union were practically unanimous for Blaine as their next candidate and that the party was "warmer and stronger" for him than it had been eight years before. Mugwumpism was "played out." The old charges of corruption were

in the Senate and then in the Presidency found him a marble statue when they asked for a recognition of their services." (*Autobiography*, p. 252.) "If you want an army to fight for you, you must feed it," was Samuel J. Randall's laconic diagnosis of Harrison's unpopularity. (S. M. Cullom, *Fifty years of Public Service*, p. 138.)

[1] New York *World*, August 20, 1891.
[2] Felix Agnus to Blaine, August 27, 1891.

forgotten. Medill took Blaine up on the mountain of ambition and showed him all the kingdoms of the world. He alone could carry New York and the other pivotal States. He need not exert himself as he had done in 1884, but might remain quietly at Bar Harbor while his devoted followers swept him into the White House. Once President, he could develop his cherished policy of reciprocity with the backing of a united party. He could place the United States on a high plane among the powers of the world in trade and influence. He could push the Isthmian Canal to completion and open the way for our dominion over the Pacific. If he would but say "Yes," he could retire betimes from the Cabinet and spend the winter between his election and his inauguration in the "balmy, sunny, health-giving, anti-malarial climate of Southern California." [1]

Not less confident was the brief note which Murat Halstead sent on the eve of his departure for Italy. The ticket must be Blaine and John Sherman (!). It was sure to win. "And I think if I were you and President, I would offer Harrison the Secretaryship of State (!), McKinley the Treasury, and Clarkson the Postmaster Generalship." [2] The next month Lynde Harrison wrote from New Haven, begging Blaine not to refuse to "save the party next year," as he only could do,[3] and George A. Halsey of Newark expressed his concern because Elkins had said that Blaine would not run: "I told him that it would be useless to run anyone *but* yourself; he did not seem inclined to talk." [4] J. S. Clarkson, Chairman of the National Committee, assured Blaine that the business men of the country were looking to him to foster the prosperity already evident in the new policy of reciprocity, and that he was the only man who could "draw from the Farmers Alliance the necessary votes to keep the party in power in the States of the Northwest." [5] Halsey wrote again from Chicago, on the eve of Blaine's sudden resignation from the Cabinet: "Your friends are full of hope that you will say nothing and let them go ahead. I have not seen a Harrison man in my visits among business houses today. The young men are wild over the prospect of your nomination. Mr. P. E. Stude-

---

[1] Medill to Blaine, November 30, 1891.
[2] Halstead to Blaine, November 25, 1891.
[3] L. Harrison to Blaine, December 5, 1891.
[4] Halsey to Blaine, December 18, 1891. Elkins had just been taken into Harrison's Cabinet as Secretary of War. Rumor had it that this appointment of Blaine's old friend was made on the assurance that Blaine would not become a presidential candidate.
[5] J. S. Clarkson to Blaine, January 15, 1892.

baker arrived home this morning after a five months' trip through Washington, Oregon, California and Colorado. He says nine tenths of the voters are for you." [1]

Meanwhile, the political schemers were doing their best to widen the breach between the President and the Secretary of State, dwelling especially on the former's ultimatun to Chile in the message to Congress of January 25, 1892, in defiance of Blaine's wish to pursue a moderate and temporizing policy with the offending South American republic. We have seen in a former chapter how little justification there was for representing the President and Blaine as antagonistic on the fundamental issue in the Chilean affair,[2] but political animus is seldom restrained by consideration for the truth. Many of the President's opponents charged him with having sent in his message against the advice of Blaine simply to aid himself politically by "firing the American heart." "If this feeling grows as rapidly all over the country as it has in Washington," wrote the correspondent of the Kansas City *Star*, "the President will find . . . that he has injured himself by his message, unless Chile absolutely refuses to apologize. If she does this and there is war, Harrison would be able to justify all he has done." [3]

The movement for Blaine for President had gained such headway by the opening of February, 1892, that the Secretary thought it time to declare his position. On the sixth of that month he wrote to Chairman Clarkson: "I am not a candidate for the Presidency and my name will not go before the Republican National Convention for the nomination. I make this statement in due season. To those who have tendered me their support I owe sincere thanks and am most grateful for their confidence. They will, I am sure, make earnest efforts in the approaching contest, which is rendered especially important by reason of the industrial and financial policy of the Government being at stake. The popular decision on these matters is of great moment and will be of far-reaching consequence." Some of Blaine's friends, like Depew and Elkins, accepted this note as definitive, and worked for Harrison's renomination. Others, including Chairman Clarkson himself, regarded it as only the usual disclaimer, often intended to advance the aspirant's prospects. Blaine had not said that he would not accept the nomination, if tendered. His statement that his name would not be presented at the

[1] G. A. Halsey to Blaine, June 2, 1892.
[2] See above, Chapter XV, pp. 422–423.
[3] Kansas City *Star*, January 27, 1892.

convention was not an injunction, but only a prophecy which might or might not be true, while his insistence on the importance of the issues to be decided at the election might be an invitation to the country to entrust their management to a tried and popular leader.

At any rate, Clarkson, Cameron, Frye, Hale, Platt and Quay only worked the more diligently for Blaine. Quay declared that he would be nominated on the first ballot and triumphantly elected. On the other hand, there were disinterested friends who saw how unwise it would be and how unfortunate it would be both for Blaine's health and for his reputation to pit him against his chief for the nomination. Collector Dow of Portland had an interview with Blaine early in 1892, which he reports as follows: "I met Mr. Blaine by his invitation at the Falmouth Hotel. He was even then evidently in poor physical health and did not appear to be mentally as alert as formerly. He told me that many of those who had always opposed him in the past were urging him to seek again the nomination for the Presidency. I asked him if he was sure that such proffered support was not as much due to the opposition to President Harrison as to friendship for himself. . . . I urged him as strongly as I could not to gratify the enemies of President Harrison in that way. For the time I thought I had made some impression on him, but stronger influences than mine prevailed with him, and action the most lamentable in his whole political career followed. That, I think, would not have been, were he then in the enjoyment of his pristine physical and mental strength." [1]

Whatever the influences that were working upon Blaine during the spring months of 1892—increasing strain in his relations with the President, waning health, the zeal of friends ambitious for his advancement,[2] the solicitation of political ax-grinders—he startled the capital and the country on June 4 (three days before the meeting of the Republican nominating convention) by sending his private secretary Louis A. Dent to the White House early in the afternoon with a brief note to the President:

---

[1] The Portland *Sunday Telegram and Press Herald*, February 9, 1930.
[2] A letter of Gail Hamilton's to Blaine's daughters, written just before the assembling of the Minneapolis convention, reveals a confidence in Blaine's destiny. "What I want now is that he (Blaine) shall go on and win. . . . Understand, if we get the nomination I don't think your father any more likely to lose his health than if we don't. Likewise with the Presidency. He may be ill, but they will not be cause and effect, judging from the past. His worst illness was his first, when he was in the prime of life. His best work has all been done since then. He has too much life in him to lay himself on the shelf for its lack." Gail Hamilton, *Biography of James G. Blaine*, pp. 718–9.

"I respectfully beg leave to submit my resignation of the office of Secretary of State of the United States, to which I was appointed by you on March 5, 1889. The condition of the public business in the Department of State justifies me in requesting that my resignation be accepted immediately. I have the honor to be, very respectfully, your obedient servant, James G. Blaine."

The President immediately replied with the same curt formality:

"Your letter of this date, tendering your resignation of the office of Secretary of State of the United States has been received. The terms in which you state your desires are such as to leave me no choice but to accede to your wishes at once. Your resignation is therefore accepted. Very respectfully yours, Benjamin Harrison."

That was all. No expression of esteem on the one side or regret on the other; no acknowledgment of consideration received or services rendered. It was noticed that the President held his Saturday afternoon reception in the East Room and greeted his two hundred guests in better spirits than usual. The reporters who hurried to the State Department and to the White House to request explanations and comments on the notes received only the prompt dismissal: "Nothing to say."

Rumor supplied the explanations which were not forthcoming from the principals in the case. According to Seth Milliken, who represented Blaine's old congressional district in Maine, the Secretary confessed that he had resigned because he "had become an object of suspicion to the other members of the Cabinet," and found the situation too "irksome" to endure. On the other hand, the Washington correspondent of the Kansas City *Times* reported a story widely credited in the capital that it was Harrison himself who forced the resignation. The President, "becoming more and more convinced from the confiding work of Quay, Clarkson and others, that Blaine was really and actively, although secretly, a candidate, determined to smoke him out. To this end Harrison instructed Elkins to tell Blaine plainly that he must either stop this hubbub of his partisans by some declaration of an intention not to run [1] or withdraw from the Cabinet. This mission Elkins performed day before yesterday while he and Blaine were on their way to the Cabinet, to which they came in the same carriage. The outcome was Blaine's resignation this afternoon." [2]

A completely satisfactory explanation of Blaine's resignation we do

---

[1] Evidently Blaine's letter of February 6 to Clarkson was not accepted by the President as a *bona fide* declination.

[2] Kansas City *Times*, June 5, 1892.

not, and probably never shall, have. Indeed, it is doubtful whether the Secretary himself really knew what his own mind was on the matter. One day in May he suddenly rose from his seat at the Cabinet table and left the room. While his colleagues were gazing at one another in embarrassed silence Secretary Elkins hastened after Blaine and found him outside bordering on a state of collapse. He got Blaine into his carriage to take him to his home across Lafayette Square, and during the short ride Blaine, who feared that the sudden attack might prove fatal, begged Elkins to tell the President that he had his confidence and his support for a renomination. At about the same time Edward Stanwood called on Blaine "in the privacy of his own home," and reports Blaine as saying to him: "The truth is I do not want that office [the Presidency]. When the American people choose a President they require him to remain awake four years. And I have come to a time in life when I need my sleep. I like my present office. I enjoy it and would like to continue in it." [1] Yet, less than a month later Blaine sent in his letter of resignation. All we can say is this: whether the resignation was voluntary or forced, whether it was premeditated or sudden, if it was made with the intention of contesting the renomination of Harrison it was a mistake which justified Colonel Dow's judgment as "the most lamentable act of Blaine's whole political career."

For Blaine was too good a politician not to know what an immense advantage the control of the patronage gave to the President in securing delegates for a renomination. To win rival delegates for his own candidacy, he should have resigned months before the convention met and let his backers work freely with his open support. Clarkson bemoaned the poor showing of the Blaine forces in the convention with the plaint, "But we had a candidate for only three days." On the other hand, if Blaine's resignation had "no connection with the proceedings at Minneapolis," as he was reported to have told Milliken, he should not have timed it so as to give the public cause to believe that it had everything to do with those proceedings. Certainly, he could have endured the "irksomeness" of his Cabinet associations just a few days longer, till the proceedings at Minneapolis were over. He could even have properly absented himself from the Cabinet meetings on the score of his health. Rhodes baldly states that "Blaine was eager for the

[1] Edward Stanwood, *James Gillespie Blaine*, pp. 339–40.

nomination." [1] The balance of the evidence inclines, in my opinion, to the opposite conclusion. He may have believed the Clarksons and the Patrick Fords that he was the only man who could save the Republican Party and the country from the menace of Populism; he may have allowed his great name and popularity to be exploited by the Quays and Platts who had political grudges to settle against Benjamin Harrison; he may even, as was reported by an alleged witness, have said that he was "determined to prevent that man in the White House from getting a renomination." But all this is conjecture. Blaine himself studiously refrained from making any explanation, public or private, of his resignation, and gave no hint to friend or foe of his expectations from the party leaders who were assembling at Minneapolis. [2]

The tenth National Republican convention had been allocated to the thriving city at the Falls of St. Anthony, partly because Chicago was willing to waive its almost vested right to the convention [3] in view of its preparations for the great Columbian Exposition of 1893, and partly because, Minnesota being one of the strongholds of Populism, it was believed that the meeting of the Republican cohorts in that State would be a help in holding the Northwest to its allegiance to the Grand Old Party. Moreover, the city had recently completed its magnificent Industrial Exposition Building, with a seating capacity of eleven thousand, and a large committee of enthusiastic citizens had raised the funds to guarantee ample entertainment. The convention sat from June 7 to 10, with Governor William McKinley, jr., of Ohio in the chair. After a long and acrimonious debate over the credentials of delegates from twenty-four States, the convention was ready, on the evening of the ninth, to listen to the platform as read by ex-Governor J. B. Foraker of Ohio, Chairman of the Committee on Resolutions. It was the usual recital of the blessings which the Republican Party had conferred upon the country and of the disasters which were certain to ensue if the Democrats were to come into power. It commended "the able, patriotic and thoroughly American Administration of President Harrison," and

---

[1] James Ford Rhodes, *From Hayes to McKinley*, p. 381.

[2] The question was only further confused by a statement of Chauncey M. Depew, in the Philadelphia *Press*, the day after Blaine's death, that a certain member of the convention had in his pocket a letter from Blaine to be read to the convention in case he was nominated—absolutely declining to run. Philadelphia *Press*, January 28, 1893.

[3] The Republican conventions of 1880, 1884, and 1888 had all been held in Chicago. So also has every Republican convention of the twentieth century, except those of 1924 (Cleveland) and 1928 (Kansas City).

reaffirmed "the American doctrine of protection," but it significantly omitted any direct endorsement of the tariff bill which bore the name of the gentleman sitting in the chair, and which had been chiefly responsible for the Democratic landslide in the congressional elections of 1890.[1]

The nominating and seconding speeches, which occupied the day session of June 10, were, with one exception, of the most ordinary caliber, often descending into the merest claptrap. Eleven speakers came to the platform, six to extol the merits of Blaine, and five to plead for the renomination of Harrison. No other names were put in nomination. Senator Edward O. Wolcott of Colorado started the oratory with the following encomium: "On this occasion there is remarkable unanimity between genuine Republicans of the West and genuine Republicans of the East as to who is needed, and his name is Blaine!" He declared that it was Blaine who had made Republican Presidents possible, and had "enriched and guided two Administrations with his sagacity and statesmanship." "We are honored and respected abroad: we owe it to his statecraft. We are gathering the Republics of all America together in bonds of closest friendship: it is because he devised the plan and shaped the policy. We are protecting our own people on the farm and in the workshop and by wise concessions are inducing the people of the world to open their gates to our products: his foreseeing and discriminating vision saw the possibilities of reciprocity and induced us to follow it. . . . No official title can add to or detract from the luster of his fame, but we may at least let history record that such as we had to give we gave with loyal and loving hearts. . . . And so, Mr. Chairman, we turn in the hour when victory is at hand to the intrepid leader who shaped for his party the policy which has lifted it above the danger of further defeat!"[2]

The Senator's speech was punctuated by "great applause," "loud and continued cheering," and cries for "Blaine! Blaine!" The white plume was borne aloft as the "Blaine legion" paraded past the sheaves of wheat and stalks of corn which decorated the walls of the convention hall. But there was something forced in the demonstration. It was anachronistic. It suggested resurrection rather than abounding life. And the five seconders from Minnesota, Missouri, New York, Ten-

[1] *Proceedings of the Tenth Republican National Convention*, by Theodore C. Rose and Jas. F. Burke, official stenographers. Minneapolis, 1892, pp. 85–88.
[2] *Proceedings*, pp. 117–9.

nessee and Wyoming only departed from perfunctory repetition of Wolcott's eulogy to fall into such fatuous assertions as that of G. Q. Boyd of Tennessee, who assured the delegates that "the ladies and the babies in the cradle want Blaine," and wound up with the peroration: "His worthy deeds alone have rendered him immortal, and when oblivion shall have swept away kingdoms, thrones and principalities and the last vestiges of human grandeur shall have moldered in the dust, eternity itself will treasure the name of James G. Blaine." [1] This apotheosis was loudly applauded; but when the final Blaine orator, a rustic delegate from Wyoming, endeavored with halting speech and grammar to carry on, the convention grew restive and interrupted him with cries of "time" and "sit down!" [2]

The only speech at all worthy of even the indifferent standard of convention oratory was that of Chauncey M. Depew of New York in support of President Harrison. Depew put aside eulogy and eschewed invidious comparisons. He paid tribute to the accomplishments of Blaine in his department, as well as to the other lieutenants of the Administration; but he insisted that it was the President, as the responsible coördinator of all ·these activities, who should be rewarded with a vote of confidence as the party chief. The platform had heartily endorsed his Administration: the delegates could do no less than ratify that endorsement. Very neatly Depew turned Blaine's own words of a dozen years before into an argument for Harrison's renomination: "The Secretary of State, in accepting his portfolio under President Garfield wrote, 'Your Administration must be made brilliantly successful and strong in the confidence of the people, not at all diverting its energies for reëlection, and yet compelling that result by the logic of events.' . . . The prophecy he made for Garfield has been superbly fulfilled by President Harrison. In the language of Mr. Blaine, the President has compelled a reëlection 'by the logic of events and the imperious necessities of the situation.' " [3]

William McKinley was not formally nominated, but Mark Hanna, who for several years had been vainly endeavoring to win the honor for John Sherman, had now transferred his allegiance to the Governor of Ohio—an allegiance which combined personal devotion with unshakable confidence in McKinley's political and economic views. Hanna

[1] *Proceedings*, p. 128.
[2] *Ibid.*, pp. 131–2.
[3] *Ibid.*, p. 125.

was not a delegate to the convention, but, at his own expense, he established McKinley headquarters at the West House in Minneapolis and worked like a Trojan to collect delegates for his candidate. While he hardly expected that McKinley could be nominated, he nevertheless thought it possible that, if enough opposition to Harrison should be developed by the Blaine forces, McKinley might be brought forward as a compromise candidate. His chief object probably was to make a showing on the ballot sufficient to draw the attention of the party and the country to McKinley as a serious contestant at the next convention. 1892 was a kind of dress rehearsal for 1896. And the 182 votes that McKinley received at Minneapolis were a heartening harbinger for Mark Hanna.

Ever since Grant's unanimous renomination at Philadelphia in 1872, the Republican conventions had been the scene of bitter struggles between factions in the party, and no Republican incumbent of the Presidency had secured a renomination, but it took only a single ballot at Minneapolis to make the choice. Perry Heath of the Post Office Department, who was in charge of the Harrison interests, had the machine so well oiled that it ran smoothly and relentlessly on the appointed track—the "Postmasters' Convention." The delegates from south of Mason and Dixon's line gave 244⅙ votes for Harrison to 45⅙ for Blaine. Nor did the States of the North and West furnish any better justification for Quay's wild prophecy, "It will be Blaine on the first ballot." The national convention of Republican Clubs at Cincinnati had written to Blaine that nine tenths of the delegates were for him, but when the roll was called at Minneapolis, Ohio gave 45 votes for McKinley and one for Harrison. Blaine was assured that he was "more popular than Harrison in Indiana" (which was the truth); but the Indiana delegation cast its solid vote for the President. Clarkson, Platt and others had declared that Blaine alone could stem the tide to Populism in the Northwest; but the states of Iowa, Kansas, Nebraska, Colorado, Minnesota, Wisconsin and the Dakotas furnished 83 delegates for Harrison and only 28 for Blaine. The only State that gave Blaine as many as 15 delegates was New York, which was divided as follows: Blaine 35, Harrison 27, McKinley 10. Indeed, though Platt of New York was supposed to be Blaine's "manager" at Minneapolis, there was really no management at all. Emmons Blaine was there, as both Emmons and Walker had been at Chicago in 1888, working in his father's interest, but his efforts resulted only in rousing demonstrations, and not in securing delegates.[1] A few days after the convention adjourned Emmons Blaine died of acute appendicitis.[2] When the first roll call was completed Harrison had 535⅙, of the 904⅓ votes (nearly 100 more than the necessary majority), Blaine 182⅙, McKinley 182, Tom Reed of Maine 4, and Robert Lincoln of Illinois 1.[3] Harrison's nomination was made unanimous and the convention adjourned till evening, when Whitelaw Reid of the New York *Tribune* was named by acclamation for the Vice Presidency. The thanks of the convention were extended to the chairman and the other officers, to the retiring National Committee and the city of Minneapolis, the committees were appointed to notify the nominees, and the convention stood adjourned *sine die*.

The renomination of President Harrison was in accord with the traditions of American party politics. In spite of his forbidding formality, his nepotism, and his too generous encouragement of pension legislation, he had given the country a dignified and able Administration. In the opinion of that rather cynical onlooker on the side lines of politics, Henry Adams, Harrison was "perhaps the best President the Republican Party had put forward since the death of Lincoln."[4] And ex-President Hayes wrote in his *Diary* for June 10, 1892: "Telephone from the *Journal* office that Harrison was nominated on the first ballot. This is well, perhaps the best possible under all the circumstances. . . . Harrison represents the best elements of the party."[5] Against these favorable judgments we may set the characteristic comment of Thomas C. Platt, eighteen years later: "Harrison's selection for a second term caused a chattering of teeth among warm blooded Republicans of the East. When there was added to it the choice of Whitelaw Reid, a persistent assailant of the New York organization for Har-

---

[1] William Allen White has the following vivid paragraph on the scene: "On the fourth day, June 10, Blaine was put in nomination by Senator Wolcott. The scene was indescribably pathetic. All knew he was at the threshold of eternity, but at the mention of his name the innumerable hosts broke into confused and volleyed thunder that for twenty-seven minutes seemed to shake the foundations of the earth and sky. Like the chorus of an anthem, with measured solemnity the galleries chanted 'Blaine! Blaine! James G. Blaine!', myriads of stamping feet keeping barbaric rhythm, while plumes and banners waved and women with flags and scarfs filled the atmosphere with motion, color and light. It was the passing of Blaine. That gigantic demonstration was at once a salutation and a requiem. The Republican Party there took leave of their dying leader and bade him an eternal farewell." W. A. White, *Masks in a Pageant*, p. 101, note.
[2] The Democratic National convention, in session at Chicago at the time of Emmons Blaine's death, paused to pass resolutions of sympathy for the family.
[3] *Proceedings*, p. 141.
[4] *The Education of Henry Adams*, p. 321.
[5] C. R. Williams, *The Life of Rutherford Birchard Hayes*, Vol. II, p. 376.

rison's running mate, many of the New York delegates, including myself, wrapped ourselves in overcoats and earmuffs, hurried from the convention hall, and took the first train for New York. I had repeatedly uttered warnings that Harrison's renomination spelled disaster. My prediction was verified." [1]

Blaine left Washington immediately after his resignation for his summer cottage at Bar Harbor, stopping over at Boston during the session of the convention, in order to get more prompt and detailed reports of the proceedings at Minneapolis, which he followed with eager interest. When the results were known, he dictated a brief statement for the press, calling upon the party to sink factional discord and rally as a unit to the support of the ticket. He spent the summer quietly at "Stanwood," seeking recuperation in walks and drives and long hours on the broad veranda overlooking the waters of the bay.

Visitors came, some to try to persuade him to enter the campaign so far as his health would allow. His old friend William E. Chandler wrote to Whitelaw Reid on June 13: "Blaine needs tender treatment. There was not enough tact used toward him. We need everybody to win, and even then the fight will be a desperate one." [2] Some blamed Blaine for having himself introduced discord into the party, and thought that he should bring forth works meet for repentance. Woodhale of North Dakota wrote to Chandler: "Blaine's ridiculous efforts to have the nomination thrust upon him by a waiting and praying party have hurt us. The only reparation that he can make is, after a while, to take the stump." [3] A zealot in the far West might not have understood how impossible it would have been for Blaine to undertake any campaigning in the summer of 1892; but even such close friends as Patrick Ford and Joseph Manley hoped that he would "make at least one speech in New York."

Blaine adhered to his determination to make no speeches (except for a single deviation near the close of the campaign), but he wrote the leading article for the *North American Review* for November, on "The Presidential Election of 1892." After calling attention to the "lack of excitement and of active interest in the campaign . . . as a feature common to both parties," and suggesting as an explanation of this apathy the increasing absorption of the country in "business transac-

---

[1] *Autobiography of Thomas Collier Platt*, pp. 246–7.
[2] *W. E. Chandler Papers*, Library of Congress.
[3] *Ibid.*

tions of immense magnitude," [1] Blaine devoted the rest of the article to a criticism of the Democrats for their advocacy of the repeal of the ten per cent tax on the issue of currency by State banks, their objections to the pension roll, and their misrepresentations of the beneficent results of the reciprocity agreements. He concluded with an exposition of the inconsistency of the Democratic platform with the principles of Thomas Jefferson, whom that party insisted on invoking as its founder and patron saint.[2] Aside from a few lines commending the clarity of Harrison's letter of acceptance, there is no mention of the Republican candidates. There is no exhortation to vote the Republican ticket. Indeed, except for the opening sentence of the article, one might never surmise that there was an election pending at all. The article is more in the nature of an essay, with references to Jefferson, Clay and Abraham Lincoln, which might have been published a month after the election as appropriately as a month before, so far as reference to that supposedly critical event was concerned.

In the middle of October Blaine yielded to the urgent invitation of Whitelaw Reid to stop on his way back to Washington for a brief visit to Reid's country estate, Ophir Farm, at Purchase, Westchester County, New York. Politics were not discussed in the invitation, but only the pleasure that it would give the Reids to entertain the Blaines and the benefit Blaine would derive from "breathing the invigorating air and viewing the glorious autumnal coloring" of Westchester. He must come "before the leaves begin to fall." [3] However, when Blaine arrived at Ophir Farm, he found that Reid had planned an elaborate house party for October 14. The guests invited to dinner included Chauncey M. Depew, William H. Robertson, Garrett A. Hobart, Patrick Egan, D. O. Mills and other Republican notables, and when the company stepped out on the broad piazza in the clear, frosty air under the brilliant stars, it was to confront a gathering of more than three thousand citizens of Westchester, escorted by Whitelaw Reid Clubs from the neighboring towns, with bands and torches. When the cheers for Blaine

[1] There were other obvious reasons for the noticeable lack of interest in the campaign. Both Harrison and Cleveland had already served a term in the White House, and their personalities and policies were familiar to the American people. Furthermore, there was in both parties a considerable amount of lukewarmness toward the candidates as well as a feeling that the issues were not very clear cut. One witty observer of the slow campaign judged that "each side would have been glad to defeat the other if it could do so without electing its own candidate."

[2] *The North American Review*, Vol. CLV, pp. 513–25.

[3] Whitelaw Reid to Blaine, October 3, 1892.

and his host had died down, Reid thanked his neighbors for their courtesy in arranging this "surprise" party for his distinguished guest, and called upon Blaine to speak.

So it was that Blaine made his only speech of the campaign, an address of about ten minutes which he read from a manuscript, by the light of two lamps held above his head. He lauded the prosperity of the country under the wise Administration of President Harrison, and attributed that prosperity to the Republican protective tariff. It was a text from which he had preached since the beginning of his political career and a faith from which he had never departed. Mr. Egan followed with a justification of his Chilean mission, and Depew kept the assembly in roars of laughter with a speech devoted mainly to twisting the lion's tail. At its close he eulogized Blaine as "an American of Americans, who for many a year has represented the best thought, the best aspirations, the best principles concentrated into measures which should be for the benefit of the American Republic . . . the one man who has distinguished himself in the two departments of the legislature and the executive, standing in the House of Representatives, peerless among its debaters and as its presiding officer unequaled in the history of the country . . . the flower and fruitage of one hundred years, the one foreign minister who has commanded the respect and fear of the whole world." If Depew had spoken thus four months before!—but Ophir Farm was not Minneapolis. When the exercises were over, the house was thrown open to the crowd who pressed in to shake hands with Reid and his guests and to partake of the refreshments served in the dining hall. It was midnight before Blaine got to bed.[1]

The Democrats also had to cope with disaffection in their ranks in this presidential year. Grover Cleveland, in spite of his defeat on the tariff issue in 1888, was still the idol of the great mass of the party, on account of his indomitable courage, his incorruptible honesty and his self-effacing devotion to the public weal as he saw it. Naturally, his independence and probity were an offense in the eyes of the most powerful political organization in his own state, Tammany Hall, and offered ex-Governor (since 1891 United States Senator) David B. Hill the temptation to block Cleveland's nomination by a tricky manœuvre. As soon as the Democratic National Committee had fixed the date for the nominating convention at Chicago, Hill got Edward

[1] See account in the New York *Tribune* of October 15, 1892.

Murphy, Chairman of the State Committee, to issue a call for the State convention for choosing delegates to Chicago to meet at Albany on February 22, two or three months before the usual date for such a meeting. The object of thus summoning the State convention in midwinter and in an eastern city was obviously to anticipate the organization of the Cleveland forces in western New York and to make it difficult for the snow and ice bound delegates from up State to attend.[1]

Hill's "snap convention" on Washington's birthday was apparently a complete success. It was dominated by Tammany and it chose a solid Hill delegation to Chicago, bound by the unit rule. But the wily Senator had overreached himself. The "anti-snappers" in New York organized a huge mass meeting at Syracuse to denounce his trickery. The Democratic press all over the country cried shame upon him. And when he sought (by a personal visit) to detach the South from Cleveland, whom he represented as a tool of Wall Street and an enemy of the agricultural interests, he found himself butting against a stone wall. State after State instructed their delegations for the old standard bearer of the party. Tammany renewed the fight at Chicago, sending its silver-tongued orator Bourke Cockran to the platform at midnight before the balloting to plead with the convention to spare New York the humiliation of nominating a man who could not possibly carry his own pivotal State and who would drag the party down to inevitable defeat. But the Cleveland forces, magnificently marshaled by William C. Whitney, held firm. On the first ballot they polled 617⅓ votes (10⅓ more than the necessary two thirds), while Hill received less than one fifth of that number (114).[2]

The campaign was somewhat "listless," chiefly because it was devoid of the factional animosities and personal abuse which had characterized the contests for a score of years. Harrison and Cleveland had each served a term in the White House, and the country recognized them both as able and honest executives. But the stars in their courses fought for Cleveland. Harrison's lack of popular appeal, Speaker ("Czar")

[1] When Cleveland, returning from a hunting trip in the South, heard at Baltimore of Hill's crafty move, he showed his indifference by remarking to the reporters who boarded his train: "The State Committee has selected an historic day. I hope the weather will be fine."

[2] Grover Cleveland thus had the unique distinction in our history of being nominated three consecutive times by a convention of one of the major political parties. But at the next national convention of the Democratic Party (1896), which was controlled by the Populists, a resolution commending "the honesty, economy, courage and fidelity" of the man who had been the head of the party for sixteen years was rejected by a vote of 357 to 564!

Reed's drastic rule of the House of Representatives, the lavish appropriations for pensions, and the general "extravagance" of a Congress which had spent half a billion dollars in a single session were all "talking points" against the Administration. Moreover, the very abundance of legislative measures in the Fifty-first Congress (made possible by the fact that for the first time in fifteen years the President had a clear majority in both Houses) offered an unusual number of facets for attack. The Sherman Silver Purchase Act of 1890, for example, was a cowardly compromise measure, which satisfied neither the staunch advocates of the gold standard nor the free silverites of the West. The attempt to revive the coercive policy of the Reconstruction Era by the proposed Federal Elections (or "Force") bill of the same year alienated large numbers of Notherners who were tired of the old device of "waving the bloody shirt." [1] Most serious of all, however, was the reaction against the high schedules of the McKinley tariff bill. It had been the chief cause of the Democratic landslide of 1890, and it was still costing the Republicans thousands of votes.[2] To cap the climax, a bitter labor war broke out in July between the powerful union of the Amalgamated Steel and Iron Workers and the Carnegie steel plant at Homestead, near Pittsburgh. Henry C. Frick, the manager of the plant, was given free hand by Carnegie (who was in Scotland) to put down the strike; and his summons of a "private army" of 300 Pinkerton detectives resulted in a battle on the banks of the Monongahela in which ten men were killed and over sixty wounded. Order was not restored until the Governor of Pennsylvania called out 8,000 militia to protect the works. The party of high protection suffered heavily from this incident of riot and bloodshed in one of the most highly protected industries of the country.

On the other hand, the Democrats closed their ranks. Under the suave management of Mr. Whitney, the Tammany leaders, Sheehan, Croker and Murphy, were subdued in a conference with Cleveland, and even David B. Hill gave his grudging allegiance to the ticket in September.

---

[1] M. Woodhale of Michigan wrote to Chandler that now was the time to stress the war service of "the gallant Harrison, as over against the record of those two notorious Copperheads Cleveland and Stephenson," whose election would mean the triumph of the "rebels" in Washington. *W. E. Chandler Papers*, Library of Congress.

[2] Senator Cullom wrote to Harrison a few days after the election: "I especially desire to say that the cause of the defeat does not lie at your door personally. Any man in the country standing on the doctrine of high protection would have been defeated. The people sat down upon the McKinley bill two years ago and they have never gotten up. They were thoroughly imbued with the feeling that the party did not do right in revising the tariff up instead of down. They beat us for it in '90 and now again." Shelby M. Cullom, *Twenty Years of Public Service*, p. 259.

Cleveland's victory at the polls two months later was complete. In addition to the solid South he carried the four doubtful States of New York, Indiana, New Jersey and Connecticut, and the "safe" Republican States of California, Illinois and Wisconsin, which, with the exception of California in 1880, had not contributed a single electoral vote to the Democratic column since the election of James Buchanan. Cleveland's popular plurality was 400,000 and the electoral vote stood 277 for Cleveland to 145 for Harrison, with 22 votes for the Populist candidate James B. Weaver.

The Republican leaders were stunned by the result. They had, with few exceptions confidently predicted victory from the beginning of the campaign. They had declared that Cleveland was the weakest candidate the Democrats could put up. They had closed their eyes to the agrarian discontent in the West. They seemed not to have sensed the significance of the drift of the "intelligentsia" to Cleveland and the defection of erstwhile prominent Republicans like Seth Low, W. Q. Gresham, and Wayne MacVeagh (Attorney General in Garfield's Cabinet). Even Blaine, for all his usual astuteness in predicting the trend of political sentiment, seems to have shared the myopic confidence of the party prophets. His devoted champion, Rowland B. Mahaney of Buffalo, wrote to him in October: "I do not agree with you that Harrison is ahead. The tide here is decidedly for Cleveland. The audience that assembled last evening in Music Hall to hear Senator Frye was a mere handful compared with the uproarious demonstrations of former days." [1]

When Blaine returned to Washington as a private citizen in the autumn of 1892, his relations with the President were naturally on a more cordial basis than they had been in the spring. It was foreign to Blaine's sympathetic nature to cherish personal resentments, and whatever disappointment he may have felt at the President's coldness to his recommendations for office was forgotten in his genuine enthusiasm for the success of the party at the polls; while the President, freed from any anxiety of Blaine as a rival, was grateful to have him as a supporter. The two men walked home from church together on the Sunday before the election, engaged, doubtless, in discussing the hopeful auguries for the day after the morrow, and parted at the White House door with a

---

[1] R. B. Mahaney to Blaine, October 4, 1892. Mahaney, as a student at Harvard in 1884, had organized the Blaine Club of the college, and by his persuasive oratory had secured a straw vote of the student mass meeting in favor of Blaine—somewhat to the annoyance of the dignified Mugwump President Eliot.

cordial handgrasp. If there was any trace left in Blaine's mind of the alleged determination to block a second inauguration of Benjamin Harrison, it was wholly wiped out by Harrison's crushing defeat two days later. Only a few more weeks of life were left to Blaine and a few more months of office to Harrison. In the inexorable vicissitudes of fortune brought by the march of time the voices of political ambition were hushed and the petty rivalries of office stilled.

Since the completion of his *Twenty Years of Congress* in 1886 and the publication the next year of his collection of *Political Addresses,* Blaine had been free from the exactions of authorship and the proddings of publishers for a season. But in the last two years of his life he was vexed with a number of demands of the sort upon his valuable time and his declining strength. On February 14, 1891, General William T. Sherman died of asthma, leaving his family in rather straitened circumstances. His son, Father Thomas Sherman, hastened home from the Island of Jersey, where he was studying in a Jesuit seminary, and on February 27 made a contract with the C. L. Webster Company for the publication of the General's *Memoirs.* A few days later he promised Webster, apparently on the basis of some rather vague encouragement from members of the Blaine family, that Blaine would write an introduction to the work. Advertisements were circulated by the publishing firm announcing that attractive selling feature. Blaine himself seems rather to have acquiesced in the arrangement than to have given it any positive endorsement. General Sherman had been his lifelong friend and for some years his near neighbor in Washington. Ellen (Ewing) Sherman, the widow, was a relative of the Blaines through the marriage of Blaine's aunt Eleanor to John Hoge Ewing. Rachel Sherman, the daughter, was almost a sister to her cousins Margaret and Harriet Blaine. She added her pleas to those of her mother and brother, begging Blaine, in a letter of February 15, to write also an appendix to the *Memoirs,* describing the last years, the death and the character of her father.

Blaine was in the midst of pressing state business in the spring of 1891, laboring at an acceptable *modus vivendi* with Lord Salisbury on the Bering Sea fisheries, answering the excited protests of the Italian Foreign Minister on the New Orleans lynchings, and directing the conduct of Minister Egan in his embarrassing post at Santiago during the civil war in Chile. And all the while Father Sherman was bombarding him (and the rest of the family) with letters and telegrams urging him to send in copy for the printers. Could he let them have by return mail the pages already done, to be set up immediately? Time was pressing. Cheap *Lives* of General Sherman were already being put on the market. "Please let us have *anything* soon!" "Margaret delights me by saying that you are pushing on with your tribute." Still the copy was not forthcoming. The advertising prospectus was changed to announce that Blaine would contribute an appendix instead of an introduction. The final outcome of the solicitation of Father Sherman, abetted by Mark Twain, was a seven page "Tribute" to the General from Blaine's pen, which apppeared in the 1891 edition of the *Sherman Memoirs* published by the C. L. Webster Company. When Webster failed and the *Memoirs* were taken over by Appleton's, the "Tribute" was omitted—for what reason I have not been able to discover.

In the spring of 1892, when the rumors of his intention to seek the presidential nomination were rife, Blaine was exasperated by various attempts of publishers to exploit his popularity. When he heard of the project of the A. K. Keller Company of Philadelphia to publish a volume of five hundred pages, edited by Willis F. Johnson, on *An American Statesman: the Works and Words of James G. Blaine,* he wrote Mr. Keller: "Did it ever occur to you that it is a great liberty you are taking and a great wrong you are perpetrating? I have not granted any permission. I hope you will well consider your course and refrain from so gross an outrage upon my rights." [1] The volume appeared, however, after Mr. Keller's assurance that it would contain only excerpts from the speeches and writings of the statesman. Blaine was even more incensed by the announcement by the Cyrus H. K. Curtis Company of a sketch to appear in the *Ladies' Home Journal* on "The Personality and Home Life of Mrs. James G. Blaine, with the First Portrait ever Printed with her Permission." In a sharp correspondence with Mr. Curtis, Blaine declared that the alleged portrait of his wife was a bogus one, that there was no "permission" for its use, and that he was prepared to take legal measures against any such "violation of the privacy of his family life." [2] "If I *have* been imposed upon," replied Mr. Curtis, "it has been by one very near and dear to your own family." [3] He enclosed the article—and ordered the presses stopped.

There was no cause of offense in the proposition made to Blaine

[1] Blaine to A. K. Keller, May 27, 1892.
[2] Blaine to C. H. K. Curtis, March 30, 1892.
[3] Curtis to Blaine, April 2, 1892.

shortly afterward by H. S. Smith of Philadelphia, President of the Hirst Publishing Company, to prepare his *Personal Recollections* in one or two volumes. The work was to be written in a popular and intimate style, quite different from the formal, objective narrative of the *Twenty Years of Congress*, in which the author had hardly mentioned his own name. It was not to deal with party politics or important historical events, but to be a series of picturesque reminiscences, anecdotes of his boyhood, stories of his family, incidents in his brilliant career, personal contacts with distinguished people at home and abroad—in short, a book to satisfy the curiosity of the mass of American readers in the "human side" of a man of great eminence.[1] What answer, if any, Blaine made to this proposition is not known. General Grant's *Memoirs* had been suggested by Mr. Smith as a kind of pattern for the work. But Blaine had no such motive as the taciturn General for the distasteful task of setting his own career before the curious public. He was in very comfortable circumstances, without a burden of debt like Grant, or of anxiety for the welfare of his family. And even if his physical strength had been sufficient for the labor of writing his memoirs, his lifelong practice of preserving his intimate family life free from the prying eyes of the public would have made Mr. Smith's proposal irksome to him. He retired to the peaceful refuge of Mount Desert for rest and recuperation after the distressing experience of the spring months. He was tired of publicity.

[1] H. W. Smith to Blaine, May 3, 1892.

THE INCESSANT rains and fogs which descended upon the Maine coast in the summer of 1892 were nature's counterpart of the gloom and anxiety which hovered over the Blaine family. "That dreadful summer!" was the way the daughters remembered it many years later. First of all was the deep shadow of Emmons Blaine's sudden illness and death in June, before his parents and sisters could start on their sad journey to Chicago. It was a blow from which Blaine never recovered. Then, too, in spite of his reiterated declarations that the analysis of the physicians revealed no trace of sugar in the blood, the increasing pallor of Blaine's face, the slowing of his gait, and the puffiness beneath the eyes all strengthened the apprehension which no amount of diverting courage or enforced cheerfulness could conceal. His family knew, even if it was not to be mentioned, that he was a very sick man. For the first time he returned to Washington (in October) from his vacation in Maine unrefreshed and uninvigorated.

He was again free from public responsibility, as he had been eleven years before, on his retirement from Arthur's Cabinet; but he lacked the vitality to resume the historical study and writing which had been beckoning to him fitfully ever since the publication of his *Twenty Years of Congress*. The plan of spending the winter in "the balmy, sunny, health-giving climate of Southern California," as suggested by Joseph Medill's letter of the previous autumn, was reluctantly abandoned in view of the strain which the long journey would be on his health. He drove out almost every day with his youngest daughter Harriet in the glory of the late autumn afternoons. On December 18 a serious warning of the end came in an attack of faintness like that which had compelled him to leave the Cabinet meeting in the spring. He rallied, and again was able to be taken now and then for a short drive. But one day early in the new year he came back to take to his bed in the southwest (Seward) chamber on the third floor. He suffered no great pain, but just grew weaker day by day as the poison sapped his vitality and wasted his flesh.

When the news of Blaine's critical condition spread through the city and the country, the public, without respect to party or section, shared the anxiety of the watchers by his bedside. Messages of sympathy and hope came from far and near. Crowds gathered in Lafayette Square before the house to get the latest news as the doctors left the door. A few minutes after eleven o'clock on the morning of Saturday, January 27, 1893, they saw the shades of the windows of his room pulled down and knew that the end had come. Fully conscious, but unable to speak, his veiling eyes turned now to one and now to another of the members of his family gathered about him, but mostly seeking the face of his devoted wife who sat by the bed with her hand in his, he fell peacefully into his last sleep. The doctors came out and announced to the waiting crowd: "Blaine is dead." Their published bulletin gave the cause of death as "chronic Bright's disease, aggravated by tubercular lungs and heart weakness." Had he lived three days longer, Blaine would have completed his sixty-third year.

Representative Boutelle of Maine was the first to call at the stricken house, followed soon by President Harrison, Secretary of State Foster and other members of the Cabinet. Representative Milliken and Senator Hale of Maine announced the sad news in brief eulogies of their fellow statesman before their respective Houses of Congress, which immediately adjourned. The Cabinet met for a few minutes shortly after noon to endorse President Harrison's proclamation: "His devotion to the public interest, his marked ability and his exalted patriotism have won for him the great affection of his countrymen and the admiration of the world. In the varied pursuits of legislation, diplomacy and literature his genius has added new luster to American citizenship." State legislatures in all sections of the country adjourned as a mark of respect to his memory. Newspapers appeared the morning after his death with mourning lines between the columns that contained long stories of his career and testimonials to his greatness from followers and opponents alike. President-elect Cleveland, hearing of Blaine's death when he was on the train from Lakewood to New York, said: "His brilliant statesmanship will always be an inspiration to the nation he has served so long and well."

The funeral was held in the Presbyterian Church of the Covenant, in which Blaine had been for some years a pew holder. The pallbearers were chosen from his intimate political friends—Hale, Frye, Reid, Boutelle, Hitt, Bingham, Ewing and Hay. Hundreds of men and women with bowed heads stood outside the church and along the way as the funeral cortège moved out to the Oak Hill cemetery in Georgetown, where the dead statesman was laid to rest beside the graves of his two children, Walker and Alice.[1]

The biographer of James G. Blaine is confronted at the outset with a startling paradox. Here was a man who for more than a score of years was the acknowledged leader of the Republican Party and the most conspicuous figure in American public life. His popularity was immense and nation-wide. His charming amiability warmed and won the hearts of almost all who met him, either in the more formal contacts of official association or in more intimate social intercourse. His extensive and detailed knowledge of history, his uncanny memory for names and faces, his confident skill in debate and persuasiveness in exposition, his proud exhibition of the statistics of our manufacturing, mining, transportation and agricultural industries, his uncompromising assertion of American rights in every controversy with a foreign government and his prophetic insistence upon the destiny of the United States as a power second to none in the world—all commended him to the masses of our citizens as the embodiment of what a later generation has called "100 per cent Americanism." He was the patriot par excellence. The mere mention of his name was enough to start thousands of men in mass meetings and conventions into a delirium of shouting and cheering. Blaine Clubs all over the country marched with songs and banners. In five successive Republican national conventions, from 1876 to 1892, he was brought forward for the presidential nomination, once to be easily successful and twice to create a deadlock which resulted in the choice of a compromise candidate. Through all these years his was the one name that the political managers of both parties could not afford to leave out of the reckoning.

[1] When Mrs. Blaine died ten years later she was buried beside her husband. In 1920 the legislature of Maine passed a resolution requesting of the surviving members of the Blaine family "the privilege of bringing from Washington the remains of himself and his beloved wife and of placing them in the family lot near Forest Grove cemetery in Augusta, and of erecting thereon . . . an appropriate memorial." On Sunday June 13, 1920, the ceremony of reburial took place in the presence of many of the officials of the State of Maine and the City of Augusta. The plot, on the summit of a hill overlooking the city (one of Blaine's favorite walks) was made into a small park surrounded by shrubbery and furnished with a curved stone bench. Twin slabs of gray slate mark the graves. On Blaine's tablet is recorded the long list of the offices which he held in the service of his country. The inscription on Mrs. Blaine's stone, contains, as her children thought she would have wished, only the words: "His Wife, Harriet Stanwood Blaine, 1827–1903."

The very extravagance of the estimates of Blaine's place in history made at the time of his death, all due allowance being made for obituary fervor, testify to the tremendous impression which he made on his contemporaries. To quote but a few of the typical tributes—Eugene Hale, in announcing Blaine's death to the Senate, said: "In all the history which may be written of his times, he will stand as the central figure." Said Chauncey M. Depew: "His name will rank with Lincoln's and Grant's; he will live in the hearts of the common people." The Chester (Pennsylvania) *Evening News* declared: "Upon the pages of history he will live when other men of his day have passed off the stage of action and entirely out of memory, and their deeds beyond recall." "He has carved his name on the rock of enduring fame," said the Washington *Evening News,* "where it will remain when the waves of countless years have rolled against it and receded from it." At a great memorial meeting held in Chicago on January 31, J. F. Finerty declared: "This generation is too near to the days of Blaine to do him full justice. His is a fame that will grow with time." [1]

The forty years and more that have passed since Blaine's death have brought little fulfilment of these prophecies of his enduring fame. His latest biographer, Charles Edward Russell, has stated curtly: "No man in our annals has filled so large a space and left it so empty." [2]

I have been astonished in my conversations with many friends in the preparation of this book, not only at the lack of knowledge of Blaine's career but also at the indifference shown toward it. Some have said, "Why don't you write about somebody interesting?" Others have recalled vaguely that he was the man "who wrote some Mulligan letters" or called the Democrats the party of "rum, Romanism and rebellion" or ridiculed Roscoe Conkling as a "turkey-gobbler." "You had better write your life of Blaine soon," said a distinguished scholar to me, "because he is being rapidly forgotten." Exaggerated as this judgment may be, it is still true that the "spread" between the forecasts of Blaine's permanent enshrinement in the hall of American fame and their fulfilment is wide,

---

[1] A few dissenting opinons were expressed, to be sure, notably in the English press. The London *Standard* wrote: "It would be idle to pretend that America is made any poorer by the loss of her great statesman . . . his life's labours will leave scarcely a memory." And the London *Chronicle* thought that America was well rid of him. "We must place him," it said, "in the category of lesser men. He typified the period in which he lived and the best we can hope for his country is that the class to which he belonged, whether brilliant and intellectual like himself, or sordid and dispirited like most of its members, may soon pass from actuality into history."

[2] Charles Edward Russell, *Blaine of Maine,* p. 432.

and perhaps widening. His form and features are not made familiar to the present generation by statues in our squares and parks. His name is not perpetuated in towns, counties, rivers, mountains, highways, and schools. While many men of far less prominence in his day have been the subject of numerous biographies, monographs and articles, there has been published in the last quarter of a century but one Life of Blaine— and that not a judicious, balanced, impartial biography, but rather a journalistic polemic in support of the thesis that Blaine was "crooked as a ram's horn." [1]

Men are still baffled by the paradox. Was Blaine "the Alcibiades of American politics," as one of my correspondents has called him, or was he the American Aristides of the unrelieved panegyric of Gail Hamilton (1895) and the more moderate eulogy of his wife's relative Edward Stanwood (1906)? "The moment I touch Blaine," writes Gamaliel Bradford in his *Journal,* "I touch something human all over. . . . He was a passionate, emotional, eager, sensitive temperament, full of desires, ambitions and hopes, vastly capable of self-delusion." And again, "I wish somebody would tell me whether this Blaine was a rascal or not. . . . I have been reading his enemies or critics, combating their excesses and prejudices, trying to keep the balance even, not to let him sink too irretrievably low in my judgment and sympathy, but all the time thinking that when I came to his advocates, to the lives by Gail Hamilton and Edward Stanwood, it would be far easier to keep the balance the other way." [2] But he found that the "special pleading" of Blaine's advocates prejudiced him "far more than all his enemies did," and was left, like Pilate, with his question unanswered.

It is the duty of the biographer of a public man, abjuring equally the spirit of adulation and of denigration, to portray the facts of his life with as complete fidelity as possible to the record, in order that an enlightened posterity may judge fairly the value of his policies and achievements. Few statesmen rise to approach the stature of a Washington or a Lincoln; few politicians sink to the depths of a Tweed or a Butler. For the vast majority the ledger shows credit and debit items. Nor is the balance easy to strike by a mere process of addition and subtraction, as the simile might imply. For the items are weighted with widely differing values. Therefore, if I venture to set down some of them, it is

[1] Referring to Charles Edward Russell's *Blaine of Maine,* published by the Cosmopolitan Book Corporation, 1931.
[2] *Journal of Gamaliel Bradford,* pp. 191, 193, 195.

with no dogmatic presumption of "fixing" Blaine's place in history, but only in fulfilment of the summary "estimate" expected of a biographer.

Blaine's first claim to remembrance rests upon his Latin-American policy. It was he who conceived the idea of transforming the unilateral Monroe Doctrine into a coöperative scheme of Pan-Americanism, which should substitute arbitration for constantly recurring warfare between the countries south of the Rio Grande and bind the nations of the Western Hemisphere in mutually advantageous ties of commercial and cultural intercourse. Each successive Pan-American Congress has been a step in the fulfilment of Blaine's pioneer project of 1881 and pattern of 1889. His, too, was the policy of reciprocity, achieved in the teeth of the Bourbon protectionists of 1890—a policy to which every subsequent mitigation of stark protectionism, in the shape of tariff commissions, flexible schedules or bargaining projects, owes its inspiration. By his insistence on retaining Hawaii as "a part of the American system," and his keeping our foothold in the Samoan Islands, he made our entrance upon "the new and untried path" of permanent power in the Pacific seem more natural and acceptable to the nation. His claims to a prestige for America in the eyes of the European countries commensurate with her rapidly mounting wealth were a prelude to the drama of the United States as a world power. He was an untiring advocate of an adequate merchant marine, of the resumption of specie payments, of the exclusion of sectarian religious teaching from the public schools. It was the "Blaine amendment" that mitigated the rigor of the Fourteenth Amendment to the Constitution as proposed by Thaddeus Stevens' extreme radicals in Congress, and held out to the South the definite promise of restitution to the Union upon the fulfilment of certain specified conditions.

To contend, in the face of these accomplishments, that Blaine was nothing but a political liability to the country is sheer nonsense. The record rather confirms the truth of Elihu Root's judgment that Blaine united to the art of the politician the vision of the statesman. That his substantial services have been too meagerly appreciated has been due partially to a bitter political animosity which was naturally directed against him as the most conspicuous and able leader of his party, and partially to the fact that he exposed himself by certain injudicious acts to a reputation for unethical conduct, which his opponents were quick to represent as the essence of his character.

Most people are only too prone to believe evil report of a public servant, and therefore a man in public life should be doubly on guard against giving any cause for suspicion of his rectitude. That Blaine was dishonest in his dealings with Warren Fisher, that he "prostituted" his position as Speaker of the House to secure favors for the Little Rock and Fort Smith Railroad, or that he sought to involve others in ruin in order to save himself, I do not, after a careful study of the evidence, believe to be true. Nevertheless, it was a calamity from every point of view (as Blaine himself confessed) that he had any part in the speculative enterprise of Mr. Fisher and his associates. As a private citizen he would not have been criticized for it, but when he insisted that his correspondence with Fisher on the subject was as much a private matter as the running of his household or the education of his children, he overlooked the moral responsibility which attaches (quite apart from his legal rights) to the business transactions of a man in high public office, especially when those transactions are in any way "affected with public interest." It was this incaution which exposed him to the slanderous attack of Mulligan and compelled him to what he called the "humiliation" of having to defend his honor on the floor of the House. It was this mistake of ever having anything to do with the prospective profits of railroad promotion that gave his friends concern for his career and furnished his enemies the opportunity to pillory him in cruelly unjust cartoons and campaign slogans.[1]

The more is the pity of this incident, which was magnified into the decisive criterion of Blaine's character, and which doubtless cost him the Presidency, because he was anything but an avaricious man. He was free-hearted and open-handed, generous to a fault. "If Blaine had been content to be poor," one critic said, "he might have been a very great man." But none who really knew him ever believed that greed warped his character. He spent freely, but he was generally so indifferent

---

[1] Edwin D. Mead, a lifelong advocate of reform in politics, wrote of the New York *Nation's* persistent and venomous attacks on Blaine's veracity: "These articles, with their ready acceptance of Mulligan's high character, are responsible for three fourths of the disaffection toward Blaine. . . . I should like to have the Independents of Boston make it clearly understood that, however it may be elsewhere, in the Boston of Samuel Adams and John A. Andrew no Independent wishes his cause to prosper on any grounds but those of justice and generosity. If there are grievances and dangers, we will discuss and deal with them like men . . . but we will not prostitute our wits to the ingenious 'manufacturing' of a case and we will not tolerate anything that is petty, trumped up, inflated or fictitious." Letter to the Boston *Traveller*, July 15, 1884.

to the sources of income that his wife had to take charge of the ways and means, as is abundantly evident from her letters to her children. Again and again Blaine declined opportunities to earn large sums of money in business enterprises, because he was intent on following his political or literary interests.

In fine, the more sympathetically one studies the character and career of Blaine, the more one becomes convinced that none of his biographers, hostile or friendly, has discovered the true key to both his strength and his weakness. That key is in the simple phrase *party devotion*. Macaulay said of James II that he "could never see immorality in any act by which he benefited." [1] For Blaine it was equally difficult to find anything reprehensible in measures which advanced the interests of the Republican Party. Those interests were identical in his mind with the interests of the country. Beginning his career as an editor in Maine at the moment of the birth of the party, he had thrown himself zealously into the crusade for its national triumph. He had attended its first national convention at Philadelphia in 1856. He had come forward as an ardent defender of Lincoln both in the State legislature of Maine and in the House at Washington. His residence of three years in Kentucky had confirmed in him two convictions which he retained to the end of his life—a real affection for the colored people and a burning hatred of slavery. In the secession of the Southern States he saw only a sinful rebellion against the best and mildest of governments, and because the "rebels" found among Democrats practically all the sympathy and support that they had in the North, he always regarded the Democratic Party, in spite of his respect and affection for some of its members individually, as a party of collusion with disunion, with "Southern outrages," and with nefarious schemes for defeating or annulling measures for the preservation of the fruits of the war: namely, the constitutional amendments guaranteeing the emancipation, the civil rights and the enfranchisement of the blacks, and the legislative and administrative acts designed to guard against any revival of disloyal projects. Because the Republican Party was the repository of these guarantees, it was in Blaine's eyes the only "American" party. He could not understand how a true patriot could belong to the Democratic camp.

That the Republican Party, its charter program of preserving the Union and eliminating slavery once accomplished, became transformed

[1] T. B. Macaulay, *History of England*, Vol. IV, p. 173.

more and more into the party of wealth and privilege; that its long term of power nurtured abuses which it was too ready to ignore or to regard with complacency, made little difference to Blaine. For him the G.O.P. was always the party of union, freedom, enlightenment and virtue. *Ex hypothesi,* its policies were beneficial to Americans of every class and condition—farmer and townsman, laborer and employer, merchant and manufacturer, rich and poor, white and colored. The zeal and eloquence, the array of statistics and historical instances, with which he propagated this doctrine of the identity of Republicanism and Americanism won for him that devoted popular following which the unfaltering and unqualified advocacy of a political faith by a persuasive leader always wins. Blaine thus came to stand in the eyes of millions of his fellow countrymen as the very incarnation of American achievement and promise.

On the other hand, his intense partisanship was largely responsible for his shortcomings. Just as heresy was the unpardonable sin in the eyes of the medieval churchmen, so was party irregularity in the eyes of Blaine. An Independent like Carl Schurz, now enjoying high office in a Republican Administration and now bitterly attacking the Republican organization, was little better than a guerrilla deserter sniping at his own comrades. Nothing in the program of the Liberal Republicans could justify the schism which they created in the party ranks. If reforms were needed in the civil service or elsewhere, they should be initiated and carried out by the party which had already accomplished the greatest reform of the country. To be a Republican in good and regular standing was something like having righteousness imputed to one, even if one had it not. Indeed Blaine's partisanship led him dangerously near to the doctrine that the worst Republican was better than the best Democrat. For the former was at least in the right fold, while the latter was in the hopelessly wrong fold.

Two considerations may be adduced in explanation, if not in extenuation, of this attitude. In the first place, partisan feeling was much more intense in the decades just following the Civil War than it is today. Political issues were sharper. The economic questions which have now come to occupy the stage of national concern were then more or less in the wings. Third party movements based on economic demands (of farmers, silverites, laborers, Socialists, and other champions of the "forgotten man"), while not proving strong enough to prevail against the highly organized regular parties, have made considerable inroads on their strength and accustomed the people to regard as meritorious rather than reprehensible a certain measure of political revolt. The "scratchers" of tickets are not so much a little band of conspirators as the leaders of a sturdy movement for independence of judgment and enlarged vision of political duty. The spectacle of a Norris or a Nye sitting on the Republican side of the Senate and working for the election of a Democratic President, of an Ickes supporting the Bull Moose ticket in 1912, the regular Republican candidate in 1916, and entering Franklin Roosevelt's Cabinet in 1933, would have been as unbelievable as the two-headed calf in the circus to the men of Blaine's generation.

Furthermore, if Blaine allowed his intense partisanship to blind him to the realities of the political situation, it may be pleaded that the blindness was widely shared. The tone of post Civil War politics was low. The scandals of the Grant Administration marked what Professor Dunning called "the nadir of national disgrace." The Tweeds, Shepherds, Butlers, Belknaps, Fisks, Goulds, Drews, and McDonalds present a rare galaxy of rascals. Plutocratic influence was rampant. The first business of private citizens and public servants alike seemed to be "Put money in thy purse"—from whatever source derived. "The time had not come," says William Allen White, "to harness the aggrandizement of organized capital with the Beatitudes nor to compass it about with the Golden Rule."[1] The astonishing amount of silent acquiescence in corrupt politics, even on the part of men who were themselves honest, was due to the debased morals of the age. Nevertheless, there were voices raised, like Schurz', Curtis', Storey's, Seeley's, Eliot's and Pattison's, against the prevailing low standards in public life.

The reason why Blaine did not come forward as a reformer, as ardent a champion of the purification of the government at Washington under Grant as he had been of the preservation of the government under Lincoln, was not because, like Conkling, he held reform in cynical contempt, nor because, like Ingalls, he thought the purification of politics "an iridescent dream," but because of a conviction, acquired in the early years of the struggle for the preservation of the Union and the elimination of slavery, and clung to with the tenacity which marked his support of men and measures, that the Republican Party could do no wrong. He judged the reformers, as his letter of December 10, 1880, to President-

[1] W. A. White, *Masks in a Pageant*, p. 80.

elect Garfield shows, not from the point of view of the merits of their program, but rather from the point of view of the effect of that program on the solidarity of the Republican Party. And he met the challenge that a great leader must be better than his party by the constant endeavor to make his party seem better than it was. The devotion of so much of his wonderful talents to this apologetic task exposed him to the reproach of "giving up to party what was meant for mankind."

As to the charges of moral obliquity, overweening ambition, and sophisticated self-aggrandizement so persistently brought against Blaine by his political opponents during his lifetime, and repeated by not a few historians and biographers of a later generation, the reader will form his own judgment of their truth, exaggeration, or falsehood from the foregoing pages, which have been written with the sincere and sole desire of presenting the statesman in the setting of his time. If the reader concurs with a Rhodes or a Russell in a condemnatory judgment, he will at least own that Blaine amply atoned for his faults in the frustration of his hopes, and will be moved to cast the mantle of charity over the frailties that are common to human nature. If, on the other hand, one shares with Blaine's many admirers the conviction of his complete rectitude, that judgment will be reinforced by its harmony with such traits of Blaine's character as his generosity, his tolerance,[1] his domestic fidelity, his capacity for making and keeping the warmest friendships, his unobtrusive religious sincerity, and the empire of his lovable nature over all who came to know him well.

But whatever praise or blame Blaine deserves in the eyes of posterity, one thing he certainly does not deserve—oblivion. He was too compelling a figure in his generation to be allowed to fade into forgetfulness. Both his achievements and his failures have too valuable lessons for Americans of today to be ignored.

---

[1] "It would be hard to name a public man of whom so much evil has been spoken and who spoke so little evil of others." Edward Stanwood, *James G. Blaine,* p. 353.

BLAINE'S BIRTHPLACE AT WEST BROWNSVILLE, PENNSYLVANIA

BLAINE AS SPEAKER OF THE HOUSE
CIRCA 1870

W. E. Chandler traces the origin of the report in the *N. Y. Sun* of Blaine's transactions with the Kansas-Pacific R. R.

EMMONS BLAINE
1857–1892

WALKER BLAINE
1855–1890

The Dupont Circle Mansion in Washington (*above*)
The Seward Mansion (in which Blaine died) at Washington (*below*)

The Augusta Residence (*above*)
The Blaine Cottage at Bar Harbor (*below*)

CONKLING A "WHITE ELEPHANT" ON ARTHUR'S HANDS, 1882

(A Gillam Cartoon)

"ONLY A 'BLIND' FOR BLAINE"

B. F. Butler's candidacy

McDougall's Cartoon in the *New York World*, Oct. 20, 1884

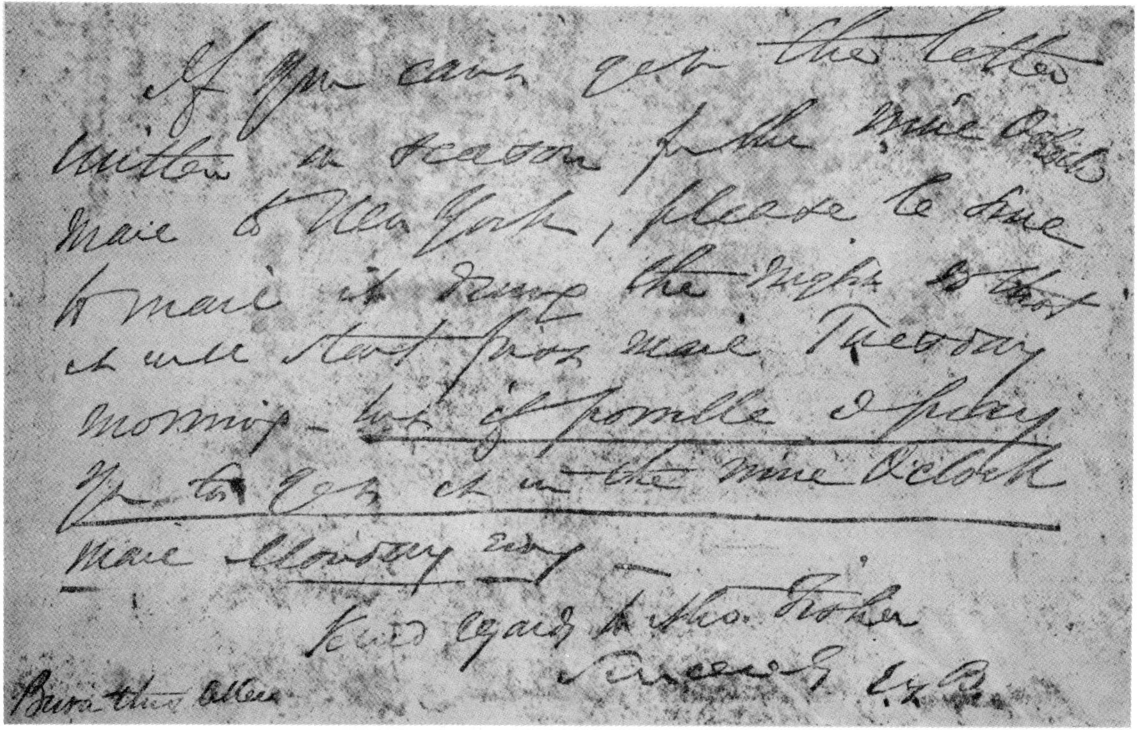
If you can get the letter
written in season for the nine o'clock
mail to New York, please be sure
to mail it during the night so that
it will start from mail Tuesday
morning — but if possible I prefer
you to get it in the nine o'clock
mail Monday evening —
Kind regards to Mrs. Fisher
Sincerely J. G. B.
Burn this letter

BLAINE'S LETTER TO FISHER, APRIL, 16, 1876

"BELSHAZZAR BLAINE AND THE MONEY KINGS"
McDougall's Cartoon in the *New York World*, Oct. 30, 1884

THE BLAINES ENTERTAIN THE HARRISONS AT BAR HARBOR, 1889

By permission of Charles Scribner's Sons, from W. Damrosch's "My Musical Life"

A PICNIC IN THE SCOTCH HIGHLANDS, 1888

(Left to right), Margaret Blaine, Mrs. Blaine, Harriet Blaine, Andrew Carnegie, Rev. Charles Eaton, Miss Dodge,
Mr. Blaine, Mr. Damrosch, Mrs. Phipps

PRESIDENT HARRISON'S CABINET

(Left to right) seated: W. H. H. Miller (Att'y Gen.), President Harrison, John Wanamaker (Postmaster Gen.), J. G. Blaine (State); Standing: J. W. Noble (Interior), William Windom (Treasury), J. M. Rusk (Agriculture), Redfield Proctor (War), B. F. Tracy (Navy)

BLAINE'S "SPIRITED FOREIGN POLICY"

(A Cartoon by Nast)

BLAINE'S LAST PHOTOGRAPH, 1892

Bibliography

A

Source Material

My sources have been pretty thoroughly indicated in the footnotes. The numerous notations "—to Blaine," with date, refer to letters preserved by the Blaine family and kindly loaned to me. Blaine's own letters, except for those few already published or in manuscript collections in the Library of Congress, are hard to come upon. He rarely made copies of his letters, and, in general, was quite careless of his correspondence. Such private letters as have been furnished to me by various individuals have been acknowledged in the footnotes.

The numerous government publications which I have used, such as the Congressional Globe, the Congressional Record, Executive Documents, Reports of Committees, United States Foreign Relations, as well as the leading newspapers of the time, have been noted by chapter and verse at their appropriate places in the text. Besides the letters of Blaine above mentioned, the most important source material has been found in

The John Sherman Papers, Library of Congress
The W. E. Chandler Papers, Library of Congress
The J. A. Garfield Papers, Library of Congress
The Israel Washburn Papers, Library of Congress
The W. Q. Gresham Papers, Library of Congress (Box C.)
The J. S. Morrill Papers, Library of Congress
The J. A. Kasson Papers, Library of Congress
The Carl Schurz Papers, Library of Congress
The J. S. Black Papers, Library of Congress
The Benjamin Harrison Papers, Library of Congress
The Baron Rosen Papers, Department of State
The Letters and Instructions in the Archives of the Department of State at Washington and the United States Chancellery at London.

B

Blaine's Published Writings

Many of Blaine's speeches in Congress and addresses in various parts of the country on public questions were printed in pamphlet form and are to be found readily in the catalogue of Blaine's writings in the Library of Congress. Occasionally he wrote for the magazines: a contribution to a symposium on Negro Suffrage in the *North American Review* for March, 1879; a defence of the Foreign Policy of the Garfield Administration in the *Chicago Weekly Magazine* of September 16, 1882; an article on the Presidential Election of 1892 in the *North American Review* for October, 1892. Blaine's *magnum opus* was

"Twenty Years of Congress: from Lincoln to Garfield" (Vol. I, 1884, Vol. II, 1886). This was followed (1887) by "Political Discussions: Legislative, Diplomatic and Popular." These two works contain the essence of Blaine's political philosophy. The "Eulogy of Garfield," delivered before the two Houses of Congress on February 2, 1882, is his most carefully prepared occasional composition. A brief essay from his pen on "Some Personal Traits of General Sherman" was appended to the first edition (1891) of the General's "Memoirs." Blaine's early "Memoir of Luther Severance" (1856) is interesting for the light which it throws on the politics of Maine.

C

BIOGRAPHIES OF BLAINE

Blaine's nomination in 1884 brought forth the usual flood of campaign biographies—by W. R. Balch, J. W. Buel, Hugh Craig, H. T. Ramsdell, R. H. Conwell, J. C. Ridpath, W. S. Vail, C. R. Williams and others. His death was the occasion for another spate of hastily written eulogies—by J. P. Boyd, H. D. Northrop, W. F. Johnson, T. H. Landis, J. W. Pierce and others. The best of the former class is C. W. Balestier's "James G. Blaine, A Sketch of His Life" (New York, 1884), and of the latter, T. C. Crawford's "James G. Blaine, A Study of His Life and Career" (Philadelphia, 1893).

Mary Abigail Dodge ("Gail Hamilton"), "The Biography of James G. Blaine," while indiscriminately eulogistic, is indispensable on account of the access which the author had, as a member of the family, to the intimate life of the statesman. The letters which Miss Dodge prints at the ends of her chapters are the most valuable part of her thick volume.

Edward Stanwood, "James Gillespie Blaine," in the American Statesmen Series (second), (Houghton, Mifflin and Company, Boston, 1905), is a popular, judicious presentation of Blaine by a more distant relative of his wife. The book is without notes or critical apparatus.

Thomas H. Sherman, "Twenty Years with James G. Blaine" (the Grafton Press, New York, 1928), makes no pretension to being a formal biography, but contains many interesting anecdotes of the statesman whom Mr. Sherman served as a beloved secretary for a score of years.

Charles Edward Russell, "Blaine of Maine: His Life and Times" (the Cosmopolitan Book Corporation, New York, 1931), is in the nature of a polemic refuting the eulogistic interpretation of Blaine's career by Gail Hamilton—on whom Russell depends for much of his material.

D

GENERAL WORKS CONSULTED

Adams, Henry. The education of Henry Adams.
Adams, John Quincy. Memoirs.

Alexander, D. S. History of the State of New York.
Andrews, E. B. The United States in our own time.
Appleton's Annual Encyclopaedia.
Badeau, Adam. Grant in peace.
Bancroft and Dunning. The writings of Carl Schurz.
Beale, Harriet Blaine. The letters of Mrs. James G. Blaine.
Bigelow, John. Life of Samuel J. Tilden.
Bolton, C. K. Memoir of Edward Stanwood.
Boston Committee of One Hundred. Mr. Blaine's record.
Bowers, Claude. The tragic era.
Boyd, T. B. The Blaine and Logan campaign of 1884.
Bradford, Gamaliel. Journal.
Bradford, Gamaliel. Wives.
Brigham, John. Blaine, Conkling and Garfield.
Bryce, James. The American commonwealth.
Conkling, A. R. Life of Roscoe Conkling.
Cortissoz, Royal. Life of Whitelaw Reid.
Crook, G. W. Through five administrations.
Cullom, S. M. Fifty years of public service.
Curtis, G. W. Orations and addresses.
Damrosch, Walter. My musical life.
Dana, C. A. Life of U. S. Grant.
Davis, W. W. Civil war and reconstruction in Florida.
Evans, H. C. Chili and the United States.
Evans, R. D. A sailor's log.
Foraker, J. B. Notes of a busy life.
Ford, W. C. The letters of Henry Adams.
Foster, J. W. Diplomatic memoirs.
Foulke, W. D. Life of Oliver Morton.
Fry, J. B. The Conkling and Blaine-Fry controversy in 1866.
Fuess, C. M. Carl Schurz, reformer.
Hall, W. H. Mr. Blaine and his foreign policy.
Hart, A. B. Practical essays in American government.
Haworth, Paul. The disputed presidential election of 1876.
Hedges, Charles. The speeches of Benjamin Harrison.
Hendrick, B. J. The life of Andrew Carnegie.
Hitchcock, Ernest. The Mulligan letters.
Hoar, G. F. Autobiography of seventy years.
Holst, H. von. Constitutional and political history of the United States.
Howe, M. A. de W. Portrait of an independent: Morefield Storey.
Hurlburt, W. H. Meddling and muddling: the foreign policy of James G.
    Blaine.
Johnson, W. F. An American statesman: the works and words of James G.
    Blaine.
Keenleyside, H. L. Canada and the United States.

Laughlin and Willis. Reciprocity.
Lewis, Lloyd. Sherman, fighting prophet.
Lodge, H. C. Correspondence with Theodore Roosevelt.
McClure, A. K. Our presidents and how we make them.
McElroy, R. M. Grover Cleveland, man and statesman.
Mitchell, E. P. Memoirs of an editor.
Moore, J. B. Digest of international law.
Moore, J. B. Four phases of American development: federalism, democracy, imperialism, expansion.
Nevins, Allan. Grover Cleveland. A study in courage.
Nicolay and Hay. Abraham Lincoln. A history.
Noyes, A. D. Forty years of American finance.
Oberholtzer, E. P. History of the United States since 1865.
Oberholtzer, E. P. Jay Cooke.
Ogilvie, J. S. Welcome home.
Peck, H. T. Twenty years of the republic.
Platt, T. C. Autobiography.
Pringle, H. F. Theodore Roosevelt.
Proceedings of the republican conventions of 1876, 1880, 1884, 1888, 1892.
Rhodes, J. F. From Hayes to McKinley.
Rhodes, J. F. History of the United States from the compromise of 1850.
Richardson, J. D. Messages and papers of the presidents.
Robertson, W. S. Hispanic-American relations.
Robertson, W. S. Rise of the Spanish-American republics.
Ryden, G. H. The foreign policy of the United States in relation to Samoa.
Sherman, John. Recollections.
Sherman letters.
Smith, T. C. The life and letters of James Abram Garfield.
Sparks, E. E. National development.
Stanwood, Edward. American tariff controversies in the nineteenth century.
Stanwood, Edward. History of the presidency.
Stevenson, R. L. A footnote to history: eight years of trouble in Samoa.
Strobel, E. H. Mr. Blaine's foreign policy.
Thayer, W. R. Life and letters of John Hay.
Tyler, Alice Felt. The foreign policy of James G. Blaine.
White, A. D. Autobiography.
White, W. A. Masks in a pageant.
Williams, C. R. Diary and letters of Rutherford B. Hayes.
Williams, C. R. Life of Rutherford B. Hayes.
Young, J. R. Around the world with General Grant.

Index